A PROPHET TO THE NATIONS

A Prophet
to the Nations

Essays in Jeremiah Studies

Edited by

Leo G. Perdue and Brian W. Kovacs

Eisenbrauns

Winona Lake, Indiana

Library of Congress Cataloging in Publication Data

A Prophet to the nations

    1. Bible. O.T. Jeremiah—Criticism, interpretation, etc.—
Addresses, essays, lectures. I. Perdue, Leo G. II. Kovacs,
Brian W.
BS1525.2.P76 1984   224′.206   83–20648
ISBN 0–931464–20–X

CONTENTS

Preface

As those who have engaged in a similar effort will attest, the selecting and compiling of essays covering a wide range of issues within a specific area of research is a complicated task. The substantial number of important essays which have shaped the currents of Jeremiah study during this century have made selection extremely difficult. Furthermore, the decision to limit the major areas of discussion to six resulted in the exclusion of many fine essays in other areas of interest, such as form criticism and theology. And efforts to obtain permission to reprint certain essays were not always successful. Nevertheless, the high quality of the reprinted essays should offset these restrictions.

It is obvious that significant contributions made by many scholars to Jeremiah research are not represented by essays in this volume: Walter Baumgartner, Sheldon Blank, C. Brekelmans, Bernhard Duhm, Georg Fohrer, Eberhard Gerstenberger, A. H. J. Gunneweg, Gerald Janzen, Herbert G. May, Sigmund Mowinckel, E. W. Nicholson, Thomas W. Overholt, H. Graf Reventlow, Claus Rietzschel, Wilhelm Rudolph, John Skinner, Winfried Thiel, Emanuel Tov, Helga Weippert, Artur Weiser, Moshe Weinfeld, and others. However, the effort has been made in the introductory essay to point to the impact their work has had on our understanding of Jeremiah.

Many people have contributed directly and indirectly to the production of this volume. Dr. Joe R. Jones, President of Phillips University, continues to support the scholar's craft by means of research grants and leaves in spite of economic pressure. A research grant from Phillips University covered the major expenses incurred from procuring reprint rights, typing, and indexing. In addition, a major portion of my work on this volume was done during my 1982–83 research leave spent in residence at Göttingen University where I worked as a Fulbright Senior Research Scholar. I am especially grateful to my host, Professor Walther Zimmerli, for his congeniality, assistance, and interest in my work; to Assistant Dr. Hermann Spieckermann for the many conversations we had about Old Testament studies and for the use of his office; and to Professors Rudolf Smend, Lothar Perlitt, and Gerd Lüdemann for their hospitality and invitation to participate in the intellectual life of the theological faculty. Special thanks also go to the German Fulbright Commission, ably led by Dr. Ulrich Littmann, for making my research leave in Germany a most pleasant one.

Thanks are also extended to Dr. Anne Winston, Professor of German Literature, and Gary Lance Johnson, Assistant to the Dean of the Graduate Seminary, two colleagues at Phillips University, who translated Gerhard von Rad's essay included in this volume. Laurie Miller, a graduate student at Phillips University, helped with the laborious task of indexing.

Finally, special thanks are offered to James Eisenbraun for his commitment to Old Testament and ancient Near Eastern research and highly professional work as publisher-scholar. His unusual insight and care were of considerable value in seeing this volume through to publication.

November, 1983   Leo G. Perdue
                                  Associate Professor of Old Testament
                                  The Graduate Seminary
                                  Phillips University

Acknowledgments

H. H. Rowley, "The Early Prophecies of Jeremiah in Their Setting," reprinted with permission from *Bulletin of the John Rylands University Library, Manchester* 45 (1962–3), 198–234.

J. P. Hyatt, "The Beginning of Jeremiah's Prophecy," reprinted with permission from *Zeitschrift für die alttestamentliche Wissenschaft* 78 (1966), 204–14.

C. F. Whitley, "The Date of Jeremiah's Call," reprinted with permission from *Vetus Testamentum* 14 (1964), 467–83.

Henri Cazelles, "Jeremiah and Deuteronomy," reprinted and translated with permission from *Recherches de Science Religieuse* 38 (1951), 5–36.

J. Philip Hyatt, "Jeremiah and Deuteronomy," reprinted with permission from *Journal of Near Eastern Studies* 1 (1942), 156–73.

Henri Cazelles, "Zechariah, Jeremiah, and the Scythians in Palestine," reprinted and translated with permission from *Revue Biblique* 74 (1967), 24–44.

Brevard S. Childs, "The Enemy from the North and the Chaos Tradition," reprinted with permission from *Journal of Biblical Literature* 78 (1959), 187–98.

C. F. Whitley, "Carchemish and Jeremiah," reprinted with permission from *Zeitschrift für die alttestamentliche Wissenschaft* 80 (1968), 38–49.

T. R. Hobbs, "Some Remarks on the Composition and Structure of the Book of Jeremiah," reprinted with permission from *Catholic Biblical Quarterly* 34 (1972), 257–75.

John Bright, "The Date of the Prose Sermons of Jeremiah," reprinted with permission from *Journal of Biblical Literature* 70 (1951), 15–35.

William L. Holladay, "A Fresh Look at 'Source B' and 'Source C' in Jeremiah," reprinted with permission from *Vetus Testamentum* 25 (1975), 394–412.

James Muilenburg, "Baruch the Scribe," reprinted with permission from *Proclamation and Presence. Old Testament Essays in Honour of Gwynne Henton Davies*. Ed. by John I. Durham and J. R. Porter. Richmond: John Knox Press, 1970, 215–38.

J. Philip Hyatt, "The Deuteronomic Edition of Jeremiah," reprinted with permission from *Vanderbilt Studies in the Humanities* 1. Ed. by Richmond C. Beatty, J. Philip Hyatt, and Monroe K. Spears. Nashville: Vanderbilt University Press, 1951, 71–95.

William McKane, "Relations Between Poetry and Prose in the Book of Jeremiah with Special Reference to Jeremiah iii 6–11 and xii 14–17," reprinted with permission from *Supplements to Vetus Testamentum* 32 *Congress Volume Vienna 1980.* Ed. by J. A. Emerton, Leiden: E. J. Brill, 1981, 220–37.

David Jobling, "The Quest of the Historical Jeremiah: Hermeneutical Implications of Recent Literature," reprinted with permission from *Union Seminary Quarterly Review* 34 (1978), 3–12.

Siegfried Herrmann, "Overcoming the Israelite Crisis. Remarks on the Interpretation of the Book of Jeremiah," reprinted and translated with permission from *Beiträge zur Alttestamentlichen Theologie* (FS Walther Zimmerli; ed. by H. Donner, R. Hanhart, and R. Smend. Göttingen: Vandenhoeck und Ruprecht, 1977), 164–78.

William L. Holladay, "The Background of Jeremiah's Self-Understanding. Moses, Samuel, and Psalm 22," reprinted with permission from *Journal of Biblical Literature* 83 (1964), 153–64.

John Bright, "A Prophet's Lament and Its Answer: Jeremiah 15:10–21," reprinted with permission from *Interpretation* 28 (1974), 59–74.

Gerhard von Rad, "The Confessions of Jeremiah," reprinted and translated with permission from *Evangelische Theologie* 3 (1936), 265–76.

Walther Zimmerli, "The Fruit of the Tribulation of the Prophet," reprinted and translated with permission from *Die Botschaft und die Boten* (FS Hans Walter Wolff; ed. by J. Jeremias and L. Perlitt; Neukirchen-Vluyn: Neukirchener Verlag, 1981), 131–46.

Bernhard W. Anderson, "'The Lord Has Created Something New': A Stylistic Study of Jeremiah 31:15–22," reprinted with permission from *Catholic Biblical Quaterly* 40 (1978), 463–78.

Robert P. Carroll, "Prophecy, Dissonance, and Jeremiah xxvi," reprinted with permission from *Transactions of the Glasgow University Oriental Society* 25 (1976), 12–23.

In the five translated articles, biblical citations are taken from the *Revised Standard Version*, except in those cases when the translation of the French and German biblical passages is necessary to capture the meaning of the original essays.

Abbreviations

A.A.A.	Annals of Archaeology and Anthropology
AB (AncB)	Anchor Bible
ABR (A.B.R.)	Australian Biblical Review
ADAJ	Annual of the Department of Antiquities of Jordan
AfO	Archiv für Orientforschung
AJSL (A.J.S.L.)	American Journal of Semitic Languages and Literatures
ANQ	Andover Newton Quarterly
ANVAO	Avhandlinger utgitt av det Norske Videnskaps-Akademi i Oslo
AR	Archiv für Religionswissenschaft
ATD (A.T.D.)	Das Alte Testament Deutsch
BA (Bib. Arch.)	Biblical Archaeologist
BASOR	Bulletin of the American Schools of Oriental Research
BBB	Bonner biblische Beiträge
BibOr (BiOr)	Bibliotheca Orientalis
BJRL (B.J.R.L.)	Bulletin of the John Rylands Library
BKAT (BK)	Biblisher Kommentar Altes Testament
BWA(N)T (B.W.A.T.)	Beiträge zur Wissenschaft vom Alten (und Neuen) Testament
BZ (B.Z.)	Biblische Zeitschrift
BZAW	Beihefte zur Zeitschrift für die alttestamentliche Wissenschaft
C.A.H.	Cambridge Ancient History
Camb. B.	Cambridge Bible
CBQ	Catholic Biblical Quarterly
Cent. B.	Century Bible
D.B.	Hasting's Dictionary of the Bible
E.B.	Encyclopaedia Biblica
EBib (E.Bib.)	Études Bibliques
EvT (EvTh)	Evangelische Theologie
ExpT (Exp Tim, E.T.)	Expository Times
FRLANT	Forschungen zur Religion und Literatur des Alten und Neuen Testaments
G.J.V.	Geschichte des Jüdischen Volkes
G.V.I.	Geschichte des Volkes Israel
HAT (H.A.T.)	Handbuch zum Alten Testament

HKAT (H.K.)	Handkommentar zum Alten Testament
H.S.A.T.	Die Heilige Schrift des Alten Testaments (Kautzsch)
H.S.A.Tes.	Die Heilige Schrift des Alten Testaments
HSM	Harvard Semitic Monographs
HTR	Harvard Theological Review
IB (I.B.)	The Interpreter's Bible
ICC (I.C.C.)	International Critical Commentary
IDB	The Interpreter's Dictionary of the Bible
IDBSup	The Interpreter's Dictionary of the Bible, Supplementary Volume
IEJ	Israel Exploration Journal
Int	Interpretation
JA	Journal Asiatique
JBL (J.B.L.)	Journal of Biblical Literature
JBR	Journal of Bible and Religion
JCS	Journal of Cuneiform Studies
J.E.	Jewish Encyclopedia
JNES (J.N.E.S.)	Journal of Near Eastern Studies
JR (J.R.)	Journal of Religion
JSOT	Journal for the Study of the Old Testament
JRAS	Journal of the Royal Asiatic Society
JTS (J.T.S.)	Journal of Theological Studies
KAT (K.A.T.)	Kommentar zum Alten Testament
K.D.	Keil-Delitzsch, Commentar über das Alte Testament
K.E.H.	Kurzgefasste exegetische Handbuch
KHC (K.H.C.)	Kurzer Hand-Commentar zum Alten Testament
LCL	Loeb Classical Library
L.O.T.	Introduction to the Literature of the Old Testament
LXX	Septuagint
MDOG	Mitteilungen der Deutschen Orientgesellschaft
MT	Masoretic Text
MVAG (M.V.A.G.)	Mitteilungen der Vorderasiatischen Gesellschaft
NICOT	The New International Commentary on the Old Testament
OTL	Old Testament Library
PG	Patrologia Graeca
PJB	Palästinajahrbuch
P.W.	Pauly-Wissowa-Kroll, Realencyclopädie der classischen Altertumswissenschaft
RA (R.A.)	Revue d'Assyriologie
RB	Revue Biblique
R.G.G.	Die Religion in Geschichte und Gegenwart
RHPhR	Revue d'Histoire et de Philosophie Religieuses
R.H.R.	Revue de l'Histoire des Religions

Riv. St. Or.	Revista degli Studi Orientali
RLA	Reallexikon der Assyriologie
RSR	Recherches de Science Religieuse
S.A.T.	Die Schriften des Alten Testaments in Auswahl
S.B.	Sacra Bibbia
SBL	Society of Biblical Literature
SBLDS	Society of Biblical Literature Dissertation Series
SBT	Studies in Biblical Theology
S.B.U.	Svenskt Bibliskt Uppslagsverk
S.D.B.	Supplément au Dictionnaire de la Bible
StTh	Studia Theologica
ThB (TB)	Theologische Bücherei
ThLZ (TLZ)	Theologische Literaturzeitung
Th.R.	Theologische Rundschau
THAT	Theologisches Handwörterbuch zum AT
ThWAT	Theologisches Wörterbuch zum Alten Testament
ThZ (Th.Z.)	Theologische Zeitschrift
TQ	Theologische Quartalschrift
TRu	Theologische Rundschau
USQR	Union Seminary Quarterly Review
VT	Vetus Testamentum
VTS (Sup. VT)	Supplements to Vetus Testamentum
West. C.	Westminster Commentary
WMANT	Wissenschaftliche Monographien zum Alten und Neuen Testament
WZKM	Wiener Zeitschrift für die Kunde des Morgenlandes
ZA (Z.A.)	Zeitschrift für Assyriologie
ZÄS	Zeitschrift für die Agyptische Sprache und Altertums- kunde
ZAW (Z.A.W.)	Zeitschrift für die alttestamentliche Wissenschaft
ZDMG (Z.D.M.G.)	Zeitschrift der Deutschen Morgenländischen Gesellschaft
ZKT	Zeitschrift für Katholische Theologie
ZSTh	Zeitschrift für Systematische Theologie
ZTK (ZThK, Z.Th.K.)	Zeitschrift für Theologie und Kirche

1
Jeremiah in Modern Research: Approaches and Issues
Leo G. Perdue

During the twentieth century, Jeremiah research has focused on several related issues which continue to be addressed by new and more refined methodologies.[1] In fact, the history of biblical criticism, including its advances and insights as well as its shortcomings, is clearly mirrored in Jeremiah studies. The issues which continue to receive the major attention of students of the prophet of Anathoth include: the date of Jeremiah's call, his view of and/or relation to the Deuteronomic reform, the prophet's identification of the enemy from the North, the substantial textual differences between the MT and the LXX, and most problematic, the composition and development of the book into its present canonical form. Though at first glance these issues may appear to be disparate in nature and concern, this is not the case. Undergirding and stimulating most Jeremianic research since the inception of modern criticism is the concern to discover the Jeremiah of history. Obviously, this concern, which has been largely responsible for the vitality of Jeremiah criticism over the years, has important parallels with the questions of historicity, history, and historiography in the study of the Gospels and the patriarchal narratives.

While it is something of an oversimplification, it may be argued at least in broad outlines that two major interpretative approaches have emerged in Jeremiah studies. The first, which has been shaped by liberal theology, is the psychological-biographical approach which argues that the Book of Jeremiah contains a significant amount of historically reliable, biographical, autobiographical, and oracular materials which allow us to reconstruct the life and theology of the prophet. On the other hand, the traditio-historical approach, largely informed by Neo-Orthodoxy, finds in the book of Jeremiah composite literary complexes which are the creation of tradition circles at work from the lifetime of the prophet well into the

---

[1]For recent surveys of Jeremiah research, see Georg Fohrer, "Neue Literatur zur alttestamentlichen Prophetie (1961–1970). VII. Jeremia," *TRu* 45 (1980) 109–21; and Siegfried Herrmann, "Forschung am Jeremiabuch: Probleme und Tendenzen ihrer neueren Entwicklung," *TLZ* 102 (1977) 481–90.

post-exilic and even exilic periods. The historical Jeremiah for the most part remains concealed behind the various traditions which have undergone a long process of reshaping and reformulation. While many scholars may be found somewhere between these two positions, this dichotomy is useful for understanding Jeremiah scholarship.[2]

II. THE DATE OF JEREMIAH'S CALL

The question of the date of Jeremiah's prophetic call (chapter 1) is an issue of considerable importance, due to its impact on other problems: the prophet's position regarding the Deuteronomic reform, the dating of the prophet's early oracles, the identity of the "Foe from the North," and the historical reliability of the prose traditions.

The prose traditions (1:2, 25:3) place the call of Jeremiah in the "thirteenth year of King Josiah" (627/26 B.C.E.) and indicate that he was active as a prophet in "the days of King Josiah" (3:6, 36:2) who reigned from 640 to 609 B.C.E. Several poetic texts may indirectly concern the issue at hand. The first is the prophet's unflattering contrast of Jehoiakim with his deceased father who practiced justice (22:15–16). However, this poetic text, usually assumed to be from the prophet himself, may indicate no more than Jeremiah's familiarity with Josiah's reputation. It does not sufficiently prove that Jeremiah either knew Josiah or that he prophesied during his reign. The second is the indictment of Israel for "going to Assyria" (2:18), probably for aid, a situation that would not occur after the fall of the Assyrian empire, the failure of Assur-uballit II to recapture Harran from the Babylonians, and Josiah's death in 609.

The majority of Jeremiah scholars have tended to accept as historically genuine the 627/6 date given to the prophet's call by the prose texts.[3] And, consequently, many attempts have been made to locate historically various oracles and other kinds of material in the last eighteen years of Josiah's reign (627/6–609). This effort is usually linked with attempts to reconstruct Baruch's scroll(s) mentioned in chapter 36. However, the prose date is not

---

[2]Robert Carroll has an important analysis of these two approaches to Jeremiah interpretation in the introductory chapter to his book, "The Quest of the Historical Jeremiah," *From Chaos to Covenant* (New York: Crossroad, 1981) 5–30.

[3]E.g., John Bright, *Jeremiah* (AB; 2d ed.; Garden City: Doubleday, 1965) xxviii; Albert Condamin, *Le Livre de Jérémie* (3rd ed.; Paris: Gabalda et Cie, 1936) vi; Thomas W. Overholt, "Some Reflections on the Date of Jeremiah's Call," *CBQ* 33 (1971) 165–184; Gerhard von Rad, *The Message of the Prophets* (New York: Harper and Row, 1962) 161; H. H. Rowley, "The Early Prophecies of Jeremiah in their Setting," *BJRL* 45 (1962–3) 198–234 (reprinted in this volume); Wilhelm Rudolph, *Jeremia* (HAT 12; 3rd ed.; Tübingen: J. C. B. Mohr (Paul Siebeck), 1968) iii; Albert Strobel, *Trauer um Jerusalem. Jeremia-Klagelieder-Baruch* (Stuttgarter Kleiner Kommentar, Altes Testament 11; Stuttgart: KBW Verlag, 1973) 7; J. A. Thompson, *The Book of Jeremiah* (NICOT; Grand Rapids: William B. Eerdmans, 1980) 56; Paul Volz, *Der Prophet Jeremia* (KAT 10; Leipzig: Deicher, 1922) xiii; and Artur Weiser, *Das Buch des Propheten Jeremia* (ATD 20/21 4th ed.; Göttingen: Vandenhoeck und Ruprecht, 1960) xv.

without its difficulties. First of all, if Jeremiah was active as a prophet during the reign of Josiah it is curious that he is presented as saying nothing to or about Josiah, except for the previously mentioned poetic oracle dating from the reign of Jehoiakim (22:15–16). Second, nowhere in the Jeremiah traditions do we find the prophet specifically referring to the Josianic reform, based on the Deuteronomic law code. The only possible exception is 11:1–17, a prose judgment oracle which condemns the people for violating the covenant, possibly in its Deuteronomic form. Third, in addition to the call in chapter one, we find only one other speech, also mainly in prose, that is dated to the reign of Josiah (3:6–14). Fourth, if the prophet is active this early and already has begun to speak of the "Foe from the North," it would not be clear who he had specifically in mind as the enemy. Fifth, there is the matter of the consultation of Huldah the prophetess (2 Kgs 22:11–20), not Jeremiah, following the discovery of the "book of the law." This consultation of Huldah instead of Jeremiah may simply indicate that the prophet of Anathoth was only an insignificant rural prophet at the time. But it could also indicate Jeremiah was not active as a prophet in 622. Sixth, and finally, those prose texts which make Jeremiah active in the period of Josiah and may imply he supported the reform may well be Deuteronomic, and as such, could represent the attempt of this school to present Jeremiah as an active supporter of the reform.[4]

Due to these problems, several scholars reject the 627/6 date as much too early for the beginning of Jeremiah's prophetic career and opt instead for a significantly later date. Resorting to textual emendation, Gordon has argued that the thirteenth year of Josiah's reign (1:2) should be read as the twenty-third year, making the call, in his estimation, coincide with the rise of the Neo-Babylonian empire and Nabopolassar's attack against Assyria.[5] Horst, Hyatt, May and Holladay have suggested 609 as a more appropriate date, since this would have the prophet's call coincide with the crises of the death of Josiah and the eventual accession of Jehoiakim to the throne.[6] Finally, Whitley points to 605 as the most likely date, since the Babylonian victory at Carchemish culminates in Babylon's unrivaled power in the Near East.[7]

---

[4]See J. Philip Hyatt, "Jeremiah and Deuteronomy," *JNES* 1 (1942) 156–73 (reprinted in this volume).

[5]T. C. Gordon, "A New Date for Jeremiah," *Exp Tim* 44 (1932/33) 562–65.

[6]William L. Holladay, *Jeremiah. Spokesman Out of Time* (Philadelphia: Pilgrim Press, 1974) 17–22; F. Horst, "Die Anfänge des Propheten Jeremia," *ZAW* 41 (1923) 111f.; J. Philip Hyatt, "The Book of Jeremiah," *IB* 5 (New York: Abingdon, 1956) 779; *idem*, "The Beginning of Jeremiah's Prophecy," *ZAW* 78 (1966) 204–14 (reprinted in this volume); and Herbert G. May, "The Chronology of Jeremiah's Oracles," *JNES* 4 (1945) 227.

[7]C. F. Whitley, "The Date of Jeremiah's Call," *VT* 14 (1964) 467–83 (reprinted in this volume).

Among this dissenting group, Hyatt and Holladay have been the most outspoken critics of the traditional date, arguing that the thirteenth year of Josiah's reign is actually a reference to the prophet's birth date. This argument is based on the language of 1:5 which refers to Yahweh's commissioning of Jeremiah to be a prophet even before his birth. In their estimation, the problems mentioned above would then be easily resolved, since Jeremiah would not have begun his prophetic task until Josiah had died and the events of his reign had come to an end.[8] On the other hand, the early date is Deuteronomic and historically unreliable.

What becomes clear in this debate is the primary concern to locate the man Jeremiah within the current of well-known, significant, historical events. The issue gains in intensity only when the individual scholar is convinced that the events of Jeremiah's life may be successfully correlated with those of Israelite and Near Eastern history. For those scholars who see the Jeremiah traditions in theological and traditio-historical rather than historical terms, the issue of dating is not so significant. In addition, the difficulties with any of the proposed dates lend added support to the traditio-historical argument that the historical Jeremiah lies hidden behind the different cycles of tradition.

One final point should be made. It is possible that the prose tradition and the poetic tradition are functioning with two different dates for the beginning of Jeremiah's prophecy. 627/6 is clearly the date posited by the prose, and the poetic speeches may possibly be interpreted as implying a 609 date. The historian's effort to judge which is more historically correct, necessarily leads to an assessment of the historical veracity of both traditions. More will be said about this issue in the later section dealing with the composition of the book of Jeremiah.

III. JEREMIAH AND THE DEUTERONOMIC REFORM

The narrative in the Deuteronomic History (2 Kgs 22–23, cf. 2 Chr 34–35) detailing the reform program of Josiah (beginning circa 622 B.C.E.), presumably based on an early Deuteronomic law-code, indicates Josiah engaged in a wide sweeping religious and social reform which seems to have ended with his death. If indeed the reform was as dramatic as the narrative describes, at least in its initial years, an obvious question scholars have raised concerns both Jeremiah's possible relationship to and attitude towards its nature and results.

As noted above, it is surprising that no text in Jeremiah directly addresses the reform. The prose tradition of Jeremianic speeches contains

---

[8]Holladay adds that 15:16, "Thy words were found and I ate them," refers both to the discovery of the law-code in the temple in 622/21 and Jeremiah's call in 609. Thus he argues the prophet must have accepted the call after the discovery of the law-code and not before ("Jeremiah and Moses: Further Observations," *JBL* 85 (1966) 21–24). It should be noted,

one text, 11:1–17, in which the prophet condemns Judah for violating the covenant (Deuteronomy?), though no date for the speech is provided. Jeremiah's temple sermon (7 and 26), also in prose and dated in the "beginning of the reign of Jehoiakim" (609), does mention some of the ten commandments as being violated, though this would suggest only that the reform had dissipated. In addition, the question of the veracity of the prose speeches has been raised by several scholars, as will be discussed later on. Hence, even if 11:1–17 is properly interpreted as an indication of Jeremiah's support for the reform, are we hearing the actual voice of the prophet or that of a later, possibly Deuteronomic, redactor?[9] Nothing in the poetic speeches clearly alludes to Josiah's program.

Because of the sparsity of evidence, several very different, though admittedly tentative, positions have crystallized in regard to this issue. A number of scholars, accepting the prose date of the call (627/26 B.C.E.), argue that when the Josianic reform began, the prophet was an active supporter,[10] and possibly even regarded it as one of the results of his earlier preaching.[11] His persecution by the "men of Anathoth," including members of his own priestly family (11:18–12:6), may have been prompted by his sympathy for the reform, its centralization of worship in Jerusalem, and the elimination of local high places. Since he was a Levite, his move from Anathoth to Jerusalem may have been occasioned by his obedience to Deuteronomy and the reform. On the other hand, several scholars, who also accept the prose date as historically accurate, argue that Jeremiah entered a period of silence which began with the initiation of the reform in 622 B.C.E. and ended only with Josiah's death in 609 B.C.E. The silence is taken as demonstrating either Jeremiah's sympathy for the ideals of the reform,[12] or his conviction that the inevitability of impending doom rendered futile any efforts at reform.[13]

Another position, also based on the prose date, considers the prophet to have been an active supporter at the beginning, but later, to have changed his position after determining that it was characterized by rampant nationalism and improper attention to the externals of religion (cult, sacrifice, and

---

however, that 15:16 is a part of one of Jeremiah's "confessions," the authorship of which is seriously contested. See section VII of this essay.

[9]André Robert ("Jérémie et la réforme deutéronomique d'après Jér. xi, 1–14," *RSR* 30 (1943) 3–16) argues that the kernel of this text (vv 6, part of 8, and 9–12) comes from Jeremiah and demonstrates his support for and even active participation in the reform.

[10]For example, H. Cazelles, "Jérémie et le Deutérome," *RSR* 38 (1951) 5–36 (translated and reprinted in this volume), who does conclude the prophet came to realize the weaknesses of the reform; and A. Strobel, "Jeremias, Priester ohne Gottesdienst?" *BZ* 1 (1957) 214–24.

[11]Weiser, *Das Buch des Propheten Jeremia*, xvi.

[12]Von Rad thinks that while Jeremiah was silent in the years following the reform, he was probably in sympathy with it. However, he cautions that the lack of evidence should limit too much speculation on this point (*Message of the Prophets*, 166).

[13]C. C. Torrey, "The Background of Jeremiah 1–10," *JBL* 56 (1937) 207.

temple).[14] This change in the prophet's position may have been occasioned by the death of Josiah and the disastrous consequences his death entailed. Perhaps Jeremiah opposed a legalistic and nationalistic orthodoxy that inhibited true reform.

A final stance is taken by several scholars who have posited a 609 date for the call of the prophet. They suggest that Jeremiah's silence about the reform is due to his being only a child when the program was enacted. Thus he did not begin to prophesy until after it had run its course.[15] Nevertheless, several of these scholars (e. g. Hyatt and May) still add that Jeremiah became a critic *post eventu* of several features of the reform, especially the undue importance placed on sacrifice and the temple. For them, the prophet believed that the essence of religion is ethics, not cult. They admit that Jeremiah was in sympathy with the reform's emphases on social justice, the rejection of apostasy, and retributive justice, but argue he stood in direct opposition to the cultic legislation. The few prose speeches that possibly imply Jeremiah supported the reform are the result of later Deuteronomic redaction which attempted to present the prophet as the champion of Deuteronomic theology.[16]

Again, the difficulty in assessing the relationship, if any, to the reform is taken by the traditio-historical approach to enhance the argument that we should move away from questions involving the life and thought of the prophet to questions involving the variety of ways the different Jeremianic traditions depict his life and thought.

IV. "THE FOE FROM THE NORTH"

A third major issue concerns the identity of "the Foe from the North." The theme of the northern enemy figures prominently in a series of poetic oracles in chapters 4–10. The description includes the following: the enemy

---

[14]John Bright, *Covenant and Promise* (Philadelphia: Westminister, 1976) 143f. (cf. his *Jeremiah*, xxxviii–xl); R. Davidson, "Orthodoxy and the Prophetic Word," *VT* 14 (1964) 407–16; E. W. Nicholson, *The Book of the Prophet Jeremiah, Chapters 1–25* (Cambridge: At the University Press, 1973) 5; Overholt, "Some Reflections on the Date of Jeremiah's Call"; H. H. Rowley, "The Prophet Jeremiah and the Book of Deuteronomy," *Studies in Old Testament Prophecy* (FS T. H. Robinson; edited by H. H. Rowley; Edinburgh: T. & T. Clark, 1950) 157–74; Rudolph, *Jeremia*, iv; and John Skinner, *Prophecy and Religion* (1st Paperback Edition, Cambridge: At the University Press, 1961) 96–137. Strobel argues that while Jeremiah did not oppose the reform, he did question its authenticity and criticized the superficial repentance of the nation (*Trauer um Jerusalem*, 25–26). In S. Granild's opinion, Jeremiah was supportive of Deuteronomy and much of its teaching, but attacked the reforming circle for using the text to promote its own self-interests ("Jeremia und Deuteronomium," *ST* 16 (1962) 135–54).

[15]Holladay, *Jeremiah*, 20–21; Hyatt, "Jeremiah and Deuteronomy," 156–73; *idem*, "Torah in The Book of Jeremiah," *JBL* 60 (1941) 381–96; Herbert May, "The Chronology of Jeremiah's Oracles," 226–27; and Whitley, "The Date of Jeremiah's Call," 482.

[16]Carroll, *From Chaos to Covenant*, 105. However, he refuses to speculate over either the prophet's view of Deuteronomy or the Josianic reform.

comes from the North and from a distant land, is an "ancient" and "enduring" nation, speaks a foreign language, is merciless, consists of great warriors, attacks unexpectedly, rides on swift horses and chariots, is armed with bows and spears, uses battle formations, and is bold enough to attack a fortified city even at noon. But when we pass beyond the description, we find no specific identification in these texts.

It is true that the northern enemy is identified in the prose tradition as Babylon (25; cf. 36), though these texts have often been attributed to a later redactor, either Baruch or a Deuteronomic editor. Even so, it should be noted this specific identity is made, according to the date given by both texts, in 605, probably immediately following the Babylonian victory at Carchemish. In addition, the language of the "Foe from the North" is utilized in chapters 50–51 to speak of the enemy (the Persians or possibly the Medes) who conquer Babylon. Most of the entire section of the "Oracles Against the Nations" has been attributed to later redactors by many scholars, and this adaptation demonstrates the fluidity of the expression even in Jeremiah.

The question scholars have often raised about the "Foe from the North" involves both the time of the oracles and the identity of the Foe. Positions taken may be separated into three major categories: an historical enemy, a mythical or eschatological enemy, and an originally unspecified enemy only later identified as the Babylonians.

A large number of scholars have pointed to either the Scythians or the Babylonians as the identification in the prophet's mind from the very beginning. The Scythian hypothesis is based on the *History* of Herodotus and cuneiform texts which speak of the *Umman-Manda*, who at times may be equated with the Scythians.[17] However, while the cuneiform texts provide some details about the movements and alignments of the Scythians, only Herodotus (Bk I, 104–6) speaks of a Scythian presence in Palestine.[18] In the context of describing a Scythian defeat of the Medes that projected them into the position of being "masters of all Asia," the Greek historian mentions a Scythian march against Egypt after their arrival in "the part of Syria called Palestine." Posed to invade Egypt, they were met by Psammetichus who bribed them not to attack. Accepting tribute, they then began to march back through Palestine, but a contingent, stopping at Ashkelon, plundered the temple of the Heavenly Aphrodite and suffered the plague of the "female sickness." It is at this point that Herodotus states the Scythians "ruled Asia for twenty-eight years," adding that they laid waste to the land because of their violence and pride.

---

[17] Those supporting a Scythian hypothesis include Otto Eissfeldt, *The Old Testament. An Introduction* (New York: Harper and Row, 1965) 348; H. H. Rowley, "The Early Prophecies of Jeremiah in their Setting," and John Skinner, *Prophecy and Religion*, 35–52.

[18] *Herodotus*, I, Trans. by A. D. Godley (LCL; Cambridge: Harvard University Press, 1946).

The identification of the foe in Jeremiah as the Scythians, based primarily on this passage from Herodotus with indirect support from cuneiform texts speaking of the Umman-Manda, is faced by several problems.[19] For one thing, establishing a precise chronology for the twenty-eight years of Scythian domination is difficult to do. In his article that follows, Cazelles has made an important attempt,[20] resulting in the following scenario: in 640–39 an offensive by Psammetichus I into Palestine was stopped by Scythian auxiliaries who were sent by a faltering Assyrian power; the beginning of the Scythian "domination" began then around 639/38 and lasted for 28 years; following the fall of Assyria, the Egyptians under Psammetichus and then Necho began an attempt to control Palestine by conquering Ashdod in 611/10 and Ashkelon, ejecting their Scythian garrisons, and then defeating and killing Josiah at Megiddo. However, in regard to Jeremiah, this reconstruction by Cazelles does pose a problem. If one accepts the 627/6 date for Jeremiah's call, the Scythians were already in control of Palestine. On the other hand, if the later 609 date is correct, the Scythians have already been defeated. In either case, the Scythians are eliminated as the "Foe from the North." Cazelles suggests that Jeremiah simply appropriated some of the language characterizing the earlier Scythian invasion to speak about a new foe, the Babylonians, when they became a powerful, threatening force later in Jeremiah's ministry.

Of course, this reconstruction depends largely on the credibility of the account by Herodotus. Whitley, for one, has argued that the entire story is replete with legendary lore, making for a good, fanciful, but certainly not historical story that amuses with the etiology of the "female sickness" infecting the Scythian hordes.[21] By contrast, both Cazelles and Vaggione give credibility to the narrative, arguing that the Scythian domination found expression in an Assyrian alliance, with the Scythians gaining in importance as Assyrian power waned.[22] In addition, Vaggione suggests the statement by Herodotus that the Scythians "ruled (ἐπέσχον) all Asia" should instead be translated: "they overran all Asia." While the Scythian presence ran in an east-west direction stretching from Persia to Asia Minor, nevertheless, they did make occasional raiding sorties into surrounding areas, including the one into Palestine. Vaggione also rejects the

---

[19]Currently no archaeological evidence exists that would support a Scythian presence in Palestine in the seventh century. Beth-shan was renamed Scythopolis, but Avi-Jonah has demonstrated that this name was first given to the site by the Ptolemies ("Scythopolis," *IEJ* 12 (1962) 123–34).

[20]Henri Cazelles, "Sophonie, Jérémie, et les Scythes en Palestine," *RB* 74 (1967) 24–44 (translated and reprinted in this volume).

[21]C. F. Whitley, "Carchemish and Jeremiah," *ZAW* 80 (1968) 42–44 (reprinted in this collection).

[22]Cazelles, "Sophonie, Jérémie, et les Scythes en Palestine," 41f.; and Richard P. Vaggione, "Over all Asia? The Extent of the Scythian Domination in Herodotus," *JBL* 92 (1973) 523–30.

interpretation that depicts Herodotus as describing an emerging Scythian empire.

It may be suggested at this point that if a Scythian-Assyrian alliance was indeed a political reality in 627/6, the call of the prophet in this same period could have included his anticipation that the Scythians, as Assyrian allies, might well invade Palestine to suppress the general uprising of the small Syro-Palestinian states, probably stimulated by the death of the powerful Assyrian king, Asshurbanipal. Obviously, this makes the prophet fallible in regard to the interpretation of current and future events, but this is a theological, not an historical problem.[23]

Two further problems are faced by the Scythian hypothesis. First, some of the description in the Jeremianic poems does not always appear to conform to the characteristics of a nomadic, tribal people: "ancient nation," use of chariots, besieging of cities, taking of captives, and fighting in battle formations.[24] And second, Jeremiah's promised threat of devastation by this enemy, if indeed he is speaking about the Scythians, would not have materialized. Consequently, he would have been discredited, reduced to silence, and eventually distraught enough to express his anger and humiliation in the "confessions." Jeremiah's credibility and prestige would have returned only after the devastating defeat of Judah and the death of Josiah in 609. It would be at this point, or perhaps later in 605, following the battle of Carchemish, that the prophet would have reinterpreted the enemy as the Babylonians.[25]

More commonly, however, those looking for an historical identity for the foe have pointed to the Babylonians, an identification clearly made in the prose (25:9). In fact, a number of scholars have argued that this identification was made from the very beginning of the prophet's ministry, whether we are speaking of the 627/26 or a 609 date. They contend that there is no other viable historical foe, the prophet's description fits the Babylonians very well, and a Babylonian foe keeps Jeremiah from being discredited by a Scythian invasion that failed to materialize.[26]

---

[23]On the basis of identifying the Scythians with the Umman-Manda in the Babylonian Chronicles, Malamat has suggested that the Scythians entered the Near East in 612 and later, in 609, made a brief raid into Palestine that lasted approximately two months ("The Historical Setting of Two Biblical Prophecies on the Nations," *IEJ* 1 (1950/51) 155–59).

[24]J. Philip Hyatt, "The Peril from the North in Jeremiah," *JBL* 59 (1940), 499–513.

[25]In his utilization of the theory of cognitive dissonance, Carroll has argued that Jeremiah, while he originally in all probability had no specific foe in mind, did come to identify this enemy as the Babylonians. However, this rather "open-ended" type of prophecy enabled the enemy to be reinterpreted mythologically and as a reference to various later historical events. He argues: "Such an adaptive approach to prediction greatly enlarged the scope of prophecy and made specific failures of predictions less important because they were capable of being reapplied to new situations and events" (*When Prophecy Failed* (New York: The Seabury Press, 1979) 173–74; also see his "Prophecy, Dissonance, and Jeremiah XXVI," *Transactions of the Glasgow University Oriental Society* 25 (1976) 12–23; reprinted in this collection).

[26]For example, Bright, *Jeremiah*, lxxxi–lxxxii; and Holladay, *Jeremiah*, 47–61.

A mythological-eschatological interpretation of the "foe from the North" has been made by Welch who argued that these poems in Jeremiah depict an eschatological judgment of a sinful world by God.[27] The North is not a geographical reference point, but rather a symbol of mysterious terror evoked by an angry God. Welch states that "the enemy was not a historical figure," but rather "the first faint hint of the conception which gave rise to the figure of Antichrist." No one has accepted this argument, at least in its present form. It is obvious that apocalyptic texts, e.g. the Book of Revelation, utilize this imagery, but do the apocalyptists capture the original nuances of the text? Paul Hanson's tracing of the origins of apocalyptic back to the sixth century may provide the basis for a re-examination of Welch's theory.[28]

Finally, a third category of argument, represented by Childs, suggests that Jeremiah originally had no particular enemy in mind, but only the impression of impending catastrophe.[29] For Childs, the prophet came to identify the enemy as Babylonia sometime after Assyria's defeat and the rise of the Babylonian empire. Accordingly, Jeremiah and other pre-exilic prophets clearly have in mind a human agent. However, in the Jeremiah tradition developing in the exilic and post-exilic periods, a coalescence occurred between "the enemy from the North" and the chaos tradition, characterized especially by the technical term רעש (8:16, 10:22, 4:22–26, and chps. 50–51). In these texts one finds a depiction of the eschatological shaking of the world, the return of chaos, and the appearance of a mythical, supra-human enemy. In this manner Childs brings together the earlier two positions.

V. THE TEXT OF JEREMIAH

Another issue of long-standing debate concerns the substantial differences between the preserved Massoretic Text (MT) and the Septuagint (LXX). The two major differences involve the length of the text and the ordering of the large literary complexes. The LXX, which contains close to 2700 fewer words than the MT, is approximately one-eighth shorter.[30] For example, several extensive sections of the MT are absent in the LXX (33:14–26, 39:4–13, 51:44b–49a, and 52:27b–30). In addition, the LXX and MT represent different redactional arrangements of materials, the most notable being the placement of "The Oracles against the Foreign Nations."

---

[27]Adam C. Welch, *Jeremiah. His Time and his Work* (Oxford: Blackwell, 1955) 110–26.

[28]*The Dawn of Apocalyptic* (Philadelphia: Fortress Press, 1975).

[29]Brevard Childs, "The Enemy from the North and the Chaos Tradition," *JBL* 78 (1959) 187–98 (reprinted in this collection). Also see, e.g., Georg Fohrer, *Introduction to the Old Testament* (New York: Abingdon Press, 1968) 391; and Thompson, *The Book of Jeremiah*, 87.

[30]Ralph W. Klein, *Textual Criticism of the Old Testament* (Philadelphia: Fortress Press, 1974) 20. For a convenient list of most of the MT words not found in the LXX, see Friedrich Giesebrecht, *Das Buch Jeremia* (HKAT; 2d ed.; Göttingen: Vandenhoeck und Ruprecht, 1907) xix–xxxiv.

While these oracles are located near the end of the MT (chps. 46–51), they are found in the middle of the LXX (i.e., 25:13af. of the MT). Furthermore the internal arrangement of the individual oracles of this same literary complex differs in both texts.[31]

In approaching the first major difference, two explanations have been offered: either the LXX translator(s) has deliberately abbreviated the Hebrew text, or the MT is expansionistic due to later scribal redaction that enlarged the shorter Hebrew manuscript tradition residing behind the LXX translation.[32] Important in this debate has been the discovery of four Qumran fragments of Jeremiah: 2QJer (beginning of the first century C.E.), 4QJer[a] (dated to the end of the third century B.C.E.), 4QJer[c] (dated no earlier than the end of the first century, B.C.E.), and 4QJer[b] (dated to the Hasmonean period).[33] The first three fragments represent a Jeremiah text that is generally the same as the MT, while the fourth, 4QJer[b], represents a shorter Hebrew text behind the Old Greek translation.[34] Thus, both the long text and the short text were present at Qumran.

For historians, the issue of which text best reflects the life and thought of the historical Jeremiah is one of great significance. Frank Cross, Gerald Janzen, and Ralph Klein have argued for the "superiority" of the short (LXX) text.[35] Janzen has concluded that the MT has experienced considerable secondary expansion which includes writing shorter names in their full form, adding titles and epithets to names, making explicit

[31] Eissfeldt provides a ready summary of the different arrangement of materials (*The Old Testament*, 348–49).

[32] Emanuel Tov, "L'incidence de la critique textuelle sur la critique littéraire dans le livre de Jérémie," *RB* 79 (1972) 189. It should not be ignored that the LXX has its own complicated problems in regard to origin and development. For a recent analysis of the Greek text of Jeremiah, see Tov's *The Septuagint Translation of Jeremiah and Baruch* (HSM 8; Missoula: Scholars Press, 1976). Here Tov argues that the first translation (Old Greek) is preserved in chapters 1–28 of Jeremiah, while 29–52 represent a major revision of the Old Greek translation. Tov's work is important in efforts to recapture the Hebrew precursor of the LXX, the so-called short text.

[33] For discussions of the Jeremiah fragments at Qumran as well as his theory of local texts, see Frank Moore Cross, Jr., *The Ancient Library of Qumran and Modern Biblical Studies* (rev. ed.; Garden City, New York: Doubleday, 1961) 168–94; "The Contribution of the Qumrân Discoveries to the Study of the Biblical Text," *IEJ* 16 (1966) 81–95; "The Evolution of a Theory of Local Texts." *1972 Proceedings. IOSCS Pseudepigrapha* (ed. by Robert Kraft; Septuagint and Cognate Studies 2; SBL, 1972) 108–26; and "The History of the Biblical Text in the Judean Desert," *HTR* 57 (1964) 281–99. These three articles are reprinted in *Qumran and the History of the Biblical Text* (ed. by Frank Moore Cross and Shemaryahu Talmon; Cambridge, Mass.: Harvard University Press, 1975).

[34] In 4QJer[b] a fragment of Jer 9:22–10:18 corresponds to the LXX in regard to three distinct features: the absence of four verses present in the MT (10:6–8, 10), the placement of v 5 of the MT after v 9, and the inversion of two words in v 4 of the MT: "hammer and nails" in contrast to the MT's "nails and hammer" (Cross, *Ancient Library of Qumran*, 187, n. 38).

[35] For Cross, see n. 33; Gerald Janzen, *Studies in the Text of Jeremiah* (HSM 6; Cambridge, Mass.: Harvard University Press, 1973); *idem*, "Double Readings in the Text of Jeremiah," *HTR* 60 (1967) 433–47; and Ralph Klein, *Textual Criticism of the Old Testament*.

pronoun subjects and objects of verbs, interpolations, doublets, and conflation. He concludes that the MT reflects "conscious scribal notation and
harmonization."[36] Following Janzen's conclusions, Klein asserts that when
doing textual criticism of Jeremiah, "preference should ordinarily be given
to the shorter LXX."[37]

Important in the work of Cross, Janzen, and Klein is the "theory of
local texts."[38] According to Cross, three textual families developed in
Palestine, Egypt, and probably Babylonia between the fifth and first
centuries, B.C.E. The Palestinian family is characterized by conflation,
glosses, synoptic additions, and other scribal changes. The Egyptian family
also represents a fuller text, but at least in the Pentateuch has not suffered
from the extensive additions found in the Palestinian textual tradition. The
Egyptian family is best undertood as a branch of the old Palestinian family.
The Babylonian family represents a short text and is known only in the
Pentateuch and former prophets. Its character varies, since in the Pentateuch it is conservative, pristine, and shows little expansion, while in
Samuel it is a poor, corrupt text. According to Cross, most of the Cave 4
manuscripts at Qumran are "proto-Massoretic" and "Palestinian" in type.
However, there are three groups of manuscripts which share some of the
characteristics of the Palestine text, but are not proto-Massoretic. In his
assessment of the textual families of Jeremiah Cross argues that the long
text, represented by 4QJer[a] and 4QJer[c], is proto-Massoretic and Palestinian.
Thus it is expansionistic. However, the third fragment, 4QJer[b], which
preserves the short text, is unique and perhaps developed in isolation,
probably in Egypt, as early as the fifth or even sixth century B.C.E. Unusual
in that it branches off from the Palestinian family very early, or even before
the Palestinian family began its special development, this text may be
"within a generation or two of Jeremiah's death in Egypt."[39] Therefore,
Cross concludes, the LXX, or better, the Old Greek translation of Jeremiah,
based on the shorter Egyptian Hebrew text, presents a more original and
thus superior textual tradition. The MT, on the other hand, preserves the
expansionistic Palestinian text that existed at least by 200 B.C.E. in Palestine.

The most provocative extension of the above arguments has been
made by Tov who agrees that the LXX's Hebrew precursor represents an
older Hebrew text than that of the MT.[40] However, he extends this
observation by arguing that the LXX and the MT are witnesses of two
distinct redactional stages in the development of the book. Tov combines
the text-critical work of Cross with the analysis of Hyatt that points to an

[36]*Studies in the Text of Jeremiah.*

[37]*Textual Criticism of the Old Testament,* 30.

[38]See n. 33. For a criticism of this theory, see George Howard, "Frank Cross and
Recensional Criticism," *VT* 21 (1971) 440–50.

[39]Cross, "The Evaluation of a Theory of Local Texts," *Qumran and the History of the
Biblical Text,* 309.

[40]Tov, "L'incidence de la critique textuelle," 189–99.

extensive redaction of Jeremiah by the Deuteronomic school.[41] In Tov's own analysis, the development of the text of Jeremiah may be explained as follows. Redaction I, represented by the LXX, was made by a redactor (perhaps Mowinkel's C) who added his comments to sources A and B. Redaction II, represented by the MT, was made by another, later redactor who had access to a text similar to but not identical with the text of redactor I. This second redactor either knew of a different arrangement of the Jeremiah text or made his own modifications. Moreover, he also added some new sections of poetry and prose, and inserted his own remarks throughout the three sources. In Tov's opinion, both redactors were members of the Deuteronomic school. Thus, he concludes that the Deuteronomic redaction of Jeremiah is more complex than previously thought. C is the result of two stages of redaction and parallels in this fashion the redactional stages of Deuteronomy and the Deuteronomistic History. Tov extends the work of Cross and Janzen by stressing that the redactional process contributes to an understanding of the issue of the differences between the shorter and longer texts.

The placement of literary complexes is a second major difference between the MT and the LXX. According to Janzen, the order of the LXX is the more original. In addressing the placement of the "Oracles against the Nations," he proposes the following scenario: after the various complexes of Jeremiah circulated for quite some time as independent units, they were brought together in an early form, and included 1:1–25:13b and 25:15–45:5. Then the collection dealing with the nations was inserted between these two larger groups because of three influences: the pattern of Isaiah and Ezekiel which have oracles against the nations in the middle of their texts, the presence of other oracular material dealing with the nations in this section of Jeremiah, and the sewing of the collection of the speeches against the nations on to earlier Hebrew leather manuscripts in a conservation effort to continue to use them.[42]

Childs also considers the LXX order to be the more original, since it probably reflects an earlier stage in the development of the book. In addition he argues that the MT represents a rearrangement of the earlier order that is due to two factors: the influence of other prophetic books which have similar oracles at the end and the concern to maintain a close connection between the oracles in 1–25 and the biographical materials in 26–45.[43]

---

[41]For a discussion of the analysis by Mowinckel and Hyatt, see section VI of this essay.

[42]Janzen, *Studies in the Text of Jeremiah*, 115–16.

[43]Brevard Childs, *Introduction to the Old Testament as Scripture* (Philadelphia: Fortress Press, 1979) 352. Carroll's remark is to the point: "Whichever may be the original arrangement, the fact that they are different indicates the freedom with which the versions developed and therefore emphasizes the significance of redaction in the Jeremiah tradition" (*From Chaos to Covenant*, 10).

The issue concerning the text of Jeremiah is of considerable importance, especially when scholars are primarily concerned to reconstruct the life and thought of the prophet. If, for example, Cross and others are correct in their arguments, the LXX, in spite of the fact that it is a translation with its own inherent problems, would provide a more historical representation of Jeremiah. On the other hand, the traditions-history approach would regard the MT as of greater value in that it provides additional material for examining how the prophet is shaped by his later interpreters. The issue is also reflected in Childs' canonical approach to the Old Testament which will be discussed below. In both his criticism of the limitations of the historical critical method and his emphasis on a canonical approach that is concerned to understand the process by which the biblical material was shaped by communities of faith, Childs does concern himself with textual criticism.[44] For Childs, the canonical approach values the MT over any other text in that the canonical text of first century Judaism is contained within this post-canonical MT. Unlike the MT, the LXX on the other hand ceased to function within the religious streams of ongoing Judaism. Obviously in his canonical approach, Childs is working with a different set of concerns than that of historians.

VI. THE COMPOSITION OF JEREMIAH

By far the most complicated and controversial issue in Jeremiah studies involves the analysis of the literary composition and development of the book.[45] In fact, the position one takes on this issue impacts dramatically on all the others. The contents of the book include four different types of literary materials: poetic oracles, prose sermons, first person narratives, and third person narratives. The interrelated questions which emerge from the various assessments of these materials involve the relationship between the poetry and prose, the distinguishing between the actual words of Jeremiah and those placed in his mouth by redactors and tradents, the reconstruction of the first (and second?) scroll of Baruch, and the transmission, growth, and final composition of the book. As will be discussed in section VII, the underlying concern is to determine which, if any, of these materials may be used to reconstruct the life, thought, and character of the prophet.

Literary Sources and Redaction

The pioneering work by Duhm was the first significant application of Pentateuchal source criticism to Jeremiah in order to explain the relation-

---

[44]Childs, *Introduction to the Old Testament*, 84–106.

[45]For recent surveys, see Siegfried Herrmann, "Forschung am Jeremiabuch," and T. R. Hobbs, "Some Remarks on the Composition and Structure of the Book of Jeremiah," *CBQ* 34 (1972) 257–75 (reprinted in this volume).

ships between the various types of literary materials.[46] Duhm concluded that the book consists of three major sources: the poetic speeches of Jeremiah (approximately 280 verses in the dirge meter, found primarily in chapters 1–25), the Book of Baruch (a biography of Jeremiah consisting roughly of 220 verses, located mostly in chapters 26–45), and a number of supplements (some 850 verses interspersed throughout the book, consisting of synagogue homilies and narrative influenced by a Deuteronomic style, and written to explain the exile).

Following this seminal analysis by Duhm, Mowinckel brought a greater literary precision to source analysis.[47] Arguing that the original book consisted of chapters 1–45 (46–52 were later additions), Mowinckel delineated four major literary sources. Source A is a collection of primarily metrical oracles from Jeremiah, found throughout chapters 1–25, which was shaped by an editor wishing to provide a comprehensive collection of the prophet's words, but at the same time avoiding extensive modifications and additions. The second source, B, is a prose narrative concerning the activities of the prophet, found in chapters 26–45. Written by an anonymous author, this source intended to demonstrate the relationship between the prophetic word and the events of history. C is the third source, and is comprised of prose speeches that reflect a Deuteronomic style and theology. Located throughout chapters 1–45, this source is made up of freely composed sermons, occasionally based on Jeremianic sayings. The fourth and final source, D, contains oracles about the future which were collected in chapters 30–31. Mowinckel concluded this last source was written by a non-prophetic author who inserted the collection into the book. Chronologically, A was written first, followed by B, C, and D. Mowinckel argued A originated in Egypt where Jeremiah and Baruch were taken and was put together by a redactor between 580 and 480 B.C.E. B also originated in Egypt, probably no later than 480 B.C.E. C was written in Palestine or Babylon around 400 B.C.E. However, for Mowinckel, D is impossible to date and locate precisely.

These two source analyses have continued to have a considerable impact on many scholars who have accepted their salient features with some modifications. Rudolph, for instance, sought to place more material into source A, argued that B was written by Baruch, and suggested that C's mostly Deuteronomic sermons are frequently based on Jeremianic sayings.[48] While not using the same nomenclature, Hyatt often agreed with Mowinckel's conclusions.[49] However, Hyatt redirected the understanding of source C into the categories of redaction criticism, arguing that this so-

---

[46]Bernhard Duhm, *Das Buch Jeremia* (Kurzer Hand-Commentar zum AT 2; Tübingen: J. C. B. Mohr, 1901) xi–xx.

[47]Sigmund Mowinckel, *Zur Komposition des Buches Jeremia* (Kristiania: Jacob Dybwad, 1914).

[48]*Jeremia*, xiv–xxii.

[49]"The Book of Jeremiah," 787–90.

called source was in actuality an extensive redaction of three earlier collections (two collections of poetic oracles—Baruch's first and second scrolls, which are similar to Mowinckel's source A, and Baruch's Memoirs which approximates Mowinckel's B source).[50] The Deuteronomic editors finished this major edition of the book around 550 B.C.E., perhaps in Egypt. The intent behind this edition, argued Hyatt, was to demonstrate that the prophet ". . . was in general agreement with the ideas and purposes of the Deuteronomic school." While the Deuteronomic editors used earlier materials, they freely added their own themes in a typically Deuteronomic style. For Hyatt the value of this edition in regard to the issue of the historical Jeremiah is mixed, since earlier material at times is preserved while much, on the other hand, is simply Deuteronomic theology placed in the prophet's mouth.

Hyatt's redactional analysis has been accepted and extended by Herrmann and, most recently, Thiel.[51] Thiel delineates in extensive fashion the major characteristics of the Deuteronomic redaction—language, key phrases, citations from Deuteronomy and the Deuteronomistic History, the use of preexisting Jeremianic sayings, the procedures of redaction, the concern to transmit without distortion earlier Jeremianic traditions, and the inclusion of Deuteronomic theology. The major new insertions included Deuteronomic covenant theology, the presentation of Jeremiah as a preacher of the law, the stressing of the old exodus tradition, the retributive interpretation of history, and oracles of future salvation for Judah. Thiel concurs with Hyatt that the redaction dates around 550 B.C.E., but places it in Judah, not Egypt.

The Prose Sermons[52]

Another understanding of C, the prose sermons, has emerged that radically differs with the one just outlined. T. H. Robinson also delineated three major groupings of materials: A (oracular poetry), B (biographical and historical prose), and C (autobiographical, literary prose or artistic poetry).[53] However, while his A and B sources are quite similar to the

---

[50]"The Deuteronomic Edition of Jeremiah," *Vanderbilt Studies in the Humanities* 1 (Nashville: Vanderbilt University Press, 1951) 71–95 (reprinted in this volume).

[51]Siegfried Herrmann, *Die prophetischen Heilserwartungen im Alten Testament* (BWANT 5; Stuttgart: Kohlhammer, 1965) 159–241. Herrmann argues Jeremiah has a conception of divine grace for the future. However, the extensive, systematic presentation of salvation for the future found in this book is the result of editing by Deuteronomic circles. Winfried Thiel, *Die deuteronomistische Redaction von Jeremia 1–25* (WMANT 41; Neukirchen-Vluyn: Neukirchener Verlag, 1973); and *Die deuteronomistische Redaktion von Jeremia 26–45* (WMANT 52; Neukirchen-Vluyn: Neukirchener Verlag, 1981).

[52]For a recent discussion, see C. Brekelmans, "Some Considerations on the Prose Sermons in the Book of Jeremiah," *Bijdragen* 34 (1973) 204–11.

[53]T. H. Robinson, "Baruch's Roll," *ZAW* 42 (1924) 209–21.

analysis by Mowinckel, it is his assessment of the C source that differs significantly. For Robinson, the sermons in C originate with Jeremiah himself, not with a Deuteronomic school. Robinson's thesis found later supporters in Eissfeldt, Weiser, Reventlow, Miller, Weippert, and Holladay.[54] In Eissfeldt's opinion, the prose sermons' Deuteronomic flavor simply indicates that the prophet on occasion used this sermonic style. Weiser agreed, adding that the preaching of Jeremiah took shape within the covenant cult in which this type of preaching flourished. Reventlow also argued that the prose sermons were liturgical-paraenetic sermons which originated within a cultic setting, and thus were a significant part of the tradition inherited by Jeremiah when he became a cult prophet.

Taking his cue from Eissfeldt, Miller even suggested that the scroll of Baruch originally consisted only of prose speeches (see below). Jeremiah, we are told, dictated these oracles to Baruch in a Deuteronomistic sermonic style, because it would be a familiar one to Baruch's listening audience.

Last of all, Weippert has argued that the artistic prose speeches have their roots in the metrically formed prophetic preaching of Jeremiah, and in fact represent an authentic Jeremianic tradition which stands closer in time to the prophet than even the biographical narratives. Indeed, these prose speeches, says Weippert, are really neither sermons nor Deuteronomic, but rather are the paraenetic portions of the prophet's proclamation designed to admonish the people to repent. For Weippert, influence actually works in the opposite direction: it is the Deuteronomists and their sermons who are dependent on the prose speeches of Jeremiah. Holladay, who has made extensive efforts to extract Jeremianic sayings from the prose sermons,[55] believes that Weippert's analysis solves the problem of the prose speeches.

---

[54]Eissfeldt, *The Old Testament*, 350–55; Weiser, *Das Buch des Propheten Jeremia*, xxxvif.; H. Graf Reventlow, "Gattung und Überlieferung in der 'Tempelrede Jeremias', Jer 7 und 26," *ZAW* 81 (1969) 315–52; John Wolff Miller, *Das Verhältnis Jeremias und Hesekiels sprachlich und theologisch untersucht* (Assen: Van Gorcum, 1955); Helga Weippert, *Die Prosareden des Jeremiabuches* (BZAW 132; Berlin; Walter de Gruyter, 1973); and William Holladay, "A Fresh Look at 'Source B' and 'Source C' in Jeremiah," *VT* 25 (1975) 394–412 (reprinted in this volume).

[55]See his "Prototype and Copies: A New Approach to the Poetry-Prose Problem in the Book of Jeremiah," *JBL* 79 (1960) 351–67; and "Style, Irony, and Authenticity in Jeremiah," *JBL* 81 (1962) 44–54. In his article reprinted in this collection ("Relations between Poetry and Prose in the Book of Jeremiah with Special Reference to Jeremiah III 6–11 and XII 14–17," *VTS Congress Volume, Vienna* (ed. J. A. Emerton; Leiden: E. J. Brill, 1981) 220–237), W. McKane has engaged in a penetrating critique of Thiel and Weippert for concentrating too much on the issue of the Deuteronomic or non-Deuteronomic character of the prose sermons of Jeremiah. Thiel is criticized for attempting to make the prose too uniform and systematic, while Weippert attempts to make the impossible case that the multivarious prose speeches could somehow derive from Jeremiah during his lifetime. Instead, McKane asserts we should spend our time understanding the ways the prose functions intrinsically within the Book of Jeremiah.

A somewhat differently nuanced assessment of the prose sermons has been made by Bright and Muilenburg.[56] Bright argued that while the style of the prose discourses is "closely akin" to the style of Deuteronomic literature, nevertheless, they still possess their own distinctive, literary character. Thus it is wrong to classify these sermons as Deuteronomic. Secondly, he concluded that the prose style of the sermons is the "characteristic rhetorical prose of the seventh/sixth centuries." Thirdly, while agreeing that the prose sermons are not the actual words of the prophet, they still had their origins in his preaching. They were then remembered, preserved, transmitted, repeated, and reformulated by later disciples. Still, Bright considered these sermons to be trustworthy representations of Jeremiah's thoughts and activities, especially since they probably achieved fixed form within several decades after Jeremiah's death. Therefore, for Bright, there are no significant differences between the Jeremiah in the poetry and the Jeremiah in the prose sermons. The point to note in this is Bright's acknowledgment of the work of tradition circles in casting the shape of these sermons. Muilenburg, on the other hand, argued that these sermons were the transformation of Jeremianic speeches into a Deuteronomistic prose style. However, the one responsible is Baruch, who, being a scribe, would have used typically Deuteronomistic (scribal) language.

The suggestion that we have in C a recasting of Jeremianic oracles into prose by either a tradition circle (Bright) or by an individual, Baruch, belonging to a specific tradition circle (Muilenburg), points in the direction of another major approach to those sermons: the traditio-historical method. The Scandinavian scholars have usually opted for a lengthy period of oral transmission of prophetic oracles before they were eventually written down. Birkeland has suggested that, in comparison with the poetic speeches, the prose sermons underwent a longer period of oral transmission that allowed for more extensive reformulation.[57] In 1946 Mowinckel revised his earlier position by choosing to speak of traditions and tradents rather than sources, authors, and redactors.[58] In this reassessment, he concluded that some of the Deuteronomic prose sermons were variants of metrically formed sayings belonging to Baruch's scroll which had undergone considerable transformation in a Deuteronomistic spirit. Thus, while the sermons on occasion may provide us with the thoughts of Jeremiah, they are not his

---

[56]Bright, *Jeremiah*, lv–lxxviii; "The Date of the Prose Sermons of Jeremiah," *JBL* 70 (1951) 15–35 (reprinted in this volume); "The prophetic reminiscence: its place and function in the book of Jeremiah," *Biblical Essays* (Proceedings of the Ninth Meeting of 'Die Ou-Testamentiese Werkgemeenskap in Suid-Afrika', 1966) 11–30; "The Book of Jeremiah: Its Structure, Its Problems, and their Significance for the Interpreter," *Int* 9 (1955) 259–78; and James Muilenburg, "Baruch the Scribe," *Proclamation and Presence* (ed. John Durham and J. R. Porter; Richmond: John Knox Press, 1970) 215–38 (reprinted in this volume).

[57]Harris Birkeland, *Zum hebräischen Traditionswesen* (ANVAO 2; Oslo: Jacob Dybwad, 1938); and "Zur Kompositionsfrage des Buches Jeremia," *Le Monde Oriental* 31 (1937) 49–62.

[58]Sigmund Mowinckel, *Prophecy and Tradition* (Oslo: Jacob Dybwad, 1946).

actual words. Mowinckel stressed that this interaction between the community and the living tradition led to the creation of new prophecies and the interpretation of older ones. While regarding the recovery of original words behind the prose speeches to be a precarious undertaking, nevertheless, he argued the attempt should still be made.

In several more recent studies, Janssen, Nicholson, and Rietzschel have extended Mowinckel's ground-breaking work of 1946, and have reached very similar conclusions about the prose sermons.[59] In general, these scholars have argued that the prose sermons of Jeremiah had their origins within a Deuteronomic preaching tradition that had its roots in the pre-exilic period. Rietzschel specifically identifies the tradition circle as country Levites whose preaching originally appeared in Deuteronomy. This same circle, appropriating some authentic Jeremianic poetic sayings, shaped them according to the major features of its own literary and theological tradition, especially during the period of the Babylonian exile. Thus, these homiletical and didactic sermons were the result of the hermeneutical efforts of the Deuteronomic preachers to enable the prophet to speak to a new generation of Judah. The specific location for this activity was probably the synagogue. However, efforts to recover the "authentic sayings" of Jeremiah behind these sermons is generally discouraged as either unsympathetic to the importance of this formulation or an impossibility. Carroll, who agrees with the major features of this approach, goes even further in removing these sermons from any direct connection with Jeremiah. He concludes these are free compositions of the Deuteronomists.[60]

The Prose Narratives

Similar differences have developed over the nature and development of the biographical narratives found in 26–45 (B). It is conceded that these narratives are not a biography, but rather include an account that provides the context for some of the speeches and activities of the prophet (26–36) and a "passion narrative" that portrays in vivid fashion his suffering (37–45).[61] Scholars who have taken the psychological-biographical approach have tended to see Baruch as the author of these narratives at least in an earlier form.[62] However, the assumption that Baruch is Jeremiah's "biog-

---

[59]E. Janssen, *Juda in der Exilszeit* (FRLANT 69; Göttingen: Vandenhoeck und Ruprecht, 1956); E. W. Nicholson, *Preaching to the Exiles* (New York: Schocken Books, 1970); and Claus Rietzschel, *Das Problem der Urrolle* (Gütersloh: Gerd Mohn, 1966).

[60]Carroll, *From Chaos to Covenant*, 12–13, 249–68.

[61]See, e.g., Martin Kessler, "Jeremiah Chapters 26–45 Reconsidered," *JNES* 27 (1968) 81–88; and H. Kremers, "Leidensgemeinschaft mit Gott im Alten Testament. Eine Untersuchung der 'biographischen' Berichte im Jeremiabuch," *EvT* 13 (1953) 122–40.

[62]E.g., Bright, *Jeremiah*, lxvii; Duhm, *Das Buch Jeremia*, xiv–xv; Eissfeldt, *The Old Testament*, 354; Hyatt, "The Book of Jeremiah," 787; Rudolph, *Jeremia*, xv–xvi; Thompson, *The Book of Jeremiah*, 43; Volz, *Der Prophet Jeremia*, xlivf.; and Weiser, *Das Buch des Propheten Jeremia*, xl.

rapher" is rarely substantiated. Generally one finds the statement that Baruch, a contemporary and companion of the prophet, would have been an eyewitness to Jeremiah's activities. In addition, since chapter 36 indicates Baruch's part in the recording of the early speeches of the prophet, it is argued he also wrote at least some of the narratives in an earlier form. This position does not always deny later redaction of the narratives, especially by the Deuteronomic school. But it does find a solid, historical kernel within many of these narratives.

However, since Mowinckel raised the issue in 1914, voices of dissent have been heard. In his 1914 book, Mowinckel chose to reject Baruch as the author, and pointed instead to an anonymous writer who composed B in Egypt no later than 480.[63] May developed Mowinckel's thesis, arguing that to identify Baruch as the "biographer" is an *a priori* assumption based on no real evidence, other than chapter 36 which presents the scribe as an amanuensis, not an author.[64] May's own identification was that of a "biographer" deeply steeped in the Deuteronomic tradition who also wrote at least some of the prose speeches. The major theme of this anonymous writer who wrote in the first half of the fifth century was the reunification of Israel and Judah under a restored Davidic dynasty. May's arguments included literary influence on these narratives by Deuteronomy and II Isaiah, some close affinities with late texts (Obadiah, Ezra, and Nehemiah), and similarities to the redactions of I Zechariah and Ezekiel.

Following the lead of May, Nicholson has presented the most significant challenge against the Baruch hypothesis. He argued that both the prose sermons and the prose narratives were shaped by a Deuteronomic circle active within the synagogue community of the Babylonian exile. Thus, the nature of the prose narratives is not historical biography, but rather theological. These narratives, filled with Deuteronomic themes, are concerned to present a prophet addressing hermeneutically the issues and concerns of a community still in exile.[65]

Finally, Wanke has made a detailed analysis of the narratives and concluded that they are not a uniform work by one author with a single point of view, but rather are the combination of three separate tradition complexes with different circles, origins, and developments: (1) 19:1–20:6, 26–29, 36; (2) 37–44; and (3) 45 and 51:59–64.[66] Wanke's arguments are based on delineating the unique form critical and theological features of each collection. In regard to theology, for example, Wanke argued complex

---

[63] *Zur Komposition des Buches Jeremias*, 30.

[64] Herbert May, "Towards an Objective Approach to the Book of Jeremiah: The Biographer," *JBL* 61 (1942) 139–55.

[65] *Preaching to the Exiles*. Carroll carries the argument by Nicholson a step further by suggesting that one concern of the tradents was to legitimate their claims in the power struggle ensuing in the post-exilic period (*From Chaos to Covenant*, 249–68).

[66] Gunther Wanke, *Untersuchungen zur sogenannten Baruchschrift* (BZAW 122; Berlin: Walter de Gruyter, 1971).

JEREMIAH IN MODERN RESEARCH

2 concentrates on Jeremiah's prophetic existence and demonstrates that through the failure of his preaching his personal existence achieved integration. By contrast complex 1 stresses the continuation of prophetic preaching in the face of persecution and inner doubts, while complex 3 indicates that the preaching of the prophet is transmitted by personalities closely connected with the prophet.[67]

The Scroll of Baruch

Jeremiah 36 narrates the story of Jeremiah's dictation to Baruch of his early oracles, from the beginning of his ministry down to the fourth year of Jehoiakim (605 B.C.). After Jehoiakim's destruction of the scroll read by Baruch, the narrative has Jeremiah dictating a second scroll recorded by Baruch and concludes with a statement that could be interpreted as indicating additional, similar words were added to the content of the original scroll.

Efforts to reconstruct the first and even a second scroll of Baruch are as different as they are seemingly endless. However, a few basic categories of interpretation have taken shape. The majority of scholars have regarded at least part of Mowinckel's source A to be the most likely candidate for Baruch's scroll(s).[68] This indicates the historical veracity attributed by these scholars to the poetic speeches: Jeremiah spoke them, remembered them, and dictated them, while Baruch, his amanuensis and companion, recorded them. A second major position has appeared which includes some or all of the prose sermons in Baruch's scroll(s). Miller presented the extreme form of this position when he argued that the prose sermons alone originally comprised the scroll of Baruch.[69]

Curiously, the historicity of chapter 36 has rarely been questioned, since it has provided such an important basis for authenticating the historicity of at least part of the Jeremiah tradition and an indication, however slight, of the origin and growth of the book.[70] However, Carroll has recently done just that, and if he is right, the implications for the

---

[67]One other redactional analysis should be mentioned: Karl-Friedrich Pohlmann, *Studien zum Jeremiabuch* (FRLANT 118; Göttingen: Vandenhoeck und Ruprecht, 1978). Pohlmann, rejecting the term Deuteronomic, argues that 21: 1–10, 24, and 37–44 are a fourth century, "*golah*-oriented," redactional complex that is concerned to condemn those who remained behind or were exiled in Egypt (i.e., Zedekiah, Jerusalem, and Judah) and to substantiate the salvation and importance of the Babylonian exiles.

[68]E.g., Rietzschel, *Das Problem der Urrolle*; Holladay, *The Architecture of Jeremiah 1–20* (Lewisburg: Bucknell University Press, 1976), 169–74; *idem*, "The Identification of the Two Scrolls of Jeremiah," *VT* 30 (1980) 452–67; and Hyatt, "Jeremiah," 780f.

[69]E.g., Eissfeldt, *The Old Testament*, 350f.; Weiser, *Das Buch des Propheten Jeremia*, xxxvif.; and Miller, *Das Verhältnis Jeremias und Hesekiels*.

[70]See, e.g., Martin Kessler, "Form-Critical Suggestions on Jer 36," *CBQ* 28 (1966) 389–401; and "The Significance of Jer 36," *ZAW* 81 (1969) 381–83. Kessler staunchly defends the historicity of chapter 36. Of course, many scholars despair of ever reconstructing the scroll(s) (cf., e.g., Bright, *Jeremiah*, lxi).

psychological-biographical approach would be severe. Carroll argues that
chapter 36 is a literary fiction written to legitimate the role of the scribes in
the formulation of the Jeremiah traditions, a procedure that parallels the
story of the discovery of the law-book in the temple during the reign of
Josiah (2 Kgs 22:8–13) which is designed to legitimate Deuteronomy.[71]
Carroll's argument receives unlikely support from an article by Charles
Isbell which demonstrates striking similarities between 2 Kgs 22–23 and Jer
36.[72] While Isbell believes the author of Jer 36 had the Kings narrative
available as a source, it is more probable that both originated within the
same Deuteronomic circle.

VII. THE QUEST FOR THE HISTORICAL JEREMIAH

As often emphasized in this essay, the stimulus behind most Jeremiah
research during this century has been the quest to discover the Jeremiah of
history.[73] The debate over this issue has been most vocal in three major
areas: the poetry-prose problem, the call, and the confessions.

The Poetry-Prose Problem

As is obvious from the discussion in the previous section, a large
number of scholars, whom we would loosely categorize under the heading
of the psychological-biographical approach, have endeavored to distill as
much historically "authentic" material from the Jeremiah traditions as
possible. Thus, it is often asserted that a particular section or passage goes
back to Jeremiah himself or at least to his scribe Baruch, an "eye-witness"
of the prophet's life. In this regard, then, the poetic oracles of judgment
usually found in Mowinckel's source A have been regarded as Jeremianic
by most scholars.[74] In addition, the "biographical" narratives (B) have
often been attributed to Baruch in an effort to substantiate their essential
historicity.[75] Furthermore, the efforts to rediscover "authentic" sayings,
motifs, and ideas of Jeremiah within the prose sermons (C) are designed
not only to glean as much material as possible for reconstructing the
Jeremiah of history, but also to emphasize that even later redactions are
based on primary material from the prophet's words and actions.[76] Several

[71]Carroll, *From Chaos to Covenant*, 15–16.

[72]Charles D. Isbell, "2 Kings 22:3–23:24 and Jeremiah 36: A Stylistic Comparison," *JSOT*
8 (1978) 33–45.

[73]For two recent discussions, see Carroll's "The Quest of the Historical Jeremiah," *From
Chaos to Covenant*, 5–30; and David Jobling, "The Quest of the Historical Jeremiah:
Hermeneutical Implications of Recent Literature," *USQR* 34 (1978) 3–12.

[74]E.g., see Mowinckel, *Zur Komposition des Buches Jeremia*, 19–20; and Hyatt, "The
Book of Jeremia," 787.

[75]E.g., see Bright, *Jeremiah*, lxvii; Strobel, *Trauer um Jerusalem*, 8–9; and Claus
Westermann, *Jeremia* (Stuttgart: Calwer, 1967) 13–15.

[76]E.g., Holladay, "The Recovery of Poetic Passages of Jeremiah."

scholars have even argued that the prose sermons are indeed Jeremiah's own preaching tradition.[77] These scholars generally conclude their investigations by stating that we possess more historical information about Jeremiah than any other person in the O.T.

On the other hand, there has been an increasing tendency (the so-called traditions-history approach) to question the historicity of each of the Jeremianic traditions, either directly or indirectly, by arguing that the nature of these traditions is theological, not historical. While Jeremiah's "authorship" of the poetic judgment speeches (A) has been an almost unassailable dogma, Herrmann has challenged even this traditional tenet, calling for a reassessment due to the presence of later poetic traditions associated with the prophet, as for example the one represented by Lamentations.[78] Secondly, Baruch's authorship of the biographical narratives (B) has at times been impugned, most seriously in Wanke's recent study which points to three cycles of tradition in B, each of which has a different author, origin, theme, development, and form. While Wanke does not eliminate Baruch as a possible author for the first cycle, he remarks that there is no compelling evidence to regard Baruch as the author.[79] In addition, Carroll has challenged the assumption behind the rather large role given to Baruch in the formation of the various Jeremianic traditions. Baruch's part really comes down to chapter 36, which could well be, in Carroll's assessment, a creation by the Deuteronomic scribes to legitimate their role in the formation of the traditions.[80] Further, the prose sermons (C) have frequently been regarded as non-Jeremianic, though how much "distortion" of the prophet's own theology occurs is vigorously contested.[81] Nicholson's sympathetic treatment points to their Deuteronomic origins as part of the effort to address the concerns of the exilic community.[82] Thus, these non-Jeremianic sermons are theological, not historical in nature. In regard to C, some scholars have questioned the possibility and at times the appropriateness of attempting to discover "actual words" of Jeremiah in these texts.[83]

---

[77]E.g., Eissfeldt, *The Old Testament*, 350–55; Miller, *Das Verhältnis Jeremias und Hesekiels*; and Weiser, *Das Buch des Propheten Jeremia*, xxxvif.

[78]Herrmann, "Forschung am Jeremiabuch," 488–89.

[79]Wanke, *Untersuchungen zur sogenannten Baruchschrift*. As noted above, Nicholson regards the narratives as Deuteronomic (*Preaching to the Exiles*).

[80]Carroll, *From Covenant to Chaos*, 15–16.

[81]Hyatt sees considerable distortion occurring on occasion ("The Deuteronomic Edition of Jeremiah," 92, *et passim*).

[82]Nicholson, *Preaching to the Exiles*. McKane prefers to speak of many layers of commentary made in prose on the earlier poetic speeches ("Relationships between Poetry and Prose").

[83]E.g., Rietzschel, *Das Problem der Urrolle*.

The Call of Jeremiah[84]

The call of the prophet in chapter 1 has been fertile ground for the psychological-biographical approach to Jeremiah. This text, assumed at least in its kernel (vv 4–10) to come from Jeremiah himself, is thought to reflect the interiority and personality of the prophet who only reluctantly entered into the role of an individual prophet not bound to an institutional office, and continued to remain in tension with this role. Skinner has argued that the call's emphasis on "personal predestination" and eventual "self-surrender to a personal Being" were formative principles which shaped his self-consciousness. According to Skinner, the impress of this privatistic call became so formidable a force that it enabled the prophet to subdue inner doubts and withstand the external hostility he was to encounter.[85] Habel and Holladay have added that this narrative, so shaped by earlier accounts of calls of charismatic figures, especially that of Moses, demonstrates that the prophet came to see himself as the prophet like Moses (cf. Dtr 18:15–22).[86]

By contrast, several scholars have challenged the cogency of this approach to the call. Also recognizing the traditional, formal structure and content of the call, Reventlow has interpreted Jeremiah's call as a typical ordination ritual for a person entering the office of cult prophet, i.e. the public mediary between God and the people.[87] Thus, for Reventlow, both the traditional form and language of the call provide no insight into the personality and ideology of the prophet himself. Gunneweg has moderated Reventlow's position by noting it is possible that the traditional form and language of the call are experienced in a personal way. Nevertheless, he is equally critical of the psychological-biographical interpretation of the call, an interpretation that retrojects scholars' own modern individualism and piety into the ancient prophets.[88] Carroll has concluded that the Deuteronomic redaction is responsible for linking Jeremiah's call to Moses and Sinai, as well as other prophetic calls. Thus, chapter one tells us more about the redactors than the interiority of the prophet.[89] Herrmann,

---

[84]For a summary of the two approaches to the call, with his own mediating position, see J. Schreiner, "Jeremiasberufung (Jer 1, 4–19), ein Textanalyse," in Homenaje a Juan Prado (ed. by L. Alvarez Verdes and E. J. Álonso Hernandez; Madrid: Talleres Gráf, 1975) 131–45.

[85]Skinner, Prophecy and Religion, 18–34.

[86]Norman Habel, "The Form and Significance of the Call Narratives," ZAW 77 (1965) 297–323; and William Holladay, "The Background of Jeremiah's Self-Understanding," JBL 83 (1964) 153–64 (reprinted in this volume); "Jeremiah and Moses: Further Observations," JBL 85 (1966) 17–27.

[87]H. Graf Reventlow, Liturgie und prophetisches Ich bei Jeremia (Gütersloh: Gerd Mohn, 1963) 24–77.

[88]A. H. J. Gunneweg, "Ordinationsformular oder Berufsbericht in Jeremiah I," Glaube Geist Geschichte (FS Ernst Benz; ed. by Gerhard Müller und Winfried Zeller, Leiden: E. J. Brill, 1967) 91–98.

[89]Carroll, From Chaos to Covenant, 31–58, especially p. 49.

speaking of the Jeremiah of tradition, including the prophet presented in the Deuteronomic redaction of the call, concludes that the redaction has made the prophet into a symbol of the exilic community's past (suffering and destruction), its present call to repentance, its future hope for redemption, and its mission to the nations.[90]

The Confessions[91]

The "Confessions" have been the source of the greatest controversy in regard to the quest for the historical Jeremiah. These prophetic dialogues with Yahweh comprise the linchpin of the psychological-biographical approach to Jeremiah, for they are considered to be the primary source for understanding the interiority of the prophet, particularly his tensions with God, religious and political officials, and the prophetic role.[92] These privatistic laments are seen as demonstrating the prophet's common human weaknesses which erupted into harsh complaints and even vigorous attacks on God, especially during periods of intense persecution. While the confessions are not specifically dated, two periods have generally been regarded as the time when he may have uttered these complaints: the period of persecution by Jehoiakim or perhaps earlier, when the "Foe from the North" did not materialize for many years. However, the recognition that these confessions are couched in the form of the individual lament has raised serious questions about whether they are indeed either the prophet's own creation or expressive of his own psychology and life. This problem is only intensified by the recognition that 20:14-18 is very similar to and possibly dependent on the lament of Job 3.[93] Nevertheless, the psychological-

---

[90]Siegfried Herrmann, "Die Bewältigung der Krise Israels," in *Beiträge zur Alttestamentlichen Theologie* (FS Walther Zimmerli; ed. by H. Donner, R. Hanhart, and R. Smend; Göttingen: Vandenhoeck und Ruprecht, 1977) 164-78. For an extensive analysis of the Deuteronomic redaction of the call, see Thiel, *Die deuteronomistische Redaktion von Jeremia 1-25*, 62-79.

[91]While minor variations exist in regard to the texts assigned to this "collection," the following are usually included: 11:18-23, 12:1-6, 15:10-21, 17:14-18, 18:18-23, 20:7-13, and 20:14-18.

[92]Walter Baumgartner, *Die Klagegedichte des Jeremia* (BZAW 32: Giessen: Alfred Töpelmann, 1917); G.-M. Behler, *Les confessions de Jérémie* (Casterman: Éditions de Maredsous, 1959); John Berridge, *Prophet, People, and the Word of Yahweh* (Basel Studies of Theology 4; Zurich: EVZ Verlag, 1970) 114f.; Sheldon Blank, "The Prophet as Paradigm," in *Essays in Old Testament Ethics* (ed. by J. L. Crenshaw and John T. Willis; New York: Ktav, 1974) 111-30; John Bright, "Jeremiah's Complaints—Liturgy or Expressions of Personal Distress?" *Proclamation and Presence* (ed. J. I. Durham and J. R. Porter; Richmond: John Knox Press, 1970) 189-214; *idem*, "A Prophet's Lament and Its Answer: Jeremiah 15:10-21," *Int* 28 (1974) 59-74; William Holladay, *Jeremiah*, 88-106; Helmut Lampartner, *Dein Wort war zu mir Mächtig. Die Bekenntnisse des Propheten Jeremia* (Metzingen: Ernst Franz, 1965); Joseph L. Mihelic, "Dialogue with God," *Int* 14 (1960) 43-50; Strobel, *Trauer um Jerusalem*, 37-40, 50-53; and Thompson, *The Book of Jeremiah*, 88-92.

[93]We should remind ourselves that Psalms criticism has debated the issue of whether there are indeed "individual" laments in the Psalms. Some have suggested, of course, that "indi-

biographical approach has articulated the view that by means of form criticism and the search for the unique in these confessions, one is able to see how the prophet adapted a traditional form and common themes to fit his own temperament, theology, and life experiences.[94]

A variation of this approach that included a significant new direction in the understanding of these texts has been made by von Rad and Zimmerli. Not only are the confessions the outpourings of Jeremiah's own inner affliction and turmoil, but also expressions of a new development in the prophetic office. Now the prophet is no longer only a mouthpiece of God, but also a suffering servant whose entire life is involved in the prophetic task. As intercessor, Jeremiah, more than the earlier prophets, bears the entire range of the human needs of his community within himself.[95] While von Rad stresses the darkest dimensions of the prophet's suffering, Zimmerli speaks of two primary results: the writing down of the prophetic word and an insight into the nature of divine suffering.

A radically different approach has been taken by Reventlow who, as noted above, concluded that Jeremiah held the cultic office of prophetic mediator. Hence, the confessions are liturgical laments in which the individual "I" is swallowed up in the collective "We." The prophet in his public laments has merged with the corporate community in voicing their complaint to God, by serving as intercessor on their behalf, and by returning the divine response to the people. This interpretation precludes the possibility of discovering any private thoughts and experiences of the prophet in the confessions.[96]

Finally, Gerstenberger's analysis of 15:10–21 has traced the growth of this lament from an original nucleus consisting of an individual complaint coupled with a priestly oracle of assurance, both of which were inserted into the Jeremianic tradition by an editor to complement the theme of the prophet's sufferings found in the biographical narratives.[97] Other later

---

vidual" laments are actually community laments, where the individual "I" is either the spokesman or a literary technique for the community.

[94]Baumgartner, Die Klagegedichte des Jeremia. Franz D. Hubmann's recent analysis follows this approach by interpreting 11:18–12:6 and 15:10–21 as the prophet's own confessions specifically arising out of his conflict with the false prophets. However, he also admits that these texts experienced later editing and eventually took on a paradigmatic function (Untersuchungen zu den Konfessionen: Jer 11, 18–12, 6 und Jer 15, 10–21 [Forschung zur Bibel 30; Würzburg: Echter Verlag, 1978]).

[95]Gerhard von Rad, "Die Konfessionen Jeremias," EvT 3 (1936) 265–76 (translated and reprinted in this volume); Walther Zimmerli, "Jeremia, der leidtragende Verkünder," Internationale Katholische Zeitschrift 4 (1975) 97–111; and idem, "Frucht der Anfechtung des Propheten," Die Botschaft und die Boten (FS Hans Walter Wolff; ed. by J. Jeremias und L. Perlitt; Neukirchen-Vluyn: Neukirchener Verlag, 1981) 131–146 (translated and reprinted in this volume).

[96]Reventlow, Liturgie und prophetisches Ich bei Jeremia, 205–57.

[97]E. Gerstenberger, "Jeremiah's Complaints: Observations on Jer 15:10–21," JBL 82 (1963) 393–408. Carroll argues that the presentation of Jeremiah as an intercessor is a

redactions were made, until this lament achieved its present form. Nothing, not even the nucleus, originated with the prophet himself. Gunneweg extended Gerstenberger's assessment to all of the confessions and concluded that all of the laments were shaped by later tradents.[98] What we have in these texts, concludes Gunneweg, is an interpretation of Jeremiah as a paradigm of righteous suffering for the later Jewish community. However, he doubts that these texts significantly distort an accurate picture of the historical Jeremiah.[99]

The Quest and the Lives of Jeremiah

In examining the various lives of Jeremiah written over the years, all of them are written by scholars who have taken the psychological-biographical approach.[100] This group, arguing that much of the biblical book reflects the historical Jeremiah, has painted a portrait of Jeremiah with the brushes of classical liberal theology. Thus, the prophet is portrayed in the guise of an individualist functioning under the impress of a private call that freed him from the constraints of institutional office. This Jeremiah was an antagonist of major political and religious institutions which had corrupted the ethical nature of true religion: kingship, temple cult, scribal interpretation of torah, and cultic prophecy. An eventual opponent of the reform of Josiah because it was primarily concerned with unimportant, religious externals, Jeremiah comes to be viewed as the father of personal religion characterized by internal, spiritual, and ethical qualities which rejected or spiritualized the external formalism of cultic religion, including tradition, sacrifice, festival, and temple. It is the personal relationship with a demanding, but loving Father God, not the communal experience of formal worship, that characterizes the apex of Jeremiah's and thus Israel's religion.

By contrast, those more inclined towards the traditions-history approach have not produced a life of Jeremiah, for obvious reasons.[101] For

---

creation of redactors that in fact expresses the experiences, thoughts, and feelings of the exiles (*From Chaos to Covenant*, 107–35). Cf. Peter Welten, "Leiden und Leidenserfahrung im Buch Jeremiah," *ZTK* 74 (1977) 123–50.

[98] A. H. J. Gunneweg, "Konfession oder Interpretation im Jeremiabuch," *ZTK* 67 (1970) 395–416.

[99] Recently, D. Clines and D. Gunn have critiqued both the psychological-biographical and the traditions-history approach and have taken something of a mediating position, at least in regard to chapter 20. According to them the two pieces are an individual lament (vv 7–13), which has a kernel (vv 7–9) originating in the prophet's own life situation, and a self-curse (14–18), which does not express the prophet's own inner despair, but rather is a conventional utterance of distress that accompanies a judgment speech or woe oracle ("Form, Occasion and Redaction in Jeremiah 20," *ZAW* 88 (1976) 390–409).

[100] Cf., e.g., Sheldon Blank, *Jeremiah, Man and Prophet* (Cincinnati: Hebrew Union College Press, 1961); J. Philip Hyatt, *Jeremiah. Prophet of Courage and Hope* (New York: Abingdon, 1958); and Moshe Weinfeld, "Jeremiah and the Spiritual Metamorphosis of Israel," *ZAW* 88 (1976) 17–56.

[101] Carroll, *From Chaos to Covenant*, 25–29.

this approach concludes that what we find in the corpus of Jeremiah traditions are in large measure the creations of later scribes and religious communities who sought to enable the prophet to speak to a variety of later issues and situations. Thus he is a proclaimer of divine judgement (A), or a priestly mediator (the confessions), or a preacher of the law (C), or a suffering servant who at least bears the sins and sufferings of the nation in himself if he does not remove them (the "passion history" in 37–45).

If the quest for the historical Jeremiah is to continue, several points articulated by Jobling should be taken into view.[102] First, Jobling admonishes Jeremiah scholars to learn from the advances as well as the pitfalls of Jesus research that has capitivated the interests of New Testament scholarship. Second, he urges scholars to become aware of their own hermeneutical positions, lest they continue to create the prophet in their own image. And third, Jobling stresses the importance of seeking out the variety of views about the prophet that were formative in the shaping of the different Jeremianic traditions.

VIII. NEW DIRECTIONS IN JEREMIAH STUDIES

Due to the impasse reached in respect to most of the issues discussed above, new methods are being applied to address old problems and to raise new questions.

Rhetorical Criticism[103]

In contrast to literary critics who have stressed the disparate nature of the text, Lundbom has attempted to argue for a well ordered, aesthetically arranged text that has kept an observable rhetorical structure, in spite of undergoing five major editions. Arguing that inclusion and chiasmus are the dominant rhetorical features of the poetic speeches, Lundbom makes them into the controlling factors that have shaped the five speech and narrative collections, each of which was made by Baruch. These five editions include: the first edition or original scroll (1–20), the second edition made by the appending of two collections—the oracles to the kings of Judah (21:11–23:8) and the oracles concerning the prophets (23:9–40), the third edition which added the "Jehoiakim cluster" (25, 26, 35, 36) and probably the "Oracles to the Foreign Nations" (46–51), the fourth edition which

<hr>

[102]"The Quest for the Historical Jeremiah," 3–12.

[103]In addition to the two extensive treatments discussed, other rhetorical analyses include B. W. Anderson, " 'The Lord has Created Something New', A Stylistic Study of Jer 31:15–22," *CBQ* 40 (1978) 463–78 (reprinted in this volume); G. R. Castellino, "Observations on the Literary Structure of Some Passages in Jeremiah," *VT* 30 (1980) 398–408; Charles D. Isbell and Michael Jackson, "Rhetorical Criticism and Jeremiah VII 1–VIII 3," *VT* 30 (1980) 20–26; David Jobling, "Jeremiah's Poem in III 1–IV 2," *VT* 28 (1978) 45–55; Burke O. Long, "The Stylistic Components of Jer 3, 1–5," *ZAW* 88 (1976) 386–90; and Phyllis Trible, "The Gift of a Poem: A Rhetorical Study of Jeremiah 31:15–22," *ANQ* 17 (1977) 271–80.

inserted the "Zedekiah cluster" (24, 27, 28, 29), and the final, fifth edition which detailed the prophet's suffering (37–44). Thus, this understanding of the book obviates any substantial rearrangement of the text. Furthermore, Lundblom has also explained that the affinity of Jeremiah's rhetoric with that of Deuteronomy is due not only to the prophet's conscious appropriation of this style in his speeches but also to the efforts of Baruch, a Deuteronomic scribe, who shaped the written collections for use in temple worship. Indeed, concludes Lundbom, this shaping of material for temple worship indicates that both Jeremiah and Baruch "looked forward to the day when a new temple would be built."[104]

In its major contours, Lundbom's work remains largely unconvincing. While the intent of rhetorical criticism may be to discover the unique literary features of a writer's particular style and through this his major ideas, how is it possible to conclude that the very general features of inclusion and chiasmus are somehow specifically indicative of a presumed style followed by Jeremiah and Baruch? Countless recent studies purport to demonstrate the presence of chiasmus and inclusion in a large variety of Old Testament texts. Further, if this style, as Lundbom admits, is close to the Deuteronomic one, could one not conclude, as many have, that much of the text has been written and edited by Deuteronomic scribes?

Holladay's rhetorical analysis of Jeremiah 1–20 is less sweeping in scope and claims far less in regard to solving the intricate problems of the composition and development of the book.[105] Beginning with Lundbom's observation that an inclusion frames chapters 1–20 (1:5 = 20:18), Holladay concluded that these chapters contain a recognizable rhetorical structure that includes assonance as a dominant feature. Since both the speeches of Jeremiah and the larger units of 1–20 are shaped by the same rhetorical features, Holladay has contended that Jeremiah was probably responsible for the larger structure of 1–20. Further, according to Holladay, the first scroll dictated to Baruch included the call (1:4–14), a harlotry cycle (2–3), and the first foe cycle (4–6), while the second scroll included the addition of the supplementary foe cycle (8–10).

One need not labor the point that both of these studies are used in order to enhance the role of Jeremiah and Baruch in the shaping of some (Holladay) or all (Lundblom) of the Jeremianic traditions. However, until more specific rhetorical features of a distinctive literary style are uncovered and until the underlying assumption that Jeremiah himself formulated the poetic speeches is examined, this method may not be convincingly used to address historical questions, but rather should be limited to such literary tasks as the demarcation of compositional units, their texture, and ultimately their meaning.

---

[104] Jack Lundbom, *Jeremiah: A Study in Ancient Hebrew Rhetoric* (SBLDS 18; Missoula, Montana: Scholars Press, 1975).

[105] William Holladay, *The Architecture of Jeremiah 1–20*. Holladay has recently updated his analysis ("The Identification of the Two Scrolls of Jeremiah").

Canonical Shaping[106]

In a creative way, Childs has attempted to demonstrate how the Jeremiah traditions underwent "canonical shaping," a process by which traditions were formed and shaped by communities of faith in order to produce a sacred text. Concentrating on the poetry-prose problem (A and C), Childs has argued that the book of Jeremiah points to two different forms of the prophet's proclamation which emerged from two different settings (25 & 36): the twenty-three years of oracular preaching probably in poetic form (627–605, source A) and the later written, prose reformulation of the materials which functioned as a call to repentance (source C). Further, the Jeremiah tradition, especially in source C, casts the prophet into the role of a Deuteronomic preacher, and it was this ". . . later role as a preacher of judgment after the mode of Deuteronomy that became the dominant pattern by which the prophetic message was shaped." This depiction became the major canonical, and thus authoritative picture of the prophet, even though it may well have been a later, secondary interpretation. Childs here gravitates somewhat to the sphere of the traditions-history approach to Jeremiah, although with a different nuance.

Social Dimensions of Jeremiah

Recently, biblical scholars have begun to return to sociology, social-anthropology, and social psychology in order to provide new insights into the prophetic traditions by dealing with such issues as social location, the nature and functions of the social roles of the prophets, charisma, support groups, ecstasy, and so forth. One of Carroll's recent books appropriates the theory of cognitive dissonance, given classical expression by Leon Festinger, in discussing the social dimensions of failed prophecy.[107] In regard to Jeremiah, Carroll points to "adaptive prediction" as one means by which the dissonance caused by the failure of the "Foe from the North" to materialize for some three decades was overcome. This adaptability of prophetic predictions of doom contained an open-ended dimension that allowed later prophetic and even apocalyptic texts to use the image of the "Foe from the North" in order to speak of coming destruction by a wide variety of historical and eschatological bearers of disaster. In addition, the depiction of Jeremiah's recognition of Yahweh's demonic deceit of individuals and communities could be used to overcome the dissonance caused by the failure of prophecy.

Robert Wilson's recent book[108] has a section on Jeremiah that makes use of social-anthropology. According to him, Jeremiah was at home in the

---

[106]Childs, *Introduction to the Old Testament as Scripture*, 339–54.

[107]Robert Carroll, *When Prophecy Failed*, 173–74, 188–96. Also see his "Prophecy, Dissonance, and Jeremiah XXVI," 12–23.

[108]*Prophecy and Society in Ancient Israel* (Philadelphia: Fortress Press, 1980) 231–52.

Ephraimite (Northern) traditions of prophecy which included stereotypical speech configurations, a distinctive vocabulary, and standard behavior patterns which were modeled after the Mosaic prophet. These traditions functioned within a support group that included Levitical priests and some of the prophet's own relatives. The Deuteronomic language used by the prophet and his own self-interpretation as "a prophet like Moses" were in accord with the Deuteronomic traditions at home in the prophet's initial support group. Wilson goes on to argue that Jeremiah was not a central prophet working within the religious establishment that was concerned to carry out Josiah's reform, but a peripheral prophet who attempted to reform society in his own way by admonishing the people of Judah to follow the Ephraimite prescriptions. However, when some of his Levitical support group moved into the Jerusalem establishment, their demands for reform became less radical. Consequently, they became disenchanted with Jeremiah and may have even convinced him to stop his activity for a time. After Josiah's death, Jeremiah's dissatisfaction with the failures of the reform led to his announcement of judgment which in turn increasingly alienated him from his original support group. When conditions changed during the reign of Zedekiah, opposition from his initial support group lessened and new support began to form inside the royal establishment, particularly in the family of Shaphan which had been instrumental in carrying forth Josiah's earlier reform. Nevertheless, Jeremiah continued to be a peripheral prophet.

One of the obvious ramifications of Wilson's interesting study is the attributing of the C prose sermons and the call to Jeremiah himself. However, the most critical question that Wilson must address in his description of Ephraimite and therefore Jeremianic prophecy is whether this is not a uniform, stereotypical creation of the Deuteronomic school that would include Deuteronomy and the Deuteronomistic History. The redactional and traditions-history approaches to the Deuteronomic materials in Jeremiah are just as cogent in accounting for the various factors to which Wilson points.

IX. CONCLUSION

The preceding survey is by no means intended to be exhaustive. Important areas such as form criticism and theology have not been addressed in any substantial way. However, at least it should have indicated the impressive vitality of Jeremiah studies during the twentieth century. The major frustration, of course, is the recognition that no dominant consensus has emerged in regard to any of the issues discussed. This does not mean that our knowledge has not been significantly advanced, but only that the complexity of this prophetic book usually precludes anything approaching certainty. However, it does seem that there is an increasing hesitancy on behalf of many scholars to assert without careful consideration that a particular text is unquestionably Jeremianic. While historians will continue to ask questions about the historicity of the variety of Jeremianic traditions, the traditions-history approach (including Childs' canonical shaping) has evoked a very new set of equally interesting and important questions. In regard to this approach there is an increasing interest in and appreciation for later recastings of so-called "authentic" materials. Willy Schottroff has emphasized that each redactional level of Jeremiah needs to be thoroughly studied annd understood and not hastily cast aside, ignored, and forgotten in the attempt to get back to the "authentic" layer.[109] Perhaps we need to learn from the tragedies of certain archaeologists who have stripped away later strata without careful documentation and analysis in the effort to get back to the "important" earlier level, whether Iron II, or Iron I, Late Bronze II, Late Bronze I, and so forth. Fortunately for us, our later levels still remain available for analysis and interpretation.

It is doubtful that the quest for the historical Jeremiah will be abandoned. However, having recognized the dangers of unquestioned assumptions and the unfortunate dismissal of later "inauthentic" materials, the quest may now be made with a more sensitive, careful, and critically aware effort. Indeed, the two approaches to Jeremiah, the psychological-biological and the traditions-history ones, have provided the creative tension that has invigorated Jeremiah studies during this century. The diminishing of the one could only lead to the impoverishment of the other.*

[109]"Jeremia 2, 1–3. Erwägungen zur Methode der Prophetenexegese," *ZTK* 67 (1970) 263–94.

*(This essay was already in press before I was able to obtain a copy of the collection of essays edited by P.-M. Bogaert, *Le livre de Jérémie: le prophète et son milieu, les oracles et leur transmission* (Bibliotheca Ephemeridum Theologicarum Lovaniensium 54), Leuven: Leuven University, 1981. The essays which are of importance for the issues treated in this introduction include H. Cazelles, "La vie de Jérémie dans son contexte national et international," 21–39; J. Scharbert, "Jeremia und die Reform des Joschija," 40–57; W. L. Holladay, "A Coherent Chronology of Jeremiah's Early Career," 58–73; E. Tov, "Some Aspects of the Textual and Literary History of the Book of Jeremiah," 145–67; P.-M. Bogaert, "De Baruch à Jérémie. Les deux rédactions conservées du livre de Jérémie," 168–73; *idem*, "Les mécanismes rédactionnels en Jér 10,1–16 (LXX et TM) et la signification des suppléments," 222–38; S. Herrmann, "Jeremia- der Prophet und die Verfasser des Buches Jeremia," 197–214; and J. Mermeylen, "Essai de Redactionsgeschichte des «Confessions de Jeremie»," 239–70).

2

The Early Prophecies of Jeremiah in Their Setting[1]

H. H. Rowley

My purpose today, as in previous lectures I have delivered in the Library, is not to propound new theories, but to examine some of the many theories which have been propounded by others, and to offer what seem to me to be adequate reasons for preferring the views I adopt. I have frequently observed that problems which appear simple on the surface often prove to be very complex on examination, and it is not seldom difficult to steer one's way through the many solutions which have been proposed. So far as Jeremiah is concerned, many English readers have been fascinated by John Skinner's superb study of the prophet in his book *Prophecy and Religion*[2], without realizing how many scholars today reject the presuppositions on which that study rests. None of the views I shall examine today was original with Skinner. Basically they have appeared in a number of other English works,[3] as well as in German[4] and other foreign[5] works, but the challenges to them are less familiar to English readers.

Let me say at the outset two things. First, that the scholars who have questioned or rejected those views deserve our thanks, whether we find their challenges to be justified or not, since it is only by questioning and constantly re-examining that our acceptance of the views that survive can be soundly established; and second, that in the matters I shall consider today the views presented by Skinner seem to me to be essentially sound.

At the beginning of the book of Jeremiah we are told that the prophet received his call when he was still but a youth[6] in the thirteenth year of the reign of Josiah,[7] which would be in the year 626 B.C. His early prophecies

---

[1]A lecture delivered in the Library series of public lectures. (This essay originally appeared in the *Bulletin of the John Rylands University Library, Manchester* 45 (1962–3) 198–234, Ed.).

[2]1922.

[3]So, e.g. in A. S. Peake, *Jeremiah* (Cent. B.); A. W. Streane, *Jeremiah and Lamentations* (Camb. B.), 1913; L. E. Binns, *Jeremiah* (West C.), 1919; G. A. Smith, *Jeremiah*, 1923.

[4]So, e.g. B. Duhm, *Jeremia* (K.H.C.), 1901; C. H. Cornill, *Das Buch Jeremia*, 1905.

[5]So, e.g. E. Bruston, *La Bible du Centenaire*, ii (1947), 449 ff.; A. Lods, ibid. pp. xxi ff.

[6]Jer. i. 6.

[7]Jer. i. 2.

speak of a peril from the north,[8] and this has long been thought by many scholars[9] to have reference to the Scythian peril, of which Herodotus gives some account. If this is true, then the predictions of Jeremiah were not fulfilled, and this has been thought to have so troubled the prophet that he relapsed into silence for some time.[10] Whether the prophet was so troubled at this time, it is certain that at some point or points in his career he was bewildered by the non-fulfilment of prophecies which he felt certain he had been moved by God to utter. The proof of this is to be found in the passages that are sometimes called the "Confessions of Jeremiah."[11] In the year 621 B.C. the Book of the Law was found in the Temple,[12] and on it Josiah based the reform he carried through. There are passages in the book of Jeremiah which have led scholars to believe that Jeremiah at first supported this reform, and the anger of his relatives against him[13] has been explained as due to his advocacy of this reform, which must have menaced the livelihood of the priestly family of Anathoth to which Jeremiah belonged.[14] Later, it is thought, the prophet perceived that the reform did not go deep enough and gave rise to false hopes. He therefore drew away from the reformers, and again we have a period of silence. Then, in the reign of Jehoiakim, when the Chaldaeans appeared on the horizon, he saw a new peril from the north, and reissued his earlier prophecies, perhaps modified to meet the new situation or to take account of the new foe.

---

[8] Jer. vi. 1; cf. i. 14f.

[9] So, e.g. H. Venema, *Commentarius ad librum prophetiarum Jeremiae*, i (1765), 142 f.; C. F. Cramer, *Skythische Denkmähler in Palästina*, 1777, pp. 22f.; J. G. Eichhorn, *Die hebräischen Propheten*, ii (1819), 9; F. Hitzig, *Jeremia* (K.E.H.), 1841, p. 33; S. Davidson, *Introduction to the Old Testament*, iii (1863), 92; H. Ewald, *History of Israel*, Eng. trans. by J. E. Carpenter, iv (1871), 226 f.; B. Stade, *G.V.I.*, 2nd edn., i (1889), 643 ff.; E. König, *Einleitung in das Alte Testament*, 1893, p. 341; R. Smend, *Lehrbuch der alttestamentlichen Religionsgeschichte*, 1899, p. 244; B. Duhm, op. cit. pp. xi, 48ff.; T. K. Cheyne, *Jeremiah: his Life and Times*, 1904, pp. 30 ff.; C. H. Cornill, op. cit. pp. 82 ff.; A. S. Peake, op. cit. i. 4 f.; V. Ryssel, *J.E.* vii (1907), 97 a; S. R. Driver, *The Book of the Prophet Jeremiah*, 1908, p. 21, and *L.O.T.*, 9th edn. 1913, pp. 252 f.; C. Steuernagel, *Lehrbuch der Einleitung in das Alte Testament*, 1912, pp. 544 f.; Streane, op. cit. pp. xii, 5; H. P. Smith, *Religion of Israel*, 1914, pp. 163, 165. A. Condamin (*Le livre de Jérémie* [E.Bib.], 1936, pp. 61 f.) observes: "Dans cet exemple on peut voir comment une hypothèse naît, se développe, se propage, passe insensiblement de la valeur de *possible* à celle de *probable*, et finit par se proclamer *certaine*, sans l'apport d'aucune preuve nouvelle, par le seul fait d'être admise et répétée un peu partout." There have, however, always been scholars who have rejected this view. So, e.g. E. F. C. Rosenmüller, *Scholia in Vetus Testamentum*, Pars VIII. i (1826), 137; C. F. Keil, *Jeremia und Klagelieder* (K.D.), 1872, pp. 77 ff. n.; R. Payne Smith, *Speaker's Bible*, v (1875), 314; F. Bleek, *Einleitung in das Alte Testament*, 4th edn., revised by J. Wellhausen, 1878, p. 359; C. von Orelli, *Jesaja und Jeremiah*, 2nd edn., 1891, pp. 222 f. (Eng. trans. of 1st edn. of Jeremiah by J. S. Banks, 1889, pp. 16 ff.).

[10] Cf. Peake, op. cit. i. 11.

[11] On the "Confessions" see below, pp. 50 ff.

[12] 2 Kings xxii. 3 ff,

[13] Jer. xi. 21,

[14] Jer. i. 1,

Of this conception of the early ministry of Jeremiah there is not a single point which has not been attacked, and in defending it I shall seek to take account of those attacks which have been first made or supported in recent years, and to deal with them as clearly as the complex nature of the often interlocked problems will allow.

We may begin with the date of Jeremiah's call. Here I would mention first and briefly the radical suggestion of C. C. Torrey, whose original views so often fluttered the dovecotes of Biblical scholarship, and whose great learning is often forgotten in the rejection of his bold theories. Torrey advanced the view that the first ten chapters of the book of Jeremiah had nothing to do with a seventh-century prophet, but that they were a pseudepigraph written in the third century B.C.[15] with no more than an imaginary connection with the age in which they are set.[16] He believed the foe from the north was Alexander,[17] on whose career the writer of the pseudepigraph looked back. But he advanced no possible motive for the throwing back of Alexander's career in this fictitious way,[18] and many of the prophecies of Jeremiah i–x bear the hall mark of real prophecy, born of a contemporary situation to which the prophet addressed himself in agony of heart,[19] and it is not surprising that Torrey's view has left no ripple on the surface of serious study of the book.

Little more is to be said for T. C. Gordon's theory[20] that we should emend the text of Jeremiah i.2 to place the prophet's call in the twenty-third year of Josiah's reign instead of the thirteenth, and thus to bring that call to the year 616 B.C.,[21] and it arises from Gordon's rejection of the Scythian hypothesis and of the association of Jeremiah with the reform of Josiah, and his consequent desire to make the call of the prophet synchronize with the rise of the Neo-Babylonian empire. The only grounds presented in support of this date[22] are that the text published by C. J. Gadd in 1923[23] showed that the fall of Nineveh occurrred in 612 B.C., and not in 607 B.C. as had been earlier supposed, and that it brought sure knowledge that Egyptian forces had marched to the help of Assyria in 616 B.C.[24] But

---

[15]Cf. *J.B.L.* lvi (1937), 193 ff.; see especially pp. 215 f.

[16]Ibid. p. 216.

[17]Ibid. p. 209. Cf. *Vom Alten Testament* (Marti Festschrift), 1925, pp. 281 ff., where Torrey refers a number of other passages in the prophets to Alexander.

[18]Torrey's view is criticized and rejected by J. P. Hyatt, in *J.B.L.* lix (1940), 503 ff. Cf. also H. G. May, *J.B.L.* lxi (1942), 146 n.

[19]Cf. A. B. Davidson, *D.B.* ii (1899), 570b: "The pathos and depth of these chs. (2–6) are not surpassed by anything in Scripture."

[20]Cf. *E.T.* xliv (1932–33), 562 ff.

[21]Ibid. p. 564b. J. P. Hyatt, *I. B.* v (1956), 798, notes that the same date is given in Jer. xxv. 1, and observes that the same corruption is not likely to have occurred in two passages.

[22]Loc. cit. p. 564a.

[23]Cf. *The Fall of Nineveh.*

[24]H. Bardtke (*Z.A.W.* liii (1935), 211 ff.) adopts a similar view of the date of Jeremiah's call.

this can in no sense be said to be evidence that Jeremiah had received his call in that year.

Horst[25] also rejects the evidence of Jeremiah i.2, on the ground that in the Septuagint form it is similar in phrasing to the opening verses of Hosea, Joel, Micah, and Zephaniah, and therefore comes from a late editor.[26] But this is not proof that it does not rest on a sound tradition, and certainly not evidence for a different date. Horst would place the call of Jeremiah after the reign of Josiah was past.[27] He is thus compelled to eliminate as secondary other verses which bring Jeremiah's ministry into the reign of Josiah. In Jeremiah xxv. 3 Jeremiah himself is represented as dating the beginning of his ministry in the thirteenth year of Josiah, while in Jeremiah iii. 6, in one of the autobiographical introductions to an oracle, and in xxxvi. 2, in a message which came to him from God, his ministry is represented as going back to the days of Josiah.[28] These cannot be dismissed on the basis of the opening verses of other prophetic books, and there is no evidence that they have been editorially altered.

J. P. Hyatt at one time[29] did not go so far as Horst, though he followed him in rejecting the evidence of Jeremiah i. 2 and xxv. 3.[30] He maintained that the prophet began his ministry in 614–612 B.C.,[31] and so towards the end of the reign of Josiah.[32] No tangible evidence for this was brought forward, and more recently Hyatt has pushed the beginning of Jeremiah's ministry into the reign of Jehoiakim[33] and suggested that the thirteenth year of Josiah was the date of the prophet's birth.[34] For this suggestion, again, there is no evidence, and the view really rests on the rejection of the Scythian hypothesis and of the idea that Jeremiah ever supported the Deuteronomic reform, and on the claim that there are no prophecies which can be dated earlier than the reign of Jehoiakim. This

---

[25]Cf. Z.A.W. xli (1923), 94 ff.

[26]Ibid. pp. 95 ff.

[27]Ibid. p. 132: "Die bisherige Chronologie, die das Auftreten des Jeremia auf 626 ansetzte, ist historisch falsch; sie beruht auf einer kultischen und tendenziösen Tradition, noch dazu sekundärer Art. Eine ursprünglichere Tradition verlegt vielmehr sein Auftreten in die Zeit unmittelbar nach der Schlacht von Megiddo."

[28]H. G. May (J.N.E.S. iv (1945), 226) also rejects all these dates, assigning them to the Biographer (on whom cf. J.B.L. lxi (1942), 139 ff.). It is not axiomatic, however, that the biographer never told the truth.

[29]Cf. J.B.L. lix (1940), 499 ff.

[30]Ibid. pp. 512 f. In J.N.E.S. i (1942), 165 f. Hyatt rejects all the four dates mentioned above.

[31]Cf. J.B.L., loc. cit. pp. 509, 511 (followed by R. Augé, Jeremias [Montserrat Bible], 1950, pp. 14 f.). According to this view the foe from the north is to be identified with the Chaldaeans and their allies—more probably the Medes than the Scythians. H. G. May (loc. cit., pp. 225 f.) thinks it complicates the problem unnecessarily to bring in the Medes.

[32]Cf. H. Winckler, Geschichte Israels, i (1895), 112, f., where the beginning of Jeremiah's ministry is assigned to circa 610 B.C..

[33]Cf. I.B. v. 799b. So also H. G. May, loc. cit. pp. 226 f.

[34]Cf. I.B. v. 779, 798.

means, as we shall see, that a good deal in the book of Jeremiah has to be explained away before the dates we are given can be dismissed.[35]

In the opening verse of the book, Jeremiah is said to have been "of the priests who were in Anathoth in the land of Benjamin." It is often assumed, though there is no direct evidence of it, that the prophet belonged to the priestly family of Abiathar,[36] the priest of David who was dismissed from Jerusalem by Solomon and who went to his estate in Anathoth.[37] Some authors, both ancient and modern, have supposed that his father Hilkiah was the Jerusalem priest who found the Book of the Law,[38] but this is

[35]J. Bright (*J.B.L.* lxx (1951), 15 ff.), while rejecting the Scythian hypothesis, argues for 626 B.C. as the date of Jeremiah's call.

[36]Cf. Lods, *Histoire de la littérature hébraïque et juive*, 1950, p. 405 ("sans nul doute"; cf. *La Bible du Centenaire*, ii, p. xxi: "très probablement"); J. T. Nelis, *Dictionnaire encyclopédique de la Bible*, 1960, p. 919 ("sans doute"); J. Steinmann, *Le prophète Jérémie*, 1952, p. 23 ("presque certain"); C. F. Kent, *The Growth and Contents of the Old Testament*, 1926, pp. 116 f. ("appears to have been"); V. Ryssel, *J.E.* vii. 96a ("probably"); A. Penna, *Geremia*, 1952, p. 5 ("con probabilità"; cf. p. 30); B. Mariani, *Introductio in libros sacros Veteris Testamenti*, 1958, p. 357 n. ("probabiliter"); B. N. Wambacq, *Jeremias*, 1957, p. 27 ("mogelijk"); W. Rudolph, *Jeremia* (H.A.T.), 2nd edn., 1958, p. 2 ("sehr wohl möglich"); H. Wildberger, *R.G.G.*, 3rd edn., iii (1959), 581 ("möglicherweise"); B. Duhm, *Jeremia*, 1901, pp. 2 f. ("nicht unmöglich"); J. Skinner, op. cit. p. 19 ("the natural, though not absolutely certain, inference"); E. A. Leslie, *Jeremiah*, 1954, p. 20 ("reasonable to suppose"); B. W. Anderson, *Understanding the Old Testament*, 1957, p. 300 ("possibly"); A. S. Peake, *Jeremiah*, i. 3 ("by no means improbable"); E. Bruston, in Westphal, *Dictionnaire encyclopédique de la Bible*, i (1932), 603b ("vraisemblablement"); J. Condamin, *Le livre de Jérémie* (E.Bib.), 1936, p. v ("peut-être"); R. Liechtenhan, *Jeremia*, 1909, p. 6 ("die Vermutung hat viel für sich"). A. Bentzen (*Introduction to the Old Testament*, 2nd edn., ii (1952), 115) contents himself with saying this is generally assumed. R. Augé (*Jeremias* [Montserrat Bible], 1950, p. 13) thinks that Jeremiah's allusions to Shiloh (vii. 14, xxvi. 6) and Ephraim (xxxi. 18–22) favour the view of his descent from Abiathar. G. Hölscher (*Die Profeten*, 1914, pp. 268 f. n.) rightly says this is "eine reine Vermutung" (cf. Hyatt, *I.B.* iii. 796). Abiathar retired to his family estate, and we have no evidence whatever that he served any shrine in Anathoth, whereas it is probable that the family of Jeremiah served in a priestly capacity.

[37]I Kings ii. 26 f.

[38]So Clement of Alexandria, *Stromata* I, xxi (*P.G.* viii (1891), 849, or ed. C. Mondésert and M. Caster, i (1951), 136; Eng. trans by W. Wilson, i (1871), 431); Kimḥi, on Jer. i. 1 (see *Miḳrā'ôth Gᵉdhôlôth*, viii (1902), 192b); P. von Bohlen, *Historical and Critical Illustrations of the First Part of Genesis*, Eng. trans. by J. Heywood, i (1862), 265, J. W. Colenso, *The Pentateuch and Book of Joshua critically examined*, vii (1879), 259 ("very probably"); F. C. Jean, *Jérémie, sa théologie, sa politique*, 1913, p. 5. C. W. E. Nägelsbach (*Jeremia*, 1868, p. x; Eng. trans by S. R. Asbury, 1871, p. 4) pronounced this to be possible, but not certainly provable, and T. K. Cheyne (*Jeremiah: his life and Times*, 1904, p. 19 n.) said it was not impossible (so also R. Payne Smith, *Speaker's Bible*, v (1875), 311 f.). P. Volz (*Jeremia* [K.A.T.], 1928, p. xi; cf. *Prophetengestalten des Alten Testaments*, 1938, p. 219) thought his father might have exercised his priesthood in Jerusalem and not at the Anathoth shrine, but without identifying him with the High Priest. Against this, however, is the hostility of Jeremiah's family to him, apparently arising from his advocacy of the newly found Law Book, which the Jerusalem priesthood would have welcomed. Rudolph (op. cit. pp. 2 f.) says it is impossible to say whether his father was High Priest, or whether he exercised his priesthood in Jerusalem, though living elsewhere, like Zechariah (Luke i. 39 f.). A. Neher (*Jérémie*, 1960, pp. 1, 3) thinks Jeremiah was from the family of Abiathar, but that his family was debarred

generally rejected as quite improbable. Meek goes farther[39] and challenges the view that Jeremiah belonged to a priestly family at all. He holds that the words "of the priests" are a gloss in the verse.[40] There is certainly no evidence that Jeremiah ever exercised the priesthood, and it is generally believed that though he belonged to a priestly family he did not do so.[41] That his whole attitude to religion was prophetic rather than priestly[42] is agreed, but this does not prove that he did not belong to a priestly family. We are told that the expression "of the priests" is found only here.[43] To this it could be replied that if every expression in the Old Testament which is found but once were eliminated as a gloss, a great deal would go. It would certainly be strange for Jeremiah to be described in this way if he actually served as a priest, but the phrase is unexceptionable as the description of one who came of a priestly family.[44] It is probable that the phrase does not recur in the Old Testament because no other member of a priestly family who did not exercise the priestly office calls for description.

Moreover, if the words "of the priests" were a gloss—and there is no textual evidence against them, and few scholars have found any reason to question them—it does not follow that they are mistaken. Meek thinks they were added by someone who jumped to the conclusion that because Jeremiah came from Anathoth he must have been a priest.[45] It might have been expected that in that case he would describe him as a priest, instead of using the expression to which objection is made on the ground of its rarity. The words could equally well have been added, if they were added, by one who knew that Jeremiah was of a priestly family of Anathoth. Further, we know that the family of Jeremiah plotted against his life,[46] and the account of this stands in the chapter which tells of the prophet's advocacy of "the words of this covenant."[47] To this we shall return, but here it may be observed that if, as many scholars have believed,[48] this is a reference to

---

from all priestly service, though the priests of Anathoth, with the exception of Abiathar's descendants, served in the Jerusalem Temple. H. Ewald (*History of Israel*, Eng. trans. by J. Estlin Carpenter, iv (1871), 233 n.) declares that Jeremiah's father was a common Levite.

[39]Cf. *Expositor*, 8th ser., xxv (1923), 215 ff. He also denies that Jeremiah lived in Anathoth (ibid. p. 217). Hyatt (*J.B.L.* lix (1940), 511) follows Meek in holding that Jeremiah was not of a priestly family. Cf. also *I.B.* iii. 795.

[40]Loc. cit. p. 216.

[41]Cf. Rudolph, op. cit. p. 3. A. Haldar (*Associations of Cult Prophets among the Ancient Semites*, 1945, p. 112) states that Jeremiah is "clearly" (cf. p. 121 "obviously") described as a member of the Temple staff. The adverb is question-begging, as K. Roubos (*Profetie en Cultus in Israël*, 1956, p. 23) points out. L. W. Batten (*The Hebrew Prophet*, 1905, p. 95) says we do not know whether he exercised the priestly office in his younger days.

[42]Cf. Meek, loc. cit. p. 218; Hyatt, *J.B.L.* lix (1940), 511.

[43]So Meek, loc. cit. p. 216.

[44]Cf. Jos. xii. 4; 2 Sam. iv. 2, xxi. 2.

[45]Loc. cit. p. 216.

[46]Jer. xi. 21.

[47]Jer. xi. 6.

[48]So, e.g. K. Budde, *Geschichte der althebräischen Literatur*, 2nd edn., 1909, p. 136; Peake, op. cit. i. 13; Streane, op. cit. pp. 75 f.; Binns, op. cit. pp. 106 f.; Skinner, op. cit. p. 21;

Josiah's Law Book and the centralization of worship that followed its discovery, the anger of a priestly family that served the now suppressed shrine of Anathoth could be understood. But if his kindred were not priests, there is no alternative explanation of their anger against him.[49] In all the questions we have before us today we must watch the converging evidence, and we should not lightly set aside evidence preserved in the book of Jeremiah which throws light on an incident recorded in the book, which there is no possible reason to doubt.

We may turn now to the Scythian question. At the time when Jeremiah received his call trouble was brewing in the north.[50] In the second of the visions he saw at the time of his call, the vision of the seething cauldron, the word came to him "Out of the north evil shall break forth upon all the inhabitants of the land."[51] It has been widely accepted, since the view was first propounded in the eighteenth century,[52] that this is a reference to the Scythian invasion of western Asia, of which Herodotus gives some account. This hypothesis is still widely accepted,[53] but during

---

Condamin, op. cit. p. 107; Bruston, *La Bible du Centenaire*, ii. 485; A. Gelin, *Jérémie* (Bible de Jérusalem), 2nd edn., 1959, p. 79; A. Aeschiman, *Le prophète Jérémie*, 1959, pp. 17, 95. T. H. Robinson (*History of Israel*, i (1932), 428) observes that this view offers a better explanation of the hostility of Jeremiah's family than any other. It is rejected by Volz (*Jeremia*, p. 137), May (*J.N.E.S.* iv (1945), 224), Steinmann (op. cit. p. 152), Hyatt (*I.B.* v. 912 f.).

[49]Volz (op. cit. p. 137) suggests that Jeremiah's family belonged to the Jerusalem priesthood, and that they acted under the instigation of the Jerusalem authorities. That Jeremiah's family served in Jerusalem is unlikely, or he would scarcely have been described as of the priests that were in Anathoth, and the assumption that the Jerusalem priests sought to kill him can only be justified by the rejection of Jer. xi. 1–14 (see below), or the linking of this incident with Jeremiah's Temple sermon (chapters vii and xxvi) instead of with its context. After Jeremiah's sermon we know that the priests and prophets proposed to condemn Jeremiah to death, but this was not a plot of his own family; and after it had been decided that Jeremiah should not suffer death for his sermon, it is improbable that his family would seek to carry out a sentence that had been rejected. It is far more likely that it was for what they regarded as family interests that they would be incensed against him.

[50]Jer. i. 13 ff.

[51]Jer. i. 14. J. Bright (*Interpretation*, ix (1955), 276 f.) would loose the second vision from any temporal connection with the call of Jeremiah. Similarly Hölscher (*Die Profeten*, p. 270) would ascribe both of the visions to the time when his oracles were gathered together in the reign of Jehoiakim.

[52]See p. 34. n. 9.

[53]So, e.g. Streane, op. cit. pp. 75 f.; G. Hölscher, *Die Profeten*, pp. 277 f.; Binns, op. cit. pp. xix, xxx, 130; J. A. Bewer, *The Literature of the Old Testament*, 1922, p. 143, and *The Prophets*, 1955, p. 185; Skinner, op. cit. pp. 35 ff.; G. A. Smith, op. cit. pp. 110 ff.; J. M. Powis Smith, *The Prophets and their Times*, 1925, pp. 106 ff.; D. G. Hogarth, *C.A.H.* iii (1925), 145 f.; R. Kittel, *G.V.I.*, 7th edn. ii (1925), 414 f.; C. F. Kent, *The Growth and Contents of the Old Testament*, 1926, p. 117; I. Piotrowicz, *Eos*, xxxii (1929), 473 ff.; T. H. Robinson, op. cit. i. 412 ff.; E. Bruston, in Westpahl, *Dictionnaire encyclopédique de la Bible*, i (1932), 604a, and *La Bible du Centenaire*, ii (1947), 451; A. Lods, *The Prophets and the Rise of Judaism*, Eng. trans. by S. H. Hooke, 1937, pp. 130, 163, and *Histoire de la littérature hébraïque et juive*, 1950, p. 405; E. Meyer, *Geschichte des Altertums*, 2nd edn., iii (1937), 142; R. H. Pfeiffer, *Introduction to the Old Testament*, 1941, pp. 482, 488; F. James, *Personalities*

the last half century it has been rejected by a growing number of scholars,[54] following the challenge of F. Wilke[55] early in the present century.

Herodotus relates[56] how the Scythians invaded Asia and conquered the Medes and then spread over Asia, which they dominated for twenty-eight years. He says they marched through Palestine with the intention of invading Egypt, but were bought off by Psammetichus. Thereupon they returned northwards, stopping especially at Ashkelon, where they robbed a temple. From cuneiform sources we learn of the activities of the Scythians so far as they affected Assyrian history,[57] but for an account of their raid through Palestine we have only the narrative of Herodotus. It is sometimes said that Scythian bands shared in the attack that led to the fall of Nineveh,[58] but it seems more probable that the Umman-Manda who shared

---

of the Old Testamemt, 1947, p. 307; I. G. Matthews, The Religious Pilgrimage of Israel, 1947, p. 146; B. D. Eerdmans, The Religion of Israel, 1947, p. 190; J. Paterson, The Goodly Fellowship of the Prophets, 1948, p. 99; P. Heinisch, History of the Old Testament, Eng. trans. by W. Heidt, 1952, p. 256; O. Eissfeldt, Einleitung in das Alte Testament, 2nd edn., 1956, pp. 421, 521, and apud T. H. Robinson and F. Horst, Die Zwölf Kleinen Propheten (H.A.T.), 2nd edn., 1954, pp. 188f.; B. W. Anderson, op. cit. pp. 301, 303. H. Wildberger (R. G. G. 3rd edn., iii (1959), 588) says: "Da die Gedichte der Frühzeit J.'s angehören, bleibt die Deutung auf den Skythensturm trotz aller Gegenargumente am naheliegendsten, wobei es möglich ist, dass J. selbst sie später auf die babylonische Gefahr bezogen hat." C. Kuhl (The Old Testament: its Origins and Composition, Eng. trans. by C. T. M. Herriott, 1961, p. 185) thinks the reference is "perhaps" to the Scythians.
[54]So, e.g. J. Lewy, M.V.A.G. xxix, no. 2 (1925), 51 ff.; L. W. van Ravesteijn, Jeremia (T.U.), i (1925), 82; Volz, Jeremia, pp. 57 f.; A. C. Welch, Jeremiah: his Time and his Work, 1928, pp. 53, 101 ff.; J. Meinhold, Einführung in das Alte Testament, 3rd edn., 1932, p. 231; R. H. Pfeiffer, in Westphal, Dictionnaire encyclopédique de la Bible, ii (1932), 648a (but cf. preceding note); F. Nötscher, Das Buch Jeremias (H.S.A. Tes.), 1934, pp. 78 ff.; A. Condamin, op. cit. pp. 61 ff.; L. Gautier, Introduction à l'Ancien Testament, 3rd edn., i (1939), 389; J. P. Hyatt, J.B.L. lix (1940), 499 ff.; J. Bright, J.B.L. lxx (1951), 28 n., Interpretation, ix (1955), 275, and History of Israel, 1960, p. 293; J. Steinmann, Le prophéte Jérémie, 1952, pp. 58 f., n.; A. Weiser, Jeremia (A.T.D.), 1952, pp. 43 f.; F. Horst, Die Zwölf Kleinen Propheten, 2nd edn., 1954, p. 195; W. Rudolph, op. cit. pp. 43 ff. A. Bentzen (Introduction, 2nd edn., ii. 121 f.) will not pronounce for or against, while K. Elliger (Zwölf Kleinen Propheten [A.T.D.] ii (1956), 56), thinks the Scythian hypothesis is very problematical. Cf. also A. S. Kapelrud, S.B.U. ii (1952), 1190.
[55]Cf. Alttestamentliche Studien R. Kittel dargebracht (B.W.A.T. 13), 1913, pp. 222 ff. On Wilke's article cf. T. L. W. van Ravesteijn, Theologische Studiën, xxxii (1914), 22 ff.
[56]Hist. i. 105 f.
[57]Cf. J. Lewy, Forschungen zur alten Geschichte Vorderasiens (M.V.A.G. xxix, 2), 1925, 1 ff.; L. Piotrowicz, Eos, xxxii (1929), 473 ff.; E. H. Minns, in C.A.H. iii (1925), 188 f.; E. Meyer, Geschichte des Altertums, 2nd edn., iii (1937), 139 ff. On the Scythians in general, cf. E. H. Minns, Scythians and Greeks, 1913, and C.A.H. iii. 187 ff.; Kretschmer, in P.W., 2 Reihe, ii. 1 (1921), 923 ff.; T. T. Rice, The Scythians, 1957.
[58]Cf. C. J. Gadd, The Fall of Nineveh, 1923, p. 14, and History and Monuments of Ur, 1929, pp. 228, 233; followed by B. W. Anderson, Understanding the Old Testament, p. 320. See also P. (E.) Dhorme, R.B. xxxiii, 1924, 230; J. Lewy, Z.A. xxxvii (1927), 135; M. Noth, History of Israel, Eng. trans., 2nd edn., revised by P. R. Ackroyd, 1960, p. 270. H. R. Hall (The Ancient History of the Near East, 7th edn., 1927, p. 511) describes the Umman-manda as "mixed hordes of Scythians, Mannai, and Kimmerians."

in the attack on Nineveh were an earlier wave of invaders from the southern steppes of Russia who had turned into Media, and by now were mingled with the Medes.[59]

That there are exaggerations and improbabilities in the account of Herodotus may be agreed.[60] It is improbable that the Scythians dominated Asia for twenty-eight years,[61] though it is not impossible that these nomadic hordes wandered over Asia for many years, spreading terror wherever they went.[62] It has been questioned whether Psammetichus bought them off in the way Herodotus records,[63] but we should not expect this to be recorded in Egyptian sources,[64] and there is no evidence against the story. It has, indeed, been suggested that Egyptian alarm at this experience may account for the Egyptian change of policy from hostility to Assyria to alliance with her, since Assyria must have seemed the only bulwark for civilization.[65] It is hard to suppose that the whole story of Herodotus was the free invention of the author. The circumstantial account of the doings of the Scythians at Ashkelon is specifically stated to be based on particular inquiry which the historian made.[66] To dismiss this on the grounds that the interest of Herodotus was in the identification of the goddess of Ashkelon with Aphrodite,[67] and that he readily accepted a legend which was current

---

[59]Cf. Piotrowicz, *Eos* xxxii (1929), 495 ff.; P. Schnabel, *Z.A.* xxxvi (1925), 82 f., 316 ff.; F. Thureau-Dangin, *R.A.* xxii (1925), 28 f. That the Umman-manda became fused with the Medes is shown by the fact that Nabonidus in one of his inscriptions refers to Astyages as King of the Umman-manda (cf. S. Langdon, *Die neubabylonischen Königsinschriften*, 1912, p. 220).

[60]Cf. S. R. Driver, *L.O.T.*, 9th edn., p. 253, where it is agreed that the extent of their rule may be exaggerated, but held that the fact of such an irruption cannot be doubted (cf. J. F. McCurdy, *History, Prophecy, and the Monuments*, ii (1896), 394); G. Ricciotti, *History of Israel*, Eng. trans. by C. della Penta and R. T. A. Murphy, i (1955), 394, where it is suggested that the period was more probably about ten years; Piotrowicz, loc. cit. p. 489, where similarly "all Asia" is held to be an exaggeration. Skinner (op. cit. p. 40 n.) says the historical perspective of Herodotus is greatly foreshortened.

[61]Skinner (op. cit. p. 41 n.) agrees that this is obviously exaggerated and so Heinisch (op. cit. p. 394).

[62]T. H. Robinson (*History of Israel*, i. 414 n.) says "they were plundering raids of a miscellaneous horde of savages who did not care who their victim was." On the Scythian reputation for cruelty, cf. Josephus, *Contra Ap.* ii. 37 (269), where they are said to be little better than wild beasts and to delight in killing people. Cf. also 2 Macc. iv. 17, 3 Macc. vii. 5.

[63]Cf. Wilke, loc. cit. p. 229; Hyatt, *J.B.L.* lix (1940), 501.

[64]H. Gressmann (*Der Messias*, 1929, p. 132) thinks the story of the Scythian approach to Egypt rests on an Egyptian tradition, which was carried from Egypt to Philistia. This is accepted by W. Baumgartner, *Archiv Orientální*, xviii (1950) (Hrozný Festschrift iii), 93.

[65]So C. J. Gadd, *The Fall of Nineveh*, p. 6; E. H. Minns, in *C.A.H.* iii. 190. Minns had earlier suggested (*Scythians and Greeks*, 1913, p. 42) that the Scythians had been sent by Assyria against Egypt. But that was before it was known from the Gadd tablet that Egypt was allied with Assyria in the last years of the Assyrian empire. Assyria would scarcely have gained an ally by inspiring an attack of this kind.

[66]*Hist.* i. 105. Baumgartner (loc. cit. p. 93) accepts the view that Herodotus' account rests on a genuine tradition preserved at Ashkelon.

[67]So Wilke, loc. cit. pp. 228 f.

in Ashkelon, will hardly do. A cult legend of Ashkelon can scarcely be assumed to have created a story of Scythian depredations through Syria and Palestine, including the account of the Egyptian purchase of relief.

It is certain that the city of Bethshan became known in the Greek period as Scythopolis, and this would more than suggest that at some time the Scythians were there, as Pliny[68] and George Syncellus state.[69] Against this it is argued that this name is known only from Hellenistic times,[70] and nothing which can be identified as Scythian has been unearthed in the excavations of Bethshan.[71] To this it may be replied that since Scythopolis is a Greek name, we should hardly expect to find it used before the Hellenistic period, and since, according to Herodotus, the Scythians marched through Palestine and back, harrying and plundering, we should not expect them to leave evidences of their presence, to be archaeologically uncovered, wherever they passed.[72] In northern Syria, where they may have remained for some time, there are evidences of their presence which archaeologists have found in modern times.[73] Moreover, whenever the name Scythopolis was first given to Bethshan, it is not likely to have been given to a town which was quite unconnected with the Scythians in tradition. That tradition was not derived from Herodotus, who does not mention the town in his account of the Scythians. If it did not arise in the period of which Herodotus writes, we are entitled to ask when it was. No other incursion of Scythians into Palestine is recorded, and it is securely known from Assyrian texts that Scythians were active within the Assyrian empire at this time. It would not seem convincing to reject the incursion that is recorded, without offering some more plausible suggestion as to how the name arose.[74]

[68]Cf. *Nat. Hist.* v. 16 [74], where it is said that a colony of Scythians settled at Scythopolis.

[69]Cf. *Chronographia*, 214 D (ed. Dindorf, p. 405).

[70]Condamin (op. cit. p. 65) dismisses the name Scythopolis, and says no serious weight can be attached to it, while Wilke (loc. cit. p. 229) says the name Scythopolis is mere "Volksetymologie". On the other hand Baumgartner (loc. cit. p. 93) thinks this has definite evidential value. So S. A. Cook, in *C.A.H.* iii. 393; R. Kittel, *G.V.I.*, 7th edn., ii. 415 n.; G. Beer, in *P.W.* 2 Reihe, ii. 1, 947. A. Legendre (in Vigouroux, *Dictionnaire de la Bible*, i, 1895, 1739) says: "L'explication la plus naturelle est celle qui est tirée d'une invasion des Scythes, mentionnée par Herodote." Cf. E. Schürer, *G.J.V.* 4th edn., ii (1907), 171; S.Vailhé, in *Catholic Encyclopaedia*, xiii (1912), 648b.

[71]Cf. A. Rowe, *The Topography and History of Beth-shan*, 1930, p. 42.

[72]If, as Pliny states (see above n. 68), a colony settled in Bethshan, it is not likely to have been large, and it would probably soon be assimilated to its environment.

[73]Cf. D. G. Hogarth, in *C.A.H.* iii (1925), 147 n.; Piotrowicz, *Eos*, xxxii (1929), 491. Cf. also C. L. Woolley, *A.A.A.* vii (1914–16), 122 f., where, however, it is said that "if we recognise a Scythian element in North Syria, it does not follow that this first appears with the Scythian invasion mentioned by Herodotus."

[74]Of improbable suggestions we may note that of Reland (*Palaestina*, ii (1714), 992 ff.), that it is derived from the name of Succoth (Gen. xxxii. 17), and that of E. Robinson (*Biblical Researches in Palestine*, 2nd edn., iii (1856), 330), that Scythopolis simply means "the town of

Further, it must be remembered that Herodotus is supported by the book of Jeremiah in setting some crisis in Palestine, due to external invasion, at this time. Herodotus does not specify precisely when this invasion fell, save that it occurred in the reign of Psammetichus some time before the destruction of Nineveh by Cyaxares. Since Egypt marched to the assistance of Assyria in 616 B.C.,[75] it must have been some time before this, and it is generally thought likely that it preceded the reform of Josiah. This would bring us close to the date given in the book of Jeremiah for the call of the prophet, though scholars differ somewhat as to the more precise dating.[76] To reject the story of Herodotus as groundless and the name of Scythopolis as irrelevant, and at the same time to dismiss the date given in the Bible for the call of Jeremiah, can be better described as the dismissal of evidence than its refutation.

---

uncultured people." Reland's view is curtly dismissed by Schürer (loc.cit.). Succoth stood on the opposite side of the Jordan to Bethshan, and it would be surprising for the name of the less important site to be transferred across the Jordan to the more important (cf. A. Legendre, in Vigouroux, *Dictionnaire de la Bible*, i (1895), 1738), to be formed into a hybrid Hebrew-Greek name and then corrupted into Scythopolis. Robinson's suggestion could only claim a measure of plausibility if the Scythians had passed through Palestine leaving a tradition of their barbarity behind.

[75]Cf. Gadd, *The Fall of Nineveh*, p. 6.

[76]Duhm (op. cit. p. 48), J. A. Selbie (*D.B.* iv (1902), 975), and Lods (*Histoire de la litt. héb. et juive*, p. 405) date the incursion in 626 B.C., while Bewer (*Lit. of the Old Test.*, p. 143) says it was threatening in 626 B.C., Robinson (*History of Israel*, i. 413) says it occurred "about 626 B.C.," and Skinner (op. cit. p. 40) shortly after 626 B.C. Erbt (*Jeremia und seine Zeit*, 1902, pp. 208 f.) dates it between 625 and 620 B.C., and Cornill (*Das Buch Jeremia*, 1905, p. 83) in 623 or 622 B.C. Some authors would put it substantially earlier, and some substantially later. Thus A. George (*Michée, Sophonie, Nahum* [Bible de Jérusalem], 2nd edn., 1958, p. 53) dates it "vers 630", and Eichhorn, op. cit. ii. 9 "um 628"; F. Schwally (*Z.A.W.* x (1890), 216) dates it not earlier than 615 B.C. (though he does not connect it with the prophecies of Jeremiah and Zephaniah); T. T. Rice (*The Scythians*, 1957, p. 45) in 611 B.C. These are very improbable dates, the first because it is known that from 616 B.C. Egypt was actively allied with Assyria and this could hardly have been so while the Scythians were marauding in Syria and Palestine, and the second because when Nineveh fell in 612 B.C. the Assyrian capital was transferred to Harran, which fell in 610 B.C., when Egypt was still in a position to claim domination over the area from the Euphrates to her own border. Rice would apparently accept Gadd's equation of the Umman-manda who helped the Babylonians at Harran with the Scythians (see above p. 41), but the Syrian raid would not appear to fit well between the fall of Nineveh and the fall of Harran, and, as Welch points out (*Jeremiah*, p. 103), it would be difficult to understand why one ally of the Babylonians should attack Egypt, another ally, at such a time. J. Lewy (*Forschungen zur alten Geschichte Vorderasiens*, pp. 51 ff.) would place the Scythian raid much later still, in 592–591 B.C., following a pact with the Babylonians. P. Pezron (*Essai d'un Commentaire littéral et historique sur les douze Prophètes*, 1693), who is described by C. F. Cramer (*Skythische Denkmähler in Palästina*, Einleitung p. 36) as "Pezron der Hypothesenmachter, der Grübler, der unkritische Historiker," held that there were two Scythian incursions, the first in the reign of Jeroboam II and the second in the tenth year of Josiah, in the time of Zephaniah (according to Cramer, op. cit. p. 22, which is my only access to Pezron's work). Cramer (op. cit. p. 23) pronounces the first of these alleged inroads "unerweislich" and the second "erweislich," and brought to this period both Joel and Zephaniah (his commentary on these two books is given on pp. 138 ff.).

The prophet Zephaniah is said to have prophesied in the reign of Josiah,[77] and the background of his prediction of woe has commonly been held to be the Scythian peril.[78] Apart from this no other known historical peril could have been in mind until the last years of Josiah.[79] Before the fall of Nineveh in 612 B.C., no one is likely to have thought of Babylon as a menace to the west, and even after the fall of Nineveh no imminent danger to Palestine from that quarter is likely to have been felt. Egypt occupied the area west of the Euphrates, through Syria and Palestine, and while Josiah lost his life in a vain attempt to oppose her,[80] it is improbable that Zephaniah thought of Egypt as the instrument of the devastation he predicted. The fact that neither he nor Jeremiah names the destroyer would well fit the rootless, roaming hordes of the Scythians. The conjecture that Jeremiah may well have named the Scythians in his oracles in their original form has not been unknown,[81] but this is idle speculation, and the absence of their name from the oracles of Zephaniah gives no support.

It has been maintained by some that Jeremiah had no particular foe in mind,[82] and that his early prophecies were vague eschatological predictions.[83] Zephaniah approached even more nearly to general eschatological prediction. But neither prophet is likely to have uttered his prophecies

[77]Zeph. i. 1.

[78]So W. Nowack, *Die Kleinen Propheten* (H.K.), 1897, p. 278; J. A. Selbie, in *D.B.* iv (1902), 975b; K. Marti, *Dodekapropheton* (K.H.C.), 1904, pp. 359 f.; S. R. Driver, *Minor Prophets* (Cent B.), ii. 119; A. van Hoonacker, *Les douze petits Prophètes* (E. Bib.), 1908, p. 500; J. M. Powis Smith, *Zephaniah* (I.C.C.), 1912, pp. 162 f.; C. Steuernagel, *Einleitung*, p. 636; A. B. Davidson and H. C. O. Lanchester, *Nahum, Habakkuk and Zephaniah* (Camb. B.), 1920, pp. 105 f.; G. A. Smith, *The Book of the Twelve Prophets*, 2nd edn. ii (1928), 39f.; E. Sellin, *Das Zwölfprophetenbuch* (K.A.T.), 1929, p. 415; G. G. V. Stonehouse, *Zephaniah* (West C.), 1929, pp. 3, 8 f.; O. Eissfeldt (in *Die Zwölf Kleinen Propheten* [H.A.T.], ii, 2nd edn., 1954, pp. 188 f., and *Einleitung in das Alte Testament*, 2nd edn., 1956, p. 521). This view is rejected by F. Horst, *Die Zwölf Kleinen Propheten* (H.A.T.), ii, 2nd edn., p. 195; G. Gerleman, *Zephanja*, 1942, p. 126; J. P. Hyatt, *J.N.E.S.* vii (1948), pp. 25 ff.

[79]König (*Einleitung in das Alte Testament*, 1893, pp. 352 ff.) and Hyatt (loc. cit.) would transfer the ministry of Zephaniah to the reign of Jehoiakim.

[80]2 Kings xxiii. 28 ff.

[81]So G. A. Smith, *Jeremiah*, p. 111. Piotrowicz (*Eos*, xxxii (1929), 492) thinks the lack of precision in Jeremiah's references may arise from the fact that he had never seen the Scythians.

[82]Cf. Nägelsbach, *Jeremiah*, Eng. trans., p. 24; J. F. McCurdy, *History, Prophecy and the Monuments*, ii (1896), 395 f. F. Nötscher, *Jeremias* (H.S.A. Tes.) 1934, p. 79; A. Gelin, in *S.D.B.* iv (1949), 879; A. Weiser, *Jeremia* (A.T.D. i, 1952), 44; E. A. Leslie, *Jeremiah*, 1954, p. 51; W. Rudolph, *Jeremia*, 2nd edn., 1958, p. 45. A. Aeschimann (*Le prophète Jérémie*, 1959, p. 63) thinks Jeremiah had no definite enemy in mind, but drew traits from both Babylonians and Scythians (cf. A. Gelin, in A. Robert and A. Feuillet, *Introduction à la Bible*, i (1957), 528, where it is suggested that the Scythians left traces on the language of the prophet). Cf. the view of van Hoonacker (op. cit. p. 500), that the Scythians were not the only cause of the apprehensions of Zephaniah.

[83]So A. C. Welch, *Jeremiah*, 1928, pp. 97 ff.; cf. A Lauha, *Zaphon*, 1943, pp. 62 ff., and W. Staerk, *Z.A.W.* li (1933), 9 ff.

without thinking of some human power that would be the instrument of the disaster God was about to bring on the world.[84] Welch suggested that the destroyer of nations of whom Jeremiah spoke was "the first faint hint of the conception which gave rise to the figure of Antichrist."[85] But Antichrist is always the enemy of God and His people, whereas the foe whose ravages Jeremiah predicted was the instrument of God to discipline His people, and so far as Zephaniah was concerned, it was the Day of the Lord, and not the Day of Antichrist, of which he spoke.

A few recent writers still hold the view, which was current before the Scythian hypothesis became current, that while the call of Jeremiah fell in the year 626 B.C., the enemy he had in mind from the start was the Chaldaeans.[86] At that time the Chaldaeans were but launching their revolt against Assyria, and were just striking for independence and not even menacing Assyria, let alone countries in the west.[87] A century earlier, Isaiah had warned Hezekiah against alliance with the Chaldaeans when they made an earlier bid for independence, and had not hesitated to name them.[88] There would seem no reason why Jeremiah should not name them in 626 B.C., if he really had them in mind. Besides, in his second inaugural vision the message that came to him was "I am calling all the tribes of the kingdoms of the north."[89] This would more naturally describe hordes which poured from the southern steppes of Russia than the Chaldaeans, even though the approach of either to Palestine would be from the north.[90]

[84]Cf. J. P. Hyatt, *J.B.L.* lix (1940), 506 f.; "Welch is undoubtedly correct in insisting that with Jeremiah the ultimate source of the doom was Yahweh. So it probably was with the other prophets, but they generally thought of Yahweh as using a human agency to carry out his will. Apart from this, the description of the foe from the north is often sufficiently detailed to make it clear that the prophet had in mind a definite people."

[85]Op. cit. p. 126.

[86]So E. J. Young, *Introduction to the Old Testament*, 1949, p. 225.

[87]Piotrowicz (*Eos*, xxxii (1929), 491) observes that it is impossible to believe that Jeremiah or Zephaniah could have thought of the Babylonians, and that the only foe that could have been in mind was the Scythians.

[88]2 Kings xx. 12 ff.; Isa. xxxix.

[89]Jer. i. 15.

[90]Condamin (op. cit. p. 63) presses the consideration that the approach to Palestine would in any case be from the north, and compares Isa. xiv. 31 and Jer. xiii. 20. But these passages are not really to be compared. They refer merely to the route of approach, and not to the source of the enemy armies. As Welch says (op. cit. p. 121), Jeremiah's expression would be a remarkable description of a people whom every man in his audience knew to live in the east. Condamin (loc. cit.) further cites Jer. xxv.9, where "all the tribes of the north" are mentioned along with Nebuchadnezzar. Here, however, we should remember that allied with the Chaldaeans in their attack on Assyria were the Umman-manda. Whether these are to be equated with the Scythians or not (see above, p. 208), they were certainly a kindred people. Throughout the seventh century wave after wave of these invading hordes had poured over the Assyrian frontiers, and for Jeremiah to refer to them as "all the tribes of the kingdoms of the north" would be more easily understandable than so to refer to the Chaldaeans or Babylonians. That Jeremiah should give the same description to Scythians in 626 B.C. and to the barbarian allies of Nebuchadnezzar at a later time would be easily intelligible, since they were of a

The initial call of Jeremiah, as expressed in the second inaugural vision, was not merely to announce disaster from the northern invader, but also judgment on the people of Judah for their idolatry and wickedness.[91] In his early prophecies we find many references to their unfaithfulness to God and the idolatry that flourished throughout the land,[92] as well as to the breaches of the moral law which were common amongst all classes in Jerusalem.[93] If these early prophecies fell before the reform of Josiah, they belonged to the time when the country shrines were still functioning. But with the reform of Josiah the country shrines were closed. It is sometimes thought that later in the reign of Josiah the reform had lost its impetus, and the old practices may have appeared afresh.[94] But there is no evidence that the country shrines were reopened during the reign of Josiah.[95] It is for this reason that those who reject the Biblical date for the call of the prophet are constrained to transfer that call to the reign of Jehoiakim. For there can be no doubt that religious conditions in the reign of Jehoiakim were as little satisfying to the prophet as those which prevailed before the reform of Josiah.[96] Early in the reign of Jehoiakim Jeremiah delivered the Temple address recorded in Jeremiah xxvi. It is usually thought that the Temple address given in Jeremiah vii is a duplicate report of the same incident, though no date is there given.[97] Torrey thinks this is unlikely,[98] and sees no reason why Jeremiah should not repeat essentially the same message at different points in his career.[99] Here, however, we have to remember that after the address of Jeremiah xxvi the prophet's life was in danger[100] and he

---

common South Russian origin. Gadd justifies his use of "Scythians" for the Umman-manda by saying they are both generic terms which may be applied indiscriminately to all the various northern Aryan tribes which overran Asia Minor and the adjoining lands at this period, though he recognizes that the actual term "Scythians" is nowhere used of the Umman-manda (*Fall of Nineveh*, p. 14 n.).

[91] Jer. i. 16.

[92] Jer. ii. f.

[93] Jer. v.

[94] Cf. Hyatt, *J.N.E.S.* i (1942), 161.

[95] Cf. C. C. Torrey, *J.B.L.* lvi (1937), 203 f.: "Neither Josiah nor his powerful supporters would have permitted any defection from the covenant while he lived." H. G. May (*J.N.E.S.* iv (1945), 226 n.) rejects the view of Hyatt, and asks if Jeremiah could have described Josiah in the terms of Jer. xxii. 15 f. if his view were right.

[96] Cf. Jer. xxii. 12–23. Nevertheless, as A. S. Peake (*Jeremiah*, i. 150) says: "Jehoiakim was a worthless king, and probably quite out of sympathy with his father's religious policy. Yet we have no explicit evidence to convict him of reinstating, or even permitting, the re-introduction of idolatry."

[97] On the Temple sermon cf. G. Fohrer, *Th.Z.* v (1949), 401 ff. See also P. F. Stone, *A.J.S.L.* l (1934), 73 ff.

[98] Cf. *J.B.L.* lvi (1937), 194 ff. Torrey calls the view that the account of Jer. vii and that of chapter xxvi refer to the same Temple discourse "a strange theory."

[99] Torrey assigns the discourse of chapter vii to the time before the finding of the Law Book (ibid. p. 199 n.). H. G. May (*J.N.E.S.* iv (1945), 223) holds that the account in Jer. vii is a much expanded version of that in chapter xxvi.

[100] Jer. xxvi. 16 ff.

was only spared when attention was drawn to the fact that Micah had not suffered when he prophesied the destruction of the Temple in the time of Hezekiah.[101] If Jeremiah had uttered a similar prophecy in the reign of Josiah without being punished for it, we should have expected this more recent precedent to be cited. It would seem likely, therefore, that we should accept the common view that chapters vii and xxvi refer to the same Temple address.

This does not mean that the whole of Jeremiah vii refers to events that fell in the reign of Jehoiakim. Jeremiah vii. 16–20 speak of the women of Judah making cakes in honour of the queen of heaven. These verses interrupt the Temple discourse of Jeremiah and contain a message from God to the prophet. They appear to be separate from their context and may not necessarily refer to the same time.[102] We remember that after Jeremiah had been carried into Egypt he found the same practice of making cakes in honour of the queen of heaven.[103] The people refused to listen to the prophet and referred to the misfortunes which had overtaken them since they had ceased to worship the queen of heaven, and boldly announced their intention of resuming that worship. This does not read as if the reform of Josiah had been completely reversed in the reign of Jehoiakim, and it would seem to imply that the worship of the queen of heaven had been interrupted from the time of the reform until after the fall of Jerusalem.[104] In that case the only earlier point in the life of Jeremiah when he could have been confronted with the practice lay before the reform of Josiah. This brings some additional evidence for the placing of his call before that reform. It is true, of course, that in the reign of Jehoiakim the court is unlikely to have shown much interest in the enforcement of the Law Book, and older practices may have begun to appear.[105] But the women of the community in which Jeremiah was in Egypt do not seem to have been aware that this particular practice had reappeared. Yet at some earlier point in the ministry of Jeremiah it had been current.

There would seem, therefore, to be strong reason to accept the date given for the call of Jeremiah,[106] the thirteenth year of the reign of Josiah,

---

[101] Jer. xxvi. 17 ff.

[102] Cf. Peake, *Jeremiah*, i. 149 f.

[103] Jer. xliv. 15 ff.

[104] Cf. Peake, loc. cit.: "The impression we gain from xliv is that this form of worship had not been resumed after the reformation of Josiah, for in reply to Jeremiah's appeal that his hearers will not practice it, they retort that all their calamities are due to neglect of it."

[105] Cf. Jer. xxii. 20–33; vii. 8 ff.

[106] J. Milgrom (*J.N.E.S.* xiv (1955), 65 ff.) argues that Jer. ii belongs to the period 627–622 B.C., and hence maintains that the date of the superscription of the book is to be accepted. He maintains (pp. 67 f.) that all the references to idolatry in Jeremiah belong to the period before the reform of Josiah. P. E. Broughton (*A.B.R.* vi (1958), 39 ff.) claims that the account of the call of Jeremiah in Jer. i. 4–10 reflects Deut. xviii. 9–22, and adds that this has some bearing on the relationship between Jeremiah and Deuteronomy. It is not clear, however, whether he

and to believe that there was some historical basis for the account of the Scythian incursion reported by Herodotus, and to find in this incursion the background of Jeremiah's prophecy of trouble from the north, as well as for the prophecies of Zephaniah. While the Scythians are not named in the books of Jeremiah and Zephaniah, this is more than an unsupported conjecture. It rests on the evidence of Herodotus and on that of the book of Jeremiah, and these are quite independent of one another.[107] The alternative views rest not on evidence but on the explaining away of the only evidence we have.

It is certain that if Zephaniah had the Scythian peril in mind, his prophecies were not fulfilled.[108] It is equally true that whatever he had in mind, his prophecy of universal desolation was not fulfilled in the seventh century b.c., though the prophecy of devastation for the cities of Philistia fits well into the story of Herodotus concerning Ashkelon. It may well be that there was a good deal more suffering for the people of Palestine and Syria than we should gather from the story of Herodotus, since he was not concerned to record all their doings. We should not, therefore, argue too much from silence. But it is certain that the Scythian peril did not bring upon Judah such miseries as the early prophecies of Jeremiah envisaged.[109] This was not unique in the experience of Jeremiah. If, as some suppose, these early prophecies followed a call after the rise of Babylon and had Babylon in mind, then it is equally true that they were not then fulfilled, and it was not until the disastrous rebellion that led to the destruction of Jerusalem that his prophecies found any real fulfilment.

Those who accept the Scythian hypothesis recognize that Jeremiah's prophecies were not fulfilled by that incursion, but many of them think it probable that, troubled though Jeremiah was, he relapsed into silence[110] until the new peril from the north in the form of the Chaldaean armies of

---

means that this has a bearing on the date of the prophet's call, or on the date of the account of it.

[107] Piotrowicz (*Eos*, xxxii (1929), 489) emphasizes the fact that the witness of Herodotus and that of Jeremiah and Zephaniah mutually confirm one another.

[108] Piotrowicz (*Eos*, xxxii (1929), 493) suggests that the retreat of the Scythians is hailed in Zeph. iii. 14 f.

[109] Skinner (op. cit. p. 41 n.) observes that the silence of the Hebrew historians with regard to this incursion is remarkable. It would not be remarkable, however, if Judah did not suffer greatly and if her people were not seriously harried in the progress and withdrawal of the invaders. Cf. Erbt, *Jeremia und seine Zeit*, 1902, pp. 208. J. F. McCurdy (*History, Prophecy, and the Monuments*, ii (1896), 395) says the terror they inspired was their most serious infliction on the people of Judah.

[110] Cf. Peake, op. cit. i. 11. After his advocacy of the Josianic reform, and subsequent disillusionment (see below) he seems to have relapsed again into silence, and we have no datable evidence of his activity from then until the reign of Jehoiakim. Cf. Vittonatto, *Geremia*, 1955, p. 14b; A. Weiser, *Introduction to the Old Testament*, Eng. trans. by D. M. Barton, 1961, p. 210. J. M. Powis Smith, who holds that the reform of Josiah did not stir Jeremiah to utterance, thinks he lapsed into silence after the withdrawal of the Scythians for fourteen years (*The Prophets and their Times*, 1925, p. 118).

Nebuchadnezzar led him to reissue the prophecies, retouched to meet the new situation.[111] Of this there can be no proof or disproof. That there are some things in the oracles which have been frequently called the "Scythian Songs," since Duhm coined the name,[112] more relevant to the Chaldaeans than to the Scythians is recognized, and that is why the oracles are believed to have been retouched.[113] Other things are thought to be more relevant to the Scythians than to the Chaldaeans, though this is disputed and the phrases are held to be paralleled elsewhere in the Old Testament, where the reference is clearly to the Assyrians or the Babylonians.[114] It is just possible that the non-mention of the Chaldaeans by name is due to the fact that the original oracles did not mention the name of the foe. But even if it be true that everything in the oracles as they now stand could have relevance to the Chaldaeans, this cannot prove that they were originally uttered in relation to them. For it is precisely what we should expect if the theory is correct. After the oracles had been retouched to fit them to the new situation, it would be expected that they would fit it. The view that these oracles have been retouched is born of the fact that Jeremiah's ministry is stated to have begun at approximately the time to which Herodotus assigns the Scythian invasion, and of the recognition that as they stand they are appropriate to the Chaldaeans, even though some things could equally well apply to the Scythians, and some things perhaps better to them.[115]

[111]So, e.g. Peak, *Jeremiah*, i. 117; S. R. Driver, *Jeremiah*, p. 21, and *L.O.T.*, 9th edn., p. 253; F. C. Jean, *Jérémie, sa politique, sa théologie*, 1913, p. 10; Streane, op. cit. p. 25; G. A. Smith, *Jeremiah*, pp. 110 f., 117, 122, 126, 382; R. H. Pfeiffer, *Introduction to the Old Testament*, 1941, p. 502; I.G. Matthews, *The Religious Pilgrimage of Israel*, 1947, p. 146 n.; J. A. Bewer, *The Prophets*, 1955, p. 185. H. Wheeler Robinson (*The Cross in the Old Testament*, 1955, p. 127) says: "It was natural that in 604, when the Babylonians . . . were first coming into the arena of Palestine, Jeremiah should make a new identification. The prophets stood for principles, not for the details of their application, and the principles of 626 received a new application in 604." L. Gautier (*Introduction*, 3rd edn., i. 390) expresses some caution about the retouching, and Skinner (op. cit. p. 43 n.) says it is possible that the poems were modified, but this assumption is hardly necessary.

[112]Cf. *Jeremia*, p. 48. On the "Scythian Songs," cf. T. L. W. van Ravesteijn, *Theologische Studiën*, xxxi (1913), 241 ff., xxxii (1914), 1 ff.

[113]Many writers have noted the inappropriateness to the Scythians of the description of the foe in Jer. v. 15 as "an ancient nation" (so, e.g. Hyatt, *I.B.* v. 779b; Aeschimann, op. cit. p. 63). T. T. Rice (*The Scythians*, 1957, p. 19) observes that many ancient Greek scholars mistakenly considered the Scythians the world's oldest race. According to Herodotus (*Hist.* iv. 5), they regarded themselves as the youngest of nations. It is improbable that Jeremiah really thought of them as especially ancient, unless he regarded barbarity as a sign of antiquity, though Peake (op. cit. i. 131) and Streane (op. cit. p. 39) see no difficulty in this. Binns (op. cit. p. 51) dismisses Peake's view as pure conjecture, and thinks the Scythians are definitely excluded here. It may be noted that the phrase is omitted from LXX.

[114]Cf. Condamin, op. cit. pp. 63 ff.; Hyatt, *J.B.L.* lix (1940), 502. N. Schmidt (*E.B.* ii (1901), 2390) suggested that there was a Chaldaean contingent amongst the Scythians, but he later modified this view (iv (1907), 4333).

[115]Cf. Skinner, op. cit. p. 42: "Jeremiah's descriptions of the unnamed foe agree *in the main* with what we know of the Scythians"; G. A. Smith, op. cit. p. 383: "the oracles in question far more closely fit the Scythian than the Chaldaean invasion."

We may next turn briefly to the question of the "Confessions of Jeremiah." These consist of a number of passages[116] in which the prophet addressed himself to God, lamenting his lot and the suffering it entailed, and in some passages complaining that the prophecies he had been driven to utter had been unfulfilled and had left him discredited. The best known of these stands in Jeremiah xx. 7 ff.,[117] where the prophet complains that God has overpowered him and compelled him to prophesy and has then made him a laughing stock by the non-fulfillment of his word, until he vowed that he would never prophesy again, only to feel a fire burning in his bones and a constraint to speak that he could not resist.[118]

This passage is not necessarily to be assigned to the later part of Jeremiah's career, and connected with the night which the prophet spent in the stocks in the reign of Zedekiah, as recorded earlier in the same chapter.[119] Skinner thinks it is more likely that the whole series of "Confessions" comes from the middle period of the prophet's ministry, in the latter part of the reign of Josiah.[120] The passage just referred to would seem to look back on a long series of unfulfilled prophecies and of consequent derision, and so would seem to be better placed towards the close of Jeremiah's career, when his sufferings were greatest and when the day of tragic fulfilment was nigh at hand.

It is improbable, however, that the whole series of "Confessions" should be brought closely together in time. The intimate communion with God which is expressed in these passages is something that was characteristic of Jeremiah's experience and likely to mark his dealings with God in all periods. In Jeremiah xi. 18–xii. 6 we have such a passage arising out of the plot against his life by his own family, and this, as I have already said, is usually connected with the time of Josiah's reform, quite early in the ministry of Jeremiah.[121] Some of the "Confessions" may well have fallen either before or after this in the reign of Josiah.

---

[116]Jer. xi. 18–xii. 6; xv. 10–21; xvii. 9 f., 14–18, xviii. 18–23, xx. 7–12, 14–18. On the "Confessions" cf. W. Baumgartner, *Die Klagegedichte des Jeremia*, 1917; Skinner, op. cit. pp. 201 ff.; G. A. Smith, op. cit. pp. 317 ff.; E. A. Leslie, *The Intimate Papers of Jeremiah*, 1953 and *Jeremiah*, 1954, pp. 137 ff.; L. Leclercq, in *Études sur les Prophètes d'Israël*, 1954, pp. 111 ff.; G. M. Behler, *Les Confessions de Jérémie*, 1959.

[117]Torrey (*J.B.L.* lvi (1937), 212 f.) suspects this passage to be of late date and not genuinely from Jeremiah, but elsewhere it is recognized to be the most poignant and moving revelation of the agony of spirit that the prophet endured. Peake (op. cit. i. 241) describes it as "one of the most powerful and impressive passages in the whole of the prophetic literature, a passage which takes us, as no other, not only into the depths of the prophet's soul, but into the secrets of the prophetic consciousness." J. W. Rothstein (in E. Kautzsch and A. Bertholet, *H.S.A.T.*, 4th edn., 1922, p. 781) says its authenticity is beyond doubt.

[118]Skinner (op. cit. pp. 201 f.) says that without these "the devotion of the Jewish Church would have been immeasurably poorer in that strain of personal piety which saves its religion from degenerating into a soulless legalism."

[119]Peake (op. cit. p. 242) and Streane (op. cit. p. 124) attribute it to the early part of the reign of Jehoiakim, and Rothstein (loc. cit.) late in the same reign.

[120]Op. cit. p. 209.

[121]Skinner (op. cit. p. 209) assigns it to the fifth or sixth year of Jeremiah's ministry.

To examine all of the "Confessions" today is impossible, and irrelevant to our subject of the early prophecies of Jeremiah if they were spread throughout his career. But there is one passage at which we should look, since it culminates in a renewal of the call of the prophet. This stands in Jeremiah xv. 10–20. Here the prophet complains that God has let him down like a wady that fails, and that he has suffered reproach and persecution because of his ministry. Then comes the renewed call, when the prophet has the assurance that if he will distinguish between the precious and the vile he shall be as the very mouth of God, and shall be made as a wall of bronze, immovable before the assaults of his enemies. This passage, which clearly belongs to a time after Jeremiah has been prophesying for some time, bears so much resemblance to the initial call of Jeremiah, when he was promised that the Lord's word would be put in his mouth[122] and that he would be delivered from his enemies if he fearlessly uttered that word,[123] and to the message that came to him in his second inaugural vision, promising him that he should be as an iron pillar and a brazen wall against the whole land,[124] that it is rightly regarded as a renewal of the call of Jeremiah. This would seem most probably to be placed at a fairly early point in his ministry. When he first received his call he was conscious of his youthfulness,[125] and he was apparently of timid nature. Many think that he could not have been more than twenty years of age when he had his call,[126] and some think he may have been some years younger than this.[127] Though he felt sure that God was calling him to prophesy and would be with him, it is likely that when the buffets he suffered through discredit and the scorn of men struck him, his timidity reasserted itself. If this could happen towards the end of his career, it is hard to suppose that it could not happen earlier, when the first failures of his prophecies exposed him to the derision of

---

[122] Jer. i. 9.

[123] Jer. i. 8, 19.

[124] Jer. i. 18.

[125] Jer. i. 6.

[126] G. Vittonatto, (*Geremia*, 1955, pp. 9, 87) suggests that he was 25–30 years old; Nötscher (*Echter Bibel*, iii (1958), 217) perhaps 20–30 years of age; A. Penna (*Geremia* [S.B.], 1952, p. 33) thinks the expression could describe one of 20–25 years of age (and so B. Mariani, *Introductio in libros sacros Veteris Testamenti*, 1958, p. 357 n.); C. H. Cornill (*Jeremia*, 1905, p. 6) suggests that Jeremiah was about 25. Cheyne (op. cit. p. 14 n.) says he was probably as much as 20, and so Orelli (*Jesaja und Jeremia*, 2nd edn., 1891, p. 228; Eng. trans. of 1st edn. of *Jeremiah*, 1889, pp. 29 f.), while J. Goettsberger (*Einleitung in das Alte Testament*, 1928, p. 295) suggests that he was not much more than 20; Skinner (op. cit. p. 24 n.) and Leslie (op. cit. p. 22) think he was probably under 20, and Pfeiffer (*Introduction*, p. 493) "not quite 20".

[127] Hyatt (*I.B.* v. 798) suggests that he was but 17 or 18 years old. The same expression is used in 2 Chron. xxxiv. 3 of Josiah when he was 16 years of age. It is also used in 2 Sam. xviii. 5 of Absalom at the time of his rebellion. Hence Binns (*Jeremiah*, p. 5) and Hyatt (*I.B.* v. 802) rightly say we cannot deduce the age of Jeremiah from this word. The fact that Jeremiah was unmarried, and that this was due to his prophetic vocation (Jer. xvi. 2), would seem to indicate that his call came when he was very young, since marriage commonly took place very early. M. D. Goldman (*A.B.R.* ii. Parts 1–2, 1952, 43 ff.) thinks this rests on a mistaken interpretation, and holds that Jeremiah did marry.

men. And the renewal of his call can most naturally be placed after his initial experience of failure. If his faith had survived the experience of failure for any considerable time, it would be surprising for doubts to begin to arise and then continue with him through the rest of his ministry. It is far more natural to suppose that he became uncertain of his call and needed it to be renewed quite early in his career, even though to the end he was troubled by what he called God's deception of him. At the time of his call trouble threatened from the north,[128] and his call bore relation to that trouble and carried a message of disaster and devastation arising from it. One of the most brilliant and at the same time gloomy oracles came from that time:

> I looked at the earth, and lo, chaos!
> At the heaven, and it shed no light.
> I looked at the mountains, and lo, they were quaking,
> And all the hills moved to and fro.
> I looked, and lo, there was no man,
> And all the birds of the air had fled away.
> I looked, and lo, the garden had become a wilderness,
> And all its cities were in ruins.[129]

Here is a picture of desolation which one day would not seem extravagant after Nebuchadnezzar's destruction of Jerusalem, but which went far beyond anything the Scythians may have been responsible for. The non-fulfilment of this prediction must have exposed Jeremiah to the taunts of men, and filled him with misgiving.

If the call of Jeremiah came towards the end of the reign of Josiah or early in the reign of Jehoiakim and had the Chaldaeans in mind, they were not wholly fulfilled, but they were not so spectacularly falsified as to discredit him entirely. Josiah, who shared in a western attempt to secure independence from Assyria that synchronized with the rising of Nabopolassar in Babylon, opposed Pharaoh Necho when he marched to the aid of Assyria, and lost his life.[130] This was such a blow to Judah that the tragic story was long remembered in song.[131] If Jeremiah had already predicted that the Chaldaeans were to bring disaster on Judah, the failure of this ill-omened attempt to play a part on the side of Babylon would not have discredited the prophet. And after the battle of Carchemish, when Nebuchadnezzar pursued the retreating forces of Necho, Jeremiah could well have uttered his prophecies of the approach of the conquering army from the north. Though Judah suffered at that time far less than the "Scythian Songs" would suggest—assuming them to have been first uttered

---

[128] Jer. i. 14.
[129] Jer. iv. 23 ff.
[130] 2 Kings xxiii. 29 f.
[131] 2 Chron. xxxv. 25, where it is said that Jeremiah composed the song.

at this time and to have had reference to the Chaldaeans, and not to the Scythians—it should not be forgotten that Judah at this time came under the yoke of Babylon. There was not, therefore, the complete discrediting of Jeremiah that would make him the butt of taunts and lead him to doubt his very call, whereas if they were spoken first of the Scythians he would be so exposed when the Scythians withdrew, leaving Judah an independent country. Skinner observes that after the Scythians withdrew, "the country settled down to peaceful pursuits, with a fairer prospect of prosperity than it had known since the days of Uzziah and Jeroboam."[132] Such a situation would have appeared to belie Jeremiah's predictions far more completely than anything at a later date, and could most fully account for his need of a renewal of his call. In the reign of Zedekiah, his sufferings were due in part to the charge of disloyalty,[133] since he urged submission to the Chaldaeans,[134] and not simply to the taunts of unfulfilled prophecy. But the "Scythian Songs" are not charged with calls to submission to the foe, but are associated simply with calls to submission to God.[135]

Hence, if the call of Jeremiah took place in 626 B.C., as is stated in Jeremiah i. 2, and if the danger from the north was linked with the Scythian incursion, and if Jeremiah uttered the "Scythian Songs" at that time, prophesying the devastation of the whole land, he must have been completely discredited[136] and exposed to the contempt of men as the false prophet *par excellence* of his time. At such a time, as nowhere else in his career, he would stand in need of a renewal of his call, and an assurance that his word had really come from God.

Let it not be forgotten that though Jeremiah's word, like that of other prophets, was related to a political and international situation, it was not simply born of that situation, and it was not an expression of his political acumen. It was a message from God, and it announced God's judgement on the nation that was flouting His will. That fundamental message was a true one, and it ultimately found its fulfilment in the disaster that came upon the nation in 586 B.C. The prophet at first mistook the time of the judgement, and more than once seems to have thought it was nearer than it actually was. But his message that the nation that forsook the will of God could only stumble forward to disaster was a true message from God, and in the end it was tragically fulfilled.

---

[132]Op. cit. p. 89.

[133]Jer. xxxvii. 11 ff., xxxviii. 4.

[134]Jer. xxxviii. 2.

[135]As H. P. Smith (*Religion of Israel*, pp. 165 f.) observes, we here have not only a picture of the invader, but of the intense sympathy the prophet felt for his own people.

[136]Cf. Peake, op. cit. i. 11: "He must have seemed to the people to have been discredited by the failure of his predictions. The foe from the north had come, but it had also gone, while Judah remained unshaken." Cf. J. M. Powis Smith, *The Prophets and their Times*, 1925, p. 117; H. Wheeler Robinson, *The Cross in the Old Testament*, 1955, p. 144.

We must now turn to the question of Jeremiah's attitude to Josiah's reform. If he did not receive his call until some years after that reform had been carried through, he could have played no part in it. On the other hand, if he received his call some years before the Law Book was found in the Temple and made the basis of the reform, we should expect Jeremiah to adopt some attitude in relation to it. Attention is sometimes drawn to the fact that the king consulted the prophetess Huldah about the Law Book, and not Jeremiah.[137] We know nothing further about Huldah, and to some it would seem incredible that she should be consulted rather than Jeremiah,[138] if he were already active as a prophet, since we recognize his stature to have been far greater than Huldah's. But if Jeremiah's prophecies concerning the Scythians had been so completely falsified as we have seen reason to believe, his stature would not seem very great to people or court, and we can hardly wonder that this prophet, who was still but young and who seemed only a false prophet, should be ignored by the king.

In Jeremiah xi we read that Jeremiah felt called to proclaim in the cities of Judah and the streets of Jerusalem the words of the covenant,[139] and to summon men to obedience to the words of this covenant.[140] The passage is full of Deuteronomic phraseology, and it has long seemed certain to most scholars that Jeremiah was here advocating the reform and its basis in the Deuteronomic law.[141] Some of those who have placed Jeremiah's call later than the reform have held that the ascription of his call

---

[137] 2 Kings xxii. 14.

[138] T. C. Gordon (*E.T.* xliv (1932–3), 563 f.) says the only way out of this dilemma is to recognize that Jeremiah was not yet on the stage of events. Cf. also A. F. Puukko, in *Alttestamentliche Studien R. Kittel dargebracht*, 1913, p. 134; Hyatt, *J.N.E.S.* i (1942), 166. Torrey (*J.B.L.* lvi (1937), 119 n.) goes so far as to suggest that the compiler of 2 Kings did not know of Jeremiah.

[139] Jer. xi. 6.

[140] Jer. xi. 3 ff.

[141] So, e.g. Orelli, op. cit. p. 216 (Eng. trans., p. 3); K. Marti, *Z.Th.K.* ii (1892), 54 ff.; F. Giesebrecht, *Jeremia* (H.K.), 1894, p. 67; Cheyne, op. cit. pp. 55 ff.; W. W. von Baudissin, in *D.B.* iv (1902), 91a; V. Ryssel, *J.E.* vii. 96b; Peake, op. cit. i. 11 ff.; S. R. Driver, *Jeremiah*, p. 65, *L.O.T.*, 9th edn., p. 255; C. Steuernagel, *Einleitung*, p. 546; Streane, op. cit. pp. 75 ff.; H. Schmidt, *Die grossen Propheten* (S.A.T.), 2nd edn., 1923, p. 240; Skinner, op. cit. pp. 89 ff.; G. A. Smith, *Jeremiah*, pp. 134 ff.; E. Bruston, in Westphal's *Dictionnaire encyclopédique de la Bible*, i (1932), 605a; Condamin, op. cit. pp. 103 ff.; Pfeiffer, *Introduction*, pp. 493, 495; A. Robert, *Recherches de Science Religieuse*, xxxi (1943), 5 ff.; J. Paterson, *The Goodly Fellowship of the Prophets*, 1948, pp. 148 ff.; A. Gelin, *S.D.B.* iv. 864 ff. and *Jérémie* (Bible de Jérusalem), 2nd edn., 1959, p. 11; R. Augé, *Jeremias* (Montserrat Bible), 1950, pp. 17 f., 117; H. Cazelles, *Recherches de Science Religieuse*, xxxix (1951), 5 ff.; G. Vittonatto, *Geremia*, 1955, pp. 12 ff.; B. W. Anderson, op. cit. p. 318. Binns (op. cit. p. 8) is doubtful. Cheyne (op. cit. p. 56) goes so far as to suggest that Jeremiah was present when the Law Book was read to the king. E. König (*Geschichte der alttestamentlichen Religion*, 1915, pp. 441 ff.) maintains that Jer. xi refers to Josiah's Law Book, but that this was not Deuteronomy. T. C. Gordon (*E.T.* xliv (1932–3), 564 n.) thinks Jer. xi. 3 refers to the ancient covenant in Egypt. Cf. Rudolph, op. cit. pp. 71 f.

to the year 626 B.C. was deliberately designed to make him appear to be a supporter of the reform, and have held that passages such as the one we are now considering were the invention of the Deuteronomic editors of the book to support that impression.[142] This at least recognizes that in the only record we have of the life and activity of Jeremiah, he is presented as a supporter of the reform. And once more it is pertinent to observe that we can only discuss his career in terms of the record that has come down to us, and we are not justified in removing without evidence whatever is inconvenient to a different view which we wish to impose on the record.

Various ways of avoiding the conclusion that Jeremiah at first favoured the reform have been proposed. Some have argued that the book of Deuteronomy was not composed until after the time of Jeremiah, and that it reflects the influence of this prophet.[143] It is unnecessary to examine this view today, partly because it would be hard to find scholars who hold it now, and partly because some years ago I examined this question in some detail and offered reasons for rejecting it.[144] That Josiah's Law Book was Deuteronomy in some form, though not wholly identical with the present

---

[142]Cf. Hyatt, *J.N.E.S.* i (1942), 158, *Vanderbilt Studies in the Humanities*, i (1951), 91 and *I.B.* v. 906. Cf. also A. Bentzen, *Introduction*, 2nd edn., ii. 118 f. Skinner (op. cit. p. 102) remarks that we know of no circumstances that called for the fictitious attribution to Jeremiah of support for Deuteronomy. C. Kuhl (*The Old Testament: its Origins and Composition*, Eng. trans. by C. T. M. Herriott, 1961, p. 188) thinks the passage was derived to a considerable extent from Jeremiah, but was revised, perhaps by disciples of Jeremiah who were very close to Deuteronomic circles.

[143]Cf. R. H. Kennett, *Deuteronomy and the Decalogue*, 1920 (reprinted in *The Church of Israel*, 1933, pp. 73 ff.), and *J.T.S.* vi (1905), 161 ff., vii (1906), 481 ff.; G. R. Berry, *J.B.L.* xxxix (1920), 44 ff., lix (1940), 133 ff.; G. Hölscher, *Z.A.W.* xl (1922), 161 ff.; F. Horst, *Z.A.W.* xli (1923), 94 ff., and *Z.D.M.G.* lxxvii (1923), 220 ff.; J. N. Schofield, in *Studies in History and Religion* (ed. by E. A. Payne), 1942, pp. 44 ff. Amongst older scholars who advocated a post-exilic date for Deuteronomy the following may be noted: C. W. P. Gramberg, *Kritische Geschichte der Religionsideen des Alten Testaments*, i (1829), pp. xxvi, 153 ff., 308 ff.; W. Vatke, *Die Religion des Alten Testamentes nach den Kanonischen Büchern*, 1835, pp. 504–9 n. ; G. d'Eichtal, *Mélanges de critique biblique*, 1886, pp. 81 ff. (see M. Vernes, *M. Gustave d'Eichtal et ses travaux sur l'Ancien Testament*, 1887, pp. 33 ff.); M. Vernes, *Précis d'Histoire juive*, 1889, pp. 468 ff., 795 n.; L. Horst, *R.H.R.* xvi (1887), 28 ff., xvii (1888), 1 ff., xviii (1888), 320 ff., xxiii (1891), 184 ff., xxvii (1893), 119 ff.

[144]Cf. *Studies in Old Testament Prophecy* (T. H. Robinson Festschrift), 1950, pp. 157 ff. On the question of the date of Deuteronomy, see the symposium by J. A. Bewer, L. B. Paton, and G. Dahl in *J.B.L.* xlvii (1928), 305 ff., 322 ff., 358 ff.; also H. Gressmann, *Z.A.W.* xlii (1924), 313 ff.; J. Battersby Harford, *Expositor*, 9th ser., iv (1925), 323 ff.; K. Budde, *Z.A.W.* xliv (1926), 117 ff.; W. C. Graham, *J.R.* vii (1927), 396 ff.; W. Baumgartner, *Th.R.*, N.R. i (1929), 7 ff. That there are links between Jeremiah and Deuteronomy is undoubted, but the direction of the influence is the point at issue. Cf. W. Gesenius, *De Pentateuchi Samaritani origine, indole et auctoritate*, 1815, p. 7; P. von Bohlen, *Historical and Critical Illustrations of the First Part of Genesis*, Eng. trans. by J. Heywood, i (1862), 270 ff.; S. R. Driver, *Jeremiah*, pp. xli–xliv. Hölscher (loc. cit.) and Horst (loc. cit.) deny the authenticity of all passages in Jeremiah which appear to show dependence on Deuteronomy, while Kennett (loc. cit.) and Schofield (loc. cit.) think Deuteronomy was influenced by Jeremiah.

book of Deuteronomy, seems to be one of the most firmly established results of Old Testament scholarship.[145]

That Jeremiah should advocate Josiah's reform has seemed to many antecedently improbable, and even incredible.[146] Jeremiah appears to have had so little use for the cultus[147] that they have felt he could not have been interested in the concentration of that cultus in Jerusalem or anywhere else. We know that in the time of Jehoiakim Jeremiah predicted the destruction of the Temple,[148] as Micah had done a century earlier,[149] and but for powerful advocacy he might have lost his life at that time.[150] He asked whether God had commanded sacrifice in the wilderness period in terms that have led many to suppose that he disapproved of any sacrifice.[151] This seems to me to be an overpressing of his words.[152] It is true that he

---

[145]Cf. J. P. Hyatt, *J.N.E.S.* i (1942), 158: "The date of Deuteronomy is one of the most assured results of modern criticism and an important keystone in the whole structure of modern views of the Old Testament."

[146]Cf. Kennett, *Deuteronomy and the Decalogue*, pp. 12 ff. (*Church of Israel*, pp. 81 ff.); Schofield, loc. cit. pp. 58 f.; Hyatt, loc. cit. p. 162. Hence many have rejected Jer. xi. 1–14 as a late addition; cf. e.g. Duhm, op. cit. pp. 106 ff.; Cornill, op. cit. pp. 143 ff.; Hyatt, loc. cit. pp. 168 ff. A. F. Puukko, in *Alttestamentliche Studien R. Kittel dargebracht*, 1913, pp. 127 ff. examines Jeremiah's attitude to Deuteronomy and concludes (p. 153) by saying that the prophet was from the beginning passive and then increasingly hostile, while A. B. Davidson (*D.B.* ii (1899), 570b) thought it improbable that Jeremiah advocated Deuteronomy, and A. Weiser (*Jeremia* [A.T.D.], i. 100 f.) thinks Jeremiah's attitude to the reform cannot be determined on the basis of chapter xi. G. G. Findlay (*E.T.* xviii [1906–7], 298n.) says that if Jeremiah had been as hostile to the reform as Duhm supposes, we should have heard a great deal more about the matter than we do. L. Dennefeld, *Les grands Prophètes* (Pirot-Clamer's Sainte Bible), 1946, pp. 277 f. says Jeremiah xi is not concerned with Josiah's law, but belongs to the time of Jehoiakim (so, earlier, J. W. Rothstein (in Kautzsch-Bertholet, *H.S.A.T.*, 4th edn., i (1922), 755); Volz, *Jeremia*, p. 130; and Nötscher, *Jeremias*, pp. 106 f.; cf. P. F. Stone, *A.J.S.L.* l (1934), 74).

[147]Cf. Skinner, op. cit. p. 105: "the disinclination to admit even a temporary co-operation of Jeremiah with the Deuteronomists rests less on the exegesis of particular texts than on the broad ground that his insight into the nature of religion makes it inconceivable that he could ever have had any sympathy with an attempt to convert the nation by a forcible change in its forms of worship." Cf. also Peake, op. cit. i. 12. Most scholars, though in varying degree, recognize that Jeremiah was critical of the cultus. At the other extreme is A. Haldar (*Associations of Cult Prophets*, pp. 112 f., 121 f.), who holds that Jeremiah was a cultic prophet on the staff of the Temple.

[148]Jer. xxvi. 6; cf. vii. 14.

[149]Mic. iii. 12.

[150]Jer. xxvi. 17 ff.

[151]Jer. vii. 22.

[152]Cf. what I have written elsewhere in *The Unity of the Bible*, 1953, pp. 31 ff., 40 f., and *B.J.R.L.* xxix (1945–6), 22 ff. J. Jocz (*The Spiritual History of Israel*, 1961, p. 71 n.) says I make every effort to deny any fundamental difference between prophet and priest. This is a complete misrepresentation of my position. I recognize a difference of function and emphasis between prophet and priest, but maintain that prophet and priest were not exponents of two totally different religions. Curiously enough, Jocz goes far beyond me when he says (p. 69), "The 'Law' is essentially prophetic and the cultic elements are used for prophetic ends." This

condemned trust in the Temple as a guarantee of security for the nation, and said it could as easily be destroyed as the shrine of Shiloh had been.[153] But it should not be forgotten that in the same speech he declared that if men would amend their ways and obey the will of God they could dwell in security in the land,[154] and it was only because they did not so obey Him that the Temple would be destroyed. This does not suggest that he disapproved of the Temple as such,[155] but only of the Temple and its cultus as a substitute for obedience to the will of God in all the relationships of life. When he condemned sacrifices, the condemnation was always linked with the condemnation of the life of the people, and this would strongly suggest that in his view the sacrifices were vain because they were empty acts and not the expression of any true devotion to the will of God.

But even if these passages were to be interpreted as others interpret them and mean that Jeremiah was utterly opposed to all sacrifice and to all the worship of the Temple and believed the Temple itself had no place in the purpose of God, it would not follow that he could not have supported the reform of Josiah. For the Temple discourse was uttered at the beginning of the reign of Jehoiakim, some seventeen years after the finding of the Law Book. We have no right to assume that Jeremiah's teaching was static throughout his career.[156]

The book of Deuteronomy was a Law Book, inculcating cultic acts. But it has long been recognized to rest also on the teachings of the eighth-century prophets, and to inculcate prophetic principles.[157] While it is hard

---

would seem to obscure the difference between prophet and priest more than anything I would say. How Jocz reconciles this with his view expressed elsewhere in the same volume (pp. 82 ff.), that the preexilic canonical prophets were opposed to the whole institution of sacrifice, I am not able to see. How the Law could use for prophetic ends cultic elements which were diametrically opposed to those ends is not obvious. On Jeremiah's attitude to sacrifice and the Temple, cf. K. Marti, *Z. Th.K.* ii (1892), 64 f.: "Neimand kann bei dieser Rede meinen, dass er den Tempel als solchen verwerfen wollte; das lag nicht von ferne in seinem Sinn. Ebenso fiel es ihm nicht ein, jedes Opfer als ein Ungerechtigkeit zu verwerfen.... Jeremia achtete den Tempel viel höher als seine Zeitgenossen, er war ihm kein Amulett, kein Talisman, und die Opfer darin hatten kein magisch wirkende Kraft." A. Robert (*Recherches de Science Religieuse*, xxxi (1943), l) refers to "le vieux préjugé protestant d'après lequel les prophètes auraient condamné le culte non seulement dans ses abus, mais pour lui-même." On Jeremiah's attitude to the cultus cf. further A. Strobel, *B.Z.*, N.F. i (1957), 214 ff.

[153] Jer. vii. 14, xxvi. 6.

[154] Jer. vii. 5 ff.; cf. xxvi. 4, where the prediction of destruction is conditional on the rejection of the prophet's word, which is introduced by the observation "It may be they will listen."

[155] Meek (*Expositor*, 8th ser., xxv (1923), 218 f.) says that to Jeremiah the Temple was a hindrance to the religious life. In that case he should have desired its destruction anyhow, and not merely if the people refused to amend their ways.

[156] Skinner (op. cit. p. 105) pertinently asks "Had Jeremiah nothing to learn?"

[157] J. Paterson (*The Goodly Fellowship of the Prophets*, 1948, pp. 148) observes: "It represented an effort to codify the prophetic spirit, to write into the statute book of the realm the ideals of Israel's great religious leaders."

to imagine Jeremiah writing the book of Deuteronomy—though even this improbable idea has found advocates[158]—it is not hard to see him welcoming the book as a great step forward.[159] He had denounced the worship of the scattered shrines, and had stigmatized it as the worship of a multiplicity of gods,[160] and hence as completely rejected by Yahweh. He would surely, therefore, welcome the suppression of these shrines and the Deuteronomic insistence on the oneness of God,[161] and, as I have already said, this would well explain the wrath of his own kinsfolk, and their plot to kill him.[162] He would welcome the purification of the Temple and the elimination of the abominations that had marked the reign of Manasseh. And he must have welcomed the emphasis on true devotion of spirit that marks Deuteronomy. While there were doubtless provisions in Deuteronomy which would not greatly appeal to him,[163] there was much which would, and, as Peake observes, "every reformer discovers that he has to be

---

[158]For references, cf. Puukko, loc. cit. pp. 126 f. See also Colenso, op. cit. vii. 12, 262. C. F. Volney (*Oeuvres Complètes*, 1838, p. 335) supposed that Jeremiah collaborated with Hilkiah in the writing of Deuteronomy. The Talmud (*Baba Bathra*, 15a) ascribed to Jeremiah the authorship of the books of Kings, and so of the story of the finding of the Book of the Law and of Josiah's reform, and this has been accepted by many authors. Cf. R. Cornely and A. Merk, *Introductionis in S. Scripturae libros Compendium*, 10th edn., i (1929), 391 f.

[159]On Jeremiah's attitude to Deuteronomy, cf. Puukko, loc. cit. pp. 94 ff.; Skinner, op. cit. pp. 89 ff.; G. A. Smith, op. cit. pp. 134 ff.; J. P. Hyatt, *J.N.E.S.* i (1942), 156 ff.; H. H. Rowley, *Studies in Old Testament Prophecy* (T. H. Robinson Festschrift), 1950, pp. 157 ff.; A. Robert, *Recherches de Science Religieuse*, xxxi (1943), 5 ff.; H. Cazelles, ibid. xxxix (1951), 5 ff.

[160]Jer. ii f.

[161]Peake (op. cit. i. 12 f.) thinks Jeremiah was never fully in harmony with the reform, but observes that there was much in the Law with which he would feel in full sympathy, and even the reform of the cultus would in many respects be pleasing to him. Cf. Streane, op. cit. p. 61: "With the moral tone of that Book he was in full sympathy, as is shown by his frequent use of its words and phrases, and persistent enforcement of its general teaching." G. A. Smith, op. cit. p. 140: "That he was in sympathy with the temper and the general truths of Deuteronomy we need not doubt." It is curious that of those who would deny that Jeremiah at first supported the Deuteronomic reform, some excise from the book of Jeremiah all that suggests that he supported it and others find in these same passages evidence that Deuteronomy is later than Jeremiah and bears the marks of his influence. Needless to say, if the book of Jeremiah is re-edited to make it fit a theory, it is not surprising that it then fits it. But the theory is not supported by the surgery to which it leads. As for the other alternative, it is hard to see why Jeremiah must be presumed to have been in irreconcilable hostility to the Deuteronomic reform, if Deuteronomy is held to reflect his influence.

[162]E. Bruston, indeed, claims (in Westphal, *Dictionnaire encyclopédique de la Bible*, i. 605a) that this incident suffices to demonstrate that Jeremiah was entirely favourable to the Deuteronomic reform. The present writer would not go so far as this, but finds in Jeremiah's support of the reform the most natural and likely reason for their anger against him.

[163]Skinner (op. cit. p. 94) observes: "The sacrificial and ceremonial legislation of Deuteronomy, which many modern critics find so obnoxious, is really a subordinate element, amounting to little more than a regulation of ancient usages too deeply bound up with the life and thought of the people to be swept away by legal enactment."

content with less than the second best, and to work with men whose motives and aims are other than his own."[164]

It is argued that Jeremiah could not have approved the political aspirations that were associated with the reform of Josiah.[165] That the king's reform was associated with his bid for independence is beyond question. But what ground have we for assuming that Jeremiah disapproved of that? The Assyrian empire was tottering to its fall. After the death of Ashurbanipal the Assyrian hold on the west was completely relaxed. That within a few years Nineveh would be destroyed could not then be forseen. But that Assyrian control of the west had collapsed was a fact of experience, and the Scythian incursion which Assyria had been powerless to interfere with was the clearest evidence of this.[166] Egypt had not yet stepped in to claim the western part of what had been the Assyrian empire. Why, then, should Jeremiah disapprove of Josiah assuming independence? Indeed, what other alternative was there? Isaiah had disapproved of the revolt against Assyria in his day, and later Jeremiah condemned the revolt against Babylon. But now the position was quite different. To whom could Jeremiah have supposed that Josiah should yield allegiance in 621 B.C.? We have no right to transfer his attitude years later, after Judah had been annexed by Babylon, and when people vainly supposed that because the Temple was in Jerusalem they were secure, to an earlier day when conditions were totally different, when there was no menace to their security from without and the Temple was being cleansed and reformed instead of blindly trusted in.

That Jeremiah later perceived that the Deuteronomic reform did not go deep enough is no proof that he did not support it at first.[167] Attention is frequently directed to the passage in which he denounces those who put their confidence in the law, and who said "We are wise, and we have the law of the Lord."[168] To them he said "Behold, the false pen of the scribes hath wrought falsely."[169] Some have supposed that this reference was to another compilation which was then in progress,[170] and it has been suggested

---

[164] Jeremiah, i. 13.

[165] Cf. Hyatt, *J.N.E.S.* i (1942), 159 f.

[166] S. A. Cook (*C.A.H.* iii. 394) thinks the Scythian invasion facilitated the bid for independence of the western states. Cf. T. H. Robinson, *History of Israel*, i. 413: "in the disturbed state of politics they exercised a decisive influence, for it was they especially who swept away the last remnants of the organized Assyrian empire." J. F. McCurdy (*History, Prophecy, and the Monuments*, ii (1896), 392) describes them as "a great disintegrating factor—one of the most influential in all Oriental history."

[167] Cf. N. K. Gottwald, *A Light to the Nations*, 1959, p. 356: "Perhaps the most interesting argument for some connection with the Deuteronomists is the fact that the clique of noblemen who were nearest to Jeremiah in the last years seem to have been sons of Shaphan, scribe under Josiah and chief figure in the reform of 621."

[168] Jer. viii. 8.

[169] Ibid.

[170] So V. Rysell, *J.E.* vii. 96b.

that this may have been the first draft of what became the Priestly law.[171] Others hold that the reference here also is to the law of Deuteronomy,[172] and that by this time Jeremiah's attitude to the Law Book had changed because his hopes of it had not been realized.[173] If this view is correct—and it seems to me to be probable—it would seem that at this time men were putting their confidence in a book, just as later they put it in the Temple, and instead of treating it as a summons to right living were regarding it as a manual of correct ordinances. They were bringing to the reformed religion the spirit that the great prophets had always condemned, the belief that correct ritual could dispense with a life of obedience to the will of God. The hopes with which he had supported the reformation were disappointed, and it is not to be surprised at that Jeremiah should change his attitude towards it. It was because his fundamental attitude to God and understanding of the real nature of religion had not changed that his attitude to the reform had changed. We have no right to put the prophets in strait jackets of our making.

I therefore come back to the view with which we started. It is based on the evidence of the book that has come down to us, and this is the only evidence of the life and thought of Jeremiah which we have. So far as the

---

[171]So G. A. Smith, op. cit. p. 155. Skinner (op. cit. p. 104) says it might be argued that the reference is to a multifarious literary activity rather than the production of a single document. Cf. Volz, *Jeremia*, pp. 77. Similarly Rudolph (*Jeremia*, 2nd edn., pp. 57 f.) says this passage is not directed against Deuteronomy, but is much more general. Streane (op. cit. p. 61) thinks it is more likely that Jeremiah here refers to the traditional directions, already committed to writing, which the priesthood claimed to possess for guidance in ritual. Peake (op. cit. i. 160) says: "It is more probable that he is referring to regulations, now no longer extant, which had been concocted by the scribes as Divine ordinances; possibly falsified copies of the Torah had been put in circulation"; while Steinmann (op. cit. pp. 132 f.) thinks the reference is to written interpretations of Deuteronomy which contradicted its substance (cf. T. H. Robinson, *History of Israel*, i. 428).

[172]So, e.g. Duhm, op. cit. p. 88; Cornill, op. cit. p. 116; Skinner, op. cit. pp. 103 f.; E. Bruston, in *La Bible du Centenaire*, ii. 474; Pfeiffer, *Introduction*, p. 495; A. Gelin, *S.D.B.* iv (1949), 865 ("Jérémie attaque visiblement une exploitation faite par des commentateurs qui faussent le sens original du Deutéronome en mettant l'accent uniquement sur tel de ses aspects, vraisemblablement cultuel, ou qui pensent que sa possession matérielle suffira à sauver"). A. Aeschimann, *Le prophète Jérémie*, 1959, p. 84, notes that Jere. viii. 8 is an allusion to Deut. iv. 6, and thinks that if Jeremiah's reference is not to Josiah's law, then it is to sacerdotal deviations from it. Cf. G. Ricciotti, op. cit. i. 400: "Syncretism did not yield to the reform of Josias without a struggle, and even after the discovery of the codex it must have tried to justify syncretistic usages by various depositions of the codex itself."

[173]So Skinner, op. cit. pp. 106 f.; T. H. Robinson, op. cit. i. 428; Paterson, op. cit. pp. 149 f. N. Schmidt (*E.B.* ii. 2367) says: "Before the end of Josiah's reign Jeremiah seems to have recognised the futility of a reform carried out by the strong arm of the state." Cf. C. F. Kent, *The Sermons, Epistles and Apocalypses of Israel's Prophets*, 1910, p. 186: "It is evident that Jeremiah was by no means satisfied with the work of those who endeavoured to present the whole duty of the nation and individual in the form of written laws." Hyatt (*I.B.* v. 883) says that Jeremiah was here objecting to the the idea that God's will can be crystallized into a book.

identification of the foe from the north at the beginning of his ministry is concerned, since the foe is not named in the book of Jeremiah any identification must be conjectural. But the Scythian conjecture is based on the only evidence we have of the activity of any foreign invaders in Palestine at the time of the prophet's call as given in the Bible. The other interpretations are not only conjectural, but are forced to discard from the book whatever is intractable. The Biblical dating of his call has to be altered wherever it is found, and the story of his advocacy of the covenant has to be excised as an addition or interpreted unnaturally of some covenant other than the Deuteronomic, and the hostility of his own family is left without any explanation. Instead of the pieces fitting together and making a whole, they are scattered to the winds, and we are offered a doctrinaire figure instead of the most human and tragic prophet of all the Old Testament story. He becomes a man who objected to independence when there was no alternative, who could not support the closing of the shrines to which he objected because every form of worship was not suppressed at the same time. That Jeremiah could enjoy a rich fellowship with God in the privacy of his own situation, even when he was in the guard house or the foul cistern, does not mean that he eschewed every form of public worship, and the fact that he believed religion could function even if the Temple should be destroyed does not mean that he thought it could only function then. He could denounce the new abuses that followed the reform as well as the abuses that preceded it, but there is no evidence that he preferred the days that preceded it, or failed to support the reform. His mission cost him infinite suffering, and he deserves sympathetic understanding from us.

3
The Beginning of Jeremiah's Prophecy*
J. Philip Hyatt

The question as to when Jeremiah began to prophesy is a very important one, for it has a bearing on several problems in his life and message. It bears upon the attitude of Jeremiah toward the reforms of Josiah. It is related to the question of the identity of the peril from the north he describes in some of his poems. It has an indirect relevance for the problem of the nature and value of the prose narratives and "sermons" in the book. And, of course, this question has great bearing upon our estimate of the nature and effectiveness of Jeremiah's prophetic career as well as its length.

Most interpreters of Jeremiah date his call and the beginning of his prophecy in 627/6 B.C., following the date in Jer i 2, which is supported by xxv 3 (cf. iii 6 and xxii 15). Others believe that the figure in i 2, "thirteenth year" of Josiah's reign, is a scribal error for "twenty-third year," and so place the beginning in 617/6.[1] Others date it in 609, at the outset of Jehoiakim's reign.

In the October, 1964, issue of *Vetus Testamentum*, C. F. WHITLEY has proposed an even later date for Jeremiah's call, apparently the latest ever suggested.[2] He thinks that the outcome of the Battle of Carchemish, which he places in May/June 605, inspired the call of this prophet; that one of Jeremiah's first public appearances was that in which he preached his so-called temple sermon; and that he dictated his scroll to Baruch (which "was not very long") the next year. According to WHITLEY, nothing in the book of Jeremiah can be assigned to a date before 605.

This proposal of WHITLEY has several arguments to commend it, and I welcome it as offering support for a beginning of Jeremiah's career after the close of Josiah's reign, as I have advocated in the past.[3] However, I

---

* Geneva Congress for O. T. Study VIII, 27, 1965. Published in the *Zeitschrift für die alttestamentliche Wissenschaft* 78 (1966) 204–214.

[1] T. C. GORDON, "A New Date for Jeremiah," *Expository Times* XLIV (1932–33), 562–65; H. BARDTKE, *ZAW* LIII (1935), 218 f.

[2] "The Date of Jeremiah's Call," *VT* XIV (1964), 467–83. Cf. his earlier view in *The Exilic Age* (Philadelphia, 1957), pp. 34–43, where he seems to place the beginning of Jeremiah's career in the outset of Jehoiakim's reign.

[3] *Interpreter's Bible* V, pp. 779 f., and elsewhere. I subsequently abandoned the view expressed in *JBL* LIX (1940), 509, which fixes the prophet's beginning in 614–12.

believe that his date is four years too late, because some of his evidence should not be interpreted in the way he has done.

The most important is his interpretation of the phrase, "in the beginning of the reign of Jehoiakim" in Jer xxvi 1. He thinks that this can mean within the early years of the reign of the king, since in xxviii 1, "the beginning of the reign of Zedekiah" is the time of events in that king's fourth year. However, the Hebrew rēʾšîth mamlᵉkûth, usually rendered simply "beginning of the reign," has no such general meaning, but is a technical term for "accession year." Furthermore, the Hebrew text of xxvii 1 and xxviii 1 is corrupt, and can be corrected or improved by reference to the LXX.

The term rēʾšîth mamlᵉkûth occurs in xxvi 1, and the related term rēʾšîth mamléketh in xxvii 1 xxviii 1, and rēʾšîth malkûth in xlix 34. The slight variants in the second word may be considered as only textual variants without significance. These are the only occurrences in the OT. The phrase is the exact equivalent of Akkadian rêš šarrûti, the technical term for "accession year"—that is, the time which elapsed between the accession of a king and the following New Year, when his year 1 was considered as beginning. Such a system of dating was employed in Mesopotamia from early times.[4] It is the opinion of many interpreters of Jeremiah, and of the great majority of those who have written on the problems of OT chronology, that the Hebrew rêʾšîth mamlᵉkûth means "accession year," and that this system of reckoning time was employed in the later years of Judah, when Assyrian and Babylonian influences were dominant, whatever the situation may have been in Israel.[5] In his translation of Jeremiah in The Anchor Bible, JOHN BRIGHT correctly renders the phrase "the accession year" in xxvi 1 and xlix 34.[6]

[4]The facts are conveniently summarized in JACK FINEGAN, Handbook of Biblical Chronology (Princeton, 1964), pp. 85 f.

[5]J. BEGRICH, Die Chronologie der Könige von Israel und Juda (Beiträge zur Historischen Theologie 3; Tübingen, 1929), pp. 91, 93; W. F. ALBRIGHT, JBL LI (1932), 102 and elsewhere; J. MORGENSTERN, "The New Year for Kings," Gaster Anniversary Volume, ed. B. Schindler (London, 1936), pp. 1–18; E. R. THIELE, The Mysterious Numbers of the Hebrew Kings (Chicago, 1951), pp. 157, 251; H. TADMOR, "Chronology of the Last Kings of Judah," JNES XV (1956), 226–30; J. FINEGAN, op. cit., p. 195; A. JEPSEN, Zur Chronologie der Könige von Israel und Juda (BZAW 88; Berlin, 1964), pp. 21–3. THIELE has given the closest attention to the problems involved in the use of the accession-year (postdating) and non-accession-year (antedating) systems. He thinks that Israel used the non-accession-year system from Jeroboam I through Jehoahaz, and then changed to the accession-year system; Judah used the accession-year system from Rehoboam through Jehoshaphat, and again from Amaziah through Zedekiah, employing the non-accession-year system from Jehoram through Joash (op. cit., pp. 281 f.). This explanation is probably too complicated; THIELE attempts to make the biblical figures harmonize too completely. In any event, however, there is no reasonable doubt that the accession-year system was used in the later years of Judah, with which we are here concerned. The only scholar known to me who does not accept this view is F. X. KUGLER, who wrote in 1922 (Von Moses bis Paulus).

[6]He is, however, incorrect in rendering šᵉnath malkûthô in lii 31 (of Evil-Merodach) in the same way. This should refer to year 1 of the reign of Amel-Marduk, who came to the

WHITLEY makes use of the phrase, "in the beginning of the reign of Zedekiah," in xxviii 1, where the reference is to that king's fourth year, to support his understanding of the term under discussion. It is significant, however, that LXX has a different text here, and also in xxvii 1, which in the Hebrew refers to the beginning of the reign of Jehoiakim (a few MSS have Zedekiah). LXX has nothing to correspond with xxvii 1. In xxviii 1 LXX reads: "And it came to pass in the fourth year of Zedekiah king of Judah. . . ." The latter is almost certainly the correct reading, for the events of Jer xxvii–xxviii occurred in 594/3 B.C., Zedekiah's fourth regnal year. A scribe incorrectly copied xxvii 1 from xxvi 1, and made a similar mistake in xxviii 1. It is significant that in a number of places in Jer xxvii LXX appears to have an earlier, more original text than the Hebrew (particularly in xxvii 7. 13–14, 21–22).[7] In xxvii 1 the Hebrew may have had a different reading originally, but we cannot satisfactorily recover it; or there may have been no indication of date at the beginning of this chapter in the original text.

We must conclude, then, that the temple sermon of Jeremiah was delivered during the accession year of Jehoiakim. I agree with WHITLEY that it was one of the first public utterances of the prophet. In fact, it was the first public utterance of any considerable length of which we have record. The only message in his book which may be earlier is the oracle concerning Josiah and Shallum/Jehoahaz in xxii 10–12. It is now possible to fix the time of Jehoiakim's accession with fair precision, thanks particularly to the publication by D. J. WISEMAN of the British Museum tablets extending the Babylonian Chronicle.[8] The relevant biblical information is in 2 Kings xxiii 28–35 and 2 Chron xxxv 20 to xxxvi 4.

In the month Du$^{\circ}$uzu of the seventeenth year of Nabopolassar, which corresponds to June 25–July 23 of 609 B.C.,[9] the city of Harran was

---

throne in Oct. 562 (cf. FINEGAN, *op. cit.*, p. 210). In Jer xxv 1 in the Hebrew text, the fourth year of Jehoiakim is equated with *haššānā hā-ri$^{\circ}$šōnith* of Nebuchadnezzar. Though this is usually translated "the first year," the fourth year of Jehoiakim does not, in the opinion of most students of OT chronology, overlap the Babylonian king's year 1, but his accession year (Sep. 7, 605–Apr. 2, 604). Thus we should probably translate here also "accession year" (so FINEGAN, *op. cit.*, p. 202; E. VOGT, *Strasbourg Congress Volume* [*Sup. VT* IV: Leiden, 1957], p. 84). However, LXX omits xxv 1b, and the words are thus very likely a gloss from a later time, when either the chronology was not clearly remembered, or the terminology was not strictly employed.

[7]See my remarks, *Interpreter's Bible* V, pp. 1010-13; cf. W. RUDOLPH, *Jeremia*, 2nd ed. (HAT I/12; Tübingen, 1958), pp. 158-63; J. BRIGHT, *Jeremiah* (The Anchor Bible; Garden City, N. Y., 1965), pp. 195–202. Concerning LXX of Jer. xxvii, BRIGHT writes on p. 202: "At few places in the book do LXX and MT differ more widely than in this chapter . . . In some cases . . . one is constrained to believe that LXX has the more original text, and that MT is a splendid illustration of the way in which the prose discourses of Jeremiah were verbally expanded in the course of transmission."

[8]*Chronicles of Chaldean Kings (626–556 B.C.) in the British Museum* (London, 1956).

[9]The equivalence with Julian dates is based on R. A. PARKER and W. H. DUBBERSTEIN, *Babylonian Chronology 626 B.C.–A.D. 75* (Brown University Studies XIX; Providence, R. I., 1965), p. 27.

attacked by Ashur-uballit, king of Assyria, and "a large Egyptian army." This city had been conquered by the Babylonians in the previous year, when the Egyptians may have been present in Syria. The course of events is difficult to reconstruct because of the lacunae in the cuneiform text, but it appears that the Assyro-Egyptian forces directed their main assault upon the garrison which had been stationed in Harran by the Babylonians, and that they were at first successful, but could not decisively defeat the defenders. They thereupon laid seige to the city for about two months, until the month Ululu (Aug. 23–Sep. 20). When Nabopolassar approached with his army, the attackers retired, apparently without meeting Nabopolassar in battle. The Egyptians returned to their own land, and nothing more is heard of Ashur-uballit.

The death of Josiah must be understood in connection with these events. He had pursued a successful anti-Assyrian policy for many years, and must have been aware that Egypt was in alliance with the Assyrians. He could not afford to see the Egyptians advance to the aid of Ashur-uballit, and so went out to meet Pharaoh Neco on his way to Syria. The laconic account of the biblical historian in 2 Kings xxiii 29 is simply, "and Pharaoh Neco slew him at Megiddo when he saw him." This encounter must have taken place before the attack on Harran by the Assyro-Egyptian forces. Since it was customary for Near Eastern kings to mount their campaigns in the spring, and since Neco needed time to make his junction with the Assyrian forces and prepare for the attack on Harran, we must place the death of Josiah no later than May, 609, and possibly earlier.

On the death of Josiah, his son Jehoahaz was placed on the throne by "the people of the land," and ruled for three months. At the end of that time he was deposed by Neco, who replaced him with his brother Jehoiakim. The three months of Jehoiakim's reign must coincide with the time consumed by Neco in his march from Megiddo to Harran and a part of the attack on that city. 2 Kings xxiii 33–34 says that it was in Riblah in the land of Hamath that Neco put Jehoahaz in bonds, and laid a large tribute on Judah. He then made Jehoiakim king of Judah and took Jehoahaz with him, eventually to Egypt. These events ought be dated soon after the initial success at Harran while the Pharoah was still in Syria, not after the approach of the Babylonian army of Nabopolassar.[10] Such actions by the Egyptian king would hardly have been possible at the latter time. Hence, we should date the dethronement of Jehoahaz and the accession of Jehoiakim in July or early August, 609.

Unfortunately there is no way to determine certainly whether the Judeans at this period counted year 1 of a new king from Tishri 1 (in the fall) or Nisan 1 (in the spring). Among those who have written on the complicated and often thankless problems of OT chronology, a Nisan beginning is favored by KUGLER, BEGRICH, TADMOR, and others; THIELE

---

[10]Cf. A. MALAMAT, *IEJ* 1 (1950–51), 11–12.

and MORGENSTERN stoutly argue for a Tishri beginning.[11] AUERBACH has sought to prove that an autumn basis was used until the fifth year of Jehoiakim, but when Jehoiakim submitted to Nebuchadnezzar in June 604 the Babylonian calendar was introduced, with a Nisan beginning of the regnal year. This required the lengthening of that year by five months.[12] The biblical data on which we must depend can all be subjected to more than one interpretation. For example, AUERBACH relies heavily upon the information in Jer xxxvi 22 that the burning of Baruch's scroll occurred in the ninth month (Kislev) of Jehoiakim's fifth year, clearly a winter month. This supports a Nisan beginning of the year; but it is quite possible (in spite of AUERBACH's statement to the contrary) that the calendar year and the regnal year were not counted from the same month. All in all, however, I am inclined to think that at the time of Jehoiakim's accession the regnal year began in Nisan.

The accession year of Jehoiakim on a Tishri basis would have lasted from some day in July or early August to September 21. On a Nisan basis we would need to extend the time to Nisan 1 = March 17, 608. The alternative view of THIELE is very unlikely. He thinks that Jehoiakim came to the throne after Tishri 1, 609, and thus his accession year extended to Tishri 1, 608.[13] This allows too long a period between Josiah's death and the accession of Jehoiakim, and, in my view, introduces confusion into later dates.

In the content of the temple sermon as reported in Jer vii 2–15 and xxvi 4–6 there is very little that can be related to a specific historic situation. Both reports come through the Deuteronomic editor and hardly represent in every detail the actual words of the prophet.[14] The main point

[11] See references in n. 5. For THIELE's later remarks, see *BASOR* 143 (Oct. 1956), pp. 26–7. W. F. ALBRIGHT in *BASOR* 100 (Dec. 1945), p. 20, n. 13, said he thought the matter should be left *sub judice*, but that he favored a Tishri beginning for the civil year; in *BASOR* 143 (Oct. 1956) p. 32, he says that Zedekiah's reign must be reckoned from Nisan.

[12] "Der Wechsel des Jahres-Anfangs in Juda im Lichte der Neugefundenen Babylonischen Chronik," *VT* IX (1959), 113–21; cf. *ibid.* X (1960), 69 f. His view is adopted by FINEGAN, *op. cit.*, p. 203. But see the criticism by JEPSEN, *op. cit.*, pp. 27 f. AUERBACH thinks the Judean New Year was on Heshvan 1 before the introduction of the Babylonian system.

[13] *BASOR* 143 (Oct. 1956), pp. 25–26. In his earlier discussion, *The Mysterious Numbers*, pp. 158f., he sought to place the death of Josiah in 608, on the assumption that Neco made a second advance through Palestine in that year; but the WISEMAN tablets do not seem to allow for such a campaign. In his later article, just cited, THIELE retreats from that position, placing the death of Josiah in early Tammuz or late Sivan (that is, approximately June) 609.

[14] Even if one adopts the view of BRIGHT that the prose sermons of Jeremiah, and related passages, are not Deuteronomic but in a rhetorical prose which was characteristic of the seventh/sixth centuries, the same judgment must be passed on the temple sermon. BRIGHT himself in commenting on Jer vii remarks that the prose discourses do not consistently provide us with the prophet's *ipsissima verba*, and that in evaluating them we must "reckon with verbal expansion, and even with the possibility of some adaptation, of the prophet's thought." See J. BRIGHT, *op. cit.*, pp. 58–59, and cf. pp. lxxi–lxxiii. There is no reason to doubt the essential authenticity of the reports of the temple sermon.

made by Jeremiah is that genuine security cannot be found in the temple and its cult, but rather in obedience to the moral commands of Yahweh. Both accounts contain the threat that Jerusalem's temple may become like that of Shiloh. A single Hebrew word in vii 10 may give a hint of the historic situation. The prophet accuses the people of committing various sins and then coming to the temple and saying "We have been delivered!" (niṣṣálnû) only to go on committing their abominations. If the deliverance which they are celebrating is a military or political deliverance, it is difficult to see how it would be appropriate soon after the Battle of Carchemish. On the other hand, many of the Judeans may have believed that the dethronement of Jehoahaz and accession of Jehoiakim represented a deliverance. Josiah had been anti-Assyrian, and we may assume that Jehoahaz was also. Jehoiakim owed his throne to the Egyptians and was loyal to them until after the Battle of Carchemish, when he submitted to Nebuchadnezzar. There were doubtless some persons at the court and among the masses who were pro-Egyptian in their sympathies and welcomed the accession of Jehoiakim. Although Neco and his Assyrian ally did not succeed in their attack upon Harran, the Egyptians still had real power, and were not decisively defeated by the Babylonians until four years later. Even in 601, as the WISEMAN tablets show,[15] they were able to fight the Babylonians to a draw when Nebuchadnezzar invaded Egypt, if they did not actually defeat them. Of course, this interpretation of the accession of Jehoiakim as a form of "deliverance" was not shared by all of the people, nor by the prophet Jeremiah.[16]

We should date the temple sermon early in the accession year of Jehoiakim, not long after he came to the throne. We have no information by which to be more precise. It need not be placed at the time of the king's coronation, nor on any particular feast or fast day—although such is possible.

The events of 609 and the subsequent dependence on Egypt are reflected in several verses of Jer ii, which are of importance for the dating of his early messages.

Jer ii 16 says:

> Moreover, the men of Memphis and Tahpanhes
> have broken the crown of your head.[17]

---

[15] WISEMAN, op. cit., pp. 29–30, 70f.

[16] I do not wish to insist that this interpretation of niṣṣálnû is the only one possible. The verb nṣl may be used of deliverance from an enemy, from disaster, or the like (e. g. Exod v 23 xii 27 Deut xxiii 15 Jer xxxix 17); or of deliverance from sin, guilt, or the like (e. g. Ps xxxix 9 li 16 lxxix 9). The former concrete meaning is far more frequent than the latter, but sometimes of course it is impossible to determine the precise significance. The latter meaning is the one usually assigned to this verb in the interpretation of Jer vii 10.

[17] This is the RSV rendering, but the obscurity of the verb makes any rendering precarious. MT has yirʿûk, which appears to mean "will pasture you," from the verb rāʿâ, but

This is most naturally interpreted as a reference to the debacle at Megiddo in 609, or—if the words are to be interpreted figuratively—to the way in which the Egyptians gained mastery over Judah at that time. This is widely recognized by commentators.[18] However, the verse is loosely related to the context, and it may be a gloss—although conceivably originating with the prophet himself.

In Jer ii 36, the prophet says:

> How lightly you gad about,
>> changing your way!
> You shall be put to shame by Egypt
>> as you were put to shame by Assyria.

The most natural date for this is the period between 609 and the time when Jehoiakim submitted to Nebuchadnezzar (605 or 604). The reference to alliance with, or dependence on, Assyria is very clearly to Judah's relationships in the past, as in the times of Ahaz, Manasseh, or other kings. The verb is perfect, and this chapter contains many references to the past history of Israel and Judah, going back even to the wilderness period. This interpretation is widely held by commentators, but those who think that Jeremiah began to prophesy in 627/6 must suppose that this verse was added by the prophet in the light of changed conditions of a later time, or that he "revised" his earlier messages for dictation to Baruch. We must notice here, however, that vs. 36 is very closely related to its context (vss. 33–37), as is not the case with vs. 16. If it is a revision by the prophet or anyone else, it is a very skilful revision. The suggestion that Jeremiah revised his own prophecies in view of the course of events is indeed curious, without parallel in other prophetic books.

The third verse in this chapter, vs. 18, is more difficult. Here the prophet says:

> And now what do your gain by going to Egypt,
>> to drink the waters of the Nile?
> Or what do you gain by going to Assyria,
>> to drink the waters of the Euphrates?

This verse is usually interpreted as coming from a time when Assyria was still a political power with whom Judah might seek alliance, and thus

---

a form of the root r^{cc} may be intended. Various emendations have been proposed. Several Hebrew mss. have *yedā͑ûk*, and this is supported by the LXX reading *egnōsan se*; the Vulgate *constupraverunt te* suggests a perfect form of the verb. Here the Hebrew root *yd͑* may well have the unusual meaning "be reduced to submission or humiliation," cognate with Arabic *wada͑a*, as suggested by D. W. THOMAS, who here translates "caused thy head to hang in shameful submission" (*JTS* 36 [1935], 410f.). This meaning is appropriate for several OT verses; see D. W. THOMAS, *JTS* 35 (1934), 298–306; 36 (1935), 409–12; 37 (1936), 59f.; 38 (1937), 404f.; G. R. DRIVER, *ibid.* 38 (1937), 48f.; J. P. HYATT, *AJSL* LVIII (1941), 410f.

[18]See RUDOLPH. *op. cit.*, pp. 15f.; BRIGHT, *op. cit.*, p. 14.

to the early part of Jeremiah's ministry following his call in 627/6. Several objections can be raised to this interpretation. In the first place we know that Josiah adopted an anti-Assyrian policy, perhaps as early as 632 B.C., if 2 Chron xxxiv 3–6 is an authentic account of the beginning of his religious reforms and his exertion of authority over what had been Assyrian territory in north Israel.[19] Of course, it may be that some members of his court and some of the people were pro-Assyrian and that this verse refers to them. If this is the case, then we may say that the Assyrians probably continued to have some power even after 609. In the Babylonian Chronicle Ashur-uballit is called "king of Assyria" at the time of the attack on Harran (609); although he is not referred to again, and his fate is not certainly known, it is not improbable that a remnant of the Assyrians retained some power up to the time of the Battle of Carchemish. MILGROM maintains that two conditions must be met in the interpretation of Jer ii 18 and 36: one, we must assume that Assyria has not yet been destroyed; and two, they come from a time when Egypt and Assyria were enemies of each other.[20] In fact, however, nothing in the two verses compels such conditions. As we have seen, ii 36 refers to Assyria in the past and assumes her destruction as a political power. I can see nothing in either verse that makes us assume that Assyria and Egypt were enemies.

The most probable interpretation of ii 18 is that which is supported by WHITLEY: "Assyria" is here a geographical rather than a political term, referring to the land (Mesopotamia) in which Assyria had held sway. WHITLEY points to several OT passages in which the word is used in such a sense (Zech x 10–11 Lam v 6 Ezra vi 22). There are other passages in which this is possibly true, but their dating is insecure. HERODOTUS uses "Assyria" as a geographical term in writing of the Persian period; indeed he seems to use "Assyria" and "Babylonia" interchangeably (*History* I, 178).

If the objection is made that all of these are later than the time of Jeremiah, then we must point out that a geographical reference for "Assyria" is more natural in ii 18 than a political one. The Hebrew does not literally speak of going to Egypt and Assyria, but of "the way of Egypt" (*dérek miṣráyim*) and "the way of Assyria" (*dérek ʾaššûr*). Furthermore, the verse mentions two *physical* features of those countries—the Nile and the Euphrates.

Difficult though it is in some respects, the interpretation of Assyria as a geographical term in ii 18 is entirely feasible. Thus interpreted, we may see in the verse a reflection of attempts or desire to secure aid from the Chaldeans on the part of some group(s) in Judah, and attempts on the

---

[19]Cf. F. M. CROSS, Jr., and D. N. FREEDMAN, "Josiah's Revolt Against Assyria," *JNES* XII (1953), 56–68.

[20]J. MILGROM, "The Date of Jeremiah, Chapter 2," *JNES* XIV (1955), 65–69. He dates the chapter to 627–616 B.C., preferably in the first half of that period. Yet he fails to discuss vs. 16.

part of others to support the alliance with Egypt, in the period between 609 and 605.

In the light of all of these data, I believe we are justified in placing the beginning of Jeremiah's prophecy in the year 609, rather than earlier, with most interpreters, or in 605 with WHITLEY. This date has been held by several others in addition to myself.[21] Many of WHITLEY's arguments for 605 apply equally well to a beginning in 609: the difficulty in dating any oracles with satisfaction within the reign of Josiah, and the lack of any reference to specific contacts between that king and Jeremiah, similar to those of later kings; the probable attitude of Jeremiah toward the Josianic reforms;[22] the identity of the enemy from the north; and so on.

Regarding the identity of the foe from the north, it is significant to cite the view of BRIGHT in his Anchor Bible volume on Jeremiah.[23] BRIGHT is a cautious and conservative interpreter of the prophet, and a careful historian. He remarks that not a few of the poems concerning the enemy from the north "seem far more appropriate to Babylonians than they do to wild Scythians," and that among recent commentators the Scythian interpretation has tended to fall from favor. Then he says that *if* there was a Scythian thrust into the western lands, "it is probably best understood as coming later in Josiah's reign, coincident with Assyria's final collapse." In his own interpretation of the early chapters of Jeremiah, he sees some passages as coming from a time well on within the reign of Jehoiakim, but does not doubt that some reflect the terror inspired by the Scythians and Medes, and that Jeremiah may even have had a premonition of invasion and doom at a much earlier period. Such an interpretation is quite different from the traditional Scythian interpretation, and contains many uncertainties.

Many interpreters of Jeremiah who begin his career in 627/6 B.C. portray him as a prophet who at the outset of his career was weak and faltering; who became very much excited over a "Scythian menace" which failed to materialize, and at first supported the Josianic reforms but then turned against them; and who found it necessary to withdraw into a period

---

[21] In addition to those named by WHITLEY, *loc. cit.*, pp. 467f. (F. HORST, H. G. MAY, and C. A. SIMPSON), add W. L. HOLLADAY, "The Background of Jeremiah's Self-understanding: Moses, Samuel, and Psalm 22," *JBL* LXXXIII (1964), 153–64; see 160f. The monograph in which C. A. SIMPSON discusses the date of the beginning of Jeremiah's career should be known more widely than it is: *Jeremiah: The Prophet of "My People"* (Inaugural Lecture of The Winslow Memorial; Evanston, Ill. 1947), espec. pp. 6–13.

[22] R. DAVIDSON advances the interesting theory that the orthodox religious leaders of Jeremiah's day used Deut xiii 1–6 and xviii 15–22 to discredit him and brand him as a false prophet ("Orthodoxy and the Prophetic Word: a Study of the Relationship between Jeremiah and Deuteronomy," *VT* XIV [1964], 407–16). He accepts the traditional view of the beginning of the prophet's career, but this theory serves to underline the gulf between Deuteronomy and its proponents on the one hand and Jeremiah on the other.

[23] Pp. xxxvii, lxxxi f. He appears to identify the *umman manda* of the Babylonian Chronicle with the Scythians. A clear-cut identification such as this is most improbable, but it is possible that they included Scythians; cf. WISEMAN, *op. cit.*, pp. 16, 81 and his references.

of silence for about a decade before prophesying again at the beginning of Jehoiakim's reign. This is not a convincing portrayal, and does not fit well with what we know of Jeremiah's career from the time of the temple sermon on. If, on the other hand, we date the beginning of his prophecy in 609 B.C., we can see him from the outset of his career as a prophet who was dynamic and confident, proclaiming with great vigor the word of Yahweh for the people of his time.

4

The Date of Jeremiah's Call*
C. F. Whitley

According to the present text of the book of Jeremiah the prophet was called to his work in the thirteenth year of the reign of Josiah (i 2). This would be about the year 627 B.C., and it is the date accepted in the standard Commentaries and Introductions.[1] We have reason, however, to doubt if Jeremiah were active at all in the reign of Josiah. Mention of this king is made in certain passages (iii 6 f.; xxii 15; xxv 3), but their authenticity is open to question. Apart from the reference to his call we have no record of Jeremiah uttering a prophecy in a definite year of Josiah's reign. And this is significant in view of the precise datings of his oracles in the reigns of Jehoiakim and Zedekiah. We hear, for example, of Jeremiah's activity in the fourth and fifth years of Jehoiakim (xxxvi 1, 9), while we likewise read of his utterances in the fourth and tenth years of Zedekiah (xxviii 1; xxxii 1). Again while we read of Jeremiah attempting to advise these kings on certain occasions (xxvi 23 f.; xxxvii 17; xxxviii 14) we hear of no such relationship with Josiah.

There is thus little in the content of the book of Jeremiah to point to the activity of the prophet in the reign of Josiah. And this is a conclusion to which more than one scholar has independently come. Rejecting the statement in Jeremiah i 2 as editorial, Friedrich HORST went on to argue that we may detect in the book an original tradition which places the prophet's call after the battle of Megiddo.[2] In a study of the chronology of Jeremiah's oracles H. G. MAY similarly maintains that we have little to substantiate the claim that the prophet began his career before the reign of Jehoiakim.[3] Arguing again that the contents of Baruch's roll contained only prophecies delivered since the battle of Megiddo, C. A. SIMPSON concluded that Jeremiah could not have entered on his task before 608.[4]

---

* Originally published in *Vetus Testamentum* 14 (1964) 467–483.

[1]E.g., R. H. PFEIFFER (*Introduction to the Old Testament*, 1941, pp. 487 f.) and A. WEISER (*Introduction to the Old Testament*, Eng. trans., 1961, p. 209). See also recently, H. H. ROWLEY, "The Early Prophecies of Jeremiah in Their Setting," *B.J.R.L.* XLVIII, Sept. 1962, pp. 198 ff.

[2]"Die Anfänge des Propheten Jeremia," *Z.A.W.* XLI, 1923, pp. 94–153.

[3]"The Chronology of Jeremiah's Oracles," *J.N.E.S.* IV, 1945, pp. 217–227.

[4]*Jeremiah: The Prophet of "My People"* (The Winslow Memorial Lecture, Illinois, 1947), pp. 6–13.

More recently J. P. HYATT expressed the view that the invasion poems were uttered in the time of Jehoiakim, and that Jeremiah did not begin his career before the reign of that king.[5]

Our contention here, however, is that Jeremiah did not only begin his ministry till the reign of Jehoiakim, but that he did not do so till after the battle of Carchemish in 605. Apart from the opening paragraph of the book we have no precisely dated material till chapter xxv. There we read that "in the fourth year of Jehoiakim . . . the first year of Nebuchadrezzar king of Babylon," the word of Yahweh came unto Jeremiah. The substance of the message was, "Behold I will send for all the tribes of the north, and for Nebuchadrezzar the king of Babylon . . . and I will bring them against this land and its inhabitants . . ." (xxv 9). The fourth year of Jehoiakim was, according to Jeremiah xlvi 1, the year in which Nebuchadrezzar defeated the Pharaoh Necho at the battle of Carchemish. Now we know from recently published Babylonian records that this battle was fought in May-June of the year 605.[6] The fourth year of Jehoiakim was therefore 605; and this accords with the recent confirmation of the view that he ascended the throne in the year 609.[7] It was probably in the months following Carchemish that Jeremiah delivered his well-known address in the temple. It is true we are told that it was "in the beginning of the reign of Jehoiakim" (xxvi 1), but in xxviii 1 we note that the editor could regard the "fourth year" as the beginning of the reign of Zedekiah.[8] There are,

---

[5] *Interpreter's Bible*, V, 1956, p. 779a.

[6] Contrary to E. R. THIELE (*The Mysterious Numbers of the Hebrew Kings*, 1951, p. 160) who places the battle of Carchemish in 604. D. J. WISEMAN's recent publication of certain Chaldean chronicles shows that Nebuchadrezzar commanded the Babylonian forces at Carchemish, as his father, Nabopolassar, was in ill-health. He died in August 605 and Nebuchadrezzar ascended the throne on the 6/7th September (1st of Elul). His "accession year" therefore lasted till the New Year Festival in the following Spring (Nisan) 604, when he began his "regnal" year. See WISEMAN, *Chronicles of Chaldean Kings* (626–556), 1956, pp. 26–27.

[7] WISEMAN's Chronicle (*op. cit.*, p. 33) reveals that Jehoiakim died on the 6/7th December 598 B.C.; and as he reigned 11 years (2 Kings xxiii 36) his accession was in the year 609. We may further note here that as far as Nebuchadrezzar's reign is concerned the biblical writer seems to think in terms of the "non-accession" system, by which a king's reign is reckoned from the year he ascends the throne. This would also seem to be the case in 2 Kings xxiv 8–12 where we find that Jehoiachin was taken captive in the third month of his reign. This was immediately after the fall of Jerusalem on the 15/16th March (2nd Adar) 597 (WISEMAN, *op. cit.*, p. 33), the end of Nebuchadrezzar's seventh "regnal" or "accession" year; but according to the writer of 2 Kings xxiv 12 it was Nebuchadrezzar's eighth year, and therefore he would seem to reckon from 605. E. R. THIELE, however, thinks that at this period the "accession" system obtained in Judah (*op. cit.*, pp. 14–41).

[8] H. G. MAY indeed thinks that mention of the fourth year may be "a scribal addition, influenced by the references to the 4th year of Jehoiakim, and added after the corruption in xxvii 1 had transferred this incident to the reign of Jehoiakim" (*loc. cit.*, p. 217 n. 4). But if this influence were operative at all we should expect it to obtain in the case of xxvii 1 where "Jehoiakim" was mistakenly written for "Zedekiah." In xxviii 1 the name "Zedekiah" remained unaltered and could hardly therefore be the cause of influencing a copyist to confuse

moreover, certain features about the temple address which suggest that it was one of the first appearances of Jeremiah in public. We notice that the people asked why he "prophesied in the name of Yahweh" (xxviii 18), an inquiry they would scarcely have made if he had been active amongst them previously. Again we hear him called "this man" rather than by his own name, as he is later in xxix 27. In saying "Yahweh has sent me to speak all these words in your ears" (vs. 15) Jeremiah also implies that he has only recently received his call. Some members of his audience remarked too "This man does not deserve the sentence of death," thereby implying that, although Jeremiah was a stranger, his claim to be a prophet of Yahweh entitled him to immunity. It is of further significance that certain elders drew attention to the case of Micah of Moresheth who prophesied against Jerusalem in earlier times but was not put to death because he spoke in Yahweh's name (vv. 17–18). The fact that this precedence of Micah was now cited indicates that Jeremiah was not yet recognised as a prophet in his own right.

Chapter xxxvi contains further evidence for our view that Jeremiah was not called before the battle of Carchemish. The opening verses pertain to the fourth year of Jehoiakim, and we learn that Jeremiah was debarred from entering the temple. He accordingly instructs the scribe Baruch to make a record of his utterances and to read them on a future occasion in the temple. We are then told that at a feast day in the following year, the fifth year of Jehoiakim (xxxvi 9), Baruch read the oracles of Jeremiah in the chamber at the entrance to the temple. When Micaiah, the son of Gemariah, heard them he deemed it his duty to report their tenure to the authorities in the royal household. They then demanded that Baruch himself should read the scroll before them, and when he had finished, they in turn regarded it of such significance that they declared "We must report all these words to the king" (vs. 16). It was thus immediately arranged that a certain Jehudi should read the scroll before Jehoiakim, who likewise considered it so ominous that he burned it leaf by leaf in the fire (vv. 23 f.).

Now it is clear from this narrative that the contents of the scroll were of specific political significance and were regarded as being dangerous to the stability of the state. It is evident too that the scroll was not very long, as it was read three times in different places in the course of one day; and it is further likely that Jehoiakim would not have listened to it unless it

---

it with a chronology which pertained to Jehoiakim. Moreover, the circumstances implied in chapters xxvii–xxviii concur with what we know of the historical situation round the period 594/3. During the 10th year of his reign (595/594) Nebuchadrezzar's authority in Babylon was undermined by a revolt in his army which was suppressed only by considerable efforts (WISEMAN, op. cit., pp. 36 f.). News of this would in due time spread to the west and might well induce the states there to consider a united revolt (Jer. xxvii 2 ff.) during the following year (594/3), the 4th year of Zedekiah. The false prophets now also declared that Yahweh "had broken the yoke of the king of Babylon" and that within two years the exiles would return (xxviii 2 ff.).

directly pertained to a political crisis. That this was indeed the case may be gathered from his remark, "Why have you written in it that the king of Babylon will certainly come and destroy this land . . ." (xxxvi 29). Contemporary Babylonian documents record that in 604 Nebuchadrezzar mounted an expedition to Syria where he remained six months.[9] This would probably have been known to Jehoiakim, but Jeremiah now emphasized its danger for Judah, and in wishing to make it public would add to the king's embarrassment. We know that in the event Jeremiah was proved right, for later in that same year Jehoiakim, in common with other western rulers, was compelled to declare his submission to Nebuchadrezzar.[10]

It would thus seem that it was the outcome of the battle of Carchemish which was the signal for Jeremiah's call, and that his address in the temple followed immediately. The people and the authorities concerned ignored his warnings and refused him access to the temple again. Jeremiah accordingly authorized Baruch to read to the temple on a convenient occasion, a written account of this address, together with oracles relating to the appearance of Nebuchadrezzar's forces in Syria. This was the substance of the roll which Jehoiakim heard with such misgiving.

When Jeremiah then referred to evil (רעה) from the north, it was the Babylonians under Nebuchadrezzar he had in mind. There are, moreover, certain instances in which he openly identified the enemy. As we know from Jehoiakim's remark, the king of Babylon was mentioned in the oracles dictated to Baruch, while we find direct reference to Nebuchadrezzar and the Chaldeans in xxxviii 28–29 and xxxiv 2. In xlvi 2 we have again definite mention of the river Euphrates being situated in the north. This verse clearly refers to the victory of the Babylonians at Carchemish and is in a context which appears to derive from Jeremiah himself.[11] It is thus the victorious army of the Babylonians at Carchemish that the prophet refers to as "a boiling pot facing away from the north" (i 16; cf. xxv 8), and it is, likewise, this army which was the subject of his invasion songs now preserved in the early chapters of the book that bears his name.[12]

---

[9] WISEMAN, op. cit., pp. 28, 69.

[10] WISEMAN, op. cit., p. 28.

[11] Although collected with the oracles against Foreign Nations the material of chapter xlvi 3–6 would appear to be from Jeremiah himself. Both HYATT (I.B. V, 1956, p. 1104) and PFEIFFER (op. cit., p. 506) also regard verses 7–12 as Jeremianic. The fact, however, that the LXX presents the oracles against Foreign Nations immediately after xxv 13 leads a number of scholars to doubt their authenticity: so, e.g., Paul VOLZ, Der Prophet Jeremia (K.A.T.), 1922, pp. 374–386; W. RUDOLPH, Jeremia (H.A.T.), 1947, pp. 228 ff. J. A BEWER considers that chs. xlvi–xlix contain at least Jeremianic material, The Book of Jeremiah, 2, 1952, p. 54. We are, of course, only concerned with xlvi 3–6 here, but even if this is secondary it is a witness to a tradition identifying Carchemish with the north.

[12] E.g., iv 5–7, 13–22, 27–31; v 15–17; vi 1–6, 22 f. These are the so-called "Scythian Songs" of Bernard DUHM (Das Buch Jeremia, 1901, pp. 48 ff.). See, e.g., the discussion by J. P. HYATT, "The Peril from the North in Jeremiah," J.B.L. LIX, 1940, pp. 499 ff.

We further learn from chapter xxxvi that Baruch's roll was the basic element in the compilation and growth of the present book of Jeremiah. The original scroll containing all that Jeremiah had uttered up to 604 was burnt by Jehoiakim, but it was again written by Baruch at the prophet's dictation, and as verse 32 notes "many similar words were added to it."[13] But this addition was effected in a disorderly and confused manner, as material was placed both before and after Baruch's nucleus. Much of the material added after is supplied with dates, but even so it is not in chronological order.[14] If we regard the kernel of chapter xxv as pertaining to the fourth year of Jeremiah's call it is probable that the contents of chapter xxvi form a sequel to it, but chapters xxvii and xxviii, as the superscriptions relate, are concerned with the reign of Zedekiah. Chapter xxix, which contains Jeremiah's letter to the exiles, was written after the first deportation in 597, and chapter xxxii is connected with the tenth year of Zedekiah's reign, the year 587. Chapter xxxv recalls us to events in the reign of Jehoiakim, while chapter xxxvi, as we have noted, refers again to the fourth year of his rule. Such instances exemplify the disorderly nature of this part of the book and show that oracles from the reigns of Jehoiakim and Zedekiah have been collected and placed together without any regard for chronological order.

Nor is there any material in chapters i–xxiv which can be regarded as pertaining to events prior to 605. The reference to Judah's association with both Egypt and Assyria in ii 18 has indeed led some commentators to connect it with the last years of Assyrian sovereignty. Thus HYATT would place it between the death of Josiah and the battle of Carchemish.[15] Egypt and Assyria were, however, allies at this time, and it is difficult to see what Judah would gain in a policy of vacillation between them. But we may further doubt if Assyria could have exercised any political influence at this period. Her last king, Ashurballit, had disappeared from the political scene in 609 when he failed in his attempt to recapture Harran from the Babylonians.[16] It was while marching northwards to help Assyria in this venture that Necho encountered and slew Josiah at Megiddo. For a few years subsequent to this Judah was under the dominance of Egypt (2 Kings xxiii 33 f.). But after Carchemish Babylon became the power of the day, and certainly from 604 onwards Judah was subject to her. We read, however, in 2 Kings xxiv 1 that after the space of three years Jehoiakim

---

[13]Cf. here, Sigmund MOWINCKEL, *Prophecy and Tradition* (Oslo) 1946, pp. 61 ff.

[14]See e.g., H. G. MAY, "The Chronology of Jeremiah's Oracles" *loc. cit.*, pp. 217–227.

[15]*I.B.* V, 1956, p. 817. Jacob MILGROM assigns Jer. ii 18, 36 to the years 627–616 ("The Date of Jeremiah, Chapter 2," *J.N.E.S.* XIV, 1955, pp. 65–69). But at this time Judah was making an effort to emerge from subjection to Assyria and to establish her own independence (cf. F. M. CROSS and D. N. FREEDMAN, "Josiah's Revolt against Assyria," *J.N.E.S.* XII, 1953, pp. 56–58). It is thus unlikely that she would wish to become involved in Egyptian politics. Certainly in 609 Josiah wanted little association with Egypt.

[16]See WISEMAN, *op. cit.*, p. 19.

rebelled against Nebuchadrezzar. Egyptian influence is doubtless to be discerned in this decision, for when Nebuchadrezzar appeared in the west to deal with the matter he found it necessary to proceed to Egypt and engage Necho in battle. The engagement was, however, indecisive, and a contemporary Babylonian chronicle states that Nebuchadrezzar withdrew his forces immediately and returned home.[17] The military strength of the Egyptians was thus considerable at this time, and this consideration may accordingly have tempted Jehoiakim to waver in his loyalty to Babylon.

These events may then constitute the historical background of Jeremiah ii 18. We would, of course, have to substitute "Babylon" for "Assyria" here; but the name "Assyria" was applied to Babylon in the post-exilic age. In Zechariah x 10–11 we read:

> I will bring them home from the land of Egypt,
> and gather them from Assyria. . .
> The pride of Assyria shall be laid low,
> and the sceptre of Egypt shall depart.

It will scarcely be questioned that while there were Israelite exiles in Assyria since the fall of Samaria (2 Kings xvii 6), Babylon and Egypt were the two main centres of the dispersion. Again in Lamentations v 6 we find mention of Assyria and Egypt in a sense in which "Assyria" can only mean Babylon. Ezra vi 22 likewise mentions the "king of Assyria" in a context dealing with the ruling power of Persia. It will further be observed that ii 18 is in a context which represents the men of Memphis and Tahpanhes exercising control over the Judeans (ii 16); and this must refer to the time when, subsequent to the fall of Jerusalem, Jeremiah and other Judean exiles were living in Egypt as related in chapters xliii–xliv. We read in xliii 7 that "they came into the land of Egypt for they did not obey the voice of Yahweh"; and ii 17 states that Judah's deplorable association with foreign nations was due to the same reason. ii 18 may, therefore, belong to such late biographical and editorial material as chapters xliii–xliv and ii 17, 19. On the other hand, the remark that Judah would "be put to shame by Egypt" as she formerly was "by Assyria" (ii 36) may have possibly been made by Jeremiah round the year 601.

It has been suggested that Jeremiah's condemnation of idolatry at the beginning of the book must be placed before Josiah's reforms, as the country shrines were then abolished.[18] We doubt, however, if in this respect Josiah's reforms were entirely successful. We read in Deuteronomy xvi 2–4 that the celebrations connected with unleavened bread should henceforth be observed in the temple in Jerusalem. If this was an article of the Josianic legislations it was not widely observed, for according to 2 Kings xxiii 9 the

[17]WISEMAN, op. cit., pp. 29 ff.
[18]E.g., MILGROM, loc. cit., pp. 65 ff.; ROWLEY, B.J.R.L., Sept. 1962, p. 215.

priests of the local sanctuaries did not go up to Jerusalem, but rather celebrated the feast of unleavened bread among their brethren.[19] If the priest could lightly disregard such legislations we have no reason to think that the populace was any less indifferent.[20] MILGROM considers Josiah's reforms as having effected "the complete and irrevocable purge of all idolatrous elements."[21] But there is scarcely any chapter in the present book of Jeremiah in which idolatry and its attendant evils are not mentioned (e.g., iii 1b, 9; iv 30; v 7; vi 15; vii 9, 18, 30 f.; vii 2, 19c; ix 14 etc.). We may accordingly doubt if we can point to any material in the book and claim that it derives from the period immediately following the reforms of Josiah on the grounds that it reflects these reforms. Nor, for this same reason, can we infer that because a passage contains a reference to idolatry it is necessarily prior to 622.

It is similarly thought that the worship of the Queen of Heaven had been abandoned from the time of Josiah's reforms till the Jews went into exile in Egypt, and that therefore the only time Jeremiah could have witnessed this worship in Judah was before the reformation.[22] A reference to the Queen of Heaven appears in chapter vii 16–20, in the context of Jeremiah's temple address, but it is likewise suggested that the reference need not necessarily belong to this context.[23] Apart, however, from this assumption it is questionable if Jeremiah chapter xliv can be accepted as offering evidence for the discontinuation of this particular kind of worship for a period after the reform. The Jeremianic authorship of the passage is in doubt,[24] but even if we accept that the prophet did rebuke the Jews in Egypt for this idolatry, there is nothing in the chapter itself to denote that it ever ceased in Judah. For Jeremiah's compatriots now declare that they would do everything, including the burning of incense to the Queen of Heaven, as their fathers did in Judah, for then they had plenty of food and encountered no misfortune (vs. 17). They then added, "But since we left off burning incense to the queen of heaven and pouring out libations to her, we have lacked everything and have been consumed by the sword and by famine" (vs. 18). The implication here is that the Judeans as a whole continued to worship the Queen of Heaven until the fall of Jerusalem when it became impracticable to do so. Verse 22, moreover, represents this

---

[19]The feast of Unleavened Bread was an ancient Canaanite agricultural festival. It was combined with the Passover in the Deuteronomic legislations; cf. also Ezra vi 19–22. See here R. H. PFEIFFER, *Religion in the Old Testament*, 1961, pp. 40–41.

[20]Cf. HYATT who remarked: "Of all the requirements of the reforms, one of the most impracticable must have been that demanding the abolition of all local sanctuaries . . . ," *J.N.E.S.* I, 1942, pp. 160 f.

[21]*Loc. cit.*, p. 68.

[22]E.g. ROWLEY, *loc. cit.*, pp. 216–217; Cf. also John SKINNER, *Prophecy and Religion*, 1922, pp. 341 f.

[23]ROWLEY, *ibid.*

[24]Cf. e.g., RUDOLPH, *op. cit.*, pp. 223 f.

idolatrous practice as the immediate cause of the disaster which overtook the city.

ROWLEY has again claimed that Jeremiah's Confessions before God, of which we read in xv 10 ff., were prompted by unfulfilled prophecies.[25] These utterances were thought to have particular reference to the "Scythian" invasions of 626, while chapter iv is regarded as being the prophet's own conception of the chaos and devastation of the invasion.[26] The passage (vv. 23–36) referring to the disorder of the earth, the blackened heavens, and the quaking mountains, is, however, scarcely Jeremianic. The expression "waste and void" (*tohu wabohu*) would appear to depend on Genesis i 2, itself as late as the P document, while the passage as a whole is reminiscent of the apocalyptic thought of later Judaism which we find in such late passages as Isaiah x 23, Micah i 3–4 and Zephaniah i 18. But aside from the question of the genuineness of the passage, we doubt if Jeremiah's spiritual conflicts in chapter xv 10 ff. arose from unfulfilled prophecy. The passage indeed represents him as experiencing some opposition, but this is due to his prophesying immediate destruction and exile for the nation: "Your wealth and your treasures I will give as spoil . . . for your sins . . . I will make you serve your enemies in a land which you do not know . . . " (vv. 13–14). His claim to have found and eaten Yahweh's word (vs. 16) is a reference to his call, and he is thus convinced in his belief of impending disaster. It is for this that he is looked upon as "a man of strife and contention to the whole land" and is regarded as a "curse" by all (vs. 10). At his call Yahweh endowed him with strength and rendered him as a bronze wall (i 8–9, 18), and he is now assured of similar support (xv 10). The office to which he is called is inevitably exacting, and he is not to be influenced by the standards of men or be discouraged by their criticisms: "They shall turn to you, but you shall not turn to them" (vs. 19). His discomfiture accordingly arises from the enmity and resentment with which people regard him, rather than from any sense of being the victim of unfulfilled prophecy.

Nor, again, can it be said that the plight of Jeremiah in chapter xx 7ff. was due to unfulfilled prophecy.[27] We read that "the word of Yahweh has become . . . a reproach and derision all day long" (xx 8), but there is no indication that this is due to the unfulfilment of that word. It is due to Jeremiah's continuing to utter it, and this he does because he cannot desist; he is under an inward compulsion. Moreover, if this passage has any thematical connection with its context it would appear that Jeremiah's despondency on this occasion was due to the treatment he received at the hands of Pashur, the chief priest of the temple. For in prophesying that destruction would come on Jerusalem he is put in the stocks by Pashur

---

[25] *Loc. cit.*, p. 221 f.
[26] *Loc. cit.*, p. 223.
[27] As e.g., ROWLEY, *loc. cit.*, p. 220.

(xx 1 ff.). Far, therefore, from regarding Jeremiah's utterances as being unfulfilled, the people of Jerusalem were deeply concerned in case they would materialize. Hence we hear them frantically expressing the hope that he would yet be deceived:

> Denounce him, let us denounce him . . .
> Perhaps he will be deceived,
> then we can overcome him,
> and take our revenge on him (xx 10).

It is common too to place xi 18–xii 6 shortly after the publication of Deuteronomy. The passage contains a further reference to Jeremiah's ministerial difficulties, and mentions in particular a threat to his life by the men of Anathoth (xi 21; cf. also xii 6). It is thus argued that Jeremiah must have at first been an advocate of the Deuteronomic reforms, thereby depriving the priests of Anathoth of their altars and livelihood.[28] The text is probably disarranged here,[29] but even so there is little basis for this interpretation. xii 6, which should probably follow xi 8, refers to the treacherous attitude of the house of his father, while xi 21 states that "the men of Anathoth said, Do not prophesy in the name of Yahweh or you will die by our hand." Hence it would rather seem that Jeremiah is threatened here because he is prophesying destruction in the name of Yahweh. His kinsfolk at Anathoth would, doubtless, have experienced much embarrassment from his utterances, and they, no less than the people of Jerusalem, would wish to silence him on this account.[30]

Those scholars who think that Jeremiah approved of the reforms of Deuteronomy immediately after its publication appeal to chapter xi 1–8 in support of their view.[31] There we read: "Hear the words of this covenant, and speak to the men of Judah and the inhabitants of Jerusalem. You shall say to them, Thus says the Lord, the God of Israel: Cursed be the man who does not heed the words of this covenant which I commanded your fathers when I brought them out of the land of Egypt. . . ." The covenant here is thought by many to be Deuteronomy,[32] and it is true that in the mind of

---

[28]Cf. e.g., Skinner, *op. cit.*, p. 109 f.; Rowley, *loc. cit.*, pp. 230–231. T. J. Meek, however, regards the words "of the priests" in i 1 as a gloss, and questions if Jeremiah were of a priestly ancestry, "Was Jeremiah a Priest?," *The Expositor*, March 1923, pp. 215–222.

[29]See Hyatt, *I.B.*, V, p. 912; Rudolph, *op. cit.*, pp. 71 f.

[30]Volz argued that the opposition to Jeremiah was probably organized by the priests in Jerusalem, *op. cit.*, pp. 136 f.

[31]E.g., Bewer (*op. cit.*, vol. 1, p. 43) who thinks that verses 1–8 speak of Jeremiah's activity at the introduction of the law in 621. so Milgrom credits the view that Jeremiah was a disciple of the reform and toured Judah and northern Israel on its behalf (*loc. cit.*, p. 68 n. 23).

[32]See e.g., Skinner, *op. cit.*, pp. 97–102; John Paterson, *The Goodly Fellowship of the Prophets*, 1948, pp. 148 ff.; A. Aeschimann, *Le Prophète Jérémie*, 1959, p. 96. Others claim to see a reference here by Jeremiah to the Sinaitic covenant; e.g., Rudolph, *op. cit.*, p. 71 f.

the writer of the passage the covenant is synonymous with this Code.[33] But despite many arguments to the contrary we have no clear indication that the passage is from Jeremiah himself. It contains so many striking parallels with the book of Deuteronomy that we can scarcely hold that it is even a development from a Deuteronomic kernel. A few examples will illustrate the force of this parallelism. In Jeremiah xi 3 we read, "Cursed be the man who does not heed the words of this covenant," while in Deuteronomy 27:26 we find, "Cursed be he who does not confirm the words of this law." The phrase "in order to establish the oath . . . to give them" in Jeremiah xi 5 corresponds with "the oath which he swore to your fathers" in Deuteronomy vii 8. The description of Canaan as "a land flowing with milk and honey" in Jeremiah xi 5b is, again, frequently found in Deuteronomy (e.g., vi 3; xi 9; xxvi 9; xv 2, 7). A number of other parallels between Jeremiah xi 1–8 and Deuteronomy may be cited,[34] but such instances as we noted point to the Deuteronomist as the source of the passage.[35]

In considering the parallelism of phraseology between Deuteronomy and the book of Jeremiah we are, of course, reminded that both in their original forms belong to the end of the seventh century B.C. We would thus expect to find in them many parallelisms of thought and phraseology, and HYATT has ventured to offer a list of certain words and phrases which, he thinks, were common to the religious vocabulary of that time.[36] The religious community of seventh century Judah doubtless used a common religious vocabulary, but it is questionable if we can claim to recognize it in the present book of Jeremiah. For the book which has been transmitted to us seems to consist of genuine prophetic utterances and material of the Deuteronomic school; and each element has its distinctive characteristic. The language of the Deuteronomist, whether that of the founders of the school or later members of the circle, is stereotyped, rhetorical and moralistic. It is, moreover, basically concerned with certain themes. Israel is reminded of her bondage in Egypt and of Yahweh's intervention which led to her Exodus and Settlement in Canaan. Her preoccupation with the Baals of the land was, however, an infringement of the covenant he made with her, and this is condemned in the most profuse and didactic language (e.g., Dt. iv 34–39; vi 12–15; xxvi 5–9). The language of the prophet is, on the other hand, succinct, direct and forceful. It is creative and is not

So Bruce VAWTER thinks that the covenant is that of Sinai, though Jeremiah spoke the words of this passage in support of Josiah's reforms, *The Conscience of Israel*, 1961, pp. 245 f.

[33]See the present writer, "Covenant and Commandment in Israel," *J.N.E.S.* XXII, 1, 1963, pp. 42 f.

[34]See the analysis of J. P. HYATT, "Jeremiah and Deuteronomy," *J.N.E.S.* 1942, p. 169.

[35]It will further be observed that verses 7–8 are not represented in the LXX, and this suggests, in addition, that the passage itself continued to attract the attention of the Deuteronomic editors.

[36]*Ibid.*, pp. 164–165. Cf. also W. O. E. OESTERLEY and T. H. ROBINSON, *An Introduction to the Books of the Old Testament*, 1941, p. 298; W. L. HOLLADAY, *J.B.L.* 1960, pp. 351 ff.

confined to particular themes. It is thus as distinct from Deuteronomy as the poet is from the mere preacher or moralist. But the language of prophecy was not, by virtue of its originality, indebted to contemporary modes of speech, so it is unlikely that it in turn exerted any great influence on the religious language of the day. For there was no continuous succession of great prophets, and their utterances were at most sporadic. These utterances were collected by the religious community. The more memorable pronouncements and phrases were preserved in their original oracular form, while other less striking comments would seem to have been handed down by the community in prose, and so represents the substance rather than the form of the prophet's utterances. Much of this latter material would also be modified in the course of transmission, and it is therefore doubtful if we can claim to recover the common religious language of Jeremiah's day. Baruch's roll in its original form may possibly have represented such language, but this too has been subjected to modification and expansion.[37]

We can hardly hope to determine the precise role of the Deuteronomists in the religious community of their day, but it is fairly certain that, whatever else their function, they were the editors of the literary documents and traditions which resided in the religious community.[38] In the course of their editing they modified and expanded the material at hand in accordance with their own theological presuppositions; and this they did in a form of language suitable for instruction and edification. When, therefore, we find in the book of Jeremiah passages which are typical of the thought and style of Deuteronomy we are naturally doubtful of their Jeremianic origin.[39]

Nor, again, have we any evidence that Jeremiah quoted Deuteronomy in the course of his ministry. Some scholars, however, claim to recognize references to that Code in certain utterances attributed to the prophet. For example, the material of chapter iii 1 is considered to be Jeremianic and, therefore, dependent on Deuteronomy xxiv 1–4.[40] The passage in Jeremiah reads: "If a man divorces his wife and she goes from him and becomes another man's wife, will he return to her? Would not that woman (with LXX) be greatly polluted?" Now Deuteronomy xxiv 1–4 states that a wife

---

[37] Cf. T. H. ROBINSON, "Baruch's Roll," *Z.A.W.* 1924, pp. 209–221.

[38] Cf. here S. MOWINCKEL who speaks of the Deuteronomists as being "associated with the learned circles of the scribes," *Prophecy and Tradition*, 1946, p. 63.

[39] MOWINCKEL thinks that the Deuteronomic passages represent "an independent, parallel transmission of the memories about Jeremiah's sayings" (*ibid.*). We have, however, but little evidence for this view. Such evidence as we have tends to associate Deuteronomists with the activity of editing and moulding the common traditions of the religious community. J. LINDBLOM would prefer to account for the Deuteronomic ideas and style in terms of "a Deuteronomistically influenced tradition" (*Prophecy in Ancient Israel*, Eng. trans., 1962, p. 426). But inasmuch as it is so influenced, the reliability of such tradition is open to question.

[40] E.g., ROWLEY in *Studies in Old Testament Prophecy* (also ed.), 1950, p. 171; HYATT, *J.N.E.S.* I, 1942, p. 164.

who is divorced by her husband, because of "some indecency" in her, may not return to him if she has in the meantime been married to, and divorced from, another man. She is then thought to have "been defiled." But however this law may find a place in the Deuteronomic legislations, we may question whether Jeremiah would have used it as an analogy to his own view of Israel's relationship with Yahweh. For Jeremiah maintained that Yahweh would receive Israel back in any circumstances, if she would only return to him (e.g., iii 12–14; cf. also xxxi 31–34), whereas the Deuteronomic law enjoins that a former wife may not return to her first husband if she has been divorced from him.[41] It is, on the other hand, noticeable that we find a characteristically Jeremianic emphasis on the notion of Israel's return to Yahweh in iii 1b:

> You have played the harlot with many lovers
> and would you return to me? says Yahweh.

It is, therefore, probable that the part of the verse referring to divorce was inserted by an editor under the influence of Deuteronomy xxi 1–4.

Chapter xxxiv 8–18 is regarded as yet another instance in which Jeremiah appeals to the Deuteronomic Code.[42] We here read of Zedekiah making with the people of Jerusalem a covenant securing the release of both male and female slaves. But this agreement was subsequently dishonoured, and the people brought their former slaves back into subjection. Jeremiah is now represented as criticizing the masters on the grounds that they are abusing a law which Yahweh is alleged to have made with the Hebrews after the Exodus from Egypt, and which now appears in Exodus xxi 2. It is to the effect that a Hebrew male servant who has served six years should be freed on the seventh. Now we find a law in Deuteronomy xv 12 which demands that both a Hebrew manservant and maidservant should be set free in the seventh year; and it is doubtless such a presupposition that the writer of Jeremiah xxxiv 8–18 had in mind, although it is strange that the law he cites as his authority is that of Exodus xxi 2. We may consequently doubt if Deuteronomy xv 12 had been written by then, else he would have quoted it. It may well be the case that the notion of freeing the Hebrew maidservant, as well as the manservant, was first conceived in the final months of Zedekiah's reign, when the impending fall of Jerusalem would suggest a greater measure of humanitarianism between Jew and Jew (xxxiv 9), and that this gesture should later find a place as an article of law in Deuteronomy. But however this may be we can hardly regard the narrative of Jeremiah xxxiv 8–18 as deriving from the prophet. Exhortatory mention of such topics as Egypt, the covenant, and the house called by Yahweh's name, denotes the presence of Deuteronomic material,

---

[41] HYATT's comment that Jeremiah is here speaking from a moral standpoint and Deuteronomy from a cultic legal standpoint scarcely makes the analogy more applicable, *ibid.*

[42] E.g., ROWLEY, *op. cit.*, p. 169.

while the passage as a whole appears as an intrusion in the context. The beginning of the chapter represents Jeremiah declaring immediate doom for Jerusalem and predicting the capture of Zedekiah and his nobles,[43] and this theme is continued in verses 20–22. Verses 8–18 would, then, appear to be an insertion here designed to explain the capture of Zedekiah and his nobles in terms of disobeying the covenant of Yahweh: "I will make you a horror to all the kingdoms of the earth. And the men who transgressed my covenant and did not keep the terms of my covenant . . . I will make like the calf which they cut in two . . ." (vv. 17–18).

The genuineness of those passages in which Deuteronomic influence on Jeremiah is claimed is thus doubtful. Nor indeed is it likely that we can establish what the prophet's attitude to Deuteronomy was. As we noted, some exegetes regard xi 1–8 as attesting to Jeremiah's early support for the Deuteronomic Code. Chapter viii 8 has, on the other hand, been interpreted as expressing his later criticism of this law.[44] The passage is:

> How can you say, We are wise,
> and the law of the Lord is with us?
> But, behold, the false pen of the scribes
> has made it into a lie.

We find the phrase "the law of the Lord" in 2 Kings xxii 8, 11 and Deuteronomy xxxii 10 where it clearly refers to the book found in the temple, and it may thus apply to Deuteronomy here. It is again true that the "law of the Lord" contrasts with "the word of Yahweh" in the following verse, and we may therefore assume that we have a written law contrasted with the vibrant prophetic word. We cannot, however, determine with any certainty whether the criticism in question applies to the activities of the scribes or to the law itself. It is possible, moreover, that the scribes here are to be identified with the priests. For we find the priests rebuked in the book of Malachi (ii 7 f.) for corrupting the covenant of Levi and showing partiality in their instruction. Accordingly it may be the law as falsified by the scribes that is condemned in this passage in Jeremiah.[45] Apart from TORREY doubts on the genuineness of the passage have not been emphatically expressed;[46] yet it is not germane to its context, while its similarity with Malachi ii 7–9 may be indicative of a post-Jeremianic age. In view, then, of such exegetical uncertainties we cannot draw any firm conclusion from Jeremiah viii 8 regarding the prophet's attitude to Deuteronomy.

---

[43]Verses 4–5, however, seem to promise a peaceful death for Zedekiah. It is thus uncertain whether they represent a tradition according to which Jeremiah offered a conditional escape to the king, or whether they are entirely editorial. Verse 19 is probably a later addition.

[44]E.g., K. MARTI, *Geschichte der Israelitischen Religion*, 1897, p. 166; DUHM, *op. cit.*, pp. 88 f.; T. H. ROBINSON, *Introduction to the Books of the Old Testament*, p. 307 f.; John PATERSON, *op. cit.*, pp. 148 ff.

[45]Cf. the comments of RUDOLPH, *op. cit.*, pp. 252–253.

[46]C. C. TORREY, *J.B.L.* LVI, 1937, pp. 196 f.

It is, of course, true that a prophet who condemned sacrifice (vii 12 ff.; xi 15; xxvi 9) and who visualized the worship of Yahweh in a foreign land (xxix 11 ff.) could have but little sympathy with a law which conceived of worship in terms of the cult.[47] It is, on the other hand, equally true that there are certain elements of Deuteronomy to which he could take no objection. Its implacable opposition to idolatry, and its attempt to regulate the worship of Yahweh at one sanctuary could scarcely have been regarded with complete indifference by him.

It must, however, be admitted that we know but little of Jeremiah's attitude to Deuteronomy. And this is all the more surprising if the prophet were called to his office in 626 or 627 and Deuteronomy published some five years later. For the publication of Deuteronomy must have been regarded by the people of the day as an event of some importance, and we should expect that, in the enthusiasm of his early career, Jeremiah should have made some reference to it. His silence may, therefore, find its explanation in the view that he did not begin his ministry till 605, some sixteen years after the publication of Deuteronomy. By this time the novelty associated with its promulgation would have passed and it would no longer be a topic of current discussion. Jeremiah rather saw the leading issue of the day as the victory of the Babylonians at Carchemish and their inevitable expansion westwards. This explains why his interpretation of these developments perturbed Jehoiakim (xxxvi 29) and why on a later occasion he was consulted by Zedekiah himself (xxxvii 17; xxxviii 14).

How, however, it will be asked, can we account for the statement in Jeremiah i 2 that the prophet was called in the year 626 B.C.? Various suggestions have been offered. It has been proposed that we may regard that date as the year of Jeremiah's birth,[48] and again that it is a textual error for the year 616.[49] K. BUDDE, on the other hand, pronounced all the material of verses 1-2 as late. Recognizing the awkward juxtaposition of phrases in this passage he commented that it was not only bad, but impossible, Hebrew. He further observed that the text of the Septuagint is shorter here and presupposes an original Hebrew text דבר יהוה אשר היה אל. The opening words of Jeremiah would then be the same as the (Hebrew) introductions to Hosea, Micah, Zephaniah and Joel.[50] But as these formalistic introductions seem necessarily to be as late as Joel they may present unreliable chronologies.[51]

---

[47]On the question of Jeremiah's relationship to Deuteronomy see A. F. PUUKKO's study "Jeremias Stellung zum Deuteronomium" in *Alttestamentliche Studien Rudolf Kittel zum 60. Geburtstag dargebracht*, ed. R. KITTEL, *B.W.A.T.* XIII, 1913, pp. 126–153.

[48]HYATT, *I.B.*, V, p. 779b.

[49]So T. C. GORDON, *Expository Times*, XLIV, 1932–33, pp. 562 ff.

[50]"Über das erste Kapital des Buches Jeremia," *J.B.L.* XL, 1921, pp. 23 ff.

[51]Cf. R. E. WOLFE, "The Editing of the Book of the Twelve," *Z.A.W.*, 1935, pp. 90–129, especially pp. 116–118.

We further notice that according to the Chronicler (2 Chron. xxxiv 3–4) Josiah initiated his reforms in Judah in the twelfth year of his reign, the year 627 or 628. On this reckoning Jeremiah entered on his prophetic career almost as soon as Josiah began his reforming movements. It is significant that the Chronicler also records that Jeremiah lamented for Josiah (2 Chron. xxxv 25).[52] There was thus a tendency in Jewish tradition to associate Jeremiah with Josiah, and we see this likewise reflected in certain passages in the book of Jeremiah (iii 16; xxii 15 f.; xxv 3). But this seems to spring from a desire to place Jeremiah's ministry in the reign of Josiah so that he would be regarded as lending support to his reforms and thus to the Code Deuteronomy.

But however we are to explain the motives of Deuteronomic editors in placing Jeremiah's call in the thirteenth year of Josiah, there is no evidence in the rest of the book to show that he was prophesying as early as this. Nor, apart from a few doubtful allusions, is there anything to connect him at all with the reign of Josiah. Not till we come to chapter xxv 1 do we find the first definite date relating to Jeremiah's activity. This was the fourth year of Jehoiakim, the year of the battle of Carchemish.

---

[52]So Josephus (*Antiq.*, x 5, 1) claims to know of such a dirge in his own day. Lamentations chapter iv is thought to be the dirge in question; cf. PFEIFFER, *Intro. to the Old Test.*, p. 722.

5

Jeremiah and Deuteronomy*
Henri Cazelles

(Translated by Leo G. Perdue)

"Jeremiah began his ministry in 627; the reform of Josiah took place in 622. In the face of such a significant undertaking, what was the reaction of the young prophet?" "This problem, declares Albert Condamin, is one of the most interesting ones in the Old Testament." The wording and citation are by A. Robert[1] who in this fashion began his study of one of the most important and at the same time one of the most contested texts: Jer 11:1–14. Before returning to this study in its entirety, it is important to set forth very briefly a kind of *status quaestionis*. To begin with, this study will set forth and evaluate the major points of contact between Jeremiah and Deuteronomy. Then, taking account of the objections of the critics, the paper will proceed with a close exegesis of the major passages. Finally, after a summary of the principal historical data, we shall then be more in position to venture a conclusion.

STATUS QUAESTIONIS

The controversy began as early as 1839, when J. L. König disputed the validity of the thesis of von Bohlen and of Knobel. The latter saw in Jeremiah, if not the editor of Deuteronomy, at least a partisan of the reform of Josiah which was inspired by Deuteronomy, as de Wette had demonstrated. J. L. König contrasted the similarities of style and vocabulary together with an entire series of topical differences.

Since then other arguments have been set forth, and the center of the debate has shifted slightly: it is less a matter of vocabulary than it is of ideas. Is the religious position of Jeremiah compatible with the reform of Josiah that centralized the cult in Jerusalem following the precepts of Deut 12?

---

*Originally appeared as "Jérémie et le Deutérome," *Recherches de Science Religieuse* 38 (1951) 5–36.
[1]"Jérémie et la réforme deutéronomique d'après Jér. XI, 1–14." *Science religieuse, travaux et recherches*, 1943, p. 1

1. Duhm,[2] Marti,[3] and Cornill,[4] followed by Kennett, Hölscher, Puukko,[5] Welch,[6] and Mowinckel all respond in the negative. The essential idea of Deuteronomy is the centralization of the cult in Jerusalem; the salvation of the people is assured by the worship practiced in the temple of Jerusalem. However, for Jeremiah, say these scholars, God has no desire for such a cult, for he did not require sacrifices at the time of the revelation at Sinai (Jer 7:21–22). What is more, Jeremiah even announced the destruction of the temple of Jerusalem after the fashion of the one at Shiloh (Jer 7–8, cf. 26). He could not therefore have supported a movement like the Deuteronomic reform of Josiah. Other arguments have been added to this fundamental one. Welch insisted that if Jeremiah had been a supporter of the reform, he, not Huldah the prophetess, would have been consulted. Puukko sought to demonstrate that Jeremiah did not have the good relationship with the supporters of the reform that the texts at first glance would seem to suppose. Duhm rejected the authenticity of certain passages as Jer 11:1–14. Cornill interpreted 8:8 as a sure witness that for Jeremiah the redaction of Deuteronomy was the falsification of the true covenant, that of Sinai. Meanwhile, in a more nuanced fashion, G. A. Smith[7] held the opinion that the prophet spoke against certain affirmations of Deuteronomy (e.g., the existence of sacrifices in the desert).

2. However, this position is not the one supported by the majority of critics. Wellhausen wrote in 1894 in his *Israelitische und jüdische Geschichte* (p. 94): Jeremiah "has contributed to the enactment (*Einführung*) of Deuteronomy." This has continued to be the opinion of Catholics such as Condamin,[8] Robert,[9] and Gelin,[10] as well as Protestants of every period and nuance (Budde, Steuernagel, von Rad,[11] Volz,[12] Rudolph,[13] Giesebrecht,[14] Rothstein in German; S. Driver,[15] Peake, Skinner,[16] Rowley[17] in

---

[2] *Jeremia* in *Handkommentar zum A.T.* Göttingen, 1892.

[3] *Jeremia* in *Kurzer Handkommentar*. Tübingen, 1900.

[4] *Das Buch Jeremia*. Leipzig, 1905, p. 144.

[5] "Jeremias Stellung zum Deuteronomium," in *Alttest. Studien R. Kittel zum 60ten Geburstag dargebracht*. Leipzig, 1913, pp. 126–153.

[6] *Jeremiah, his Time and his Work*. Oxford, 1928, pp. 76–96.

[7] *Jeremiah*. London, 1923, pp. 134–161.

[8] *Le livre de Jérémie*[3]. Paris, 1936, pp. 103–106.

[9] *Op. cit.*, pp. 1–16.

[10] Art. "Jérémie" in Supplément au *Dictionnaire de la Bible*, IV, col. 864f.

[11] *Das Gottesvolk im Deuteronomium*. Stuttgart, 1929, pp. 90–100.

[12] *Der Prophet Jeremia*[2]. Leipzig, 1928, pp. 103–105.

[13] *Jeremia* in *Handbuch zum alten Testament*. Tübingen, 1948, p. iv, 67–69.

[14] *Das Buch Jeremia*. Göttingen, 1907.

[15] *Deuteronomy* in *International Critical Commentary*. Edinburgh, 1902, pp. xcii–xciv, and *The Book of the Prophet Jeremiah*. London, 1906, pp. xli–xliv.

[16] *Prophecy and Religion*. Cambridge, 1922, 1936, pp. 165–184.

[17] "The Prophet Jeremiah and the Book of Deuteronomy," in *Studies in Old Testament Prophecy*. Oxford, 1950, pp. 157–174.

English; and Lods[18] and L. Gautier in French). But, though they adhere to this basic point, their assessments are infinitely diverse. For some, Jeremiah did not go back on his support. So argues Condamin as well as von Rad who has endeavored to set forth in detail the meaning of the Deuteronomic reform. For others such as A. Lods, the prophet at a later time came to realize the insufficiencies of the reform: "He was not long in recognizing that the improvements provoked by the royal edicts were extremely superficial and did little more than sustain the illusions."[19] This position is very close to that of Wellhausen: "But he was by no means satisfied with the results of the reform."

3. Other scholars go further and recognize a change in the position and conduct of Jeremiah. This is true for Skinner and for Rudolph: "Without any doubt, Josiah had the young prophet of Anathoth among his supporters," but the passages where Jeremiah rejects the cult and the temple demonstrate to us that Jeremiah "rejected Deuteronomy" (p. 69). There had been a shift in the life of the prophet ("einer Wandlung in der Einstellung des Propheten"). If he makes an appeal to observe the law in certain passages (e.g. 6:19) and if it is necessary to preserve something of chapter 11 where the prophet exhorts respect for "the words of the covenant," it is not necessary to see there an allusion to Deuteronomy, but only to the covenant of Sinai. On this point Rudolph is in agreement with Volz and König. But there is room in this category for a wide variety of opinion.

These last two categories have tended to make ground in spite of the weight of the proponents of the first. This first, more radical position requires that the problem be examined in a more detailed fashion. Moreover, it is only in this manner that one is able to make a study of some interest, seeking a clearer understanding of that significant period in the history of religions—the 6th century B.C. and the fall of Jerusalem. But the difficulty is a difficulty of method: how does one exactly pose the problem?

THE COMMON POINTS BETWEEN JEREMIAH AND DEUTERONOMY

It is always necessary to appeal to the texts, but we shall come to see that their interpretation is more difficult than elsewhere. When one consults with some care a concordance, one is able to glimpse a double connection: one between Ezekiel and part of Leviticus (in particular the Holiness Code of 17–26) and other priestly documents of the Pentateuch, and one between Jeremiah and Deuteronomy. But if one easily admits that Ezekiel and Leviticus participate in the same current of thought, one hardly ever discusses their respective anteriority. However, in the case of Jeremiah and

---

[18] *Les Prophètes d'Israël.* Paris, 1935, pp. 163f., 175, and *Histoire de la littérature hébraïque et juive.* Paris, 1950, pp. 405ff.

[19] *Les Prophètes . . .* , p. 165.

Deuteronomy, not only does one discuss their dates, but one even goes so far as to ask whether the prophet is not himself opposed to the Deuteronomic current of thought. P. Dumeste has written: "We do not think that Jeremiah may have taken an active part in the elaboration and diffusion of the Deuteronomic Code. . . . The institutional aspect of religion is, so to say, alien to his thinking" (*Vie spirituelle*, May 1938, p. 156f., cited by A. Gelin, *S.D.B.*, IV, 165), a statement that summarizes in a forceful fashion the position of an entire school.

A precise comparison of the vocabulary and the style of these two works is necessary then before proceeding any further. The similarities of vocabulary, expression, and doctrine have already been noted by Movers[20] in 1840. In 1873, Zunz[21] had placed in parallel form more than two pages of concordant formulae (of which, it must be added, a page and a half refer to Deut 28:21ff.). In his commentary on Deuteronomy, S. Driver[22] has preserved the more common ones, while noting with Zunz that he has found 66 passages in Deuteronomy that are echoed in more than 86 passages in Jeremiah. On the one hand they may be brief formulas as "so that they may fear me all the days" (Deut 4:10, cf. Jer 32:39) or "that it may be well with you" (Deut 5:26, cf. Jer 7:23). On the other hand some are longer: "do not go after other gods to serve or worship them" (Jer 25:6; Deut 8:19). Sometimes it is an entire passage of Jeremiah which seems to depend upon one from the Deuteronomic law: thus Jer 34:8–14 could be an application of Deut 15:2 to the liberation of slaves after seven years of service.

These lists of Movers, Zunz, and Driver ought, however, to be closely examined for the following reason. There are two preliminary questions to resolve. The first will not be addressed in this study: is the law discovered under Josiah actually Deuteronomy? In spite of some sporadic resistance, the affirmative response appears to be secured ever since the study of de Wette. But another comes into view that one cannot elude: are there literary contacts between the "Book of Jeremiah" and the "Book of Deuteronomy" from which conclusions may be drawn about the relations between the "person of Jeremiah" and the reform movement carried out under Josiah? Some other data in fact are to be taken into account:

1. Some data relative to the Book of Jeremiah. It is certain that not everything is from Jeremiah himself, and it is therefore necessary to conclude that a very large part is the result of redactional activity, due no doubt to the work of Baruch (see for example Podechard in *R.B.*, 1929, pp. 181 ff., and A. Gelin in the *S.D.B.*, IV, 870). Now, this post-Jeremianic redaction is produced within the mental framework of Deuteronomy and often even in the same style. Of course, it should not be concluded that all

---

[20] *Zeitschrift für Philosophie und katholische Theologie*, cahiers 1, 2 and 4. Cologne.
[21] *Zeitschrift der morgenländischen Gesellschaft*. 1873, pp. 670–673.
[22] *Op. cit.*, p. xliii.

which is Deuteronomic in the Book of Jeremiah is the work of the Deuteronomic redactor. That would be to beg the question. But, whenever we see a parallel in a text that for other reasons we are led to believe is redactional, we are not permitted to draw any conclusion about the relationship between Jeremiah and Deuteronomy. One may only infer from the mass of these parallels that the disciple of Jeremiah had to admit a spiritual kinship between the two works that would allow him to present one for the other.

2. The data relative to Deuteronomy. This book is as diverse as it is unified. Steuernagel distinguished two Deuteronomists (D^1, D^2), plus some additions and a redaction (R).[23] Perhaps it will suffice to admit a double edition of the book, one pre-Jeremianic and the other post-Jeremianic.[24] This hypothesis, which is based on disparate materials, repetitions, adaptations of the text, and the fact that certain passages (e.g. Deut 4:25ff.; 32) presuppose the exile, allows curious coincidences to be explained. The observation has been made that "heart" is generally *lēbh* in Jeremiah (58 of 65 times) and *lēbābh* in Deuteronomy. However, there are three exceptions: Deut 4:11, 28:65, and 29:3. These three passages properly belong to the second edition of the book. They should not then be taken into account in the discussion. In this specific case, the matter is of no interest, except at best to underline a difference between the two authors; but it is not always so.

We should accordingly be suspicious of any parallel in vocabulary or wording when one of the two passages involved may be found either in the second edition of Deuteronomy (at least 1–4; 28:47 to the end) or in the redactional passages of Jeremiah. However, the redactional sections of Jeremiah are not delineated with such certainty that no questions remain. It appears that one should include the passages of Mowinckel's C source which Rudolph lists as follows: 7:1–8:3; 11:1–14; 16:1–13; 17:19–27; 18:1–12; 21:1–10; 22:1–5.[25] This is not absolutely certain, but nevertheless it provides a sufficient approximation. If we encounter some passages where the density of the expressions common to the two works is particularly great, we shall be surprised if one of the two texts is not redactional. Nevertheless, that will only be one indication.

From these basic points, what then remains of Driver's list? Only three passages: Deut 6:24 and Jer 32:39; Deut 8:19 and Jer 25:6; Deut 28:25 and Jer 15:4, 24:9, 29:18, cf. 34:17. In sum, only three passages remain from the sixteen that Driver took as the best from the list of Zunz! Let us examine them more closely.

---

[23] *Deuteronomium.* Göttingen, 1900.

[24] *Le Deutéronome* in *La Sainte Bible traduite en français sous la direction de l'École biblique de Jérusalem.* Paris, 1950. Introduction, pp. 13f.

[25] In addition, all the texts relative to Jeremiah which begin in chapter 25, except for the authentic citations of the prophet.

The first parallel rests upon the expression "in order that you may fear me always." It is found again in Deut 14:23, and the theme of the fear of Yahweh is a frequent one in this book. This expression, by contrast, is not a customary one in Jeremiah. Fear for this prophet conveys a more physical than religious quality (3:8). However, some passages such as 5:22, 24, which entail a type of fear that has a rather mediocre quality, still possess a truly religious scope. This parallel is not then deprived of all value.

The second parallel is more typical, for the expressions "to go after other gods" or "to serve other gods," "to worship other gods," "to belong to other gods" abound in Jeremiah (19 times) and in Deuteronomy (18 times). Since it is obviously a doctrine common to both writers, one should not see it as merely an expression of later redactors. One finds the expression "other gods" in only 24 other passages of the Bible, most of which belong to the Deuteronomic redaction (10 times in the Book of Kings). However, neither Jeremiah nor Deuteronomy is the only source of this doctrine. It is already present in Hosea (3:1), the Decalogue (Ex 20:3), and the Covenant Code (Ex 23:13). This parallel does not prove in our opinion a case of dependence, but rather it is a simple case of common heritage.

The third expression is properly Jeremianic: "I will make them an object of horror to all the kingdoms of the earth." Jeremiah uses this expression four times. By contrast, in Deuteronomy one encounters it only a single time, and even here one may ask if it is not a later insertion. This chapter of curses formally presupposes the exile beginning with v. 47, but the exilic addition may properly begin before this. Movers already noted that the paragraph where this expression is found contains a high density of Jeremianic characteristics: 28:26 is found in Jer 7:33, 16:4, 19:7, 34:20; Deut 28:37 in Jer 25:9, 18 and 44:12; and last of all Deut 28:39 in Jer 12:13; cf. 29:5. Therefore we continue to have some doubts.

Since the list by Driver is rather disappointing, it is necessary for us to return to the one by Zunz. It will show itself to be a rather fertile one.

1. $ᵓᵉlōhîm$ $hayyîm$ in Deut 5:23; Jer 10:10, 23:36. This formula is rare. Before Jeremiah one finds it only in I Sam 17:26, 36. It does not occur in J, E, Isaiah, or the other prophets who precede Jeremiah. Being aware of the importance that Deuteronomy places on life and its continuation, one could be inclined to see here Jeremiah's dependence upon the book of Josiah.

2. "To rebel against Yahweh and not listen to his voice": Deut 9:16, 23; Jer 40:3. This is a more difficult expression to analyze. It involves two features, the first of which at least goes back to Hosea (4:8, 10:8, 13:12. . .) and the second of which evokes a specifically Deuteronomic conception (5:21. . .).

3. $Yāgôr$ $mippᵉnê$—Deut 9:19; Jer 22:25, 39:17. The expression recurs in Deut 28:26 and in three later texts. Jer 39:17 is redactional. The two

texts that remain do not appear to demonstrate literary dependence, but rather indicate merely a common literary climate.

4. "The land which I swore to their fathers to give them." Deut 10:11; Jer 32:22. This expression is a typically Deuteronomic one that occurs in a slightly different form (6:10, 23; 7:13. . .). However, it is by contrast quite rare in Jeremiah. We shall have other occasions to verify that chapters 30–33 of Jeremiah are more laden than others with Deuteronomic formulae.

5. The circumcision of the heart: Deut 10:16; Jer 9:25; 4:4. The image is peculiar to these two books (cf. Deut 30:6). It is quite improbable that so original an image would have been invented by two authors at the same time. It is supported in Deuteronomy by an alliteration (^{c}rl = foreskin; ^{c}rph = back of the neck). Jeremiah appears to presuppose that the image is well known, and it is one of those rare instances where *lēbābh* (= Deuteronomy) is used, not *lēbh*. So many indications point to Jeremiah's dependence on Deuteronomy.

6. "Under every green tree." Deut 12:2; Jer 2:20; 3:6, 13; 11:16; 17:2, 8. This expression is very typically Jeremianic, for it does not occur in either the earlier prophets or the rest of Deuteronomy. However, the expression in Deuteronomy occurs in the later redactional context of the law of the altar (cf. Welch) and thus belongs to the post-Jeremianic redaction of Deuteronomy.

7. "Gives you to inherit." Deut 12:10; Jer 3:18, 12:14. The context in Deuteronomy which pertains to centralization of worship in the sanctuary indicates this expression is dependent upon Jeremiah.

8. "To utter rebellion against Yahweh," Deut 13:6, cf. 19:16; Jer 28:16, 29:32. It appears that the occurrence of this expression in both books may be due to a dependence on Isaiah (1:5, 31:6).

9. "And it shall be a ruin forever." Deut 13:17; Jer 49:2, cf. 30:18. This expression does not occur in earlier writings. Nothing precludes the possibility that the prophet may have been inspired by the threats of Deuteronomy.

10. *rah^{a}mîm w^{e}riḥamkhā*. Deut 13:18; Jer 42:12. This "mercy" is an expression relatively more frequent in Jeremiah than in Deuteronomy, but both are dependent on Hosea (particularly 2:25).

11. The prophet who speaks what God has not commanded him to speak. Deut 18:20; Jer 29:23. This tenet of the divine commandment is very Deuteronomic (17:3). It is likewise found in Jeremiah outside of this passage (which may be due to Baruch): 17:22 and 19:5. While it does not occur in Hosea, Jeremiah may have appropriated it from Amos, Isaiah, or Deuteronomy.

12. "Yahweh brought Israel out of Egypt with a mighty hand, an outstretched arm, signs and wonders, and great terror, and led them into a land flowing with milk and honey." Deut 26:8–9; Jer 32:21 and 22. These expressions frequently recur in Deuteronomy 5:15, 6:21, 7:8, 9:26, 7:19, 11:2). They are rare in Jeremiah, since 21:5 appears to be redactional.

Jer 32:22 belongs to the Book of Consolation where the contacts with Deuteronomy are especially numerous. The hypothesis by Volz, who discerns an important nucleus here that belongs to the prophecy of Jeremiah while he enthusiastically awaits during the reform the return of Ephraim (30:10, 31:18 ff.), could explain this more intimate dependence of the prophet on Deuteronomy.

One could continue this effort by taking up one by one the eighty-nine words or expressions regarded by Steuernagel[26] as typically Deuteronomic. But this effort suffices to prove that, even by eliminating certain suspect passages, the contacts between the two are too numerous to deny a definite connection between the prophet and the law discovered in the temple. It would seem then, when closely examined, these parallels should lead one to think that Jeremiah is dependent upon this law.

However, it is not correct to make the young man of Anathoth simply a disciple of the law. J. L. König and later Driver and Puukko have underlined some important differences in the vocabulary itself. Not only does one use $l\bar{e}b\bar{a}bh$ and the other $l\bar{e}bh$, but Deuteronomy often adds the epenthetic ג to the plural which Jeremiah avoids (except for five occurrences). Deuteronomy is fond of the pronoun $^\jmath\bar{a}n\bar{o}kh\hat{\imath}$ for the first person singular, whereas Jeremiah prefers $^{\jmath a}n\hat{\imath}$. Deuteronomy uses $h\bar{e}m$ for the third person plural, while Jeremiah has $h\bar{e}mm\hat{a}h$. The prophet's $^\jmath\hat{e}kh$ and $l\bar{a}kh\bar{e}n$ are missing in Deuteronomy, while reciprocally raq in the latter is absent in Jeremiah. Deuteronomy says that Yahweh is a jealous God ($qann\bar{a}^\jmath$ 4:24, 5:9, 6:14), compassionate ($rah\hat{u}m$ 4:31),[27] faithful ($ne^{\jmath e}man$ 7:9), fearful ($n\hat{o}r\bar{a}^\jmath$ 7:21, 10:17), and a devouring fire (4:24, 9:3), expressions which are never uttered by Jeremiah. On the contrary, he speaks of Yahweh's hosts, an expression not found in Deuteronomy.

Other differences are less precise, but very much to the point. Deuteronomy speaks with insistence about the love of God for Israel and Israel's for God. This is more rare in Jeremiah (2:2, 31:3). In similar fashion, Jeremiah mentions only once Yahweh's election of Israel (33:24), that significant Deuteronomic theme. The observation of the law ($\check{s}\bar{a}mar$) which Deuteronomy insistently requires is mentioned by the prophet only in 16:11 and 35:18, while he refers to the possession of Canaan only in 30:3 and 32:23. He never uses the phrase "to prolong the days." While he speaks of "the children of Israel" and "the house of Israel," he does not use the phrases "the holy people," "the people of inheritance," and "the portion of Yahweh" ($nah^al\hat{a}$, but see 10:16; cf. 3:18 and 12:14).

These differences need not be multiplied. They prove only that Jeremiah underwent a religious formation prior to the discovery of the law. In actuality this entire preceding paragraph suggests at least as many parallels as differences. Even if he speaks very little about the love and jealousy of

---

[26] *Einleitung zum Hexateuch.* Göttingen, 1900, p. xxxiii–xli.

[27] But for this idea, see section 10, p. 95.

Yahweh, the prophet is still animated by that love. His preaching is permeated by it, in regard to both his call for the faithless wife to return and his personal life itself (20:7—"I have been seduced"). As for the differences in vocabulary, they are very well explained by peculiarities of dialect. This would be an additional argument in favor of Welch's theory that Deuteronomy is the work of men of the Northern Kingdom who are addressing the faithful of the Kingdom of Israel. Jeremiah remains a Judean speaking to Judeans, even if he has taken part in a reform based on Deuteronomy. Likewise, if one admits that "Yahweh's hosts" designates the worship of Yahweh in the temple of Jerusalem, one discovers why Jeremiah may have used the expression while Deuteronomy had avoided it. Speaking to the people of the North in order to convince them that the only valid cult must take place in Jerusalem, it was prudent to avoid an appellative that brought to their mind the rival state rather than the God common to the tribes.

In brief, these differences are those that one would expect from two different temperaments who were addressing different audiences and different circumstances. The Deuteronomist systematized in chamber pre-existing legislative texts. He was able to attend to his style and his sentences. It was Israel who was in view. By contrast, Jeremiah was an orator who was to write down the entirety of his oracles late in life, and he lived in a Judean milieu. When we add that his call went back to 627–626, while the discovery of the law occurred in 622–621, the influence of Deuteronomy is exerted upon a Jeremiah already shaped to a large extent. Therefore it is quite remarkable that such a significant number of parallels that indicate an influence of the book on the prophet appear.

In fact, it is in the area of doctrine, more than vocabulary, that the resemblances are the more apparent. De Wette and Schrader have already noted five of these: 1. the insistence on an interiorization of the law; 2. the words of God are to be inscribed on the heart; 3. God requires that one seek him will all of his heart (Deut 4:29; Jer 29:13); 4. the battle against the cult of the stars and the queen of heaven; 5. and elimination of the popular doctrine of retribution (Deut 24:16; Jer 31:29). This last point is extremely important. It is all the more curious, because this feature hardly squares with either book in its entirety. Both lay stress upon the idea of collective retribution: one emphasizing the notion of the people of God, and the other the punishment of the people. Nevertheless, both lend themselves to that individualization which Ezekiel would sanctify, Deuteronomy by its appeal to the human heart and Jeremiah by his exhortations to a conversion which the masses do not want.

Von Rad prefers, however, not to take into consideration this aspect of their doctrine in his comparison of the ideologies of the two (pp. 97f.). Robert summarizes von Rad's position: "The same similarities with Hosea, the same way of looking at history, the same conception of the chosen people, the same polemic against the nature cults, and the same moral requirements deriving from a spiritually resolute conception of service to God" (p. 16). "One may assess Deuteronomy only with the viewpoint of Jeremiah," concludes von Rad (p. 99).

We have in both books the identical movement of thought in regard to the design of God and divine action. For both, the point of departure for everything is Yahweh's election of his people in the desert. And this Yahweh is the only power, the only master of nature, the only one who has the ability to save. It is to convert, to open the eyes of his people, that he may chastise. Conversion is less certain, for Israel-Judah appears incapable of escaping the destruction which threatens her (Jer 3:13, 25; 4:5; 9:10; it is less apparent in the first edition of Deuteronomy; see however 8:19f., 9:13f.). The false prophets are active and corrupt the people. Yet there is some hope; beyond the punishment there reside some prospects for life. And even there the first edition of Deuteronomy, optimistic in its basis, is closer to Jeremiah 30–33 than the rest.

We are now able to conclude this part of our study by stating: if the second edition of Deuteronomy is clearly dependent on Jeremiah and his vocabulary, the resemblances of vocabulary and doctrine between the first edition of Deuteronomy and the oracles of Jeremiah suggest rather a dependence of the prophet on the text discovered by the high priest Hilkiah.

THE TEXTS OF JEREMIAH

Our task is no longer one of searching for parallels in regard to vocabulary or doctrine. Rather now we are to investigate the principal texts of Jeremiah which are summoned by the critics. Do these texts of the prophet establish the fact that he had known Deuteronomy and actively supported it? Or, on the other hand, do they indicate that he has rejected this book and the reform it inspired? In favor of the first hypothesis, one invokes 3:1, 11:1–14, 34:8, 44:17f. In favor of the second, one calls forth 3:6–13, 7:21f., 8:8, 9:12. We shall begin with the second group of texts.

A. Texts of Jeremiah Which Could Imply a Rejection of Deuteronomy

1. 3:6–13.

Welch places emphasis on these verses which deal "with the conditions of national reform" (p. 78). They "warn Israel against following the example of its sister-nation, Judah," and then in v. 12 God tells her, "return." This is the call to conversion, not an ironic invitation to return from exile that would be impossible to carry out. Israel is guilty, but Judah is even more so. Why? "It is because the Southern people, warned by the fate which befell its neighbour in 721, carried out a reform, but a reform which was in *šeqer* (v. 10)," that is to say, "falsity or treachery" (pp. 84–85). Thus for Welch v. 10 means that Judah has not returned to Yahweh in her heart, but rather in treachery. This "return" implies a reform, and it can be no other than that of Josiah. It is this reform, says Welch, which Jeremiah sees as treachery, the reform itself, and not its unsatisfactory results: "The movement has been bad in itself, since it was wrought in falsity or was false in principle."

The exegesis by Welch is at this point less solid than it first appears. In fact, is it true that Jeremiah here is reproaching Judah (as Israel elsewhere)? It is idolatry, the "committing of adultery with the tree and stone" (v. 9), "the profligate walking towards every green tree." Now this position is exactly that of Deuteronomy in chapter 12. If Jeremiah had truly wished to censure the Deuteronomic movement, he would have said: your transgression is going to the altars, is the offering of tithes. However, he does not say this. Instead he casts the blame on the high places, the cult of the false gods. The conversion to which he alludes and about which he speaks takes place not in the heart, but rather in treachery. Why is one to see in this the reform of Josiah? Could it not simply be the tendency to increase the acts of external worship instead of effectuating an internal conversion (*bᵉkhōl-lēbh*)? This is a recurring phenomenon that happens each time conditions worsen. Now, in 622 conditions were not bad; rather on the contrary they were good. For Assyria was on the eve of destruction, and Judah was in the process of experiencing the rebirth of national independence. This false return appears to concern something other than the reform. What? Perhaps it is not necessary to decide. Here as elsewhere, the young Jeremiah is an outlet of Hosea, and in 5:15–16 this prophet has already alluded to these false returns of the people of Yahweh. The prophet reproaches them for a "devotion which is like a morning cloud, like the morning dew which goes away" (Hos. 6:4): "Come, let us return to Yahweh," said the Israelites after a catastrophe (Hos 6:1), but Yahweh did not accept the integrity of a superficial conversion. It seems that Jeremiah does not fully take up again this theme of his predecessor, and this would restrict the efforts to see here an allusion to the reform of Josiah.

2. 7:21f.

The most important verse is v. 22: "For in the day that I brought them out of the land of Egypt, I did not speak to your fathers or command them concerning burnt offerings and sacrifices."

How would this be compatible, one asks, to Deuteronomy which devotes 12:1–16:7 to the code of sacrifices, tithes, and annual festivals? Such is the objection.

Certainly Jeremiah is not here in accord with Leviticus which places at Sinai the revelation of the ritual of sacrifices, a revelation made directly by God. But Jeremiah is entirely in line with Deuteronomy. This text places at Sinai only the Decalogue and its moral requirements. It transfers to Moab the revelation of ritual and takes great care in distinguishing the two features. There was, on one hand, the exodus from Egypt which led to the revelation at Sinai, made directly by God. But there was, on the other hand, later in Moab the communication of the Deuteronomic law, a revelation mediated through Moses. This Deuteronomic law is given in a single "day" (v.g. 11:32), that is to say in Moab. Elsewhere, v. 23 which follows in chapter 7 is Deuteronomic, as is the remainder of the chapter which Mowinckel attributes to his C source.

If then Jeremiah appears to engage in polemics (in this context) against sacrifices, it is not in order to castigate Deuteronomy. Rather he wishes to demonstrate to the Jews that in comparison to the event where God's power is manifested with such brilliance (the exodus from Egypt), sacrifices are nothing. What is important is to obey the prescriptions of Yahweh, for the rest do not have the same value. We return at this point once again to Hosea: "I desire steadfast love (*hesedh*) and not sacrifice, the knowledge of God more than burnt offerings (6:6)." And in this verse, the first line with its strong semitic antithesis is explained and made precise by the second where one sees not a negation or a rejection, but rather a simple comparison. Knowledge of God for Hosea is the following of the Decalogue (compare 4:1 and 4:2). Deuteronomy has the same teaching. It places the Decalogue in the paramount position, and it proclaims with greater insistence the necessity to obey the commandments than it does to offer sacrifices.

3. 8:8

"How can you say, 'We are wise, and the law of the Lord is with us'? But behold, the false pen of the scribes has made it into a lie."

Marti, Welch, and above all Cornill see in this passage the affirmation that the law of Yahweh has been falsified by the scribal redactors of Deuteronomy. In this period, only Deuteronomy could be a written law that is at issue here. And indeed this book presents its law as the true wisdom of Israel (4:6). Skinner himself is persuaded by this text (p. 104).

In fact, according to v. 9, the wisdom in question is not linked to the law in the text. Rather, the sages are said in effect to have rejected the word of Yahweh and thereby lost their wisdom. Deut 4 has the same teaching.[28] In another connection, the term "sages" is paralleled to "scribes," and this must be the ordinary meaning of the word in Jeremiah (cf. 18:18). It is a term that designates officials: the law depends upon the priest and the counsel of the wise man. These scribes-sages are not those who compose various articles of the law, but rather draft decrees, as in the case of Isa 10:1. And the word *šeqer* (falsehood) is precisely employed in the legislative texts (Ex 23:7; Deut 19:18) in regard to justice, witnesses, and judgment (also for oaths: Jer 5:2, 7:9). Jeremiah indeed appears to say that the law has been falsified by the application made by the judges. This is the opinion

---

[28] And let us not forget that this chapter belongs to the post-Jeremianic redaction of Deuteronomy.

of Puukko (p. 149) who, in regard to this point, differs from Cornill. "The single import of Jer 8:8 causes one to see that what is of concern is the falsification of the law relative then to certain clauses or alterations of the law selected for selfish purposes." Ever a disciple of Hosea (4:6–8), Jeremiah fights against justice based on social class (*Klassenjustiz*).

While this solution appears to be the proper one, other authors have looked for different ones. Giesebrecht thinks it is impossible that Deuteronomy is at issue, and proposes instead certain additions to the law made by the priesthood of Jerusalem.[29a] Along the same line von Rad thinks the law may be the Holiness Code though strong reasons militate against dating this text in this period. But v. 10 indicts the greed of these scribes in the same way as Mic 3:3 and Isa 5:8. It seems then that Jeremiah may be more concerned with official avarice than legislation. Legislation has never given license to this type of malfeasance, whether one appeals to the Holiness Code or Deuteronomy. Even if one may see in Deut 12 an encouragement of the greed of the priests of Jerusalem, they still are excluded from being landholders by v. 12. And one knows how much such an exegesis of Deut 12 is disputable and disputed. Even there Jeremiah seems, in our opinion, not to be in opposition, but rather in conformity with Deuteronomy (15:2, 11; 16:18–20).

4. 9:12

Yahweh says: "Because they have forsaken my law which I set before them, and have not obeyed my voice, or walked in accord with it."

For argument's sake it could be that the prophet had considered Deuteronomy to be an abandonment of the law of Sinai. But nothing indicates that is the case. The vocabulary is Deuteronomic (14:27, except for the word law, but cf. 17:10, 11, 19; 5:28; 8:20; 28:15), even though the expressions may not be entirely Deuteronomic. Leviticus 16, which follows and continues the development, is, as it were, Deuteronomic in the view of writers like von Rad who see here a gloss.

In any case, in accord with Hosea (8:12) the attack is against idolatry, and nothing supposes an assault by Jeremiah against that which is specifically Deuteronomic. Indeed, it is just the opposite. This verse, as well as the others, points toward a Jeremiah who is in accord with the law discovered five years after his call.

B. Texts Invoked in Support of Jeremiah's Dependence on Deuteronomy

1. 3:1

This text of Jeremiah assumes it is impossible for a man to take back his wife, once he has renounced her and she has belonged to another. Now,

---

[29a] "Further additions . . . which at that time were cited by the priests."

we know the text of law which formulates this interdiction. It is Deut 24:1–4.

Jeremiah does not quote the text, but there are some rather striking coincidences of vocabulary: *šalaḥ* for "send away," *ʾîš* for the man, *ʾiššâ* for the woman (actually *ʾēšet*), the preposition *min*, *halᵉkhâ* for departure, *šûbh* for returning to the first home, and finally *wᵉhāyᵉtâ lᵉʾîš ʾāḥēr* is copied word for word. Yet, there are some differences. The *mēm* is shifted to another place, and above all Jeremiah replaces *tāmēʾ* in Deuteronomy with *ḥānaph* right at the time when he has the occasion to make use of *tāmēʾ*. But this is insignificant in comparison to the parallels.

Since this law is not present in the Priestly code, it is improbable that this custom would have had much of an application to Jerusalem. Jeremiah in this verse brings to mind the teaching of Hosea in regard to the second marriage of Yahweh and Israel. If he takes up that image (which is an objection), it is because Deuteronomy has been superseded. Or rather it is more of an indication of overturning a legal stipulation.

2. 34:8

This pericope has as its object an illegal action taken against Hebrew slaves. They have not been set free after seven years as they ought to have been. This text of Jeremiah is composed of two parts: an introduction (8–11) and an oracle (13:22) which is preceded by a redactional verse.[29b] Now, the oracle cites the same text of the law in v. 14. We are able to draw more closely to the question and determine which law or which unwritten custom Jeremiah invokes. Before concluding that the law in this context could only be Deuteronomic, one must not ignore other legislative texts in the Pentateuch which have a similar provision. In addition to the Deuteronomic text (15:12–18), one also has to consider Ex 21:2–11 (the Covenant Code), and Lev 25:39–46 (the Holiness Code).

Jeremiah obviously does not agree with this last text which permits the departure of a slave only during the year of Jubilee. In addition, the person is not actually a slave, but rather a hireling. By contrast, one is more hesitant to choose between the other two texts, both of which provide for the release of slaves after seven years. Let us look at the vocabulary.

miqqēṣ šebaʿ šānîm initiates Jeremiah 34:14. Deut 15:12 does not begin in this fashion, since it is only one paragraph in a more general law dealing with release. However, 15:1 does begin with these exact words.

tᵉšallᵉḥû (MT) or *tᵉšallaḥ* (LXX) = "you will release." The same word occurs in Deuteronomy at the end of verse 12.

ʾîš ʾeth ʾāḥîw (MT) or *ʾāḥîkhā* (LXX). Jeremiah uses here terminology for Israelite brotherhood which is characteristic of Deuteronomy (22:1–4; cf. Ex 23:4f.), and the expression is also found in 15:12.

[29b] In regard to this passage, see M. David, "The Manumission of Slaves under Zedekiah," in *Oudtestamentische Studiën*, V, pp. 74ff.

hāᶜibhrî, cf. Deut 15:12.

ᵓªšer—yimmākhēr lᵉkhā. These words form the beginning of Deut 15:12. Jeremiah only replaces the initial *kî* with *ᵓªšer*, a change that suits better the present context of the clause.

waᶜªbhādhᵉkhā šēš šānîm is found word for word in the final line of Deut 15:12.

wᵉšillaḥtô hŏphšî mēᶜimmākh is identical to Deut 15:13a, except that the imperfect in Deuteronomy, which is preceded by a conditional *kî*, is changed to a *wāw* conversive perfect in Jeremiah.

The vocabulary and expression of Jeremiah in this case is identical to Deuteronomy. The prophet has simply made a slight abridgement. By contrast, the passage in Exodus presents matters in a very different manner. It does not use the verb *šālaḥ*; it does not call the Israelite "brother"; it does not use *mēᶜim* to express the concept of separation as do Jeremiah and Deuteronomy; and finally it inserts the term *mākhar* (to sell) only in the section relative to the woman, while Jeremiah used the verb in reference to the slave, a term that infers both male and female slaves in accordance with the historical introduction that comes no doubt from Baruch.

Therefore, Jeremiah depends upon the Deuteronomic text to the extent that even its vocabulary bears a significant impress. Evidently we are here in the chapters where the hand of the Deuteronomic redactor is especially visible. But it does not appear that this citation may be his work. In this chapter the distinction between the historical introduction and the oracle is very sharply drawn. This redactor has felt the need to take up in his own account and in his own way the text of Deuteronomy, and he has insisted on making three references in these short verses to the liberation of the slave (vv. 9, 10, 11). If he had intruded into the redaction of v. 14, he would have in all likelihood placed emphasis on this point which was so essential to him. But if he does not, it is due to his respect for the earlier text, being content to specify at the beginning a point he considered to be important. In all probability then, Jeremiah relied upon Deuteronomy itself in regard to the matter of the liberation of the slaves during a time of seige.

3. We will place little emphasis on such texts as Jer 44:17, 25 which rather sharply brings into relief this business of doctrinal parallels, inasmuch as the contribution of the redactor is quite considerable here, and it is necessary to remark that Deut 17:3 is the oldest text which has prohibited the worship of celestial beings. One has the impression that the aging prophet still continues the battle begun during his youth.

4. Jer 11:1-14

We now come to the principal text. After all that we have said, it does not surprise us that the assessment of this text is not certain. Duhm has rejected it in its entirety, seeing it instead as a kind of haggadah, a pious development that presents Jeremiah as a missionary of the Law, but he has offered few arguments to support this position. Puukko ended with a similar type of conclusion in that he "disputed vv. 1–8 and has doubts about vv. 9–14" (Robert). Many other writers make similar drastic cuts. Erbt and Skinner excise vv. 1, 3b, 5b, 6aa¹b, 8bb¹, 9, 10ba¹, 11 and 12. Volz eliminates 6–8, while Rudolph is less specific.

Robert has sought out an objective principle of discrimination. This appears to be necessary, for the brief introduction, "the word which was addressed to Jeremiah by the Lord," is unique in this first part of the book. Being in the third person, it invites one to discern in these verses redactional activity. Robert rejects that which is a patchwork, an accumulation of Deuteronomic stock terms. This style is in fact not Jeremiah's. Thus he dismisses the authenticity of vv. 1–5 which are replete with Deuteronomic expressions. He also repudiates vv. 7–8. These verses are absent from the LXX (save for the last words which Robert keeps), and they take up in substance and even number expressions which are spoken in 7:24–26. As for the rest, 6, 8bb¹, 9–12, which flow quite well, have the style and the vocabulary of Jeremiah. One has no a priori reason for suspecting their authenticity. This text suffices to establish Jeremiah's position concerning the issue which has preoccupied us. Yahweh has sent him to proclaim in Judah and Jerusalem the words of the covenant, i.e. Deuteronomy (cf. Deut 28 and 29). But the men of Jerusalem and of Judah have not observed the covenant, they have "returned" to the iniquities of their ancestors, they have violated the covenant into which they had entered, and they will not be saved. Thus, in this passage Jeremiah has indicated both his support for the reform and its subsequent failure. Robert aligns himself, then, with the position of Wellhausen, Lods, Rowley, and many others. The "return" (*šābhû*) of which Rudolph is unwilling to press the meaning appears to him to have a very real importance. In any case he would have the prophet engaged in an activity that has the same sense as the reform.

This position appears to be very certain. The following considerations serve only to reinforce it.

a. Verses 1–5 are perhaps not so "piecemeal" as they may seem at first. Many of the references attributed to Deuteronomy concern texts which belong to the second edition of Deuteronomy. Thus, one reads in v. 2: "the words of this covenant." This expression is found only in Deuteronomy, specifically 28:69 and following, all texts of the post-Jeremianic edition. In the first edition, in 17:19, one has only "the words of this law," which is not the same thing. We could discover here the very free way in which Jeremiah handles the texts of Deuteronomy. Even the curse of v. 3 refers back almost word for word to Deut 27:26. But this verse either properly belongs to the curses of Shechem which have been inserted after the event in Deuteronomy, or rather it is the work of the redactor who has himself made this insertion. "Which I commanded" (v. 4) is not present as such in Deuteronomy which prefers to have Moses speak rather than God. While this book often states that God has sworn to the fathers, or that he has given to the fathers, it never says that God has commanded the fathers (ṣāwâ). As for the expression, "the covenant which Yahweh has commanded," it is encountered only in post-Jeremianic redacted texts (4:13, 23; 28:69). Likewise "the iron furnace" is found only in Deut 4:20. The presence of "and you will be my people" and "even to this day" in some suspect passages indicates that they belong to that same second edition. It is then extremely possible that our text may be much more in the customary style of Jeremiah, freely citing Deuteronomy without being too bound to its exact language.

The force of Robert's position comes especially from the curious redaction of the introductory verse which suggests it is an editorial creation. The somewhat clumsy repetition of "hear the words of this covenant" (2, 3, 5, 8) hints that this is not a writing composed by a single hand. But perhaps the redactor has indeed strongly felt very little freedom in the presence of the literary material which is offered to him. Would he not have wanted to group here different appeals of Jeremiah, propagandist of Deuteronomy, conserved by memory or by writing? He would have made that collection serve the verses which Robert has recognized as authentic.

b. Verses 7 and 8 seem to take up 7:24–26. There are in fact many common expressions with the exception of one or two ("I have called to witness," v. 7). The difficulty derives from the argument by Rudolph and Mowinckel that chapter 7 is the product of the Deuteronomic redactor. One would then be led to ask whether 11:7–8 may not have been the basis for the work of the redactor. The objection that vv. 6–8 reiterate 1–5 is not decisive proof against their authenticity, if we admit that the redactor of chapter 11 has appropriated different phrases of Jeremiah relative to the same subject. Robert believes 7:24–26 to be authentic, since they belong to a development concerning sacrifices which would be difficult to imagine for the pen of a redactor, even after the explanations that one has been able to provide (*op. cit.*, pp. 11f.). More especially the argument of textual criticism serves at this point to reinforce Robert's position: these verses are absent in the Septuagint. The position would even be irrefutable if the following translation was obligatory: "And I have brought upon them all the words of this covenant." The execution of "all" the threats had not occurred by the time of the exile, and these verses would seem to presuppose the exile. But wā³ābhî³ is more probably a future than an imperfect conversive; otherwise one would more commonly have in fact the apocapated wā³ābhē³. We would find ourselves within the perspectives of threat as one has it in Deut 29:27 (still the second edition of Deuteronomy), and thus a slight doubt remains in regard to this point.

In any case, whether one admits or not the authenticity of these two pericopes, Robert has demonstrated that vv. 6–9 testify to Jeremiah's active support of Deuteronomy, and one may subscribe to the following words of Lods: "The hypothesis which appears to give the best account of the facts is the one in which, immediately after the intervention of the king (Josiah), an entire army of benevolent missionaries, recruited from among the disciples of the prophets, are put into action, in Jerusalem and in Judah, in order to 'proclaim the words of this law,' to commend its observation, to set forth the understanding of its spirit, and to specify its consequences. Jeremiah was 'one of these preachers of the reform'; and it is by means of him that we are acquainted with that interesting movement."[30]

Even if one agrees with Rudolph, Volz, Hölscher, and König that "this covenant" is not Deuteronomy, the text to which an array of writers increasingly are attributing an historical basis, we have to see a Jeremiah calling again for fidelity and obedience to the covenant and to the law in the manner and style of Deuteronomy. So it is that Jeremiah has worked within the meaning of the reform.

JEREMIAH AND THE DEUTERONOMIC REFORM

One may add to these literary observations several pieces of historical data that are of considerable interest.

1. The relationship of Jeremiah with the men of the reform.

Von Rad has underscored the importance of these very unusual relationships. Puukko has recognized the force of this point and is forced to attack the argument.

We know that in the time of Jehoiakim, thus between 608 and 598, a long time after the discovery of Deuteronomy and the reform which had followed, Jeremiah escaped death thanks to the protection of a certain Ahikam, son of Shaphan (Jer 26:22). Then, after the first exile of 598, under Zedekiah, he entrusted an important message to the exiles to "Elasah the son of Shaphan and Gemariah the son of Hilkiah" (29:3). Are not Elasah and Ahikam the two sons of the same Shaphan? In addition we find Hilkiah and Shaphan, priest and scribe, acting in concert in II Kgs 22:8–10 when the law is discovered. Moreover, Ahikam, son of Shaphan, is mentioned on the same occasion (vv. 12 and 14). He appears already to be an important personage, without doubt fully mature, for thirty-four years later, in 588, at the time of the fall of Jerusalem, it is not to him, but rather to his son, Gedaliah, son of Ahikam, son of Shaphan (II Kgs 25:22; Jer 39:14), that Nebuchadnezzar entrusted the government of the land. Jeremiah was allowed freely to choose to remain with him in order to attempt to save what was left of Judah, something he would continue to do until the assassination of Gedaliah by the anti-Chaldean party (cf. 40:5, 41:2, 43:6). By now Ahikam must have been dead. He already had under Josiah a post of first rank, and it is this that may explain why he would be mentioned

---

[30] *Les Prophètes d'Israël*, p. 265.

before his father Shaphan, the "scribe" (*sôphēr*). Ahikam may have exercised a superior position, perhaps that of *šôkhēn* or *ʿal-bayith* (cf. Isa 22:15, 20). All of this in spite of the fact he had not been more directly placed in charge of the contacts with Huldah the prophetess. It is then a family deeply attached to the reform of Josiah and opposed to the anti-Chaldean party that triumphed under Jehoiakim and Zedekiah. Jeremiah was intimately bound to that family.

There is more. When he gave the order to Baruch to read publicly in the temple the report of his prophecies, this reading took place in the *liškha* of Gamariah, "son of Shaphan the scribe," and this same Gamariah along with Elnathan, son of Achbor, intervened to prevent Jehoiakim from burning the scroll (36:25). Moreover, we find an Achbor among the supporters of the reform of Josiah (II Kgs 22:12), and this Gemariah could well have been a third son of Shaphan. Here then are two families, supporters of the reform, who protected Jeremiah at a critical moment.

Puukko has sought to break the force of this cluster of observations. He distinguishes two Shaphans and two Hilkiahs (without counting the father of Jeremiah). Ahikam had nothing to do with Shaphan the scribe, and also would have been found to be much less involved in the reform. His friendship for Jeremiah, dating only from the reign of Jehoiakim, would have been motivated not by a common religious action, but by a common political action—both judged the war against the Chaldeans to be sheer folly. Puukko does agree that Elasah may have been the brother of Ahikam, even as Elnathan, the son of Achbor, may have been the son of the minister of Josiah. Gemariah, the son of Shaphan the scribe, the one before whom Baruch read the scroll of Jeremiah, would also be, according to Puukko, the son of the minister of Josiah. But this Shaphan the scribe is not the same Shaphan who was the father of Ahikam, for this latter Shaphan is not designated by the title scribe (in fact in 36:11, Shaphan is not designated with a title, but if the author had wished to distinguish the two would he have repeated the same name here?). Finally there was another Shaphan, the one in Ezek 8:11f., but in some very different circumstances.

The hypothesis of two Shaphans may have a certain basis, for it would be an anomaly to find the son listed before the father in II Kgs 22:12, 14 (but one is able to provide some reasons for that anomaly). The theory of two Hilkiahs appears to be much more gratuitous. In any case, the fact remains that Ahikam, the son of Shaphan and protector of Jeremiah, is the same Ahikam in II Kgs 22:12, 14, who had a significant role at the time of the reform of Josiah and a son, Gedaliah, by whom Jeremiah would wish to stay after the destruction. To suppose with Puukko that this friendship had begun only at the time of Jehoiakim and that it was animated "only by socio-political, but not cultic circumstances," rests in the final analysis on the two-fold presupposition that Jeremiah adhered to a religion that rejected cult and an essentially cultic Deuteronomy, two assumptions that are rightly placed in question. Puukko modified in another place his affirmation by a *vorwiegend* ("predominantly") and a *kaum* ("hardly") which demonstrate both his critical judgment, and the weakness of this position. In that period, politics and religion are one. It suffices to admit that Jeremiah and the reformers may have had in view a politico-religious program having a very clear cultic dimension. In any case, the cluster of indications collected in the preceding paragraph holds good even after the suppositions of Puukko and the distinction between two Shaphans. Jeremiah has cast his lot with that of the reformers: Ahikam, Gedaliah, Elnathan, Achbor, and Gemariah.

2. The departure from Anathoth.

Jeremiah, as we know, was born in Anathoth, that village situated an hour and a half's walk from Jerusalem. The prophet had to conserve some relationship with this area. His parents would have been dead before the siege of Jerusalem, since he was the one to whom Hanamel his cousin came to offer the purchase of a field. Without doubt it was to Anathoth that he wished to go between the two sieges, an effort for which he was imprisoned (Jer 32 and 37). It is probable that at the time of the symbolic action recounted in chapter 13 (the rotten waistcloth), he was still at Anathoth, for the source of the Euphrates (*ph^{e}rāth* in Hebrew) is closer to that small town than to Jerusalem. Had he already been in the capital, Jeremiah would have more simply been able to go to the Gihon and give there more publicity to his action. But very soon he had to enter Jerusalem (under the protection of Ahikam?), for the great discourse of chapters 7–8 (cf. 26), another that deals with the sanctification of the Sabbath (17:19ff.), and the episode of the broken flask (19) presuppose he had settled in Jerusalem.

When and why does he make this move? The most simple explanation one can make is that Jeremiah had complied with Deuteronomy and the reform of Josiah. Deuteronomy in 18:6 allowed any Levite of Israel to dwell "in the place that Yahweh had chosen," i.e. Jerusalem, and to serve there with the same rights, but with a provision difficult to specify. The reform of Josiah made that measure not only a right, but an obligation. The king "brought all the priests out of the cities of Judah, and defiled the high places where the priests had burned incense, from Geba to Beersheba" (II Kgs 23:8). Now, Anathoth was not far from Geba, and the father of Jeremiah, Hilkiah, was priest (1:1). If one admits that Jeremiah supported the reform, then everything falls into place. He left Anathoth in order to settle in Jerusalem where, however, the reform of Josiah did not provide him with all the rights stipulated by Deuteronomy, no doubt because of the resistance of the Jerusalem priesthood. Perhaps this resistance of the Jerusalem clergy had prevented Deuteronomy from appearing under Hezekiah and had obligated Josiah to attenuate that measure. We would have in this one of the origins of the tension between the Zadokite priests, i.e. the clergy of Jerusalem, and the other Levites. The Priestly code makes a distinction that Deuteronomy had not made. Jeremiah is a man of Deuteronomy and fell into difficulty with the Jerusalem clergy, particularly with Pashhur.

Consequently, Jeremiah participated in a reform that gravely injured the interests of the local priestly families, and those of his own family. Whatever the origins of his family's discontent, they wished to kill one of the members who had betrayed their interests. The men of Anathoth, Jeremiah tells us in 11:21, wished to prohibit him from speaking in the name of Yahweh, but he could not do otherwise than to obey that which was commanded him and related at the beginning of the same chapter (11): preaching in favor of the reform against the local cults and high places (v. 13: "you have as many gods as cities, O Judah"). It is without doubt the period when he renounced marriage (16), and when he was ashamed of his mother's giving birth to him (20:14–18). These are indications of his disaffection from his parents. He found refuge only in Yahweh. It seems that he may have taken up residence in Jerusalem and had exercised his ministry only after the reform of Josiah reuniting in Jerusalem the local Yahwistic priests (the others were massacred, II Kgs 23:20, at least in Samaria). One understands very well then why he was not consulted at the time of the discovery of Deuteronomy by Hilkiah. He was unknown in Jerusalem. In fact, we have very few means to distinguish between his career in the period 627–622 and that which followed, for the oracles are not presented in a regular order. Some oracles as the one dealing with drought (14:2–6) may very well have originally been intended for the little town in Judah and only later extended to Jerusalem when Baruch and Jeremiah would compose the scroll that was to be read before the king. But the activity of the prophet may have been sharply curtailed between his call and the reform. The international events of 626, the death of Assurbanipal, the independence of Babylon, and the general shaking of the Assyrian empire conspicuous by the ratification of the independence of Egypt, taken together were able under divine inspiration to stimulate within him the feeling that the destiny of Judah was linked to the destiny of the nations and that he would be the prophet to the nations. But a very long period of time may have elapsed between this divine call and his entry into the scene. In the same way we know very little about Isaiah between his call in 740 and the Syro-Ephraimitic war. It should not surprise us then that Huldah, a citizen of Jerusalem, was consulted instead of the young prophet of Anathoth. Puukko has not succeeded in his attempt to undermine these facts: a *na*ᶜ*ar*, perhaps 25 years old (that which in Cornill's mind remains doubtful), would be only a young man without authority. That one knows nothing more about Huldah does not negate the possibility that she may have had great authority for her time. One needs only recall how little the Bible tells us about a king as important as Omri!

It is thus the Deuteronomic reform that provides the best explanation for Jeremiah's departing Anathoth and coming to Jerusalem.

3. A very important point remains. After his arrival in Jerusalem, did the prophet not change his mind about the reform of Josiah? For Skinner, "very soon its defects became apparent: its superficiality, its inability to cope with prevalent immorality, and the surviving tendencies to polytheism and superstition; and Jeremiah began to suspect the inherent impotence of the legal method of dealing with national sin. At a later time he detected a worse evil in the new-born spirit of self-righteousness based on a formal acceptance of the Covenant and an outward compliance with its demands. Against this spirit Jeremiah protested in the way we have seen. . . . But we need not suppose that Jeremiah, any more than Jesus and Paul, repudiated the law, which was the occasion of this evil, as in itself of no authority. And in spite of differences there are close affinities between the school of Deuteronomy and the teaching of Jeremiah." These modified lines (pp. 106f.) correct the declaration of p. 105: "He must have been aware of the essential discordance between the spirit of law and the spirit of prophecy,—between the ideals of the Deuteronomists and his own." Perhaps it would be suitable to distinguish two aspects of the question.

a. Has Jeremiah rejected Deuteronomy? While Rudolph believes this to be the case (109), it does not appear to us to be so. We see the prophet rely upon several texts of this law during the reigns of Jehoiakim and Zedekiah (34), and even when he is in Egypt (44). Why would the failure of the reform of Josiah urge him to abandon this book? With Rowley, von Rad, and all of the Catholics, we do not think that the purpose of Deuteronomy was principally the centralization of the cult and salvation by means of religious reform. We are aware of certain indications that lead one to ask if the clergy of Jerusalem had been so favorable to this law. In fact, von Rad appears to have an excellent formula when he centers the preoccupations of Deuteronomy on the "concept of the people and not on the problem of the cult" (p. 96). Thus, it is the unity and the salvation of the elect people that Deuteronomy has in view. The men of the North sought for this unity and salvation in the sanctuary of Amos (1:2) and of David after the fall of Samaria. In another respect, this movement fought against the nature cult by replacing it with the true religion of the divine will: what matters is Yahweh's election of his people, the election he had established in a place where he had guaranteed his presence when other sacred places of the patriarchal period, more celebrated than Jerusalem (Bethel), had all failed. Deuteronomy saw salvation in obedience to the revealed Law, preserved in the ark of the covenant in the temple of Jerusalem. If Jeremiah envisioned the disappearace of the ark (3:16) and the destruction of the temple (7:6), it is because he regarded the covenant as broken. But he did not reject the great Deuteronomic themes involving divine election and faithfulness to God which he took up in every period of his life. His task was to elaborate them when the conversion of Israel appeared more improbable each day and the covenant of Sinai more futile. And the prophet came to see clearly the necessity of divine action in the area of the human will itself: the writing of the law of God on the human heart and no longer only on tablets.

b. Did the prophet finally disapprove of the reform? We have seen that the texts require nothing of the kind, and his loyalty to such reformers as Ahikam and Gedaliah seems to imply that also here he did not radically alter his behavior. However, he and his friends had both experienced the loss of some of the illusions of youth. In the light of all kinds of opposition encountered by the reform, in Anathoth as well as Jerusalem following the death of Josiah at Megiddo, they had come to see the inherent deficiencies in the ancient covenant. A political reform does not transform the heart, for men are overwhelmed by political and social conditions which they are not able to control. Jeremiah was a prophet to the nations, and thus he had to demonstrate the insufficiency of nationalism in order to assure the divine plan of salvation for humanity. All would perish, including Israel and Judah. A new covenant was outlined where God would place his will into the human heart (31:32). Jeremiah had hardly considered including the nations, but he knew, however, that he was sent not only to destroy but also to plant and to build (1:10). This new covenant did not exclude the cult and the Levites (33:18, 22), for Jeremiah had a place for them. But he still awaited a divine action to be effectuated on the human heart, something that had been lacking in the reform of Josiah. Ezekiel, Zadokite priest of Jerusalem, would see in the priesthood a centerpiece of the new covenant (which for him would also require an interior renewal, but joined with ritual action, 36:25). He depended upon the Holiness Code and the traditions of Jerusalem. This point of view does not occupy the thought of Jeremiah. He remains the man of Deuteronomy where priests and Levites are only one feature. For him, the king, the anointed one, held vis-a-vis the priesthood a privileged place (23:5; cf. Deut 17:14–20 to compare to 18:1f.), whereas Ezekiel, while reserving the rights of the future David (34:23), in his vision of the future knew only of a prince (44:3, 46:2) with powers limited by those of the priesthood.

All of these perspectives are perfected and enlightened by the messianic fulfillment in the New Testament. But one more time we may remark that the perspectives of Jeremiah are those of Deuteronomy. One understands that the editor of Jeremiah had extensively utilized Deuteronomy and that the second edition of Deuteronomy had so often made recourse to the images and thoughts of the prophet. Thus, each work permeates the other, with the result that together they provide the full range of meaning that the fall of Jerusalem has allowed one to discover ever since. If this was possible, it is due to the fact that both had already possessed a unity of thought and direction.

6
Jeremiah and Deuteronomy*
J. Philip Hyatt

It has long been observed that there is a close similarity between certain verses or portions of Jeremiah and of Deuteronomy. This similarity has been accounted for in a variety of ways.

Some critical scholars of the nineteenth century believed that Jeremiah had a part in the production of Deuteronomy; if not the author himself, he was one of a group who wrote the book. For example, C. F. Volney surmised that Jeremiah was a confidant and perhaps even collaborator of Hilkiah the priest in the production of the Pentateuch, the book discovered in the eighteenth year of Josiah's reign, of which Deuteronomy, chapters 27–28, were read in the presence of the king.[1] P. von Bohlen, after pointing out certain expressions common to Deuteronomy and Jeremiah, advanced the theory that Jeremiah may have had a part in revising the Pentateuch for the public eye. He referred to II Macc. 2:1–13 in partial support of his theory.[2] The most extreme view of this kind was held by Bishop Colenso, who sought to prove that Jeremiah not only was the author of Deuteronomy but also was the "Deuteronomist" who edited many of the historical books of the Old Testament.[3] The improbability of these theories was made evident by the demonstration, especially by J. L. König[4] and P. Kleinert,[5] that there are very important differences in vocabulary and grammar between the Book of Jeremiah and Deuteronomy.

At the opposite extreme, those scholars who think of Deuteronomy as being of Exilic or post-Exilic date have sought to show that Deuteronomy borrows from Jeremiah or that the dependence of Jeremiah upon Deuteronomy lies only in late passages of the prophetic book. Berry thinks that the dependence is entirely of Deuteronomy upon Jeremiah, who "was a man of much greater originality of thought and expression than the writer of Deuteronomy, and he would be particularly unlikely to be materially indebted to the thought and expression of D which moves largely in a circle

*Originally published in *Journal of Near Eastern Studies* 1 (1942) 156–173.
[1] *New Researches on Ancient History*, Trans. from the French (London, 1819), I, 82–86.
[2] *Genesis* (Königsberg, 1835), pp. clxvii–ix (Eng. ed., I, 270–77).
[3] *The Pentateuch and Book of Joshua Critically Examined*, Part VII (London, 1879), 12, 225–27, 259–69, and Appen. 149.
[4] *Alttestamentliche Studien*, Heft II (Berlin, 1839), 22–113.
[5] *Das Deuteronomium und der Deuteronomiker* (Bielefeld and Leipzig, 1872), 185–94.

of ideas quite different from his own."[6] A very similar view was held by R. H. Kennett.[7] Hölscher denies that any genuine passages of Jeremiah show acquaintance with Deuteronomy, but only later additions to the prophetic book.[8] The theory of an Exilic or post-Exilic origin of Deuteronomy has not met with general acceptance among modern scholars, although the views of the above-named scholars have brought to light a number of important considerations and have led to a re-examination of the problem of the date of this book.[9] In the case of R. H. Kennett especially, the view rests upon highly conjectural theories regarding the history of the Hebrews.

The view which seems to be held by a majority of critical scholars today is as follows: Jeremiah began his public career in 626 B.C., five years before the reforms of Josiah, which were based upon the original edition of the Book of Deuteronomy. When the reforms were instituted in 621, Jeremiah found much in them in agreement with his own ideas and was at first an enthusiastic supporter of them. He even went to the extent of going about the cities of Judah and the streets of Jerusalem exhorting people to support Deuteronomy, which he referred to as "this covenant" (Jer. 11:1–8). Later, however, when Jeremiah became more mature and when the Deuteronomic reforms failed to live up to his expectations, he turned against them and so came to predict even the destruction of the Jerusalem Temple itself, in which the Deuteronomists sought to centralize all worship.[10]

None of these views seems adequate to express the relationship between the work and ideas of Jeremiah the prophet and the reforms of Josiah and the relationship between the Book of Jeremiah and the Book of Deuteronomy. It is the purpose of the present paper to consider in detail these relationships and to advance a new theory for their explanation. My thesis may be briefly stated in advance as follows: Jeremiah did not begin his public career until about a decade after Josiah's reforms of 621 B.C.[11] He was acquainted with the original edition of Deuteronomy but never expressed approval either of the principles or of the methods of the Deuteronomic reforms. Indeed, his outlook was on many important questions diametrically opposed to that of the writers of Deuteronomy. The Book of Jeremiah as we now have it, however, has received expansion and redaction at the hands of "Deuteronomic" editors, whose purpose in part was to claim for Deuteronomy the sanction of the great prophet.

---

[6] *JBL*, XXXIX (1920), 46; cf. *JBL*, LIX (1940), 133–39.

[7] *JTS*, VI (1905), 182 f.; in detail, *JTS*, VII (1906), 481–86.

[8] *ZAW*, 1922, pp. 233–39.

[9] See esp. Bewer, Paton, and Dahl, *JBL*, XLVII (1928), 305–79, and Graham, *JR*, VII (1927), 396–418.

[10] See, e. g., T. H. Robinson, *A History of Israel*, I (Oxford, 1932), 427–28; Bewer, *Literature of the Old Testament* (New York, 1922), 147–52; Skinner, *Prophecy and Religion* (Cambridge, 1922), chap. vi.

[11] Cf. my article, "The Peril from the North in Jeremiah," *JBL*, LIX (1940), 499–513.

I

Before proceeding to a detailed discussion of this view, it is necessary to consider first a few questions regarding the Book of Deuteronomy and Josiah's reforms.

1. A majority of critical scholars are agreed that the first edition of Deuteronomy, *Urdeuteronomium*, formed the basis of Josiah's reforms. The attempts of some (Welch, Staerk, Oestreicher, *et al.*) to prove that the book is earlier than Josiah have not been successful, although it is by no means impossible that some parts of the book are of comparatively ancient origin. On the other hand, it cannot be held that the book is Exilic or post-Exilic. Thus the date of Deuteronomy is one of the most assured results of modern criticism and an important keystone in the whole structure of modern views of the Old Testament.

But what constituted *Urdeuteronomium?* The general opinion is that the kernel of the book is chapters 12–26, to which chapters 5–11 may have formed an introduction and chapter 28 a conclusion. It is very significant, however, that the reforms of Josiah as recorded in II Kings, chapters 22–23, could well have been based only upon Deuteronomy, chapters 12–18. All the reforms described in detail there, with the possible exception of that concerning the $q^e d\bar{e}\check{s}\hat{i}m$ in 23:7, are commanded in chapters 12–18; as for the $q^e d\bar{e}\check{s}\hat{i}m$, the prescription of Deuteronomy 23:18 is not precisely the same as the action carried out in II Kings 23:7. At any rate, the reforms of Josiah described in detail have to do mainly with cultic purification and have nothing to do with provisions for judicial procedure, family life, business affairs, etc., as described in Deuteronomy, chapters 19–26. There are three logical possibilities of explanation of this fact: (i) *Urdeuteronomium* consisted only of Deuteronomy, chapters 12–18; (ii) II Kings, chapters 22–23, is an incomplete account of Josiah's reforms; or (iii) the emphasis in the reforms was primarily if not exclusively upon cultic rather than moral reform. In view of the general unity of Deuteronomy, chapters 12–26, recognized by most critics, it is dangerous to suppose that the first of these possibilities is the correct one. Rather it is more likely that a combination of the second and third offer the correct solution. Jeremiah may well have felt himself in agreement with the attempts of Deuteronomy to establish social justice in matters of legal, commercial, and domestic relations; but the *emphasis* of the reformers of 621 was apparently upon the cultic features of national life, and the prescriptions of Deuteronomy regarding social justice were allowed to become largely a dead letter.

2. Insufficient attention has usually been given to the motivation of the Josianic reforms. It seems most probable that the motives of Josiah and his supporters were partly political—to unify the nation around Jerusalem as both the political and the religious capital and to establish independence of Palestine from Assyria. The account of the reforms in II Kings, chapters 22–23, has received expansion at the hands of later editors, but there is no adequate reason for doubting that Josiah actually did attempt to make

religious reforms in Bethel and other parts of the northern kingdom, as related in 23:15, 19 f. (see also the reference to Bethel in 23:4). We learn in Jer. 41:4 ff. that, on the day after the murder of Gedaliah, a large group of men were making a pilgrimage from Shechem, Shiloh, and Samaria to the Jerusalem Temple. The international situation at the time was favorable to Josiah's attempt.[12] The Assyrian Empire was gradually breaking up, certainly after the death of Ashurbanipal in 626. Assyria was too busy elsewhere in 621 to prevent Josiah from extending his influence over the northern kingdom and centralizing both political and religious authority in Jerusalem. There is no implication that the king's motives were insincere; there is only recognition of the fact that in ancient Israel no careful distinction was made between political and religious affairs. There was close union between what we should call church and state—terms which an ancient Hebrew would hardly have understood.

If these remarks are correct, we may see one of the reasons for Jeremiah's attitude toward the Deuteonomic reforms. He was never an ardent nationalist and constantly disapproved of isolationism and intense nationalism. He would not have approved of the Assyrian influence in religious life which was maintained during Manasseh's reign, but he strongly disapproved of defiance against the power of the Neo-Babylonian Empire which succeeded to the place of the Assyrian Empire.

3. A third question which needs to be asked concerning the reforms of Josiah is: How successful were they? It may be noted at once that the provision regarding the local priests which is commended in Deuteronomy 17:6–8 was not actually carried out, according to II Kings 23:9. It has often been remarked that the law of battle in Deuteronomy 20:5–8 and 24:5 is not practical. Indeed, the impracticality of many of the laws of Deuteronomy impressed Hölscher so much that it led him to date the book in post-Exilic times.[13] It is probably quite true that the requirements of Deuteronomy regarding centralization of worship in Jerusalem were not capable of being carried out in their entirety until post-Exilic days, when the Jewish community was small and compact.

The recognition of this fact has led Budde to assert that Deuteronomy was not a lawbook but a program.[14] However, such a distinction is hardly valid. In almost every country and in every age a law is a program; it is an ideal which is more or less capable of attainment. One could easily point to laws of the United States today or in recent times which have been too idealistic for attainment (e.g., the Volstead Act). This would have been especially true of a law promulgated by the king in a state such as Israel was. It so happened that the Deuteronomic law was in many respects too

---

[12]Cf. Welch, *Jeremiah* (London, 1928), pp. 18 ff.

[13]*ZAW*, 1922, pp. 227 ff.

[14]*ZAW*, 1926, p. 180.

idealistic and too far advanced for it to be put into practice in every detail. But this is not a valid argument against the book's having been written in the seventh century.

Of all the requirements of the reforms, one of the most impracticable must have been that demanding the abolition of all local sanctuaries. While it is entirely possible that these were abolished temporarily, it is very improbable that they remained in disuse and were not rebuilt—at least that they were not soon visited by members of the local communities for purposes of worship. The history of worship in Palestine, not only in Jewish times but also in Christian and Mohammedan eras, shows that it is impossible permanently to prevent worship at small local sanctuaries.[15]

It seems very likely, therefore, that the reforms attempted by Josiah were only partially and temporarily successful. Perhaps even before the time of his death the local sanctuaries were partly rebuilt and used for worship. At any rate, a reaction must have set in against his reforms after his death during the reign of Jehoiakim. The death of Josiah would have been understood by the people as showing divine disapproval of his work, and the character of Jehoiakim was not such as to carry on the reforms. There is evidence in the Book of Jeremiah itself that some of the Deuteronomic laws were not obeyed. Both Jer. 16:6 and 41:5 show that the prohibition in Deut. 14:1 against self-laceration in time of mourning was not obeyed. Also, we may see from Jer. 44:19 that the Jewish women must have resumed the worship of the Queen of Heaven even before they had left Palestine to go to Egypt.

If the reforms of Josiah were not very successful, it is possible to explain Jeremiah's frequent references to idolatry and worship at high places even without supposing that he lived before the time of the reforms. They may quite easily have been appropriate during the reign of Jehoiakim if not in the last years of Josiah, after Jeremiah had begun his preaching.

II

It is very difficult to offer thoroughly convincing proof that Jeremiah did not, or could not, approve of the Deuteronomic reforms, especially since so many critics have pointed out specific elements in them that Jeremiah must have found congenial to his own thinking.[16] But one must consider not only specific elements in the thought of the prophet and of the reforms but the whole general religious outlook and program of each. With these in mind it is very difficult to believe that Jeremiah could ever have approved of Josiah's reforms. There are a few specific passages which may

---

[15]Cf. Paton, *loc. cit.*, p. 335. A similar difficulty faced Akhnaton and his supporters in their attempted reforms in Egypt many centuries before this time (cf. Breasted, *The Dawn of Conscience* [New York and London, 1933], pp. 303–5).

[16]See, e. g., Peake in the Century Bible, *Jeremiah*, I, 12–13; Cornill, *Das Buch Jeremia* (Leipzig, 1905), pp. 143–44.

be cited as expressing a religious outlook diametrically opposed to that of the Deuteronomists.

The first is the Temple sermon as reported in chapters 7 and 26. Here Jeremiah declares that the Temple will be destroyed unless the people show true moral reform. Such a prediction must have been wholly incomprehensible and utterly abhorrent to anyone imbued with the spirit of Deuteronomy, with its emphasis on the Jerusalem Temple and its cult, as the treatment of Jeremiah following the sermon shows. In chapter 7 one should notice particularly verses 21–23:

> Thus said Yahweh of hosts, God of Israel: "Add your burnt-offerings to your sacrifices and eat flesh; yet I did not speak with your fathers and did not command them in the day I brought them from the land of Egypt concerning burnt-offering and sacrifice, but this is the word I commanded them, 'Hearken to my voice and I will be to you a God and ye shall be to me a people, and ye shall walk in all the way which I shall command you that it may be well with you.'"

Another passage is Jer. 11:15. I have elsewhere[17] suggested that this oracle should be translated:

> What right has my beloved in my house?
> She has done wickedness!
> Can fatlings and holy flesh avert
> From thee thy doom?

Again, consider 6:20, in which Yahweh speaks to Israel as follows:

> What to me is incense from Sheba
> And sweet cane from a far land?
> Your burnt-offerings are not to my liking,
> And your sacrifices please me not.

In addition to these passages, there are two passages in which Jeremiah seems to express (veiled?) opposition to Deuteronomy—8:8–9 and 13 and 2:8. Since I have discussed these fully elsewhere, I need only list them here.[18]

When one considers carefully the import of these passages (all unquestionably genuine) in connection with the general religious position of Jeremiah, and when one remembers that there is no evidence for vacillation and compromise in that part of Jeremiah's life for which we have surprisingly full biographical information, it is difficult to believe that Jeremiah ever expressed approval of the Deuteronomic reforms or supported them in any way. R. H. Kennett has well summed up the matter in these words: Jeremiah "regarded the king's [Josiah's] enactments as an unsatisfactory

---

[17]*JBL*, LX (1941), 57–60.
[18]*JBL*, LX (1941), 382–87.

compromise—the good seeds which they contained were sown in the midst of thorns of sacrificial worship."[19]

III

We may now discuss the interrelationship between the work of Jeremiah the prophet, on the one hand, and the original Deuteronomy and the "Deuteronomists," on the other, as shown by the literary relations between the Book of Deuteronomy and the Book of Jeremiah. A discussion of this nature is fraught with many perils, and it must be frankly admitted that subjective judgments are likely to play a part. It is often extremely difficult to determine the *direction* of literary influence. But it is surely not sufficient simply to list the parallel or similar passages of the two books and then conclude that the influence was all in one direction—as has often been done. Due regard must be had for the context of each verse or passage, and careful attention must be paid to the question as to what is original and what is secondary in each book. It is here that subjectivity is likely to enter in. The best one can do is to be as careful and objective as possible in considering what is characteristic of the style and thought of the prophet Jeremiah, on the one hand, and of Deuteronomy and the Deuteronomists, on the other.

The most complete listing of the parallel and similar passages of the two books may be found in Colenso's *The Pentateuch and Book of Joshua Critically Examined.*[20] Many of the examples there given, however, are based on only superficial resemblances, and Bishop Colenso drew too sweeping a conclusion from the list.[21]

A. JEREMIAH'S ACQUAINTANCE WITH THE ORIGINAL EDITION OF DEUTERONOMY

I have said above that Jeremiah was acquainted with the original edition of Deuteronomy. A priori we should expect this to be true, whether Jeremiah began his career in 626 or in *circa* 614–612. There are at least two passages which show rather clearly that this was the case:

1. *Jer. 3:1 and Deut. 24:1.*—There can be little doubt that Jer. 3:1–5 is genuine, since it is a fine poetic passage and is strongly prophetic in tone. Jer. 3:1 should be translated (following LXX in important points where MT represents interpretation) as follows:

> If a man send away his wife, and she leaves him
> And becomes another man's, can she[22] return to him[22] again?
> Has not that woman[22] committed adultery?

---

[19] *Deuteronomy and the Decalogue* (Cambridge, 1920), p. 16.

[20] Part VII, Appen. 149, pp. 85–110.

[21] See also Driver, *Deuteronomy* ("I.C.C."), pp. xcii ff.; Carpenter and Harford-Battersby, *The Hexateuch*, I, 88 ff.

[22] Following LXX.

Deut. 24:1–4 contains the law of divorce. The similarity of expression in both passages (cf. especially Jer. 3:1b and Deut. 24:1 [end]) is close enough to make it probable that Jeremiah knew the passage; but Jeremiah is speaking primarily from a moral standpoint and Deuteronomy from a cultic legal standpoint: Deuteronomy is concerned with the fact that the woman becomes "defiled" (vs. 4); Jeremiah, with the fact that she has committed adultery. It is impossible that the passage is a Deuteronomic "insertion" in Jeremiah. On the other hand, Jer. 3:8 betrays clearly the hand of a Deuteronomic editor; it is most probable that all of 3:6–12a is secondary (see below).

2. *Jer. 28:9 and Deut. 18:22.*—Here the same test of prophecy appears in both books, but there is no reason to doubt the genuineness of the Jeremiah passage.

B. COMMON TERMINOLOGY IN THE ORIGINAL BOOK OF JEREMIAH AND THE ORIGINAL EDITION OF DEUTERONOMY

The original Book of Jeremiah as well as the original edition of Deuteronomy was written in the seventh century, and all of Jeremiah's work was done in the latter part of the seventh or the early part of the sixth century. We should expect, therefore, that both books would show many similarities in vocabulary and syntax which would not necessarily come from influence of one upon the other. Many of the phrases which scholars have listed as showing such influence must be due to this factor. It is possible, of course, that some of these are due to influence—especially to the fact that Jeremiah was acquainted with Deuteronomy—but it is safer to consider them as due rather to what we may call the terminology of the time.[23] The following may be listed as belonging to this group: "circumcision of the heart" (Jer. 4:4; 9:25; Deut. 10–16; 30:6; cf. Lev. 26:41; Ezek. 44:7, 9); "the stranger, the fatherless and the widows" (Jer. 7:6; 22:3; Deut. 10:18; 14:29; 16:11, 14 and frequently; cf. Exod. 22:21 f.); "go after other gods whom ye know not" (Jer. 7:9; Deut. 11:28); "the place where I (he) cause(s) my (his) name to dwell" (Jer. 7:12; Deut. 12:11; 14:23; 16:2, 6, 11; 26:2; cf. Neh. 1:9; Ezra 6:12); "walk in all the way which I (Yahweh) commanded you, that it may be well for you" (Jer. 7:23; Deut. 5:33; for the latter part of this expression see Deut. 4:40; 5:16, 29; 6:3, 18; 12:25, 28; 22:7; II Kings 25:24); "the inheritance which I (Yahweh) gave (gives) thee" (Jer. 17:4; Deut. 12:9); "mighty hand and outstretched arm" (Deut. 4:34; 5:15; 7:19; 11:2; 26:8; cf. "outstretched hand and mighty arm" [Jer. 21:5]); "give to you (thee) and have pity on you (thee)" (Jer. 42:12; Deut. 13:18); "stiffen the neck" (Jer. 7:26; 17:23 [not genuine!]; 19:15; Deut. 10:16); "and thine eyes seeing" (Jer. 20:4; Deut. 28:32).

---

[23]Of course Jeremiah may well have been influenced, consciously or unconsciously, by the terminology of Deuteronomy without approving of the book as a whole. One often owes a greater debt to his enemies than he can realize!

C. THE DEUTERONOMIC EDITORS

We come now to the most important and most extensive group of passages—namely, those in Jeremiah which are due to the activity of Deuteronomic editors. Here the term "Deuteronomic editor" or "Deuteronomist" is used in a broad sense as applying to any editor of the Book of Jeremiah who shows strongly the influence of the style and thought of the Book of Deuteronomy. We cannot be certain of the identity of such editors with men who actually wrote the original editions of Deuteronomy or some later portions of it, but it is probable that in some instances such identity existed.

One of the main purposes of these editors, as stated above, was to attempt to show that Jeremiah did approve of the Deuteronomic reforms, or, in other words, to claim for Deuteronomy the sanction of the prophet. Here the passages may be classified under divisions which will in the main indicate the motives of the editors.

1. *Dates in the Book of Jeremiah intended to make Jeremiah begin his public career before the time of the Deuteronomic reforms.*—These dates are in 1:2, 3:6, 25:3, and 36:2. I have already discussed these passages in *JBL*, LIX (1940), 511–13. I need here only add a few additional remarks to emphasize the probability that Jeremiah did not begin his career until near the end of Josiah's reign or even until the beginning of the reign of Jehoiakim.

In an extended and valuable discussion of the relationship of Jeremiah to Deuteronomy, A. F. Puukko[24] had pointed out that it is impossible to prove a close relationship between Jeremiah and the men who were primarily concerned in the institution of the Deuteronomic reforms of 621, as they are listed in II Kings, chapter 22. It is most improbable that Hilkiah the high priest was the father of Jeremiah, as scholars once assumed. Jeremiah does seem to have been friendly with sons of the Shaphan of II Kings 22:12 (probably not identical with Shaphan the scribe), but this friendship was based upon agreement on social and political questions rather than on purely religious ones and dates from the time of Jehoiakim and Zedekiah. Puukko remarks upon the fact that Jeremiah never stood in as close a relationship with Josiah as Isaiah, for example, did with Hezekiah. This is important, and we should note further that Jeremiah did not occupy so close a position with reference to Josiah as he himself did with later kings of Israel, especially Jehoiakim and Zedekiah. In fact, Jeremiah appears in the role of adviser to these kings as Isaiah did to Ahaz and Hezekiah; both stand in the tradition of the older "royal prophets" of the type of Nathan, Elisha, Micaiah son of Imlah, and others. If Jeremiah actually did begin his career in 626 B.C., as these "Deuteronomic" dates of

---

[24] "Jeremias Stellung zum Deuteronomium," in *Alttestamentliche Studien Rudolf Kittel zum 60. Geburtstag dargebracht* ("Beiträge zur Wissenschaft vom Alten Testament," ed. R. Kittel, Heft 13 [Leipzig, 1913]), pp. 126–53; see esp. pp. 134–40.

the book would have us believe, it is extremely difficult to see (i) why he was not called upon to place the prophetic stamp of approval on the book found by Shaphan the scribe, rather than the otherwise obscure Huldah the prophetess; (ii) why he was never summoned by Josiah for advice on other occasions; and (iii) why it is so difficult to date oracles of Jeremiah in the period between 621 and the beginning of Jehoiakim's reign.[25]

2. *Passages inserted in Jeremiah to emphasize the existence of pre-Deuteronomic sins during the prophet's early career.*—These passages have to do mainly with the sins of Topheth in the Valley of Hinnom, which was a symbol to the Deuteronomists of the worst heresy of Manasseh. Now, although it has been pointed out above that the worship in the local sanctuaries may easily have been resumed in the last years of Josiah and certainly in the reign of Jehoiakim, it is not probable that the pagan sanctuary of Topheth was rebuilt and worship there resumed. The priests of Jerusalem doubtless could exercise supervision over the worship in Jerusalem and its vicinity to a degree impossible for the outlying villages; also, considerable time and labor would have been involved in the restoration of this place of worship.[26] But the Deuteronomic editors have used this place in trying to prove Jeremiah's knowledge of the great sins of Manasseh's time.

a) Jer. 19:2–9, 11b–14a.—Chapter 19 clearly consists of two different messages: one given in connection with the breaking of the pottery flask, and the other in the Valley of Hinnom. The two have been closely combined, but there are many inconsistencies in the narrative which show clearly that we have here an original account in which a secondary narrative has been inserted. The portion which is secondary, dealing with the message of the Valley of Hinnom, is in verse 2, "the valley of Ben-Hinnom, which," and in verses 3–9 and 11b–14a. The rest is the original portion describing the symbolic action with a flask. For the strong Deuteronomic flavor of the language compare verse 7 with Deut. 28:26 (but see below), verse 8 with Deut. 29:22, and verse 9 with Deut. 28:53. Furthermore, verses 6–9 and 11b–14a, beginning with the formulistic "Therefore, behold, days are coming . . . ," is of the nature of *vaticinium post eventum*.

b) Jer. 7:31–8:3.—This again emphasizes the sins at Topheth. It is probable that verse 30 is original and that all that follows, through 8:3, is secondary. Verse 30 begins with a construction which is usually late: perfect with *wāw* copulative instead of imperfect with *wāw* consecutive. Verses 32–33 are parallel with 19:6–7 (cf. 7:31 with Deut. 12:31 and 18:10 and 8:2 with Deut. 17:3).

c) Jer. 32:35 mentions briefly the offerings in Hinnom. This is in a long section, a prayer of Jeremiah, which is almost universally recognized by critics as secondary (at least, 32:17–23, 28–44), with strong Deuteronomic

---

[25]Cf. Skinner, *op. cit.*, chap. vii.
[26]Cf. Torrey, *JBL*, LVI (1937), 204.

influence in many verses (cf. Jer. 32:18 with Deut. 7:21; 10:17; 5:9 f.; Jer. 32:20–22 with Deut. 4:34; 10:11; 26:8 f., 15 etc.; Jer. 32:37 with Deut. 29:27; and Jer. 32:41 with Deut. 28:63; 30:9).

d) *Jer. 15:4* predicts future ruin to the nation, so that it will be "a horror to all the kingdoms of the earth, because of what Manasseh, king of Judah, did to Jerusalem." This verse is hardly from Jeremiah; he did not explain the coming destruction primarily on the basis of the sins of past kings, Manasseh or anyone else, but of the people of his own day. The verse is strongly reminiscent of II Kings 23:36 and 24:3 and of Deut. 28:25.

e) *Jer. 3:6–12a* is a prose passage recognized by many critics to be editorial (e.g., Skinner).[27] The resemblances to Ezek. 16:44 ff. and 23 are striking. Verse 8 strongly betrays the hand of the Deuteronomist (see above). Verse 6 contains a Deuteronomic formula, "on every high hill and beneath every spreading tree," symbolic of the sins which Josiah sought to destroy (cf. Deut. 12:2; I Kings 14:23; II Kings 16:4 and 17:10). The same formula has been inserted by a Deuteronomist in Jer. 2:20, where the figure is not in accord with the figures used in the original poem and where it overloads the meter; and in 3:13, where it also overloads the meter. In Jer. 17:2 a somewhat similar expression, but not so formulistic, occurs; the text is corrupt, but it may be that the passage is original.

3. *Jer. 11:1–8 written to prove that Jeremiah was an active supporter of the Deuteronomic reforms.*—This passage is a *crux interpretum* in the study of our problem. Nearly all interpreters have recognized that it was intended to show that Jeremiah supported Deuteronomy and even became an itinerant evangelist for the reforms of Josiah; they have been divided on the question as to whether the passage is genuine or secondary.

That there is strong Deuteronomic influence on the language of the section is apparent from the parallels cited on the following page. These parallels are very striking. They have led Duhm, Cornill, Kent, and others to consider the whole section as editorial. Puukko, after a careful analysis, pronounced 11:1–14 a free composition of a later writer who built it upon Baruch's book (esp. 7:16–28) and Deuteronomy (esp. 27:14–26). Other critics (including Giesebrecht, Driver, Peake, and Condamin) consider the passage as genuine, at least in part.

These extensive parallels between 11:1–8 and Deuteronomy must mean either that the whole section is editorial or that the section is an expansion of a Jeremianic kernel. While the latter is a possibility, the former is much more likely to be true, for the following reasons: in verse 2 the expression "the words of this covenant" is introduced very abruptly without any previous reference to a covenant; Deuteronomic vocabulary and ideas pervade the whole passage more than any other single passage in Jeremiah; important parallels to the passage in genuine parts of the prophetic book are lacking; and the motivation of the passage can easily be

[27] *Op. cit.*, p. 82.

Jeremiah	Deuteronomy
11:3: "Cursed (be) the man who shall not hearken to the words of this covenant. . . ."	27:26: "Cursed (be he) who shall not establish the words of this *Torah* to keep them. . . ."
11:4: ". . . on the day that I brought them from the land of Egypt, from the iron furnace . . . that ye may be to me a people and I may be to you a God."	4:20: "And you Yahweh took, and brought you from the iron furnace, from Egypt, to be to him a people of inheritance. . ." (cf. I Kings 8:51 ". . . from the midst of the iron furnace . . .").
11:5: "In order to establish the oath which I swore to your fathers to give to them	7:8: ". . . the oath which he swore to your fathers. . . ."
	8:18: ". . . in order to establish the word which Yahweh swore to thy fathers. . . ."
	9:5: ". . . and in order to establish the word which Yahweh swore to thy fathers, to Abraham, to Isaac and to Jacob."
a land flowing with milk and honey,	6:3; 11:9; 26:9, 15; 27:3; 31:20: ". . . a land flowing with milk and honey."
as at this day.	2:30; 4:20, 38; 6:24; 8:18; 10:15; 29:27: ". . . as at this day."[28]
And I answered and said, 'Amen, Yahweh.' "	27:15: "And all the people shall answer and say, 'Amen' " (similarly in following verses).
11:8: ". . . this covenant which I commanded to keep. . . ."	4:13: ". . . his covenant which he commanded you to keep. . . ."

explained as a desire on the part of a later writer (or writers) to secure for the Book of Deuteronomy and the Josianic reforms the support of the great prophet Jeremiah. (Although 11:9–14 may well be genuine, it is not important for the present study).

4. *Passages designed to explain the Exile and its misfortunes as due to disobedience of Yahweh and worship of foreign gods.*—Jer. 5:19, 9:11–13, 16:10–13, and 22:8–9 are very similar both in style and in thought. In each case a question is asked concerning the reason for Yahweh's bringing misfortune upon the Israelites, in the laying waste of the land, destruction of Jerusalem, and the like; and the answer is given—that Yahweh brought

[28]This occurs elsewhere but is characteristic of Deuteronomy (cf. Driver, *op. cit.*, pp. 43 f.).

this upon them because they have forsaken him, or his law or covenant, and served other gods. Very similar passages, both in wording and in idea, are to be found in Deut. 29:21–27 and I Kings 9:8–9 (in the vision of Solomon, clearly Deuteronomic). All of these passages doubtless come from the same editor or editorial school, writing after the destruction of Jerusalem in 586 for the purpose of giving the Hebrews a ready explanation of the disaster (cf. Jer. 9:15 with Deut. 28:64; 4:27 [all of Jer. 9:11–16 is secondary]; and Jer. 16:13 with Deut. 28:36). Deut. 29:21–27 is especially close in vocabulary and style to Jer. 22:8–9.[29]

5. *Passages which definitely predict restoration from Exile and future prosperity.*—In many chapters of our present Book of Jeremiah, especially in chapters 30–33, are passages which describe in definite terms the conditions of the Exile and predict future restoration and final triumph for the Hebrews. It is extremely difficult to determine how many of these are genuine; no doubt some of them are, since Jeremiah may well have entertained a hope for future restoration, albeit in vague and imprecise terms. Of those passages which are secondary, as shown by their formulistic nature and the general similarity of the predictions, some show the influence of the Deuteronomists. Without asserting that these necessarily come from the same scribes as those who wrote other Deuteronomic passages, we may note the following parallels: (i) In Jer. 3:14–18 compare verse 17 with Deut. 29:19 and verse 18c with Deut. 1:38, 3:28, 12:10, 19:3, and 31:7. (ii) Compare Jer. 29:10–14 with Deut. 4:29 and 30:3 and 5. (iii) Compare Jer. 30:3 and 33:26b with Deut. 30:3 and 5. (iv) The long prayer of Jeremiah in 32:16–44 is secondary either wholly or in large part; even so conservative a scholar as Condamin considers verses 17–23 and 28–36 as secondary. It is probable that in this section only verses 24–25 are genuine. This prayer is a résumé of Hebrew history in Deuteronomic style, culminating in promises of future restoration. The following parallels should be noted: compare Jer. 32:18 with Deut. 5:9 and 10, 7:21, and 10:17; Jer. 32:20–22 with Deut. 4:34, 6:22, 7:19, 10:11, and 26:8–9 and 15; Jer. 32:37 with Deut. 29:27; and Jer. 32:41 with Deut. 28:63 and 30:9.

6. *Legalistic passages inserted to prove that Jeremiah knew the laws of Deuteronomy.*— In two passages the Deuteronomists have made it appear that Jeremiah knew two specific laws of the original Deuteronomy and, by inference, that he approved of them.

a) Jer. 3:8 contains a reference, indirectly, to Deut. 24:1, with the use of two technical terms, "to send away, to divorce," and "bill of divorce." As noted above, Jer. 3:6–12a is secondary; it was added at this point to make it appear that in 3:1 Jeremiah had in mind the Deuteronomic law of divorce. However, the whole style and tenor of verses 6–12a is different from that of verses 1–5.

---

[29]See also my article cited in n. 18 above.

b) Jer. 34:13b-14.—The account in Jer. 34:8-22 of the release of Hebrew slaves is apparently in large part genuine; yet the release was obviously not the sabbatical release prescribed in Exod. 21:2 ff. or Deut. 15:1 ff. but a release by special royal decree because of an emergency situation. As the account now stands, however, it is made to appear that it was in fulfilment of the Deuteronomic law. This has been accomplished by the insertion of verses 13b and 14, with an almost direct quotation of Deut. 15:1a and 12 in verse 14; for the expression "out of the house of bondmen" see Deut. 5:6, 6:12, 8:14, and 13:5 and 10. The omission of this verse and a half removes the difficulties in the account.[30]

7. *Miscellaneous.*—These passages do not exhaust the extent of Deuteronomic editorial activity in the Book of Jeremiah. There are other passages of less importance. For example, Jer. 13:11 is apparently a Deuteronomic addition to the parable of the loincloth; it makes a wholly new point to the whole parable, and the language of the latter part of the verse is like that of Deut. 26:19. Jer. 33:9 also is closely parallel to Deut. 26:19; it is probable that most, if not all, of chapter 33 is non-Jeremianic. Two post-Septuagintal additions to Jeremiah, under the influence of Deuteronomy, may be seen in Jer. 28:16 and 29:32, where the clause, "for he (thou) has(t) spoken rebellion against Yahweh," does not appear in LXX but has been added twice to the Hebrew from Deut. 13:6.

D. INFLUENCE OF JEREMIAH UPON DEUTERONOMY, CHAPTER 28

It has often been noted that Deuteronomy, chapter 28, especially abounds in parallels to passages in the Book of Jeremiah. Now, this chapter presents a number of problems. It is usually considered as forming the conclusion to the original edition of Deuteronomy. For several reasons, however, it is probably nearer the truth to consider that verses 1-6 and 15-19, which are mostly poetic, formed the original nucleus of this chapter and that the remainder constitutes only prose expansion of this nucleus, written, at least in part, soon after the siege of Jerusalem.[31] If this theory is correct, may we not expect to find in this expanded portion traces of the influence of the original Jeremiah, composed by Baruch some years earlier? This I believe to be the case. The following are examples: (1) The phrase in verse 20, "the evil of your doings," is borrowed from Jer. 4:4, 21:12, 23:2 and 22, and 26:3; it has in turn been used by an editor in Jer. 25:5 and 44:22.[32] (2) The expression "a horror to all the kingdoms of the earth" in

---

[30]The same editor has probably also inserted in vs. 9 *hā-ibrî wᵉhā-ibriyyāh*, which is awkward in the context and is not elsewhere used by Jeremiah.

[31]See W. A. Irwin, "An Objective Criterion for the Dating of Deuteronomy," *AJSL*, LVI (1939), 337-49. Irwin credits the theory regarding the original nucleus to Valeton.

[32]For a clear instance of the influence of genuine portions of Jer. upon an editorial portion see Jer. 32:17-23 and the parallel passages listed in Condamin's commentary, p. 249, n. 2.

verse 25 has been borrowed from Jer. 24:9 and 34:17 and used in turn by an editor in Jer. 15:4 and 29:18. (3) Verse 26 is taken from Jer. 34:20 and then used in Jer. 7:33, 16:4 (or is this verse genuine?), and 19:7. (4) The description of the Neo-Babylonians in verses 49–51 shows acquaintance with Jeremiah's description of the "foe from the North," especially with Jer. 5:15–17 and 6:22–23. That Jeremiah is original and Deuteronomy secondary is shown by the fact that Jeremiah's passages are poetic and in general more vigorous and original; furthermore, the description of the horrors of the siege in Deut. 28:52 ff. is more specific and reveals acquaintance with the actual happenings.[33] To complete the description of the relationships between the Book of Jeremiah and Deuteronomy, chapter 28, we may note that parallels have been pointed out above between verse 36 and Jer. 16:13; verse 53 and Jer. 19:9; verse 63 and Jer. 32:41; and verse 64 (cf. Deut. 4:27 and 30:3) and Jer. 9:15. Also, verse 37 has influenced the editor of Jer. 25:9 and 18. It may indeed be that the editor of the secondary portions of Deuteronomy, chapter 28, was also the editor of many of Deuteronomic passages in the Book of Jeremiah.

The Deuteronomic editors did their work well. The best measure of their success is the general prevalence of the view that Jeremiah once approved of the Deuteronomic reforms and later changed his attitude. But, in order to understand the true Jeremiah, we must discount the Deuteronomic passages. We shall then see that the prophet was not given to compromise or to fundamental change of mind.

[33]Cf. Irwin, *op. cit.*

7
Zephaniah, Jeremiah, and the Scythians in Palestine*
Henri Cazelles

(Translated by Leo G. Perdue)

We are not lacking in sources which pertain to the last three decades of the Assyrian empire, a period which lasts *grosso modo* from 640 to 612 B.C. However, it is a matter of some anxiety for the historian who must translate and order them into precise dates and movements of specific peoples. One of the most sensitive questions, and yet one of considerable interest for the historian of Israel, is that of the Scythian invasion which would have wrested the provinces of the West (Syro-Phoenicia) from Assyrian domination long before the fall of Nineveh. For good reasons, certain contemporary historians agree such an invasion occurred but others are more cautious.[1] The difficulty stems from the heterogeneous nature of the sources. Only Herodotus speaks of a Scythian invasion. But the cuneiform texts are most explicit about certain movements of the Scythian population. As for the biblical sources, if they say nothing about the Scythians, they are still capable of furnishing some ideas about the invasions of the period. And as for the hieroglyphic texts, are they totally silent?

HERODOTUS

In Book I (Clio), 11. 104–106, Herodotus speaks explicitly of a Scythian domination extending to the borders of Egypt which would have

---

*Originally published as "Sophonie, Jérémie, et les Scythes en Palestine," *Revue Biblique* 74 (1967) 24–44.

[1] J. Boulos, *Les peuples et civilisations du Proche-Orient*, II, p. 260, Paris 1962, and W. F. Albright in *Historia Mundi*, II, 374, Munich 1953, acknowledge this invasion. J. Bright is very cautious about the witness of Herodotus, *A History of Israel*, London, 1963, p. 293, as also Sidney Smith, *Cambridge Ancient History*[1], III, p. 196, and É. Dhorme who hardly takes this point into account in the different cases where he has had to speak of the Scythians (*Recueil Dhorme*, Paris 1951, see the index). O. Eissfeldt (*Einleitung*[3], Tübingen 1964) admits the possibility (pp. 468, 573) and suggests a connection with the "Day of the Lord" in Zephaniah, but he is very uneasy about the rather general character of that prophetic schema. A more elaborate historical study is set forth by A. Deissler (and M. Delcor), *Les Petits Prophètes* II, p. 438, Paris 1964.

lasted 28 years. He employs the aorist, ἦρχον, of the verb which clearly signifies political domination.[2] This political power of the Scythians in the area which Herodotus calls "Syria-Palestine" followed some complex movements. Pursuing the Cimmerians whom they had chased from Europe, they reached Media. But they did not follow the customary route of the Maeëtian lake (Sea of Azov) to Media by way of the river Phasis and the land of the Colchi (Georgia). Instead they took a detour, a road situated higher up and "often longer." This is a route about which Herodotus obviously lacks information, except to say that they had the Caucasian mountains "on their right." Defeated by the Medes, the Scythians spread over "all Asia" and from there made for Egypt where Psammetichus stopped them with presents. Herodotus' idea of Asia is not delimited in a precise fashion. It is one of three parts of the world along with Europe and Libya (II, 16). Thus Herodotus includes Egypt in Asia and places the frontier of Asia at the Arabian Gulf where Libya begins (IV, 41). Asia is the domain of the "Barbarians" (I, 4), more or less identified with the Achaemenid empire (I, 192; III, 88). Asia stops at the Indian Ocean (IV, 40, the Erythre Sea), the Indus river (III, 98), the Phasis river, and the Caspian Sea. Also in Clio, when he points out that the Greeks designate the Cappadocians as Syrians (I, 72), he does not name Asia purely and simply Anatolia between the Cyprian and Euxine seas, but rather he specifies: πάντα τῆς Ἀσίης τὰ κάτω. The manner in which he expresses himself about the invasion assumes then a very large dispersion of these Scythians over the area which would one day constitute the Achaemenid empire, when Assurbanipal was still on the throne of Nineveh.

This passage refers to a defeat of the Scythians in Media and without other explicit details moves on to a specific event, the plundering of the temple of the Heavenly Aphrodite at Ashkelon by a rear guard of Scythians at the time of their withdrawal which Psammetichus (644–610)[3] obtained by means of a payment of gold. As in the case of Sennacherib, Herodotus seems duly dependent here on his informants from the temples of Egypt. According to Diodorus (II, 4) the Heavenly Aphrodite was Derceto, one of the epithets of Anat in the Ugaritic texts, and a goddess well known in Egypt.[4]

It is proper to attribute to that same Egyptian source two other pieces of information from Herodotus that we find this time in Book II (Euterpe). Speaking of Psammetichus (II, 157), he tells us that this king besieged not only Ashkelon, but also another Philistine city, Ashdod. The siege lasted 29

---

[2]For example, *History* I, 127; III, 8; V, 1. . . . (English translations are taken from or based on the *LCL*, Ed.).

[3]These are dates of J. Parker, *Festschrift Junker* I, pp. 208–212, in *Mitt. Deutsch. Arch. Inst. Kairo*, Wiesbaden 1957, assured by the dates of the solar eclipse of September, 610 (E. Hornung, in *ZÄS*, XCII, 1965, pp. 38–39).

[4]Remark by C. Virolleaud in reference to the title of Anat, $b^c lt\ drkt$ in RS 24.252.

years and was terminated by the taking and destruction of the city. This siege of Ashdod began then the year preceding the Scythian domination recorded in reference to Ashkelon. One may not disassociate this information from that which is told us in II, 159. Psammetichus has died, and we are in the reign of Necho II (610–595). Herodotus speaks from the outset of the canal excavated by this Pharaoh in order to connect the Nile and the Red Sea. Then he adds: "He used these ships at need, and with his land army met and defeated the Syrians at Magdolus, taking the great Syrian city of Cadytis after the battle."[5] What is the identity of each of these two towns? In III, 5 of his *History*, Herodotus speaks once more of Cadytis and specifically states that it is a maritime city in the South of Palestine: "the road runs from Phoenice as far as the borders of the city of Cadytis, which belongs to the Syrians of Palestine, as it is called." It is thus impossible not to identify this town with Gaza, an identification which all of the commentators make.[6] As for the victory of Necho at Magdolus over the "Syrians," no longer the Scythians, one may see here nothing but the victory of Necho of Josiah at Megiddo. The Greek historian, who is not familiar with Palestine, has confused this rare term with the numerous places called Migdol-Magdolus in the eastern Delta. We know that Necho ascended the throne between January 23rd and September 20th of a year which used to be regarded as 609, but now, following Parker, is perhaps 610. The Babylonian Chronicle, published by Gadd and corrected by Wiseman, permits the battle of Megiddo to be dated with certainty to the 17th year of Nabopolassar, for in the autumn there was already close to Assur-uballit an Egyptian army, *ummani*[mât] *Mi-sir*.[7] The fall of Gaza to Necho is linked to the fall of Ashdod to Psammetichus, and the data of Herodotus furnish the following chronological schema:

a) The offensive by Psammetichus stimied for 29 years at Ashdod;
b) The Scythian domination for 28 years to the borders of Egypt, which is ended by the fall of Ashdod. Psammeticus was still alive.

---

[5]In regard to this campaign, see J. Yoyotte, in *Suppl. Dict. Bible*, "Néchao," especially VI, 365. It has also been studied by A. Malamat, "The Last Wars of the Kingdom of Judah," in *JNES*, IX, 1950, pp. 218–227. In *Herodotus over de 26ste Dynastie*, H. De Meulenaere treats the Scythian matter on pp. 30–33. A. Malamat accepts the witness of Herodotus, but places the Scythian invasion at the end of the reign of Psammetichus, after the fall of Harran (cf. above all "Two Prophecies on the Nations," in *IEJ*, I, 1951, p. 11; the two prophecies were those of Zach. 9 and Jer. 47). J. Lewy, *Forschungen zur alten Geschichte Vorderasiens*, in MVAG, 1924/2, pp. 51ff., pushes forward the invasion under the reign of Psammetichus II. These positions take account of the difficulty one has in reconciling Herodotus with the Israelite and Assyrian data for the period 640–610, but we shall see that another solution is possible.

[6]In the Herodotus edition of the Budé collection, E. Legrand says only "probably," Paris 1939, p. 40, note 4. But no other town corresponds so exactly to the data; cf. J. Yoyotte, "Néchao," in *SDB*, VI, 389.

[7]D. J. Wiseman, *Chronicle of Chaldaean Kings* (626–556), London 1956, p. 63.

c) The capture of Gaza, another Philistine city, by his successor Necho, after a victory over the "Syrians," not the Scythians (that is, the defeat of Israel at the battle of Megiddo).

With the battle of Megiddo occurring in 609 or 610, the capture of Ashdod is at the end of the reign of Psammetichus (611 or January, 610), and the offensive of Psammetichus would have begun 29 years earlier, around 640/39 B.C. The Scythian domination begins a year later in 639/8.

Now, the date of 640/39 is an important date in Israel. It marks the accession of Josiah, still a youngster after the assassination of his father Amon, an event that was the occasion of a violent clash between the "officers" (literally "servants," II Kgs. 21:23) and the "people of the land."[8] The Book of Kings is very laconic, and one would like to know if, in a Jerusalem so open at the time to foreign influences, that drama of court is not the reaction to some disruption of harmony, such as the offensive of Psammetichus in Philistia. This Saite prince gained his independence from a formidable Assyria at an unknown date, but sometime before 653. For, after the death of Tanatumun in approximately 655, Psammetichus energetically proceeds to Thebes and installs Nitrocis as the divine votery of Amon.[9] Assurbanipal tells us of his intrigue with Gyges of Lydia before Gyges' defeat by the Cimmerians and death in 652.[10]

But 639 is also the date when the great inscriptions of Assurbanipal cease.[11] His reign lasts for at least eight more years. One has some contracts

---

[8]This expression has been the object of many discussions. See in particular R. de Vaux, "Le sens de l'expression « peuple du pays » dans l'Ancien Testament et le rôle politique du peuple en Israël," in *RA*, LVIII, 1964, pp. 167–172 with the bibliography of p. 172. A. Alt in *Kleine Schriften*, II, 237 note 1; Amussin in *Vestnik drievni istorij*, 1955/2, pp. 14–36; R. J. Coggins, in *JTS*, XVI, 1965, pp. 125–127; J. A. Soggin, in *VT*, XIII, 1963, pp. 187–196; J. Nicholson, in *JSS*, 1965, X, pp. 59–66, who concludes that the term has no "fixed and rigid meaning."

[9]Stela of adoption translated in J. Breasted, *Ancient Records of Egypt*, IV, §§ 935ff; concerning the role of Montuemhat, cf. J. Leclant, *Montouemhat quatrième prophète d'Amon*, Le Caire, 1961, pp. 260f., 266f., 274f. Unfortunately, one knows the Libyan (cf. H. Goedicke, "Psammetik I und die Libyer," in *Mitt. Deutsch. Arch. Inst. Kairo*, 1962, pp. 26–49) and Theban policies better than his Asiatic policy. One cannot draw many conclusions from the bronze ring in the cartouche of Psammetichus recovered at Carchemish. The arguments of F. K. Kienitz, *Die politische Geschichte Ägyptens vom 7. bis 4. Jahrhundert vor der Zeitwende*, Berlin 1953, pp. 16–20, rest upon an essentially extra-Egyptian documentation. He connects the beginning of the Scythian invasion to the alliance of Psammetichus with Gyges and the date of 650. He acknowledges another around 620, regarding the attack as historical, but objects to a continuous blockade. Consult S. Sauneron and J. Yoyotte, "Sur la politique palestinienne des rois saïtes," in *VTS*, II, pp. 131–36.

[10]Approximate date, allowed by Boulos (*op.cit.*, p. 262) and *Peuples et Civilisations* by Halphen and Sagnac, Paris 1950, I, 613. The Texts of Assurbanipal concerning Gyges and Psammetichus (*Pisimilki*) are found in Luckenbill, *Ancient Records of Assyria*, II, Number 785 (read Tushamilki); Streck, *Assurbanipal und die letzten assyrischen Könige*, II, p. 23 (Rassam Cylinder, II, 114ff.).

[11]H. Tadmor, *Congrès (XXVe) des Orientalistes* held at Moscow in August 1960; summary in the Moscow publication 1964, I, pp. 240f.; R. Labat, *Annuaire der Collège de*

dating from the 38th year of the king[12] and, at the beginning of 631, Assurbanipal is still king. According to the inscription of the mother of Nabonidus, he would have reigned for 42 years,[12] thus theoretically until 627. But since this inscription acknowledges only 3 years for Assur-etil-ili (sic) between Assurbanipal and Nabopolassar and confirms the length of the latter's reign (21 years) and the reigns of his successors, it has Assurbanipal die three years before the accession of Nabopolassar to the throne of Babylon (626). It is approximately in 630 that it dates the end of Assurbanipal's reign, taking account of the accession year of his successor. The fact still remains that during this period, which involves almost a decade, we lack information precisely at the time when Herodotus places the Scythian invasion. Nevertheless, due to the Neo-Babylonian inscriptions and chronicles, we are not completely lacking in information. Are the Scythians mentioned in these documents?

SCYTHIANS, CIMMERIANS, AND THE UMMAN-MANDA

The population which Herodotus designates as Scythian is not so easily identifiable as one might believe. P.-E. Legrand had to group under two rubrics the references to the Scythians in the analytical index of his

---

France, 1962/3, pp. 294ff.; 1963/4, pp. 298ff.; 1964/5, pp. 333–337, over the problems relative to the dating of Assurbanipal; J. M. Aynard, *Le Prisme du Louvre AO 19 39*, Paris 1957, gives a synchronic table of the campaigns, pp. 91–94, and a general introduction to the texts and their dating on pages 2–5. It is Louis F. Hartman, *JNES*, 1962, p. 25, who is the most hesitant over the dates of Gyges, whose engagement with the Cimmerians, and then alliance with Psammetichus, is situated "somewhere between 664 and 649."

[12]The data relative to the reign of Assurbanipal and his successors have been gathered by R. Borger, "Mesopotamien in den Jahren 629–621 V. Chr.," in *WZKM*, LV, 1959, pp. 62–76, and "Der Aufstieg des neubabylonischen Reiches," in *JCS*, XIX, 1965, pp. 59–77. He has attempted to resolve the problems of chronology in identifying Sin-šar-Iškun and Assur-etil-ilani as the same person. The first is in fact ignored by the mother of Nabonidus, "author" of the stele of Harran (C. J. Gadd, "The Harran Inscription of Nabonidus," in *Anatolian Studies*, VIII, 1958, p. 47), as well as Sinšumlišir. J. van Dijk and W. von Soden (bibliography *JCS*, XIX, p. 59) have some different views. One is not able to enter here into this complex problem. It is difficult to attribute 42 years to the reign of Assurbanipal in accordance with the stele of Harran. The latter wishes to ignore every Assyrian king, from the liberation of Babylon by Nabopolassar, but the 45 (or 46) years that it reckons between the succession of Nabopolassar and the one of Assurbanipal (42 plus the 3 of Assur-etil-il(an)i) would bring the succession of the latter back to 671 (626 + 45). This is incompatible with Assyrian chronology, barring a sharing of the throne by Assurbanipal and Esarhaddon which is badly documented. The problem is taken up again by J. Oates in *Iraq*, XXVII, 1965, pp. 135–159, who accepts the integrity of the stele of Harran, and has Assurbanipal reign from 669 to 627, Assur-etil-ilani from 627 to 623, and Sin-šar-Iškun from 623 to 612 after a short interregnum by Sin-šum-lišir. Some recent texts from Warka (Uruk) suggest once again the identification of Assurbanipal of Nineveh and Kandalanu of Babylon. The major objection to a reign of 42 years results from the absence of contracts dated from Assurbanipal after the 38th year of his reign. At Nippur one has two contracts from the 36th year, one from the 37th, one from the 38th, and quite a series from Assur-etil-ilani: the year of accession, 1st, 2nd, 3rd, and 4th year, and after that another series for Sin-šar-iškun (cf. M. Falkner, in *AfO*,

edition.[13] One speaks of the Scythians of southern Russia of whom Herodotus narrates in Book IV. Coming from Asia and passing over the Araxes, they drove the Cimmerians out of southern Russia where they settled. They consisted of several groups which Herodotus distinguishes (IV, 17). On the other hand, there are the Scythians of Book II who invaded Media at the time of Cyaxares. These are the ones who would have submitted to the Egyptian king Sesostris (II, 110), realizing an achievement here where Darius would have failed. This Sesostris, who would have left his monuments in Syro-Palestine (106), attacked the land of the Scythians and Thracians (103), and would have returned with numerous prisoners, seems to result from a confusion between the Sesostris of the Middle Kingdom and the campaign of Thutmosis III reaching the Euphrates and the region of Harran. Here and there Herodotus appears to attempt to make these two categories of Scythians identical. It is plain in IV, 1, but it is possible that the long, uncertain detour between the Sea of Azov and Media corresponds to the same end. Those who encounter Darius are in Russia, and the peninsula of Kertch is in Scythia (IV, 99). But in VII, 64 there are the Amyrgian Scythians identified with the Sacae and living in Bactra. These are the Saka (in the Persian language) at the end of the Behistun inscription (V, 20–30). They have a painted headdress, live near a sea, and their chief is called Shuka. One may be all the more hesitant as in the inscription of Naqs-i-Rustam (§ 3, 15–30),[14] Darius distinguishes three types of Scythians: he mentions at first the Saka in the vicinity of Sind and of Gandara—these are the Amyrgian Scythians; then follow the Scythians with the pointed headdress, very near to the first, but closer to Babylon and Assyria; and finally, after referring to Cappadocia, Sardis, and Ionia, the Scythians (Sakas) who are beyond the sea, clearly the Euxine Sea.

We are at the end of the 6th century. What can the earlier texts tell us? I know of no mention of the Scythians before Esarhaddon (680–669). In the dedicatory inscription of Nineveh[15] the 11th episode is devoted to the Mannaeans and to the Scythians: "I dispersed the men of the land of the Mannaeans, the disorganized Guti (la sanqu)[16] and their troops, Ispaka of the Scythian country, an ally who bore him no aid, I killed with weapons." Text B and the inscription of Til Barsib express a little differently the relation between the Mannaeans and the Scythian chief: ". . . Mannaeans,

---

XVI, pp. 308ff.). How may one explain the disappearance of the name of Assurbanipal in that city which continues to be in subjection to Assyrian domination, if he is still king?

[13]Paris 1954, pp. 145 and 146.

[14]Cf. R. G. Kent, *Old Persian*, New Haven 1950, pp. 137–138; F. H. Weissbach, *Die Inschriften der Achemeniden*, Leipzig 1911, pp. 88–89 with the trilingual text (Elamite, Persian, Babylonian).

[15]R. Borger, *Die Inschriften Asarhaddons Königs von Assyrien*, Graz 1956, p. 52.

[16]Or "nomad," "no enclosure." In regard to *šanâqu*, see A. R. Millard, in *Iraq*, XXVI, 1964, pp. 28f.

who are the troops (*ummanati*) of Ispaka of the land of the Scythians, an ally who bore him no aid, I killed. . . ."[17] The connection between the Scythians and Mannaeans is certain, and quite a series of Sargonide texts place the Mannaeans in Media-Atropatene, to the south and southeast of the lake of Urmiah, (north)east of Assyria. The Scythians are called the Išguzay, or Ašguzay, which corresponds to the Hebrew Ashkenaz. While the Septuagint does not make the identification, it does translate Elam by Scythians in Gen. 14:1 and 9.

The Scythians reappear in several oracles that favor Esarhaddon. These are not the oracles of Ishtar of Arbeles, but rather are the responses of the god Shamash at the time of consultation.[18] The king of the Išguzay is threatening, but he sends a messenger carrying peace proposals to Esarhaddon, *dibbi kinûtu šalmûtu*: he will keep the *adê*[19] which the Assyrians will impose upon him, but he demands an Assyrian princess (of the *bît ridûti*) in marriage. What does Shamash think of that proposal? The consultation of the liver follows. Another consultation (no. 30) puts the Išguzay in league with the Medes, the lands of Bitkari and Saparda, while another (31) with the Mannaeans. One has identified with reason[20] this Partatua with the Protothyes of Herodotus (I, 103), the father of Madyes who plays a role at the time of the first Median offensive against Nineveh.[21]

The term Išguzay (Ašguzay) then disappears from cuneiform, and one does not find it in the inscriptions of Assurbanipal. But one does have it in the form Aškenaz in three biblical texts (Gen. 10:3, Jer. 51:27, I Chron. 1:6). The first text, of which the third is only a summary, belongs to the priestly redaction of the Table of Nations.[22]

[17]R. Borger, *op. cit.*, pp. 52 and 100.

[18]J. A. Knudtzon, *Assyrische Gebete an den Sonnengott*, Leipzig 1893, pp. 119ff., nos. 29 to 36.

[19]The *adê* or *adî*, Aramaean and Assyrian, are some of the stipulations imposed under oath upon a vassal.

[20]Since H. Winckler (*Forschungen*, I, 488), cf. *Rec. Dhorme*, p. 181; Sidney Smith in *Camb. Anc. Hist.*, III, p. 82; Streck, *Assurbanipal*, I, p. ccclxxv.

[21]Madyes is also known by Strabo (*Géographie*, I, 3, 21). Evidently there was a very great variation in the proposition of Partatua that supposes Esarhaddon was still active in the North (cf. Sidney Smith, p. 82) before he turned toward the Egyptian expedition. This is perhaps a sign that he desired appeasement in the North, and the event may date around 673 in the context of the vassal treaties with Ramatya (672). The offensive of Madyes against Nineveh may not be dated from 653 as R. Labat has pointed out ("Kaštariti, Phraorte et les débuts de l'histoire mède," *JA*, 1961, pp. 1–9); confirmed by E. Cavaignac (*ibid*, pp. 153–162). The latter interprets the mutilated lines 34–37 of the Wiseman chronicle, for the year 624/3, as a victory of the Assyrians over the Medes (*RA*, 1957, pp. 28–29, cf. *JA*, 1962, p. 157). There would be 50 years between the proposals of marriage of Partatua and the action of his son against the Medes, which is impossible. But if one dates this offensive against the Assyrians and their Scythian allies to 614, these 59 years are no longer improbable.

[22]See É. Dhorme, "Les peuples issus de Japhet d'après le chapitre X de la Genèse," in *Syria*, 1932, pp. 28–49 (*Recueil*, pp. 167–189). This priestly recension dates probably from the 6th century B.C. (cf. *SDB*, VII, col. 830ff.).

Ashkenaz is a Japhethite of the first branch—Gomer, that is to say the Cimmerians, about whom we shall return. Gomer precedes Magog, the Medes, and the Greeks (Javan); and among the Cimmerians Aškenaz is the first born, preceding Riphath (the Paphlagonians according to Josephus) and Togarmah, considerably better known[23] in the loop of the Euphrates. This text could be tending towards the placement of Askenaz as a Cimmerian branch between Paphlagonia (near the Black Sea and Bithynia) to the west and the Euphrates to the east. But Jer. 51:27 celebrates a coalition against Babylon under the direction of the "king" of Media with Ararat, Minni, the Mannaeans[24] near Lake Urmiah, and Aškenaz. Thus Aškenaz is more to the east. No one attributes this text to Jeremiah, not only because of its anti-Babylonian fervor which does not correspond to the prophet's own attitude, especially in his last years, but it also is close to the time of the city's fall. Rudolph[25] believes it is prior to the fall in 538. This last text appears to be properly spoken in Palestine, but as in the preceding cases, Aškenaz is certainly not close by. It is a remote tribe of the North, cited in passing in the midst of others.

It is probable that the term Išguzay-Aškenaz is already an archaism when the Israelites employ it in the 6th century. The texts of Assurbanipal in the 7th century know the Scythians by the term Saka, at least in one of the most recent formulations of the Annals (probably from 640–639), the one from the 1931/2 excavations of Nineveh, published by Campbell-Thompson.[26] In line 146 (Thompson, pp. 88 and 96), he speaks of Dugdamme or Tugdamme, king of the Sakay-Ugutumki. He campaigned on the borders of Assyria, fell ill (he spat up blood) and had to return "into his land." He paid tribute and submitted with an oath. We have some other details about his illness, even about his clan, "a race of Halgate." But neither the Ugumtuki nor Halgate are exact equivalents to what the Greeks and Persians tell us of the Scythians.[27]

---

[23]It is Hittite Tegarama, Assyrian Til-garimmu near Melitene, close to the loop of the Euphrates.

[24]Concerning the Mannaeans, see Kinnier-Wilson, in *Iraq*, XXIV, 1962, p. 111 in reference to the Kurba'il statue of Shalmaneser III; Rainer. M. Boehmer, "Volkstum und Städte der Mannäer," in *Baghdader Mitteilungen*, III, 1964, pp. 11–24. They disappeared after 616 (Wiseman Chronicle), while still the allies of the Assyrians. The Neo-Babylonian texts ignore them, an indication that one cannot date the text of Jeremiah after the 6th century B.C.

[25]*Jeremia*, Tübingen 1947, p. 257.

[26]*AAA*, XX, Liverpool 1933, p. 79. The text has been discovered in the temple of Ishtar. It appears to be subsequent to the Nassouhi Prism (*Archiv für Keilschriftforschung*, II, pp. 97–105) which dates from the 30th year of the reign; cf. E. Weidner, *AfO*, VII, pp. 1–7; J. M. Aynard, *Le prisme du Louvre*, p. 5.

[27]So the Chicago Dictionary (A, 131b) and R. Pfeiffer see a common name in this expression ("rabble, mob"). But W. von Soden (313b) and Herbert B. Huffmon (*BASOR*, 181, 1966) p. 33, see it as "nomads." The expression is interesting for the Hebrew "my father was a wandering Aramean" (Deut 26:5) seems to be an echo of it. Sidney Smith (*JRAS*, 1934, 576), displeased with *Sak-a-a*, "tentatively" proposed: *šarru šad-da-ai-u Gu-tu-um KI* (improbable).

But this Tugdamme is known elsewhere. Strabo knows him as Lyg-damis.[28] He could have taken Sardis from Gyges, and pillaged the Temple of Artemis at Ephesus. The goddess would have punished him with illness, even as Assurbanipal tells us that Assur, Ishtar of Arbeles, Ninlil, Bel, and Nabu had punished him in the same way. The taking of Sardis and the death of Gyges, ally of Psammetichus of Egypt, occur in 652. But the offensive of Tugdamme may have been several years later. Tugdamme is already known from the inscriptions of Assurbanipal, but with another titulary. Of concern is a dedication to Marduk in the Esagila,[29] consisting of 50 lines on a golden, incense altar. It makes allusion to a campaign in Elam where he had ruined the land (1, 18). Winckler and Streck see the campaign against Teumman, who died in 655. One may, with H. Tadmor,[30] date it in 641/640; in this case the two inscriptions would point to the same campaign, but the date of 655 appears to me to be required.[31] The main

---

[28]I, 3, 21. It was Sayce who made the first connection (*Academy*, 1893, p. 277) that has since been recognized by all (Campbell-Thompson, p. 106; Sidney Smith, *Camb. Anc. Hist.*, III, p. 189; Streck, I, p. ccclxxiii).

[29]Text in Streck, *Assurbanipal*, II, pp. 276–286, after Strong and Craig. Translation only in Luckenbill, *Ancient Records*, II, pp. 384–386. The essential lines (14–25) are in Streck, pp. 281f. with some important notes. The edition by T. Bauer (in the *Assyriologische Bibliothek*, N. F., 1–2, p. 29) adds nothing of importance.

[30]See note 11.

[31]I am very tempted to follow the chronology of Tadmor (and of P. Naster, *L'Asie Mineure et l'Assyrie aux VIII[e] et VII[e] s.*, Louvain 1938, p. 99, who places the death of Tugdamme between 637 and 626), for it is curious that, for this dedication to Babylon, neither Shamash-shum-ukin nor Kandalanu may be named when the two cover the entirety of the reign of Assurhanipal. Generally in the inscriptions of Babylon which precede the revolt of Shamash-shum-ukin, Assurbanipal names him, but sometimes in a very brief manner, and precisely at the moment where there ought to be found the mention "of the beloved brother" (Rev. 19, to compare with L[1] line 21, L[2] line 22, Streck, pp. 226–233) we have some lines filled with lacunae. Certain restored lines as those of Streck, p. 351, very brief it is true, also mention only Assurbanipal. Contrary to Rassam and the plaque of Nineveh, no allusion is made to the revolt of Shamash-shum-ukin. Elam is spoken about in very general terms, not like prisms F and Nassouhi, or the plaque of Nineveh in another literary genre, all texts subsequent to the taking of Susa by 646. *For the text of Nineveh (line 160) as for the Greeks, it is in Anatolia, allied with Mugallu of Tabal, that Tugdamme-Lygdamis died.* His relations *with Elam* in the East, *having provoked Babylon* where one felt more the need to be protected against Elam and its allies, *are placed then before 652*, the date of the passage from the East into the West after he had had to abdicate in favor of his son. Above all it is necessary to remark that all of the restoration works of Assurbanipal at the Esagila, constructions and furniture, are placed in 655. See Unger, "Babylon," in *RLA* I, 356ff.; the chronicle published by Millard, *Iraq*, XXVI, 1964, pp. 14–35 and Millard's commentary on p. 22; and B. Landsberger, "Brief des Bischofs von Esagila an König Asarhaddon," in *Mededelingen der kon. Niederlande Ak. Wet.*, N. R. 28, Amsterdam, 1965, p. 25. One includes some new works in 639 based on the Nassouhi prism (I, II. 2–3) which speak of the offering of a bed to Marduk, replacing perhaps the one which had been made in 655 and had arrived at Babylon in 654 (Millard, *op. cit.*, p. 23 note; cf. Unger, *Babylon*, col. 356), but the Nassouhi text, although found at Babylon, speaks neither of Babylon nor of the Esagila. B. Landsberger, who dates the return of the bed of Marduk to the Esagila in the 27th year of Assurbanipal

point for us is that Tugdamme is here called the king of the Umman-
Manda, a title which is repeated in a fragmentary inscription found at
Nineveh in the same campaign as the first and mentioned only in a note by
Campbell-Thompson.[32]

Ought one to identify the Umman-Manda with the Scythians in the
time of Assurbanipal? In fact they appear very frequently, whereas the
Išguzay have disappeared. But the problem is more complicated, for the
Umman-Manda are one of the fluctuating categories of nomenclature of
peoples in the cuneiform texts. Studied by Forrer[33] and E. Dhorme,[34]
among others, F. Cornelius has recently devoted to them a long note[35] and
sees them as a "band of horseman" by connecting *manda* with the Indo-
European word for the horse. But J. R. Kupper makes the observation that
the term appears well before the arrival of the Indo-Europeans.[36]

The Umman-Manda are mentioned as early as the period of Naram-
Sin in the third millennium in the texts of the *Nâru* literature. Several
samples of this have already been published.[37] O. Gurney has recovered

---

(*op. cit.*, p. 26), was not yet aware of the study of Millard on the colophon of K 2411. The
eponym of Awianu dates from 655/4; cf. Weidner, *AfO*, XIII, 1940, p. 207. The restoration
"in Babylon" is likely, for Nassouhi 1, 2 and 3 is not the beginning of the column, and it is a
matter concerning Marduk. The Weidner fragment adds nothing, except that often Elam,
Cyrus I of Persia, and the adjoining lands are of concern. But there is nothing of Tugdamme.
After much hesitation, I believe I must abandon the dating of Tadmor, reattach the offering of
the incense altar to the restorations well attested in 655/4, and argue that Tugdamme had
been in the East before abdicating in favor of his son Sandakšatru and fleeing with his
supporters towards the West where he would die after having beaten Gyges severely. Mugallu
of Tabal is still living in Cilicia since the defeat of Tugdamme and not his son (whose name is
perhaps given at the mutilated beginning of line 141, and ends in *ussi*); this son, as well as the
daughter in the preceding line, is sent to the king of Assyria. In regard to Mugallu,
D. Kennedy calls to my attention the interesting omen of Thompson, *Report of the
Magicians* . . . 64 B, which places him in contact with Itu²a and Ahlamu. Mugallu of Tabal
has made Esarhaddon uneasy, and probably even Sennacherib, for Assurbanipal has his
subject use the plural "my fathers." One could consider identifying Sandašarme of Cilicia in
the Rassam Cyl. with the Cimmerian of the text of Harran (Luckenbill, II § 911), but the text
refers to the 3rd campaign of Assurbanipal as a consequence of the activities of Gyges: it is
still at the beginning of the reign and not at the end.

[32] *Op. cit.*, p. 107, note 1.

[33] *ZDMG*, LXXVI, pp. 248ff.

[34] *Recueil*, pp. 173, 318ff., 365 *et passim*.

[35] *ERIN-Manda*, in *Iraq*, XXV, 1963, pp. 167–170. Concerning the Umman-Manda and
the Indo-Europeans, see the bibliography in M. Mayrhofer, *Die Indo-Arier im alten Vodera-
sien*, Wiesbaden 1966, p. 149.

[36] "Northern Mesopotamia and Syria," in *Cambridge Ancient History*[2], fasc. 14, p. 41,
Cambridge 1963.

[37] *Chronicles concerning early Babylonian Kings*, London, 1907, II, pp. 87–96 (*Cuneiform
Texts from the Babylonian Tablets in the British Museum*, XIII, 42–43). The *nâru* literature,
which is presented as some copies (apocryphal) of texts from ancient stelae, has been studied
by H. G. Güterbock in *ZA*, 1934, XLII, pp. 62ff; E. A. Speiser, in *The Idea of History in the
Ancient Near East*, Yale, 1955, pp. 55ff.

some new copies at Sultan-Tepe.[38] The Umman-Manda had their camp at Shubat-Enlil (rather than in the "residence of Enlil"),[39] well known by the Mari texts in the north of Mesopotamia. From there they ravaged Subartu (towards the loop of the Euphrates), and, more to the east, the land of the Guti and Elam. A fragment published by Scheil shows that this "Legend of the King of Cutha" (or Naram-Sin) was known since the Old Babylonian period, and, strictly speaking, one could see in it an indication of Indo-European movements which led to the establishment of Mitanni.[40] In fact, if we take the most recent texts concerning the Umman-Manda, from the time of Nabonidus and Cyrus, it is certain that they portray the Medes with an Astyages as king.[41] But this identification is not correct for all the texts. Some of the Umman-Manda may have been Indo-Europeans who fought the Hittite King Ḫattusilis I,[42] but one is not able to determine those who conquered Ammi-saduqa of the First Dynasty of Babylon,[43] nor those who were targeted by a hepatoscopic tablet of the same period though this portends in conformity with another over a "levy of Subartu."[44]

One does not easily know how to interpret the "report of pay or of gratification"[45] from the Mari archives which was published by J. Bottéro. In this text one jointly finds four "men of Manda" and three Elamites, as well as a typically West Semitic person: Habdu-ni-ša, that is *servant*. . . . Continuing on to the west of Mesopotamia we have the Hittite laws (I § 54) which tell of a privileged category, relieved from the corvée and characterized by its armament. This could perhaps be calvary for Cornelius, but Friedrich does not commit himself.[46] If Otten[47] appears to parallel the text, "Zuladi, lord of the Umman-Manda," with "the chief (UGULA) of the UKUŠ troops," who are in fact characterized by heavy armament, the Hittite laws have the Manda followed by a series of other "warriors"

---

[38]*Anatolian Studies*, V, 1955, p. 101.

[39]A. Goetze, *JCS*, VII, 1953, p. 58, proposes to see here Chagar Bazar.

[40]This is the position of E. Forrer, *Forschungen*, V, 21, 1947.

[41]See further page 9.

[42]The Hittite text published by Otten (*MDOG*, 86, Dec. 1953, pp. 60f.), where it is a question of the campaigns of a certain Zaludi, "chief of the Umman-Manda" in liaison with Zukraši, head of the *UKUŠ* troops, and in relation with Aleppo and Ḫaššu, is perhaps from the period of Ḫattusilis I. But Otten does not exclude the possibility of the period of Mursilis I. He prefers, however, the first hypothesis. W. F. Albright (*BASOR*, 146, p. 30) dates the text from 1670. Bibliography relative to this text is in H. Klengel, *Geschichte Syriens in 2 Jahrt. v. u. Z.* I, Berlin 1965, pp. 143, 147, 167 (notes 69 and 71).

[43]S. Langdon and J. K. Fotheringham, *The Venus Tablets of Ammizaduga*, Oxford, London 1928, p. 9 (line 27).

[44]J. Nougayrol, 1950, p. 14. The "levy" (*tibût*) may be a "thrust," an "offensive."

[45]J. Bottéro, *Arch. Royales de Mari*, VII, Paris, 1957, pp. 113 and 224 (no. 221, 10); cf. A. Falkenstein, *BiOr*, XVII, 1960, p. 176.

[46]*Hethitische Gesetze*, Leiden 1954, p. 35 (Commentary p. 100).

[47]See note 49. Over the meaning of *UKUŠ*, cf. J. Friedrich, *Hethitisches Wörterbuch*, Suppl. 1, p. 29.

determined by their city, before speaking at the end of the list of archers, carpenters, and carriers. A geographic or ethnic meaning is more probable for the texts of that epic, and is confirmed by the statue of Idrimi,[48] that minor prince of Northern Syria who had to flee from Aleppo (about the 15th century) and make his peace with Suttarna, "king of Hurri and king of the ERIN.MEŠ (= Umman) [Dinger] wa-an-da." This is close to the time when Thutmosis III defeated the Mitanni and passed over the Euphrates. We have seen that the tradition of Herodotus about Sesostris may be an echo of this. In the 13th century the Umman-Manda are the enemies of Ugarit and have some relations with Bentesina of the Amurru.[49]

It is certainly the case that the Umman-Manda reappear under the Sargonides. At first, they appear during the reign of Esarhaddon, though episodically. They are mentioned in the eighth episode of Borger,[50] which is positioned in all the recensions prior to the episode relative to the Išguzay. Here, there is a Cimmerian (*Gimiraya*), Teušpa-Teispes, described as the "distant Umman-Manda," who was conquered by the Assyrians in the land of Hubušna, not far from the Cilicia cited afterwards in the same campaign, perhaps Cabissos (Luckenbill).[51] Still the fact remains that Herodotus knows this Teispes[52] as a Persian name and as an ancestor of the Achaemenids. This does not simplify the identifications.

In any case, the identification of the Cimmerians with the Umman-Manda appears to be made in the curious, astrological report ABL 1391.[53] After having mentioned in 1.15 the destruction of the Umman-Manda (*šalpù-tim* Umman-Manda), the scribe draws a line and says: "Umman-Manda Cimmerian man" (*amêl* gim-ra-ya). Then he draws a new line and resumes the astronomical observations. Some similar explicative notations enclosed in two lines are found in lines 6 and 22. We suggest that this identification of the Umman-Manda with the Cimmerians may perhaps only be a kind of "actualization" of the omen.[54] In fact, the beginning of the text opens by evoking a threat, not against the Umman-Manda, but over the "land of the Cimmerians," and it is the West, the *mât Amurri* which is threatened.

---

[48]Sidney Smith, *The Statue of Idrimi*, London 1949, p. 16, line 46. The alternation *wa/ma* is attested for the period and the region. Thus Iluwer and Ilu-mer represent the same person.

[49]J. Nougayrol, *Palais Royal d'Ugarit*, IV, p. 180 (RS 17.286 line 6). Bentesina lived around 1280 (M. Liverani, *Storia d'Ugarit*, Rome 1962, Tavola I, p. 158).

[50]*Inschriften Assarhaddons . . .*, Graz 1956, p. 51. Nineveh A III, 43–46. It is the fifth episode of recension B and the sixth of recension C.

[51]Sidney Smith dates this campaign from 679 and places Hubušna in Tabal (*Camb. Anc. Hist.*, III, p. 83).

[52]Herodotus (VII, 11) knows two persons by this name.

[53]Publication by Harper. The text has been copied again in *Cuneiform Texts From the Babylonian Tablets in the British Museum*, XXXIV, 10–11, London 1914, nos. 10–11 and studied again by Louis Hartman, "The Date of the Cimmerian Threat against Ashurbanipal According to *ABL* 1391," in *JNES*, 1962, pp. 25–37, who pushes the date proposed by Olmstead back five years (657 in place of 652).

[54]The method of *pesher* already existed well before the demotic Chronicle and Qumran.

In *l'Astrologie chaldéene*,[55] the treaty Enuma Anu Bel, compiled under the Sargonides but containing some data going back to the Sumerians,[56] there are frequent references to the Umman-Manda and some forebodings concerning "thrusts" (ZI, *tibût*), incursions, or revolts. It is an evil occurrence for the "land" (Sin III, 7; Ishtar XXI, 42; see also Sin XXXIII, 30; Ishtar XXI, 95). The case of the *tibût* of the *Umman-Manda* in Adad XI, 10 is interesting for it is near the *tibût umman dadme* of X, 11. The *dadme* are the places of settlement, and this could prompt one to see in the Umman-Manda a different quality, that of nomads, which has been proposed. One may recall here that in a letter to Esarhaddon it is said of the Cimmerians that they are of the *zêr halqati*,[57] even as Assurbanipal said the same of Tugdamme.

The Umman-Manda still play a role in the land of the successors of Assurbanipal. But it is necessary to observe that there are some Babylonian sources. The Umman-Manda appear in line 38 of Gadd's Chronicle; they are united (*ana tarṣi*) with Nabopolassar at the fall of Nineveh. One hesitates to see here the Medes who are called ^{mât}*mada-a* in the preceding lines (23 and 24). It is tempting, however, for Cyaxares, king of the Medes, is mentioned two lines further on; but some words are missing. The Umman-Manda (without their king) returned two years later as allies of Nabopolassar when in the 14th year Cyaxares went back to his land and is no longer mentioned. In fighting against Assur-uballit and (probably) Egypt, the Umman-Manda and Nabopolassar took Harran. This is the date that the mother of Nabonidus reports as the time of the destruction of the temple of Sin at Harran. Nabonidus himself attributes this destruction to the Umman-Manda in the Cylinder of Sippan and the stele of Babylon.[58] Now, for Nabonidus the Umman-Manda who have destroyed the temple of Sin are certainly the Medes. He objects to the god who requires him to rebuild the temple about the presence of the Umman-Manda who "surround the temple and are powerful." But then the god reveals to him (I, 26–32) the victory of Cyrus, King of Anshan, over Astyages, king of the Umman-Manda. It follows that the Umman-Manda of the Chronicle (Rev. 59–75), at the time of the taking of Harran in 610 and the "sacking" of the temple and the city, are the Medes. Consequently, one does not see how the Umman-Manda of 612, in spite of the lacunae of the text, would not be those who have Cyaxares for their king, mentioned two lines further down, and thus are identified with the Medes. Nevertheless, the difference of

---

[55]Édition C. Virolleaud, Paris 1908–1912.

[56]B. Meissner, *Babylonien und Assyrien*, II, pp. 247f., Heidelberg, 1925.

[57]See note 27 over the meaning of the expression. This letter, *ABL* 1237, lines 15–16, has been translated by R. Pfeiffer, *State Letters of Assyria*, New Haven 1935, pp. 224–225.

[58]S. Langdon, *Die neubabylonischen Königsinschriften*, Leipzig 1912, pp. 218f. I, 12; pp. 284f. X, 14; pp. 272f. II, 14; P. Garelli, "Nabonide" in *SDB* VI, 279; A. L. Oppenheim, *The Interpretation of Dreams in the Ancient Near East*, Philadelphia 1956, p. 250 and commentary p. 203.

terminology in the report of the campaigns of 615 and 614 (11th and 12th years of Nabopolassar), where it is a question of the land of the Medes (Madaa), and those of 612 and 610 (the 15th and 16th years of Nabopolassar), where it is a question of the Umman-Manda, urges one to admit that there had been a change in the composition of the Median army. While the cylinder of Nabonidus keeps us from seeing a Cimmerian raid in the conquest of Harran, it does not stop us from recognizing a Scythian invasion at the time of the destruction of Nineveh.

Now this is what Diodorus Siculus tells us. In his history (II, 26) he attributes the fall of Nineveh to an army coming from Bactra. We have seen that Herodotus is acquainted with the Scythians of Bactra. In two places (I, 103 and 106), he mentions a victory of Cyaxares over the Scythians before the taking of Nineveh.[59] The better explanation of the long detour which he attributes to the Scythian army, "having on their right the Caucasian mountains" (I, 104), supposes that he knew that the Scythians, defeated by Cyaxares before the fall of Nineveh, came from Bactra and not from Europe. The change of terminology in the Chronicle derives from the victory of Cyaxares which had taken place between 615 and 612. He attacked Nineveh again, this time with some contingents of Umman-Manda or Scythians who were missing earlier.

The Chronicle does not mention Cyaxares before the 12th year of Nabopolassar. That year he took Assur, but failed to take Nineveh. He had taken the initiative in his operations, but once in Assur, Nabopolassar "comes to his aid." Elsewhere, Herodotus tells us that while laying siege to Nineveh, Cyaxares was attacked by a "great army of Scythians, led by their king Madyes son of Protothyes" (Partatua). Cavaignac and Labat[60] have shown that there could not have been a Median attack against Nineveh in 653 as some have proposed. One has no precise indication of an assault by the Medes against Nineveh before 614, and at that time the Scythians are still on the side of the Assyrians. But, if the facts given by Herodotus blend well with the Babylonian Chronicle, its chronology is still disconcerting, for its order has the Median victory occur before the 29 years of Scythian domination in Syria-Palestine. It is even more disconcerting, if one takes account of what Herodotus says in I, 74. Here the conflict between the Scythians and Cyaxares is this time linked to the war with the Lydians, dated by the eclipse of Thales in either 610 or 585,[61] but at a time well before Labynetus (Nabonidus) would come to the throne. In any case, these Scythians are no longer the eastern Scythians of Bactra, but rather the Scythians of Asia Minor. One is even tempted to see in this case the

---

[59]In confusing it with some other elements; not without value it must be added.

[60]See note 21. It is this change of terminology by the Chronicle which causes one to hesitate to accept the date of 623 proposed by E. Cavaignac for the first attack by Cyaxares.

[61]One chooses rather the date of 585 (cf. R. Labat, op. cit., p. 10 note). In 610 Cyaxares is occupied elsewhere.

Umman-Manda, not as Scythians and Medes, but rather as Cimmerians who have been in the region since they had severely beaten Gyges to the great delight of Assurbanipal about 653.

There is nothing astonishing in the fact that the scribes of Assurbanipal, and then those of the Neo-Babylonian kingdom, may have extended to some of the barbarians of the East the name Umman-Manda, a name more commonly attributed up to that point to some nomads of the confines of the loop of the Euphrates. And perhaps it is from this that Herodotus has drawn in giving the name Scythian to some very diverse groups. But we have noticed that the Achaemenid inscriptions extended the term *saka* to others besides the barbarians of the Elamite region even as one of the last annals of Assurbanipal was doing. This extension of the terminology is not without connection to the real facts. Cimmerians and Scythians are obviously two groups barely distinguished by a number of Assyrian scribes.[62] And the trilingual inscription of the Behistun stone calls the same land *gimirri* in Babylonian, *saka* in Persian, and *sakka* in Elamite.[63] The Cimmerians, who appear as adversaries of Urartu in a letter prior to 714 B.C., crossed into the West in Cappadocia, before establishing themselves at Sinope, conquering Gyges, and going as far as Ephesus.[64] One may observe a gradual movement of the Cimmerians from the East to the West. Before 655, at the time of the campaign against Teumman, the Assyrians encountered Tugdamme, king of the Umman-Manda, who had to flee and leave his "place" to this son, who had a good Iranian name—Sandakshatru. One will find him in Lydia referred to as Saka-Ugutumki, (thus a Scythian). He entered into intrigue with the King of Tabal, Mugallu. He paid tribute to Assurbanipal and overthrew Gyges who had negotiated with Psammetichus about 652. We would date then with Hartmann the Cimmerian-Scythian threat to about 657 either in Amurru or in Elam. Afterwards they became the allies of Assyria and made some raids into Anatolia.

Around 639, save for one year, the Annals fall silent, so that we know of the following years of Assurbanipal's reign only from the dates of contracts and later witnesses, such as the inscription of the mother of Nabonidus. The above date is important, for we have seen that it was the time of the accession of Josiah, the offensive of Psammetichus into Philistia, and the beginning of the Scythian domination according to Herodotus. As R. Labat[65] has demonstrated the Scythian domination overlaps with at least a part of the reign of Cyaxares, for the better

---

[62]This is the opinion of Streck (*Assurbanipal* I, p. ccclxxvi; III, p. 784.).

[63]Cf. Weissbach, *Inschriften der Achemeniden*, pp. 12f. (Behistun), 82ff. (Nakš-i-Rustam). We have not forgotten that Tugdamme, dispossessed, has left his place to his son, then with some Cimmerians.

[64]E. Cavaignac recalls (*JA*, 1962, p. 156) that the common reckoning dates the foundation of Sinope to 630.

[65]See note 21.

manuscripts of Herodotus do not say: "The Scythians, then, ruled Asia for twenty-eight years, . . . after which Cyaxares who had reigned 40 years died," but "after which Cyaxeres died, who had reigned 40 years, including the time of the Scythian domination." The death of Astyages dates between 553 and 550.[66] The 75 years which elapsed between the death of Astyages and the accession of Cyaxares dates the beginning of the latter's reign to 628–625. This confirms at least the partial concurrence proposed by R. Labat between Cyaxares' reign and the Scythian domination that, at the latest, concludes at the battle of Megiddo in 610 or 609.[67]

ZEPHANIAH AND JEREMIAH

The Scythians have left some traces of their passage into the North and in Anatolia. One may locate them not only at Ziwiye,[68] but also at Hasanlu,[69] and at Neapolis of the Scythians, Karmir-Blour,[70] at the beginning of the 6th century. Scythian art is even present at Sardis, which gives witness to the defeat of Gyges.[71] But by contrast traces of the Scythians are very meager in Syria and in Palestine.[72] One used to be able to believe that the name of Scythopolis given to Beisan in the Greek epoch was derived from the presence of the Scythians in the region. But Tcherikover[73] has challenged that, and Avi-Yonah thinks that the name comes from a κληρουχία established by the Ptolemies.[74] It is in fact the epoch of the Hellenization of Palestine by the Diadochi, though in other regions. As for the Bible, it only mentions the Ashkenaz in three texts of the 6th century. Here, these people are considered to be of the same stock as the Cim-

---

[66]There are some uncertainties in the Median chronology. Herodotus fixes the reign of Cyrus at 29 years (I, 214), but certain other authors say 30 or 31 years (cf. E. Legrand, op. cit., p. 202, note 1). The date of the death of Cyrus is now fixed in the summer of 530 (R. Parker and W. Dubberstein, Babylonian Chronology, Providence 1956, p. 14). His victory over Astyages, before the taking of Harran by Nabonidus, perhaps dates between the 3rd and 6th years of the latter, thus between 553 and 550 for a reign beginning in 556.

[67]One usually says 609, but as a consequence of the works prior to the article by Parker who traces the death of Psammetichus to 610 and the presence of an Egyptian army at Harran in the 16th year of Nabopolassar (610). J. Yoyotte has proposed (SDB, VI, 380) the connection between Megiddo and Harran. But some doubts remain over the accession of Nabopolassar, consequently his "1st year" began probably in the spring of 626.

[68]André Godard, Le trésor de Ziwiyé, Haarlem 1950, who is not very convinced of the "Scythian" character of this treasure.

[69]Robert H. Dyson, in JNES, 1965, p. 207.

[70]B. B. Piotrovsky, P. N. Schultz . . . S. P. Tolstov, Ourartou, Neapolis des Scythes, tr. fr. A. Belkine. Paris 1954, p. 56.

[71]David Gorden Mitten in Bib. Arch., XXIX, 1966, p. 45.

[72]One has some examples, for instance, at Tell el Šafi, H. Thiersch, Die neuen Ausgrabungen in Palästina, in Archaeol. Anzeiger, 1908, p. 374.

[73]V. Tcherikover, Die hellenistischen Städtegründungen, Leipzig 1927, pp. 71f.; F. M. Abel, Géographie de la Palestine, II, p. 281.

[74]M. Avi-Yonah, "Scythopolis," in IEJ, XII, 1962, pp. 123–134.

merians, appear as a distant nation, and by no means seem to occupy any land. The Book of Kings, finished in the sixth century with some seventh century sources, does not mention them.

More curious is the fact that we have for the second half of the seventh century some relatively well dated prophetic books, and yet at first glance they do not appear to allow a Scythian hiatus between the collapse of the Assyrian menace which occurs for Nahum around 614–612 and the Chaldean threat which by the time of Habakkuk is already realized. Only Jeremiah in the oracles of his youth (4:5–5:21, 6:1–26, 14:7–15:6) speaks in general terms of an invasion coming from the North, of a "great nation stirring from the farthest parts of the earth; they lay hold on bow and spear, they are cruel (ʾakzârî) and have no mercy" (6:22). It is not customary for pre-exilic prophets to leave people unnamed in this way. Some have thought of an anticipation of the Chaldean invasion, but Jeremiah knows very well how to name them, as in the oracles where he personally speaks of the Chaldeans (24:5) or of Nebuchadnezzar their king (40:2f.). Others have thought about an apocalyptic invasion, but the apocalyptic genre has not hindered Ezekiel from giving a name to the invader, Gog (probably Gyges), King of Magog. It was Venema in 1765 who first associated this coming invasion from the North with the Scythian invasion of Herodotus. He was followed by Duhm and many others, including Skinner.[75]

One is able to follow its stages on the map. The danger begins in Dan and Ephraim (4:15), but it is Jerusalem which is threatened. That army of "horsemen and archers" (6:23) attacks Benjamin in chapter 6 with the siege of Jerusalem beginning at v. 3. Supposing that Beth-haccherem is rightly Ramat Rahel,[76] so the city of Jerusalem is blockaded. Many of the villages are destroyed together with their populations (4:5–9), but the city is not

[75] *Prophecy and Religion*, 1922, pp. 35ff. In the same sense, H. H. Rowley, *Prophecy and Religion in Ancient China and Israel*, London, 1956, p. 30; Ewald, Eichhorn, Cornill, and others cited by A. Condamin, *Jérémie*, Paris, 1936, pp. 62f. Condamin himself is opposed, pp. 61–67, as also Rudolph, *Jeremia*, Tübingen 1947, pp. 41–43; O. Eissfeldt in Robinson-Horst, *Die zwölf kleinen Propheten²*, Tübingen 1954, pp. 188–189; A. Penna, *Geremia*, Rome-Turin, 1952, pp. 84f.; F. Wilke, *Das Skythenproblem im Jeremiabuch* (*Alttest. St. Kittel*, Leipzig 1913, pp. 222–254). Certain ones like Volz and others have an undetermined enemy, others an apocalyptic enemy. Most, above all J. Hyatt, point to the Chaldeans as fitting better the description made by Jeremiah. But certain features do fit (calvary and archers). To transfer with Hyatt (*JBL*, 1956, pp. 277–284) all the oracles to the Babylonian period does violence to the structure of the book and does not consider the difference between the Jeremiah of Anathoth (v.g. 11:21) under Josiah and the Jeremiah of Jerusalem under Jehoiakim. The prophet frequently inserts his oracles into events. It remains to detect what these events were. The texts which speak of a ministry under Josiah (1:2, 3; 3:6; 22:11, 18; 25:1, 3 . . .) are numerous enough to merit an historical investigation.

[76] Y. Aharoni, "Excavations at Ramat-Rahel," in *IEJ*, VI, 1956, p. 152; J. T. Milik, *ADAJ*, IV/V, 1960, pp. 151f. For another position see G. Garbini, "Sul nome antico di Ramat Rahel," in *Riv. St. Or.*, XXXVI, 1961, pp. 199–205.

taken. One should note the analogy of certain expressions of Jeremiah with those which were used by Isaiah to describe the Assyrian invasion (Isa. 5:27f., 8:7f., 17:12–14, 28:27; cf. Jer. 5:22 and 30; Isa. 28:11 and Jer. 5:15). Jeremiah seems to place his thoughts into some pre-existing categories pertaining to the fall of Nineveh, and S. Mowinckel appears to me to have reason to suggest[77] that the Chaldeans and the Scythians are the two groups being evoked.

This is explained by the stages of the placement of the oracles of the prophet into writing.[78] The first of these redactions is made by Baruch according to the order of Jeremiah in 605/4, when Jehoiakim is king and the Chaldeans of Nebuchadnezzar are the threatening enemy. But these oracles put into writing are those of his youth, oracles which do not allude to the Chaldeans. The threat was the same, but the enemy has changed. From this comes the use of a deliberately imprecise expression: an enemy coming from the North, from Syria, the area through which the Chaldeans will come even as the Assyrians or the Scythians who preceded them had come. It remains to be seen whether the Scythians had come for their own account, since Assyrian power could have already collapsed in the region, or whether the Scythians had come as auxiliary troops of the Assyrians.[79] We should not forget the submission of Tugdamme, the Scythian-Cimmerian, at the fall of Gyges, and the Scythian fidelity which made the first attack of Cyaxares against Nineveh to fail. It is in 614 or 623 (Cavaignac) that this attack occurred, but we have seen that Cyaxares became king of the Umman-Manda according to the terminology of the Chronicle of Gadd. We should no longer forget that Herodotus' information about Palestine is limited and linked to Ashdod and the sanctuary of Ashkelon.

How then are the succession of events and the role of the Scythians to be described?

There was at the first the murder of Amon who was subservient, as was Manasseh, to Assyrian domination. The coup d'etat of his "servants" was contemporaneous with the beginning of the siege of Ashdod by Psammetichus. And A. Malamat has correctly connected the two events.[80] One well knows the extent to which the pro-Egyptian party had grown during the reigns of Hezekiah, Jehoiakim, and Zedekiah. One can with great likelihood attribute to this party the murder of Amon.

---

[77] *VT*, 1962, p. 287: "There is no sufficient reason to eliminate all the account of Herodotus as legendary."

[78] Cornill already has thought of these two aspects of the question.

[79] W. Cannon already has suggested that we should see the Scythians as some auxiliary troops, but he made them auxiliaries of the Chaldeans (*ZAW*, 1925, p. 81), whereas the understanding between Assurbanipal and the Cimmerians, which originates between Esarhaddon and the Išguzay and continues until the attack of Madyes against Cyaxares, makes me believe that they are the auxiliaries of the Assyrians. This better suits the chronology.

[80] *Israel Expl. Journal* III, 1953, p. 25–29; see also *idem.*, I, 1950/1, p. 156.

The beginning of the activity of Zephaniah is best situated at this point. It has been noted that the superscription of the book recounts his genealogy unto the fifth generation in order to emphasize that he descended from Hezekiah. Prophecy, silent since the disappearance of Isaiah, is revived after several decades in a dynastic and nationalistic sense. The attack is sharp against Assyrian influences at the court of Judah, ". . . officials, and the king's sons and all who array themselves in foreign attire" (1:8).[81] We shall not dwell here upon the opposition, the outcry which comes from the "new town," men of Mortar, near to the Fish Gate.[82] That town, or quarter, is the one where Josiah would have the prophetess Huldah sought out (II Kgs 22:14), the "daughter of Zion" (Zeph 3:14), which consisted essentially of refugees from Samaria (a remnant from "Israel") who eagerly supported Assyrian domination over Israel and a pro-Assyrian policy. But more interesting is the external situation,[83] as it is described in chapter 2. The first country mentioned is Philistia, and the first three towns threatened by the war are Gaza, Ashkelon (mentioned twice in vv. 4 & 7), and Ashdod, precisely the same three towns that interest Herodotus. The prophet expresses the customary tone for prophecies against the nations which follow in the line of execration texts and treaty curses in the case of infidelity. But he announces a restoration of this maritime confederation to the "remnant of the house of Judah" (and no longer Israel). Each of the terms should be carefully weighed, but this is not the place.

We lack enough details to determine the exact range of meaning of the oracle against Moab and Ammon.[84] But the matter concludes with these two nations who are disputing over influence in Palestine. However, the great adversary is still Assyria, with its two cities, Assur and Nineveh. It is still Assyria who is the enemy that threatens the kingdom and its dynasty and imposes disagreeable officials. Zephaniah returns again to this in 3:3.

But what is more suggestive is the manner in which he expresses himself about Egypt. He does not even mention it by name. But he has one verse (2:12) dealing with Ethiopia: "You also, O Ethiopians, slain by my sword them(selves)!" There is no verb; it is noun phrase which is not to be

---

[81] There are some other allusions difficult to catch.

[82] In respect to the "Mishneh," see our communications in the Fourth Congress of Jewish Studies (Jerusalem, July, 1965), "Histoire et Géographie en Mic., IV." This makes it identical to the city of Zion, not in terms of the population of the city, but rather like "the daughters of Heshbon," the "daughters of Yazer," . . . a city or dependent, fortified quarter.

[83] It is this international situation which unfortunately is not studied by the commentators of Zephaniah, v.g. *JNES*, 1948, pp. 25–29.

[84] The threat against Moab and Ammon is best explained, however, if it is near to the campaign of Assurbanipal against Uate^c (or Iaute) of Sumu-il (Ismael) and Qedar which dates from 643/2. It will not be renewed before the fall of the Assyrian empire, and that leads one to date the oracle of Zephaniah close to the beginning of Josiah's reign, three or four years after the event.

understood as referring to the future. Zephaniah here tolls the bell for the Ethiopian dynasty. Tirhakah was dead by 663. Tanatumun, after an initial success, had to run away and died shortly after 655 when he had lost suzerainty of Thebes where Psammetichus made Shepenwepet II and Montuemhat acknowledge Nitocris.[85] The political position of Zephaniah is now clear. He does not have a single word against Psammetichus and the Saites. On the contrary he celebrated his victories at Thebes and in Philistia and awaited from his action a change in the government of Jerusalem, the ruin of Assyria, and the deliverance of Israel.

But we know that the hopes of Zephaniah and the coup d'etat by the servants of Amon were short-lived. In one of those brief accounts, to which only it has the secret, the Book of Kings tells us that "the people of the land slew all those who had conspired against King Amon, and the people of the land made Josiah his son king in his stead (II Kgs 21:24)." The rather clumsy repetition of the "people of the land" gives the impression of two distinct acts, and it is not impossible that it may be the redactor of the Book of Kings who had preferred to place the proclaiming of Josiah king after the punishment of the murderers. For the redactor, evidently much later, of the superscription of the Book of Zephaniah, Josiah is already king when the prophet intervenes. But it is possible that Josiah may not have been the oldest son of Amon and that the conspirators may have proclaimed as king another older son.

Josiah was only eight years old, and he would be a minor for a long time. In any case, the assassination of Amon had alarmed the loyalty of a population very attached to the dynasty, especially since the adventurism of Athaliah.

But there was not only an internal reaction against the conspirators. We know according to Herodotus that the offensive of Psammetichus was checked in 638 at the city of Ashdod. It is the Scythian invasion, or more probably the sending of Scythian and other contingents by a faltering but not defeated Assyrian power. The young Jeremiah who would still have been a *na^{c}ar* in 626, the 13th year of Josiah, was at this time a child, perhaps about ten years old. A member of the family of the local priesthood of Benjamin, he was at Anathoth when the invaders passed through. He would have heard the invitation to escape to Jerusalem (6:1). He would have heard the trumpet blast, signalling the call to escape into the fortified cities. The news came from Dan and Ephraim. The signal is raised at Beth-haccherem. These are the reminiscences of the Assyro-Scythian response to the efforts of the murderers of Amon who were allied with Psammetichus. The prophet would recall and use these reminiscences in evoking the Chaldean threat some thirty years later. Assyria is always there. It is Assyria that Nahum will attack and not the Scythians. From the point of

[85]See Drioton-Vandier, *L'Égypte*[4], Paris 1962, pp. 674ff., and J. Leclant, *Montouemhat* (cf. note 9).

view of the Israelite sources, the Scythians may have only been some of Assyria's allies, and we have noted in the Greek and cuneiform texts features of their understanding with Assyrian power. That power would be truly shaken in the West only in 626, with the independence of Babylon, and that is the date of Jeremiah's call. As early as the 8th year of his reign (II Chr 34:3), the approximate date of the death of Assurbanipal, Josiah returned to the God of his fathers, an important sign in a period where religion and nationalism were still bound together. According to the same Book of Chronicles, he had begun his reform as early as 627/6. The call of Jeremiah may be an echo of the reform. But it is in the eighteenth year (perhaps after the first offensive of Cyaxares against Nineveh according to M. Cavaignac, in any case after the death of Assur-etil-ilani), that he extended his power over Israel by means of a religious and national revival. The Egypt of Necho became the enemy capable of ejecting the meager Scythian garrisons remaining at Ashdod and Ashkelon. In the North as well as the South the Assyrians were abandoned by their auxiliaries for 50 years. In the light of all these texts one may conclude that there was a "Scythian domination" in Syro-Palestine, but it had only been a last reflection of Assyrian control.[86]

[86]I thank M. R. Labat, professor at the Collège du France, who has consented to read over this text and suggested certain corrections. (I have returned to this subject in the article, "La vie de Jérémie dans son contexte national et international" (*La Livre de Jérémie, Le prophète et son milieu, les oracles et leur transmission,* Leuven 1981, 21–39) where I inadvertently allowed three mistakes to escape my attention: p. 21, line 6, read "2 de Adar" (and not 16; cf. p. 35, line 7); p. 21, line 22, read "26ème dynastie (saïte)" (and not 25ème); and p. 34, line 22, read "4ème année" (and not 5ème; cf. p. 24). Now, to draw attention to my new positions:

1. P. 25, note 17: I have been won over to the position of F. M. Cross and D. N. Freedman who date the revolt of Josiah against Assyria in 628/7.

2. P. 25, note 18: I now accept the date of 644 for the death of Gyges, as proposed by A. Spalinger.

3. P. 25, note 19: the date of 655 appears to me to be in fact too early for the death of Tugdamme (see the studies by A. R. Millard and A. Spalinger).

4. P. 34, note 41: The position of E. Lipinski in regard to the *magdôlos* of Herodotus appears to me to be solid, as well as the date of 601/600 for the taking of Gaza that is mentioned in Jer 47:1).

8

The Enemy from the North and the Chaos Tradition[1]
Brevard S. Childs

I. THE PROBLEM

The "enemy from the north"[2] has long been a controversial subject in the history of OT scholarship. The great quantity of literature on the subject has concerned itself, by and large, with the problem of the identification of the enemy.[3] Because the subject has been dealt with chiefly as an historical problem, the important literary side of the development of the enemy motif within Israel's tradition has not been adequately treated. Wellhausen[4] suggested that the enemy in the pre-Exilic period was a concrete historical enemy which varied according to the political scene, but in the post-Exilic period took on a fanciful apocalyptic coloring. This, however, was more of a suggestion than a proof. The precise development of the enemy-from-the-north tradition into an eschatological motif remained unclear.

The purpose of this paper is to attempt a clarification of that problem. The method of approach is as follows:

[1]Grateful appreciation is expressed to the Editorial Committee for the many helpful suggestions given to improve this paper, especially to G. Ernest Wright and David Noel Freedman. (This paper originally appeared in the *Journal of Biblical Literature* 78 (1959) 187–198, Ed.).

[2]We understand by the term "enemy from the north" those passages in which an attacking nation from the north is mentioned (e.g. Jer 4:6). Included also are those passages in which the northerly direction of the enemy can be ascertained without the specific mention of the word (e.g. Isa 5:26 ff.). Finally, we feel justified in treating those passages in which the description of the enemy evidences such similarity with the above passages that a sharing of a common tradition is presumed (e.g. Isa 13:4 ff.).

[3]For an exhaustive bibliography, cf. J. P. Hyatt, "The Peril from the North in Jeremiah," *JBL*, LIX (1940), 499 ff. To this should be added: K. Meuli, "Scythica," *Hermes*, LXX (1935), 128 ff.; A. Lauha, *Zaphon. Der Norden und die Nordvölker im Alten Testament*, in *Annales Academiae Scientiarum Fennicae*, XLIX, 2 (1943); R. de Langhe, *Les textes de Ras Shamra-Ugarit et leurs rapports avec le milieu biblique de l'Ancien Testament* (Gembloux, Paris, 1945), II, 217 ff.; A. S. Kapelrud, *Joel Studies* (Uppsala, 1948), 93 ff.

[4]J. Wellhausen, *Prolegomena to the History of Israel* (Eng. trans.; Edinburgh, 1885), 419.

1) To give evidence that the verb רעשׁ (shake) evolved into a technical term within the language used to depict a return, or threatened return, of chaos at the end of the current era;

2) To give evidence that the enemy-from-the-north tradition was assimilated into the "chaos myth"[5] as shown by its use of רעשׁ.

II. רעשׁ AND THE CHAOS TRADITION

The verb רעשׁ, meaning "to shake," appears 29 times in the OT: the *qal* form appears 21 times, the *nifal* once, and the *hifil* 7 times. The appearance of the verb in Ps 72:16 should not be included in this study since, as Köhler suggests,[6] it is probably derived from another root. The noun רעשׁ occurs 17 times.

The verb has the meaning of "quake, tremble, or shake." It is used in the majority of cases with reference to the quaking of the earth (Judg 5:4; II Sam 22:8; Isa 13:13), parts of the earth (Jer 4:24; Nah 1:5), or the heavens (Joel 2:10). It is used of buildings, but usually accompanied by the shaking of the earth (Amos 9:1). It seldom occurs in reference to man, and then its reference is to man as part of the inhabitants of the earth (Ezek 38:20). Only in the *hifil* does it acquire a psychological connotation of shaking from fear (Ezek 31:16).

The noun has as its primary meaning "earthquake" (I Kings 19:11, 12; Amos 1:1; Zech 14:5). Its meaning is expanded to include the rattle of javelins (Job 41:21), the rumbling of wheels (Jer 47:3), and the trembling of a horse (Job 39:24). Isaiah uses the noun to encompass all the tumult of war (9:4). Ezekiel employs the word once in the sense of quaking from fear (12:18). The word appears twice in Ezekiel in an attempt to describe unique sounds: the departure of the glory of Yahweh (3:12, 13), and the coming together of the dry bones (37:7). Finally, the word is used to denote the eschatological event of the "great shaking" (Ezek 38:19).

---

[5]The terms "chaos myth" or "chaos motif" are used throughout in a neutral way to designate the traditions dealing with the struggle between Yahweh's creative activity and the primeval forces of disorder which oppose him. Although the motif has well-known roots in Near Eastern mythology, it exhibits a uniquely Hebraic character within the OT.

The problem of tracing the sources of the OT chaos motif has greatly increased in complexity since Gunkel's epoch-making book, *Schöpfung und Chaos* (Göttingen, 1895). In Canaanite mythology the dragon fight theme existed in various forms, e.g. the smiting of Lôtân (C. H. Gordon, *Ugaritic Handbook* [rev. ed.; Rome, 1947], 67:1–5), the battle between Baal and Yam (*UH*, 68:1 ff.), "the crooked serpent" (*UH*, ᶜnt: III: 38). In these myths the battle often appears unconnected with the original creation of the world. The prophets also reflect dependence on this Canaanite tradition without reference to the creation (Amos 9:3; Isa 27:1; Nah 1:3 ff.; Hab 3:8). Nevertheless, the Canaanite mythology has been fused with the Babylonian within the OT. Cf. P. Humbert, *AOF*, XI (1936), 235 ff.; A. Lods, *RHPhR*, XVI (1936), 113 ff.; O. Eissfeldt, *Ras Schamra und Sanchunjaton* (Halle, 1939), 144 f.; W. Baumgartner, *Theologische Rundschau*, XII (1940), 188; XIII (1941), 163; J. Gray, *The Legacy of Canaan* (Leiden, 1957), 19 ff.

[6]L. Köhler, *Lexicon in Veteris Testamenti Libros* (Leiden, 1953), 903.

Very early in Israel's history the verb became associated with the theophany of Yahweh, when he revealed his power over the creation in a quaking or shaking of the earth (Judg 5:4; Ps 18:8). In both these instances the reference to the Sinai theophany is apparent. It was natural that this power of Yahweh over his creation would be expressed in terms of the defeat of the primeval chaos, when the latter was introduced into Israel from contemporary pagan mythology. Gunkel[7] was the first to point out clearly the chaos motif in Psalm 46. The waters roar and foam against Zion. The mountains *quake* (vs. 13), but the city is secure against the onslaughts of the chaos, because God dwells in her midst. In this psalm the reference to the chaos is not to Yahweh's primeval victory, as in Pss 104:6 ff., 89:10, nor is it to an eschatological chaos, as in Isa 17:12 ff.[8] Rather, within a liturgical framework, the chaos is conceived as a present force in opposition to Yahweh, and being held in submission by him.

The verb רעש appears also in Ps 77:19 in connection with the chaos theme. The waters are afraid; the deep trembles before Yahweh. The defeat of the chaos waters has been historicized and used to portray the Exodus event (cf. Isa 51:9 ff.). The shaking no longer stems from the chaos, but from Yahweh himself whose power overcomes the waters. Similarly, in Ps 18:8 and Nah 1:5 it is Yahweh who has assumed the powers once attributed to chaos; he it is who shakes the earth.

The first clearly eschatological usage of the chaos theme, again connected with רעש, occurs in Jer 4:23 ff. The coming judgment is a return to the original state of תהו ובהו before the creation.[9] To this chaos belong the return of darkness, utter silence, and the shaking of the earth.

When we enter the Exilic and post-Exilic periods, the eschatological usage of רעש in connection with the final judgment through a returned chaos is everywhere evident. In fact, it is our contention that the term has become a *terminus technicus* within the language of the return of chaos. The writer of Ezekiel 38–39 describes the approaching end of the world when distant, anti-godly nations descend upon helpless Jerusalem. At that time Yahweh ushers in his "day" (vs. 18) with the "great shaking" (רעש גדול, vs. 19). The verb appears again in vs. 20, when Yahweh shakes the world and destroys the demonic forces of Gog with rain, fire, and brimstone.

The book of Isaiah contains two non-genuine passages in which the verb is joined to the eschatological chaos. The writer pictures the day of

---

[7]H. Gunkel, *op. cit.*, 100.

[8]Cf. H. G. May, "Some Cosmic Connotations of *Mayim Rabbîm*, 'Many Waters,'" *JBL*, LXXIV (1955), 9 ff.

[9]In vs. 23, *tōhû wā* is deleted by the majority of commentators on the grounds of meter and the LXX reading (Duhm, Erbt, Cornill, Rothstein, Volz, Rudolph). There are difficulties, however, to this emendation since *bōhû* never appears alone in the OT. Duhm feels forced to emend to *pānōh*. In our opinion, the LXX reading οἰθὲν is an adequate translation of the Hebrew. The Greek can hardly be expected always to provide the same number of words as the Hebrew. The MT has rightly been retained by Gunkel, Schmidt, Nötscher, and Weiser.

Yahweh as a *shaking* of heaven and earth (13:13). Similarly, in 24:18 f. the end comes with the concomitant cosmological disturbances. In Haggai the verb רעשׁ appears three times in reference to the end of the old age when the "heavens and the earth" will be shaken (2:6, 7, 21).

Finally Joel uses the verb twice, both times in reference to the final judgment through a returned chaos. In 2:10 the locust plague has reached demonic proportions and become the eschatological judgment. Not only does the earth quake, but the heavens tremble and the sun and the moon are darkened. Joel 4 is drawn from a tradition similar to Ezekiel 38–39. Again the day of Yahweh is preceded by the assembly of the multitudes around Jerusalem. Then begins the final convulsions, as Yahweh *shakes* the heavens and the earth to end the old age (vs. 16).

We feel that this evidence supports the conclusion that the word רעשׁ became embedded in the chaos tradition of Israel, and developed into a technical term for the eschatological chaos during the post-Exilic period.

III. THE ENEMY-FROM-THE-NORTH AND THE CHAOS TRADITION

We shall now examine the passages in which the enemy-from-the-north appears. We believe that it is sound procedure to begin with Jeremiah, because the enemy appears most frequently here and in sharpest outline. The following are the genuine Jeremiah passages dealing with the enemy: 1:13–15, 4:5b–8, 11b–17a,[10] 19–21, 29–31, 5:15–17, 6:1–5, 22–26. We shall treat 8:16 and 10:22 separately because they pose particular problems. Chap. 4:23–26 will also be discussed below.

These passages depict the enemy in the following way: he comes from the north (1:14 f., 4:6, 6:1, 22), from a distant land (4:16, 5:15, 6:22). It is an "ancient" and "enduring" nation (5:15) speaking a foreign tongue (5:15). All of them are mighty men (5:16) and without mercy (6:23). The suddenness of the attack is emphasized (4:20, 6:26). The enemy rides upon swift horses (4:13, 4:29) with war chariots (4:13) and is armed with bow and spear (4:29, 6:23). He uses battle formations (6:23) and attacks a fortified city at noon (6:4, 5). While a very plastic picture is given, there is no direct evidence by which to identify it with an historical nation. Certain expressions stand out by their frequency such as the "evil from the north" (4:6, 6:1; cf. 1:14). The recurrence of the expressions "from a distant land" (4:16), "from afar" (5:15), "from the farthest parts of the earth" (6:22), is characteristic. So also is the encircling of the city (4:17, 6:3).

W. Staerk, in an important article,[11] felt that central to an understanding of Jeremiah's enemy was its mythical character: "Es geht in dieser Bildsprache immer um eine mythische Gestalt und um einen Weltunter-

---

[10]There is general disagreement as to length of this passage. Duhm includes 11b–18 (omit 14) as the unit, Erbt and Schmidt 15–18, Rothstein and Hyatt 13–18, Volz 15–17. The unit can hardly begin at 15 since it is related to 13. We are inclined to agree with Duhm.

[11]W. Staerk, "Zu Habakuk 1:5–11. Geschichte oder Mythos," *ZAW* LI (1933), 1 ff.

gangsmythos" (p. 12). In our opinion, however, there is nothing in these passages which can be termed as mythical. Expressions such as "chariots like the whirlwind" (4:13) are common in the OT, describing suddenness and terror (Job 27:20; Prov 1:27). While the term *gibbôrîm* can have a mythical meaning (Gen.6:4; Ezek 32:27), very often it means simply elite, trained soldiers (Josh 1:14; I Sam 2:4). With the exception of Jer 8:16, there is no indication that the enemy in Jeremiah possesses superhuman characteristics.

The central passage in Isaiah is 5:26–29. This passage gives no direct evidence by which we can identify the enemy. Other passages indicate that Isaiah had Assyria in mind as the enemy from the north (10:5, 12, 10:28 ff.); nevertheless, there remains a certain element of indetermination in his description. We hear of a "storm coming from afar" (10:3), "smoke out of the north" (14:31), "thunder of many peoples" (17:12). The enemy comes from afar (5:26), with tremendous speed (vs. 26). It is a well-trained and prepared army (vss. 27–28) with chariots and horses (vs. 27).

The similarity of Isaiah's description with that in Jeremiah is noteworthy. The enemy comes from "afar" (Isa 5:26; Jer 4:16, 5:15), from the "end of the world" (Isa 5:26; Jer 6:22). He approaches swiftly (Isa 5:26; Jer 4:13) with chariots like "the stormwind" (Isa 5:28; Jer 4:13). Isaiah's description in 5:27, "none is weary, none stumbles," is a picture of the *gibbôrîm* (Jer 5:16).

Again we feel that there are no mythical elements attributed to the enemy in the genuine Isaiah passages, although there is admittedly a difficulty in distinguishing mythical expressions from mere hyperbole. The mention of Yahweh, who "whistles for it from the ends of the earth" (5:26), certainly promotes a strange and terrifying atmosphere while not being actually mythical. The later gloss in 5:30 is interesting, however, in this regard. In spite of the difficulty in syntax, we have an example of cosmological disturbance joined to that of the enemy.

The enemy appears once again in Hab 1:5–11. We learn of a ruthless nation (vs. 7), coming from afar (vs. 8), riding horses at great speed (vs. 8). He gathers many captives (vs. 9) and is able to conquer fortresses by regular war tactics (vs. 10). The similarity in the description of the enemy with that of Jeremiah and Isaiah should again be noted. He comes from afar (vs. 8) as in Jer 4:16, 5:15 and Isa 5:26. He comes swiftly (vs. 8) as in Jer 4:13, Isa 5:26. His horses are compared to eagles (vs. 8) as in Jer 4:13. The enemy is bitter, dreadful, and terrible (vss. 6–7), which is similar to Jer 6:23.

The identification of the enemy is unusually complicated in Habakkuk due to the textual and literary problems.[12] Specifically, the LXX reading in 1:6 has increased the difficulty. Regardless of what one decides textually to

---

[12] Cf. the thorough handling of the problem by C. L. Taylor, Jr., *Interpreter's Bible*, VI, 975 ff.

have been the original reading, the picture of the enemy or rather the symbolic language employed in depicting him, does not appear to rest upon an historical description of either the Babylonians or the Assyrians. In this observation Staerk was surely correct. Rather, the close similarity to Isaiah and Jeremiah in the description of the enemy indicates a dependence upon an older tradition which has been used to portray a contemporary enemy. Staerk is in error, however, in supposing the framework to be the *Welt-untergang* myth. There is nothing here to suggest a mythical enemy. To argue from vividness of language is to confuse colorful figures of speech with mythology.

It is a question as to whether one can rightly include Nah 2:2–10 and 3:1–3 within this cycle of enemy passages. We feel the same indefiniteness in regard to the identification of this enemy as in previous passages. However, Nahum's description has few significant words in common with the enemy tradition. The recurrence of words such as "soldier," "chariot," "horses," is to be explained from the common subject matter, rather than from a specific tradition. Perhaps the passages stand on the periphery of the cycle. For our study they are significant in that they lack mythical features.

We should like to summarize our evidence up to this point. In the pre-Exilic passages dealing with the enemy-from-the-north we have found no sign of the mythical interpretation of the enemy, but throughout the enemy has retained the characteristic of a human agent.[13] We feel it is very significant that in none of these passages does the root רעשׁ appear.

There are, however, certain apparent exceptions to this evidence which, upon first glance, cast grave doubts on the validity of the proposed theory. The enemy appears twice in Jeremiah in connection with the verb רעשׁ (Jer 8:16, 4:24), and once with the noun (10:22). The explicit reference in 4:24 to the returning chaos caused by the enemy, makes the interpretation of this passage crucial. Do these passages belong to the pre-Exilic oracles of Jeremiah?

---

[13]This does not rule out the possibility that the theme of the enemy-from-the-north may originally have been a mythical motif. Lauha, *op. cit*, 53 ff. has pointed out many parallels in comparative mythology in which the north is conceived of as the source of evil. Eissfeldt, *Baal Zaphon, Zeus Kasios und der Durchzug der Israeliten durchs Meer* (Halle, 1932), 22 ff., has argued convincingly from the Ras Shamra material that the northern enemy motif stems from the Syrian-Canaanite mythology associated with Baal Zaphon. However, no direct evidence has been produced which proves conclusively the source of the enemy tradition. Eissfeldt's suggestion remains an attractive theory on how such a tradition might have arisen. Lauha objects to finding a mythical source to the tradition on the ground that the enemy is too deeply anchored to "men of flesh and blood" (p. 85) to have been originally mythical. This argument is tenuous as W. Baumgartner has indicated, *Theologische Zeitschrift*, III (1947), 223 f. We conclude that the source of the tradition remains uncertain. This uncertainty, however, does not affect the concern of this paper which deals with Israel's use of the tradition. Our point is that the enemy tradition, regardless of its origin, evidences no mythical elements when it occurs in pre-Exilic literature. For the latest discussion of Baal Zaphon, cf. W. F. Albright, "Baal Zaphon," *Festschrift Alfred Bertholot* (Tübingen, 1950) 1 ff.

In Jer 8:16 the רַעַשׁ appears in a fragmentary oracle. At the sound of their horses "the whole land *shakes*." This is the first time in which the enemy has been associated with an earthquake. Does this verse belong to the enemy cycle of Jeremiah 4-6? Years ago Cornill[14] pointed out a significant difference: "Dort nervöse Unruhe, leidenschaftliche Erregung; hier dumpfe Resignation, völlige Verzweiflung." Likewise, Rudolph[15] misses in this passage "jede Mahnung zur Umkehr" and assigns it to a later period in Jeremiah's life. We are not suggesting that these arguments establish the case against the Jeremianic authorship of 8:16, but we are merely noting a difference in tone and approach from the earlier prophecies. Jer 10:22 is too fragmentary a passage to allow for any sure judgment. It could have originally belonged to the cycle in 4-6, or it could be a later imitation of these earlier poems.[16]

Finally, the Jeremianic authorship of 4:23-26 has been defended by most commentators (Duhm, Cornill, Elliot-Binns, Peake, Rudolph, Weiser). However, serious questions have been raised by some (Giesebrecht, Volz, Hyatt). The argument against the Jeremianic authorship rests on two chief points. First, the passage contains an apocalyptic portrayal of cosmic destruction which is unusual for Jeremiah. Secondly, there is a marked change in style which separates this passage from the other enemy passages.

While we feel that these arguments are cogent, one cannot deny the large element of subjectivity involved in their usage. It would be rash to deny the Jeremianic authorship merely on such evidence, especially when a theory of interpretation is involved. The danger of circular reasoning is apparent. Even the compromise theory in which these verses belong to a later state of Jeremiah's thinking remains unsupported without more objective proof. Is there any further evidence which would point to an Exilic dating of this passage? We suggest that there is neglected evidence to be found in Jeremiah's oracles against the nations (25, 46-51).

Critical judgment on the authenticity of 46-51 has varied considerably. A large number of scholars have followed the lead given by Schwally,[17] who denied the possibility that any Jeremianic content could be recovered (Wellhausen, Duhm, Volz, Skinner, Hyatt). However, there have always been those who attempted to find a kernel of genuine oracles.[18] In one of the most brilliant sections to his commentary, Rudolph returns to this

---

[14]C. H. Cornill, *Das Buch Jeremia* (Leipzig, 1905), 19.

[15]W. Rudolph, *Jeremia* (Tübingen, 1947), 55.

[16]Hyatt allows for both possibilities without passing a judgment (p. 902). Cornill notes its excessive length (p. 141), Volz its "kompilatorischen Charakter" (p. 126), Rudolph its awkward style (p. 65).

[17]F. Schwally, "Die Reden des Buches Jeremia gegen die Heiden. XXV. XLVI-LI," *ZAW*, VIII (1888), 177 ff.

[18]Cf. especially H. Bardtke, "Jeremia der Fremdvölkerprophet," *ZAW*, LIII (1935), 209 ff.; W. Rudolph, "Zum Jeremiabuch," *ZAW*, LX (1944), 95 ff. Rudolph's article can also be found in the introduction to his commentary.

problem and tries to establish criteria for distinguishing genuine oracles from the secondary. In our opinion, his efforts have been eminently successful.

Rudolph has almost universal support in eliminating as secondary the oracles against Babylon (50:1–51:58), as well as chap. 48 (against Moab) and 49:7–22 (against Edom). His arguments appear to us convincing in holding, as generally authentic, the oracles against Egypt (46:3–12, 13–26), Philistia (47:1–7), Ammon (49:1–5), Damascus (49:23–27), Arabic tribes (49:28–33), and Elam (49:34–38). The extent of the genuine oracles in chap. 25 remains controversial, although few would deny the close connection between 25 and the oracles in 46 ff. The majority of commentators regard 25:15, 16, 27–29 as genuine, but again Rudolph breaks new ground in defending vss. 32, 34 ff. with convincing evidence.[19]

The recovery of a body of genuine oracles in 46–49 bears directly on our study. The fourth year of Jehoiakim saw the defeat of the Egyptians at Carchemish (605), and the beginning of a new era for the Near East. Up to this event Jeremiah had concealed the name of the enemy-from-the-north. Now he makes it explicit: it is Babylon. Jer 25:32 picks up the earlier language of 6:22 to indicate its fulfilment.[20] In a similar fashion, 46–49 are characterized by their explicit play on the vocabulary and motifs of 4–6. Egypt shall be delivered "into the hand of a people from the north" (46:24; cf. also vss. 10, 20). Philistia shall be overwhelmed by "waters rising out of the north, etc." (47:2; cf. 6:22). The description of Damascus: "Anguish and sorrows have taken hold of her, as of a woman in travail" (49:24), reflects 6:24. The cry "terror on every side" (6:25) returns in 49:29.

We feel it is highly significant that a strong continuity exists in the concept of the enemy found in 46–49 with those classified with certainty as genuine in 4–6. Although the enemy has been named in 605, there are no significant changes in his description. The judgment executed by Babylon is thoroughly this-worldly. Moreover, in none of these passages does the verb רעשׁ appear.[21] The importance of this omission is heightened when we compare the description of the enemy in the generally acknowledged Exilic oracles against Babylon (50:1–51:58).[22] Once again earlier motifs are reworked, but with the crucial difference that now the verb רעשׁ appears. Jer 50:41–43 cites 6:22–24 almost *verbatim*, but concludes the oracle with the

---

[19]Rudolph, *Jeremia, loc. cit.*

[20]Cf. Rudolph's note on 25:38.

[21]The appearance of the noun in 47:3 does not vitiate this evidence. The common usage of the noun meaning "earthquake" or "rumble" appears in all periods of the OT. Its occurrence is frequent within a series which describes violent action (Jer 47:3; Isa 29:6; Nah 3:2). This usage is to be contrasted with those cases in which the word assumes an absolute, technical connotation as in Jer 10:22 and Ezek 38:19.

[22]The Exilic dating of 50–51 is held by Volz, Eissfeldt, Weiser, and Rudolph. Post-Exilic dating is preferred by Duhm, Hyatt, etc. Our preference is with the former, but the issue is not crucial for our thesis.

verse: "At the sound of the capture of Babylon the earth shall shake . . ." (vs. 46). The violent apocalyptic nature of Babylon's fall appears even clearer in 51:29: "The earth *trembles* and writhes in pain." The final usage of the verb appears in 49:21 against Edom, a passage whose secondary nature has already been established.

Armed with the evidence from Jer 46–49 and 50–51, we return to the question of the authorship of Jer 4:23–26. What now seems clear is the unbroken continuity which exists between the concept of the enemy found in the genuine passages of 4–6 studied above, and the concept in the genuine oracles in 46–49. The enemy has been identified, but his description as an historical enemy remains constant. There is no evidence that Jeremiah ever departed from this earlier concept,[23] even after 605. We know, however, that a new understanding of the enemy did arise from the description in Jeremiah 50–51. (This will be further corroborated when we study Ezekiel.) The evidence clearly focuses on the Exile as the decisive event which produced the change. The enemy has taken on a trans-historical, apocalyptic coloring. While we do not insist that this finally disproves the Jeremianic authorship of 4:23–26, it certainly casts doubt on its pre-Exilic dating. The passage, along with 8:16 and 10:22, reflects the catastrophic experience of Jerusalem's destruction. We leave the issue open as to whether it could possibly stem from Jeremiah. Our concern is only with the Exilic setting.

We turn to the Exilic period and find in Ezekiel's oracles against foreign nations (25–32) clear allusions to the enemy tradition.[24] Explicit reference is made to Nebuchadrezzar, "from the north," who will destroy Tyre (26:7). In striking contrast to its absence in the pre-Exilic oracles of Jeremiah against the nations, the verb רעשׁ appears four times, three times in reference to Tyre (26:10, 15, 27:28), once to Egypt (31:16). In all passages Babylon appears as the enemy, although in 31:11 f. he is described rather than named. These oracles have pictured the destruction wrought by the enemy in terms of the verb רעשׁ, but the nature of the enemy has not been appreciably altered. He is still a human enemy on the plane of history.

The marked change in the essential nature of the enemy, as well as his function, appears first in Ezekiel 38–39.[25] We hear of a great army

---

[23]We cannot agree with the attempt to date the oracles in Jer 4–6 in the same period as chap. 25, and, thereby, to obliterate the distinction between the earlier and later usage of the enemy motif. (Cf. J. Bright, "The Book of Jeremiah," *Interpretation*, IX [1955], 275 f.). This theory rests on the unproved hypothesis that Jeremiah always had the Babylonians in mind as the enemy (contra Hyatt, footnote 3). Also it fails to recognize the conscious return in chaps. 25 and 46–49 to the earlier motifs in order to demonstrate the fulfilment of the prophetic word.

[24]We are aware of the difficulty involved in dating these oracles precisely. Nevertheless, it is becoming increasingly clear that objective literary or historical criteria are missing by which to distinguish between primary and secondary levels.

[25]We have no new evidence to add to the complex problem of the authorship and dating of Ezekiel 38–39. The strongest case against the authorship of Ezekiel is made by H. Gressmann,

gathering from the "uttermost parts of the north" (38:6, 15, 39:2), a great host, riding horses, coming up "like a cloud" to plunder (38:10). They are well-equipped *gibbôrîm* dressed in full armor with shield and bucklers (38:4). Not only are the peoples of the north involved, but it would appear that the whole world is mustering for the attack (38:5–6). The appearance of Gog falls "in the latter years" (38:8, 16), which indicates that the events described have passed from the plane of history and entered the apocalyptic age. The battle is considered the final stage before the coming of the new age in 38:19 ff. Yahweh decides the outcome by destroying the enemy with rain, hail, fire and brimstone. Significantly, these events are designated as the day of the "great shaking" (רעש גדול, vs. 19), in which the world's inhabitants *shake* before Yahweh (vs. 20). The description which began on the nebulous fringes of history has been elevated into the trans-historical, into an arena beyond direct relation to contemporary reality. Gog has become the representative of the cosmic powers of the returned chaos which Yahweh destroys in the latter days, powers which cannot be described as historical, though presented partly in historical dress.

A similar transformation of the old enemy tradition appears in Isaiah 13. There is almost unanimity in assigning this oracle against Babylon to the Exilic period.[26] The *gibbôrîm* (vs. 3) are summoned; there is a tumult on the mountain (vs. 4); the nations gather together (vs. 4). They come from a distant land (vs. 5), from the end of the heavens (vs. 5). This mythical army comes from the "end of the heavens," not simply to destroy one land, but the "whole world" (vs. 5).The darkness of the heavens and the cosmological shaking witness to the end of the world with the threatened return of the primeval chaos.

Isa 14:12 ff. is a taunt against the king of Babylon and not directly related to the enemy tradition. Nevertheless, it is quite remarkable that the king who dared to "sit on the mount of assembly in the *far north*" is described as the one "who made the earth tremble, who *shook* kingdoms."

The book of Joel describes a locust plague which ushers in the day of Yahweh (2:1, 11). Gressmann[27] noticed the many features which do not fit into the picture of an ordinary locust plague. The burning fire (2:3), the trembling of the earth and the heavens (2:10), the blackening of the stars (2:10), these stem from another tradition. Our suspicions are confirmed by 2:20: "I will remove the *northerner* far from you...."[28] The foreign

---

Der Messias (Göttingen, 1929), 118 ff. G. Fohrer, *Die Hauptprobleme des Buches Ezechiel* (Berlin, 1952), 93 ff. and *Ezechiel* (Tübingen, 1955), 212 ff. vigorously defends Ezekiel's authorship.

[26]Duhm, Skinner, Gray, Procksch, Eissfeldt, Pfeiffer, Rost.

[27]H. Gressmann, *Der Ursprung der israelitisch-jüdischen Eschatologie* (Göttingen, 1905), 187 ff. and *Der Messias* (Göttingen, 1929), 134 ff.

[28]The frequent attempts to emend the text have been refuted in Kapelrud's study, *op. cit.*, 93 ff. After a thorough review of the problem, he affirms the mythical interpretation of the

elements appear due to the fact that the locust plague, which enters ordinarily from the south, has been described in the language of the enemy-from-the-north tradition. The relation between the locusts and the trans-historical cataclysm is clearly evident in 2:10: "The earth *quakes* before them, the heavens tremble, the sun and moon are darkened and the stars withdraw their shining." In chap. 4 the parallel to Ezekiel's picture is striking. Again the attacking nations descend in the latter day upon helpless Zion. Yahweh intervenes at the last moment to *shake* the heavens and the earth (4:16). Clearly the enemy-from-the-north has become identified with the return of chaos. The occurrence of the verb רעשׁ in 2:10 and 4:16 would appear to confirm this conclusion.

We should like to summarize our evidence. The root רעשׁ appears to have developed into a technical term for the final shaking of the world at the return of chaos. In tracing the tradition of the enemy-from-the-north, however, we discovered that, within the great body of pre-Exilic writings, the enemy remained on the plane of human history, and, significantly, the word רעשׁ is never used. A transition appears to take place in the early Exilic period, when the enemy took on superhuman characteristics and could be depicted with the aid of language drawn from the chaos myth. In the late Exilic and post-Exilic writings the enemy tradition appears invariably with the "great shaking"; the two must have been fused together.

IV. CONCLUSION

This study of the development within Israel's tradition is of interest for several reasons. First, it throws light on the perennial problem of the shift from prophetic to apocalyptic eschatology,[29] and indicates, within a controlled area, some of the essential differences. Secondly, the study supports the view that, in expressing apocalyptic eschatology, Israel reversed her usual handling of mythical traditions. Whereas throughout her earlier history, Israel had reacted against the intrusion of mythical material by historicizing the broken myth within her tradition,[30] in this case, Israel has not "demythologized" the myth, but instead has "mythologized" an historical tradition. This has not been done unthinkingly, but was effected as a testimony to her deepened understanding of the full dimensions of divine judgment and redemption arising out of the experience of the Exile.

---

verse. His defense of a pre-Exilic dating, however, has not succeeded in refuting the traditional arguments for a post-Exilic date (cf. O. Eissfeldt, *Einleitung in das Alte Testament* [2 Aufl.; Tübingen, 1956], 477 ff.).

[29]Cf. Th. C. Vriezen, "Prophecy and Eschatology," *Supplements to Vetus Testamentum*, I, (1953), 199 ff.

[30]The subject of Israel's handling of the myth is treated by the author in *Myth and Reality in the Old Testament*, SBT 27 (London: SCM Press, 1960).

9
Carchemish and Jeremiah*
C. F. Whitley

I.

The date of the beginning of Jeremiah's ministry has long been debated by Old Testament scholars. In a recent article in "Vetus Testamentum" I briefly sketched the history of this debate, and suggested that the battle of Carchemish in 605 B.C. was the signal for the prophet's call.[1] More recently, however, in the pages of "Zeitschrift für die Alttestamentliche Wissenschaft" J. P. Hyatt, while welcoming my proposals as a whole, questioned some of my arguments, and re-stated his own view that Jeremiah began his ministry in the year 609.[2]

In my article I observed that, apart from the superscription to the book of Jeremiah, we have no precisely dated material till chapter xxv. We there read that "in the fourth year of Jehoiakim ... the first year of Nebuchadrezzar king of Babylon" the word of Yahweh came to Jeremiah. The fourth year of Jehoiakim was, according to Jer xlvi 2, the year in which Nebuchadrezzar defeated the Egyptians at Carchemish, which in turn, as we know from Babylonian sources, was the year 605.[3] The substance of Jeremiah's utterance on this occasion was the impending invasion of the land of Judah by Nebuchadrezzar and the tribes from the north (v. 9). The fact that the threat of invasion becomes more urgent in chapter xxvi, where the prophet speaks to the people in the temple, leads me to think that this temple address followed shortly after the utterance recorded in chapter xxv. The events of chapter xxvi are indeed described as taking place "in the beginning of the reign of Jehoiakim" (v. 1). But, as I noted in my article, the writer of chapter xxviii 1 could regard the "fourth" year as falling within the beginning of a king's reign.

Hyatt finds difficulty in accepting this date of 605 for the events of chapter xxvi and doubts if appeal may be made to the evidence of xxviii 1. He believes with some scholars that the term בראשית ממלכות (in the beginning of the reign) in xxvi is to be equated with the Akkadian reš

---

*Originally published in the *Zeitschrift für die alttestamentliche Wissenschaft* 80 (1968) 38–49.

[1] 14 (1964), 467–483.

[2] "The Beginning of Jeremiah's Ministry," 78 (1966), 204–214. Cf. also his remarks in: Interpreter's Bible, V 1956, 729a.

[3] See D. J. Wiseman, Chronicles of Chaldean Kings (626–556), 1956, 25.

šarruti, and is therefore to be taken as a technical term for the "accession year."[4] This involves acceptance of the view that the Babylonian system of dating was adopted in Judah by the time of Jehoiakim. According to this system the period which elapsed from the king's accession to the next New Year (Nisan) was known as the "accession year," and his first "regnal" year began only with the New Year. Thus while Nebuchadrezzar ascended the throne in the first of Elul (August-September) 605, his first year in actual office did not begin till the New Year 604.[5] But while we have little definite evidence that the Babylonian method of dating obtained in Judah at this time, it is significant that the biblical references to Nebuchadrezzar's reign are calculated in terms of the "non-accession" method; that is, in terms of direct reckoning from the time he ascended the throne. The passage in Jer xxvi which correlates the fourth year of Jehoiakim with the first year of Nebuchadrezzar presupposes the "non-accession" system; for the fourth year of Jehoiakim, or 605, was according to Babylonian reckoning the "accession year" of Nebuchadrezzar. The "non-accession" system is similarly apparent in II Reg xxiv 8–12. We know from Wiseman's Chronicles that in the month Kislev (Nov.-Dec.) of the seventh year of his reign, Nebuchadrezzar arrived in Jerusalem and immediately took Jehoiakim captive. Jehoiakim was then succeeded by Jehoiachin, who after a three months reign was replaced by Zedekiah on the 2nd of Adar (Feb.-March).[6] But while according to the Babylonian Chronicle all this took place within Nebuchadrezzar's seventh year, the writer of II Reg xxiv 12 states that Jehoiachin was taken prisoner in the eighth year of Nebuchadrezzar, and therefore reckons his reign from 605.

In so far then as we are able to compare Hebrew chronology with instances of precise and definite contemporary Babylonian chronology it would appear that the Hebrews made their calculations on the basis of the "non-accession" year. If, moreover, בראשית ממלכות were a technical term for "the accession year" we should expect that it would be used without variation of form. Instead we have the variants בראשית ממלכת (xxvii 1 and xxviii 1) and בראשית מלכות (xlix 34), suggesting that the expression could be used in a general sense.[7]

Hyatt is again prepared to accept the text of the LXX rather than that of the Hebrew in Jer xxviii 1. The LXX reads, "and it came to pass in the fourth year of Zedekiah king of Judah, in the fifth month. . . ." It thus does not contain the phrase "In the beginning of the reign," and this phrase is also lacking in its text of xxvii 1. Both Hyatt and May accordingly regard this phrase in the Hebrew text of chapters xxvii and xxviii as a scribal

---

[4]ZAW loc. cit. 205–206.

[5]Wiseman op. cit. 46–47. 69.

[6]Wiseman op. cit. 73.

[7]Certainly in some cases the Hebrew chronology is imprecise (and it is with some justification that Hyatt describes it as "complicated and often thankless"!, loc. cit. 208).

repetition from xxvi 1.[8] But as the Hebrew text of xxvii 1 stands it is not a mere repetition of xxvi 1. It begins with the words ויהי בשנה ההיא. It may be argued that these words are likewise an editor's insertion, but his motive could only have been to note that the significant events of chapter xxvii took place in the same year as those of chapter xxviii. And from what we know of ancient Near Eastern history, it is likely that the events of chapter xxvii, as well as of chapter xxviii, took place in the period 594/93, that is, in Zedekiah's fourth year as stated in both the Hebrew and LXX texts of xxviii. During Nebuchadrezzar's tenth year (595/94) his authority at home was weakened by a revolt among his troops.[9] Reports of this rebellion naturally reached the west, and were probably the basis for a group of western states to consider revolting against Babylonian sovereignty (Jer xxvii 2ff.). Such developments likewise encouraged false prophets such as Hananiah to proclaim that the yoke of Babylon was broken and that within two years the exiles would return to Jerusalem (xxviii 2ff.). Now it will be observed that although the events of chapter xxvii were critical, the LXX does not attempt to date them. It indeed assigns the events of chapter xxviii to the fourth year of Zedekiah, but the compiler or editor of the Hebrew text could say that it was "the same year" as that in which the events recorded in chapter xxvii took place. Further, while the Hebrew text of xxv 1 correctly mentions that the fourth year of Jehoiakim was the first ("non-accession") year of Nebuchadrezzar, the LXX makes no such correlation. However, then, we may account for the chronological details of the Hebrew text they are not inconsistent with what we know of historical events.

It may, however, be more profitable to inquire whether the events depicted in Jer xxvi are more likely to have occurred in 609 or in 605. It is clear that the contemporary political scene was one of crisis; for as the people resort to the temple Jeremiah warns them of impending and immediate disaster. But could he envisage such a situation in 609, immediately after the accession of Jehoiakim? Hyatt maintains that the historical situation of chapter xxvi was precisely that.[10] He thinks that a single word נצלנו (we are delivered) provides the clue, and that when Jeremiah addressed the people in the temple they were celebrating a political deliverance; for the unpredictable Jehoahaz had been deposed by Necho and had been replaced by Jehoiakim who would be loyal to the wishes of Egypt. It will be observed that Hyatt bases his argument on a word from Jer vii which is the latest and most Deuteronomic account of the temple address.[11] But even so, there is not the slightest indication that the people in chapter vii

---

[8]Hyatt loc. cit. 206; H. G. May, "The Chronology of Jeremiah's Oracles," JNES 1945, 217 n. 4.

[9]Wiseman op. cit. 36 and 37.

[10]Loc. cit. 210.

[11]See my article, loc. cit. 472ff., where I draw attention to the lateness of the material of chapters i–xxiv.

are celebrating a military victory. The prophet is represented as going to the temple where some people are professing to worship Yahweh. But Jeremiah is aware that these people commit murder, stealing and such like, and now hope that an expression of confidence in the temple is sufficient to "deliver" them from the effects of their sins. The Hebrew text reads ואמרתם נצלנו למען עשות את כל־התועבת האלה (vii 10, and ye say, we are delivered, to do all these abominations). The Syriac version is, however, grammatically preferable: ואמרתם הצילנו ועשׂיתם (and ye say *deliver us* and yet ye do . . .). Now the expression הצילנו occurs in Ps lxxix 9 in the sense of deliverance from sin: "deliver us and forgive our sins." We again find it in Ps xxxix 9: "from all my transgressions deliver me"; and also in other places in the Old Testament (e. g., Ps li 16; Ez iii 9; xxxiii 9). What therefore the people are vainly requesting in Jer vii 10 is "deliverance" from their sins and short-comings.

Nor can we imagine that the danger foreseen by Jeremiah in chapter xxvi would spring from Egyptian quarters. For at that same time a prophet called Uriah preached a similar message of disaster and fled to Egypt for refuge. Jehoiakim with the co-operation of the Egyptian authorities, success-fully extradited him and put him to death (Jer xxvi 20–23). But this he could scarcely have done if Uriah had been predicting an Egyptian invasion of Judah; for Egypt now exercised a nominal control over Judah, and it would clearly be in her interests that propaganda of this nature should flourish. Altogether, then, there is little evidence to connect the events of chapter xxvi with the year 609.

There is, on the other hand, much to suggest that they pertained to the year 605. Chapter xxv contains the threat that Yahweh will bring Nebu-chadrezzar and the tribes of the north againt Jerusalem (v. 9). This threat of invasion becomes more ominous in chapter xxvi where Jeremiah is able to foretell the destruction of the temple and the depopulation of the city (v. 9). Again we read in chapter xxvi that Jeremiah is "debarred from going to the house of Yahweh" (v. 5), and was consequently compelled to commit to a scroll all the oracles he had hitherto uttered so that his scribe Baruch might read them in public on a future occassion. This Baruch did, and it is significant that the burden of his message was the destruction of Jerusalem by the king of Babylon (xxxvi 29).

Now it is highly unlikely that Jeremiah could have known of Nebu-chadrezzar's intentions in 609. For it was not clear then whether the Egyptians or the Babylonians would emerge as the eventual rulers of Syria-Palestine. The Egyptians had been in the region of the Euphrates for some time, and had been helping the Assyrians to maintain themselves against the Babylonians and their allies. But the decisive clash between the two great powers did not take place till 605 at Carchemish. Even Nebuchad-rezzar, whom Jeremiah mentions by name as the invader of Judah (xxv 9), did not appear on the military scene till immediately before the battle, when, owing to his father's illness, he acted as commander-in-chief, and he was not actually king of Babylon till a few months later.[12] But immediately following his defeat of the Egyptians, Nebuchadrezzar, as the Babylonian Chronicle testifies, conquered the whole of Syria-Palestine,[13] and according to II Reg xxiv 7 marched even as far as the Egyptian borders. It is therefore in this context of the result of the battle of Carchemish and the events which immediately followed that we must place Jeremiah's call and early ministry.

II.

The outcome of the battle of Carchemish also accounts for the appearance of the enemy known as "the foe from the north" in the prophecies of Jeremiah. And it is the mistaken identity of this people which more than any other factor has contributed to a misunderstanding of the dating of Jeremiah's work.

The most common interpretation of this ominous force is that it refers to the Scythians.[14] But this arises from an uncritical acceptance of the material in chapter i 2 which represents the prophet's call as taking place in the year 627/26 B.C. As, therefore, we have no historical evidence of an invasion of Judah at this time exegetes readily identified the evil from the north with Scythians mentioned by Herodotus in Book i 104–106. We there read that, having conquered the Medes, the Scythians "marched against Egypt; and when they were in the part of Syria called Palestine, Psammetichus king of Egypt met them and persuaded them with gifts and prayers to come no farther. So they turned back, and when they came on their way to the city of Ascalon in Syria, most of the Scythians passed by and did no harm, but a few remained behind and plundered the temple of Heavenly Aphrodite. This temple, as I learn from what I hear, is the oldest of all the temples of the goddess ... But the Scythians who pillaged the temple, and all their descendants after them, were afflicted by the goddess with the 'female' sickness, insomuch that the Scythians say that this is the cause of their disease, and that those who come to Scythia can see there the plight of the men whom they call 'Enareis.' The Scythians then ruled Asia for twenty-eight years."[15]

---

[12]Wiseman 23–27.

[13]Wiseman 25 and 69.

[14]Hence B. Duhm's "Scythian Songs," Das Buch Jeremia, 1901, 48ff.; cf. A. Condamin, Le Livre de Jérémie, 1936³, 61f., for a survey of the "Scythian" interpretation. So also the standard commentaries and introductions such as W. Rudolph, Jeremia, 1947, 3; R. H. Pfeiffer, Introduction to the Old Testament, 1941, 487 ff.; A. Weiser, Introduction to the Old Testament (Eng. trans.), 1961, 209; A. Aeschimann, Le Prophète Jérémie, 1959, 16 and 42. See, again, more recently, H. H. Rowley, "The Early Prophecies of Jeremiah in Their Setting," BJRL 48 (1962), 198ff.

[15]Translation by A. D. Godley (The Loeb Classical Library), 1921, 137. Godley comments that although the derivation of "enareis" is uncertain, it is agreed that the disease was a loss of virility, ibid. n. 2.

The Scythians were a tribe of horsemen who began migrating south-
wards from their homeland in the Eurasian steppes during the early
centuries of the first millennium B.C.[16] We hear of them in the region of
Lake Urmia in the time of Sargon II (722–705),[17] and we later read of their
alliance with Esarhaddon (680–669) in his struggles against the Medes.[18] As
the Assyrian empire declined, the Scythians penetrated still farther south
and doubtless contributed to the fall of Nineveh in 612.[19] But apart from
the reference in Herodotus we have no record of their appearance in
Palestine. The Egyptian king he mentions could have been Psammetichus I
(663–609); but it is questionable if this able ruler, who founded the twenty-
sixth dynasty and who in the early years of his reign expelled the Assyrians
from Egypt,[20] would have found it necessary to treat with the Scythians in
the manner described by Herodotus. There is, moreover, no indication in
Herodotus as to what period the twenty-eight year rule of the Scythians
covered. He does indeed say that, having subdued the Scythians, the Medes
under Cyaxeres reduced the Assyrians into subjection (i 106). Now Cyaxeres
launched his attack on the Assyrians in about 614,[21] so that the Scythians
must have been subdued before that time. The beginning of a twenty-eight
year domination would therefore be as early as 643. But at this time
Ashurbanipal (668–633) exerted his strong rule over Syria-Palestine, and
Judah, which had been a vassal of Assyria since about 700, would have
been protected by him. But even if the story in Herodotus rests on some
historical basis, and we are to accept the possibility of a Scythian invasion
of Palestine round 643, it is difficult to see how such an event could have
aroused Jeremiah to prophesy in 626 B.C.

It has, of course, been suggested that while we may accept Herodotus's
account of the Scythian invasion of Palestine, his figure of a twenty-eight
year hegemony over Asia is to be regarded as an exaggeration. Thus G. E.
Ricciotti considers that the period of their activity in the west is to be
limited to the years 632–622 B.C.[22] But there is, again, no evidence for this,
while those scholars who place their incursion round 626 appeal to no
other evidence than the books of Jeremiah and Zephaniah.[23] Accepting, on

---

[16]See Tamara Talbot Rice, The Scythians, 1958[2], 39ff.; M. Rostovtzeff, A History of the
Ancient World, 1926, 121.

[17]Rice op. cit. 44.

[18]J. Laessøe, People of Ancient Assyria (Eng. trans.), 1963, 116.

[19]See C. J. Gadd, The Fall of Nineveh, 1923, 13f.; H. Schmökel, Ur, Assur und Babylon,
1955, 141.

[20]Cf. F. K. Kienitz, Die politische Geschichte Ägyptens vom 7. bis zum 4. Jahrhundert
vor der Zeitwende, 1953, 12f.

[21]Gadd op. cit. 9.

[22]History of Israel (Eng. trans.), i 1955, 394.

[23]So T. H. Robinson wrote: "Two prophets, Zephaniah and Jeremiah, testify to their
presence and to the terror which they inspired. Both seem to have owed their initial prophetic
call to this invasion," A History of Israel, 1932, 413. See also J. Skinner, Prophecy and
Religion, 1922, 39ff., and J. A. Bewer, The Book of Jeremiah, i 1951, 21.

the other hand, that the Scythians ruled over a large part of western Asia for twenty-eight years, T. Tamara Rice thinks that they reached Egypt in 611 B.C.[24] The activities of the Scythians immediately after the fall of Nineveh are obscure. Whether or not they are to be considered an element of the Umman-Manda who were a major ally of the Babylonians against the Assyrians on this occasion, it is likely that they were present during the fall of the city.[25] But we have no evidence that they penetrated westwards towards Egypt in the following year. The Egyptians, who had been allies of the Assyrians since 616,[26] would probably be in a position to prevent any westward movement of hostile forces at this juncture. Moreover, the Scythians were themselves present in full strength at the fall of Harran in 610, and they were doubtless now in 611 preparing for this onslaught.[27]

We cannot therefore place historically the story in Herodotus i 105 that the Scythians appeared in Palestine during a period of dominion over western Asia.[28] And this is not surprising in view of what Herodotus himself says elsewhere. In Book iv 1 we read: "The Scythians, as I have before shown, ruled the upper country of Asia for twenty-eight years; they invaded Asia in their pursuit of the Cimmerians, and made an end of the power of the Medes, who were the rulers of Asia before the coming of the Scythians. But when the Scythians had been away from their homes for eight and twenty years and returned to their country after so long a time, there awaited them another task as hard as the Median war. They found themselves encountered by a great host. . . ."[29] In other words the Scythians ruled over that part of Upper Asia once dominated by the Medes. An incursion into Iranian territory seems therefore to have been the extent of their predations.[30]

But Herodotus is known to have been misleading in other instances too. For example, he exaggerates the part played by the Medes in the capture of Nineveh; and from his account one would scarcely think that the armies of Babylon were concerned in the event at all, his only reference to Babylon being that the Medes "brought all Assyria except the province of Babylon under their rule" (i 106). The legendary and romantic, again, appealed to him, and he included much material of this nature in his works.[31] Hence as F. Wilke pointed out Herodotus would have heard of the story that the Scythians suffered from "female sickness" and also of the

[24]Rice op. cit. 45.

[25]Wiseman op. cit. 15f.

[26]Gadd op. cit. 5f.

[27]Gadd op. cit. 21f.

[28]It is significant that in endeavouring to comment on this passage in Herodotus many Classical scholars can do little more than refer to the books of Jeremiah and Zephaniah; e. g., W. W. How and J. Wells, A Commentary on Herodotus, 1912, 106; T. R. Glover, Herodotus, 1924, 95.

[29]As translated by Godley op. cit. 199.

[30]Cf. A. T. Olmstead, The History of the Persian Empire, 1948, 32 n. 87.

[31]Cf. e.g., How and Wells op. cit. 44f.

aetiological explanation that at one time they visited Syria-Palestine where some of them sacked the temple of Aphrodite at Ascalon and, recognizing it as a remarkable tale, included it in his writings.[32]

But however we may regard the evidence of Herodotus there is little in the invasion poems of Jeremiah to identify the evil from the north with the Scythians. These poems may originally have constituted a separate entity, but they are now dispersed throughout the first ten chapters of the book. We recognize them, however, as comprising in the main chapters iv 5–7, 13–22, 27–31; v 15–17; vi 1–6, 22–26; viii 14–16; x 22.[33] The opening lines of the first poem suggests that an enemy is on the march from the north intent on invading Judah:

> Blow the trumpet through the land,
> cry aloud and say,
> Assemble, and let us go into the fortified cities . . .
> for I will bring evil from the north
> and great destruction.

The enemy is then referred to as a lion and a destroyer of nations. His chariots are as whirlwind and his horses swifter than eagles (iv 13). Proceeding from Dan to Mount Ephraim he hastens to lay siege to Jerusalem (iv 15–16) whose inhabitants scatter for safety (iv 29). In v 15–17 we read that the nation which comes from afar

> is an enduring nation,
> it is an ancient nation,
> a nation whose language you do not know,
> nor can you understand what they say.

Chapter vi 1–6 continues the theme of an evil looming from the north which will reach and destroy Jerusalem. V. 22–23 represent this evil as a great nation whose people

> lay hold on bow and spear
> they are cruel and have no mercy,
> the sound of them is like the roaring sea;
> they ride upon horses . . .

In viii 14–16 we have, again, a portrait of inescapable doom. The appearance of the enemy is imminent, and his approach is described thus:

---

[32]"Das Skythenproblem im Jeremiabuch" (in: Alttestamentliche Studien für R. Kittel zum 60. Geburtstag dargebracht, ed. R. Kittel), BWAT 13, 222–254. Cf. here also the comments of J. P. Hyatt, "The Peril from the North in Jeremiah," JBL 59 (1940), 499ff.

[33]Some exegetes, however, differ slightly in their estimate of the extent of the poems; see, e.g. Skinner op. cit. 33–37. 38n.; R. H. Pfeiffer op. cit. 482; Hyatt ibid. 499.

> The snorting of their horses is heard from Dan;
> at the sound of the neighing of their stallions
> the whole land quakes.
> They come and devour the land and all that fills it . . .

Finally in x 22 we read of a commotion in the north country which is destined to make the cities of Judah a desolation.

The question which now arises is whether this portrait of the enemy applies exclusively to the Scythians. It is true that from what we know of the Scythians they were accomplished horsemen and skilled in the use of the bow and spear.[34] It could therefore probably be said of them that their "horses are swifter than eagles" (iv 13) and that "they lay hold on bow and spear" (vi 3). We read, however, of a similar description of the Chaldeans in Hab i 6–11:

> For lo, I am rousing the Chaldeans,
> that bitter and hasty nation,
> who march through the breadth of the earth,
> to seize habitations not their own.
> Dread and terrible are they . . .
> Their horses are swifter than leopards,
> more fierce than the evening wolves;
> their horsemen press proudly on.
> Yea, their horsemen come from afar;
> they fly like an eagle swift to devour.
> They all come for violence . . .
> they sweep by like the wind and go . . .

Again, the expression וכסופה מרכבותיו (and his chariots as whirlwind) in Jer iv 13 is reminiscent of וגלגליו כסופה (and his wheels as whirlwind) in Is v 28. This is in a context which relates to the Assyrians, if not to the Babylonians. At any rate the author sees the enemy as "a nation afar off," who "comes from the ends of the earth," whose "arrows are sharp" and whose "horses hoofs seem like flint" (Is v 26–28). The great nation which Yahweh rouses from a far country in Jer vi 22 (וגוי גדול יעור מירכתי־ארץ) again reminds us of the great tempest which he arouses in Jer xxv 32 (וסער גדול יעור מירכתי־ארץ) where the people in question are obviously the Chaldeans. With reference to the invaders in Jer v 15 Yahweh says: הנני מביא עליכם גוי ממרחק . . . הוא גוי לא תדע לשונו ולא תשמע מה ידבר (Behold I bring upon you a nation from afar . . . a nation whose language you shall not know and you shall not understand what he says). But this similarly recalls Dtn xxviii 49 where we read ישא יהוה עליך גוי מרחק . . . גוי אשר לא תשמע לשננו (Yahweh will bring against you a nation from afar . . . a nation whose language you shall not understand). It is clear from the context that

---

[34] Cf. Rice op. cit. 39. 74–75.

this passage in Deuteronomy refers to the Chaldeans. For in v. 36–37 we find a reference to the Babylonian invasion and deportation, and to the sons and daughters who "shall go into captivity" (v. 41). Such considerations, then, indicate that there is little in the invasion poems of the book of Jeremiah to identify the evil from the north with the Scythians.

Some scholars indeed recognised the weakness of the Scythian theory, but, still accepting the traditional date of Jeremiah's call, resorted to other interpretations of the foe from the north. Thus according to P. Volz Jeremiah entered on his task believing that judgment was about to overtake Israel and that this would materialize through the convulsive movements of nations in the north. The prophet himself did not, however, connect this with any definite people. He was satisfied that Yahweh had called him to declare this message and was not interested further.[35] The view that Jeremiah thought of the foe from the north in the context of the turmoil amongst many nations was again proposed by Lauha and Rudolph, and more recently countenanced by Leslie and Lindblom.[36] A. C. Welch, on the other hand, thought that we should interpret the evil from the north in an eschatological sense. Doom is impending on the whole world and Jeremiah is entrusted with declaring it. Welch claims to recognise this theme of universal catastrophe in at least three passages (iv 23–26; iv 27–31; xxv 1–29) and concludes that the evil from the north was not an historical figure any more than the North from which he came was a point of the compass. We are rather to see in this destroyer of nations a faint indication of the figure of the Antichrist.[37] More recently A. Bentzen favoured an interpretation which is at once both historical and eschatological. The enemy in the prophet's mind was a threatening political force from Mesopotamia as well as an "actualization" of mysterious forces coming from the north.[38] Recognizing, again, that there are many features of the invasion poems which may be applied to the Chaldeans rather than the Scythians, some scholars have proposed that Jeremiah began his work in 626 expecting an invasion from the north, but when it did not materialize he recast his oracles to make them applicable to the Babylonians.[39]

But none of these views does justice to the nature of prophecy as a whole and to Jeremiah in particular. For to maintain that Jeremiah was unaware of the identity of the foe from the north overlooks the fact that the prophets were keen observers of the contemporary political scene and

---

[35]Op. cit. p. 58. Cf. also Aeschimann op. cit. 63.

[36]A. Lauha, Zaphon, der Norden und die Nordvölker im Alten Testament, 1943, 62ff. and 72ff.; W. Rudolph op. cit. 41ff.; E. A. Leslie, Jeremiah, 1954, 51; J. Lindblom, Prophecy in Ancient Israel, 1962, 371.

[37]Jeremiah: His Time and His Work, 1951 (reprint), 110–126.

[38]Introduction to the Old Testament, II 1949, 122. A. Haldar saw the foe from the north entirely in terms of cultic ideology. It was the sham fight enacted at the New Year Festival of the ancient Near East, Associations of Cult Prophets Among the Ancient Semites, 1945, 157f.

[39]E. g., Pfeiffer op. cit. 494f.; Bewer op. cit. 21. Cf. also Skinner op. cit. 230ff.

spoke a relevant word to the situation of their day. To suggest, again, that Jeremiah spoke in terms of eschatology attributes to him a doctrine not characteristic of his teaching.[40] To suppose that Jeremiah was mistaken in his first utterances and was compelled to modify them in accordance with later developments likewise overlooks the efficacy of the divine word. For as we read in Is lv 11 the word of Yahweh is powerful in itself and accomplishes all its purposes.[41]

In view of the relevance of the prophetic word to the events of history we must attempt to place the invasion oracles of Jeremiah against a tangible historical background. He began his ministry with an expectation of the immediate appearance of the foe from the north (xx 9 cf. i 14–15). The interpretation of this foe cannot therefore be indifferent to the time and circumstances of his call. Earlier in this article we have argued that Jeremiah did not assume his office till after the battle of Carchemish. And as the victor of Carchemish cannot be dissociated from the tribes of the north, it was also this event which provoked the invasion poems. For the prophet was now able to discern that the victorious Babylonians were intent on conquering the west and that the subjugation of Judah was part of their policy. It may be that in the reference to the "tribes from the north" we recognize certain elements of the Umman-Manda which had earlier aligned themselves with the Chaldean forces, but it was this impatient, invincible army which Jeremiah described as "a boiling pot facing away from the north" (i 13). Under Nebuchadrezzar's dynamic leadership this military force was a veritable "evil from the north," capable of "great destruction" (iv 6). Emerging in 605 it was to constitute a menace to Judah till the fall of Jerusalem some twenty years later.

[40]See here the present writer, The Prophetic Achievement, 1963, 217f.
[41]Cf. H. W. Robinson, Inspiration and Revelation in the Old Testament, 1946, 170.

10

Some Remarks on
the Composition and Structure
of the Book of Jeremiah*
T. R. Hobbs

I. SURVEY OF EARLIER ATTEMPTS AT SOLVING THE POETRY-PROSE PROBLEM
OF THE BOOK OF JEREMIAH

Since the publication of the epoch-making commentary on Jeremiah in 1901 by Bernhard Duhm,[1] almost all critical scholars are agreed that the book of Jeremiah contains at least two types of literary material, poetry and prose. However, once the problem of interpreting this phenomenon is approached, this unanimity disappears. Well known by now is Duhm's own extreme opinion that only a small number of verses within the present book, two hundred and eighty, were authentic to the prophet. The main characteristic of these verses was the dirge, or Kinah metre. Of the rest, two hundred and twenty were written by the prophet's friend and scribe, Baruch, and the remainder, some eight hundred, were attributed to a succession of editors and glossators (*Ergänzer*), who continually added to the original words of the prophet throughout the long history of transmission up to the second century B.C.[2] Duhm[3] also recognized that much of what he regarded as "secondary" material was similar in style to the Deuteronomistic literature.

Duhm's views have left a marked impression on the vast majority of studies on the book since 1901.[4] Before this time, although the difference in

---

*Originally published in the *Catholic Biblical Quarterly* 34 (1972) 257–275.
[1]B. Duhm, *Das Buch Jeremia* (*HKAT* 11; Tübingen: J. C. B. Mohr, 1901).
[2]*Ibid.*, xxff.
[3]The adjective "Deuteronomistic" is used throughout this study of the dominant theological viewpoint which developed during and after the exile, and which gave rise to the so-called "Deuteronomistic literature," the bulk of which is contained within the Deuteronomistic History, Jos–2 Kgs. The adjective "Deuteronomic" is taken to apply exclusively to things pertaining to the book of Deuteronomy.

[4]For example, cf. the comments of L. Gautier, *Introduction à l'Ancien Testament* (2d ed.; Lausanne: Payot & Cie., 1910) 382. S. R. Driver, *Introduction to the Literature of the Old Testament* (9th ed.; Edinburg: T. & T. Clark, 1913) 272, readily acknowledged the widespread influence of the work of Duhm upon the study of the book of Jeremiah, but does not adopt

style within the book may have been acknowledged, it was never really taken very seriously, and the significance of the difference was overlooked. More attention was given to the equally complicated problem of the relationship between the Greek and Hebrew recensions of the book and the question of priority. Apart from a few minor exceptions, most of the words recorded in the book were seen as the result of a combined effort at collecting the oracles of the prophet by Jeremiah himself, and his scribe Baruch.[5]

The influence of Duhm can be traced in the works of Sigmund Mowinckel,[6] whose unique contribution to the study of the book was to trace three basic literary sources now incorporated into the present book. These he saw as the authentic oracles of the prophet, mostly poetry (A), the biographical narratives from Baruch (B), and the autobiographical prose sections (C). The last of these three is the least authentic and owes its origin to the Deuteronomists.[7] With relatively few modifications, this position has been subsequently adopted by Volz,[8] Rudolph[9] and Hyatt.[10]

There are other scholars, notably T. H. Robinson[11] and O. Eissfeldt,[12] who accept the three-fold division of material by Mowinckel, but who see in the autobiographical material, Mowinckel's source C, the authentic words of the prophet which were included in the scroll whose history is told in ch. 36.

Duhm's position himself. Cf. also the works of Mowinckel, Volz, Hyatt and Rudolph mentioned below.

[5]For example, cf. K. F. Keil, *Lehrbuch der historischen-kritischen Einleitung in die kanonischen Schriften des Alten Testaments* (Frankfurt-am-Main: Heyder & Zimmer, 1853) 283–301; S. Davidson, *The Text of the Old Testament Considered* (London: Longman, Brown, Green, Longman and Roberts, 1856) 868–885; F. Hitzig, *Der Prophet Jeremia* (Leipzig: S. Hirzel, 1866) ix, who notes the similarities of style between Jeremiah and the book of Deuteronomy, but without elaboration. Cf. also C. von Orelli, *The Prophecies of Jeremiah* (tr. J. S. Banks; Edinburgh: T. & T. Clark, 1889) 20ff.; F. Bleek, *Einleitung in das Alte Testament* (3d ed.; Berlin: Reimer, 1870) 468ff.

[6]S. Mowinckel, *Zur Komposition des Buches Jeremia* (Kristiania: Dybwad, 1914); *Prophecy and Tradition* (Oslo: Dybwad, 1946).

[7]*Komposition*, 31ff. Mowinckel also detected a later source (D) which included such optimistic material as chs. 30–31 (*ibid.*, 47).

[8]P. Volz, *Der Prophet Jeremia* (Leipzig: Tauchnitz, 1928).

[9]W. Rudolph, *Jeremia* (*HAT* 12; Tübingen: J. C. B. Mohr, 1947); also in subsequent editions of the same commentary in 1958 and 1968.

[10]J. P. Hyatt, "Jeremiah: Introduction and Exegesis," *Interpreter's Bible*, vol. 5 (Nashville: Abingdon, 1956) 777–1142.

[11]T. H. Robinson, "The Structure of the Book of Jeremiah," *The Expositor*, 8th series, 20 (1920) 16–31; "Baruch's Roll" *ZAW* 42 (1924) 290–221; cf. also his contribution in W. O. E. Oesterley and T. H. Robinson, *Introduction to the Books of the Old Testament* (London: SPCK, 1936).

[12]O. Eissfeldt, *The Old Testament: An Introduction* (tr. P. R. Ackroyd; Oxford: Blackwell, 1965) 250ff.; this view was also espoused by C. H. Cornill, *Das Buch Jeremia* (Leipzig: Tauchnitz, 1905) xli.

In view of the obvious differences of style within the book, the suggestions that the prose and poetry have separate points of origin would seem to be a natural conclusion to draw. The style of Mowinckel's source C, which is closely akin to the style of Deuteronomy and the Deuteronomistic history (Jos–2 Kgs), has provided for many the clue needed to discover the origin of the prose. A number of scholars are prepared with Duhm to see the prose as the result of the activity of Deuteronomistic editors upon the original words of the prophet. There have been a few notable exceptions to this since Duhm. A. S. Peake[13] was content to see the differences in style as evidence of the versatility of the prophet. The differences have also been ignored,[14] and in some cases refuge was sought in the theory that Jeremiah was influenced by the style of Deuteronomy,[15] or in the more plausible, but still improbable theory that the prophet was using typical sixth-century Hebrew speech style.[16] The problem has also been tackled on form-critical grounds, notably by Weiser[17] and von Reventlow.[18] The former sees typical cultic language, particularly from the covenant renewal festival, in the prose, whilst the latter has sought to identify the prose of chs. 7 and 26 as examples of "Temple entrance

[13]A. S. Peake, *Jeremiah*, vol. 1 (Edinburgh: T. C. & E. C. Jack, n.d.) 51. But Peake does attribute the biographical passages to Baruch (*ibid.*, 62).

[14]E. J. Young, *An Introduction to the Old Testament* (London: Tyndale Press, 1960).

[15]Suggested by S. R. Driver, *Introduction*, 257; also cf. Y. Kaufmann, *The Religion of Israel from Its Beginnings to the Babylonian Exile* (tr. M. Greenberg; Chicago: University of Chicago Press, 1960) 415.

[16]Oesterley & Robinson, *Introduction*, 219ff.; B. W. Anderson, *Understanding the Old Testament* (Englewood Cliffs: Prentice-Hall, 1958) 311; J. A. Thompson, "The 'Deuteronomic' Editors and the Covenant Gattung in the Old Testament," *Tyndale Bulletin* 37 (1963) 5–10. This is also hinted at, but never fully developed in W. L. Holladay, "Prototype and Copies: A New Approach to the Poetry and Prose Problem of the Book of Jeremiah," *JBL* 79 (1960) 351–357. The basic objection to be leveled at this viewpoint is the question why Jeremiah on certain occasions chose to employ one style of speaking, and on others without any apparent reason, employ another so different. The sum of the evidence for this view is the number of linguistic affinities in the book with Deuteronomy, and the similarities with the Lachish Letters, both dated in the 7th century B.C.

As regards the first comparison, suffice it to say here that this style is by no means limited to the 7th century. It is characteristic of the Deuteronomistic History (5th century), parts of the book of Ezra (cf. ch. 9) and with the book of Daniel (cf. ch. 9). On the second comparison, it seems as though too much has been concluded from too little evidence. The similarities of style are not precise enough to draw any definite historical conclusions.

[17]A. Weiser, *Das Buch des Propheten Jeremia* (*ATD* 20–21; 4th ed.; Göttingen: Vandenhoeck & Ruprecht, 1960) xxxvii. In his *The Old Testament: Its Formation and Development* (tr. D. Barton; New York: Association Press, 1961) 217f., Weiser does admit that the style is Deuteronomistic ". . . and was the regular usage for the cultic recitals of the prophetic writings (in the synagogue)," but he also maintains that the content of this material, especially ch. 7, is both anti-cultic and anti-Deuteronomistic, and therefore pre-exilic. It is ". . . phraseology of public worship, employed already before the 'Deuteronomic' view of history and revision, and used by Jeremiah himself, or by Baruch."

[18]H. Graf von Reventlow, "Gattung und Überlieferung in der 'Tempelrede Jeremias' Jer 7 und 26," *ZAW* 81 (1969) 315–352.

Torah."[19] The greatest difficulty with Weiser's position is that the use of the prose is not consistent enough to locate it in the cult, especially the covenant renewal festival. What then becomes of the poetry? Von Reventlow's position is also to be criticized. Granted that such a form as the entrance liturgy existed in which law was cited, this does not explain the presence of the prose in chs. 7 and 26. Every other example of this form in the OT is in poetry,[20] and the attempts of Fohrer[21] to reduce the style of ch. 7 to "Kurzvers" poetry have been unsuccessful.

Attempts at a more precise location of the origin of the prose "Deuteronomistic" tradition of the book have varied. Duhm, followed closely by Gautier,[22] saw the origin of the prose in the undisciplined additions of the pious *Ergänzer* over a long period of time. Their intention is characterized thus ". . . sie wollten in ihrem Jeremiabuch einen Beitrag zu einer Art Volksbibel liefern, ein religiöses Lehr—und Erbauungsbuch, das dem Laien zu einem besseren Verständnis seiner Religion und Geschichte verhelfen sollte. . . ."[23] Apart from the very literary character of this work, this conclusion may not be too far from the truth, but the method envisaged leaves much to be desired. The *Sitz im Leben* of this kind of activity was seen as postexilic Judaism, centered around the synagogue. Mowinckel[24] contented himself with the description of the prose as "Deuteronomistical" (sic!) and made little attempt to evaluate its *Sitz im Leben*. Rudolph[25] attributed this style to "der exilischen Deuteronomiker," and H. F. May[26] saw it as the creation of an anonymous "Biographer" who lived long after the death of Jeremiah. Bright[27] acknowledges the existence of the two traditions, poetry and prose, but avoids any sharp differentiation between them. According to him, both had separate existences until their

---

[19]This form had been previously investigated by K. Koch, "Tempeleinlassliturgien und Dekalog," *Studien zur Theologie der alttestamentlichen Überlieferungen* (Neukirchen: Neukirchener Verlag, 1961) 45–60; also cf. G. Östborn, *Tora in the Old Testament: A Semantic Study* (Lund: Ohlsson, 1945) 137ff.

[20]Pss 15, 24:3–6; Mic 6:6–8; Am 5:14ff.; Isa 1:6ff.

[21]G. Fohrer, "Jeremias' Tempelwort 7, 1–15," *ThZ* 5 (1949) 401–417, esp. 407.

[22]*Introduction*, in loc.

[23]Duhm, *Jeremia*, xvi.

[24]*Prophecy and Tradition*, 62. While Mowinckel abandoned his earlier three source theory, this rejection of literary criticism was tempered by speculation regarding the possible later *literary* incorporation of the "Deuteronomist Jeremiah tradition" (*ibid.*, 63) into the book written by Baruch. Thus he slips back into viewing the compilation of the book as a combination of documents.

[25]*Jeremia*, 3d. ed., xvii.

[26]H. G. May, "Towards an Objective Approach to the Book of Jeremiah: The Biographer," *JBL* 61 (1942) 139–155; "Jeremiah's Biographer," *JBR* 10 (1942) 195–201. F. Augustin, "Baruch und Das Buch Jeremia," *ZAW* 67 (1955) 50–56, also sees one hand at work in the prose, but that of Baruch.

[27]J. Bright, "The Date of the Prose Sermons of Jeremiah," *JBL* 70 (1951) 15–35; *Jeremiah* (*AB* 21; New York: Doubleday, 1965) lxff.

inclusion into the present book, but as far as the circles of tradition in which they were transmitted are concerned, Bright[28] is cautious.

A problem related with the detection of two different literary styles within the book of Jeremiah is whether in both he is seen from the same theological perspective. For those who see both the prose and the poetry as originating with the prophet himself,[29] the problem does not exist. But if the possibility of the different origins and *Sitze im Leben* of the two traditions is open, then the possibility of a different picture in each also becomes very real. To such as Duhm and Mowinckel the differences were indisputable. Also for Hyatt[30] the Deuteronomists did the prophet a great disservice by making him into something he obviously was not, a supporter of the reform of Josiah. To a similar extent, May's "Biographer" made the prophet a mouthpiece of his own idea. This is still an open question. To Duhm, Mowinckel, and a later critic like Bentzen,[31] it was axiomatic that the different origins of the two traditions implied a distortion of the prophet and his words in the prose. But Bright, whilst acknowledging the existence of the two traditions, sees both as authentic developments of the Jeremiah tradition, and therefore does not admit to any significant distortion of the prophet.

II. CRITIQUE OF SOME RECENT APPROACHES

The majority of studies thus far examined have presupposed the difference in style, origin and intent of the poetry and prose of the book of Jeremiah. Thus, either one is seen as "authentic" or "inauthentic"; more often than not this division corresponds to "poetry" and "prose" respectively, the latter frequently being denied any value in an assessment of the prophet's message.[32] Some of the more recent studies dealing with the growth of the book of Jeremiah in particular, have tended to play down this extreme distinction between the poetry and prose, which was so characteristic of the work of Mowinckel and Duhm, without losing sight of the obvious differences.

W. L. Holladay[33] has produced work on the book of Jeremiah over the last decade which is full of promise in this direction, promise, however,

---

[28] *Ibid.*, lxxii.

[29] Such as Weiser, von Reventlow and Young.

[30] J. P. Hyatt, "Jeremiah and Deuteronomy," *JNES* 1 (1942) 156–173, esp. 158; "The Deuteronomic Edition of Jeremiah," in *Vanderbilt Studies in the Humanities*, vol. 1 (Nashville: Vanderbilt University Press, 1951).

[31] A. Bentzen, *Introduction to the Old Testament*, vol. 2 (Copenhagen: Gad, 1958) 119. Cf. also S. Granild, "Jeremia und das Deuteronomium," *StTh* 16 (1962) 135–154, esp. 136.

[32] Duhm (*Jeremia*, xviii) saw nothing in common between the real Jeremiah and the prose. Likewise, Mowinckel (*Komposition*, 63–64) regarded the prose as having weakened, watered down and completely distorted the real Jeremiah.

[33] Two of the most important studies of Holladay in this area have been "Prototype and Copies: A New Approach to the Poetry and Prose Problem in the book of Jeremiah," *JBL* 79

which is not always fully realized. Nevertheless Holladay has done some extremely valuable spade work in detecting some relationship between the two traditions of poetry and prose within the book. Holladay has examined some of the many doublets, or passages of similar content or phrasing which appear in both poetry and prose. His basic conclusion is that where this occurs the prose passages are based on poetic "prototypes" which served as the inspiration for the larger and more expanded prose. As examples of these "prototype-copy" passages he cites 22:19 which is repeated in prose form in 1:15; 17:19–27; and 5:31 which is repeated in 14:14; 23:25–6; 27:10ff.; 29:9, 21, etc. Holladay's work has gone far in determining some kind of continuity between the poetry and the prose in the book of Jeremiah, which is a healthy correction to the sometimes frustrating scepticism of a commentary like Duhm's.

But Holladay's work does stop short of attempting an answer to some of the obvious questions which arise in connection with the composition of the book of Jeremiah. He makes no attempt at all to define the *Sitz im Leben* of the prose tradition, nor does he seek to ascertain how or why this development from prototype to copy took place. In a later article he uses language which provides some hints in this direction, but nothing more, when he speaks of a "prose editor," or mentions that the prose was composed "for liturgical purposes."[34] These hints are unfortunately never followed through, and this has resulted in what appears to be a regression, when at the end of the essay under discussion he lists for further study some of the basic questions which have nagged at students of the book of Jeremiah ever since the publication of Duhm's commentary in 1901.[35]

A stimulatingly new approach to the growth of OT literature has been given by the so-called "traditio-historical school" which consists of a number of Scandinavian scholars, chief of whom was, until his death in 1965, Ivan Engnell. One characteristic of this school is an outright rejection of the "classic" literary critical approach to OT literature.[36] This rejection is at times rather harsh, and tinged with sarcasm,[37] but dominated by the belief that whatever literary critical criteria may be used, it is impossible to come to any sound results in terms of "sources" in the area of the growth of

---

(1960) 351–367, and "The Recovery of the Poetic Passages of the Book of Jeremiah," *JBL* 85 (1966) 401–435.

[34]*JBL* 85 (1966) 418 (and n. 43).

[35]E.g. "How much influence has the Jeremiah prose material had on the 'Deuteronomic' style, and how much did it inherit from the D-tradition?," "To what extent does the prose tradition (a) reflect accurately, (b) distort the message of Jeremiah? How did the prose material arise, and when and where?" (*JBL* 79 [1960] 367).

[36]I. Engnell, *The Call of Isaiah* (Uppsala: Luneqvistska, 1949) 6 begins with a ". . . total disengagement of all preconceived notions of literary criticism."

[37]Mowinckel's monograph, *Prophecy and Tradition*, for example, is characterized rather unfairly as ". . . an evolutionary pipedream, based upon purely subjective reasoning." Cf. I. Engnell, "Jeremias Bok," *Svenskt Bibliskt Uppslagsverk*, vol. 2, 1098–1106, esp. 1101.

literature. It is through the book, directly or indirectly, that the prophet speaks to us, either through his own words, or those of his disciples. Which is involved is impossible to determine. The very existence of a piece of literature bearing the name of "Jeremiah" is testimony to the vigorous and creative personality of the prophet, a personality which it is impossible to reconstruct. Coupled with this rejection of literary criticism is a thoroughgoing dependence upon the fidelity of oral tradition.[38]

In an article in the 2d edition of the *Svenskt Bibliskt Uppslagswerk*, Engnell[39] applies the methods of this school to the Book of Jeremiah. He begins where most literary critics do, at ch. 36, but this is not in the attempt to reconstruct the contents of the scroll described therein, but rather in an attempt to discover the theological (Engnell—"ideological") thrust of the whole passage. Two main points are brought out. On the one hand, the theological thrust of the passage is seen in the growing opposition between the prophet and the king, and the royal reaction in cutting up and burning the scroll is an attempt by Jehoiakim to invalidate the prophetic word. On the other hand, the passage is seen as illustrating the importance of oral tradition in the ancient world in that the prophet could recall to memory twenty years of his preaching. The writing down of the words by Baruch does not provide any evidence for an early written tradition of the prophet's words, rather it is part of the thrust of the passage in that it gives greater effect and a permanence to the words which Baruch later spoke. Hence the re-writing of the scroll after the incident (vs. 32).

Using this kind of approach Engnell detects several "tradition complexes" which have arisen out of similar or varied theological motives. These tradition complexes were drawn together in the process of oral tradition by a common subject matter, common intention and a common milieu. During the course of oral transmission they have been continually improved upon and reshaped to suit the changing historical context. Thus the actual *ipsissima verba* of the prophet recede further into the background as his voice becomes fused with that of his disciples who keep alive his spirit, if not his voice, in this process of adaptation. The final combining of these tradition complexes into the present book is again through the process of oral tradition, and the "tradition analysis" as outlined above cuts right across the traditional literary critical source theory of the book. The date for this final stage is given as the exilic or immediate postexilic period, and the bearers of these tradition complexes were a particular group of the disciples of the prophet who came to have definite affinities with the Deuteronomists.

---

[38] A good characteristic study in English of this approach is to be found in E. Nielsen, *Oral Tradition* (*SBT*: 1/11; London: SCM Press, 1951). Cf. Engnell's own essay, "The Traditio-Historical Method in Old Testament Research," *A Rigid Scrutiny* (Nashville: Vanderbilt University Press, 1969) 3–11, also his "Methodological Aspects of Old Testament Study," *VTSup* 7 (1959) 13–30.

[39] *Svenskt Bibliskt Uppslagswerk*, vol. 2, 1089–1106.

Another significant study dealing with the growth and composition of the book of Jeremiah is that of Claus Rietzschel[40] which appeared in print in 1966. There are some interesting similarities with, but also some basic differences from, the work of Engnell.[41] Rietzschel accepts the usual poetry-prose division of the book. The former was the first to be committed to writing, and the latter underwent a longer period of oral tradition. By virtue of this it is hardly possible to find the *ipsissima verba Ieremiae* within the prose. Rietzschel agrees that the scroll described in ch. 36 is to be found within the present poetry with the rest of the authentic words of the prophet. However, on the method of combination of the poetry and prose Rietzschel tends to differ from most before him, with the possible exception of Engnell. There are two ways of viewing the problem.[42] The first is based on the assumption that the poetry and prose had separate histories before their inclusion into the present book. If this were the case, the final task of combining the two must be attributed to one man who threaded the different materials together. The second comes close to Engnell's theory. It would be possible to regard the poetry and prose as having been collected into smaller units before their inclusion into the present book. These smaller units are the "tradition complexes" outlined by Engnell.[43] The oracles, biographical data and the sermonic prose material which make up these complexes have been drawn together by reason of their ". . . thematischen Gesichtspunkten oder Stichwortverknüpfungen."[44] It is this latter approach which Rietzschel adopts, and the greater part of his monograph is concerned with the growth and limits of these tradition complexes.

In an attempt to discover the *Sitz im Leben* of these complexes Rietzschel follows the thesis of E. Janssen,[45] that the sermons which characterize the prose sections of the book are products of the influence of the book of Deuteronomy upon the exilic and postexilic synagogue. In neither style nor form are these speeches prophetic, the first appearance of such style is with the book of Deuteronomy. Thus the prose is not seen so much as a literary source in the strictest sense of the term, but is rather a collection of homiletical and didactic comments on poetic "texts."

Rietzschel's contribution to the solution of the complicated problem of the growth and structure of the book of Jeremiah is fresh and full of keen insight. On the one hand it is an unconscious modification of the extreme

[40] *Das Problem der Urrolle: Ein Beitrag zur Redaktionsgeschichte des Buches Jeremia* (Gütersloh: Gerd Mohn, 1966).

[41] While the approach is somewhat similar to that of Engnell, the Scandinavian is not mentioned throughout.

[42] *Urrolle*, 19.

[43] Chs. 1–24; 26–36; 37–45; 25, 46–51.

[44] *Urrolle*, 24.

[45] E. Janssen, *Juda in der Exilszeit: Ein Beitrag zur Frage der Entstehung des Judentums* (*FRLANT* 51; Göttingen: Vandenhoeck & Ruprecht, 1956).

approach of Engnell in that it relies to a very large extent on the results of earlier literary criticism of the book. On the other hand, it supports the thesis outlined by many that the so-called biographical and autobiographical prose material, Mowinckel's sources B and C, are to be united. These, however, are some of the minor results of Rietzschel's thesis. The division of the book of Jeremiah into "tradition-complexes" and the implication of this for the nature of the composition of the book will be examined in more detail below. At present there are some more basic criticisms of the work of both Engnell and Rietzschel which need to be set out.

Engnell's position is so extreme that it is not difficult to criticize. The first criticism is directed against the insistence on oral tradition as the medium for the handing on of the words and deeds of the prophet as *opposed* to a written tradition, and the utter reliability of the former. In view of the fact that both the memorizing of the words of the prophet *and* the writing down of the same figure so prominently in the narrative of ch. 36, it would be far more reasonable to assume that both methods were used, side by side, as was insisted on, for example, by Mowinckel's[46] later work on the subject, and Rietzschel.[47] If, however, oral tradition is as reliable as Engnell and Nielsen[48] maintain, would it not be possible to trace alterations, glosses, and additions to an oral "text" in virtually the same way as a literary critic would work, and thus arrive at a possible reconstruction of the prophet's original words?[49] In this process of transmission there would be little to distinguish between what were originally written and what were spoken words. Both, presumably, would reflect the age in which they were added to the original and the theological position of their authors. On the other hand, if it is impossible to reconstruct the original words of the prophet in this way, does this not indicate a fundamental failure of oral tradition to transmit the prophet's words correctly? Engnell has created a dilemma for himself on this point which he makes little or no attempt to avoid.[50]

A second criticism is related to the first. Engnell had outlined four tradition complexes within the book on grounds of style and theology, but saw the whole process of combination and expansion as oral. One could ask at this stage whether one is not permitted to speak of each tradition as a "source." Whether written or oral is a point of dispute, but this is really irrelevant since it appears that Engnell detects the tradition complexes by the use of style, vocabulary and ideology, in other words, with the same

[46] *Prophecy and Tradition.*

[47] *Urrolle.*

[48] *Oral Tradition,* passim.

[49] Cf. C. R. North, "The Place of Oral Tradition in the Growth of the Old Testament," *ExpT* 61 (1949–50) 292–296; and "Oral Tradition and Written Documents," *ExpT* 66 (1954–55) 39.

[50] This dilemma is evident also in *Call of Isaiah,* 58–59, where Engnell is caught between the "remodelling function" of oral tradition, and its "capacity for resisting corruption."

tools that the literary critic uses. However, one can take this a step further, and this applies to both Engnell and Rietzschel. If one can detect material common to more than one tradition complex, on grounds of style, vocabulary and ideology, surely one is then allowed to speak of "sources" used by the compilers of these complexes, and which in fact cut right across the lines drawn by Engnell and Rietzschel.

A third criticism is of an implied point in both authors, but more explicit in Rietzschel. Since there is a homogeneity to the prose, whether it occurs in the first or third complex, the division of the book into complexes rests mainly on grounds of the theological or ideological *pointe* of the defined complex. But does this difference in theological intention indicate that each complex owes its form to different *Tradenten* from those who handled the other three? The answer must surely be in the negative. There are distinct features of style, vocabulary and theology which are common to at least three of the tradition complexes defined by both Engnell and Rietzschel. If this is true, then there are good grounds for understanding this phenomenon in terms of common "sources" used in the complexes. However, in the light of the work of Rietzschel in particular and his location of the *Sitz im Leben* of the prose of the book, perhaps the meaning of the word "source" in this context needs some considerable qualification. These comments on some of the more recent studies devoted to the composition of the book of Jeremiah point out the weaknesses of those studies, and serve to pave the way for our own contribution to the problem.

III. TOWARDS A SOLUTION TO THE PROBLEM

The four tradition complexes which have been detected within the present book of Jeremiah are 1–24; 25, 46–51; 26–35; 36–45. Of these four, 25, 46–51 is the least important for the present study, since it is composed almost entirely of poetry, and the material contained within this section has a common "ideology," namely, the defeat of Israel's enemies. The problem of the dating of the individual oracles, however, is an extremely complicated one, too complicated to be dealt with here. With Rietzschel there is good reason for seeing ch. 25 as a prose introduction to the collection of oracles against the foreign nations since there are definite points of contact between the two.[51] Ch. 52 poses a problem all of its own, but this will be treated below.

Each of the three remaining complexes has a certain degree of homogeneity which marks it off from the other two. For example, the collection 1–24, a collection of oracles, sayings and sermons, with a few didactic narratives, is composed of material of diverse kinds directed almost entirely against Jerusalem. Ch. 1 can be seen as an introduction to the whole book,

---

[51]Allowing for appositional phrases, etc., in the list of nations in ch. 25, there is little difference in the order of nations in the chapter and in chs. 46–51.

and the heading of ch. 2 (vss. 1–2aA) is probably the heading for the collection 2–6, or even 2–24. This verse and part of a verse have long been seen as redactional,[52] not quite suiting the material which immediately follows in ch. 2, since that chapter is directed more toward Israel as a whole, rather than to Jerusalem. But it admirably fits the role as a heading for the whole collection.

Chs. 26–36, which seems a more desirable division than Rietzschel's 26–35 in view of the obvious climax which comes at the end of ch. 36, is also another collection of common intent.[53] In these chapters, the focus of attention seems to be the personnel of the city of Jerusalem, who had been generally attacked in the first section. Now the accusations become more specific, and the reaction of various groups within the capital city to the prophet and his word becomes clear as the section progresses. A possible exception to the overtly pessimistic nature of 26–36 is the section 30–33. This may be explained as a later collection, also dealing in part with Jerusalem, which has been inserted into its present context, in much the same way as 46–51 were added as the last word to the exiles. But the reason for the present context of 30–33 still remains something of a mystery.

37–45, with its dramatic narrative unfolding of the word of Yahweh through the prophet in the history of the people, would also seem to be a unit whose main intention is to retell the fulfillment of the prophetic word which Jeremiah had proclaimed before the exile.[54] Each of these complexes begins with what could pass for a distinct heading, which marks it off from the rest of the book. There are also indications that within these units there are even smaller ones which have been attracted together on the basis of "catchwords," or because of closely similar content. 3:1–4:8 is a collection united round the theme of "Return." 2–6, which contains the so-called "Scythian Songs," deals exclusively with Jerusalem. 21:1–23:5 is a collection directed against the royal house of Judah, and 23:9–40 is another collection directed against the prophets of Jerusalem. Each of these latter sections begins with a distinct heading ". . . concerning the. . . ."[55]

It is difficult, however, to see each of these complexes apart from the others, either in their present form, or in the process of compilation. While 26–36 can be looked upon as a unit which seeks to present a particular theological point, there are indications in this section of a knowledge of at least some of the contents of 1–24. Two examples can be given for this. In

[52]Cf. most recently the discussion in W. Schottroff, "Jeremia 2, 1–3: Erwägungen zur Methode der Prophetenexegese," *ZThK* 67 (1970) 263–294.

[53]Cf. on ch. 36 M. Kessler, "Form-Critical Suggestions on Jer 36," *CBQ* 28 (1966) 389ff.

[54]For a more detailed study of the narrative sections of Jeremiah cf. M. Kessler, *A Prophetic Biography: A Form-critical Study of Jer. 26–29; 32–45* (Diss. Brandeis University, 1965); also "Jeremiah Chapters 26–45 Reconsidered," *JNES* 27 (1968) 81–88.

[55]Cf. 22:6 and 23:9.

ch. 36 the focus of attention is the scroll which Jeremiah and Baruch made, and the royal reaction to the contents of that scroll, namely the prophecies concerning the destruction of Judah and Jerusalem at the hands of the Babylonians. The contents of the scroll are described in one half-verse:

> ... the king of Babylon will destroy this
> land and cut off from it man and beast (36:29b).

This is obviously a summary statement which presupposes a wider knowledge of the preaching of the prophet, as contained for example, in chs. 1–24. But for the sake of the purpose of the narrative of ch. 36, only the briefest reference is made to it. Similarly in 26:1–6 the incident of the prophet in the temple court is retold. As in ch. 36, the narrative of this chapter does not concentrate so much on what the prophet is supposed to have said on this occasion, but again on the official reaction to his words, which is a common theme of 26–36. To this end, the announcement of judgment made by the prophet on this occasion is confined to one verse:

> ... I will make this house like Shiloh,
> and I will make this city a curse for
> all the nations of the earth (26:6).

In contrast to this, in ch. 7, where the focus of attention is on the words of the prophet, the actual prophecy has some considerable space devoted to it.

In 37–45, which is predominantly historical narrative and biographical data on Jeremiah, so much is left unsaid that this whole complex would make little sense on its own without some detailed reference to the words and deeds of the prophet as recorded, for example, in chs. 1–24. Some questions are never fully answered in this last section, such as, Why is Jeremiah the prophet so abused by the authorities? What is the word of which the royal house and its entourage are so afraid? There are brief allusions to some of the answers, but they are in the form of summaries of a much larger body of preaching (37:7ff.; 38:2f., etc.), and Jeremiah appears right at the outset as a man who had uttered many words of doom that had so far gone unheeded:

> ... But neither he nor his servants nor
> the people of the land listened to the
> words of the Lord which he spoke (or
> had spoken) through Jeremiah the prophet (37:2).

This statement makes little sense unless one sees it in the context of the preceding chapters which contain much of the prophet's preaching. Such notices as these would indicate that the circles in which these complexes were transmitted were closely associated, if not, the same ones.

While these observations indicate that there is a unity in the present form of the book, they do not provide a complete answer to the problem of the nature of the prose in the book and its purpose. What is to be noted in this regard is first, that the prose is common to all of the "complexes." It is more predominant in 26–36 and 37–45, but this is to be expected in view of the nature and purpose of these sections. Second, the prose has a characteristic sameness about it wherever it occurs. This had been advocated long before by N. Schmidt,[56] was revived by May[57] and Holladay,[58] and most recently by Rietzschel.[59] The differences between the sermonic prose of the first complex, and the narrative prose of the second and third are to be expected in view of the purpose of each complex. Sermonic prose does occur in the second and third complexes and narrative prose does occur in the first, where needed. Any rigid separation of the two, as was done by earlier scholars such as Mowinckel and Robinson, often leaves a meaningless narrative. The two belong together.

Since Duhm, the exilic synagogue has been seen as the origin of the prose sections, although the method of the joining of poetry and prose has been imagined from many different angles. Rietzschel's monograph keeps this *Sitz im Leben* to the fore, and his emphasis on the preaching and instruction of these communities has proved very fruitful. There are several points in favor of the identification of the prose as typical exilic preaching and didactic material. The style is unlike any other prophetic texts. The theology of the prose makes more sense against the background of the exilic period than any other. There are some very striking parallels between the prose passages of the book of Jeremiah and, for example, midrashic texts dealing with the same period of Israel's history. As in midrashic interpretation, sermonic material and narrative have didactic and homiletic intentions.[60] This is one further argument in favor of the unity of the prose. Thus, allowing for the different historical backgrounds for some of the prose, one can see the prose, as a whole, as a product of the exilic or postexilic synagogue. Generally speaking, the purpose of the prose was to recreate for the exilic generations the significance of the life and prophecies of a man like Jeremiah. Hence many ideas, terminology and concepts which would have been foreign to the prophet himself, have been used in the prose. The nomenclature "Deuteronomistic" has been applied to the prose because of the similarities with other Deuteronomistic literature

[56]N. Schmidt, "Jeremiah (Book)," *Encyclopedia Biblica*, vol. 2, 2372–2395.

[57]*JBL* 61 (1942) 139–155; *JBR* 10 (1942) 195–201.

[58]*JBL* 79 (1960) 351–367.

[59]Rietzschel, *Urrole*. J. Bright ("The Prophetic Reminiscence: its place and function in the book of Jeremiah," *Biblical Essays*, Proceedings of the ninth meeting of Die Ou-testamentiese Werkgemeenskap in Suid-Afrika [Potchefstroom: Pro Regepers Beperk, 1966] 11–30) suggested that the author of the biographical narratives (B) was a member of the circle who transmitted the more stereotyped prose, sermonic passages (C). If this is the case, then the reason for keeping them separate disappears.

[60]Cf., e.g., *Pesikta Rabbati*: Psika 26 which deals with the fall of Jerusalem.

found elsewhere in the OT. As more detailed studies of this literature are showing, such an identification is not wrong.[61]

The above ideas have been gained from discussion with the more recent studies on the composition and structure of the book of Jeremiah, and they go some way in providing some sound clues as to the origin of the prose of the book and the nature of some parts of the book of Jeremiah. Behind both the "tradition complexes" and the final edition of the book we find, according to both Engnell and Rietzschel, a living religious community. Both scholars reject the idea that the final form of the book is due to the work of one man. However, the present writer is of the opinion that the present form of the book is to be attributed to one editor. This statement is considerably strengthened when the overall structure of the book is examined.

In spite of some of the earlier, yet still current objections,[62] it is possible to trace a clearly defined theologically oriented structure to the book of Jeremiah as it now stands. The first chapter, as with the book of Isaiah, provides a summary of the contents of the rest of the book. A careful statistical study of the first chapter yields the following results.[63] The original form of the call-narrative was probably vss. 1–2, 4–5a, 6–9. The rest of the verses in this section, vss. 5b and 10, contain elements typical of the prose tradition of the rest of the book, but which are quite uncharacteristic of the poetry elsewhere in the book. Of the present form of the account of the two visions, which may or may not have been experienced by the prophet at the time of his call, only vss. 11–15a are characteristic of the poetry, whilst the remainder, vss. 15b–19, also contain typical prose tradition terms and ideas. This would indicate that the present form of the call-narrative is composite. In the original call-narrative we have the kind of call-narrative found elsewhere in the OT, particularly dealing with the old heroes of the Yahwistic faith, Moses and Gideon.[64] Like their call-narratives, Jeremiah's contains the elements of objection and reassurance. The additions to the call-narrative (vss. 5b, 10) extend the work of the prophet, (i) to include the nations other than Israel, (ii) to include a program of reconstruction, after the announced judgment. In the visions that are attached, the original forms are of visual announcements of

---

[61]This position has been most recently advocated by E. W. Nicholson, *Preaching to the Exiles: A Study in the Prose Tradition of the Book of Jeremiah* (Oxford: Blackwell, 1970).

[62]Cf., e.g., H. W. Robinson, *The Cross in the Old Testament* (London: SCM Press, 1955) 130f.; and the implied criticism of the present order of the book in Bright, *Jeremiah*, and E. A. Leslie, *Jeremiah* (Nashville: Abingdon, 1954), both of whom attempt a chronological reconstruction of the material in the book.

[63]Cf. F. Augustin, "Baruch und das Buch Jeremia," *ZAW* 67 (1955) 50–56.

[64]Cf. Ex 3 and Jgs 6. A valuable study on the call-narratives of the OT is to be found in N. Habel, "The Form and Significance of the Call Narratives," *ZAW* 77 (1965) 297ff. However, the failure in this essay to distinguish between the calls of Moses and Gideon and the other calls of Isaiah, Amos, tends to detract from the work.

judgment, found elsewhere in the prophetic literature.[65] The additions (vss. 15b–19) take up a theme of the call-narrative, namely that the prophet will experience opposition. This time, however, the opposition is specified quite clearly. It will come from the important people of Jerusalem and Judah (vs. 18). One could characterize the theological themes of the combined material in ch. 1 as (i) the prophet and the word, (ii) the prophet and the nations, (iii) the prophet and the nation. It is not difficult to see that these themes are taken up in the body of the book proper, and constitute the main thrust of the whole. With the first, both the content of this word (1–24), and the prophet's relationship to the word are taken up in the rest of the book. The contents of 1–24 correspond to the contents of the prophetic word given the prophet in ch. 1. The prophet's own love-hate relationship to the word, which is picked up again in the so-called "confessions" and in some of the autobiographical narratives, is already present in his objections given at the call. With the second, the extension of the prophet's mission to foreign nations is not unique with Jeremiah. What is unique with the book of Jeremiah is the intensity of these oracles, and the concentration of them in chs. 46–51. They are however, as at the call, combined with the task to the nation of Israel itself, and their position in the LXX, after ch. 25, does correspond to the order in the call-narrative. The prophet's relationship to his own nation which is so meticulously worked out in the biographical narratives of 26–45, is mirrored in the few verses devoted to it in ch. 1. Everything in the first chapter that is said about the prophet and the nation is worked out in some detail in the rest of the book.

Ch. 52 presents a problem of its own. That it is not from the Jeremiah tradition is evident, not only from its parallel in 2 Kgs 24:18–25:30, but also from the comment which ends ch. 51 "... thus far the words of Jeremiah" (vs. 64b). It is obviously then from the Deuteronomistic tradition. It has one significant deviation from the texts from which it is derived, which unfortunately does not come out clearly enough in the edition of BHK, but which still exists in most English translations and the LXX. The final verses of 2 Kgs 25 read:

So Jehoiachin put off his prison garments.
And every day of his life he dined regularly
at the king's table; and for his allowance,
a continual allowance was given to him from
the king, every day a portion, every day of
his life (vss. 29–30).

To this the last chapter of the book of Jeremiah adds significantly: "... until the day of his death" (25:34). The editor of the BHK text suggests an emendation to bring the Kings text into line with the Jeremiah

---

[65]Cf. the series of visions in Am 7:1–8:2.

text. Neither the LXX nor any other textual tradition, however, provides for such a possibility. The significance of this addition is obvious. The prose editor of the book of Jeremiah used a text which was most probably written while Jehoiachin was still living and thus the object of considerable hope in the defeated city of Jerusalem.[66] A recorded word of the prophet, however, mentions the death of this same king (22:26), and with his death ends the Davidic dynasty. The present form of Jer 52 confirms this oracle. Thus the chapter falls into line with the bulk of the narrative material in chs. 37–45, with its stress on the working out in history of the despised word of the prophet Jeremiah. By implication, of course, the word of this true prophet concerning the foreign nations (46–51) will also come true. This in turn gives rise for the hope in the rebuilding of Israel (cf. 1:10).

IV. CONCLUSIONS

This examination of the structure of the book is, to be sure, brief. Space prohibits any further detail at this point. It is hoped, however, that it has been demonstrated that the present book of Jeremiah does possess a clear message, carefully thought out, and which cannot have been the result of the kind of "floating together" of tradition complexes as envisaged by Rietzschel, and particularly by Engnell. Such a structure must be the work of an individual theologian, who sought, as did the tradition in which he was at home, to interpret the meaning of the exile for those in exile.[67]

There is one further problem associated with the composition of the book of Jeremiah. This is whether the prophet has been correctly interpreted by the Deuteronomistic exilic interpreters, and by the final editor of the book. One can ask whether this is the correct way to put the question, but this is the form it has taken through the years. When dealing with subjects like this, degrees of "correctness" and "authenticity" are relative, since the historical context in which the prophet is being interpreted often demands different modes of expression and different concepts from those used by either the prophet himself or by the twentieth century interpreter. Hence the appearance of "distortion" of the prophet by these later interpreters to those who live centuries after both the event and the interpretation. But such "distortion" may well have been the most acceptable way of looking at the prophet then. True, the interpretation may tell us more about the age in which it was carried out than the age in which the prophet lived, but this is true of all interpretation of history and examples of this are innumerable.

Biblical studies are not unacquainted with such "distortion" particularly in the realm of NT research, and recent emphases upon the variety of the witness to Jesus in the NT alone reminds us that the issue is still very much

---

[66]This is the background to the hope of Hananiah in Jer 28.
[67]Cf. Nicholson, *Preaching*.

alive.[68] The prophets themselves have not escaped "distortion" within the last decades. They have long been seen as the champions of socialism,[69] just as in the age of a stern Germanic Protestantism, they were seriously regarded as forerunners of the Protestant Reformation.[70] Apart from these modern interpretations, the Jewish tradition itself has embellished the words and deeds of the prophets and other heroes of her faith in a quite uninhibited way.[71] Of course, that this could have happened within the book of Jeremiah does not mean that it did, and only a detailed examination of the poetry and prose traditions of the book will yield any fruitful results in this direction. Suffice it to say at this stage that all the signs point to the fact that such reinterpretation and "distortion" did take place.[72]

But what does this have to say to us? Does this mean that part of the book of Jeremiah, and judging by the division of prose and poetry the largest part, is closed to the modern reader or preacher? To a certain degree Engnell's comments are surely helpful here. The existence of such a body of material, which interprets the prophet Jeremiah to a particular age and to particular historical circumstances in the concepts and ideas of that age, enable us to see that the so-called "Jeremiah tradition" was not a static thing but a living testimony to the creative genius of a man like Jeremiah. No new prophet was looked for by the exilic interpreters to bring the word of God home to the people of God. Rather the old word that was once spoken was revived and reapplied as a control on the life of God's people as they faced new situations and new threats. Such reapplication was valid *hermeneia* of the word of the prophet in the exilic and postexilic age, and opens the way for the modern, in terms understandable to his contemporaries to interpret the same word today. Having said this, one has said everything and nothing. This is the task of the modern interpreter, but the mechanics of the task cover an enormous area. The warrant for such interpretation is found within the book of Jeremiah itself, and so is the inspiration. Those who affirm the words of another unknown exilic interpreter in Isa 40:8b are bound to take such a task of interpretation seriously.

---

[68]The current emphasis upon *Redaktionsgeschichte* has revealed that even within the so-called "Synoptic Gospels" one has to deal with different presentations of Jesus. The title of a recent book by Eduard Schweizer also reflects this present climate of NT research, cf. E. Schweizer, *Jesus Christus im vielfältigen Zeugnis des Neuen Testaments* (Munich: Siebenstern Taschenbuch Verlag, 1968).

[69]Cf. the tone of the essay by T. H. Robinson, "The Hebrew Prophets and their Modern Interpretation," *ExpT* 40 (1929) 296–300.

[70]The remarks made by Paul Volz in "Die radikale Ablehnung der Kultreligion durch den alttestamentlichen Propheten," *ZSTh* 14 (1937) 63–85, esp. 84, illustrate this unbelievable assertion.

[71]The evidence for this is vast. A brief glance at many of the Midrash passages dealing with prophetic personnel and events during their lives will substantiate this statement.

[72]Cf., e.g., Nicholson, *Preaching.*

11

The Date of the Prose Sermons of Jeremiah*
John Bright

The process by which the book of Jeremiah was collected and edited was certainly a long and involved one. It presents the student with more than its fair share of problems some of which, it is safe to say, will never be satisfactorily solved. Of all these problems none is of more crucial importance than that of the prose sermons. These, marked by a distinctive style, are found both interspersed among the poetic oracles of chs. 1–25, 30–31 and embedded in the biographical sections, chs. 26–29, 32–45. It was Duhm[1] who first called attention to their presence, assigning them to an *Ergänzer* of Deuteronomic character who had worked over both Jeremiah's book and Baruch's. Duhm's criteria were further developed and applied by Mowinckel, who designated the three major types of material in the Jeremiah book as sources A (the poetic oracles and confessions), B (the biographical narrative) and C (the prose sermons in Deuteronomic style).[2] Without entirely agreeing with Mowinckel's (or Rudolph's) allocation of the material, it is in general the last group to which we refer here.

Any sound exegesis must come sooner or later to an evaluation of this material. One's whole reconstruction of the life and message of Jeremiah will depend on the answer given. Does it contain the actual words of the prophet? Can it be relied upon to give an accurate picture of the man and his message, or does it to a greater or lesser degree distort that picture? The question is peculiarly acute in that some of the noblest and best loved passages in the book (e.g. the Temple Sermon of ch. 7, the New Covenant passage of 31:31–34) are included in it. While the poetry (once a relatively small amount of late material has been subtracted) is generally conceded to

---

*Originally published in the *Journal of Biblical Literature* 70 (1951) 15–35.

[1]B. Duhm, *Das Buch Jeremia*, (*Kurzer Hand-Commentar zum A. T.*), 1901, pp. xvi–xx and *passim*.

[2]S. Mowinckel, *Zur Komposition des Buches Jeremia*, 1914. W. Rudolph (*Jeremia* [*Handbuch zum A. T.*], 1947, pp. xiii–xvii) follows Mowinckel in general. Recently Mowinckel (*Prophecy and Tradition*, 1946, p. 62 f.) has somewhat modified his position. Source C is no longer spoken of as a literary "source," but as a circle of tradition in which certain sayings of Jeremiah have been transmitted in, of course, the Deuteronomic style and viewpoint of that circle.

yield a true picture and as close an approach to the *ipsissima verba* as is possible,[3] and while most scholars would agree that the Biographer's[4] narrative affords a reliable and circumstantial account, no such favorable verdict has generally been awarded the prose sermons.

These have, as we have said, a distinctive style. It is verbose, repetitious, and loaded with stereotyped expressions. It is, as has long been recognized, closely akin to Dtr.[5] This fact, plus the arguable assumption that it is too impoverished for Jeremiah even at his prosiest, and that it expresses sentiments of which neither Jeremiah nor Baruch would have been capable, has led scholars to regard it as the product of Deuteronomic schools which flourished in the exile and after. As a rule, a greater or less distortion of the message and ministry of Jeremiah is posited.[6] Some go so far as to relegate the entire body of this material to a date well beyond the exile.[7] Of those who do so perhaps none is more thoroughgoing and drastic than H. G. May.[8] He maintains that the prose of Jeremiah is not the work of a school but of a single hand, that of the Biographer, who is not Baruch but who lived not earlier than the first half of the 5th century. It is he who gave us the book of Jeremiah in much its present form. He is influenced by the style of D_2, II Isaiah, the editor of Ezekiel (whom May apparently places after the exile) and I Zechariah, and exhibits associations with Ezra and Nehemiah. His picture of Jeremiah is, needless to say, considerably out of focus.

Such a question can only be decided by an objective examination of the evidence. As May quite correctly insists,[9] our point of departure must

---

[3]The search for the *ipsissima verba* may become a chasing of a will-o-the-wisp, especially if radical textual surgery is involved, but that fact need not drive us to the nihilism regarding them currently voiced especially by certain Swedish scholars, notably Engnell. Cf. the criticisms of Engnell et. al. in the last-named work of Mowinckel; also A. Bentzen, *Introduction to the O.T.*, Vol. I, 1948, p. 102 ff. and *passim*.

[4]We shall so refer to him. We see no reason why he may not have been Baruch but, as May (cf. note 8, below, *op. cit.* p. 139) has recently pointed out, it cannot be proved. So we will make no issue of it.

[5]For the sake of brevity we shall in this paper arbitrarily use this symbol for the Deuteronomic literature as a whole.

[6]E. g. Duhm, (*op. cit.*, p. xvii f.), who finds it historically worthless; recently J. P. Hyatt ("Jeremiah and Deuteronomy," JNES 1–2 [1942], p. 158, etc.), who believes that Deuteronomists sought to capture the sanction of Jeremiah for their ideas and programs; A. Bentzen (*op. cit.* Vol. II, 1949, p. 118 f.), "deuteronomistic zealots who used him in their propaganda," etc. On the other hand, Rudolf (*op. cit.* p. xv f.), though assigning the material to exilic Deuteronomists, seems to see in it relatively little distortion.

[7]E.g. G. Hölscher, "Komposition und Ursprung des Deuteronomiums," ZAW, XL (1922) p. 161 ff. (cf. pp. 233–239); id. *Die Profeten*, 1914, p. 384 ff.; F. Horst, "Die Anfänge des Propheten Jeremia," ZAW, XLI (1923), pp. 94–153 (where this material, in various strata, is placed ca. 530–500 b.c.); Mowinckel also put his source C in the time of Ezra (cf. also H. H. Rowley, *The Growth of the O.T.*, 1950, p. 102), but his later position (cf. note 2 above) seems to be somewhat of a modification.

[8]May, "The Biographer of Jeremiah," *JBL*, LXI (1942), pp. 139–155.

[9]*Op. cit.* p. 142.

be the prose sermons themselves. Our task must be to examine this material as a whole, to study its characteristic clichés in their wider relationships, to analyze it for historical allusions and other internal evidence that might throw light on its date. Only so can we hope for constructive results. What one would like to believe about Jeremiah has no place in such a discussion. If the evidence points to a late exilic or post-exilic date, one must simply give in to it and adjust his ideas accordingly. But the writer, while admiring the consistency and clarity of May's argument, finds himself driven by the same evidence to radically different conclusions. He is unable to find in this material the slightest evidence of dependence on post-exilic writers, or any other proof that it is the product of that period. He is even convinced that the assumption of dependence on a school of exilic Deuteronomists is open to the gravest question.

Our investigation must proceed from the demonstrable premise (see Appendix A) that, in style and form, the prose sermons are one. Any attempt to separate "genuine" Jeremianic words from "non-genuine" accretions within this material will run head on into this stubborn fact. To search, therefore, here for *ipsissima verba* in the traditional manner is to plunge into a subjective discussion of what, in one's opinion, Jeremiah could or could not say. When Duhm long ago rejected all of it he was at least logical, even if he severely truncated Jeremiah in the attempt.[10] Commentators who, unwilling to be so drastic, tried to save some of the prose for Jeremiah by pruning away editorial expansions[11] were perhaps nearer the truth than Duhm, but they completely burked the fact that both in style and viewpoint this material is so much of a unit that objective canons for separating "genuine" from "non-genuine" are largely lacking. It must, therefore, be borne in mind in the present discussion that the question is not: could or did Jeremiah say it? but: what date for it seems to be required by the evidence?

I

An analysis of the characteristic expressions of the prose Jeremiah yields no evidence of dependence on any post-exilic style, and much to the contrary. A table of typical expressions will be found in Appendix A. Similar tabulations have, of course, been made before and the present one may seem *de trop*. It seemed to the writer, however, that a new analysis of this material is in order, for it does not seem to him that it points at all to some of the conclusions it has been widely assumed to support.[12] A total of

---

[10]*Op. cit.* xvi ff. He left Jeremiah ca. 280 verses, Baruch ca. 220, while the *Ergänzer* was awarded ca. 850.

[11]E.g. J. Skinner, *Prophecy and Religion*, 1922, A. S. Peake, *Jeremiah* (*New-Century Bible*), 1910, *passim*.

[12]Older analyses pointed out similarities to, and divergencies from, the style of Deuteronomy: e.g. P. Kleinert, *Das Deuteronomium und der Deuteronomiker*, 1872, pp. 185–194;

47 entries is included but, counting the sub-heads, the total is 56. All are taken from the prose sermons both in chs. 1–25, 30–31 and attached to the Biographer's work. They include all clichés which occur five or more times in this material and which seemed to the writer characteristic of it, plus a dozen or so others which occur less frequently but which seem likewise to be characteristic. While others could be added, and while the evidence in particular cases could be interpreted variously depending upon the position adopted regarding certain critical problems, the writer is confident that the total picture would remain much the same.

A study of Appendix A will lead one to the conclusion that the Jeremiah prose is emphatically *not* stylistically dependent on II Isaiah, the editor of Ezekiel,[13] I Zechariah, or any other post-exilic literature. Statistics can be misleading, but the concerted evidence of the following cannot be brushed aside. a) Of the 56 clichés listed (counting sub-heads), 25 (1, 2, 3, 4, 5a, 6, 7, 8ab, 9, 10, 11, 12, 13, 14, 15ab, 16, 17, 18, 19ab, 20, 28, 35) occur *never* in II Isa, Ezek, I Zech, and very rarely or never in any later literature. Three more (30, 45, 47), which are found with some frequency in later literature, are not found in II Isa, Ezek and I Zech. b) Of the 28 (or exactly half) which do occur in II Isa, Ezek and I Zech, 15 (5b, 8c, 19c, 21, 22, 23, 24, 25, 31, 34, 36, 37a, 39, 44, 46) occur *not over twice* in any one of these books, and so are hardly typical, while only 9 or 10 of the 28 occur over 3 times in all of these books. Of the same 28, in *all but two* (33, 41) the Jeremiah prose occurrences equal or outnumber all occurrences in these books (usually by over two to one). *In every case* the Jeremiah occurrences exceed occurrences in any one of the above books, usually overwhelmingly. Furthermore, in all but 9 (25, 26, 29, 32, 33, 34, 38, 39, 41) the Jeremiah occurrences equal or exceed all occurrences in all later literatures. To be sure, this sort of statistic is treacherous, but it has here a certain validity since the field of evidence of *all* post-exilic literature is vastly wider than that of the prose Jeremiah. At least these clichés are far more typical of the prose Jeremiah than of any later literature. c) Of the 56 listed, 12 (1, 3, 5a, 7, 8a, 9, 15a, 17, 18, 19ab, 20) are virtually peculiar to the prose Jeremiah. Of the 44 that remain, all but *one* (27a; and here the Jeremiah occurrences exceed all later ones by 15 to 8) are instanced in literature contemporary

---

L. Zunz, ZDMG, 1873, pp. 671–673; S. R. Driver, *Deuteronomy* (ICC), 1903, p. xciii f. The recent tabulation of May (*op. cit.* p. 154 f.) does not list occurrences outside the Jeremiah "Biographer." The only tabulations of which the writer knows that do so are: S. R. Driver, *Introduction to the Literature of the O.T.*, 1913, pp. 275–277, and G. Hölscher, *Die Profeten*, 1914, p. 382 ff. The value of the former for our purposes is vitiated by the fact that Driver listed characteristic expressions of both prose and poetry in Jeremiah, together with their occurrences, indiscriminately. Hölscher's list, while most comprehensive, is burdened with a number of expressions that hardly seem typical of the Jeremiah prose, while the listing of occurrences elsewhere is not always complete, nor is the significance of the statistics analyzed.

[13]The writer by no means concedes that Ezekiel is the creation of late editors, but he is willing to grant it here for the sake of argument.

with or prior to the prose Jeremiah (i. e. Dtr, 7th and 8th century prophets, JE, Jeremiah poetry, etc.)[14]—a fact which makes assumption of dependence on later literature more than risky. d) On the contrary, some 33 of the total occur in Dtr, 15 of these (4, 12, 22, 23, 24, 26, 33, 34, 37abc, 39, 41, 43, 46) five or more times.

The force of the evidence is overwhelming. The assumption that the Jeremiah prose depends on II Isaiah or other literature of the Restoration is *not* supported by an analysis of its style. As one would expect, its closest kinship is to Dtr. Indeed it seems to the writer that if one would assign a post-exilic date to the Jeremiah prose, one is logically compelled to relegate the entire Deuteronomic literature to the same period.[15] This is not the place to debate the problem of Deuteronomy. The writer cannot believe that the Deuteronomic histories were completed much after 561 (the last event recorded). Certainly there is no evidence that any of this literature knew of the Restoration.[16] But if Dtr be given its usual date, it becomes very difficult to believe in schools of otherwise unattested post-exilic Deuteronomists who worked over the book of Jeremiah. Who were they, and what was their purpose in advancing the cause of a reform now over a century old and with an ocean of history between? The conventional date for Dtr virtually requires a date for the prose Jeremiah prior to the Restoration.

Since this conclusion is quite opposed to that of May and others, a further word is in order. May[17] gives an impressive list of passages to prove dependence of his "Biographer" on II Isaiah and some of the later Psalms (e.g. 14:1–9, 10:2–16, 23–25, 16:19–20, 30:9–11, 31:4 ff., 7–9, 16:14–15, 12:14–17, 17:5–8, 12–18, 12:1–4). In some of these cases such kinship is at least highly debatable, but in others (especially 10:1–16, 30:9–11, 31:7–9, etc.) it is obviously present.[18] The point is, however, that of all the passages cited by May in this connection only 16:14–15 (= 23:7–8) and 12:14–17 are

---

[14]A different interpretation of the evidence in some cases might alter these statistics, but the overwhelming force of them cannot be escaped.

[15]As Hölscher, Horst, *et. al.* have done; cf. note 7 above. For full bibliography cf. H. H. Rowley, "The Prophet Jeremiah and the Book of Deuteronomy" in *Studies in Old Testament Prophecy*, 1950, p. 157, note 3.

[16]Cf. Rowley, *op. cit.* p. 160. It is the writer's opinion that the bulk of the Deuteronomic histories were written before 587 (cf. Driver, *Introd. to the Literature of the O.T.*, 1913, p. 198; Pfeiffer, *Introd. to the O.T.*, 1941, p. 410), if only because of the unlikelihood that all the sources incorporated in them would have survived the debacle and been available to an exilic writer. Certainly the later Chronicler did not have them. After making this note the writer observes that W. F. Albright has taken the same position; cf. "The Biblical Period" in *The Jews: Their History, Culture and Religion*, L. Finkelstein, ed., 1949, note 108.

[17]*Op. cit.* pp. 145–148.

[18]Rudolph, *op. cit., ad. loc.*, following P. Volz (*Der Profet Jeremia* [*Kommentar zum AT*] 1928, *ad. loc.*), argues, as did Graf long ago, that the style of Jeremiah in the poetry of chs. 30–31 influenced II Isaiah. The writer is inclined to believe that Jeremianic material has here received expansion in the style of II Isaiah.

in prose. The rest are poetry, frequently passages commonly conceded to be later additions to the Jeremiah book (e.g. the selections from chs. 10, 30 31). As such they have no relevancy to the question of the date of the prose whatever, unless one grant the assumption (which May asserts but does not prove) that the prose of Jeremiah is of a single hand; that this hand is that of the 5th century Biographer; *that this Biographer gave us the book of Jeremiah approximately in its present form; and that the book received no further expansion after he did so.* Only then may one assume that the Biographer (and so the prose sermons) stand later than whatever material the book contains.

This is not the place for the writer to express his views on the composition of Jeremiah. But he can grant none of the foregoing assumptions. While he is prepared to grant the possibility that the prose sermons could be the work of one hand, mere unity of style cannot alone prove identity of authorship. Dtr has a style so similar throughout that separation of strata on that basis alone is impossible, yet no one would ascribe all of Dtr to a single hand. On the contrary, the structure of some of the prose sections seems to argue that a complex process has been at work: e. g. 7:1–8:3, where the prose oracles (7:2b–15, 21–26, etc.) and poetry (7:28b–29) are bound together in a prose framework of autobiographical style (v. 2a, 16 ff., 27–28a); or places where a prose discourse seems to have received expansion (e.g. 19:3–9, 11:7–8b$^\alpha$, 32:17a$^\beta$–23), yet the style of original and of supposed expansion are the same. Evidence of this sort points rather to a *prose tradition* than to a single prose hand.

It is equally difficult to believe that the Biographer is responsible for all the prose sermons. The fact that some of them are embedded in a biographical framework, supplied with the characteristic chronological data of the Biographer, while others (of identical style) entered the book without any evidence that they passed through his hand, argues the contrary. It seems more likely that a prose tradition of Jeremiah existed, some of which entered the book through the agency of the Biographer, some without his help. In 7:2–15 and 26:2–6 we have a case where the same material entered the book in parallel forms, one briefer and in a biographical narrative, the other independently and longer. It does not seem likely that the Biographer created both, yet the style and substance is the same.

That the Biographer, or any one hand, put the Jeremiah book into its present form is unbelievable. Its well-nigh total chronological and topical disarray argues strongly against planned editing of the sort. No editor in his right mind would have perpetrated such disorder. This chronological confusion is especially plain in the biographical material of chs. 26–29, 32–45, as well as from the fact that biographical material, for no apparent reason, found its way into chs. 1–25 (19:14–20:6, 21:1–10, etc.). This is not to be explained by saying that the Biographer, concerned to present a "person" and not a "life," did it on purpose.[19] This is to brush aside a

---

[19]So May, *op. cit.* p. 142.

complex problem too lightly without explaining how a planned confusion *does* better present a "person" than chronological order would have done. An explanation along the lines of that of H. Birkeland[20] is, to the writer's mind, far more plausible.

But to return to the prose sermons. While a number of them have been alleged to exhibit the influence of Ezekiel, II Isaiah, etc., the evidence is at best flimsy. Influence of Ezekiel has been seen in 3:6–12a,[21] in 18:6 ff.,[22] and in 31:27–30[23] etc. Whatever this alleged dependency may consist of it is not of style. The last two mentioned are thoroughly in the style of the prose Jeremiah (which does not depend on Ezekiel). The diction of 3:6–12a has qualities of its own which we have analyzed in Appendix B. It is quite without the characteristic clichés of the Jeremiah prose, and exhibits only one which is characteristic of Dtr. But it is emphatically not dependent on Ezekiel. On the contrary, its diction is closer to the Jeremiah poetry and to Hosea than anything else. This means that whatever kinship exists between these passages and Ezekiel is of the idea only, a peculiarly hard thing to pin down. One can allege that the dependency ran either way, according to his taste, but positive proof is lacking. The writer is strongly inclined to believe that what dependency is present ran from Jeremiah to Ezekiel.[24] In the case of 3:6–12a there is only the idea of the two bad sisters (cf. Ezek 23). But the idea is scarcely recondite and the germ of it (the adulterous wife) had been in Hebrew prophecy since Hosea. In the case of 31:29–30 the common factor is a popular proverb which is here given a somewhat different twist than in Ezek 18. In addition, vs. 29–30 (in contrast to vs. 27–28) exhibit *none* of the style of the prose Jeremiah and may be an addition. As to 18:6 ff., the writer is quite unable to see much connection with Ezek 18. Both stress the conditional nature of judgment (as what prophet did not?), but Ezekiel's characteristic individualizing of the problem is quite absent from the Jeremiah passage.

Passages cited to prove dependence of the prose sermons on II Isaiah, once the bulk of those cited by May are gotten rid of, are few. II Isaiah's "universalism" has been seen in 12:14–17.[25] Here again there is no question of stylistic dependence, that being confined, as we have seen, to certain poetic passages. One has, then, only to raise the question if II Isaiah either invented "universalism" or had a monopoly on it. On the contrary, it exists already in Dtr (e.g. I Kings 8:41–43) and has roots as far back as Amos (9:7) and JE (e.g. Gen 12:3, 22:18). It is, therefore, most subjective to make

---

[20] *Zum hebräischen Traditionswesen*, 1938, pp. 41–53.

[21] E.g. Duhm, *op. cit. ad. loc.* Hölscher, *Die Profeten*, 1914, p. 385; recently Hyatt, *op. cit.* p. 168.

[22] E.g. Hölscher, *ibid.*; recently May *op. cit.* p. 150.

[23] E.g. May, *ibid.*; cf. Peake, *op. cit.*, Rudolph, *op. cit.*, *ad. loc.* For further such passages, cf. Hölscher, *ibid.*

[24] So, e.g. Oesterley and Robinson, *Introduction to the Books of the O.T.* 1934, p. 305.

[25] May, *op. cit.* p. 148, note 12; cf. also 3:17.

all passages which hint of such an idea dependent on II Isaiah. The same must be said of such passages as 16:14–15 (= 23:7–8) which have a "New Exodus" doctrine. While it is true that II Isaiah developed this theme to the fullest (as he did many another), there is no proof that he invented it. In fact, the unquestionably genuine Jeremiah poetry of 31:2–6, 15–22 has it, and germs of it may be seen in Hosea (e.g. 2:14–15). It is inevitable that the calamity of 587 would have brought such an idea to the minds even of lesser men than Jeremiah and II Isaiah.

Our conclusion, then, to this point is:[26] the prose Jeremiah exhibits no stylistic or other dependence on the literature of the Restoration. On the contrary, the style does not indicate a date much after the completion of Dtr (i.e. mid-6th century). This does not, of course, say that a style so stereotyped and so easily imitable (the writer believes that either he or the reader could imitate it) could not have been expanded at a later date. But the style itself is definitely not characteristic of the late exilic or post-exilic periods.

II

An examination of historical allusions within the prose sermons drives us to the same conclusion as does the style. While there is a host of references to show that the prose tradition of Jeremiah did not solidify until after 587 (e.g. 3:16–18, 9:11–15, 11:7–8, 23:1–4, 7–8, 32:36–44, ch. 33, to say nothing of the material embedded in the biographical sections chs. 40–44), there is little convincing evidence that this material (any more than did Dtr) knew of the Restoration.[27] Indeed, the writer will be bold enough to say that very little of it need have been written more than a few years, or at most a decade or so, after 587 (although the possibility, if not the probability, of a development and expansion in the tradition in subsequent years must not be denied).

The writer is aware that certain, if not all, of the prose sermons have been widely assigned to the age of Ezra and Nehemiah, but he finds the evidence for this most inconclusive.[28] It cannot be stated too emphatically

---

[26]Further discussion is forbidden. May (*op. cit.* p. 151, note 16, 17) see resemblances between 17:21–22 and Neh 13:19, 22; between 32:16–27 and Neh 9:6–37, Ezr 9:6–15 etc. (cf. also Hölscher, *op. cit.* p. 385). We must simply point out that resemblance and dependence are not synonyms. The style in both cases is characteristic of the Jeremiah prose and kin to Dtr. [On 17:19–27 see below, p. 23.]

[27]Not even in such passages as 31:38–40. Surely not all the passages that predict a glorious hope for Israel can be called *vaticinia ex eventu* of the Restoration unless one is prepared to say the same thing, which the writer is not, of similar passages in Dtr (e. g. Deut 4:25–31).

[28]The effort of May (*op. cit.* p. 148 f.) to assign ch. 24 to this period is a case in point. All v. 7 ("Egypt") proves is what has just been pointed out: that the prose tradition solidified after 587—if it proves that. Jews had quite possibly begun to settle in Egypt even before that date. In any case, regardless of the relationship of this chapter to Jeremiah (the writer sees no essential disharmony), positive evidence for relegating it to Ezra's day is totally lacking.

that the mere fact that a given section might plausibly be fitted into a later context is no proof that it belongs there. So many prophetic sayings might fit so many situations. Duhm was able to place Habakkuk plausibly in the Greek period, and certain Psalms have been assigned with equal plausibility to the age of David and to that of the Maccabees. Nothing is more treacherous than a procedure of this kind.

Our remarks at this point might well center about 17:19–27, a passage which has been since Kuenen,[29] and in most commentaries, assigned to the age of Ezra. Now one might well question if Jeremiah would have said such a thing in such a way. Certainly it would have been unlike him to do so. But the present question is not whether Jeremiah could or did say it, but whether there is evidence that it could have been said only as late as Ezra. In style the section is typical of the Jeremiah prose and consists of one cliché after another. The possibility of imitation at any age is therefore not to be excluded. But the assignment of it to Ezra's day seems to rest chiefly, as far as one can judge, on the assumption that such stress on the Sabbath is unthinkable sooner. The Sabbath, however, is an old institution. It is clearly enjoined in the Decalogue (Exod 20:8, Deut 5:12).[30] Amos (8:5) rebuked the breakers of it (on moral grounds to be sure), and it is not unlikely that Jeremiah would have done the same.[31] But if Dtr laid the exile to the breach of law and covenant, and if Sabbath was a part of that covenant law, then the present passage is no more than a development of good Deuteronomic theology. In short, it leads us into the world of Dtr and Dtr is quite enough to account for it. It may be added that v. 26 ("from the Shephelah, the hill country and the Negeb," cf. 32:44, 33:13) is remarkably like similar formulae in Dtr (Josh 9:1, 10:40, 11:16).

Positive evidence, while admittedly meagre, does not support a very late date for the prose sermons. The last dateable notice afforded is the prediction of the death of Hophra (which occurred ca. 570) in 44:30, and the oracle in 43:8–13 which must refer to Nebuchadrezzar's invasion a few years later. Evidence that the prose tradition solidified into its definitive form much after this time is lacking. It is doubtful, for example, if such a passage as 27:7 (itself perhaps an expansion; LXX>) would have been worded so if written after the assassination of Amel-marduk and the end of Nebuchadrezzar's dynasty in 560. An oracle such as 34:2–5 leaves one with the impression that the prose tradition had begun to solidify even in Jeremiah's lifetime, for it is doubtful that it would have been put so if composed later, when the events did not so fall out, and when subsequent oracles to Zedekiah are so much more severe.

---

[29] Cf. Peake *op. cit.*, *ad. loc.* The majority of commentators do so, with Rudolph (*op. cit.*, *ad. loc.*) apparently an exception.

[30] Why May (*op. cit.* p. 151) assigns Deut 5:12 to D₂ is not clear. But even if correct, this puts it long before Ezra.

[31] The writer agrees with Rudolph (*ibid.*) that the passage may well be a development of Jeremiah's preaching as understood (and partly misunderstood) among his disciples.

In this connection, it is somewhat of a disappointment that the Lachish Letters, our most important extra-Biblical source for the last days of Judah, throw little direct light on our problem. While they are written in a classical Biblical Hebrew closely akin to that of Dtr (and the Jeremiah prose),[32] they are quite free of the characteristic clichés of either (to "weaken the hands of the people," Jer 38:4 and Lachish VI: 6, being perhaps the only exception). But too much must not be made of this. As Ginsberg points out, it may be well enough explained by the utter difference in the types of material. If this causes surprise, let it be noted that very few of the clichés of the prose sermons occur at all, and these rarely, in the strictly narrative portions of Jeremiah's biography itself. The Lachish Letters do, however, further fortify our confidence in the circumstantial accuracy (and, by inference, in the early date) of the biographical prose. It is very hard on the surface of it to read the intimate, highly circumstantial narrative of the Biographer and believe that it was written over a century later. A contemporary, even eyewitness flavor runs through it (e.g. chs. 26, 36, 37) that can only be credited to one in the circle of the prophet's most intimate friends. The Lachish Letters add to this impression. The situation of 34:7 is paralleled by Lachish IV: 10, a detail no later writer could possibly have known. The personal names found in the Lachish Letters are far more common in the age of Jeremiah, specifically in the Jeremiah biography, than anywhere else.[33]

But if the Biographer be a contemporary of Jeremiah it becomes very difficult, from an observation of the relationship between the two, to relegate the prose sermons to a late date. The Biographer now gives an extended account of events with a minimum of discourse (e.g. chs. 26, 28, 36, 37:11 ff.), now merely supplies the framework for a prose sermon (e.g. 21:1–10, 34:1–7, 8–22, 37:3–10). The very fact that he does this, of course, is proof that the prose tradition existed when he wrote, for much of it entered the book through his hands. If, then, the prose tradition (or parts of it) were at the disposal of the Biographer, and if the latter was a contemporary of Jeremiah, then it follows that the prose tradition had begun to exist *even in the prophet's lifetime* and that much of it was incorporated by the Biographer in approximately its present form not long after his death. This, of course, is not to say that the Biographer's work may not have been expanded after he had completed it by the addition of yet other prose material.[34] But it does forbid us to regard the prose tradition as a post-exilic, or late exilic creation.

[32]W. F. Albright, *BASOR* 70 (1938) p. 17; H. L. Ginsberg, *BASOR* 111 (1948) p. 24 note 1.

[33]Cf. Albright, *op. cit.* p. 12. Of some 20 names in Lachish I–VI, some 15 occur in the Bible of which 9 or 10 are found in the biographical portions of Jeremiah.

[34]For example, ch. 27 may well have been placed before ch. 28 secondarily (note the confusion in 28:1) thereby suppressing the Biographer's original introduction. Cf. also the situation in ch. 32.

III

But if the evidence has clearly argued against a post-exilic date for the prose sermons, it has equally clearly pointed out that their closest kinship is to Dtr. Does this fact, then, drive us to the conclusion that they are the work of the exilic Deuteronomists (D_2) and must we, therefore, regard them as the more or less distorted picture of Jeremiah which these Deuteronomists have chosen to give us?[35] We make bold to question it.

Without for a moment denying the kinship of the Jeremiah prose to Dtr, or even dependence upon Dtr, both in style and idea (after all Deuteronomy was an epoch-making document and one would expect it to have influenced its age), we should like to raise the question if dependence *specifically on D_2* can be proved. While an analysis of the style cannot finally settle the matter, a study of Appendix A will serve at least to cast grave doubt on the common practice of speaking of a Deuteronomic book of Jeremiah. Let the following statistics be noted: a) of a total of 56 entries, 23 (1, 3, 5a, 7, 8ab, 9, 11, 13, 15ab, 17, 18, 19abc, 20, 27ab, 32, 35, 45, 47) do not occur in Dtr at all. And of the 33 which do, 13 (5b, 6, 10, 14, 16, 25, 28, 29, 30, 31, 36, 38, 44) occur not over twice in all that literature, and so are hardly typical of it. It may be added for what it is worth that most of these are also instanced in earlier literature, and that in each of these cases the Jeremiah prose usage outnumbers the meagre Dtr usage (a much wider field of reference) never less than 3 to 1, and in most cases from 7 to 1, to 14 to 1. If the marks of a style are not merely the words and phrases used but also the frequency with which they are used, it is most risky to speak of a dependence on Dtr here.[36] b) We see, then, that 36 of the 56 entries occur never or rarely in Dtr. On the other hand, a glance at any tabulation of the characteristic style of Dtr[37] will reveal a host of clichés which are common there, but rarely or never occur in the Jeremiah prose. It is true[38] that the resemblance between Jeremiah and Dtr is especially marked in II Kings 17, 21, 22. But it cannot be insisted upon too strongly that resemblance and dependence are not synonyms. And if there was dependence, it is at least legitimate to ask which way it ran. Nor is the question to be answered dogmatically. c) There are, however, 33 entries common to prose Jeremiah and Dtr, of which 15 (listed above, [p. 197]) occur in Dtr five or more times and are certainly characteristic of it. But, in the writer's opinion, not one of these can be regarded as the exclusive property of D_2,[39] while all but one or

---

[35]Cf. note 6, above.

[36]For example, if I use a given rare word over and over again in my speech, that word is a mark of my style. The fact that it might be instanced once or twice in a late-Victorian poet scarcely makes my style dependent on his.

[37]E. g. Driver, *Introduction to the Literature of the O.T.*, 1913, p. 99 ff., 200 ff.

[38]Driver, *op. cit.* p. 203.

[39]One realizes that judgment in each case will depend on one's views of the composition of Dtr and its various strata. For example, one who places the whole of the Deuteronomic

two are also instanced in contemporary or earlier literature other than Dtr. In fact, of all 33 in question here, all but about 7 (2, 24, 25, 30, 31, 33?, 44) are so instanced, and in most of these cases the incidence in Jeremiah far exceeds that in Dtr. d) Finally, to balance the 33 clichés occurring in both the Jeremiah prose and Dtr, are 29 (of which 11 do not occur in Dtr) which occur exactly or somewhat similarly in Jeremiah poetry (3, 5ab, 6, 8bc, 10, 13, 14, 15ab, 16, 19abc, 22, 23, 24, 26, 27b, 28, 29, 32, 36, 40, 42, 43, 45, 46). While in some of these cases the similarity is not close enough to be pressed too far, and while some might be explained as glosses, the impression of a definite kinship between the prose sermons and the genuine Jeremiah is inescapable. To excise all of these as glosses would require a most severe textual surgery which, in the writer's opinion, would be no tribute to objective scholarship.

The foregoing points up the fact that, while there is profound resemblance between the Jeremiah prose and Dtr, there are differences almost as marked as the similarities. This alone should warn us against speaking too glibly of dependence. For, if there is a certain dependence, there is also independence. In other words, the prose of Jeremiah is a style in its own right, akin to Dtr but by no means a slavish imitation of it. It must be repeated that we do not seek to deny or obscure the obvious fact of that kinship, or even of a degree of dependence. We simply wish to raise the question if there is anything like a clear case for a dependence specifically on the exilic edition of Dtr which would force us to place the Jeremiah prose later than that work, and to regard it as an edition of Jeremiah colored (not to say distorted) by "deuteronomistic" ideas. We should like also to raise the question if, granting a dependency between prose Jeremiah and Dtr, the chain of dependence did not run from D_1 to prose Jeremiah to D_2, or from D_1 to prose Jeremiah *and* to D_2. In the writer's opinion, however, it is far better to regard both the style of Dtr and of Jeremiah prose (while not denying cross influence) as but examples of the rhetorical prose of the late 7th and early 6th centuries in Judah.[40] This would certainly not force us to minimize the influence of Deuteronomy on Jeremiah and his whole generation, but it would make us chary of explaining all similarity of diction and idea in terms of literary dependence. To take a similar case, the David Biography (II Sam 12–20, I Kings 1–2), the other narratives of the Samuel-Saul-David cycles, and to a great extent JE, exhibit great similarity of style. But this is explained by the fact that all represent the classic narrative prose of the Golden Age. It would take great hardihood to argue identity or even kinship of authorship, or to trace a line of literary dependence between them.

The writer certainly would not like to argue that the prose gives us the *ipsissima verba* of Jeremiah. While he fondly believes that Jeremiah must

---

histories in the exile will get a different picture from one who, like the writer, does not. But, in any case, dependence of the prose Jeremiah specifically on D_2 will be most difficult to prove.

[40]So Oesterley and Robinson, *op. cit.* p. 304 f.; Albright, Ginsberg, cf. note 32 above.

in off moments have spoken prose (even Shakespeare did) and that, if he did so, it was the prose of his age and thus heavily "Deuteronomic," and while he firmly believes that genuine words of Jeremiah underlie the prose tradition (some of it is simply "uninventable" unless one posit a Deuteronomist of equal stature with the prophet), he would not like to engage in textual surgery in the effort to recover them. In short, the terms "genuine" and "non-genuine" as conventionally used are out of place here. What we have is a prose tradition of Jeremiah which grew up on the basis of his words, partly no doubt preserving them exactly, partly giving the gist of them with verbal expansions, partly (e.g. 17:19–27) those words as understood or misunderstood in the circle of his disciples. The origin of it must be sought among Jeremiah's intimates (but that term and "Deuteronomist" are *not* mutually exclusive!). It may be assumed to have been well developed in Jeremiah's lifetime and, if our reasoning has been correct, it was solidified into its definitive form (again allowing for subsequent expansion), whether by one hand or several we cannot decide, not many years after his death.[41]

IV

But if we are at all correct on this point it drives us to a very actual conclusion: is it thinkable that so soon after the prophet's death, in the lifetime of hundreds who knew him well, there could have taken place the fundamental falsification of his ministry, specifically of his early ministry, so widely assumed?[42] We need not boggle at some misunderstanding of his message on the part of his disciples which might have thrown it out of focus at certain points (17:19–27?). This need not require a late date, or even one after Jeremiah's death. Were not the disciples of Jesus capable of misunderstanding his message even in his lifetime? But a fundamental distortion which falsified the whole beginning of his ministry (among other things) is another thing entirely. The writer does not believe it took place. He is in hearty agreement with those who, on the basis of internal evidence, place certain of the poetic oracles of Jeremiah (e.g. 2:4–13, 18–19, 3:1–5, 19–25, 4:1–2) before 621. If the prose tradition places the beginning of Jeremiah's ministry in 626 (25:3, cf. 3:6), it but agrees with the poetry and the facts.[43]

---

[41]On this point we are very close to the position of Pfeiffer (*op. cit.* p. 504 f.) who ascribes these speeches to Baruch. We feel, however, that it was not quite the simple literary process which Pfeiffer depicts.

[42]Cf. note 6, above.

[43]A discussion of the Foe from the North, so vital to the question, is impossible here. While the writer sees no Scythians lurking among them, and while he would date these poems from ca. 612 on into the reign of Jehoiakim, he does not see that this requires a late date for Jeremiah's call. Ch. 1 is an editorial unit. The two visions in vs. 11–16 (the latter heavily overlaid with the prose style) do not necessarily refer to the same time as the account of the call in vs. 4–10 (17–19?). In fact, the words "second time" (v. 13) indicate that the two originally stood together but apart from the experience introduced in v. 4 (had vs. 4, 11, 13

One must protest the effort to have the prose both ways. On the one hand, it is the product of Deuteronomists who sought to annex Jeremiah for Josiah's reform, on the other it contains sentiments which the same scholars find abhorrent to any Deuteronomist (e.g. the Temple Sermon of ch. 7).[44] But the Temple Sermon has precisely the same style as the most "Deuteronomic" passages. It was clearly passed into our book in the characteristic "autobiographical" framework of the prose (e.g. v. 2a, 16 ff., 27, 28a). If it be objected that the Temple Sermon contains "genuine" Jeremiah, it is nevertheless true that our prose "Deuteronomist" gave it to us in its present form. But if the prose writer was a "Deuteronomist" who desired to make Jeremiah "Deuteronomic," why did he include such an "un-Deuteronomic" passage? Presumably he included what he believed in. It is the writer's conviction that, whatever divergencies in detail there may be, the prose tradition did not purpose to distort Jeremiah at all. He is further prepared to maintain that, whatever expansion of Jeremiah's thought it presents, it presents a picture of him not *essentially* different from that of the poetry. The writer must interject his feeling that the differences between classical prophetic theology and Deuteronomic theology, once the verbiage has been scraped away, have been vastly exaggerated. It has been widely assumed, on the one hand, that the primary emphasis of Deuteronomy was cultic, and on the other that Jeremiah (if not most of the prophets) was totally anti-cultic. This has forced the conclusion, if we may put it flippantly, that a self-respecting prophet would rather be dead than Deuteronomic. The writer is quite unable to grant such an extreme dichotomy between cult and ethics, priest and prophet, either in ancient Israel or in any other age.

This would lead us to a discussion particularly of the attitude of Jeremiah to the reform of Josiah which is quite out of the question here. Whatever Jeremiah's attitude toward Deuteronomy, the prose, far from making him out to be an enthusiastic reformer,[45] leaves his precise relationship to the reform quite as ambiguous as does the poetry. The complete lack of unanimity among scholars is proof enough of the point. If Deuteronomists wished to capture Jeremiah for the reform they did not do their work well,[46] they did it very poorly indeed. Had the prose desired to falsify Jeremiah it would have done it ever so much more unequivocally. It is the

---

originally stood together we would expect "third time"). Vs. 13 ff. do not, therefore, locate the Foe from the North oracles immediately after the call (*contra* May, "The Chronology of Jeremiah's Oracles," *JNES* IV [1945] p. 225; Hyatt, "The Peril from the North in Jeremiah," *JBL*, LIX [1940] p. 499).

[44] E.g. Hyatt, *op. cit.* (JNES 1942) p. 162.

[45] Provided only that one does not interpret 11:6 as making a peripatetic evangelist of Jeremiah. The writer would date 11:1–17 to Jehoiakim's reign (cf. vs. 9–10), with expansions after 587 (vs. 7–8). In v. 6 Jeremiah merely protests wherever he goes the necessity of keeping the covenant.

[46] *Contra* Hyatt, JNES 1942, p. 173.

writer's settled conviction that no falsification was intended. The prose sought, as well as it understood him, to present Jeremiah as he was.

APPENDIX A

CHARACTERISTIC EXPRESSIONS OF THE PROSE SERMONS OF JEREMIAH*

1. "Rising up early and sending / speaking," etc. (השכם ושלוח etc.): Jer prose 11 (7:13, 25, 11:7, 25:3, 4, 26:5, 29:19, 32:33, 35:14, 15, 44:4). Except for II Chron 36:15, not elsewhere.

2. To "provoke me / him with the work of your / their hands" (כעס אתי במעשה ידיכם): Jer prose 4 (25:6, 7, 32:30, 44:8). Elsewhere 3 in Dtr (Deut 31:29, I Kings 16:7, II Kings 22:17=II Chron 34:25).

3. To "turn every man from his evil way" (שוב איש מדרכו הרעה): Jer prose 6 (18:11, 25:5, 26:3, 35:15, 36:3, 7). Except for Jonah 3:8, not elsewhere, although similar expressions (always without איש, often with adjective הרע or הרשע) occur 5 in Ezek (13:22, 33:11 etc.), 1 in Zech (1:4), 1 in Jonah (3:10), 1 in Chron (II Chron 7:14); but also 2 in Dtr (I Kings 13:33, II Kings 17:13) and 1 in Jer poetry (23:22).

4. "Other gods" (אלהים אחרים): Jer prose 18 times. The expression is a favorite of Dtr (over 35 in all parts of Deut and the Deuteronomic histories). Earlier occurrences: Exod 20:3, 23:13, I Sam 26:19, II Kings 5:17, Hos 3:1. No later occurrences except II Chron 7:19, 22, 28:25, 34:25 (all based on Dtr). It is to be noted that while in Dtr the expression always occurs with verbs "serve" or "go after," Jer more often uses others: "bow down to," "burn incense to," "pour drink offerings to."

5. a) "Amend your ways and your doings" (היטיבו דרכיכם ומעלליכם etc.): Jer prose 5 (7:3, 5, 18:11, 26:13, 35:15). Not elsewhere, although verb alone occurs with similar meaning in Jer poetry (13:23, 4:22).

   b) If we include all cases where מעללים (with various suffixes) is used in conjunction or parallelism with דרכים (with various suffixes), we have 6 occurrences in Jer prose (7:3, 5, 18:11, 25:5, 26:13, 32:19), 1 in Dtr (Judg 2:19), but 3 in Jer poetry (4:18, 17:10, 23:22) and 2 in Hos (4:9, 12:3). Later occurrences are confined to 1 in Ezek (36:31) and 2 in Zech (1:4, 6).

6. "Stubbornness of their / his heart" (שררות לבם / לבו): Jer prose 7 (3:17, 7:24, 9:13, 11:8, 13:10, 16:12, 18:12); in a poetry context once (23:17). Other occurrences confined to Deut 29:18 and Ps 81:13.

7. "Sitting upon the throne of David" (ישב על־כסא דוד / לדוד על־כסאו). The exact expression 7 in Jer prose (13:13, 17:25, 22:2, 4, 30, 29:16, 36:30; in addition 33:17, 21 are very similar). Nowhere else, although the same construction (participle of ישב but without "David") occurs I Kings 8:25 (Dtr) and Prov 20:8.

8. a) "The cities of Judah and the streets of Jerusalem" (בערי יהודה ובחוצות ירושלם): Jer prose 8 (7:17, 34, 11:6, 33:10, 44:6, 9 ["land of Judah"], 17, 21); nowhere else.

   b) "Streets of Jerusalem" alone: twice in Jer prose (11:13, 14:16) and once in Jer poetry (5:1); nowhere else.

   c) "Cities of Judah" alone: Jer prose 12 (1:15, 11:12, 17:26, 25:18, 26:2, 32:44, 33:13, 34:7, 22, 36:9, 40:5, 44:2); 3 in Jer poetry (4:16, 9:10, 10:22); also II Isa 2 (40:9, 44:26), Zech 1:12, Ps 69:39. In virtually all of these instances Jerusalem is mentioned in the immediate context. "Cities of Judah" occurs *passim* in the Deuteronomic histories and the Chronicler, but usually in a definite sense.

9. "That enter in by these gates" (הבאים בשערים האלה): Jer prose 3 (7:2, 17:20, 22:2); not elsewhere.

---

*The symbol Dtr will here again stand for the whole of the Deuteronomic literature. II Isa will stand for the whole of Isa 40–66. This does not commit the writer to the unity of all this material, but for our present purposes it may be lumped together.

10. "Behold, days are coming" (הנה ימים באים): Jer prose 10 (7:32, 9:24, 16:14, 19:6, 23:7, 30:3, 31:27, 31, 38, 33:14); 1 in poetry context (23:5) as well as 4 in chs. 46–51 (48:12, 49:2, 51:47, 52). Elsewhere: 1 Sam 2:31 (Dtr), II Kings 20:17=Isa 39:6 and 3 in Amos (4:2, 8:11, 9:13).

11. "They that seek their / thy life" etc. (מבקשי נפשם / המבקשים את־): Jer prose 9 (11:21, 19:7, 9, 21:7, 22:25, 34:20, 21, 38:16, 44:30); also 2 in chs. 46–51 (46:26, 49:37). Elsewhere JE 1 (Exod 4:19), Ps 3 (35:4, 38:13, 40:15=70:3); I Sam 20:1, II Sam 16:11 are similar.

12. "That it may be well with you / them," etc. (וייטב / למען ייטב לכם): Jer prose 4 (7:23, 38:20, 40:9, 42:6). Elsewhere: Dtr ca. 9 (Deut 4:40, 5:16, 29, 6:3, 18, 12:25, 28, 22:7, II Kings 25:24) JE 2 (Gen 12:13, 40:14), Ruth 3:1.

13. To "receive correction" (לקח מוסר): Jer prose 4 (7:28a, 17:23, 32:33, 35:13). But in Jer poetry 2 (2:30, 5:3) and Zeph 2 (3:2, 7). Elsewhere only Prov 1:3, 8:10, 24:32.

14. "The evil of their / your doings" (רע מעלליהם, usually מרע or מפני רע): Jer prose 4 (23:2, 25:5, 26:3, 44:22). Also Jer poetry 3 (4:4, 23:22, 21:12 [LXX[b], Arabic omit]). Elsewhere Isa 1:16, Hos 9:15, Deut 28:20, Ps 28:4. A very similar expression, כפרי מעלליהם (and the like) is found in Jer prose (32:19), in Jer poetry (21:14, 17:10) and also Isa 3:10, Mic 7:13.

15. Certain constructions with נביאים. a) "The prophets that prophesy" (הַנְּבִיאִים הַנִּבְּאִים): Jer prose 4 (14:15, 23:25, 27:15, 16, plus 29:21, very similar). One occurrence in poetry context (23:16) may be a gloss (LXX, Lat omit). Otherwise nowhere, although Ezek has a similar construction 3 times (13:2, 16, 38:17). It should be noted that the Jer prose has a fondness for the ptcp. plu. (הַ)נִּבְּאִים)), which occurs there 12 times as against 6 in the rest of the O.T. On the contrary, the use of the impv. (הִנָּבֵא) which occurs 24 times in Ezek (and once in Amos) is absent from Jer.

b) "Your / their prophets" (נביאיכם etc): Jer prose 5 (27:9, 16, 29:8, 32:32, 37:19); Jer poetry 2 (2:26, 30); not elsewhere.

16. The two unusual expressions, sometimes used in conjunction with one another: "their dead bodies shall be food for the birds of the heaven and the beasts of the earth" and "dung on the face of the ground." One or the other occur 7 in Jer prose (7:33, 8:2, 16:4 [both] 19:7, 25:33, 34:20); once similarly in the poetry (9:21). Elsewhere only II Kings 9:37 (not Dtr), Deut 28:26 and Ps 79:2, 83:11.

17. "The voice of mirth and the voice of gladness, the voice of the bridegroom and the voice of the bride": Jer prose 4 (7:34, 16:9, 25:10, 33:11); not elsewhere. Although the bracketing of ששון and שמחה is especially popular in later literature (e. g. Isa 35:10, 51:3, Jer 31:13, Zech 8:19, Ps 51:10, Esther 8:17; cf. also קול בכי וקול זעקה in Isa 65:19), its occurrence in Jer poetry (15:16) and Isa 22:13 forbids us to assume dependence on later literature.

18. "His / thy life for a prey" (נפשו לשלל etc.): Jer prose 4 (21:9, 38:2, 39:18, 45:5); not elsewhere.

19. שקר in various constructions. a) To "trust in lying words / a lie" (/ בטח על־שקר על־דברי השקר): Jer prose 4 (7:4, 8, 28:15, 29:31); not elsewhere save once in Jer poetry (13:25 [בטח בשקר]).

b) To "prophesy lies" (נבא שקר): Jer prose 8 (14:14, 23:25, 26, 27:10, 14, 16, 29:9 [בשקר], 21 [id]; in addition 23:32 is similar). Not elsewhere, except that נבא בשקר occurs once in Jer poetry (5:31).

c) To "speak a lie" (דבר שקר): Jer prose 3 (29:23, 40:16, 43:2); Jer poetry once (9:4). Elsewhere Mic 6:12, Isa 59:3, Zech 13:3, Ps 63:12.

20. To "present my / our / their supplication" (נפל תחנתי). An unusual expression: 5 in Jer prose (36:7, 37:20, 38:26, 42:2, 9), and once in Dan (9:20); not elsewhere. Dan 9:18 has the similar expression נפל תחנונינו. Of 24 occurrences of the word תחנה in the O.T., aside from the 5 in Jer prose, 9 are in Dtr (8 of these in I Kings 8–9); and, of the 10 remaining, 4 are in II Chron 6 (// I Kings 8).

21. "My / his / thy servants the prophets" (עבדי הנבאים etc.): Jer prose 6 (7:25, 25:4, 26:5, 29:19, 35:15, 44:4). Later occurrences: Zech 1:6, Ezra 9:11, Dan 9:6, 10 (Ezek 38:17 is

similar). On the other hand, 4 in Dtr (II Kings 17:13, 23, 21:10, 24:2) and II Kings 9:7 (not Dtr), Amos 3:7.

22. "(to / with) you / we / they and your / our / their fathers" (ואבותיכם אתם and the like): Jer prose 12 (7:14, 9:15, 16:13, 19:4, 23:39, 24:10, 25:5, 35:15, 44:3, 10, 17, 21); Jer poetry once (3:25), Dtr 6 (Deut 13:7, 28:36, 64, Josh 24:17, I Sam 12:7, 15 [but cf. LXX]) and JE 4 (Gen 46:34, 47:3, Exod 13:11, Num 20:15). Later occurrences only Ezek 2:3 and II Chron 6:25.

23. "The land (place, city, inheritance) which I gave to you (them, your / their fathers, to you and your fathers)." Expression with נתתי אשר 7 in Jer prose (7:7, 14, 16:15, 23:39, 24:10, 30:3, 35:15, with 25:5 making a possible 8th [LXX, Lat]); Jer poetry once (17:4), Dtr 5 or more (Deut 3:19, 20, 9:23, I Kings 9:7, II Kings 21:8, cf. I Kings 8:34, 40, 48, 14:15, etc., Deut 26:15). Other occurrences: Ezek (20:15, 36:28, cf. 28:25, 37:25), P (Num 20:12, cf. 20:24, 27:12, Gen 35:12), Amos 9:15, II Chron 7:20. If occurrences with יהוה נתן אשר be included, the total for Jer prose stands at 8, for poetry Jer at 1, while that of Dtr is raised to ca. 18, but no later ones are added. If, further, occurrences with (יהוה נשבע) נשבעתי אשר be taken into account, the only effect is to add 1 from Jer prose (32:22, cf. 11:5), 20 or so from Dtr, plus 4 or 5 from JE, but no later ones.

24. "To provoke me to anger" (להכעיסני / הכעיסני למען): Jer prose 7 (7:18, 11:17, 25:7, 32:29, 32, 44:3, 8); Dtr (I Kings 14:9, 16:2, II Kings 22:17). Later occurrences confined to 2 in Ezek (8:17, 16:26), 2 in Chron (II 34:25, 33:6) being parallel to Kings. If occurrences of להכעיס את־יהוה / להכעיסו (not in Jer) are counted, the effect is simply to raise Dtr total to 14. If occurrences of vb. כעס in perf., impf., and ptcp. of Hiphil, with similar meaning, be included, 3 occurrences in Jer prose are added (7:19, 25:6, 32:30), 1 in Jer poetry (8:19), 7 in Dtr (Judg 2:12, I Kings 14:15, 15:30, 21:22, 22:54, II Kings 21:15, 23:26), and 1 in Hos (12:15). Elsewhere: Isa 65:3, Neh 3:37, II Chron 28:25 (// Kings), Ps 106:29, 78:58, Deut 32:16, 21.

25. To "incline the ear" (אזן נטה [Hiphil]): Jer prose 8 (7:24, 26, 11:8, 17:23, 25:4, 34:14, 35:15, 44:5). Nowhere else in prophets except Isa 55:3. Elsewhere: II Kings 19:16 (Dtr)=Isa 37:17, Dan 9:18 and 14 in Ps and Prov. It is to be noted that the form the expression takes in Jer (ולא הטו את־אזנם etc.) is instanced nowhere else save Prov 5:13, practically all the other occurrences being in prayer or entreaty.

26. "I / who brought you / your fathers out of the land of Egypt" etc. (מצרים מארץ with vb. עלה or יצא): Jer prose 9 (7:22, 25, 11:4, 7, 16:14, 23:7, 31:32, 32:31, 34:13), and once in a poetry context (2:6). The spread of occurrence is probably too wide to point to anything. The expression (or like ones) occurs in all strata of the Pentateuch: ca. 25 in P, but ca. 20 in Dtr and several in JE. In earlier prophets: Amos 2:10, 3:1, 9:7, Hos 2:17, Mic 6:4. Elsewhere Ezek 3 (20:6, 9, 10), Isa 11:16, Mic 7:15, 2 in Chron, 1 each in Ps and Dan.

27. "Sword, famine, pestilence" (the linking of חרב, רעב, דבר, and sometimes other words): a) In series of 3 or more: Jer prose 15 (14:12, 21:7, 9, 24:10, 27:8, 13, 29:17, 18, 32:24, 36, 34:17, 38:2, 42:17, 22, 44:13). A similar thing is found only in Ezek 6 (5:12, 6:11, 12, 7:15, 12:16, 14:21), Isa 51:19 and II Chron 20:9.

b) If we count series of two or more, the total for Jer prose is 25 (adding to the above: 14:13, 15, 16, 16:4, 42:16, 44:12, 18, 27, cf. 43:11, 15:2), with 4 in a poetry context (5:12, 14:18, 18:21, 11:22). Elsewhere: Ezek 9; II Isa, Chr, Lam 1 each.

28. "Men of Judah and inhabitants of Jerusalem" (יושבי ירושלם יהודה איש): Exactly so 7 in Jer in prose context (11:2, 9, 17:25, 18:11, 32:32, 35:13, 36:31), with 2 more in poetry context (4:4, and 4:3 [cf. Vrs]). Elsewhere only II Kings 23:2=II Chron 34:30 and Dan 9:7. If very similar expressions (omitting איש, or substituting for it עם, ערי, מלכי, כל־) are counted, the total for Jer is now 14 (adding 11:12, 17:20, 19:3, 25:2, 35:17), Dtr 1 (II Kings 23:2), Zeph 1 (1:4), Chron 6, Dan 1.

29. "Remnant of Judah / Israel," etc. (יהודה שארית etc.): Jer prose 13 (23:3 [my flock], 24:8 [Jerusalem], 25:20 [Ashdod], 40:11, 15, 41:10 [people], 16 [id], 42:15, 19, 43:5, 44:12, 14, 28); Jer poetry 1 (6:9). Elsewhere II Kings 21:14 (inheritance); Jer 31:7, 47:4 f. (sim.); Ezek 9:8, 11:13 (cf. 25:16, 36:3, 4, 5); Isa 46:3, Amos 1:8, 5:15, 9:12; Mic 2:12, 5:6, 7; Zeph 2:7, 9, 3:13; Hag 1:12, 14, 2:2; Zech 8:6, 11, 12; I Chron 12:38, II Chron 34:9, Neh 7:72. That "remnant"

should be much used in literature of exile and after should hardly cause surprise. That it is not exclusively a late term is shown by occurrences in Zeph, Amos, etc., not all of which are late, and by occurrences in Jer poetry.

30. "All the kingdoms of the earth" (כל־ממלכות הארץ): Jer prose 6 (15:4, 24:9, 25:26, 29:18, 34:1, 17 [cf. 1:15, 26:6]). Elsewhere: Deut 28:25, II Kings 19:15, 19 (Dtr)=Isa 37:16, 20; also Isa 23:17, Ps 68:33 (sim.), Ezr 1:2=II Chron 36:23. Chron has 4 other times (I 29:30, II 12:8, 17:10, 20:29) with plu. ארצות.

31. "Whither I have driven them," etc. (נדח שם [usually Hiphil] אשר): Jer prose 10 (8:3, 16:15, 23:3, 8, 24:9, 29:14, 18, 32:37, 40:12, 43:5). Elsewhere: Deut 30:1, Jer 46:28, Ezek 4:13, Dan 9:7.

32. "Man and beast" (אדם־ובהמה): Jer prose 10 (7:20, 21:6, 27:5, 31:27, 32:43, 33:10 [twice], 12, 36:29, 51:62 [also 50:3]). Jer poetry has similar expression (4:25, 9:9). Pentateuch incidence (Gen 6:7, 7:23, Exod 8:13, 14, 9:9, 10, 19, 22, 25, 11:7, 12:12, 13:2, 15, 19:13; Lev 27:28; Num 3:13, 8:17, 18:15, 31:11, 26, 47) is fairly divided between JE and P, but not in D. Elsewhere: Zeph 1:3, Ezek 7 (14:13, 17, 19, 21, 25:13, 29:8, 36:11), Hag 1:11, Zech 2:8, Jonah 3:7, 8, Ps 36:7, 135:8.

33. "N. N. my servant" (דוד עבדי etc.). This is the order in all 6 occurrences in Jer prose (33:21, 22, 26, 25:9, 27:6, 43:10 [the last 3, which have "Nebuchadnezzar—my servant," are all omitted or altered by LXX; cf. BH³]). Elsewhere exactly so. Ezek 4 (34:23, 24, 37:24, 35), II Isa 3 (41:8, 44:1, 45:4, with 52:13 another?), Hag 2:23, Mal 3:22, Ps 89:4, 21, I Chron 17:4. But also Dtr (but not in Deut) 10 (Josh 1:2, 7, II Sam 3:18, I Kings 11:13, 34, 36, 38, 14:8, II Kings 19:34=Isa 37:35, 20:6); and Gen 26:24 (JE). If incidence of "my servant N. N.," "to my servant, to N. N." (neither in Jer prose) be included, there are added the occurrence in Jer 30:10 (=46:27, 28?), 2 in Ezek, 1 in II Isa, 1 in Zech, 4 in Job, 1 in Chron; while total for Dtr is 14, for JE 4, plus 2 in Isa (20:3, 22:20).

34. To "do that which is evil / right in the eyes of—" (עשה הרע / הישר בעיני): Jer prose 8 (7:30, 18:4, 10, 26:14, 32:30, 34:15, 40:4, 5 [52:2=II Kings 24:19]). Incidence is particularly heavy in Dtr (50 or 60 times). Also occurs in older narratives (e. g. Judg 17:6, 21:25, II Sam 12:9). Later occurrences: Isa 65:12, 66:4 and ca. 20 in Chron (many // Dtr).

35. "Yahweh of hosts, God of Israel" (יהוה צבאות אלהי ישראל). Very frequent (ca. 30 times) in Jer prose, plus 4 in chs. 46–51; very rare elsewhere (I Sam 17:45, II Sam 7:27, Isa 21:10, 37:16, Zeph 2:9). It is interesting that LXX deletes all or part of the expression in every occurrence in the Jer book, but in no case does so elsewhere.

36. "Which is called by my name" (אשר נקרא שמי עליו) and the like: Jer prose 7 (7:10, 11, 14, 30, 25:29, 32:34, 34:15). Similarly in Jer poetry: 14:9, 15:16; also Dtr 2 (Deut 28:10, I Kings 8:43=II Chron 6:33), Amos 9:12, Isa 63:19, II Chron 7:14, Dan 9:18, 19; cf. also II Sam 12:28.

37. Expressions such as the following (cited by May, op. cit. p. 155) probably prove little. a) "In those days" (בימים ההמה / ההם): Jer prose 6 (3:16, 18, 5:18, 31:29, 33:15, 16), plus 2 in chs. 46–51 (50:4, 20). Elsewhere in prophet books only Ezek 38:17, Joel 3:2, 4:1, Zech 8:6, 23. But its use (not always referring to the future) is widespread, from JE (Gen 6:4, etc.) to Esther, Dan and Chron, with over 15 in Dtr.

b) "in that time" (בעת ההיא): Jer prose 4 (3:17, 8:1, 31:1, 33:15); also 1 (4:11) in poetry context and 2 (50:4, 20) in chs. 46–51. Use is general, from Amos (5:13), Micah (3:4) to Esther and Dan, with over 30 in Dtr (frequently in old narrative).

c) "In that day" (ביום ההוא): Jer prose 4 (25:33, 30:8, 39:16, 17); also 1 (4:9) in poetry context and 4 (48:41, 49:22, 26, 50:30) in chs. 46–51. But incidence through O.T. is so multitudinous (ca. 60 in Dtr, many in old narratives) as to prove nothing ("at the end of days" [באחרית הימים], cited by May, is not relevant since it does not occur in prose Jer at all [only 23:20=30:24 and 48:47, 49:39]).

38. To "restore the fortune of—" (שוב שבות): Jer prose 7 (29:14, 30:3, 31:23 [poetry?] 32:44, 33:7, 11, 26): also 30:18, 48:47, 49:6, 39. Elsewhere: Ezek 16:53, 29:14, 39:25; Joel 4:11,

Job 42:10; Ps 14:7, 53:7, 85:2, 126:4; Lam 2:14; Amos 9:14; Zeph 2:7, 3:20; but also Deut 30:3, Hos 6:11. That the expression should have been popular in and after the exile is understandable. While the passages in Amos and Zeph are frequently regarded as late, Deut 30:3 attests use of term by Dtr, and Hos 6:11 attests its use much earlier.

39. "A land flowing with milk and honey" (ארץ זבת הלב ודבש). Two occurrences in Jer prose (11:5, 32:22) scarcely make it characteristic. But since May (*op. cit.* p. 150) calls it a "good D₂ expression," and uses it to support the dependence of Jer prose on D₂, it may be included. It certainly cannot be proved that, of 7 occurrences in Dtr (Deut 6:3, 11:9, 26:9, 15, 27:3, 31:20, Josh 5:6), all are of the exilic edition, while other Pentateuch occurrences (Exod 3:8, 17, 13:5, 33:3; Lev 20:24; Num 13:27, 14:8, 16:13, 14) show its occurrence in JE and P. Ezek (20:6, 15) is the only other prophet to use it. It seems to be a popular cliché, and one scarcely coined by D₂.

40. "Behold, I bring—" (הנני / הנה אנכי מביא): Jer prose 6 (11:11, 19:3, 15, 35:17, 39:16, 45:5); but also Jer poetry (5:15, 6:19), and also 31:8, 49:5. Elsewhere: Ezek 5 (6:3, 26:7, 28:7, 29:8, 37:5), Zech 3:8; also Gen 6:17, Exod 10:4 (JE); Dtr 4 (I Kings 14:10, 21:21 [from old narrative], II Kings 21:12, 22:16=II Chr 34:24).

41. "covenant" (ברית). The word is frequent in Jer prose (almost 20), but occurs only once in poetry context (14:21, where a liturgy is quoted?). It is strikingly absent from the pre-exilic prophets (although Hosea uses it: 2:18, 8:1), while common in later ones (e. g. Ezek over 15, II Isa 8 or 10). It is used in all strata of the Pentateuch and is especially frequent in Dtr (ca. 26 in Dt alone, by no means all of which are D₂).

42. חרפה etc., שרקה, שמה, אלה, קללה, זעוה, often two or more in series, with נתן ל, שים ל (שית ל), היה ל ("I will make them / they shall be a curse," etc.): Jer prose ca. 13 (15:4, 19:8, 24:9, 25:9, 11, 18, 26:6, 29:18, 34:17, 42:18, 44:8, 12, 22; cf. 23:40, 29:22). Also in Jer poetry (2:15, 4:7, 18:16 [cf. 25:38, 48:9, 49:13, 17, 50:3, 51:37]). Later literature: Ezek 5:14, 15, 22:4, 23:46 (cf. 23:33, Zech 8:13, 7:14); II Chron 29:8, 30:7; cf. also Num 5:21 (P), Joel 2:19, Isa 13:9, Dan 9:16. But also Dtr 3 (Deut 28:25, 37, II Kings 22:19), Hos 5:9, Mic 6:16. The tabulation could be extended. Occurrences in Jer prose not only far outnumber those in any other book, but 5 or 6 of them have 4, 5 or 6 of the words in question in series (elsewhere only Ezek 5:15 has as many as 4).

43. To "give into the hand of—" (נתן ביד): ca. 26 in Jer prose; not in poetry (though 12:7 has same idiom with בכף). Nowhere else in prophet books save 7 or 8 in Ezek. Expression a special favorite of Dtr (ca. 30), but also Gen 27:17, 30:35, 32:17, 39:22 (JE). Elsewhere ca. 10 in Chr (some // Kings), with 3 or 4 in P (H), Job and Ps.

44. To "make bondmen of—" (עבד ב). A rare expression: Jer prose 5 (25:14, 27:2, 30:8, 34:9, 10). Elsewhere: Ezek 34:27, Lev 25:39, 46 (H), Exod 1:14 (P?), Isa 14:3; but also Deut 21:3 (of an animal), 21:4 (of a field).

45. To "visit upon, punish" (פקד על): ca. 11 in Jer prose (9:24, 15:3, 23:2, 34, 25:12, 27:8, 29:32, 36:31, 44:13 [twice], 29). Also in poetry context (11:22, 21:14, 13:21 [?]); also 30:20, 46:25, 50:18 [twice with אל], 51:44, 47, 52. Usage is widespread, from the oldest strata of the Pentateuch (e. g. Exod 34:7, Num 14:18, 16:29) to the latest (Lev 18:25, 26:16), but not in Dtr (except Deut 5:9=Exod 20:5). In prophetic books from Amos (3:2, 14) and Hosea (1:4, 2:15, 4:9, 14) to Zech 10:3, Isa 24:21, 26:21, etc., but not in Ezek, II Isa or I Zech.

46. To "hearken to / obey my (thy) voice" etc. (שמע בקול): Jer prose 18 (7:23, 28, 9:12, 11:4, 7, 18:10, 26:13, 32:23, 35:8, 38:20, 40:3, 42:6 [twice], 13, 21, 43:4, 44:23). Rare in later prophets (only Isa 50:10, Hag 1:12, Zech 6:15); but Jer poetry 3 (3:13, 25, 22:21), Zeph 3:2, ca. 50 in Dtr (of which a number in old narratives), ca. 12 in JE. Not in P, but 5 in Ps, 1 in Prov, 1 in Chron, 3 in Dan.

47. To "repent of the evil / good which I thought to do," etc. (נחם על־הטובה / הרעה) Jer prose 6 (18:8, 10, 26:3, 13, 19, 42:10); not in Jer poetry (but cf. 8:6). Elsewhere: Exod 32:12, 14, II Sam 24:16=I Chron 21:15, Jonah 3:10, 4:2, Joel 2:13; cf. also Ezek 14:22, Job 42:11, Zech 8:14 f.

APPENDIX B

THE DICTION OF 3:6–12a

1. משובה ישראל: 3 times (vs. 6, 8, 11); elsewhere only 3:12b (poetry). Use of word in any form rare: 2 in Hos (11:7, 14:5=Jer 3:22); 6 in Jer poetry (2:19, 3:12b, 22, 5:6, 8:5, 14:7); not in Ezek. Elsewhere only Prov 1:32. (Characteristic of Jer poetry and Hosea).

2. תחת כל־עץ רענן ("under every green tree," usually with "on every high hill"): v. 6. In Jer elsewhere: 17:2, 2:20, 3:13 (all poetry, though the last two have been called glosses [Hyatt, *op. cit.* p. 168]). Otherwise Ezek 6:13, Isa 57:5; but 4 in Dtr (Deut 12:2, I Kings 14:23, II Kings 16:4=II Chron 28:4, 17:10). A Dtr formula, but not characteristic of Jer prose.

3. Verb זנה (to "play the harlot"): vs. 6, 8. Word very frequent in Ezek (ca. 20, mostly in chs. 16, 23). But frequent use in Hos (ca. 12) and in Jer poetry (6, four in ch. 3) preclude dependence on Ezek.

4. כל־אלה: v. 7. Elsewhere: 4 in Ezek, 3 in II Isa, but in Jer prose (5:19) and 2 in Jer poetry (2:34, 14:22). Later dependence most questionable.

5. בגודה (adj.) and בגדה (ptcp. f. sing.): vs. 7, 8, 10, 11. Not elsewhere. Verb בגר occurs 2 in Hosea (5:7, 6:7), 7 in Jer poetry (3:20 [twice], 5:11 [twice], 9:1, 12:1, 6); never in Ezek. A word from Jer poetry and Hosea.

6. על־אודות: v. 8. Not elsewhere in prophets. Elsewhere confined to old narratives (Judg 6:7, II Sam 13:16, Josh 14:6) and JE (Gen 21:11, 25, 26:32, Exod 18:8, Num 12:1, 13:24). No late occurrence.

7. נאף: vs. 8, 9. Verb and derivatives spread through O.T.: in Ezek 4 or 5 in chs. 16, 23; but 5 in Jer poetry (5:7, 9:1, 13:27, 23:10, 14), and 2 in Jer prose (7:9, 29:23), plus 5 or 6 in Hosea. Line of dependence Hosea to Jeremiah poetry to Jeremiah prose?

8. זנותה: v. 9. Elsewhere 3 in Ezek, but 2 in Jer poetry (3:2, 13:27) and 2 in Hosea (4:11, 6:10). Dependence again Hosea to Jeremiah poetry to Jeremiah prose?

12

A Fresh Look at "Source B" and "Source C" in Jeremiah*
William L. Holladay

G. WANKE, *Untersuchungen zur sogenannten Baruchschrift* (BZAW 122). Walter de Gruyter & Co., Berlin & New York, 1971. XII + 156 pp. DM 42,—/approx. $17.50.

H. WEIPPERT, *Die Prosareden des Jeremiabuches* (BZAW 132). Walter de Gruyter & Co., Berlin & New York, 1973. VIII + 256 pp. DM 88, —/approx. $36.70.

Here are two important recent studies on the composition of the book of Jeremiah: that of WANKE is a Habilitationsschrift for the University of Erlangen-Nürnberg in 1969/70; that of WEIPPERT is a revised form of a dissertation presented at the University of Basel in 1970/71.

In 1914 S. MOWINCKEL, building on the work of B. DUHM, presented his well-known solution to the problem of the composition of the book of Jeremiah, a solution which commanded widespread support for several decades.[1] There he separated the three main literary categories in the book—prophetic oracles in poetic form, historical narratives about the prophet, and speeches in a kind of repetitive prose, and he asserted that these categories were literary "sources," which he called "A," "B," and "C" respectively. And though subsequent commentators have differed from MOWINCKEL and from each other in many details, this general analysis has become basic; O. EISSFELDT could write in 1951, "It does now appear that here we have reached a fairly permanent verdict."[2] Commentators have taken the "Source A" material to be *ipsissima verba* of Jeremiah, and most of them go on to assume this material to have made up the first dictated scroll (Jer. xxxvi)—though MOWINCKEL himself did not assume this; and again, though MOWINCKEL rejected an attribution of "Source B" to Jeremiah's scribe Baruch, most have made that attribution (thus DUHM, GIESEBRECHT, VOLZ, RUDOLPH, HYATT, BRIGHT ["it is altogether likely"], WEISER;[3] and finally, most commentators have posited a Deuteronomistic

---

*Originally published in *Vetus Testamentum* 25 (1975) 394–412.
[1] *Zur Komposition des Buches Jeremia*, Kristiania 1914.
[2] "The Prophetic Literature," in H. H. ROWLEY (ed.), *The OT and Modern Study*. London 1951, p. 151.

circle for the origin of the material in "Source C" (DUHM, MOWINCKEL himself, RUDOLPH; and HYATT and BRIGHT with modifications).

But during the past fifteen years or so this *opinio communis* has been attacked with ever-increasing convincingness. One important scholar in the attack was C. RIETZSCHEL,[4] who analyzed the present book of Jeremiah into several "tradition-blocks," which were combined, he suggested, one at a time to make up the present corpus of material: and he pointed out that there was no *a priori* reason why a "tradition-block" would have to be made up solely of a single "source": indeed his tradition-blocks did contain more than a single "source." If RIETZSCHEL's contention is correct, then of course one must conclude that the idea of "sources" does not automatically lead us to understand the steps by which the book came into existence, and indeed raises the question as to whether MOWINCKEL's supposed "sources" are really sources at all. And though many readers were not persuaded that RIETZSCHEL's close-knit reasoning was entirely persuasive,[5] nevertheless the theoretical questions which he raised were necessary and important ones.

Now come the two studies under review, the first of which successfully challenges the consensus about "Source B" (i.e. that it is to be attributed to Baruch), and the second of which successfully challenges the consensus about "Source C" (i.e. that it is to be attributed to a Deuteronomistic circle). WANKE's study comes essentially to a negative conclusion, namely that "Source B" is made up of three different "cycles," of different origins, none of which can be attributed with any confidence to Baruch, while that of WEIPPERT comes to a more positive conclusion, namely that "Source C" has no connection at all with the literary circles associated with Deuteronomy or the Deuteronomistic historical work, but rather shows a close connection with Jeremiah's own poetic diction and theological work. Both these studies are of prime importance, moving the discussion of the origin of the book of Jeremiah forward into fresh territory. Since there is no way really to summarize these studies in short compass, I shall offer here a rather full summary of the conclusions of each book, appending to each some suggestions of my own.

First, WANKE's work. It is plain, to begin with, that the narrative material about Jeremiah breaks into two main sections: chs. xxxvii–xliv form a continuous narrative on the events connected with the fall of Jerusalem in 587 B.C., while the material up through ch. xxxvi is both broken up by other material, particularly collections of poetic oracles, and at the same time is not organized chronologically (WANKE sees this latter collection to comprise xix 1–xx 6, xxvi, xxvii–xxviii, xxix, xxxvi).

---

[3] In their respective commentaries on Jeremiah. The quotation from BRIGHT is found in his commentary ("The Anchor Bible"), p. LXVII.

[4] *Das Problem der Urrolle*, Gütersloh 1966.

[5] See, for example, my review in *VT* 18 (1968), pp. 399–405.

In dealing with chs. xxxvii–xliv he depends heavily on the work of H. KREMERS, found both in an unpublished dissertation[6] and in a later published discussion of the theological data of that dissertation;[7] but I shall not here attempt to separate KREMERS' conclusions from WANKE's. WANKE outlines the material in xxxvii 11–xliii 7 into ten narratives, each consisting of three parts—a short introduction giving the details of time, situation, and/or person, and often the reasons for his appearance; then a main body offering a conversation and its consequences; and finally a closing remark, often *wayyēšeb yirmiyyāhû* . . . or the like. He finds further that these ten narratives group themselves into five pairs in sequence, the narratives of each pair being closely associated with each other. It is worthwhile to reproduce this analysis here (see pp. 94–95):

first pair:
    xxxvii 11–16:   a) introduction: vss. 11–12
                    b) main body: vss. 13–16a
                    c) closing remark: vs. 16b,
       closely associated (note the suffixes in vs. 17) with:
    xxxvii 17–21:   a) introduction vs. 17aα
                    b) main body: vss. 17aβ–21a
                    c) closing remark: vs. 21b;
second pair:
    xxxviii 1–6:   a) introduction: vss. 1, 3 (vs. 2 is probably inserted
                        from xxi 9)
                    b) main body: vss. 4–6bα
                    c) closing remark: vs. 6bβ,
       closely associated (reference in vs. 7 to vs. 6) with:
    xxxviii 7–13:   a) introduction: vs. 7
                    b) main body: vss. 8–13a
                    c) closing remark: vs. 13b;
third pair:
    xxxviii 14–28a: a) introduction: vs. 14a
                    b) main body: vss. 14b–22 + 24–27
                    c) closing remark: vs. 28a,
       closely associated (note the time reference in vs. 28b) with:
    xxxviii 28b—xl 6: a) introduction: xxxviii 28b
                    b) main body: xxxix 1—xl 6a
                    c) closing remarks: xxxix 14b and xl 6b;
fourth pair:
    xl 13–xli 2:   a) introduction: xl 13
                    b) main body: xl 14—xli 2aβ
                    c) closing remark: xli 2aγb,

---

[6] *Der leidende Prophet*, submitted at Göttingen in 1952, and thus far available only in typescript.

[7] "Leidensgemeinschaft mit Gott im AT. Eine Untersuchung der 'biographischen' Berichte im Jeremiabuch," *Ev Th* 13 (1953), pp. 122–140.

closely associated (reference in xli 4 to vs. 2 [vs. 3 seems secondary, taken from 2 Kings xxv 25]) with:

xli 4-9:   a) introduction: vss. 4-5
                 b) main body: vss. 6-8
                 c) closing remark: vs. 9;

fifth pair:

xli 10-15:   a) introduction: vs. 10
                 b) main body: vss. 11-15a
                 c) closing remark: vs. 15b,

closely associated (vss. 16-18 refer to earlier material) with:

xli 16-xliii 7: a) introduction: xli 16—xlii 1
                 b) main body: xlii 2—xliii 5
                 c) closing remark: xliii 7.

This tenfold cycle has been enlarged by several secondary additions. The material in xxxviii 1-10 is difficult to analyze, but appears to have been added at a later stage on the basis of xxi 1-7 rather than being an originally separate incident (pp. 100-102). The sixth narrative in the above analysis, namely xxxviii 28b—xl 6, seems to have undergone secondary enlargement: two narratives seem to be interwoven here, an original one (xxxviii 28b, xxxix 3, 14a, xl 6) and an additional one (xxxix 14b + 11-12, xl 1-5) which was enlarged at a later stage by further material (xxxix 1-2, 4-10); and all of this was then extended by xl 7-12, a doublet parallel to 2 Kings xxv 23-24 (p. 110). The tenth narrative in the cycle, xli 16—xliii 7, was enlarged by xlii 10-18 (p. 130); and finally the total cycle was enlarged by xliii 8-13 and xliv (pp. 131-2). This total cycle, it would seem, consists largely of set speeches.

Now this cycle is the product of conscious literary work; nothing in the OT narrative exceeds it in skill. The individual units are not loosely strung together, but each builds toward the total climax (pp. 151-2). WANKE rejects the notion that this material is the work of Baruch. If Baruch had written it, he reasons, then one must assume it arose in Egypt, since Baruch went to Egypt with Jeremiah. But in this case Baruch would surely have rounded it off with some account of Jeremiah's further experience in Egypt. Instead, WANKE is inclined to identify the author as someone in Gedaliah's administration at Mizpah, since so many details are given of that circle of officials (p. 146). The cycle has one overriding purpose: to highlight *the reality of what it is for Jeremiah to be a prophet* [*die Wirklichkeit der prophetischen Existenz Jeremias*]; the details are told with an astonishing sobriety, and there is no attempt to claim a black-white dichotomy between Jeremiah's opponents and the prophet himself. Here, for the first time in the OT, we find a connection between the life of faith and suffering: the suffering of the messenger of God is the consequence of the rejection of his proclamation (pp. 155-6).

It is quite otherwise with the other large cycle of narrative material, namely xix 1-xx 6 xxvi xxvii-xxviii xxix xxxvi, which has had a very complicated tradition- and redaction-history. He suggests that the core of this material is xxvii–xxviii and xxix (p. 149). Chs. xxvii–xxviii are built up of three sections:

(1) action of Jeremiah: xxvii 2–3 (4–8) 12b xxviii 5–9
(2) counteraction of Hananiah: xxviii 1–4 10–11a (b)
(3) confirmation of Jeremiah and threat [*Drohwort*] against Hananiah: xxviii 12–17.

Indeed there is a symmetry in the subsections of this material:

xxvii (1) 2–3 (4–8) 12b: ⌐report of the symbolic act of Jeremiah
xxvii 1–4:   ⌐⌐ reply of Hananiah
xxviii 5–9:   ⌐ ⌐reply of Jeremiah
xxviii 10–11:   ⌐ report of the symbolic act of Hananiah
                              + preliminary closing remark
xxviii 12–14:   ⌐confirmation of Jeremiah, and
xxviii 15–17:   ⌐valid threat against Hananiah (p. 34).

In the original core of ch. xxix we likewise find a parallel threefold structure:

(1) action of Jeremiah: vss. 1, 3–7
(2) counteraction of Shemaiah: vss. 24–29
(3) condemnation of and threat against Shemaiah: vss. 30–32 (p. 58).

WANKE finds great difficulty in analyzing ch. xxvi; it manifests unevennesses and has had a complicated tradition-history. He tentatively suggests a conflict story of Jeremiah in opposition to the priests and prophets, vss. 1–19, to which has been appended the Uriah narrative, vss. 20–23, and a closing remark, vs. 24. But he is troubled by the meaning of the word ʿam; it surely does not belong in vs. 8, but beyond that fact he is uncertain whether the "people" are a mob inimical to Jeremiah or folk essentially on his side (pp. 82–90). In any event at some point in its transmission the chapter was prefixed to the corpus of opposition stories in chs. xxvii–xxix (p. 149).

He believes that this small collection, xxvi–xxix, was later enlarged by two other additions, xix 1–xx 6 and xxxvi (pp. 147–9). I shall deal first with his analysis of the structure of each of these additions and defer for a moment his answer as to whether all of this made up a unified cycle.

First, then, xix 1–xx 6. The material in this passage manifests the same kind of threefold structure:

(1) action of Jeremiah: xix 1–2a* 10–11a 14–15
(2) counteraction of Pashhur: xx 1–2
(3) threat against Pashhur: xx 3 (4–6) (p. 19).

Now ch. xxxvi; this chapter has a more complicated structure. Here WANKE has based his analysis on that of E. NIELSEN:[8] the passage is divided into three sections, vss. 1–8, the exposition; vss. 9–26, the report of the public reading of the scroll; and vss. 27–32, the closing. The opening section in turn divides into two parallel subsections:

		statement of time, vs. la	
introduction of an order from Yahweh:	vs. 1b	introduction of an order from Jeremiah:	vs. 5a
order to Jeremiah:	vs. 2	order to Baruch:	vss. 5b–6
reason for the order (*ûlay):	vs. 3	reason for the order (*ûlay):	vs. 7
execution of the order:	vs. 4	execution of the order:	vs. 8.

In symmetrical fashion, the closing section has a similar structure:

statement of time, and introduction of a word from Yahweh:	vs. 27
order to Jeremiah:	vs. 28
execution of the order:	vs. 32.

The central section, the public reading, divides into three subsections, each with a parallel threefold structure:

public reading:	vss. 10	15	21b–22
reaction to the reading: reporting to others (and, in the final instance, destruction of the scroll):	vss. 11–13	16–18, 20	23
reaction to the report: fetching of the scroll (and, in the final instance, fetching of Jer. and Baruch):	vss. 14	21a	26a

This basic structure was evidently enlarged at a later time by two additions, both stimulated by 2 Kings xxii: Jer. xxxvi 24–25, which state that Jehoiakim did not do as Josiah had done (stimulated by 2 Kings xxii 11–13), and Jer. xxxvi 29–31, a judgment against Jeremiah's opponents (stimulated by 2 Kings xxii 16–20). This second addition brings the general pattern of Jer. xxxvi into conformity with the threefold pattern within xix 1–xx 6, xxvii–xxviii and xxix which we have already set forth:

(1) action of Jeremiah: vss. 1–20
(2) counteraction of Jehoiakim: vss. 21–26
(3) confirmation of Jeremiah with judgment and threat against Jehoiakim: vss. 27–32.

---

[8] *Oral Tradition*, London 1954, p. 65.

It would seem then that these additions were made at the time when the narrative of ch. xxxvi was incorporated into this cycle (pp. 63–72).

Now WANKE plainly has a true cycle in chs. xxxvii–xliv, but to what extent does he believe that xix 1–xx 6 xxvi xxvii–xxix xxxvi made up a unified cycle, given the fact that this material now lodges in three separate passages? He could assume of course that an original unity has been split by subsequent insertions, but he does not say this. He states (and it seems obvious) that xix 1–xx 6 is where it is because of the catchword association ("potter") with ch. xviii (p. 149); and he believes that ch. xxxvi served as the conclusion of either chs. i–xx or of xxv + xlvi–li (we note, though it may be too obvious to him to say so, that he follows RIETZSCHEL in assuming that the LXX offers the original location of the oracles against foreign nations [MT xlvi–li], p. 149). How, then, was the cycle split? All he says is that "units of tradition which were originally joined to each other could fall apart again" (p. 149); but this does not strike me as particularly convincing.

There is no doubt, however, that he has demonstrated that the material in this collection shows a unified, common concern: *the truth of the proclamation of the prophet Jeremiah*. The basic point in these narratives is not the experiences of Jeremiah as a result of his proclamation but rather the accomplishment of that proclamation against all hostility and challenge. There *is* a common scheme to this material, then: proclamation, challenge, and confirmation (p. 156). The narratives of this "cycle" do not move to a sequential climax as do the narratives in chs. xxxvii–xliv; each unit has had a tradition-history of its own, and the material has coalesced only gradually (cf. pp. 148–9). It would seem plausible that chs. xxvi–xxviii and xxxvi are the product of a single hand: the diction, the structure, and the point of view of the narrative demand it (p. 145); since WANKE has rejected an identification of Baruch as the author of chs. xxxvii–xliv (see above), he is open to the possibility that Baruch is responsible for chs. xxvi–xxviii and xxxvi; but he feels that the argumentation is about equally for and against such a specific identification (p. 147).

He discusses a third "cycle," namely xlv (Baruch's lament) + li 59–64 (the instructions given by Jeremiah to Zedekiah's delegation to Babylon in 594 B.C.). WANKE associates these in a "cycle," both because of the likeness of the introductory words of each passage, *haddābār ᵃšer* VERB *yirmiyyāhû ᵓel-*, which are not found elsewhere in the book of Jeremiah, and because the recipients of the two pronouncements, Baruch and Seraiah, are brothers, both sons of Neriah (xxxvi 4, li 59) (pp. 133, 140); but these two short passages, though no doubt associated, are hardly to be dignified by the term "cycle."

WANKE makes an attempt to trace the steps by which these three collections of material were fitted together with the remainder of the material of the book of Jeremiah. His tentative suggestion is as follows:

(1) chs. i–xx were combined with xxv + xlvi–li;
(2) xlv + li 59–64 came into existence alongside the first collection, and ch. xxxvi was added as a closing;
(3) between xx and xxv, xxi–xxiv was added; between xxv and xxxvi, the complexes xxx–xxxi and xxxii–xxxv were added; and between xxxvi and xlv, chs. xxxvii–xliv were added;
(4) chs. xxvi–xxix were inserted (p. 150).

My own feeling is that this study has contributed greatly to our knowledge of the origins of the book of Jeremiah: most of what WANKE has given us I find quite convincing. He is correct, I believe, in separating chs. xxxvii–xliv from xix 1–xx 6 xxvi xxvii–xxix xxxvi, and in depicting the contrasting patterns and purposes of these two bodies of material, and therefore I am forced to agree with him that xxxvii–xliv, at least, cannot be from Baruch.

But I should like to raise the question whether this curiosity of a "cycle" which comes together and then breaks up again, i.e. the broken material from xix to xxxvi, could not better be explained as precisely the freedom of Baruch in literary work. Here is material of self-consistent purpose, at least at a particular stage of tradition-history. Might not these units, now separated, always have been so, and have been framed and inserted into a previous Jeremianic corpus by an author-editor who was party to the events or had first-hand knowledge of them?

I am not prepared to offer any counter-proposal for a step-by-step sequence of the building up of the book of Jeremiah. I think much more work must still be done by all of us. I may say, though, that I am still attracted to RIETZSCHEL'S suggestion[9] that ch. xlv originally stood after ch. xx, as Baruch's "post-script"—there is, after all, the plausibility of the catchword association of *yāgôn* (xx 18, xlv 3).

Now WEIPPERT'S work. She deals with a topic about which I myself had been intending to write an extended study for a number of years but never found time to do; but now she has done a better job than I would have done, so I am very glad it has turned out as it has. Fifteen years ago I worked systematically at the problem of the repeated phrases of the sterotyped prose ("Source C") and had made my own lists, as so many others have done, from COLENSO in the nineteenth century to HÖLSCHER in the twentieth. My interim report was published in 1960;[10] my conviction was that the prose phrases were in many cases prosaicized copies of prototype phrases found in Jeremiah's poetry or in other prophetic poetry, or in some cases in other earlier traditional lore. And I assumed (though I did not publish the assumption) that the prose was Baruch's adaptation of Jeremiah's poetic message.

---

[9] *Op. cit.*, p. 128.
[10] "Prototype and Copies: A New Approach to the Poetry-Prose Problem in the Book of Jeremiah," *JBL* 79 (1960), pp. 351–67. The references to COLENSO and to HÖLSCHER are in notes 1 and 2 respectively of that study.

WEIPPERT refers to this study of mine a good deal, often critically, and more often than not her criticism is justified. My own conviction is that she has written the definitive work on the problem of the stereotyped prose in Jeremiah, and though questions remain, I believe we can consider that this issue is now solved.

What she insists upon in her analysis, particularly in extended passages, is to do what neither I nor HÖLSCHER nor any other listmaker had ever done, and that is to pay close attention to the *context* within which these phrases appear. Let me repeat here two simple examples which she cites. The first (p. 23, note 108) she draws from S. HERRMANN, but he did not draw the conclusion from the example which she does: "with all one's heart and with all one's soul" appears in Jer. xxxii 41, and is always considered a "Deuteronomistic phrase," since it appears eight times in Deuteronomy and four times in the Deuteronomistic historical work. But in the Jeremiah passage the phrase refers to *God*, while in the Deuteronomic-Deuteronomistic corpus it refers only to the faithful *Israelite*. This theological contrast is of capital importance; it means that we cannot label the phrase "Deuteronomistic" in the book of Jeremiah without further ado. Again (p. 25) the verb *qṭr* piel is common both in the Deuteronomistic work and in Jeremiah in comparison with other portions of the OT. But in the Deuteronomistic work the verb is used of the illegitimate Yahwistic cultus, while in Jeremiah it is used for idolatrous worship. This attention to context should be an obvious aspect of any analysis of the material in "Source C," but to my knowledge the task had not previously been carried through with any consistency.

Since it is manifestly impossible to cover the whole corpus of "Source C" material in this way, what she has done in this study is to analyze both extensive and intensive samples. The extensive samples are made up of four passages which are universally adjudged to be specimens of "Source C," each manifesting a typical issue in the problems of the prose style: vii 1–15 (evidencing a presumed exilic or post-exilic date); xviii 1–12 (where the content suggests a Deuteronomistic origin); xxi 1–17 (manifesting a monotony and verbosity of style); and xxxiv 8–22 (offering problems of the organization of the prose addresses) (p. 26). Then the intensive samples are five shorter passages which contain a variety of the typical repeated phrases, parallels for which she then investigates throughout the book of Jeremiah and beyond: xxvii 10, 14–16, concentrating on *nbʾ* nif. + *šeqer* (+ *bišmî*) "prophesy a lie (in my name)" and *(han)nebîʾîm* + *nbʾ* nif./*lōʾ* + *šlḥ* "prophets who prophesy/but I did not sent them" and the like; xxxv 15, concentrating on *škm* hif. "persistently," *lōʾ* + *nṭh* nif. + *ōzen* + *lōʾ* + *šmʿ* "did not incline his ear nor listen" and the like, and *šwb* + *midderek* + *yṭb* hif. + *maʿᵃlālîm* "turn from his evil way and amend his doings" and the like; xxxiv 17–20, concentrating on *ḥereb*, *rāʿāb*, *deber* "sword, famine, pestilence"; xviii 7–10, concentrating on the six verbs also found in i–10, *ntš*, *nts*, *hrs*, *ʾbd* hif., *bnh*, *nṭʿ* "pluck up, break down, destroy, overthrow, build, plant," and on the contrast of *rāʿâ* "evil" with *ṭôbâ* "good" or *šālôm* "welfare"; and xxxii 29b–32, concentrating on *ʾelōhîm* *ʾaherîm* "other gods" and *kʿs* hif. "provoke to anger."

Her treatment of the diction offered in all this material is exemplary. Thus with regard to the Temple Sermon, vii 1–15, she first compares the passage with xxvi 4–6 and concludes, as have most commentators, that xxvi 4–6 is an abbreviated form of the discourse and that vii 1–15 is nearer to the presumed original wording (pp. 32–34); that is to say, "Source C" (i.e. vii 1–15) has priority over "Source B" (ch. xxvi) in written fixing of the material. The occurrence of many of the phrases in vii 1–15 is limited, or largely limited, to the book of Jeremiah, e.g. "amend your ways and your doings" (vss. 3, 5), "trust in deceptive words" (vss. 4, 8), "the house which is called by my name" (vss. 10, 11, 14). Other phrases have ties with various other corpora within the OT: thus "alien, fatherless, widow" (vs. 6) is an old triad (Exod. xxii 20–21) which may well be implied in Isa. i 17 (see p. 42 n. 70). It is true that "walk after other gods" (vss. 6, 10) is a Deuteronomic-Deuteronomistic formula; but the total phraseological variety of the Temple Sermon does not press us to see here the specific editorial work of a Deuteronomistic writer (pp. 41–42). Further, the total *content* of vii 1–15 does not reflect the theological assumptions of the Deuteronomistic school. Jeremiah does not reject Yahweh's *possession* of the Temple: "the house which is called by my name" (vii 10, 11, 14) reflects xi 15 ("my house," in a fragment of poetry) and xxiii 11. What Jeremiah is criticizing in the Temple Sermon is the people's adherence to the Temple itself instead of an adherence to Yahweh who may be found there: in Jeremiah's mind the Temple becomes a barrier between Yahweh and his people. His message is thus in direct opposition to any high estimate of Temple-*cum*-Yahweh such as might emerge from a reading of Deuteronomy (cf. Deut. xii 5). She concludes then that vii 1–15 is consistent with Jeremiah's message in his poetic oracles and not to be construed as a product of exilic or post-exilic editorial work by the Deuteronomists (pp. 46–48).

She draws a similar conclusion with regard to the next passage with which she deals, xviii 1–12, the visit to the potter's house. If it is not an example of a typical prophetic symbolic action (it is, after all, really a prophetic *observation*. p. 52), nevertheless it has the outward marks of a symbolic action, and it offers word-play (the double meaning of *yôṣēr*, see vs. 11). She refutes the analysis of S. HERRMANN, who was convinced that Jeremiah's presentation of alternative courses of action, as in vss. 7–10, was a matter of theoretical reflection appropriate to the Deuteronomists (p. 60); rather, such alternatives are found elsewhere in Jeremiah, in his poetry (xiii 15–17, xvii 5–8, etc.) (p. 61), and as a matter of fact in Isa. i 19–20. Indeed she suggests quite acutely that when alternative courses of action are presented in Isaiah, either alternative is really possible; in Jeremiah, either is theoretically possible but the prophet expects the people to make a specific choice which he anticipates; and in Ezekiel, the alternative is unreal, since he knows how the people will decide (pp. 61–62). Again, then, this material gives every evidence of reflecting Jeremianic tradition, even though couched in prose (p. 66).

Her analysis of xxi 1–7 elicits the existence of the specific *type* of prose which occurs here, a mannered and stylistic sort of prose which she refers to as *Kunstprosa* (an English translation might be "formal prose"). *Kunstprosa* is characterized by the irregular occurrence of *parallelismus membrorum* and by the presence of word-groups (almost like lists) of two, three, or four members. Thus Jer. xxi 4–7 offers

(1) the following parallelisms:

    (a) "behold, I will turn back the weapons of war [. . .] outside the walls, and I will bring them together into the midst of this city" (vs. 4);

    (b) "and I will smite the inhabitants of this city, and of a great pestilence they shall die" (vs. 6);

and (2) the following pairs and triplets:

    (a) pairs:

        (i) "which are in your hand
              and against which you are fighting" (vs. 4),

        (ii) "against the king of Babylon
              and against the Chaldeans" (vs. 4),

        (iii) "with outstretched hand
              and strong arm" (vs. 5),[11]

        (iv) "both man
              and beast" (vs. 6);

    (b) triplets:

        (i) "and in anger,
              and in fury,
              and in great wrath" (vs. 5),

        (ii) "Zedekiah king of Judah,
              and his servants,
              and the people" (vs. 7);

        (iii) "from sword,
              from famine,
              and from pestilence" (vs. 7);

        (iv) "into the hand of Nebuchadnezzar king of Babylon,
              and into the hand of their enemies,
              and into the hand of those who seek their life" (vs. 7),

        (v) "he shall not pity them,
              or spare them,
              or have compassion" (vs. 7) (p. 75).

---

[11]This arrangement of words is unique: the normal Deuteronomic-Deuteronomistic wording reverses the adjectives. The book of Isaiah offers *yād nĕṭûyâ* in the refrain of v 25 and four additional passages.

One may add that quadruplets are found for example in xiv 14 ("lying vision, and divination, and worthlessness, and deceit of their own minds") and 16 ("them, their wives, and their sons, and their daughters") (p. 79).

WEIPPERT describes the process that gave rise to this *Kunstprosa* as the "demetrification of prophetic discourse" [*eine Entmetrisierung des Prophetenwortes*] (p. 78). She admits that *Kunstprosa* is also found in the Deuteronomistic historical work (cf. 1 Sam. xii 7–25, 1 Kings viii 14 ff.) (p. 77 and note 221) but insists that we cannot call the Jeremiah prose "Deuteronomistic" because of such formal-stylistic analogy but instead must find the common origin of such prose (p. 77): and the origin is clearly in poetry (p.78). She does not declare herself whether the development of *Kunstprosa* is a debasement or an evidence of fresh creativity but suggests that in Jeremiah's case, at least, there was a loosening from the linguistic norms of proclamation [*die Loslösung von der gattungsmässig genormten Sprucheinheit*] as he "demetrified" his addresses (p. 78).

She next notes the *parenetic* content of much of the prose (i.e. its basis in moral appeal). She wonders whether Jeremiah is encouraged in his parenetic discourse by similar parenesis within Deuteronomy[12] and comes to no conclusion, since we know neither the scope of *Urdeuteronomium* nor the extent to which Jeremiah knew the text of Deuteronomy (p. 81); for a different perspective on this problem, see my constructive remarks below.

She has an intricate analysis of her fourth extensive passage, xxxiv 8–22, a passage with a controverted relationship to the law of liberation from debt slavery, Deut xv 12–18. I shall not reproduce her discussion in detail but simply offer her conclusion: that vss. 13–22 cannot be due to a Deuteronomistic editor but are quite likely of Jeremianic origin (pp. 99–100)—the same kind of word-groups, pairs and triplets appear as in passages discussed earlier (p. 95), as well as traces of parallelism, notably between clauses in vss. 15 and 16, where *wattāšūbû* has a double meaning (p. 96); and that vss. 8–12 are a secondary introduction added later (p. 100).

She summarizes her analysis of these four extended addresses in her insistence that we must reject any theory that sees them as non-Jeremianic, indeed non-prophetic; they are built up as other prophetic speeches are built up (p. 106).

This conclusion is only reinforced by the detailed analysis which she then makes of shorter passages in which the "stereotyped" phrases occur with particular frequency, those which I earlier referred to as her intensive samples. Typical is her treatment of the expression $(han)n^e b\hat{i}^{\circ}\hat{i}m + nb^{\circ}$ nif. "prophets who prophesy" with or without the expression $l\bar{o}^{\circ} + \check{s}l\dot{h}$ "I did not send" and the like. The occurrence of this noun with the cognate verb is confined in Jeremiah to passages which involve a confrontation with other

---

[12]Cf. here G. VON RAD, *Studies in Deuteronomy*, London 1953, pp. 12 ff.

prophets; it is thus a pejorative combination. (She notes that the expression *hann^{e}bî$^{\circ}$îm* + *nb$^{\circ}$* nif./hitp. in 1 Kings xxii 10, 12 [the Micaiah episode] likewise refers, at least in the narrator's mind, to illegitimate prophets.) In Jeremiah the verb is in most cases a participle, *nibb$^{e\circ}$îm*, and so participates in the double use of a root in assonance of which Jeremiah is so fond. In many cases the verb is associated with *bišmî* "in my name" and/or *šeqer* "lie;" and in three instances "did not send" is associated with "lie" (and/or "in my name"). Now all of this is not to be understood as prolixity; rather it is the solution to the necessity to indicate the illegitimacy of the prophets who call upon Yahweh but whom Yahweh did not call. This shaping of formulas is grounded in an exegetical and homiletic interest: the confrontation with the false prophets was a real one, a constant concern of Jeremiah's. Now none of this has any connection with Deuteronomistic literature; the relations with Deuteronomistic literature in regard to this cluster of phrases are weak and problematic, and the assumption of a connection with Deuteonomistic literature was simply based on the assumption that formulaic language was characteristic of that literature (pp. 120–1).

To sum up: WEIPPERT concludes that the prose addresses (i.e. the material of the presumed "Source C") represent a tradition that stands nearer to Jeremiah than do the third-person narratives (i.e. the "Source B" material), near enough to call them a Jeremianic tradition (pp. 228–9). Detailed investigation of specific phrases indicates that the ties to Deuteronomic-Deuteronomistic speech are weak: only in a few cases (e.g. "walk after other gods") do we have a direct line to Deuteronomistic phraseology, and in most of such cases the material in Jeremiah gives a distinctive turn to the phrases. Indeed at some points the Deuteronomists seem themselves to be dependent on Jeremiah rather than the reverse. But the prose material does not simply imitate the poetry; it has its own integrity and distinctiveness (p. 229). She further concludes that these prose addresses are not really *sermons*; they are the parenetic portion of the Jeremianic proclamation of Yahweh's word, that portion which calls on the people to repent. That parenesis is exemplified by the phrase *šûbû $^{\circ}$îš middarkô hārā^{c}â*, and we note in passing that the individualizing *$^{\circ}$îš* is typical of Jeremianic, not Deuteronomic or Deuteronomistic proclamation (pp. 232–3, cf. 97–98). All this parenetic appeal is central to the prophetic task and is implied by prophecy outside Jeremiah as well. Finally, then, the prose addresses must be analyzed one by one for authenticity just as the poetic oracles have been: thus xvii 17–27 uses some of the stereotyped phrases, but it is doubtful if the passage is authentic to Jeremiah (pp. 233–4). In general, then, the prose addresses are not from the hand of a redactor.

This is an impressive and convincing study and one which in most respects coincides with conclusions toward which I myself have been moving during the past few years. One gains the sense with this book that one has moved appreciably closer to the truth in the matter of the origins of Jeremianic tradition.

I should like, however, to add a few impressionistic comments of my own to this survey, suggesting some fresh perspectives from which these old issues might be approached.

I believe WEIPPERT is quite acute in her indication of the existence of the category of *Kunstprosa* and her attribution of this material to the prophetic Jeremiah in some sense, but the problem still remains how it is that this stylistic category, with parenetic content, appears for the first time in the tradition of Jeremiah and not in any earlier material. She has established that *Kunstprosa* is a "demetrification" of poetry; good. And she has established that parenesis is central to the prophetic concern; good. But why do we have parenetic *Kunstprosa* in Jeremiah but not in Isaiah? The clue, I believe, is the advent of Deuteronomy and the concomitant necessity we face to posit a lower chronology for the prophet Jeremiah than the traditional one, a chronology which focuses his self-image more sharply. Now I am well aware that such a lower chronology, sponsored by several scholars besides myself in recent years, has not won general approval. I maintain, however, that this hypothesis solves many problems in the study of Jeremiah which continue to bedevil us; and it may be that I for my part have not stated my viewpoint with enough clarity.[13] Let me say, then, that I accept the accuracy of the datum of the "thirteenth year" of Josiah (i 1) as the crucial event in Jeremiah's life, as the time when the word of Yahweh "happened" to him; but that I take that event to be the year of his *birth*, just as i 5 says ("before I formed you in the womb I knew you"), rather than the year of Jeremiah's acceptance of his call. I suggest then that whenever Jeremiah was asked when the word of Yahweh had come to him, he answered, "in the thirteenth year of Josiah," i.e. the year of his birth: he took the verbalization of the event of his call (as recorded in i 5) as more than hyperbole. By this reading Jeremiah would have been a boy of five years of age when the Deuteronomic scroll was read in public, to become the basis of Josiah's reform; he would have been a young man of seventeen years of age when Josiah was killed at Megiddo, an occasion which is a plausible one to trigger Jeremiah's acceptance of a call from Yahweh. This sequence of events is at least indirectly supported by the curious wording of the MT of xv 16aα, *nimṣeʾû deḇārékā wāʾōkelēm*, "thy words were found and I ate them": the only other occurrences in the OT of *deḇārîm*, meaning "words," with *mṣʾ* nif. are in 2 Kings xxii 13 ("the words of this book that has been found") and xxiii 2.[14] "Thy words were found," Jer. xv 16, I

---

[13]Cf. my "The Background of Jeremiah's Self-Understanding: Moses, Samuel, and Psalm 22," *JBL* 83 (1964), pp. 153–64, and "Jeremiah and Moses, Further Observations," *JBL* 85 (1966), pp. 17–27.

[14]The combination is also found in 2 Chron. xix 3, but "good things (*deḇārim ṭôḇîm*) are found in thee" does not refer to "words."

suggest, implies the finding of the Deuteronomic scroll, and the subsequent action "and I ate them" suggests Jeremiah's acceptance of his call (cf. i 9). His acceptance of the call was then likely at the time of the death of Josiah: there would thereafter be no royal guarantor of the reform which had been based on Yahweh's words to Moses, and Jeremiah, I further suggest, understood himself to be the prophet like Moses anticipated in Deut. xviii 18; hence the likeness of the wording of Jeremiah's call in Jer. i 7, 9 to the wording of that verse in Deuteronomy, and hence the curious fact that the early prophetic oracles of Jeremiah contain so many reminiscences to Deut. xxxii, the so-called "Song of Moses." WEIPPERT affirms what is obvious, namely that we cannot be sure of the extent of *Urdeuteronomium* (p. 81), but I strongly urge the possibility that Deut. xxxii was known to Jeremiah and understood by him as a poem sung by Moses: thus when Jeremiah wished to offer prophetic oracles in his role of the prophet like Moses, he had a model already before him of what he took to be Mosaic poetry. Further, we have here a motive for Jeremiah's dictation of a scroll (Jer. xxxvi). Of course there were other motives: Jeremiah had been debarred from the Temple area (xxxvi 5), probably since the time of his Temple Sermon, so that the scroll was a means by which he could spread Yahweh's word indirectly. But the model of the earlier scroll was there, and he was the prophet like Moses. And the narrator (Baruch, no doubt) highlighted the parallels in the promulgation of the two scrolls (cf. 2 Kings xxii–xxiii).

Now in this lower chronology and consequent clarification of Jeremiah's self-image, that of the prophet like Moses, we not only solve many of the old puzzles (why do the early oracles seem not to fit Josiah's time?—because there really were none at that time; why does Jeremiah not seem to speak any assessment of Josiah's reform?—because it was in relative desuetude during his time of prophesying; who is the foe from the north, if not the Scythians?—the Babylonians), but we also have an explanation for the existence of the category of *Kunstprosa*, with its parenetic content, precisely in the Jeremianic tradition. If Moses was a model for the mode by which Jeremiah spoke out Yahweh's words, then just as Deut. xxxii became a model for the poetic oracles, so the parenetic prose passages in Deuteronomy, prose which is specifically structured prose, *Kunstprosa*,[15] became a model for a new mode of recorded prophetic discourse, a mode liberated from the canons of strict poetic structure; hence the parenetic addresses of Jeremiah in vii 1–15 and elsewhere. WEIPPERT is uneasy about the issue of dating: she assumes that *Kunstprosa* emerged in post-Josianic times—that Jeremiah used poetry for his proclamation in Josiah's time, a mixture of poetry and prose in Jehoiakim's time, and then at a subsequent stage used pure *Kunstprosa* (p. 81). But this appears to me to be an

---

[15]Cf. GEORG BRAULIK, "Aufbrechen von geprägten Wortverbindungen und Zusammenfassen von stereotypen Ausdrücken in der alttestamentlichen Kunstprosa," *Semitics* 1 (1970), pp. 7–11.

artificial evolutionary model; I suggest that my own view, clarified by the lower chronology, is more plausible.

There is a further consideration here which to my knowledge has not heretofore been discussed. Poetry can be dictated word by word: poetry has its own precise structure—every word is in place. When Jeremiah came to dictate his oracles to Baruch, then, he could do so word by word. But prose is another matter, even *Kunstprosa*: its looser structure does not force every word to be in place. This fact means that in the process of dictation the phraseology will be shaped to a greater or lesser degree by the patterns of writing to which the scribe has become accustomed. The training of a scribe involved the dictation to the scribe, and the copying by the scribe, of texts which exemplified the prose style of his period. Jeremiah's dictation of *Kunstprosa* to Baruch, or alternatively Baruch's recollection of Jeremiah's *Kunstprosa*, would inevitably conform to some degree at least to the conventions of seventh/sixth-century scribal style. Thus when W. O. E. OESTERLEY and T. H. ROBINSON many years ago stated that the prose of this material was "simply the form which Hebrew rhetorical prose took in the latter part of the seventh century and the first part of the sixth,"[16] they were avoiding what we now know to be a most complex issue, but they were nevertheless stating at least a half-truth. What happened when Jeremiah's *Kunstprosa* was recorded by Baruch may perhaps be compared to a more extreme instance in the present-day Near East: when one gives oral testimony to a police clerk in an Arab country, the reports ends up in the clerk's version of classical Arabic, whatever may have been the oral phraseology at the beginning. It may come as a surprise, then, that WEIPPERT has in fact identified as many features of Jeremiah's own diction and thought in the *Kunstprosa* as she has.

One might still wish to have a clearer conception of the *Sitze im Leben* of the poetic oracles on the one hand and of the *Kunstprosa* on the other. A semi-trance state for the poetry, we assume; in contrast to this, a deliberate public appeal for the *Kunstprosa* ("Stand in the gate of Yahweh's house, and proclaim there this word," vii 2). But we would wish to be more precise. In any event, though a large range of questions remain, one has nevertheless the sense that this is an adventurous time in which to be doing research on Jeremiah.

[16] *An Introduction to the Books of the OT*, 1934, p. 298.

13
Baruch the Scribe*
James Muilenburg

The historical period extending from the reign of Ashurbanipal, the last of the great Assyrian monarchs (663–627 B.C.), to the accession of Cyrus as ruler over the Persian Empire in the year 538 B.C. is one of the most amply documented as it is one of the most culturally significant in the history of the ancient Near East. It is also one of the most literate and articulate. Thanks chiefly to the discovery of the library of Ashurbanipal by Hormuzd Rassam in 1853, we have at our disposal today a wealth and variety of literary works and inscriptional remains to which it would be difficult to adduce a parallel. The long period of Assyrian hegemony over Western Asia was slowing drawing to a close, and forces of great vitality were challenging not only the structures of Assyrian imperial organization, but also the mentalities and interior dispositions of the peoples of the Near East. New ideas were beginning to stir in the world, and everywhere men were animated by historical forces and psychological drives more potent than anything that had been known since the period of "the first internationalism" seven centuries earlier.[1] The perplexities and dishevelments of the age, its fears and forebodings, its malaise and nostalgia for tradition are reflected in one fashion or another in the literature of the times, not only in Assyria, but also throughout the vaster ranges of its empire.[2] Ashurbanipal

---

*Originally published in *Proclamation and Presence. Old Testament Essays in Honour of Gwynne Henton Davies*. Ed. by John I. Durham and J. R. Porter. Richmond: John Knox Press, 1970, 215–238.

[1]The phrase is Breasted's. Compare S. A. Cook, "The Fall and Rise of Judah," *The Cambridge Ancient History*, eds. J. B. Bury, S. A. Cook and F. E. Adcock (Cambridge: at the University Press, 1929), vol. III, p. 394: "There was an interconnection of peoples, for a parallel to which we must go back to the Amarna Age."

[2]W. F. Albright, *From the Stone Age to Christianity* (Baltimore: The Johns Hopkins Press, 1940), pp. 240–55. "It is not surprising that this age of growing insecurity, when the very foundations of life were trembling, should give rise to an earnest effort to find a cure for the increasing *malaise* of the social organism" (pp. 240f.). "The question of theodicy always

was a scholar and a scribe, and boasts of his proficiency as copyist and decipherer of the ancient Sumerian and Akkadian records.[3] His reign marks the zenith of Assyrian art and literature, and it is to him more than to any other that we owe our knowledge of the age.[4] He dispatched royal scribes throughout Assyria and Babylonia in order that they might assemble the ancient texts, copy and translate them, and prepare them for deposit in the library. Business texts and letters appear in profusion, but also omen texts, reflecting the distraughtness and insecurity of the men of that age,[5] lengthy chronicles or annals,[6] administrative documents of different kinds, treaties and rituals and much else. It was a period of *Sturm und Drang* in which men sought to overcome the incoherence and uncertainty of the times by appealing to astrologists and magicians to discern the signs of the times, or by recourse to the ancient texts, whether cosmological or mythological, to encounter the end of one age and the beginning of another, or by reflecting upon the great cultural deposits of the remote past to discover resources for the present. It was a scribal age, an age of many scribes, in which the monarch himself played a central role and provided an impetus to learning and education which extended far and wide throughout his realm.

---

comes to the fore during prolonged times of crisis, when human emotions are winnowed and purified by a sustained catharsis" (p. 252).

[3] Jack Finegan, *Light from the Ancient Past* (Princeton: Princeton University Press, 1946). Note the following words of Ashurbanipal: "I received the revelation of the wise Adapa, the hidden treasure of the art of writing . . . I read the beautiful clay tablets from Sumer and the obscure Akkadian writing which is hard to master. I had my joy in the reading of inscriptions on stone from the time before the flood" (p. 181). See also E. Speiser, "Mesopotamia Up to the Assyrian Period: Scribal Concepts of Education," in *City Invincible*, eds. Carl H. Kraeling and Robert M. Adams (Chicago: The University of Chicago Press, 1960), p. 107 and B. Landsberger, *ibid.*, pp. 110f., for an estimate of Ashurbanipal's claims.

[4] A. T. Olmstead, *History of Assyria* (New York: Charles Scribner's Sons, 1923), pp. 489ff.

[5] *The Reports of the Magicians and Astrologers of Nineveh and Babylon in the British Museum*, ed. R. Campbell Thompson (London: Luzac & Co., 1900), vol. II; François Thureau-Dangin, *Rituels accadiens* (Paris: Ernest Leroux, 1921); *ANET*, 2nd ed. (Princeton: Princeton University Press, 1955), pp. 334–8, 349–52. Note the comment of Campbell Thompson, *op. cit.*, p. xv: "The astrologer or the prophet who could foretell fair things for the nation, or disasters and calamities for their enemies, was a man whose words were regarded with reverence and awe . . . The soothsayer was as much a politician as the statesman, and he was not slow in using the indications of political changes to point the moral of his astrological observations."

[6] D. D. Luckenbill, *Ancient Records of Assyria and Babylonia* (Chicago: University of Chicago Press, 1927), vol. II, pp. 290ff.; D. J. Wiseman, *Chronicles of Chaldean Kings, 626–556 BC* (London: Trustees of the British Museum, 1956). Note Luckenbill's comment, *op. cit.*, p. 290: "In the reign of Ashurbanipal (668–626 B.C.) we reach the high-water mark of Assyrian historical writing—as regards quantity and literary merit . . . Furthermore, the great literary activity of Ashurbanipal seems to have come in the second part of his reign, after the overthrow of Shamash-shum-ukîn in 648 B.C., and even when our documents are dated by eponyms we are in doubt as to their sequence, since the order of the eponymous years from 648 on is in doubt." See also Olmstead, *loc. cit.*

It should occasion no surprise that the corrosive forces at work throughout Western Asia during this period should exact their toll from the kingdom of Judah, the last buffer state between Assyria and Egypt, the ultimate goal of Assyrian imperialist aggression, not only politically and economically, but also psychologically and culturally. From an early period Israel's faith was governed by the conviction that the sequences of history were embraced by an all-controlling purpose and an ultimate sovereignty. It is significant, therefore, that a substantial part of the Old Testament was composed during this period of the decline and fall of one empire and the emergence and rise of another.[7] Even if we make full allowance for later accretions and supplementations, the amount of the literary precipitate is very impressive.[8] There was, first of all, the so-called great Deuteronomic work, extending from Deuteronomy through II Kings, a work which sought to explain why it was that the two kingdoms of Israel and Judah were destroyed, why the Lord of history had decreed his judgment upon the historical people κατ᾽ ἐξοχήν.[9] The great prophetic books of Jeremiah, Ezekiel, and Second Isaiah also come from this time, as do the smaller prophetic works of Zephaniah, Nahum, Habakkuk and Malachi.[10] The book of Lamentations too must be assigned to the period shortly after the downfall of Judah and the end of the monarchy.[11] If the book of Job belongs to this time, as some scholars hold, the situation becomes even more impressive.[12] Just as Ashurbanipal and later Nabonidus sought to find in the past some threshold into the inchoate future, some ποῦ στῶ from

---

[7]Compare Hermann Gunkel, in "Kultur der Gegenwart," *Die orientalischen Literaturen*, herausgegeben von Paul Hinneberg (Leipzig and Berlin, 1925), Teil I, Abteilung vii, p. 96: "*Die Literatur hatte vor den grossen Katastrophen ihre klassische Zeit erlebt. Das geistige Leben stand damals fast auf allen Gebieten, die Israel überhaupt gepflegt hat, in höchster Blüte.*" See also John L. McKenzie, s.j., "Reflections on Wisdom," *JBL* 86 (March, 1967), p. 8: "The scribes of Israel who were also the sages of Israel were not the first to collect in writing the memories of their people. The libraries of Nippur and of Ashurbanipal were obviously deliberate efforts to collect entire literary traditions. It is not without interest that both collections were made shortly before political collapse; and one wonders how much scribal activity was instigated by Josiah, who attempted a revival of the Davidic monarchy." For an authoritative account of the latter, see *inter alia* R. de Vaux, "Titres et fonctionnaires égyptiens à la cour de David et de Salomon," *RB* 48 (1939), pp. 394–405.

[8]If one undertakes to count the pages in Kittel's edition of the Masoretic Text, it will be recognized that almost four hundred pages out of the 1,434 may well come from our period.

[9]Gerhard von Rad, *Studies in Deuteronomy*, SBT 9, trans. David Stalker (London: SCM Press, 1953), pp. 74–91.

[10]Bruce T. Dahlberg, "Studies in the Book of Malachi" (Dissertation, Union Theological Seminary, New York, 1963).

[11]Norman K. Gottwald, *Studies in the Book of Lamentations*, SBT 14 (London: SCM Press, 1954).

[12]R. H. Pfeiffer, *Introduction to the Old Testament* (New York: Harper & Brothers, 1941), p. 677; S. L. Terrien, "Introduction to Job," *IB* 3, pp. 884–91; "Quelques remarques sur les affinités de Job avec le Deutéro-Isaïe," *SVT* 15, Congrès de Genève (Leiden: E. J. Brill, 1966), pp. 295–310.

from which to withstand the agitation of stormy political seasons, so the composers of Deuteronomy had sought to comprehend the turbulence of the present within the context of the age of Moses and the words attributed to him. It has too long been our practice to speak of Deuteronomists, traditionists, and redactors. But such terms are nondescript. In all probability it is in not a few instances with scribes with whom we have to do, scribes who were not only copyists, but also and more particularly composers who gave to their works their form and structure, and determined to a considerable degree their wording and terminology.[13] In Judah as in Assyria we are living in a scribal age, an age of scribes who occupied a strategic position in the royal house of David and were entrusted with the archives of both palace and Temple.[14] The names of most of the scribes during the history of the monarchy are unknown to us, but it is not without significance that they appear more conspicuously and frequently in the latter part of the seventh century and the beginning of the sixth than they do either during the United Monarchy of David and Solomon, or, for that matter, at any other time in the history of the monarchy. It seems probable that Josiah's policy of reviving the United Monarchy also involved the restoration of the officials of the royal court.[15]

If we leave the book of Job out of account, since its date is still much controverted, there are two books which occupy a position of pre-eminence above all others. Ever since the publication of Duhm's commentary on Jeremiah in 1901, it has been recognized that Jeremiah contains not a few passages which are closely related in style, terminology, and representation to Deuteronomy.[16] The affinities are not limited to these passages, however, but are to be recognized in other prose narratives as well. The best

---

[13]McKenzie, *loc. cit.*: "The Israelite wise men who were the scribes of Deuteronomy knew that the past is not meaningful unless it is continuous with the present . . . " Moshe Weinfeld, "Deuteronomy—the Present State of Inquiry," *JBL* 86 (Sept., 1967), pp. 249–62, especially p. 254, where Weinfeld attributes the crystallization of Deuteronomy to the scribes of Hezekiah and Josiah. See also his article on "The Origin of the Humanism in Deuteronomy," *JBL* 80 (Sept., 1961), pp. 241–7.

[14]Salo W. Baron, *A Social and Religious History of the Jews*, vol. I, 2nd rev. ed. (New York: Columbia University Press, 1952), p. 153: "We would know few priests or scribes by name were it not for their accidental appearance in the political arena, but their anonymous contributions, however slow and imperceptible, were as vital and lasting as the more spectacular contributions of the others. There is no means of measuring human greatness. Would one venture to decide who was greater, the anonymous author of Deuteronomy, or Jeremiah, the prophet, the tragic grandeur of whose life has been so rich a source of inspiration? As it happened, both these men were priests."

[15]See *inter alia* de Vaux, *loc. cit.*, Joachim Begrich, "Sōfēr und Mazkīr; ein Beitrag zur inneren Geschichte des davidisch-salomonischen Grossreiches und des Königreiches Juda," *ZAW* 58 (1940–41), pp. 1–29.

[16]See above all Sigmund Mowinckel, *Zur Komposition des Buches Jeremia*, Videnskapsselskapets Skrifter II. Hist.-Filos. Klasse, 1913, No. 5, Kristiania, 1914 and *Prophecy and Tradition*, Avhandlinger Utgitt av Det Norske Videnskaps-Akademi in Oslo, II. Hist.-Filos. Klasse, 1946, No. 3.

explanation for these affinities is that we are dealing in both works with a conventional mode of composition.[17] We encounter much the same style in the Deuteronomic history as we do in Deuteronomy, though there are differences in representation and theology. It has been suggested by more than one scholar that it is to the scribal family of Shaphan that we are to turn for the authorship of the Deuteronomistic history,[18] and while this can be little more than a conjecture it has much to commend it. That is to say, in both instances we are dealing with scribal style and with a scribal *modus scribendi*. What is more, it has been frequently pointed out that Jeremiah is to be understood as a second Moses or that he performs the functions of the Mosaic office (compare Deut. 18.15ff. and Jer. 1.4–10).[19]

The importance of Jeremiah in the history of Israel's religion and more especially of Israel's prophecy is generally recognized. It is often pointed out that we know Jeremiah more intimately than any other of the prophets. But this has often led to the mistaken conclusion that it is his interior self disclosures that mark his uniqueness. On the other hand, we are frequently informed today that he is only following conventional and traditional literary forms derived from the cult.[20] That Jeremiah was indeed an important person in his age cannot be legitimately questioned, indeed far more important than we are wont to think. Once we have recognized wherein his true importance lies we are on our way to solving some of the most contended and controversial issues which the man and his book pose for us. We must view the prophet first of all and above all as a major figure in the political, cultural, religious, and indeed international life of the period. His call to be a prophet does not overstate matters. He is appointed to be a prophet over the nations, and this was how he was meant to be

[17]John Bright, "The Date of the Prose Sermons of Jeremiah," *JBL* 70 (March, 1951), pp. 15–35.

[18]A. Jepsen, *Die Quellen des Königsbuches* (Halle: Max Niemeyer Verlag, 1956), pp. 94f.; Weinfeld, "Deuteronomy—the Present State of Inquiry," *JBL* 86 (Sept., 1967), p. 255, n. 35. Weinfeld rightly points out that a distinction should be made between Deuteronomy and the historiography of the Deuteronomic history and the "editorial part of Jeremiah. But these three literary strands have a common theological outlook and identical stylistic features and therefore must be considered as a product of a continuous scribal school. In my opinion this school is to be connected with the family of Shaphan the scribe who took an active part in the discovery of the book in the time of Josiah."

[19]H. J. Kraus, *Die prophetische Verkündigung des Rechts in Israel*, ThSt 51 (Zurich: Evangelischer Verlag AG, 1957); P. B. Broughton, "The Call of Jeremiah: the Relation of Deut. 18.9–22 to the Call of Jeremiah," *ABR* 6 (1958), pp. 37–46; James Muilenburg, "The 'Office' of the Prophet in Ancient Israel," *The Bible in Modern Scholarship*, ed. J. Philip Hyatt (Nashville: Abingdon Press, 1965), pp. 74–97; Norman Habel, "The Form and Significance of the Call Narratives," *ZAW* 77 (1965), pp. 297–323; W. L. Holladay, "The Background of Jeremiah's Self-Understanding," *JBL* 83 (June, 1964), pp. 154ff. See also W. Zimmerli, *Ezechiel*, BKAT XIII (Neukirchen-Vluyn: Verlag der Buchhandlung des Erziehungsvereins, 1955), pp. 13–37.

[20]Henning Graf Reventlow, *Liturgie und prophetisches Ich bei Jeremia* (Gütersloh: Gütersloher Verlagshaus Gerd Mohn, 1963).

understood. If we may trust our text, as I think we may, then Jeremiah was summoned to be Yahweh's covenant mediator, the royal emissary from the heavenly court, the divinely accredited spokesman to an age in radical ferment.[21] He is to address his nation and other nations with the word that has been committed to him to proclaim. He is endowed with the charismatic gift and is given authority and power over kingdoms and nations to pluck up and tear down, to build and to plant. The awareness of this great commission animates the prophet's mind throughout his career. Precisely because he was ordained for such a destiny he incurred the wrath of all those in high places he dared to oppose. Precisely because he is representative of the divine sovereignty or government he ventures to attack the corruption of all the venerable institutions by which his contemporaries sought to order their lives.

The cultural milieu of Jeremiah's ministry is international. The confusion and chaos within the kingdom of Judah have their source in remote lands, and Jeremiah finds himself destined to speak to that situation. The threat or actual presence of war persists throughout the ancient Near East during the period of his ministry. The book throughout bears witness to the precariousness of the international crisis, most notably in the year of the Battle of Carchemish in 605 B.C. (25.1–13; 36; 45; 46) and during the long period between the two deportations of 597 and 587. Jeremiah appears in the Temple at the beginning of Jehoiakim's reign and delivers his great sermon (7.1–15; 26.1–24); he confronts the envoys as they leave a plenary session of the emissaries of the nations surrounding Judah at the beginning of Zedekiah's reign (so the true text of 27.1); again and again he excoriates the delinquencies of Jehoiakim, and engages in bitter polemic against the leaders of the nation and Temple. He contends with other prophets and denies their accreditation since they have not stood in the heavenly council (23.18). Most significantly he is recognized by Nebuchadnezzar and the Chaldean commander after the fall of Jerusalem, is shown extraordinary preferential treatment, and is given the choice of determining his own future either by accompanying Nebuzaradan, the captain of the guard, personally (note *with me* in 40.4) to Chaldea, or by joining his fellow-

---

[21]G. Ernest Wright, "The Fruit of a Lifetime," *Interpretaion* 18 (July, 1964), p. 362: "The prophet was an officer of the heavenly government whose function, comparable to that of the royal herald in both Egypt and Israel, was to be the line of direct communication between the divine Suzerain and his vassal, Israel ... In other words, it is most important in our attempt to understand the office to stress not simply the psychology of ecstasy but the Israelite understanding of God's government of Israel and the manner in which the human phenomenon of ecstasy was taken up and transformed in that government." Compare Georg Fohrer, "Remarks on Modern Interpretation of the Prophets," *JBL* 80 (Dec., 1961), p. 310: "The herald's message is originally not prophetic but typical for the royal messenger. Prophecy did not create it, but borrowed it from that source—probably by way of the prophets of the royal court, as we know them from Mari and Byblos ... The basic form of the prophetic oracles was certainly not exclusively bound to the cult or to the law, but could be sought and given everywhere and in all contexts."

countrymen at Mizpeh (39.11ff.; 40.1ff.; 42.1ff.). Nothing could illustrate better the importance of Jeremiah in the politics of his age or the dominating position that he held, whether in the royal councils or in the affairs of state. Unfortunately, the prestige of the prophet's office is obscured for us in the *ipsissima verba* of chs. 1–25, for here chronological and biographical data are all but wanting, and we are left in the dark as to the occasions when his words were spoken, as, for example, in connection with the oracles on the foe from the north or the lawsuits or the self-disclosures. It is when we pass from these chapters to those that follow that the situation changes strikingly, for here the mode of reporting is of quite a different order. We turn, therefore, to ch. 36, the single chapter in the book which casts light upon the history of its composition.

The thirty-sixth chapter of the book of Jeremiah brings to a culmination the sequence of prose narratives beginning with ch. 26.[22] That the two accounts are designed to form the beginning and ending of the literary complex is demonstrated by the many stylistic and linguistic features they share in common. Both chapters begin with a superscription, the occasion of both is a popular assembly in a time of great national crisis, in both we listen to the prophet's solemn and public indictments, and the motivation of repentance and forgiveness is common to both. In both the prophet's life is imperilled, in both the princes are favourably disposed to Jeremiah, in both the members of the house of Shaphan play a significant role, and throughout both the stress is constantly upon speaking and hearing.

In the fourth year of Jehoiakim Jeremiah receives a command from Yahweh to take a scroll and to write upon it all the words he had spoken to him from the time of his call in the reign of Josiah, presumably 627 B.C. (25.3) to the present. It was in that year that the armies of Chaldea under Nebuchadnezzar had delivered a decisive defeat to the Egyptian foe under Pharaoh Neco. The turning-point in the history of the Near East thus coincides with what was doubtless a turning-point in the prophet's career. It is not too much to suppose that the two events were closely related. If so, it is a remarkable witness to the fatefulness of the issues which were involved for Judah and for the other peoples of the Near East.

Jeremiah summons Baruch, the son of Neriah, and he writes at the prophet's dictation. Thereupon Jeremiah informs Baruch that he has been debarred from the Temple, but that he is to go and read there all the words he had written. Baruch complies with the prophet's demand. In December of the following year a fast is proclaimed. Precisely what it was that motivated the event we are not told, but it may well be that it was related to the victory of Chaldea at Carchemish and to the prophet's conviction that his oracles on the foe from the north had at long last been fulfilled. In the hearing of all the people and then the princes, Baruch reads from the

---

[22]Martin Kessler, "Form-Critical Suggestions on Jer. 36," *CBQ* 28 (Oct., 1966), pp. 389–401.

scroll in the לִשְׁכָּה or cabinet room of Gemariah, the son of Shaphan, the secretary of state, perhaps in exactly the same place where Jeremiah had delivered the Temple speech some years previous (26.10, cf. 7:2).[23] The presence of all these princes more than suggests that they were quite aware of the impending crisis. The atmosphere was doubtless electric. When Micaiah, the grandson of Shaphan, heard all the words of Jeremiah from the mouth of Baruch, he goes to the cabinet room of the secretary in the royal palace to report to the princes who were gathered there. The latter order a certain Jehudi whose genealogy is traced back to the third generation to command Baruch to come to them. The words here are ironically much the same as those which Yahweh has employed in his command to Jeremiah (cf. v. 2). So Baruch comes, scroll in hand. The narrative at this point is dramatic. The princes say to Baruch, "Sit down and read it" (sic!). Baruch accedes to their demands, and the princes turn to each other in fear and tell Baruch that they will have to report what has happened to the king. Significantly they enquire, "Was it at his dictation?" and Baruch acknowledges that it was he! The princes then counsel Baruch that he and Jeremiah should go into hiding so that no one may know where they are. It is obvious that Baruch has fallen into friendly hands and it may be assumed that they were friendly to Jeremiah too. But what is more they recognize the validity of their credentials.

We are informed that the scroll was placed in the cabinet room of Elishama the secretary. It is not improbable that it was the repository of other documents. The princes report to the king, who orders Jehudi to procure the scroll, and the latter brings it to the king. Again the narrative is graphic and extraordinarily compressed, without any show of emotion. It is winter, and the king is seated before the open hearth. As Jehudi reads, the king cuts with a pen knife every three or four columns and consigns them to the flames. There is no terror or show of grief, in striking contrast to the time when Josiah had listened to the Book of the Covenant (II Kings 22). The supporters of Jeremiah of whom we have heard previously—Elnathan and Delaiah and Gemariah—urge the king not to burn the scroll, but to no avail. Jehoiakim gives orders that Baruch the secretary and Jeremiah the prophet be seized, but his designs are thwarted because "Yahweh had hid them" (cf. 26.24).

The account is notable for several reasons. Nowhere else in the Old Testament do we have a comparable report of a prophet dictating all his prophecies over a period of many years, nowhere else do we hear of a prophet employing an amanuensis for the purpose of transcription, nowhere else do we have a narrative so rich in graphic and circumstantial detail. The book is addressed to Israel, Judah, and all the nations. Since several manuscripts of the Greek (see BH ad loc.) read Jerusalem for Israel, many

---

[23]Kurt Galling, "Die Halle des Schreibers," Palästinajahrbuch des Deutschen evangelischen Instituts 27 (1931), pp. 51–58.

scholars emend the text accordingly, but the procedure is unwise since the whole phrase is meant to mark the momentousness of the event—an event, as we have seen, which is commensurate to the solemnity and gravity of the national and international crisis. We are informed that the book was read three times in the course of a single day, so it cannot have been very long (compare the similar case in II Kings 22). It may have been a summary or condensation of the prophet's utterances. The question naturally arises why such a document needed to be put in writing at all. Why could not a single utterance or speech have sufficed for the particular purpose in view? The fact that the words were addressed to Israel, Judah, and all the nations when Assyrian power had come to an end and Chaldea was now in ascendant—a circumstance of which the prophet could not but be aware—may offer some explanation. But there is a deeper reason. The words of Yahweh are for the particular hour, to be sure, but they are more. They are at once a witness to the fulfillment of past predictions, notably the oracles on the foe from the north,[24] and a witness for the future, the time that is still to come (Isa. 30.8; 55.10f.; Jer. 32.14).[25]

The momentousness of the event is further demonstrated by another consideration of the first importance. Jeremiah summons to his service a scribe or secretary by the name of Baruch, the son of Neriah. Speculations are numerous as to why the prophet needed someone to whom he could dictate his prophecies. Was it that he could not write, as some have supposed, or that his handwriting was poor, as has been suggested by others? We are not informed how it was that Jeremiah came to know Baruch, how long and in what capacity he had known him previously, or anything about his past history. But we are plainly told that Baruch was a scribe or secretary. On the face of it, of course, the designation could indicate that he was only an amanuensis or private secretary. But a careful inspection of our narrative and the fact that Baruch appears in other

[24]Douglas Jones, "The Traditio of the Oracles of Isaiah of Jerusalem," *ZAW* 67 (1955), p. 229: "There can be little doubt that the motive which led Jeremiah to dictate the oracles of his life's ministry was to demonstrate how old predictions were on the point of fulfilment. The foe from the North could now be identified."

[25]Johannes Pedersen, *Israel: Its Life and Culture* I–II, trans. Aslaug Møller (London: Oxford University Press, 1926), pp. 167f.; H. Wheeler Robinson, *Inspiration and Revelation in the Old Testament* (Oxford: Clarendon Press, 1946), pp. 170f.; Aubrey R. Johnson, *The One and the Many in the Israelite Conception of God*, 2nd ed. (Cardiff: University of Wales Press, 1961), pp. 1ff.; *The Vitality of the Individual in the Thought of Ancient Israel*, 2nd ed. (Cardiff: University of Wales Press, 1964), pp. 87f.; Isaac Rabbinowitz, "Towards a Valid Theory of Biblical Hebrew Literature," *The Classical Tradition: Literary and Historical Studies in Honor of Harry Caplan*, ed. Luitpold Wallach (Ithaca: Cornell University Press, 1966). Note p. 324: "The utterance of prophetic words, in fine, is for the purpose of getting them into the world so that they may act upon that world; as such they are conceived as transcending the limits of communication, and do not necessarily require an audience." In the present context, the words of Jeremiah do indeed have an audience, but their range of meaning extends far beyond it into the history of the time.

notable contexts of the prose narratives suggest that he was a man of some importance and was well known and highly regarded by his confreres and peers. The most plausible explanation for Jeremiah's summoning of Baruch is precisely that the occasion called for one who could represent him in the Temple, one who would have ready access to the chamber of Gemariah, son of Shaphan,[26] to whom Jeremiah was bound by many years of friendship, esteem, and mutuality of respect. That is to say, Baruch was more than a private secretary. He was a person of some eminence, one who was favourably known to his professional colleagues. The cabinet room would be an advantageous locale from which he could address the assembled throng in the outer court.

We are singularly fortunate in having the twofold reference to the cabinet room of the scribe, in the first instance in the Jerusalem Temple (36.10) and in the second in the royal palace (36.21). The two were closely connected, and we may be confident, quite intentionally.[27] The men who are gathered in the chambers are in both cases שָׂרִים or royal officials. To be sure we hear elsewhere of chambers or rooms belonging to private persons or eminent families (35.4), and they are also referred to later in Ezekiel, Ezra, Nehemiah, and I–II Chronicles. But the לִשְׁכָּה of the scribe referred to in 36.10 is certainly to be distinguished from these, in the first place because it was immediately connected with the royal palace and in the second because it bore the title of a distinctive office.[28] Among the other peoples of the Near East from ancient times the training of the scribe was connected with the Temple and his service associated with the royal house. We hear frequently of scribal schools and of the training that was

[26]G. G. Findlay, "Baruch," *Dictionary of the Bible*, ed. James Hastings, rev. ed. Frederick C. Grant and H. H. Rowley, eds. (London: Thomas Nelson and Sons and New York: Charles Scribner's Sons, 1963), p. 91: "He belonged to the order of 'princes,' among whom Jeremiah had influential friends (26.16; 36.25); Baruch's rank probably secured for Jeremiah's objectionable 'roll' (ch. 36) the hearing that was refused to his spoken words."

[27]Galling, *op. cit.* pp. 51–56. See especially the excellent chart on p. 53. Cf. Adolf Erman, *The Literature of the Ancient Egyptians*, trans. M. Blackman (London: Methuen & Co., 1927), p. 185: "It [the scribal school] was attached to the temple which Ramesses II built for Amūn on the west bank of Thebes, the so-called Ramesseum." See also C. F. A. Schaeffer, *The Cuneiform Texts of Ras Shamra-Ugarit*. The Schweich Lectures of the British Academy, 1936 (London: Oxford University Press, 1939), pp. 34–35: "The library was housed in a building situated between the two great temples of Ugarit, one dedicated to Baal and the other to Dagon. . . . As was usual at this time, a school of scribes was attached to the library. Here the young priests were set to copy documents and were instructed in liturgical and sacred literature." For its royal connections, see p. 34. Cf. S. Mowinckel, "Psalms and Wisdom," *Wisdom in Israel and in the Ancient Near East*, H. H. Rowley *Festschrift*, eds. M. Noth and D. W. Thomas, *SVT* 3 (Leiden: E. J. Brill, 1955), p. 207: "There is every reason to believe that the school for scribes in Jerusalem, as elsewhere in the Orient, was closely connected with the temple; this is apparent from the very fact that the 'wisdom literature' of Israel was considered to belong to the canonical writings." Aage Bentzen, *Introduction to the Old Testament* (Copenhagen: G. E. C. Gad, 1948), vol. I, p. 171, refers also to a temple school at Mari.

[28]Galling, *op. cit.*, p. 54.

received there.[29] Such training was closely related to what falls under the general category of wisdom, at least as it was understood in Egypt and Mesopotamia.[30] That is, the scribes were wise men because they had been reared in the wisdom school and had mastered its curriculum, not only in calligraphy, though this was to be sure of the first importance, but in other disciplines associated with governmental administration and finance as well. That the United Monarchy under David and Solomon was profoundly influenced by the organization of the Egyptian court is now well known,[31] and there is every reason to believe that the same is true of the period with which we are concerned. Egyptian influence is doubtless primary, but it is probable that Mesopotamian influence also made itself felt, particularly in the period of Assyrian domination. It could scarcely have been otherwise when one takes into account the international character of the age and, indeed, the international character of wisdom. In any event, it is clear that the office of the scribe was one of distinction. He was the most eminent and influential of the royal officials and was charged with governmental affairs as well as many other functions.

It is not exceeding the limits of evidence to contend that both the northern and southern kingdoms had scribal schools similar to those among the other peoples of the Near East,[32] and one may venture to assert with some confidence that they were associated with the royal house and the national sanctuaries.[33] Sigmund Mowinckel maintains that Solomon

---

[29]In addition to the foregoing, see Lorenz Dürr, *Das Erziehungswesen im Alten Testament und im Antiken Orient*. Mitteilungen der Vorderasiatischen-Aegyptischen Gesellschaft (E.F.) 36 Band, 2 Heft (Leipzig, 1932); de Vaux, *op. cit.*, pp. 394–405; Millar Burrows, *What Mean These Stones?* (New Haven: American Schools of Oriental Research, 1941), p. 183; R. de Langhe, *Les textes de Ras Shamra-Ugarit et leurs rapports avec le milieu biblique de l'Ancien Testament* (Paris: Desclée de Brouwer, 1945), vol. I, pp. 332ff.; Samuel N. Kramer, *The Sumerians; Their History, Culture, and Character* (Chicago: University of Chicago Press, 1963), pp. 230f.; A. Leo Oppenheim, "A Note on the Scribes in Mesopotamia," *Studies in Honor of Benno Landsberger on his Seventieth Birthday*, Assyriological Studies No. 16 (Chicago: The Oriental Institute of the University of Chicago, 1965), pp. 253–6; William McKane, *Prophets and Wise Men*, SBT 44 (London: SCM Press, 1965), pp. 36f.; John Gray, *Archaeology and the Old Testament World* (London and New York: Thomas Nelson and Sons, 1962), pp. 80ff. See also W. G. Lambert, *Babylonian Wisdom Literature* (Oxford: Clarendon Press, 1960), p. 8: "One point of organization on which we are regrettably ill-informed is the relation of the scribes to the temple. General considerations would lead us to suppose that the scribal schools were attached to a temple, but we are in no position either to affirm or to deny if all scribes were *ipso facto* priests."

[30]McKenzie, *op. cit.*, p. 4: "We know that wisdom literature is associated with scribal schools in Egypt and Mesopotamia, and we can assume that the same association existed in Israel." Cf. G. Fohrer, *Introduction to the Old Testament*. Initiated by E. Sellin, trans. D. E. Green (New York: Abingdon Press, 1968), p. 315: "Baruch, Jeremiah's scribe and biographer, was at least educated in the wisdom school."

[31]de Vaux, *loc. cit.*; Begrich, *loc. cit.*

[32]So de Vaux, Mowinckel, and others.

[33]Cf. *inter alia* R. B. Y. Scott, "Priesthood, Prophecy, Wisdom, and the Knowledge of God," *JBL* 80 (March, 1961), p. 10.

founded a school for scribes in Jerusalem and there introduced the international poetry of wisdom of the Orient.[34] I am inclined to support this contention as a real possibility, but would go somewhat farther perhaps by contending that wisdom in this case should be construed as broadly as it was among other Near Eastern peoples, to include such works as the Yahwist and the court history which teems with wisdom motifs. The training in the scribal schools was of a diversified kind. There were doubtless, too, many different kinds of scribes as there were different kinds of priests and prophets in Israel.

As we have already had occasion to observe, it was with the scribal family of Shaphan that Jeremiah was on intimate terms. The former were among the central figures associated with the Reform of Josiah,[35] and it is likely that in the early period of his ministry Jeremiah was favourably disposed to the movement.[36] Both Shaphan and his son Ahikam are members of the delegation sent to Huldah (II Kings 22.11–13), and Elasah, another son of Shaphan, serves as an agent in connection with the letter to the exiles (29.3). Finally, it was a grandson of Shaphan with whom Jeremiah was on friendly terms during the trying period after the fall of Jerusalem (43.1–7). What relationship Baruch may have had to Shaphan and his family we do not know, but it is not unlikely that it was similarly intimate. Baruch could enter the cabinet room of the scribe because he had a rightful place there and was himself a member of the royal officials who had come together on the crucial occasion of the public reading of the scroll. He was among colleagues.

Many attempts have been made to reconstruct the scroll which Jeremiah dictated to Baruch.[37] We are not left without some clues as to its probable content. It must have contained the oracles of judgment preserved in 1.1–25.13 from the thirteenth year of Josiah to the year 604 when the scroll was dictated. But what are we to say of the prose narratives? While absolute certainty is in the nature of the case excluded, the probabilities

[34]Mowinckel, "Psalms and Wisdom," *Wisdom in Israel and in the Ancient Near East*, p. 206.

[35]H. J. Katzenstein, "The 'ʾAsher ʿal ha-bayith' from the Days of the United Kingdom to the Downfall of Samaria," *Memorial Volume to Eliezer Shamir, Sdeh Elijahu*, 1957, pp. 120–8; "The Royal Steward Asher ʿal ha-Bayith," *IEJ* 10 (1960), pp. 149–54; "The House of Eliakim, a Family of Royal Stewards," *Eretz Israel* 5 (Jerusalem: Israel Exploration Society and the Hebrew University, 1958), pp. 108–10 (in Hebrew). Katzenstein maintains that the position was hereditary in one family and that there was a direct line of succession from Hilkiah (Isa. 22.20–24; II Kings 18.18; 19.2) to Gedaliah.

[36]H. H. Rowley, "The Early Prophecies of Jeremiah in their Setting," *BJRL* 45 (1962–63), pp. 225ff. or *Men of God: Studies in Old Testament History and Prophecy* (London and New York: Thomas Nelson and Sons Ltd., 1963), pp. 158ff.

[37]Note, for example, Otto Eissfeldt, *The Old Testament: an Introduction*, trans. Peter R. Ackroyd (New York: Harper and Row and Oxford: Basil Blackwell, 1965), p. 351.

strongly favour the assumption that they are the work of Baruch.[38] It is certain that Baruch continued to be the companion of Jeremiah until after the fall of the nation in 587. It is in these narratives, if anywhere, that we have an authentic exhibit of the scribal mode of composition. They open with the accession of Jehoiakim to the throne of Judah in 608, the occasion for the Temple speech (26.1). The account merits careful inspection because we can compare it with the report given in 7.1–15. The scribe gives the speech in his own way, abridging it by omitting details, but adding others such as the exact temporal locus, transforming the probably poetic form of the original into prose, and above all by recounting the sequence of episodes which followed upon its delivery. There is every reason to believe that he composed the other speeches or proclamations of Jeremiah in the same way. We move from the prophet's poetic formulations to the scribe's prose. It is noteworthy that all the speeches reported by Baruch, whether Jeremiah's or those of others, have the same style and terminology.[39] Following the practice of ancient historians, he reports what was spoken in his own style and language. We are fortunately not at a loss to learn whence he derives this manner of speaking. We encounter the same style elsewhere in Deuteronomistic contexts; the manner of Baruch is the manner of the scribes, not only of his own time, but long before.[40]

It is probable that Baruch and his professional confreres have been influenced by the official state or temple archives. The numerous superscriptions (26.1; 27.1; 28.1; 29.1–3; 32.1; 34.1; 36.1; 39.2; 40.1; 41.1, etc.) suggest as much.[41] They are to be compared with the formal openings of the reigns of the kings of Judah and Israel reported in the books of Kings. While different literary types are to be recognized in the complex of Jer.

---

[38]For reconstructions of Baruch's work, see T. H. Robinson, "Baruch's Roll," *ZAW*, Neue Folge Erster Band, 1924, pp. 209–21; Pfeiffer, *op. cit.*, p. 502; Mowinckel, *Prophecy and Tradition*, pp. 61f; Norman K. Gottwald, *A Light to the Nations: an Introduction to the Old Testament* (New York: Harper and Brothers, 1959), p. 353; Fohrer, *Introduction to the Old Testament*, p. 436.

[39]Leonhard Rost, "Zur Problematik der Jeremiabiographie Baruchs," *Viva Vox Evangelii, Festschrift für Landesbischof D. Hans Meiser* (Munich: Claudius-Verlag, Oskar Koch and Co., 1951), pp. 241–5.

[40]Mowinckel, *Prophecy and Tradition*, p. 63: "Baruch was a 'scribe' and belonged to 'the learned': that the 'Deuteronomists' are also associated with the learned circles of the scribes, is obvious; already Jeremiah offers us a piece of evidence that 'the law,' the *tora*-tradition, and the pursuit of it, belongs to the 'scribes' (Jer. 8.8)."

[41]Hans Schmidt, *Die grossen Propheten übersetzt und erklärt* in Die Schriften des Alten Testaments, Zweite Abteilung, Zweiter Band (Göttingen: Vandenhoeck & Ruprecht, 1915), p. 377: "*Als Vorbild für sein biographisches Werk haben dem Baruch wahrscheinlich offizielle Staats—oder Tempelchroniken gedient. Die Art, wie er jedes Ereignis mit einem Datum versieht, die in solchen öffentlichen Urkundenführung zu Hause ist, legt diese Vermutung nahe.*"

26–45, it is the biographical narrative that predominates.[42] These should not be confused with the legends that are reported concerning Elijah and Elisha.[43] Complaints that are often registered against Baruch that his style is monotonous or ponderous are quite beside the point as are the characterizations which speak of his "popular narrative art."[44] To be sure there is considerable diversity in the style of the narration, but nowhere is it alien to the scribal manner of reporting. Notable among its features is the proclivity to cite words of the participants in the events (26.2–6, 13–15; 27.5b–11, 12b–15, 16b–22; 28.2–4; 29.4–23, 24b–28; 32.17–25, 27–44; 33.2–17, etc.). Even more striking and more central to the narrator's interest is his profound interest in the person of Jeremiah. Nevertheless, despite his intimate association with the prophet and his affection for him, he nowhere indulges in subjective words of sympathy. Jeremiah does not appear as a hero or saint. The events that are recorded tell their own story. It was a long career of suffering and apparent defeat.[45] Dramatic elements are not wanting. Note the finales of 26.6, 24; 27.22c; 28.9, 16c, 17; 29.9b, 23d; 32.5b, 8d, 15b, 25; 35.19b; 36.19, 26b, 31d, etc. The canvas upon which the scribe portrays the events of the prophet's career is crowded with many *dramatis personae*. Kings, princes, priests, prophets, scribes, and others appear upon the stage, and Jeremiah moves in the midst of them, a solitary and often tragic figure. From our modern point of view, it is amazing that Baruch makes his appearance so seldom in the narratives, though where he does appear, it is clear that he must have played a not insignificant role.[46]

But there are other features in Baruch's prose narratives that demand our attention. While we have insisted that he writes in the characteristic manner of the scribe, there are a number of indications that he is deeply

[42]For a form-critical study of the narratives, see Martin Kessler, "A Prophetic Biography: A Form-critical Study of Jeremiah: Chs. 26–29, 32–45" (Dissertation, Brandeis University, Boston, 1965), ch. II.

[43]*Contra* Klaus Koch, *Was ist Formgeschichte?* (Neukirchen: Neukirchener Verlag des Erziehungsvereins, 1964), pp. 224ff.

[44]So Johannes Hempel, *Die Althebräische Literatur und ihr hellenistisch-jüdisches Nachleben* (Wildpark-Potsdam: Akademische Verlagsgesellschaft Athenaion M.B.H., 1930), p. 155: "*Stilistische Vorzüge weist dies Buch nur in beschränktem Masse auf. Seine Darstellung ist oft reichlich schwerfällig.*" But note Hempel's comment on the same page: "*Überragend in ihrer Wahrhaftigkeit, einzigartig in ihrer Verbindung tiefster-menschlich-persönlicher Anteilnahme mit einer sicheren Erfassung sachlich entscheidender Züge am Werk des dargestellten Meisters, stehen die Erzählungen Baruchs von Leben und Leiden des Jeremia in der altorientalischen Literatur . . .*"

[45]Heinz Kremers, "Leidensgemeinschaft mit Gott im Alten Testament: Eine Untersuchung der 'biographischen' Berichte im Jeremiabuch," *EvTh* 13 (Aug., 1953), pp. 122–40.

[46]Note the central role that Baruch plays in the account of the purchase of the field in 32.6–25 and in the crisis after the city's fall in 43.1–7 where he is censored for having influenced Jeremiah in his counsel to the people. On the former passage see Jones, *op. cit.*, pp. 227–9.

immersed in the ancient traditions and formulations of the covenant. He is a faithful reporter of his master's covenant-faith. He employs the classical messenger's formula כֹּה אָמַר יהוה with very great frequency as he does the formula for the reception of the divine word, *The Word of Yahweh came to me saying*. He follows the schemata of the revelatory forms with consistency, and employs the characteristic phrase נְאֻם יהוה and more especially the strategic and characteristic transitional phrase וְעַתָּה precisely in the manner of Jeremiah's *ipsissima verba*. His profuse use of the terminology of hearing is very striking. But dominating all else are the frequent conditionals, so crucial and central to the covenantal and legal formulation, most notably in the book of Deuteronomy. Nowhere are the affinities of Baruch with the latter more in evidence than here (compare *inter alia* Jer. 33.20f., 25f.; 37.10; 38.6, 17f.; 40.4bc, 5; 42.5, 6, 9f., 15f.).[47]

The sequence of prose narratives comes to a dramatic and moving finale in ch. 45.[48] It is probable that the Greek text has preserved the right order in placing it at 51.31–35. It is surely quite singular that an oracle should be addressed to an individual (cf., however, the divine word addressed to Ebed-melech in 39.15–18). The precise date and occasion are carefully given, the fourth year of Jehoiakim, at the time that Jeremiah dictated the scroll to Baruch. A number of scholars, offended by the sharp break in chronology here, have deleted the entire temporal reference, but there is no legitimate support for the procedure (1) because it is dominated by western views of compilation and editing and (2) because the passage as we have it makes very tolerable sense. For one thing, it may have been purposely designed as part of the framework with ch. 36. It is very probable that it was meant to be the divine word which illuminated all the foregoing narratives, the single divine disclosure to Baruch which had guided and directed him through all the travailing years, ever since the time, now many years ago, when the word of Yahweh had come to him. As he had written the terrible words of judgment upon the royal house and the people of Judah, line after line, he must have been torn with anxiety and sorrow. If he was closely related to the inner circle of royal officials as we have contended, we can readily grasp the depth of his feelings.

Those who were closest to Baruch would be the first to bear the brunt of Chaldean hostility, and he would surely himself be among them. The oracle opens with unusual solemnity: "Thus says Yahweh, the God of Israel, to you, O Baruch." Interestingly, Yahweh cites Baruch's own words of lamentation. The oracle is at once a rebuke and a word of comfort. In a supremely moving divine self-disclosure Yahweh tells Baruch what he is

---

[47]James Muilenburg, "The Form and Structure of the Covenant Formulations," *VT* 9 (Oct. 1959), pp. 354–7.

[48]Kremers, *op. cit.*, pp. 128–40; Artur Weiser, "Das Gotteswort für Baruch und die sogenannte Baruchbiographie," *Theologie als Glaubenswagnis*. Karl Heim *Festschrift* (Hamburg: Furche-Verlag, 1954), pp. 35–46.

doing in the earth, breaking down what he has planted and plucking up the whole land. It is highly revealing that the last words to which we are to listen echo the words of Jeremiah's call (1.10, cf. 31.28). The sorrows and griefs of Baruch are here mastered by the sorrows of God.[49] It was not a time in Judah for one to expect the realization of his ambitions and aspirations. Baruch was not to seek vindication for himself; he is to rest only in the assurance that there was an agony deeper than his own and that his life would be spared. The words accompanied him from the hour that he had read the scroll aloud before the members of the royal cabinet and the gathered crowd of Judeans. Throughout all the vicissitudes of the years he had been upheld by the momentous word from God.[50] It is surely clear why he placed the chapter at the close. It belonged with ch. 36 certainly, but it belonged even more profoundly at the point where he had completed the record of Jeremiah's trials and rejections, the end of the *via dolorosa* he had been fated to walk with the prophet. It tells us much about Baruch. In the rest of the narratives we hear of him but seldom; here a flash of unexpected light illumines the page.

It has been the purpose of the foregoing account to call attention to the importance of Baruch in the prophetic activity of Jeremiah and more particularly to set forth some of the characteristic features of scribal composition. It is very possible, indeed probable, that Baruch had a major hand in the compilation and editing of the original work extending from 1.1 to 45.5. If so, it is probably to him that we are to look for such prose additions as we find in 1.15–19, 3.6–12a, and elsewhere. It has been our contention that the so-called "Deuteronomic additions" by no means represent a separate source, but conform to conventional scribal composition and are therefore to be assigned to Baruch. The ambitions of Baruch to which reference is made in ch. 45 suggest that he may well have been a person of some eminence, corresponding to the prestige of his master. This is confirmed by the fact that his brother Seraiah served as the royal quartermaster (51.59). But it is also confirmed, in my opinion, by a circumstance of even greater significance. The traditions associated with Baruch, brief as they are, did not end with his deportation to Egypt after the fall of the nation. It has sometimes been averred that he was Jeremiah's literary executor, and if our contentions concerning his part in the composition of the book have any force in them, then this is probably true. But Baruch was to outlive his own career. He was remembered and became the inspirer of elaborate traditions and legends. The literature connected with

---

[49]Cf. G. von Rad, *Old Testament Theology*, vol. II, trans. D. M. G. Stalker (Edinburgh: Oliver and Boyd and New York: Harper and Row, 1965), p. 208: ". . . here a human being has in a unique fashion borne a part in the divine suffering." See also Abraham J. Heschel, *The Prophets* (New York: Harper and Row, 1962), pp. 256ff.

[50]W. Rudolph, *Jeremia*, HAT (Tübingen: J. C. B. Mohr [Paul Siebeck], 1958), p. 245.

his name is surprisingly large.[51] He moves into the future as few others in the history of Israel's traditions. It is surprising that he should find so eminent a place in the Jewish apocalypses. It is easy to understand why such protological figures as Enoch, Noah, Abraham, and Moses should play a central role in these compositions. Not so with Baruch. It is indeed true that he had survived the destruction of the Temple, the end of the Davidic monarchy, and the fall of the nation, but this can hardly suffice as an explanation of his continuing importance in the history of tradition. Rather, if I am not mistaken, we are to see in these ancient compositions an authentic witness to the importance of Baruch during his own lifetime. His distinction, all but suppressed in the biblical records, is recovered in legend and apocalypse and wisdom. This is not to credit these narratives with historical authenticity, though there are indeed many authentic echoes which derive from historical memory. The perplexities which seared his heart, the griefs which laid him low, the search for a wisdom that could withstand the threat and torment of inchoate times, the wrestlings with the demands of the *Torah* upon his people's life, all these have their source in Baruch's own life, a life that was lived courageously and often agonizingly in company with the prophet Jeremiah.

[51]R. H. Charles and W. O. E. Oesterley, *The Apocalypse of Baruch* (London: SPCK, 1917), pp. vii–viii: "It may be wondered why there was such a considerable Baruch-literature, for we can hardly suppose that the books mentioned represent more than a part of those written under the pseudonym of Baruch; but the fact is that, whatever may have been the reason, a good deal of legend clustered round the name of Baruch in ancient times among the Jews, and it was one which evidently enjoyed much popularity."

14

The Deuteronomic Edition
of Jeremiah*
J. Philip Hyatt

Few questions in Old Testament criticism are as interesting and as
difficult as the problem of the composition of the Book of Jeremiah.
Superficially this appears to be an easy problem. In chapter 36 we have a
very valuable account of the dictation by Jeremiah of many of his oracles
to his scribe Baruch. The book contains biographical information concerning the prophet which seems to have been written by an eyewitness; the
majority of scholars have long thought that eyewitness was Baruch. Furthermore, there are three other references to "books," in addition to those
of chapter 36, which ought to be helpful, 25:13; 30:2; 51:60. Certain
sections of the Book of Jeremiah seem to belong together: chapters 27–29
have striking stylistic peculiarities in common; chapters 30–31 constitute a
"book of comfort"; and chapters 46–51 contain oracles directed against
foreign nations.

Beneath the surface, however, there are many difficulties. Although
chapters 1–24 are mostly poetry and 25–45 are mostly prose, the former
contain extensive prose passages, and the latter some poetry. In chapters
1–24 the first person is usually employed by Jeremiah, and in chapters
25–45 the third person is ordinarily used in speaking about him, but there
are disconcerting changes of person that are hard to explain. The book
contains many duplicate passages (thirty-seven in the Massoretic text,
thirty in the Septuagint, according to Workman[1]), and a number of
passages appear to be parallel accounts of the same event. A chronological
order apparently is sometimes employed, as mostly in chapters 1–20, but a
topical order is followed in chapters 21–24, 30–31, and 46–51. Finally, the
Septuagint presents many problems in the study of the composition of
Jeremiah. It contains about one-eighth less material than the Massoretic
Hebrew text, with numerous omissions, some additions, and some changes.
Some of the passages appear in a different order in the Septuagint from

*Originally published in *Vanderbilt Studies in the Humanities* 1. Ed. by Richmond C.
Beatty, J. Philip Hyatt, and Monroe K. Spears. Nashville: Vanderbilt University Press, 1951,
71–95.

[1]*The Text of Jeremiah* (Edinburgh, 1889), pp. 50–51.

that of the Massoretic text, especially the foreign oracles, which come after 25:13.

In view of these facts it is not surprising that Old Testament scholars have reached no consensus of opinion regarding the composition of Jeremiah, and numerous theories have been offered to explain how the book reached its present condition.

I

Every commentator on Jeremiah has had to deal with the problem of its composition, and several articles and monographs have been devoted to the subject. Without attempting to give an exhaustive history of the discussion of our problem, we shall consider a few of the views that have been advanced to explain the composition of Jeremiah, particular attention being given to those which have noted Deuteronomic elements in the book.

In 1901 Bernhard Duhm published a commentary which, although radical in many of its conclusions, showed unusual religious and literary appreciation and has greatly influenced all subsequent work on Jeremiah.[2] Duhm thought that the book consists of three types of material: Jeremiah's own words, almost exclusively poetry in Qina metre, comprising 280 Massoretic verses; Baruch's life of Jeremiah, 220 verses; and later additions, 850 verses. These later additions are from many different *Ergänzer* or *Bearbeiter*, some from as late as the early part of the first century B.C. Duhm recognized that many of the additions in the third group have much in common, in both form and substance, with the Deuteronomistic parts of the Former Prophets and may come from the same hands.

C. H. Cornill[3] thought it was possible to recover the original words of Jeremiah, including the scroll dictated in 604, and the memoirs of Baruch, but recognized that the book contains much secondary material and expansions at many points. He did not attempt to classify the secondary material. He believed that the author of the oracle against Babylon, 50:2–51:58, knew the work after the words of Jeremiah and the memoirs of Baruch had been combined, somewhat in the form that we have them now; this oracle against Babylon was composed in the postexilic period before the Chronicler.

A. S. Peake has written one of the best commentaries on Jeremiah in English.[4] He distinguished the original utterances of Jeremiah, including those in Baruch's scroll, the series of narratives by Baruch, and supplements to these. Although not a few passages were attributed by him to the Supplementers, he did not classify them; he did recognize, however, that

---

[2] *Das Buch Jeremia erklärt* (Kurzer Hand-Commentar z. A. T., ed. by Marti, XI), Tübingen, 1901; see especially pp. xvi–xx.

[3] *Das Buch Jeremia erklärt*, Leipzig, 1905.

[4] *Jeremiah and Lamentations* (The New-Century Bible), 2 vols., Oxford, 1910.

the Deuteronomic phraseology tends to be pronounced in additions made by the Supplementers.[5]

Paul Volz[6] recognized in the Book of Jeremiah four sources: (1) Jeremiah's own writing (for he himself made some small collections of material, e.g., 22:1–23:4 and 23:13–32); (2) Baruch's writing at Jeremiah's dictation; (3) Baruch's independent work; and (4) later additions. Many of the passages in the fourth group were added in order to make the Book of Jeremiah, like other prophetic books, useful for reading in synagogue services and usable by synagogue preachers. Volz thus speaks of *homolieartige synagogale Erweiterung* of the work of Jeremiah and Baruch. This was apparently the result of the labors of many scribes and editors.

In 1914 Sigmund Mowinckel published a monograph on the composition of Jeremiah which contains much insight but has not received as much attention as it deserves.[7] He distinguished four principal sources in Jeremiah, designated as A, B, C and D. A was a collection of Jeremianic oracles, loosely placed together by someone living in Egypt between 580 and 480 B.C. The foundation of this was Baruch's scroll. It is contained now within chapters 1–24, and is the most authentic part of the book. It is mostly poetry, and largely in the first person. B was a personal history of Jeremiah, contained within chapters 19–20, 26–45. It was written by an admirer of the prophet, but was not genuine biography or history, properly speaking. This material existed for a time in an oral stage, and was written down by someone in Egypt in the same period as A. It was not Baruch's work. This source is valuable for events in Jeremiah's life, but does not give his words in their original form. The third source, C, is the Deuteronomic source. It consists mainly of the following: 3:6–13; 7:1–8:3; 11:1–5, 9–14; 18:1–12; 21:1–10; 22:1–5; 25:1–11a; 27; 29:1–23; 32:1–2, 6–16, 24–44; 34:1–22; 35:1–19; 39:15–18; 44:1–14; 45. This material is mostly prose, and consists largely of speeches by Jeremiah. It is characterized by a monotonous style and relatively small vocabulary. Its theme is the uninterrupted sinfulness of Judah and her punishment. It is close to Deuteronomy in form and conception of religion, and has far less value than A and B. D is the book of comfort in 30:1–31:28. Chapters 46–51 are still later, as well as some scattered portions of the book in its present form.

In a recent work, *Prophecy and Tradition*,[8] Mowinckel indicates that his view of the composition of Jeremiah has changed somewhat since he wrote his monograph in 1914. Instead of "sources" he would now speak of "traditionary circles," by which presumably he means circles in which oral tradition was preserved.

[5] *Ibid.*, pp. 59–60.

[6] *Der Prophet Jeremia übersetzt und erklärt* (Kommentar z. A. T., ed by Sellin, X), 2d ed., Leipzig, 1928.

[7] *Zur Komposition des Buches Jeremia* (Videnskapsselskapets Skrifter. II. Hist.-filos. Klasse, 1913, No. 5), Kristiana, 1914.

[8] Oslo, 1946, see especially pp. 61–65, 105–106.

In the same year as Mowinckel's monograph, Hölscher published his *Die Profeten*, in which a section is devoted to the composition of Jeremiah.[9] He advanced the theory that our Book of Jeremiah, excluding 50:1–51:58, comes largely from a single redactor who lived in the Persian period. He made use of two *Vorlage*: an "I" source, and a "He" source, the latter being the work of Baruch. The redactor put these two sources together and edited them to a large extent, as can be seen by the number of stereotyped phrases with which the book is filled, listed by Hölscher on pp. 382–384. Many of these phrases he calls Deuteronomic, but he does not term the redactor a Deuteronomic editor.

Somewhat similar to Hölscher's view, although apparently independent, is that of H. G. May.[10] He thinks that Baruch was not the author or editor of any part of Jeremiah, but only the prophet's amanuensis. The book comes to us for the larger part from the hand of one person, whom he terms "the Biographer," a man who used many stereotyped expressions and was steeped in the Deuteronomic tradition. He employed as his materials genuine oracles of the prophet, Jeremiah's memoirs, and other materials which tradition ascribed to the prophet, and sometimes he freely composed as he went along. He lived in the period between 500 and 450 B.C., being influenced by Second Isaiah, Ezra-Nehemiah, and others. His dominant theme was the coming restoration of the Davidic line and the union of Israel and Judah.

R. H. Pfeiffer has devoted to the composition of the Book of Jeremiah a very stimulating and important section of his *Introduction to the Old Testament*.[11] He distinguishes three types of material: words dictated or written by the prophet himself, a biography by his secretary Baruch, and miscellaneous contributions from later redactors. He is impressed by the large number of stereotyped expressions listed by Hölscher, and thinks that Baruch prepared an edition in which he combined the prophet's book with his own, and rewrote or revised many of his master's speeches in his own Deuteronomistic style.

The author of the latest full-scale commentary on Jeremiah, Wilhelm Rudolph,[12] follows the analysis of Mowinckel to a large extent, employing Mowinckel's symbols A, B, and C for the three principal sources. However, he differs from Mowinckel in a number of details. His Deuteronomic source "C" differs at several points from Mowinckel's; to it he assigns the following: 7:1–8:3; 11:1–14 (17); 16:1–13 (18); 17:19–27; 18:1–12; 21:1–10; 22:1–5; 25:1–14; 34:8–22; 35.

---

[9]Leipzig, 1914, pp. 379–405.

[10]"Towards an Objective Approach to the Book of Jeremiah: the Biographer," *Journal of Biblical Literature*, LXI (1942), 139–155; "Jeremiah's Biographer," *Journal of Bible and Religion*, X (1942), 195–201.

[11]New York, 1941, pp. 500–511.

[12]*Jeremia* (Handbuch z. A. T., ed. by Eissfeldt, Erste Reihe, 12), Tübingen, 1947; see especially pp. XIII–XIX.

Of others who have written on the composition of Jeremiah, we mention briefly only two. Nathaniel Schmidt's article on Jeremiah in the *Encyclopedia Biblica* is one of the most radical treatments of the book. Not only does he relegate much of the book to late editors, but he denies that Baruch was anything more than the prophet's amanuensis. E. Podechard's article, "Le livre de Jérémie; structure et formation," *Revue Biblique*, 37 (1928), 181–197, contains some important insights, especially on the nature of chapters 26–45.

This survey should make it clear that one of the basic problems in the study of the composition of the Book of Jeremiah is the determination of the precise nature of the Deuteronomic element in the book. We cannot say, as Bishop Colenso said in the nineteenth century, that Jeremiah was both the author of Deuteronomy and editor of many of the historical books of the Old Testament.[13] There is too great a difference between the prose passages which show Deuteronomic diction and the best poetry of Jeremiah for this to be true. Yet there are many questions relating to the Deuteronomic element in Jeremiah that are still the subject of controversy. How extensive is this element? Is it a source, either oral or written, used by an editor; or should we speak of a Deuteronomic edition of the book? If it was a source or edition, when was it made and by whom? Was Baruch the Deuteronomist? What is the value of the Deuteronomic material for recovering the life and teachings of the prophet Jeremiah?

The present writer published an article several years ago which dealt with the relationship between Jeremiah and Deuteronomy.[14] In that article I was principally concerned with the relationship of the prophet to Josiah's reforms, but gave some attention to the Deuteronomic editing of the Book of Jeremiah. My view concerning Jeremiah's relationship to the Deuteronomic reforms has remained unchanged, but I have come to a clearer opinion than was then expressed of the extent and nature of the Deuteronomic element in the Book of Jeremiah. I now believe that D was responsible for making an edition of the book in one of its early stages. The purpose of the present paper is to discuss the extent, the characteristics, the date, and the value of the Deuteronomic edition of Jeremiah.

II

The contribution to the Old Testament made by that individual whom we call the Deuteronomist, or the "school" of writers we call the Deu-

---

[13] *The Pentateuch and Book of Joshua Critically Examined*, Part VII (London, 1879), pp. 12, 225–227, 259–269, and Appendix 149.

[14] "Jeremiah and Deuteronomy," *Journal of Near Eastern Studies*, I (1942), 156–173. For a recent study of the subject, see H. H. Rowley, "The Prophet Jeremiah and the Book of Deuteronomy," in *Studies in Old Testament Prophecy Presented to Professor Theodore H. Robinson*, edited by Rowley (Edinburgh, 1950), pp. 157–174.

teronomists, was very great.[15] Since we must distinguish at least two stages in the work, designated by the symbols D₁ and D₂, it is best to think of a "school" and to speak of them in the plural; for the sake of convenience, however, we shall designate them simply by the symbol D.

D not only wrote the first and later editions of Deuteronomy, but edited in one way or another Joshua, Judges, I–II Samuel, and I–II Kings. D exhibits a remarkable uniformity of style and thought, remarkable though not of course complete.

The literary style of D is distinctive and easy to recognize. It shows a tendency to use a limited number of words and phrases over and over, and the general tone is parenetic. The style sometimes has great beauty, but is frequently repetitious and monotonous. D worked with a variety of methods. Sometimes they excerpted material from their sources without change; sometimes they rewrote older material (as in Joshua); sometimes they were content to provide a framework for older material (as largely in Judges); and sometimes they composed freely, especially in speeches and prayers.

The ideas of D are likewise distinctive and very pervasive. Their most important ideas were the following. Yahweh alone is to be worshiped by Israel, and that with a pure worship cleansed of pagan elements, with legitimate sacrifice only in the Jerusalem temple. Idolatry, the worship of foreign deities, is one of the greatest of sins. D had great interest in working out a theology of history, with special emphasis on the doctrine of divine retribution: Yahweh always punishes the wicked and rewards the righteous. A high social morality is demanded, with social justice for all, and with humanitarianism directed toward the unfortunate members of society.

The presence of Deuteronomic words and phrases in the Book of Jeremiah has frequently been pointed out. In order that we may have a sound basis for our discussion of the work of D, we shall list the more important D words and phrases appearing in Jeremiah, those which are of special significance in identifying D passages.[16]

(1) The following are brief D phrases which occur in Jeremiah: *a mighty hand and outstretched arm; provoke me* (or, *Yahweh*) *to anger,* especially in the infinitive *lᵉhakᶜîsēnî* and the like; *the stranger, the fatherless, and the widow; serve* (or, *go after*) *other gods; make his name dwell there; gods* (or, *people,* or *land*) *which thou knowest not; the land* (or, *place*) *which I gave to you and your fathers; when I brought them from the land of Egypt; house of bondage; hearken to his voice; do that which is*

---

[15]The contribution is well set forth by Lindsay B. Longacre, *The Old Testament: Its Form and Purpose* (New York-Nashville, 1945), chs. I–II.

[16]For further details and scriptural references, cf. the lists given by Hölscher, *op. cit.,* pp. 382–384; May, *Journal of Biblical Literature,* LXI (1942), pp. 154–155; and S. R. Driver, *Deuteronomy* (International Critical Commentary), pp. lxxviii–lxxxiv. My lists are not exhaustive.

right (or, *evil*) *in the eyes of Yahweh;* (*all*) *that he commanded you; the evil that he pronounced against you; a taunt, a reproach, a desolation, a proverb, a curse, a hissing,* etc., in a series, in various forms; *with all the heart and all the soul; the work of the hands* (i.e., idols); *sent unto you all his servants the prophets.*

(2) Longer phrases which show very close relationships to Deuteronomy, especially chapter 28, are the following: *the dead bodies of this people shall be food for the birds of the sky and the beasts of the earth, with none to frighten them away* (Jer. 7:33; 16:4; 19:7; Deut. 28:26); *behold, I will bring evil on this place, so that whoever hears it, his ears shall tingle* (Jer. 19:3; II Kings 21:12); *I will rejoice over them to do them good* (Jer. 32:41; Deut. 28:63); *I will cause them to eat the flesh of their sons and the flesh of their daughters . . . in the siege and in the distress with which their enemies shall distress them* (Jer. 19:9; Deut. 28:53); *I will make them a terror to all the kingdoms of the earth* (Jer. 15:4; 24:9; 29:18; cf. Deut. 28:25); *to a land which you have not known, neither you nor your fathers, and there you shall serve other gods night and day* (Jer. 16:3; Deut. 28:36); *why has Yahweh done thus to this great city?* (Jer. 22:8; cf. 16:10; Deut. 29:24; I Kings 9:8); *you shall seek me and find me when you seek me with your whole heart* (Jer. 29:13; Deut. 4:29); *you shall walk in all the way I command you, in order that it may be well with you* (Jer. 7:23; Deut. 5:30); *to fear me all the days, for their good* (Jer. 32:39; Deut. 4:10; 6:24); *when I brought them from the land of Egypt, from the iron furnace* (Jer. 11:4; Deut. 4:20).

(3) In addition to these, a number of stereotyped phrases occur in Jeremiah, often in association with the above, and are therefore to be considered as characteristic of D in Jeremiah although they do not appear (or appear only very rarely) in D writing elsewhere: *amend your ways and your doings; into the hand of those who seek their life; they did not hearken, and did not incline their ear; this house which is called by my name; for I am with thee to save thee and deliver thee; king, princes, priests, and prophets; walk in my law which I have given them; men of Judah and inhabitants of Jerusalem; his life shall be given* (or, *I will give*) *to him for a prey; sword, famine, and pestilence; turn now, each from his evil way; voice of joy and voice of gladness, voice of the bride and voice of the bridegroom;* and the contrasting ideas in the verbs, *build and plant, pull down and uproot.*

In identifying the D elements of Jeremiah, we must not employ the criterion of diction in a mechanical way, and we must use other criteria along with those of diction. Some of the phrases listed above may occur sporadically in genuine passages, but when several of them occur in a given passage, it is doubtless the work of D. Some of the phrases may in fact have been borrowed in the first place from genuine portions of Jeremiah. In addition to diction, we must use the criteria of style and of ideas, and we must give consideration to the motive of D in adding, or editing, a given passage.

The work of D in the Book of Jeremiah, as I conceive it, may be set forth as follows, beginning with the first chapter and working through to the end of the book.

In chapter 1, D has added vss. 15–16, 18–19 to the account of the call of Jeremiah and his two visions, which were in Baruch's scroll. Vss. 15–16 are the counterpart of 25:1–13a, also written by D, as we shall see below. Vs. 16 in particular shows D phraseology. Here it is predicted that the nations will come to surround Jerusalem and the cities of Judah to witness the judgment which God will pass on them; in chapter 25 they are the agents of the judgment. Vs. 15 may have originally read, not "all the families of the kingdoms of the north," but "a kingdom of the north" as was originally the case in 25:9. In 25:9 the Septuagint reads πατριὰν ἀπὸ βορρᾶ; in 1:15 it reads πάσας τὰς βασιλείας ἀπὸ βορρᾶ τῆς γῆς. Chapter 25 has been expanded and its general purport changed, as we shall show later; after the change was made there, a corresponding change was made in 1:15–16. Both were prophecies after the capture of Jerusalem by the Babylonians in 587 B.C. 1:18–19 borrows from 15:20, but is a prosaic piling up of figures and listing of the various classes in Judah, very characteristic of D. It is D's judgment on the life of Jeremiah written after his death. These verses have been appended to vs. 17, which originally stood in Baruch's scroll immediately after vs. 14.

In chapter 3, vss. 6–18 are widely considered secondary in whole or in part. Vs. 19 is a good continuation of vs. 5, but not of vs. 18. 3:6–14 is by D. It has little D diction, but does emphasize the sin of worship on the high places which D abhorred, and vs. 8 recalls the law of Deut. 24:1–4. D has derived the idea that Judah is worse than Israel from Ezekiel; see Ezek. 16:44–63; 23. D has incorporated a genuine oracle of the prophet, vss. 12b–14a, in the latter part of the section, but has misunderstood the meaning of the word "return," taking it to mean return from exile rather than repentance. 3:15–18 is also secondary, but from another editor, living during the exile or in the postexilic period; the ideas are similar to those found in Isa. 2:2–4; Micah 4:1–4; Ezek. 34; 37:16–28; Zech. 8:1–8, and elsewhere; to 3:17, cf. Jer. 14:21; 17:12 (also secondary).

5:18–19 is D's explanation of the exile in a form and in words very similar to those of Jer. 9:12–16; 16:10–13; 22:8–9; Deut. 29:22–28; and I Kings 9:8–9. Anyone who will compare all of these passages should be readily convinced that they are all from the same pen. They are designed to give a ready explanation for the desolation of Judah in 587 B.C., written after Nebuchadnezzar's invasion and his capture in Jerusalem.

7:1–8:3 is the first long section contributed by D to the Book of Jeremiah. The whole section is filled with D phraseology, and is in D's characteristic prose style. It contains several verses that are duplicates of, or clearly parallel to, other D passages: 7:16=11:14 (cf. 14:11–12); to 7:24 cf. 11:8; to 7:30–33 cf. 32:34–35; 19:6–7; to 7:34 cf. 16:9; 25:10. D has collected here various teachings of Jeremiah dealing with cultic places and practices. Mowinckel has appropriately compared the collection with Matthew's Sermon on the Mount. The teachings were not all given at one place and one time, but they constitute some of the most important of Jeremiah's messages. We do not have here the actual words of the prophet, since D style pervades the whole section, but we do have for the most part the substance of his teachings, for they agree in the main with his sayings elsewhere. The "temple sermon" probably extends only through 7:15. 7:21–26 may have been spoken on the same occasion, but more probably it was not. The parallel account of the "temple sermon" in 26:4–6 contains only the substance of 7:2–15, and the prophet's words reach their climax in 7:14–15; it is unlikely that the religious leaders would have allowed him to continue had he wished to do so. 7:29 is poetry, and may be a direct quotation from the prophet's sayings.

8:19b is a D gloss which breaks into the context. The poem places in the mouth of the people the question in 19a and the statement in 20. Vs. 19b is clearly a prosaic gloss in which Yahweh speaks rather than the people. The idea and phraseology are Deuteronomic.

9:12–16 is by D, comparable to 5:18–19. See the discussion above of that passage.

11:1–17 is another long contribution by D. This passage has been much discussed by critics and is very important for the study of the relationship between Jeremiah and Deuteronomy. The whole section is of D origin, though verses 15–16 have been taken unchanged from a collection of Jeremiah's own words, from either Baruch's scroll or some other collection. For detailed proof of this view, see my remarks in *Journal of Near Eastern Studies*, I (1942), 168–170. D wrote this section for a twofold purpose: (1) to show that Jeremiah was one of a line of prophets who had called on Israel to obey "the words of this covenant," as the Deuteronomists understood them (that is, the decalogue in Deut. 4:13; 9:9, 11, 15; the Deuteronomic code itself in Deut. 29:1, 9, 21—but between these two there was no contradiction in their minds); and (2) to say that because the people had not obeyed the covenant the evils pronounced for disobedience (as in Deut. 28:15–68) had come upon them. This section is therefore prophecy after the event. It is largely a free composition of the Deuteronomic editor, and we cannot recover a Jeremianic kernel with any certainty. D's incorporation of a genuine poem by the prophet (vss. 15–16) may be compared with his method in 1:15–19, where vs. 17 is a genuine saying, and with 7:1–8:3, where 7:29 is a genuine saying.

In 13:1–11, the parable of the waist-cloth, D has appended verse 11, thus making an unnecessary application of a single detail of the parable; cf. Deut. 26:19, and the use of the verb "cleave" in Deut. 10:20; 11:22; 13:4; Jos. 22:5; 23:8; II Kings 18:6.

14:1–15:4, which purports to be a word of Yahweh concerning the drouth, offers many puzzles to the interpreter. Several of the verses have to do with other subjects than drouth, some of them suggesting invasion or the like (see especially vss. 12, 13, 18). The heading in 14:1 is very late, being similar to the headings in 46:1, 47:1 and 49:34, all undeniably late. Within this congeries, 14:11–12 and 15:1–4 may be of D origin. 14:11 is closely parallel to 7:16 and 11:14, both in D sections; and D phraseology is very evident in 15:4. The emphasis on the sin of Manasseh is such as we find in II Kings 21:11–15; 23:26–27; 24:3–4. 14:13–18 is very likely genuine, but the editor who put the whole section together lived later than D.

In chapter 16, vss. 1–13, 18 are from D, as correctly pointed out by Rudolph. In vss. 1–13 D has revised a genuine account of Jeremiah's celibacy; his terminology is especially evident in vss. 4, 9, and 10–13. On 10–13, see the remarks above on 5:18–19. The whole is written from the standpoint of one who lived after the events of 587. It is not hypercritical for us to doubt that D gives the correct reason for Jeremiah's celibacy; the true reason may be that his complete and wholehearted devotion to his prophetic misson left no room for devotion to a wife and family. 16:14–15 is virtually a duplicate of 23:7–8, the original position of the passage; the verses have been inserted here (after D) in order to soften to some degree the preceding prediction of exile. If we then consider the whole section, 16:1–13, 16–18, we see that D has included a genuine poem of Jeremiah's (vss. 16–17) along with material of his own composition. The method of D here is thus similar to that which he employed in 11:1–17, where D included a genuine poem (11:15–16) with material of his own composition.

17:2b–3a is a gloss by D. Jeremiah says in vss. 1–2a that the sins of the people are written in two places: in their hearts and in the cultus. The prophet means that the cultus itself is a source of sin to the people, but D here adds a series of specific objects used in the cultus which are intended to convey the idea that it is not the cultus *per se* which is wrong, but a false variety of it. The gloss consists of the words "their altars and their Asherim by the green trees on the high hills, the mountains in the open country."

17:19–27, on Sabbath observance, is in the style and diction of D, as recognized by Rudolph. Its phraseology should be compared with that of other Deuteronomic passages, particularly Jer. 7:2, 24, 26; 11:8; 22:2, 4, 5. Nearly all critical scholars consider the passage secondary, and non-Jeremianic in its extreme emphasis of the importance of the proper observance of the Sabbath. It is not necessary to date it in the time of Nehemiah, as some scholars have done, comparing Neh. 13:15–22. It is possible, and even probable, that such interest in the Sabbath arose during the exilic period. Similar interest may be seen in Isa. 56:2–6; 58:13–14. The date of these passages has been the subject of much debate; W. S. McCullough has recently presented strong arguments for dating Isa. 56–66 in the period between 587 and 562.[17]

---

[17] *Journal of Biblical Literature*, LXVII (1948), 27–36.

In chapter 18, D has added his own interpretation of the parable of the potter, vss. 7–12. The most obvious and simple meaning of the parable in vss. 1–6 is that Yahweh has good plans for Israel and wishes to make her a good nation; if he does not succeed at first, as a potter spoils a vessel, he will remold her according to his designs. The initiative and the plans are God's; ultimately, the parable said, God will make of Israel what he wishes. The interpretation given in vss. 7–12 changes the underlying thought and makes the fate of the people depend upon what *they* do, not God. In addition to the fact that vss. 7–12 contain D phraseology is the fact that it sets forth D's fundamental doctrine of divine retribution. We may suppose that D found the parable in one of his sources and left it intact up to vs. 7; then he simply added vss. 7–12 or substituted them for the application made in his source.

In 19:1–20:6 we have an account of a symbolic action and speech by Jeremiah which led to his being placed in stocks by Pashhur. As the text now stands, two things have been combined in this section: (1) an account of the symbolic action in which the prophet broke an earthen flask, his address to the people in the temple court, and his imprisonment (19:1–2a, 10–11a, 14–15; 20:1–6), and (2) a "sermon" on Topheth (19:2b–9, 11b–13). The first of these is authentic and probably came from Baruch's memoirs; D has inserted into this his own long speech about Topheth, and has slightly revised the account of the arrest and punishment of Jeremiah. D phraseology is especially evident in vss. 3 (cf. II Kings 21:12), 7 (cf. Deut. 28:26), and 9 (cf. Deut. 28:53). D inserted the sermon on Topheth at this point because of the similarity in Hebrew between "the earthen flask" and "the potsherd gate"; he has played on the name Topheth, and in vss. 7–9 on the word *baqbūq* ("flask"). The abominations committed at Topheth in the valley of Hinnom are referred to by D also in Jer. 7:31ff.; 32:35.

21:1–12 is D's version of the incident reported in 37:3–10 (which stood in Baruch's memoirs). The relationship of these two sections to each other has been variously conceived by critics. Some believe that both refer to the same event, and combine parts of both to secure one complete account. Others accept them as accounts of two separate missions from Zedekiah. It would be dogmatic to deny that Zedekiah could have sent two separate missions to Jeremiah, one at the beginning of the Babylonian siege of Jerusalem (21:1–12) and the other during the interval when Egyptian help was coming to the city and the Babylonians temporarily lifted their siege (37:3–10). It is more likely, however, that 21:1–12 is simply D's rewriting of the incident which is more accurately reported in chapter 37, for the following reasons: Zephaniah the son of Maaseiah appears as an envoy in both; the time of the mission in chapter 21 is vague; D phraseology and ideas pervade 21:1–12; and the account is artificially constructed, in that vss. 3–7 are addressed to Zedekiah through the envoys, whereas vss. 8–10 are addressed to the people (although the conference presumably was secret), and verses 11–12 are directed to the royal house in general and consist of general admonitions based on 22:3 and 4:4.

22:1–5 is D's introduction to the group of oracles about the kings of Judah in 22:1–23:6. Since D furnishes the introduction, it was probably he who collected most of these oracles as we now have them (23:1–6 are probably later than D). They were not in Baruch's scroll, because they include oracles against kings who lived later than 604. In addition to the fact that 22:1–5 has D diction and ideas, we should observe that the admonitions are directed to the royal house in general rather than to a specific king, that they are conventional in tone, and that the promises attached are greater and more materialistic than Jeremiah usually made.

Within the group of oracles against Judaean kings, 22:8–9 was written by D (see the remarks on 5:18–19 above), and 22:24–27 may be his work. The latter has some D phrases, and is to be considered as prophecy after the event.

Chapter 24 must be assigned wholly to D. The difficulties in this chapter have been noted by critics, but most accept it as genuine, a few bracketing certain verses as secondary. Duhm declared it to be the work of an editor; May assigns it unequivocally to the Biographer. The attitude expressed here about the exiles accords well with the attitude of later times which saw in the Jews who had gone into Babylonian exile and later returned the true Israelites, and with the view of those who considered the exiled Jehoiachin as the legitimate king and opposed the claims of Zedekiah. It does not accord with Jeremiah's ideas expressed elsewhere, and is filled with D phraseology, most noticeably in verses 6, 7, 9 and 10. It is difficult to believe that Jeremiah thought God's favor depended on whether one were exiled or not, rather than upon repentance and obedience. In chapter 5 he expressed the opinion that all classes in Jerusalem were sinful. The viewpoint of chapter 24 is not consonant with Jeremiah's viewpoint in the letter to the exiles in chapter 29, nor with his general attitude toward Zedekiah. That king was friendly to the prophet and apparently wished to follow his counsel, but was weak and unwilling to risk the disfavor of the pro-Egyptian party among his officials. The view of this chapter does not accord with Jeremiah's decision at the fall of Jerusalem in 587 to remain in Palestine. We do not need, however, to date chapter 24 in the time of Ezra-Nehemiah. The mention of the exiles in Egypt suggests that the Egyptian exile chronicled in Jer. 43–44 was of recent occurrence, and the general tenor suggests that opposition to Zedekiah was of vivid memory. It is noteworthy that D frequently displays a friendly attitude toward Babylonia and her rulers. Whether D freely composed this chapter or rewrote some material which he found, we do not know; but in its present form it is his product and not Jeremiah's.

Chapter 25 is one of the most interesting and important portions of the Book of Jeremiah for the study of D. Here we must assign verses 1–13a *in their original form* to D. He wrote the section to form the conclusion to what he believed was Baruch's scroll of 604 (as shown by the reference to the fourth year of Jehoiakim in 25:1). We must recall that he had written

1:15–16 at the beginning of the book. The words "this book" in vs. 13 refer backward, not forward, and this section originally concluded with those words. Compare the "book" of 51:60, which refers back to the oracles against Babylon. The differences between the Massoretic text and the Septuagint in 25:1–13 are very striking: the Septuagint omits the references to Babylon and Nebuchadnezzar, having in verse 9 πατριὰν ἀπὸ βορρᾶ; vs. 12 is much shorter than in the Hebrew; and the Septuagint uses first person instead of third person in vss. 4–5. The Septuagint represents a more nearly original form of this passage than the Massoretic text, but not quite the original, since some changes were made in the Septuagint *Vorlage* in the same direction as the present Hebrew text. Skinner has printed a translation of what he believes to have been the original text.[18] He is certainly correct in the main. In its original form, as it came from the pen of D, 25:1–13a was directed against Judah and Jerusalem, not against Babylonia and other nations; this is clearly pointed out at the outset in vs. 2, and is implied in the nature of the sins for which punishment is promised. There is only a vague reference to the coming of a "family from the north," such as D believed possible in 604. This section was edited at a later time, after D, in order to make it serve as an introduction to the oracles against the foreign nations, probably by the editor of 25:13b–38. In the Septuagint the oracles against the foreign nations stand after 25:13; this was probably their original position, though it is possible that 25:13a–38 once stood just before the foreign oracles, even in the Hebrew text.

There is no doubt that D phraseology and ideas pervade 25:1–13a in their original form. D has not, however, worked over 13b–38; vs. 18, which has some D phrases, either is misplaced or is imitation of D phraseology. The foreign oracles show no trace of D redaction. We must conclude, then, that when the oracles against foreign nations were collected, 25:13b–38 was written (probably with the inclusion of some authentic sayings of the prophet) as their introduction, and 25:1–13a was revised to make it apply to the foreign nations rather than to Judah.

Chapter 26 is D's report of the temple sermon of Jeremiah and his subsequent arrest and trial. His rewriting is confined almost entirely to the summary of the sermon in vss. 4–6, which is filled with D phrases. Since D had given what he considered a full report in chapter 7, he was satisfied with only a brief résumé here; the account of subsequent events bears few marks of D redaction (see vss. 13, 19). For the whole chapter, D used as source a part of Baruch's memoirs.

Chapter 27 is D's version of a symbolic action and message of the prophet. It is not, however, merely a parallel to chapter 28, as Mowinckel thought. D has here taken from Baruch's memoirs an account of the action

---

[18] *Prophecy and Religion* (Cambridge, 1922), pp. 240–241. Skinner accepts the conjecture that these verses were the conclusion (rather than the introduction, as some scholars have thought) of the volume of prophecies dictated by Jeremiah to Baruch.

and words of Jeremiah and expanded them; his diction is especially evident in vss. 5, 8, and 13. The account as we now have it is repetitious, being addressed in turn to the foreign envoys, to Zedekiah, and to the priests and all the people; there is careless interchange of first and third persons.

Chapter 29, containing Jeremiah's letter to the exiles, was originally in Baruch's memoirs, but has been revised somewhat by D. His ideas and phraseology are evident in vss. 10–20, especially is vss. 16–20, which have been considered by most critics as secondary. For evidence of D phraseology, the following comparisons should be made: cf. vs. 13 with Deut. 4:29 and I Kings 8:48; cf. vs. 14 with Deut. 30:3, 5; and cf. vs. 18 with Deut. 28:25. Within vss. 10–14 there may be some of the prophet's own words and ideas (particularly verse 11), but the passage has been revised to such an extent that we cannot recover his words with precision.

Chapter 32 is an excellent example of the method of D. He found in Baruch's memoirs (32:1, 6–15) a straightforward account of Jeremiah's purchase of a field at Anathoth with a simple "word of the Lord" appended as explanation of the significance of the act (vs. 15). To this D has added a long section, vss. 16–44, repeating some of the genuine material in vss. 43–44. (32:2–5 is probably from a later editor.) Nearly all critics see in this chapter some secondary material after vs. 16; even Condamin admits that vss. 17–23 and 28–35 are secondary. Mowinckel assigns vss. 1–2, 6–16 and 24–44 to his "C," but D phraseology is as evident in vss. 17–23 as in other parts of the long section. Vss. 17–44 are an excellent summary of D's theology of history, including his interpretation of the Babylonian exile and his hope for the future. His hope for the future is expressed in positive terms, but it is more general than is found in later eschatological passages which have been included in the Book of Jeremiah.

In chapter 33, vss. 1–13 may be D's revision of some incident which is now obscurely preserved in vss. 4–5, where the text is difficult to understand. D phraseology is not strong, but may be present in such verses as 9 and 11. On the other hand, the whole passage may be much later than D, with some imitation of D terminology. Vss. 14–26 are not in the Septuagint and are probably later than D.

In chapter 34, D has rewritten vss. 8–22, the account of the release of Hebrew slaves during the Babylonian siege of Jerusalem. Not only is D phraseology abundant, but the release is confused with the sabbatical release of slaves according to the law of Deut. 15. In the nature of the case it must have been a release by special proclamation, since the sabbatical release of so many slaves could not have fallen at one time. D's hand is particularly evident in vss. 13–15 and 17. It may be that D has not preserved the real motive for the prophet's condemnation of the people's release of their slaves and then taking them back when danger seemed past. He may well have condemned them for their hypocrisy; the release of slaves during the siege would have been to the economic advantage of the owners, relieving them of the burden of feeding and caring for them when food was scarce. Mowinckel assigns the entire chapter to "C," but there is no trace of D in vss. 1–7.

In chapter 35, D has rewritten and expanded the speech of Jeremiah in vss. 12–19 and slightly retouched the early part. In addition to the strong diction of D in vss. 13, 15, 17, note the recurrence of the words *miṣwāh* and *miṣwōth* so frequently employed by D, and the idea of retribution which was so often emphasized by D. The original oracle of the prophet may be preserved in vss. 18–19.

In chapter 36, vss. 28–31 are D's rewriting of the word of Yahweh to Jeremiah concerning the dictation of a second scroll. Duhm pointed out a number of artificial elements in this section: Jehoiakim is addressed as if Jeremiah were not at the time in hiding with Baruch; the king is condemned for burning the first scroll as if that were the worst thing he had done; and the prediction that Jehoiakim would have no descendant overlooks the fact that his son Jehoiachin did rule. The whole has the tone of one of D's freely composed speeches. 36:27–28, 32 gives all the authentic information we need about the writing of the second scroll.

37:1–2 may be a historical note by D, giving a general estimate of Zedekiah and his reign of the type familiar in the Books of Kings. D has not touched the rest of the chapter, but 21:1–12, as noted above, is his version of the incident of 37:3–10.

In chapter 38, vss. 2 and 23 are from D. The former has the diction and the ideas of D; the genuine verse is 3. Vs. 23 is a prosaic explanation of the preceding verse.

Chapters 39–40 present a number of difficulties, as all commentators have recognized, but an easy and simple solution is possible. The two stories of the treatment of the prophet by Babylonian officials in 39:14 and 40:1–6 cannot be harmonized. In chapter 39, only vss. 3 and 14 are original, but they give all the information needed concerning the release of Jeremiah: he was released from prison by the officials named in vs. 3 (Nebuzaradan not being among them, for he did not appear in Jerusalem until a month later, according to Jer. 52:12), and he was then placed in the custody of Gedaliah. 39:1–2, 4–13, 15–18; 40:1–6 is all from D. 39:1–2, 4–10 is a shortened account of the events narrated in Jer. 52:4–16 (=II Kings 25:1–12). The latter is Deuteronomic, but the material in Jer. 39 is from the D editor of Jeremiah, who used the same sources as the editor of II Kings 25. 39:11–13; 40:1–6 is a legendary account of the treatment of the prophet; this account tends to elevate the standing of the prophet and to justify the actions of Nebuchadnezzar and Nebuzaradan. It is hard to see how anyone can believe that Nebuzaradan spoke the words reported in 40:2–3, where he is made to expound the Deuteronomic doctrine of retribution. 39:15–18 is also by D. His diction occurs here, and the story is told because D could not allow Ebed-melech to go unrewarded.

40:7–42:6 has been untouched by D, but his revision is clearly evident in 42:7–22. The section is repetitious and burdensome, and has many conventional D phrases. The kernel of the prophet's answer to those who wished to go to Egypt is contained in vss. 9-14, but even that shows traces of D revision.

Chapter 44 has been rewritten by D. It probably rests upon authentic words of Jeremiah, preserved in Baruch's memoirs, but the phrasing is D's and the theme is a favorite of his. It is not worthwhile to attempt to recover the prophet's original words, since the whole section has been worked over by D.

Chapter 45 has caused critics much labor in interpretation. Its subject matter seems insignificant, and the date given in vs. 1 seems to most commentators open to question. Erbt saw in the chapter the last words of Jeremiah before he sent Baruch to the Gola in Babylonia to be his witness.[19] I believe Mowinckel is right in assigning the chapter to D; he does not give strong reasons for his opinion, but seems to reach his decision by a process of eliminating the chapter from other sources. The chapter does have some familiar D phrases, particularly in vss. 4 and 5b. This is D's final word in the Book of Jeremiah, a word in which he pays tribute to Baruch, whose memoirs and collection of Jeremiah's sayings he had used. By D's doctrine of retribution, the faithful Baruch must have his reward. But he says that Baruch must not seek too great things for himself: such great things as attempting to influence Jeremiah to stay in Palestine (43:3).

IV

The date of D's work on Jeremiah can be fixed within fairly close limits. The following data bear upon this question:

(1) The fall of Jerusalem, the period of Gedaliah's governorship, and the flight to Egypt are chronicled in the latter part of the book. Jerusalem fell in 587, but we do not know how long the governorship of Gedaliah lasted. The impression given by chapters 40-41 is that it lasted for a very brief time. However, if the third deportation, of which the date is given in Jeremiah 52:30, was connected with the punishment inflicted on Judah for the murder of Gedaliah, the governorship may have lasted for about five years, to 582.

(2) 44:30 predicts that Hophra, the Egyptian Pharaoh, will be given into the hands of his enemies, as Zedekiah had been given into the hand of Nebuchadnezzar. Hophra was overthrown by Amasis about the year 570 B.C. The passage in Jeremiah is probably prophecy after the event; it has been written by D, or at least left standing by him.

(3) 22:26 is a prediction of the death in exile of Jehoiachin. This is probably from D, and again prophecy after the event. Jehoiachin was taken out of prison and given preferential treatment by Amel-Marduk, as

---

[19] *Jeremia und seine Zeit* (Göttingen, 1902), pp. 83-86.

we know from Jer. 52:31–33 and from cuneiform sources. This was in the first year (not the accession year) of Amel-Marduk, 561–60. It is not known how long after this Jehoiachin died.

(4) Chapter 24, as we have seen, seems to come from a time when the exile in Egypt had occurred and opposition to the legitimacy of Zedekiah's rule was active, or at least of vivid memory.

(5) Very instructive for the dating of D—particularly the determination of his *terminus ad quem*—is a comparison of the Massoretic text and the Septuagint in chapters 25 and 27. In both cases it seems very probable that the Septuagint is nearer to the original text than the Hebrew; it is much easier in both cases to account for the addition to the Septuagint *Vorlage* than to account for the intentional omission by the Septuagint translators. In chapter 25 the Septuagint omits the references to Babylon and Neb-uchadnezzar, and has a much shorter text in vs. 12, not referring to the punishment of the king of Babylon and the Chaldeans. In chapter 27, the Septuagint omits vs. 7, which says that the "time" of Nebuchadnezzar is coming, when his kingdom will be overthrown; and the Septuagint has a shorter version of vss. 20–22 in which there is no reference to the return from exile of the vessels taken by the Babylonians from Jerusalem. In their original form, then, both of these passages came from the time of the exile, not after the exile was over, when Babylon had been overthrown and Jews had returned to Palestine.

(6) In general accord with this is the fact that the prophecies of return from exile in D are vague and general. This is best and most clearly seen in 32:36 ff. If D is responsible for the figure "seventy years" in 25:12; 29:10 (and that is open to question), even that is no indication that he knew how long the Chaldean kingdom or the Jewish exile lasted. It is a vague number—probably two generations or "the days of one king" as in Isa. 23:15.

(7) The attitude of D towards the Babylonians and Nebuchadnezzar is in general friendly. For example, he speaks of Nebuchadnezzar as the servant of Yahweh (27:6; cf. 25:9) and justifies the actions of Nebuchad-nezzar and Nebuzaradan in 39:11ff; 40:1ff. The hatred of Babylon shown in the oracles against Babylon (chs. 50–51) is absent.

(8) The D editor of Jeremiah has his closest affinities, both in style and in substance, with the exilic D editor of Deuteronomy, Kings, Joshua, and other books edited by the D school. There are very close affinities with the exilic portions of Deuteronomy 28.[20] The similarity extends to long phrases, especially those in which the sufferings endured by Jerusalem in the time of the Babylonian siege are described. For the "predictions" of the taking of Jerusalem and the exile, one should compare also the following: I Kings 8:46–53; 9:1–9; II Kings 17:19–20; 21:7–15; 22:14–20; 23:26–27.

---

[20]See the list of Driver, *op. cit.*, p. xciii.

In the light of these data we must conclude that the D editor of Jeremiah lived during the time of the Babylonian exile; a date around 550 B.C. cannot be far wrong. Not only is there no evidence in his work of the end of the exile, but there is also no evidence of the influence of II Isaiah and early postexilic writers. II Isaiah's influence can be best seen in Jer. 10:1-16; 16:19-20; 30:10-11; 31:7-14, 35-37, but these passages show no trace of D diction and were not in his edition.

V

We may now give a summary statement describing the Deuteronomic edition of Jeremiah—its purpose, leading themes, sources, methods, and values.

The primary purpose which led D to make an edition of Jeremiah was to show how Jeremiah, the outstanding prophet at the time of Judah's decline and downfall, was in general agreement with the ideas and purposes of the Deuteronomic school. In actuality Jeremiah probably never gave active support to the Deuteronomic reforms, if indeed he was prophesying in 621 and the immediately following years; at some points he was more likely an active antagonist of those reforms. Yet, to the Deuteronomic school it was unthinkable that Jeremiah should have been out of harmony with them. Hence, his book was edited to show that he was generally in agreement with their ideas and at one time was an ardent evangelist for the Josianic reforms (11:1-17).

In his edition of Jeremiah the outstanding theme of D is that all of history is under the control of Yahweh. He had led Israel out of Egypt and into the land of Canaan. But there they fell into the worship of false gods. Nevertheless Yahweh gave them many opportunities to repent, sending them many prophets, among whom Jeremiah was one. But Israel persisted in its idolatry, and Yahweh gave them into the hand of Nebuchadnezzar, who destroyed Jerusalem and exiled many Jews. But Yahweh's ultimate plans for Israel are good rather than evil, and so he will ultimately restore them to their land. Writing about 550, his hopes for the future are positive, but expressed in vague terms.

In his edition of Jeremiah D seems to have a special fondness for the use of symbolic actions, and for composing "sermons" and prayers. One must recall that Deuteronomy itself consists of several long speeches by Moses and that in Kings and elsewhere the Deuteronomists were given to the free composition of speeches and prayers. D used the same methods in compiling his edition of Jeremiah as were used elsewhere. Sometimes he excerpted original material from his sources without change; at other times he revised or rewrote his sources; and at still other times he composed freely. Particularly instructive examples of passages in which D incorporates original materials unchanged within sections composed or revised by him are the following: 1:15-19 (17 being genuine); 7:1-8:3 (7:29 being a direct quotation); 11:1–17 (15–16 being genuine); and 16:1–13, 16–18 (16–17 being authentic).

In making his edition of Jeremiah, D employed at least three sources: (1) Baruch's scroll written at Jeremiah's dictation in 604; (2) a collection (or collections) of genuine oracles of the prophet, made by Baruch and/or others; and (3) Baruch's memoirs.

It is not possible to recover each of these sources in our present book with complete confidence. However, some tentative conclusions may be reached by careful consideration of the probable date and background of the individual passages and oracles, and by attention to literary form. The present writer has attempted to separate these various sources, and his conclusions will be given below; it is not possible within the scope of this paper to give the detailed evidence for these conclusions.

Baruch's scroll consisted of the messages spoken by Jeremiah from the beginning of his career to the time of dictation, 604. It must have consisted primarily, if not exclusively, of oracles of condemnation and threat, as the account of its dictation in chapter 36 implies. The materials in the scroll incorporated in our present book by D are probably contained within the first six chapters, consisting at least of the following: 1:4–14, 17; 2; 3:1–5, 12b–14a, 19–25; 4; 5:1–17, 20–30; 6.

D also had at his disposal a collection, or collections, of genuine oracles of Jeremiah which had been made by Baruch or others. In this group we must place all genuine oracles uttered after the dictation of Baruch's scroll, and those which are not oracles of condemnation and threat. It is entirely possible that a few passages which we list in this group were in Baruch's scroll, but most of them can definitely be excluded from it because they are later than 604, or they are lamentations, confessions of the prophet, or lyrical poems. In this group there is evidence for the collection of some of the oracles by subject matter, as in 23:9–33. To this second group we assign the following: 8:4–9:26 (9:10–11, 17–22 suggest the invasion in 602 by bands of Chaldeans and others described in II Kings 24:2); 10:17–22 (probably 598); 10:23–24; 11:15–16; 11:18–12:6 (a confession); 12:7–13 (probably 602); 13:1–11 (probably late Jehoiakim); 13:12–14 (probably reflects the civil strife in Zedekiah's reign); 13:15–19 (597); 13:20–27 (between 605 and 598); 14:2–6, 13–18; 15:5–9 (a lamentation); 15:10–21 (confession); 16:16–17; 17:1–2a, 3b–4, 9–10, 14–18 (partly confession); 18:1–6, 13–23; 20:7–18 (confession); 21:13–14; 22:6–7, 10–12, 13–23, 28–30; 23:9–33.

Baruch's memoirs do not really constitute a biography; they do not cover a sufficient portion of Jeremiah's life to be that. Baruch was concerned largely to record Jeremiah's conflicts with priests and false prophets, and to record the last days of Jeremiah, from the time of the Babylonian invasion to the flight into Egypt. Volz properly calls the latter a *Leidensgeschichte*, comparing it in fullness of detail with the passion narratives of the gospels. Baruch's memoirs consisted of materials now found within the following, in some cases revised at length by D: 19:1–2a, 10–11a, 14–15; 20:1–6; 26–29; 32:1, 6–15; 34–36; 37:3–21; 38; 39:3, 14; 40:7–42:13; 43; and 44. Our discussion above should make it clear that we do not consider Baruch to be the Deuteronomist, as suggested by Pfeiffer. It is possible at a number of points to see clearly the difference between Baruch's work and that of D; perhaps the best examples are the difference between 32:6–15 (Baruch) and 32:16–44 (D); and between 37:3–10 (Baruch) and 21:1–12 (D). Also, we must deny that Baruch was only the amanuensis of the prophet, as maintained by May and Schmidt. Not only is Baruch the most likely candidate for the authorship of those portions of the book which seem to come from an eyewitness (which we call Baruch's memoirs); there is evidence within the Book of Jeremiah that Baruch was more than a professional amanuensis. In 36:19 he is advised by the officials to hide with Jeremiah after the reading of the scroll. This would hardly have been necessary if he were only a hired agent of the prophet, not his disciple and associate. In 43:3 Baruch is accused of unduly influencing the prophet in the decision about flight to Egypt. Whether he sought to exert such influence or not, it is significant that he was accused of doing so. We should, therefore, consider Baruch as more than Jeremiah's hired scribe; he was his disciple and companion.

Our present Book of Jeremiah was not complete when the Deuteronomic edition was completed. A number of passages, and collections of material, were added to D's edition before the book reached its present form. These consisted of eschatological predictions which show the influence of later prophets, brief poems from "Wisdom" teachers, oracles against foreign nations, and the like. The following passages are post-Deuteronomic additions to the book of Jeremiah: 1:1–3; 3:15–18; 10:1–16 (showing II Isaiah's influence); 10:25 (=Ps. 79:6–7); 12:14–17; 14:7–9, 19–22; 16:14–15 (=23:7–8); 16:19–21; 17:5–8, 11–13; 23:1–8, 34–40 (the latter a very late "rabbinic" play on the word *massāʾ*) and 33:14–26 (or all of 33). Chapters 30–31 in their present form were collected later than D, for some passages show the influence of II Isaiah (30:10–11; 31:7–14, 35–37) and possibly of Nehemiah's time (31:38–40). It is entirely possible that these two chapters include genuine poems of the prophet, such as 30:12–15; 31:2–6, 15–20. The oracles against foreign nations now preserved in chapters 46–51 were collected later than D; yet, some of them may be authentic, such as the first oracle against Egypt. Chapter 52 was taken from II Kings 24:18–25:21, 27–30. Jer. 52:28–30 is missing both in II Kings and in the Septuagint of Jeremiah, but seems to be a reliable list.

A final word may be said about the value of the Deuteronomic edition for the student of Jeremiah's life and thought. We can only make a few general remarks and give a few examples, for a complete evaluation of D would require minute consideration of every passage.

The value of D's work in Jeremiah varies as it does in other books edited by the Deuteronomists. Where he incorporates older material from his sources, that material may be quite authentic. Material from the sources listed above as (1) and (2) is generally the most authentic and most valuable in the book. Baruch's memoirs are usually reliable for the narration of events, but he did not attempt to give Jeremiah's own words; he reports Jeremiah's sayings in his own style. The least valuable of D's work consists of the freely composed speeches found in his edition. Sometimes he retains ideas of the prophet, or his own ideas agree with those of the prophet, but at other times his ideas vary from those of Jeremiah.

As examples of the varying value of D's work we may compare chapters 7 and 26 on the one hand with chapter 24 on the other. Chapter 7 is D's work, but in the main it preserves Jeremiah's thoughts, though not in his own words. In chapter 26, D has rewritten only the temple sermon, the rest being left virtually intact. Chapter 24, on the other hand, is not true to the thoughts of Jeremiah, as we have seen, but gives only the idea of D and others like him.

Our final statement regarding D's edition of Jeremiah must be an expression of gratitude. He has preserved for us the larger portion of our present Book of Jeremiah, and without his work much of this material might well have sunk into oblivion.[21]

[21] Much of the research on this paper was carried on with the assistance of a Carnegie summer grant in 1947 made by the Nashville University Center Research Council. It is a pleasure to acknowledge the valuable aid afforded by this grant.

15

Relations Between Poetry and Prose in the Book of Jeremiah with Special Reference to Jeremiah iii 6–11 and xii 14–17*

W. McKane

I

A consideration of the relation between poetry and prose in the book of Jeremiah may have the form of a general lexicographical enquiry in which an attempt is made to examine the stock of vocabulary which is common to poetry and prose. If this is to be more than a mere cataloguing, in which presumably one would not go very far wrong but would have difficulty in saying anything that commanded attention or awakened interest, certain assumptions have to be incorporated into the enquiry. The assumption that the poetry is a reservoir for the prose is, in general, a reasonable one: it does not commit us to the proposition that all the poetry in the book is attributable to the prophet Jeremiah and that none of the prose is attributable to him, or that the prose is always later than the poetry. If, however, we say that the poetry is a reservoir for the prose, there is an implication that the authors of the prose who use the poetry of the book in this way are distinct from the author(s) of the poetry. There is an assertion that the poetry is a nucleus of the *corpus* and that in the process of enlarging and complicating that *corpus* writers other than the authors of the poetry make use of its vocabulary.

The principal competing assumption would be that the presence of vocabulary common to poetry and prose is an indication that the author of the poetry is also the author of the prose or of some of it. It is doubtful whether lexicographical or linguistic criteria by themselves will enable us to decide these matters: to determine the nature of the relationship between constituent parts of the Jeremianic *corpus*, whether interest is mainly focused on the prose or whether it is more precisely the relation between poetry and prose which is under consideration. This assertion, however,

---

*Originally appeared in *Supplements to Vetus Testamentum* 32, *Congress Volume. Vienna 1980*. Ed. by J. A. Emerton, Leiden: E. J. Brill, 1981, 220–237.

may seem to be contradicted by the pronounced lexicographical orientation of books which deal with the prose of the book of Jeremiah. The objection may be made that the books of W. Thiel[1] and H. Weippert[2] are marked by the attention which they have given to linguistic details and that the conclusions which are reached in them are founded on lexicographical considerations. There is a sense in which this is true, but, perhaps, a more significant and profound sense in which it is untrue. These books are principally concerned with the prose of the book of Jeremiah, but an examination of the lexicographical arguments which are used in them has a bearing on the interpretation of the relation between poetry and prose in that book.

When close attention is given to these books by Thiel and Weippert, it becomes evident that methods so different that they must necessarily lead to contrary conclusions are being encountered. Thiel and Weippert are at cross-purposes, sometimes for obvious reasons, sometimes for reasons which are more subtle, but their disagreement is inevitable and they are set on a collision course. The clearest and simplest expression of this is given where Thiel is evaluating prose vocabulary which does not occur outside the book of Jeremiah, but which he classifies as Deuteronomistic and which he assigns to an editor with the *siglum* D. It will be obvious that this involves arguments different in principle from those which he uses when he is seeking to establish affinities between the prose vocabulary in the book of Jeremiah and the vocabulary of the book of Deuteronomy or the Deuteronomistic historical books. The latter operation may be fairly described as a linguistic one, and we are in a position to set out the alleged parallels, scrutinize them and consider to what extent Thiel's account of the resemblances and the construction which he places on them commends itself to our judgement. It is in this area that the critical engagement of Weippert and Thiel is most interesting and fruitful, and it is here that her methods and interests are most clearly lexicographical and semantic. That this should be so is not surprising, because this comparative activity principally involves lexicographical skills and a range of linguistic judgements.

So far as Weippert is concerned to impose more refined evaluations on crude statistics her efforts are to be applauded. There is a danger in making too much of comparisons between vocabulary in the prose of the book of Jeremiah, on the one hand, and in the book of Deuteronomy and the Deuteronomistic historical literature on the other. If these comparisons are too general, they do not have the significance which is sometimes attached to them, and there is a skill involved in deciding when they have a degree of particularity sufficiently striking to require us to raise the question of direct literary connections. For example, if no more is being done than the

---

[1] *Die deuteronomistische Redaktion von Jeremia 1–25,* (Neukirchen, 1973).
[2] *Die Prosareden des Jeremiabuches, BZAW* 132 (Berlin, 1973).

cataloguing of isolated items of vocabulary (single words) which are common to the two areas being compared, there is a danger of ending up with statistics which do not have much significance and which are not capable of supporting the arguments into which they are pressed. An extreme statement of this point of view, which is, perhaps, a caricature, but which makes the point forcefully, is that we may be demonstrating no more than that the prose of the book of Jeremiah and the prose of Deuteronomy or the Deuteronomistic historical literature are both written in Hebrew. For the most part, arguments of the kind which are being considered will have a more substantial character, but if they rest on observations which involve only individual words, it is hardly possible to reach conclusions about direct literary relationships on such a foundation. This is so even if the words in question occur only or principally in prose of the book of Jeremiah, in the book of Deuteronomy and the Deuteronomistic historical literature. It is reasonable to regard this as a significant statistic, but to determine what kind or degree of significance is to be attached to it is a matter of the greatest difficulty. It may indicate affinities which are to be expessed in terms of a cultural or theological consensus—sympathies of a broad kind which are shared but are not necessarily limited to one organized religious party or movement. Certainly connections of this kind may represent a state of affairs which cannot be expressed as direct literary relationships between two bodies of literature.

Identical phrases or word-strings in different *corpora* constitute resemblances with a higher degree of particularity, on the basis of which questions about literary relationships can more reasonably be raised. Thiel's arguments for the Deuteronomic or Deuteronomistic affiliations of the prose in the book of Jeremiah are often occupied with entities of this kind, and the counter-arguments of Weippert seek to establish that the word-strings in the *corpora* which are being compared are significantly different in nuance or function, despite a general appearance of resemblance or even identity. It will be obvious that, when phrases or strings of words are being compared with a view to establishing a literary connection between different Old Testament books, the degree of distinctiveness possessed by these combinations, or the extent to which they have striking idiomatic qualities, enhances the probability that such a special significance should be attached to them. This is something more than simple terminological identity, because equations involving several items of vocabulary in a string do not necessarily, if the vocabulary is ordinary and the nature of the grammatical association pedestrian, enable us to conclude that there is a particular, literary relationship between the *corpora* in which they occur. We may find that we have not transcended the generality and relative insignificance of statistics which consist of the cataloguing of individual items of vocabulary common to different *corpora*. If the manner of combining these items is grammatically ordinary, we are not in a position to go beyond the kind of conclusions which have already been suggested: the combinations may indicate affinities of a cultural and theological kind, but they do not have the striking particularity which is necessary to create a probability that there is a direct literary relationship. As with comparisons of individual words, these word-strings might, at the point where their terminological particularity is minimized and they fade into insignificance, tell us no more than that the language in the two cases being compared is Biblical Hebrew.

The most interesting aspect of Weippert's treatment of parallels which are supposed to demonstrate the terminological dependence of the prose of the book of Jeremiah on Deuteronomy and the Deuteronomistic historical literature is the attention which she gives to the semantic functioning of the same vocabulary in different contexts, and the efforts which she makes on this foundation to establish significant distinctions of nuance which disengage terminology in the prose of the book of Jeremiah from identical terminology in Deuteronomy and the Deuteronomistic historical literature. This is indicative of an exegetical interest and it is in principle a legitimate way of refining statistics which consist of a mere listing of items of vocabulary common to different *corpora*. Exegetical enquiry directed to a context may elicit important lexicographical nuances for the same words in different bodies of literature. To put the matter simply, the same word may not be used in the same way or have precisely the same sense in one *corpus* which it has in another. It may be that Weippert tries too hard on occasions to drive a wedge between the prose of the book of Jeremiah and Deuteronomic or Deuteronomistic prose with the help of these considerations. The concern to separate the prose of the book of Jeremiah from Deuteronomic and Deuteronomistic connections becomes all-consuming and there is a danger of enforcing hair-splitting distinctions. Even where the lexicographical nuances are genuine, it is not necessarily true that an absolute semantic distinction between an item of vocabulary in the prose of the book of Jeremiah and the same item in Deuteronomy or the Deuteronomistic literature has been established, so that all postulated connections have to be severed.

There are thus positive and negative judgements which may be made about this sphere of Weippert's activity. On the negative side it can be said that the methods which she uses are not capable of supporting the conclusions which she wants to reach. Her objective is to show that the *Prosareden* of the book of Jeremiah are, for the most part, nothing less than the prose style of the prophet Jeremiah. It would need arguments of striking particularity and great finesse to achieve this, and it is unlikely that the available evidence, however superbly marshalled, could ever be made to support such a conclusion. The demonstration that hitherto unnoticed differences of nuance exist between lexical items common to different *corpora* is a valuable contribution. Between this and the unbelievably bold assertion that the distinctiveness of the prose-speeches of the book of Jeremiah is the distinctiveness of the prose style of an individual prophet, there is set a gulf as unbridgeable as that which separates the rich man from Lazarus.

The positive aspect of Weippert's approach consists in the possibility which it opens up of wooing us away from a too great pre-occupation with the Deuteronomic and Deuteronomistic affiliations of the prose of the book of Jeremiah. It was said earlier that Thiel and Weippert, given their respective methods, were inevitably at cross-purposes and the reason why this is so may now be clear. Weippert *prima facie* might seem to have the better case, since from her point of view Thiel has a way of arguing which amounts to heads I win and tails you lose. The absence of parallels to prose vocabulary of the book of Jeremiah in Deuteronomy and the Deuteronomistic literature does not deter him from identifying this prose as Deuteronomic or Deuteronomistic. A state of affairs which for her is evidence of a distinctive Jeremianic prose—prose disengaged from Deuteronomic or Deuteronomistic connections—is explained by him as the vocabulary of his Deuteronomistic editor of the book of Jeremiah. If the prose of the book of Jeremiah has external connections, he uses these in order to demonstrate that it is Deuteronomic or Deuteronomistic and is the work of a Deuteronomistic editor. If it does not have these external connections, he still maintains that it is derived from this editor, but the mode of argument is one which is internal to the prose of the book of Jeremiah and might be regarded as an argument in a circle. It depends on the discernment of affinities between different passages of prose, their constitution as a group and the conclusion that they all have the marks of the editor D. This is a case which is built up gradually by proceeding from one passage to the next and it has cumulative force only if one is persuaded of the validity of earlier conclusions all the way through. It leans heavily on the identification of the literary habits of the postulated D editor, on a claim to discern his attitude and objectives which sometimes seems exaggerated, and on the assumption that there is a comprehensive, systematic orientation under which all the passages can be subsumed. If one is unconvinced near the beginning and follows the argument from passage to passage, it takes on the appearance of a superstructure which has been raised on a foundation of sand.

The intention is not to take sides with either Thiel or Weippert, but to suggest that an attempt should be made to overcome the antitheses which arise from the confrontation of their respective methods. It does not seem reasonable to deny that there are affinities between Deuteronomic and Deuteronomistic prose and the prose of the book of Jeremiah, but a precise definition of these affinities will always be difficult to achieve. Even where the prose vocabulary of the book of Jeremiah is not represented in Deuteronomy and the Deuteronomistic literature, the significance of the state of affairs should not be magnified and absolute distinctions should not be imposed on such a foundation. It does not contribute meaningfully to a conclusion that the prose-speeches of the book of Jeremiah represent, for the most part, the prose style of the prophet Jeremiah. The same statement holds good for the vocabulary which is common to the *corpora* in question, but where differences of nuance are discernible from one *corpus* to another.

To Weippert it should be said that it is not surprising that these differences are noticeable, because the lexicographical constituents and the nuances of the prose of the book of Jeremiah are influenced by the *corpus* of which they are part. This does not constitute a demonstration that the prophet Jeremiah wrote the prose, but it is an indication that there is a Jeremianic nucleus which is distinctive, so that the prose which is generated by it, in connection with the processes of growth and aggregation which produce our extant *corpus*, is, in greater or lesser degree, influenced by this distinctiveness. Hence we might expect vocabulary identical with items in Deuteronomy or the Deuteronomistic literature to have different nuances, because it serves the interests of a *corpus* which has its own particular character and orientation. The concept of a *corpus* is, however, introduced with an awareness of the difficulties which cling to it and the false expectations which may be raised by it. There is not an intention to assert that the book of Jeremiah presents an aspect of form and comeliness or that its parts are fitly joined together to make a well-rounded, literary whole. It is introduced along with the caveat that there is a tendency to underestimate the untidy and desultory character of the aggregation of material which comprises the book of Jeremiah, and to invest it with architectonic properties which it does not possess. It is introduced along with what might seem to be a counter-assertion, that the processes which brought about the final product are only partially and imperfectly understood by us and that we make a mistake when we suppose that they are always susceptible of a rational explanation, or that they necessarily contribute in an orderly way to a thoughtful, systematic redaction.

The objection may be made that the notion of a *corpus* which is being invoked is ambiguous, vague and ill-defined, and the only defence which can be offered is that it, nevertheless, serves the end which is in view. We may find that there is no comprehensive framework of literary arrangement or theological system within which the parts of the book of Jeremiah are fitted together; that there is more of accident, arbitrariness and fortuitous twists and turns in the growth of the book than has been generally allowed; that the processes are dark and in a measure irrecoverable, and that we should not readily assume them to possess such rationality that they will yield to a systematic elucidation. The process of generation or triggering which enlarges the pre-existing material of the *corpus* is not necessarily related to a grand theological scheme and, perhaps, does not look beyond the verse or verses which set it in motion. Even so, and even if there is no systematic expression of the term *corpus* on offer, its use is justified in so far as growth is generated and its shape to a greater or lesser degree determined by the pre-existing material which triggers it.

This adds up to something much less than the systematic Deuteronomistic redaction which Thiel discerns in Jer. i–xxv, but it is a different aspect of Thiel's work which claims our attention, since it has a particular relevance to the overcoming of the opposition discerned in the rival methods of Thiel and Weippert. The time has come—and this is a departure which Weippert has made—to concentrate more on the internal relations of the material in the *corpus* constituted by the book of Jeremiah and to be less bothered about comparisons between the prose of the book of Jeremiah and the prose of other *corpora*. It is important, however, that this statement should not be misunderstood. It should not be taken as a denial that there are significant resemblances between the prose of the book of Jeremiah and the prose of Deuteronomy and the Deuteronomistic literature. It does not arise out of an apologetic concern to demonstrate that the prose of the book of Jeremiah is clearly distinct from the prose of other *corpora*. It simply gives expression to a feeling that arguments about which labels are to be attached to the prose of the book of Jeremiah, while they possess historical and critical importance, may have the effect of distracting us from matters which are more intrinsic to the study of the book, namely, the internal relations of its constituent parts. A correct appreciation of the way in which the prose functions within the Jeremianic *corpus* and how it serves the ends of the *corpus* is more important than the attachment of particular labels to it. As matters stand, with continuous cross-references to Deuteronomy and the Deuteronomistic literature the fashion of scholarship, one is always in danger of succumbing to a condition of distraction and disorientation.

The general part of this article is almost complete and the second part will deal with particular cases of the relation between poetry and prose in the book of Jeremiah. There is still, however, a transition to be made and some justification of the relevance of the long, general section to the particular task in hand has to be attempted. It will have been noticed that the argument in its final form was not strictly lexicographical or linguistic. Although it was urged that the lexicographical evidence available to Weippert was incapable of supporting the conclusion that the prophet Jeremiah was the author of the prose-speeches of the book of Jeremiah, it would be disingenuous to represent that this was the only consideration which made her conclusion unpalatable. It is likely that she too had an extra-linguistic concern which commended to her the construction which she put on the lexicographical material which she handled, a concern to attribute the prose-speeches of the book of Jeremiah to the prophet Jeremiah. At any rate the extra-linguistic perception which puts her conclusions out of court is that they imply a view of the inner relations of the constituent parts of the book of Jeremiah and of the processes of growth and composition which is altogether incredible. We are dealing with a long, complicated, untidy accumulation of material extending over a very long period, to which many people have contributed. The supposition that a major part of it, including much of the prose, was already in existence in the lifetime of the prophet Jeremiah is a literary judgement which seems to take no account of the problems which arise when one considers in detail the baffling inconcinnities of the constituents of the book. In this regard the account which Thiel gives of the growth of the Jeremianic *corpus*, with the prominence attached to a Deuteronomistic redaction and the allowance for large post-Deuteronomistic accretions (for example, the oracles against foreign nations), shows a more realistic grasp of the long period of time over which the book was in the process of formation. The question-mark which has been raised against Thiel's account is whether there is a redaction of the far-reaching and systematic kind which he claims to discover in chapters i-xxv. The concern of the foregoing discussion has been to focus attention on the concept of a Jeremianic *corpus* and to ask what kind of internal relationships we should envisage between its constituent parts. One of the most interesting aspects of this is the relations which obtain between the poetry and prose of the book, and the examination of this which follows will, perhaps, compensate for the necessarily general character of the preceding part of the article and illustrate in a less rarified manner some of the views which have been expressed.

II

It has been argued that the prose of the book of Jeremiah should not, for the most part, be attributed to the prophet Jeremiah, because this is not compatible with long drawn-out processes which we must assume to have attended the formation of the *corpus*. In connection with the relations between poetry and prose different exegetical considerations will be introduced, designed to show that there are cases where the prose is triggered by the poetry and is derivative. First of all, however, it should be observed that when W. L. Holladay[3] speaks of poetic prototypes and prose copies he is making this kind of assumption, and it is in accord with the attitude which has generally prevailed in critical operations directed at prose passages in the book of Jeremiah. These have usually had a particular character and a specific exegetical aim, whereas Holladay's work has the form of a more comprehensive, lexicographical enquiry. In the tradition of critical scholarship the aim has sometimes been to discover a metrical nucleus or core in a prose passage and to show how this has been enlarged and overlaid by subsequent prose elaboration. This is a way of dealing with prose compositions which is still influential in the work of Thiel. He is aware of the considerations raised by Holladay, and in considering the sources of the vocabulary of his editor D he looks not only to Deu-

---

[3]"Prototypes and Copies: A New Approach to the Poetry-Prose Problem in the Book of Jeremiah," *JBL* 79 (1960), pp. 351–67.

teronomic and Deuteronomistic sources, but also to the poetry of the book of Jeremiah. He has, however, a closer accord with earlier critical procedures in that he is always alive to the possibility that a prose composition attributed to D may have been formed around a fragment of poetry, and his tendency is to assign such a fragment to the prophet Jeremiah. There are thus two ways in which a relation between prose and poetry is envisaged by Thiel: in the first case the prose composition is wholly created by D, but he has quarried single words or phrases from the poetry of the book of Jeremiah; in the second case he has formed a composition around a verse or verses of poetry whose metrical structure is identified or restored.

The kind of relation between poetry and prose in the book of Jeremiah of which two examples are now to be given is different from those which have just been described. It does not involve extracting a metrical nucleus from a prose composition; it deals not with a hypothetical core which has been encapsulated in prose, but with a relation of adjacency or contiguity between poetry and prose. The argument is that the prose has been generated by the poetry and has the character of exegesis or comment. The implication is that the enlargement of the Jeremianic *corpus* in these cases has taken place through prose additions which are exegetical, which are limited and particular rather than systematic and general, because they are a specific response to small pieces of text.

The first passage is iii 1–13 and a question is asked about the relation of *vv.* 6–11 (prose) to *vv.* 1–5 and 12–13 (poetry). The reasons why *vv.* 6–11 rather than *vv.* 6–13 are regarded as a unit will appear presently; the latter is normally regarded as the correct delimitation. That *v.* 1 is seminal in relation to *vv.* 6–11 is indisputable, since the model of divorce, interpreted as the exile of the northern kingdom, supplies the author of *vv.* 6–11 with his theme. The treatment of the theme is certainly influenced by the supposition that *vv.* 12–13 are also addressed to the inhabitants of the former northern kingdom, but *vv.* 6–11 are not more intrinsically related to *vv.* 12–13 than they are to *vv.* 1–5, although they have been editorially connected to *vv.* 12–13 with greater deliberation. It is unlikely that the interpretation of *vv.* 1–5 which is assumed by *vv.* 6–11 is the right one, since there is no reason to suppose that *vv.* 1–5 relate so particularly to the former northern kingdom. If *vv.* 1–5 are from the prophet Jeremiah, it would be more natural to conclude that they were spoken to Judah. Nor should it be assumed that the interpretation which has been put on the poetry in *vv.* 12–13 by the connecting piece in *v.* 12 ("Go and proclaim these words to the north, saying"), which associates these verses with *vv.* 6–11, is necessarily a correct indication. The expression *mešûbāh yiśrā'ēl* is common to *v.* 12 and *vv.* 6–11, but it does not follow from this that there is an original literary continuity between *vv.* 6–11 and *vv.* 12–13. Another possible explanation is that *mešûbāh yiśrā'ēl* was appropriated by the author of *vv.* 6–11 from *v.* 12 in the same way as he took the idea of "divorce" from *v.* 1 and developed it.

The logic of what has just been said is that if *vv.* 1-13 are all attributable to the prophet Jeremiah (Graf,[4] Giesebrecht, Cornill, Volz, Rudolph, Weiser), there are no better reasons for making a unit out of *vv.* 6-13 than there are for making a unit out of *vv.* 1-13, because the connection between *vv.* 6-11 and *vv.* 12-13 is no more intrinsic than the connection between *vv.* 1-5 and *vv.* 6-11. Hence, given his assumptions, H. W. Hertzberg[5] is entirely logical in making a unit out of *vv.* 1-13 by embracing *vv.* 1-5 and supposing that these verses too were addressed by Jeremiah to the inhabitants of the former northern kingdom. It might be objected that *v.* 5 connects impressively with *v.* 19, and this has often been said, but it will not stand up to close scrutiny. If, however, we go along with the view that *vv.* 6-13 constitute a unit, we have to suppose that the historical notice in *v.* 6 is to be taken seriously and that we have an indication of Jeremiah's concern for those who were inhabitants of the former northern kingdom, whether expressed before or after Josiah's reform in 621, and perhaps related to the political interest which the king had in this territory. It is then a matter of dispute whether in *vv.* 12-13 we have an address to exiles, as most suppose, or whether *šûbāh* excludes the nuance of "Return" and is to be understood as a call to repentance issued to those who were not deported to Assyria and were still resident in Palestine.[6]

Another view disengages *vv.* 6-11 from the prophet Jeremiah, while maintaining that *vv.* 6-13 constitute a significant unit. In the case of Holladay[7] and Thiel (pp. 85-91) this goes with the assertion that *vv.* 6-13 are the composition of a Deuteronomistic editor. J. P. Hyatt, who also holds that *vv.* 6-13 are a Deuteronomistic composition, takes a different view of *vv.* 12-13, since he doubts whether these verses had an original reference to the inhabitants of the former northern kingdom. Rudolph notes that Hyatt himself has conceded that *vv.* 6-11 have "little D diction", and Thiel, for his part, acknowledges that there is little Deuteronomistic vocabulary in *vv.* 6-12aα. There is an important respect in which Thiel's view of *vv.* 6-11 is the right one. Whoever composed these verses borrowed his ideas and quarried his vocabulary from surrounding passages. Thiel has overdone his demonstration that *vv.* 6-11 are a *pastiche*, but his understanding of their secondary character is essentially correct. Once it has been established that the ideas of divorce and harlotry are derived from *vv.* 1-5 and that the working out of these in a comparison of degrees of guilt attaching to Israel and Judah is suggested by the assumption that *vv.* 12-13 are an offer of reconciliation to Israel, the case has been sufficiently made.

---

[4]Commentaries to which reference is made are listed below.

[5]"Jeremia und das Nordreich Israel," *ThLZ* 77 (1952), pp. 598 f.

[6]A. C. Welch, "Jeremiah and Religious Reform," *The Expositor* (1921), p. 467.

[7]*The Root Šûbh in the Old Testament with particular Reference to its Usages in Covenantal Contexts* (Leiden, 1958), pp. 132-4.

Thiel is right to suppose that $m^e\check{s}\hat{u}b\bar{a}h$ $yi\acute{s}r\bar{a}^{\,\jmath}\bar{e}l$ has been derived from *v.* 12, that the "divorce" idea has been developed in *v.* 8 in dependence on Deut. xxiv 3 and that the epithet $b\bar{a}g\hat{o}d\bar{a}h$ or $b\hat{o}g\bar{e}d\bar{a}h$ (*vv.* 7, 8, 10) has been suggested by iii 20.

Verses 6–11 come into existence as a kind of exegesis of preexisting texts; we are dealing with an exegetical activity and the primary answer to the question how a passage like this arises must be a literary one. The content of *vv.* 6–11 is determined by a particular interpretation which has been put on *vv.* 1–5 and *vv.* 12–13. Whether one can go any further than this and establish the particular historical circumstances and theological concerns which promoted such exegesis is doubtful. Giesebrecht believed that the organization of the argument about Israel and Judah in *vv.* 6–11 implied that the exile of Judah still lay in the future, and Cornill, comparing *vv.* 6–11 with Ezek. xvi 51 f., maintained that the dependence was on the side of Ezekiel. Both these scholars were certainly influenced by their conviction that *vv.* 6–11 were to be assigned to the prophet Jeremiah. Without this premise and the historical anchorage which it affords, one cannot tell from an examination of *vv.* 6–11 whether the exile of Judah is envisaged as in the past or in the future, nor can one pronounce on priority and dependence as between the Jeremiah and Ezekiel passages. The argument that the polemical situation which had developed between Jews and Samaritans rules out the post-exilic period (Thiel, p. 90) depends for its effectiveness on the assumption that the type of exegetical activity represented by *vv.* 6–11 has to be related significantly to a historical moment and a theological climate.

It would be dogmatic to assert that the interest which is reflected here is purely exegetical and that *vv.* 6–11, being no more than an attempt to deal with problems which were thought to inhere in existing texts (What did the "divorce" of Israel signify? Why did Jeremiah address an offer of reconciliation to Israel?), do not require an explanation in terms of appropriate historical circumstances. This having been said, it should be appreciated that it may not be so easy as has been supposed to demonstrate the appropriateness of the exilic period and the inappropriateness of the post-exilic period. The derivative character of *vv.* 6–11, and the circumstance that their interpretation of the texts out of which they arise (*vv.* 1–5, 12–13) is almost certainly wrong, establishes that they are not the work of the prophet Jeremiah and that they are at least as late as the exilic period. It is probable that the "divorce" model and the description of harlotry attached to it (*vv.* 1–5) has been wrongly referred to the apostasy of the northern kingdom and the subsequent exile. It is certain that $m^e\check{s}\hat{u}b\bar{a}h$ $yi\acute{s}r\bar{a}^{\,\jmath}\bar{e}l$ (*v.* 12) has been wrongly identified with the northern kingdom and that *vv.* 12–13, misinterpreted as a gracious offer of reconciliation to those who once constituted that kingdom, has awakened reflections on the comparative culpability of Israel and Judah. A purely exegetical account of *vv.* 6–11 may be inadequate, because the correspondence between these verses and Ezek. xvi 51 f. is close and impressive. Samaria was not half the sinner that Judah was; the sins of Judah are so much greater that her sister, Samaria, by comparison appears almost innocent. It appears that these ideas were abroad among Jews in Babylon consequent on the fall of Jerusalem (according to W. Zimmerli, Ezek. xvi 51 f. is exilic), and it is a reasonable conclusion that behind the particular, exegetical operations of the author of vv. 6–11 there is this more general current of speculation and questioning.

The understanding of vv. 6–11 which is being recommended is that they represent secondary, exegetical development which arises from vv. 1–5 (especially v. 1) and vv. 12–13. A commentary in prose is generated by these two passages and is inserted between them. It is supposed wrongly by the exegete that vv. 1–5 refer to northern Israel and "divorce" is interpreted by him as the exile of the northern kingdom. The invitation to return and repent in vv. 12–13 is also thought to have been addressed to the inhabitants of the former northern kingdom in exile, and the exegete develops the idea that the lesser guilt of Israel over against Judah justifies this offer of forgiveness and reconciliation. His primary interest is in understanding texts which are available for interpretation. It is a difficult task to recover the historical circumstances and theological tendencies which might have promoted such exegesis, but the similar ideas which appear in Ezek. xvi 51 f. suggest that there was a more general climate of theological pondering which spurred the particular, exegetical activity.

The other example to be investigated is xii 14–17, and some attention must be paid to ⁾ettôš mittôkām, although no attempt will be made to deal with all the complexities of this piece of text. A broad distinction can be made between those who take ⁾ettôš mittôkām as a reference to the deliverance of Judah (Kimchi, Calvin, Lowth, Duhm, Ehrlich[8]) and those who suppose that it is an allusion to exile (Hitzig and most of the recent commentators). Kimchi comments, "Those (of my people) who went into exile in their midst I will root out from them, when I restore the fortunes of my people." It is not entirely clear what Kimchi means by this. It could be urged that he envisages Jews exiled in neighbouring lands who are to be repatriated to Judah—this is the exegesis of the passage favoured by Duhm and Volz. It is more probable that Kimchi refers to Jews in exile in Babylonia who are mixed up with Edomites, Moabites and so on. What he is then saying is that after the exile Jews will be effectively separated from their neighbours, and so he has the post-exilic Jerusalem community in mind. In connection with v. 15 he cites passages in the oracles on foreign nations which refer to the restoration of Moab (xlviii 47) and Ammon (xlix 6). When Judah and Benjamin return from exile, their former neighbours will also be restored. The conditions, however, are those set out in v. 16 on which Kimchi comments, "For after the Israelites returned from exile they

---

[8]A. B. Ehrlich, *Randglossen zur hebräischen Bibel* 4 (Leipzig, 1912), pp. 276 f.

did not worship idols nor swear by Baal." If the neighbouring nations learn Israel's ways in this regard, it will amount to the abolition of idolatry. On $w^e nibnû b^e tôk \ ^c ammî$ (v. 16) he remarks, "For many of them will become *gērîm* when they return from exile and will reside among the Israelites." On v. 17 he refers to an exegesis of xlix 6 according to which the promise of restoration is confined to Ammonites who "learn the ways of Israel".

It is interesting and significant that Kimchi interprets *vv.* 14–17 in a post-exilic context. There are, of course, no critical implications in this: he regards these verses as a prophecy about the shape of the future by the prophet Jeremiah and not as an *ex eventu* prophecy composed in the post-exilic period. Apart from this, his perception of the historical setting in which sense can be made of the passage is one to which we should attend carefully, and, in particular, his explanation of the enigmatic $w^{e\rangle} et$-*bêt* $y^e hûdāh \ ^\rangle ettôš \ mittôkām$ could be the right one. The obvious criticism to be applied to the latter is that *ntš* is used in *vv.* 14 and 15 of "uprooting" (exiling) Judah's neighbours and that a different sense of *ntš* ("separating") is difficult to maintain in $w^{e\rangle} et$-*bêt* $y^e hûdāh \ ^\rangle ettôš \ mittôkām$. This is a cogent but perhaps not a fatal objection, because it is possible that *ntš* may have been used to play on the preceding occurrences and to convey the stringency of Jewish separation from neighbouring nations—the "uprooting" of all associations.

According to Thiel (pp. 162–8) *vv.* 14–17 are an *ex eventu* prophecy composed by D. He has latched on to *nah^{a}lāh* in *vv.* 7, 8, 9, but he has also undertaken to refer to events which he regards as the sequel of those described in *vv.* 7–13. The "evil neighbours" whose exile is predicted in v. 14 are the $rô^c îm \ rabbîm$ of v. 10 and the $šôd^e dîm$ of v. 12. D's prophecy is founded on the events of 582 B.C. (cp. Nicholson) when, according to Josephus (Ant. x 181 f.) Nebuchadrezzer marched against Coele-Syria, occupied it, subdued Moab and Ammon, and carried off Jewish captives to Babylon. The last part of this can be correlated with Jer. lii 30, according to which seven hundred and forty-five Judaeans were deported by Nebuzaradan in Nebuchadrezzar's twenty third year (582—this agrees with the date given by Josephus). The assumption that an exilic editor knew about events involving Moab and Ammon in 582 is a vote of confidence in Josephus, and Thiel brushes aside the questions which R. Marcus[9] asks about the sources available to Josephus. He may have used Jer. lii 28–30 for the latter part of his notice, although he does not mention Nebuzaradan. What sources did he have for his references to Moab and Ammon? Marcus says that these are loosely founded on the notices in the foreign oracles about the uprooting of these nations. Since Josephus was writing centuries after 582, we need to know more about his sources before we can found on his statements a conclusion that an exilic editor was alluding to a punitive Babylonian expedition against Moab and Ammon in 582 B.C.

[9]*Josephus VI, Loeb Classical Library* (London-Cambridge, Mass. 1937), pp. 258 f.

A historical anchorage of this kind should not be sought for vv. 14–17: vv. 14–15 are a late, artificial prophetic composition to which qualifications have been subsequently added in vv. 16–17. It is a composition in the sense that it is composed from pre-existing passages of scripture, especially the definition of Jeremiah's prophetic office in the call narrative (i 10—a prophet to the nations who is to uproot and to build), and the notices about the restoration of Judah's neighbours in the foreign oracles of the book of Jeremiah. This awareness of the connection of vv. 14–15 with other Old Testament passages is already present in Kimchi and can be seen also in Lowth. Kimchi notes that the restoration of Moab is prophesied in xlviii 47 and that of Ammon in xlix 6. The expression used in both passages is wᵉšabtî šᵉbût, "And I will reverse the exile of" or "And I will restore the fortunes of." This is recorded as a decision of Yahweh without reference to the repentance or conversion of those who are restored, and in that respect it is comparable with ʾāšûb wᵉriḥamtîm wahášîbôtîm in v. 15. Cornill, who postulates a saying of the prophet Jeremiah consisting of vv. 14–16*, cites xvi 19 f. as another passage where repentance is attributed to gôyim. But vv. 14–15 have nothing to say about repentance which is introduced only in the secondary qualification of v. 15 in vv. 16–17. Lowth too was aware that the oracles on foreign nations prophesied Yahweh's judgement against them. He cited Jer. xlix 1 ff. (Ammon); Ezek. xxv 3, 6 (Ammon), 8 (Moab), 12 (Edom); Zeph. ii 8 (Moab and Ammon). The last mentioned has a special affinity with Jer. xii 14, because it has a reference to encroachment on Judah's territory (wayyagdîlû ʿal-gᵉbûlām).

Verses 14–15 are generated by the poetry in vv. 7–13 and naḥálāh (vv. 7, 8, 9, 14, 15) serves as a stitch. The invaders who execute Yahweh's judgement on Judah are identified as neighbouring nations and a prophecy is composed on the foundation of the notices about the uprooting and resettlement of these neighbours in the oracles on foreign nations (xlviii 47, xlix 6). The vocabulary is influenced by the account which is given of Jeremiah as a prophet to the nations in i 10. Verses 16–17 are a subsequent qualifying of the promise of restoration, and it is interesting that we know from Kimchi that there was a discussion about the right exegesis of xlix 6: that, according to one interpretation, it was not to be understood as an unconditional promise but as one made to those who would "learn the ways of Israel." We may conclude that vv. 16–17 arise out of this kind of interest and concern: v. 15 is one exegesis of wᵉšabtî šᵉbût ʿammôn (môʾāb) and vv. 16–17 is another. As Kimchi observed, "learning the ways of my people" (v. 16) presupposes a community of Jews purified of idolatry and every other form of disloyalty to Yahweh. wᵉʾet-bêt yᵉhûdāh ʾettôš mittôkām, on the interpretation which has been adopted, is indicative of the effective separation of the Jews from surrounding Gentiles. Such a state of affairs could perhaps be said to exist in a Jewish community in Babylon, enforcing its separation and apartness from its Gentile environment by a stringent interpretation of Yahwism, but the geographical area which is envisaged in *vv.* 14–15 is Judah and its surroundings. Hence we should think in terms of the post-exilic Jerusalem community: *vv.* 14–15 are post-exilic and *vv.* 16–17 are post-exilic *a fortiori*. This is a judgement which differs from Kimchi only in so far as it assumes that *vv.* 14–17 are *ex eventu* prophecy and a post-exilic composition. Otherwise it supposes like Kimchi that *vv.* 14–17 are to be referred to a post-exilic setting. The neighbours who gloated over Judah's misfortunes and took advantage of her weakness when she suffered dismemberment and exile (cp. Obad. 10 ff.; Zeph. ii 8) themselves suffered in turn, as the prophet Jeremiah was believed to have predicted. The post-exilic Jerusalem community, separated from the corrupting influences of her neighbours, has nothing to fear, even when these are restored to their former territories, as scripture predicted that they would be. But, according to *vv.* 16–17, their restoration is to be entertained only so far as they swear allegiance to Yahweh and are integrated in his community.

Wherever the kind of activity uncovered in iii 6–11 and xii 14–17 is present in the book of Jeremiah, the hypothesis that there is a poetic nucleus is justified. Moreover, this is a type of enlargement and elaboration which operates within narrow contextual limits and does not have the comprehensive, systematic theological objectives which it is customary to ascribe to prose redactions of the book of Jeremiah. The general contention of the article is that we should take more account of expansions of such limited scope in our efforts to understand the complicated and untidy processes by which the Jeremianic *corpus* was developed. A type of expansion through commentary or exegesis which attaches itself to pre-existing elements of the *corpus* has been neglected or, at least, underestimated. In so far as the growth of the *corpus* was achieved by processes of this kind we should not expect too much in the way of coherence or artistic unity from the end product. Those who claim a systematic theological activity for a Deuteronomistic editor and identify compositions in which this is realized are perhaps professing to know more of the inner workings of his mind than can be gathered from the text. They are in danger of creating systematic theological aims for the editor whom they postulate rather than extracting these from the text. In general they exaggerate the coherence of the book and underestimate its lack of cohesiveness and obscurities.

Commentaries

J. Calvin, *Praelectiones in Librum Prophetiarum Jeremia et Lamentationes* (Geneva, 1589[3]).

C. H. Cornill, *Das Buch Jeremia* (Leipzig, 1905).

B. Duhm, *Das Buch Jeremia* (Tübingen and Leipzig, 1901).

F. Giesebrecht, *Das Buch Jeremia* (Göttingen, 1894, 1907[2]).

K. H. Graf, *Der Prophet Jeremia* (Leipzig, 1862).

F. Hitzig, *Der Prophet Jeremia* (Leipzig, 1866²).

J. P. Hyatt, "The Book of Jeremiah", *IB* 5 (New York and Nashville, 1956).

W. Lowth, *A Commentary upon the Prophecy and Lamentations of Jeremiah* (London, 1728).

W. Rudolph, *Jeremia* (Tübingen, 1968³).

P. Volz, *Der Prophet Jeremia* (Leipzig, 1928²).

A. Weiser, *Das Buch Jeremia* (Göttingen, 1969⁶).

W. Zimmerli, *Ezechiel* i (Neukirchen, 1969).

Kimchi is cited from *Miqrāʾôt Gᵉdôlôt*.

16

The Quest of the
Historical Jeremiah:
Hermeneutical Implications
of Recent Literature*
David Jobling

A survey of recent literature on the Book of Jeremiah shows striking resemblances, both in method and in results, to modern research on the Gospels and the "Life of Jesus." These resemblances have important hermeneutical implications for further work in the two Testaments, and we shall draw conclusions and make suggestions at this level. Our survey of recent books and articles will be directed to this specific end; we shall attempt neither to cover all of the important Jeremiah studies of the last few years, nor to deal with all facets of those we do mention. Our concern is with specific hermeneutical implications, which in some cases are discussed by the authors themselves, but more often not.

RECENT JEREMIAH RESEARCH

There are few Old Testament figures who have sat for as many portraits as Jeremiah. Liberal biblical scholars brought to Jeremiah, as to no other prophet, what we may call a "psycho-biographical" approach.[1] They gave a chronological account of his life and laid bare his innermost thoughts. This approach, of which, in English, John Skinner's work is perhaps the highpoint,[2] seemed to liberalism promising not merely because of the liberals' own assumptions, but also because of the apparent unusual interest in the person of Jeremiah in the book itself. The "biographical" part of the book is uniquely long, and the prophetic "I" is uniquely prominent, above all in the so-called "confessions," which for liberals were the very nerve-center of the book. An important subsidiary factor was the presence of a considerable number of dates, which encouraged the hope

---

*Originally published in the *Union Seminary Quarterly Review* 34 (1978) 3–12.

[1]For a list of such monographs and literary works about Jeremiah, cf. E. Gerstenberger, "Jeremiah's Complaints: Observations on Jer 15:10–21," *JBL* 82 (1963) 393.

[2]John Skinner, *Prophecy and Religion: Studies in the Life of Jeremiah* (Cambridge: The University Press, 1922).

that all the material might be brought into a firm chronological sequence: that a particular lament, for instance, might be firmly identified as the prophet's response to a particular experience or event.[3]

The extreme psycho-biographical approach is no longer an option—it has gone the way of the liberal lives of Jesus. Some recent authors, for instance, Bright, Holladay, Berridge, and Weippert, are still very much concerned to let Jeremiah shine forth as a unique individual,[4] but they are far removed from Skinner. And much of the recent Jeremiah research has been in conscious and extreme reaction to the traditional approach. There are two forms of attack, and they move in opposite directions.

a. "Thoroughgoing liturgiology"

The first continues to center its attention on the historical Jeremiah, but challenges the entire liberal understanding as anachronistic, romantic and individualistic. The *summa* of this point of view is Reventlow's *Liturgie und prophetisches Ich bei Jeremia*.[5] Reventlow's Jeremiah is a cultic functionary, and, as the title suggests, the use of the first person singular in the book directs us not to the prophet's "personality", but to cultic situations in the Temple, such as we know primarily from the Book of Psalms, in which the "I" was formally required. "Personal testimonies ... are not to be found in the Book of Jeremiah, at least not in the area ... where one usually seeks them. Not even in the confessions, which rank as the outstanding source for such statements."[6] In the confessions, the prophet expresses not his own, but the people's prayers: "The 'I' that appears there has passed over completely into the 'we,' it is nothing other than representation and embodiment of the community."[7] In addition to the confessions, Reventlow deliberately turns his attention to the other solid pillars of the psycho-biographical view; the call vision becomes an ordination ceremony, with another clergyman playing the part of Yahweh; the anguished cry of the sensitive soul over the fate of his people, which the liberals found in the communal laments, becomes the "prayer in time of

---

[3]For which the text provides some basis; cf. Jer 11:18–12:6.

[4]John Bright, "The Date of the Prose Sermons in Jeremiah," *JBL* 70 (1951) 15–35; "The Prophetic Reminiscence; its Place and Function in the Book of Jeremiah," *Die Ou-Testamentiese Werkgemeenskap in Suid-Afrika, Papers* 9 (1966) 11–30; W. L. Holladay, "Prototypes and Copies: A New Approach to the Poetry-Prose Problem in the Book of Jeremiah," *JBL* 79 (1960) 351–367; "The Recovery of Poetic Passages of Jeremiah," *JBL* 85 (1966) 401–435; J. M. Berridge, *Prophet, People, and the Word of Yahweh: An Examination of Form and Content in the Proclamations of the Prophet Jeremiah* (Zurich, EVZ-Verlag, 1970); Helga Weippert, *Die Prosareden des Jeremiabuches, BZAW* 132 (Berlin, Walter de Gruyter & Co., 1973).

[5]Henning Graf Reventlow, *Liturgie und prophetisches Ich bei Jeremia* (Gütersloh, Gerd Mohn, 1963).

[6]Ibid., 259.

[7]Ibid.

drought" which the prophet's job requires him to recite.[8] In a word, we know as much of the personality of Jeremiah from his oracles as we could find out about a Roman Catholic priest from a transcript of his saying mass![9]

b. *The Jeremiah tradition and its redaction*

More widespread, and taking a variety of forms, is the second reaction, that we must see the Book of Jeremiah first of all as a product of the post-Jeremianic believing community, and only from this perspective go on to ask what it may tell us about the prophet himself. The title of Nicholson's book *Preaching to the Exiles*[10] expresses the author's belief that the whole prose tradition of Jeremiah is the deposit of preaching activity, in Babylon, and after the prophet's death. Any religious initiative which hoped for a hearing from the exiles had to address the anguished questions, "Why did it happen? Why did the promises of God prove false?" Nicholson holds that there was a group of deuteronomistic theologians who preached to these questions out of a long tradition, one which not long before the Exile had produced the Book of Deuteronomy and Josiah's reform. When reform failed and exile came, the school continued its work, the main products being the "Deuteronomic History" and the Book of Jeremiah. The aim of all this work was to show, within the terms of the Sinai covenant, that all of Israel's good fortune was the result of obedience, all her misfortune the result of faithlessness, and that punishment even to the extent of the exile had been clearly threatened by Yahweh when the covenant was made. The answer to "Why did it happen?" was "Because of the sins of the ancestors."

The preaching ascribed to Jeremiah exhibits a paradox; doom is certain, but repentance is possible. In Jeremiah's own situation the contradiction would be irresoluble; but in Nicholson's view the true audience is the exilic one, and for them the two sides of the paradox are equally necessary.[11] Before the Exile, the punishment was sealed. But the possibility of repentance *now*, after the blow has fallen, is the only basis of hope. Thus Jeremiah is *allowed* to say what he said to his own time, and is simultaneously *made* to say a new word for a new time. We possess the Book of Jeremiah only because the exiles found in the Jeremiah traditions meaning

---

[8]Ibid., 24–77 and 149–187, respectively.

[9]For important critiques of Reventlow in English, cf. Berridge, *Prophet, People, and the Word of Yahweh*, and John Bright, "Jeremiah's Complaints—Liturgy or Expressions of Personal Distress?" in *Proclamation and Presence, Old Testament Essays in Honour of Gwynne Henton Davies*, edited by J. I. Durham and J. R. Porter (London, SCM Press, 1970) 189–214.

[10]E. W. Nicholson, *Preaching to the Exiles: A Study of the Prose Tradition in the Book of Jeremiah* (New York, Schocken Books, 1971).

[11]Ibid., especially 71–93.

out of meaninglessness. But in the prose of the book, what the prophet says is what the deuteronomic preachers perceived him to say to *their* situation; and the presentation of the person Jeremiah is dictated by the need of the exiles for a paradigm.

With certain important differences, W. Thiel follows a similar line.[12] He sees the present book as the product of deuteronomistic activity, although he follows Noth in locating this activity in Judah, after the deportation. He finds in Jer. 1–25 a very careful deuteronomic redaction of the Jeremiah tradition, and moves beyond Nicholson in the great detail in which he attempts to demonstrate not only the editors' composition of the prose, but also their organization of the poetry. They have, in Thiel's view, expressed their theological point of view not only in their own words, but also, more subtly, by the arrangement of Jeremiah's authentic oracles; the whole first half of the book has been organized in sections, in which poetry and prose illuminate each other.

Nicholson and Thiel both still assume the Jeremianic authorship of the great bulk of the poetic oracles. But the poetry has not remained exempt from a similar treatment; Gerstenberger and Gunneweg, whom we shall consider in a different connection, have held the confessions to be redactional compositions.[13] The view that much of the Book of Jeremiah is secondary to the prophet is, of course, far from new. Already at the turn of the century, Duhm freely employed his scalpel, and found only a small amount of authentic Jeremiah material.[14] The greatest change has been in the value attached to the secondary parts. The liberal critics saw their task as rescuing the kernel of the authentic from the shell of the secondary. Duhm, for instance, was extremely disparaging of the religious value of the secondary parts of Jeremiah,[15] and the full implications of the fact that, but for the traditioners, we would have no Jeremiah, seem not to have occurred to him. Recent work on the Jeremiah tradition and its redaction, on the other hand, has rated the secondary extremely highly, both in itself, and as casting light for us on the theology of the exilic period. Gunneweg strikingly exemplifies the change in attitude:

> It becomes clear that this prophet too, about whose personal life scholarship considered itself so well informed, remains hidden much further behind his proclamation and its interpretation by the traditioners than one previously supposed. But this is only superficially a loss. The Prophecy of Jeremiah, and also its secondary interpretation, contain less piety to be psychologically

[12]Winfried Thiel, *Die deuteronomistische Redaktion von Jeremia 1–25, WMANT 41* (Neukirchen-Vluyn, Neukirchener Verlag, 1973).

[13]Gerstenberger, "Jeremiah's Complaints," A. H. J. Gunneweg, "Konfession oder Interpretation im Jeremiabuch," *ZTK* 57 (1970) 395–416.

[14]Bernhard Duhm, *Das Buch Jeremia erklärt, Kurzer Hand-Commentar zum Alten Testament*, XI (Tübingen und Leipzig, J. C. B. Mohr, 1901).

[15]Ibid., XVII–XX. On Duhm's point of view and its influence, cf. Thiel, *Redaktion*, 7–8.

illuminated, but in its place the more kerygma to be theologically comprehended.[16]

An article by W. Schottroff carries the discussion even further.[17] It is
an exegesis of Jer. 2:1–3, but the subtitle, "Remarks on Method in
Exegeting the Prophets," implies aims far beyond one brief pericope. These
three verses, Schottroff argues, though usually held to be central to
Jeremiah's *earliest* theology, can in fact be explained only as an addition to
the rest of the chapter, at a late stage of the redaction. That is as it may be;
what concerns us is that he uses this conclusion to argue for a complete
reversal of accepted method. Prophetic research has assumed

> that each unit, of which it cannot be proved that there is no possibility of its
> coming from the prophet to whom it is ascribed, is to be claimed as probably
> authentic to that prophet. Redaction-critical suggestions normally form the
> last stage of the exegetical procedure.[18]

On the contrary, he claims, "Appropriate exegesis of the prophets must
proceed first of all redaction-critically. . . . Only when the redactional contribution to a given text-complex has been clarified may we ask about the
individual traditions which have been worked into it, and their origin."[19]
The exegete should initially assume the probability that a given pericope is
secondary and "assume as authentic only that material which can be
understood simply and solely out of the concrete conditions of a given
prophet's time."[20] It is one thing to doubt the authenticity of the Jeremianic
prose, even of this or that poetic oracle. It is quite another to assume that
we know nothing of the historical Jeremiah until there appears compelling
proof that we do have such knowledge!

Has the redaction given us a consistent picture of Jeremiah? For some
researchers it has not. G. Wanke, in a study of the "biographical" parts of
the book (the third-person narrative), makes a sharp differentiation between
two kinds of material, which he believes to have had quite different

---

[16]Konfession oder Interpretation," 416. For positive evaluation, in English, of the theological work of the redactors, see primarily Nicholson, *Preaching to the Exiles*, and P. R.
Ackroyd, e.g. "Aspects of the Jeremiah Tradition," *Indian Journal of Theology* 20 (1971)
1–12.

[17]W. Schottroff, "Jeremia 2, 1–3: Erwägungen zur Methode der Prophetenexegese," *ZTK*
67 (1970) 263–294.

[18]Ibid., 293.

[19]Ibid.

[20]Ibid., 294.

[21]G. Wanke, *Untersuchungen zur sogenannten Baruchschrift*, BZAW 122 (Berlin, Walter
de Gruyter & Co., 1971), especially pp. 144–156. Martin Kessler works in a similar direction,
without going so far as Wanke: *A Prophetic Biography: A Form-Critical Study of Jeremiah
26–29, 32–35*, (Diss., Brandeis, 1965) and "Jeremiah Chapters 26–45 Reconsidered," *JNES* 27
(1968) 81–88.

histories.[21] The main reason is that, in his view, they give pictures of Jeremiah so different as to be incompatible. The Jeremiah of the long connected section chs. 37–44 is one whose word meets rejection at every turn, who interprets this as rejection of the word of Yahweh, and who simply submits to the terrible consequences of rejection. We leave him in the abyss of hopelessness opened up by the people's folly. In contrast, the Jeremiah of the conflict stories (19.1–20.6, chs. 26–29, 36) is a hero of the word who, encountering resistance in high places to his proclamation, enters the fray; the turn of events vindicates him and discomfits his enemies.

These two Jeremiahs, whom Wanke finds incompatible with each other, live out of different literary forms. Chs. 37–44 are unique in prophetic literature; they may not inappropriately be called a "passion narrative."[22] But the second group of passages belong to the familiar form of the "prophetic legend," in which the prophet of Yahweh is characteristically triumphant, more than a match for the counsel of kings by the word that he bears. Do other literary forms present us with yet other Jeremiahs? Recent articles suggest that, in at least two other cases, they do. The Jeremiah of the "individual lament" (that is, of the confessions) is, for those who deny the authenticity of these sections, an example of the nature of prophetic existence, or, more generally, of a life of faithfulness to Yahweh:

> The confessions are interpretations of Jeremiah's proclamation and person; they interpret his fate along the lines of the exemplary "I" of the lament psalms; what Jeremiah suffers is the fulfillment and concretization of what the lament-formula already expressed; Jeremiah is the exemplarily suffering righteous one.[23]

Gunneweg is far from suggesting that the confessions have no historical referent; the traditioners related them both to Jeremiah's experience as they knew it, and to their own. But it is the use of the form of the individual lament which has given the decisive cast to these passages.[24] The Jeremiah of the "communal lament" is, on the other hand, the prophet *pro patria*, absolutely one with his people, speaking their prayers even in the fact of the certainty of divine rejection. Hertzberg has suggested that this is a Jeremiah who stands altogether outside the prophetic role, which did not include intercession.[25]

---

[22]Wanke, *Untersuchungen*, 4; but, for reservations about this name, cf. pp. 155–156.

[23]Gunneweg, "Konfession oder Interpretation," 399. Cf. Gerstenberger, "Jeremiah's Complaints," 408.

[24]Gunneweg, "Konfession oder Interpretation," 412–414. As he points out, there is a close relationship between the Jeremiah of the confessions and the Jeremiah of chs. 37–44 (pp. 414–415).

[25]H. W. Hertzberg, "Sind die Propheten Fürbitter?" in *Tradition und Situation: Studien zur alttestamentlichen Prophetie Artur Weiser zum 70. Geburtstag ... dargebracht*, edited by

What is important is not so much the degree of compatibility between these Jeremiahs, but the fact that the very use of a certain literary form to such an extent dictates the portrait that emerges. Have the modern biographers of Jeremiah, in attempting to present a coherent individual out of all parts of the book, been engaged in a task which is in principle impossible?

Our final question about the Jeremiah tradition is closely related to the form-critical one. There are hints, at least, that the tradition has been shaped at some points by a theology of Jeremiah himself, as a figure unique in prophecy and in Israel's history. We consider two points. First, Nicholson claims that Jeremiah has been conformed, in the tradition, to the "prophet like Moses" of Deut. 18:15–18, most obviously in the call narrative, but, also in the central importance given to his conflict with "false prophets."[26] Was Jeremiah understood after his death as the prophet *par excellence*, the second Moses (or, as 15:1 suggests, the third in a triumvirate with Moses and Samuel)? Second, what significance is to be read into the concentration on Jeremiah as the suffering one, which we have found both in the confessions and in chs. 37–44? The question cries out to be asked, although the scholars we have considered do not pursue it far. It must be stated that no doctrine of redemptive suffering is put forward in the Book of Jeremiah. But the word upon which Jeremiah was broken was the same word which meant life to the survivors of exile. We cannot know whether speculation about the meaning of Jeremiah's suffering is any part of the background to the Servant of Second Isaiah; but in view of the intense interest in the theological significance of Jeremiah which Gunneweg, Nicholson and others have ascribed to the post-Jeremianic community, it is a possibility which must be considered.[27]

JEREMIAH RESEARCH AND JESUS RESEARCH

Broad resemblances between the above trends in Jeremiah research and the history of research on the Life of Jesus will not have escaped the reader, and in what follows it will not be necessary at every point to spell them out. It will, however, be illuminating to demonstrate some of them in

---

E. Würthwein and O. Kaiser (Göttingen, Vandenhoeck & Ruprecht, 1963), especially pp. 72–73. It is a noteworthy point, however, that there are many more references to the fact (or possibility) of Jeremiah's interceding (7:16, 11:14, 14:11; 15:11, 18:20; 42:2–4, 37:3; and cf. 27:18) than there are instances of his actually speaking the people's prayers in the communal lament (3:22–25, 14:7–9, 19–22). This already suggests that "Jeremiah the intercessor" belongs more to interpretation than to history.

[26]Nicholson, *Preaching to the Exiles*, 113–115, and cf. 44–58, 93–103.

[27]The suggestion that the Servant is, or is in some way related to, Jeremiah, has, of course, a considerable history. Cf. C. R. North, *The Suffering Servant in Deutero-Isaiah: A Historical and Critical Study* (London, Geoffrey Cumberlege, 1948) 20–21, 27, 41, 57, 70, 99–101, 112.

more detail, particularly where the Jesus research has been based on more clearly defined hermeneutical principles.

a. Reventlow as an "anti-life" of Jeremiah

Our dubbing of Reventlow's approach "thoroughgoing liturgiology" is, of course, intended to recall the "thoroughgoing eschatology" of Johannes Weiss and Albert Schweitzer in Jesus research. Positively, the resemblance is not great—no one has claimed that Jesus was a functionary of the Second Temple—though both the Jesus of Weiss and Schweitzer and the Jeremiah of Reventlow are religious figures of a type familiar in their respective times. Negatively, they have played similar roles in the history of research; in relation to the "psycho-biographical" approach they are "anti-lives." The "anti-life" meets the liberal "life" on its own ground and does battle with it there; it takes the same evidence available to the liberals and shows how it must be assessed in a diametrically opposite way, that the figure to be reconstructed from history is a figure quite alien to us. Weiss's and Schweitzer's apocalyptic preacher was in liberal terms an anti-Jesus, and Reventlow's Temple functionary is an anti-Jeremiah. Both make it clear that theological construction will need to be something much more than historical reconstruction. Reventlow's work has met with some partial acceptance and much outright rejection; but it is not coincidental that since its publication there has been such a turning of attention from the historical Jeremiah and towards the post-Jeremianic community.

b. Tradition and redaction

The acceptance of our lack of biographical sources, the awareness of the shaping effect on tradition of the community of faith, with its social situation, and of the theology of redactors; these methodological principles, which we have found in Nicholson and others, are, of course, well known from Synoptic studies.[28] So is the theological shift from a "kernel and husk" model, where critical work has the aim of separating the authentic and valuable from the secondary setting in which it has been placed, to a deep appreciation of the theological significance of the "secondary."[29] It is striking how Jeremiah research has followed, in general trends, the course set by Jesus research. But we can be more specific.

The principle which Schottroff wants us to adopt in exegeting the prophets is recognizably the "criterion of dissimilarity" of Synoptic research, formulated as follows by Perrin: "The earliest form of a saying we can

---

[28] For convenient summaries, cf. E. V. McKnight, *What is Form Criticism?* (Philadelphia, Fortress Press, 1969), Norman Perrin, *What is Redaction Criticism?* (Philadelphia, Fortress Press, 1969), R. H. Stein, "What is Redaktionsgeschichte?" JBL 88 (1969) 45–56.

[29] For provocative discussion of the hermeneutical issues, cf. Perrin, *Redaction Criticism*, 64–79.

reach may be regarded as authentic if it can be shown to be dissimilar to characteristic emphases both of ancient Judaism and of the early Church."[30] Assume inauthenticity until authenticity is plausibly demonstrated! To carry out such a program obviously means dealing with the redactional levels first, not last. If these principles, so widely (though far from universally) accepted in New Testament studies, have anywhere else been so clearly applied to the Old Testament as by Schottroff, we are not aware of it.

The different Jeremiahs presented to us by different literary forms, and the effect on the shape of the tradition of emerging beliefs *about* Jeremiah, call to mind irresistably the recent work of two scholars in particular on the Jesus tradition. E. Trocmé[31] takes five familiar form-critical categories from the Synoptics, "dominical sayings," "apothegms," "biographical narratives," "parables," and "miracle stories," and analyzes the Jesus presented in each. He finds evidence that each was treasured by a different group in a different social setting, and that they only came together after a lapse of decades. In a final chapter Trocmé asks "Who was Jesus?" and answers that, in the last analysis, we do not and cannot know, and that any attempt at an answer must be out of an absorption of the full impact of several Jesuses, each depicted with intensity and *completeness.*[32]

Two essays by H. Koester in the book *Trajectories Through Early Christianity*[33] extend and deepen this line of thought. In the first, "One Jesus and Four Primitive Gospels,"[34] he also works form-critically on the Jesus tradition, particularly in the Gospel of Thomas. After discussing a large number of the literary forms found in the tradition, he points to the unique form of the "gospel" as possessing the power "to digest gospel literature and traditions of a different type and christological orientation, and to make these subservient to its own creed of Jesus' death and resurrection."[35] But this process "reflects at every stage the explicit or implicit controversy with different christological options."[36] In the second essay, "The Structure and Criteria of Early Christian Beliefs,"[37] he takes these "different christological options" of the primitive Church as his starting point: "Jesus as the Lord of the Future," "Jesus as the Divine Man," "Jesus as Wisdom's Envoy and as Wisdom," and "Jesus Raised from the Dead." Our Gospels, he claims, developed out of these christologies

---

[30]Norman Perrin, *Rediscovering the Teaching of Jesus* (New York, Harper & Row, 1967) 39.

[31]Etienne Trocmé, *Jesus as Seen by his Contemporaries*, trans. by R. A. Wilson (Philadelphia, The Westminster Press, 1973).

[32]Ibid., 121–126.

[33]J. M. Robinson and H. Koester, *Trajectories Through Early Christianity* (Philadelphia, Fortress Press, 1971).

[34]Ibid., 158–204.

[35]Ibid., 198.

[36]Ibid., 199.

[37]Ibid., 205–231.

and their interaction with each other, christologies which go back to the earliest time we can discern after Jesus' death. Diverse theological models for understanding Jesus in terms of the activity of God have profoundly shaped the tradition about him.

HERMENEUTICAL CONCLUSIONS AND IMPLICATIONS

We have examined trends, rather than argued a case. What the recent Jeremiah literature gives us is hypotheses, needing to be argued and tested both as to methods and as to results. But the similarities we have discerned to the history of Jesus research suggest that, in refining and extending our understanding of the Book of Jeremiah, and by implication, of other parts of the Old Testament, scholars may have to learn from, and should at least listen more closely to, their New Testament colleagues. It has been pointed out that new methods in biblical research have usually been applied first to the Old Testament, and only later to the New.[38] At the hermeneutical level, New Testament scholars are perhaps in a position to repay some of this debt!

a. "Hermeneutically open" exegesis

In Old Testament, though both have flourished, the debate over hermeneutics and the work of exegesis have tended to be isolated from one another—hermeneutical positions have been established in theory and then applied in practice.[39] In New Testament, especially under Bultmann's influence, there exists a style of exegesis which is "hermeneutically open," which accepts as one of its aims the tackling of thorny hermeneutical problems, which accepts its contingence on hermeneutical assumptions, and expects that hermeneutics may have to be rethought in the light of its results. One thinks of Ernst Käsemann and Norman Perrin as two exegetes whose style this is. In Schottroff particularly, and to some extent in other recent work on Jeremiah, one recognizes this style, but more often one wishes that an author might be clearer about his or her hermeneutical assumptions.[40]

---

[38]The most striking example is the development of form-criticism, but the statement holds for early literary and source-criticism, and for sociological and religio-historical approaches to the Bible. Cf. Herbert F. Hahn, *The Old Testament in Modern Research* (Philadelphia, Fortress Press, 1966) and W. G. Kümmel, *The New Testament: The History of the Investigation of its Problems*, trans. by S. M. Gilmour and H. C. Kee (Nashville, Abingdon Press, 1972).

[39]For instance, in the collection of essays edited by Claus Westermann, *Essays on Old Testament Interpretation* (London, SCM Press, 1963), there is strikingly little basis to the discussion—though Bultmann's essay is an exception!

[40]To take simply one example, Helga Weippert's *Prosareden*, the latest attempt to establish the essentially Jeremianic origin of the "Prose Sermons," contains wording which seems to suggest a downgrading of the secondary material over against the authentically Jeremianic: "foreign material (*Fremdberichte*)" (pp. 1, 228), "the suspicion of deuteronomic origin" (p. 228), "traces (*Spuren*) of a deuteronomic reworking" (p. 234).

b. *Method in Old Testament and in New*

The hermeneutical debate over what we may loosely call "the relationship between event and interpretation" has been carried out in each Testament in isolation from the other.[41] In New Testament, the discussion has obviously centered on Jesus, and this problem has seemed a unique one, above all on account of the factor of "christology," the exploration in the early Chruch of what later would be called Jesus' divinity. In Old Testament, the debate has been mostly concerned with Israel's earliest traditions,[42] and this is the area least likely to bring out similarities to the New Testament issues—in the case of Moses or the Patriarchs we are dealing with traditions whose historical origins are so obscured by the mists of time that we are obliged to make special assumptions and to use special methods.

But the similarities of the problems facing Jesus and Jeremiah researches are considerable, and suggest the need for more collaboration both on method and on hermeneutical implications. The problem of christology may not be unique; Jeremiah research, it seems, must face the factor of "Jeremialogy," beliefs *about* the prophet, in the creation of the book. But for the analysis of such factors, Old Testament scholars simply may not disregard the immense methodological gains of the Jesus researchers. Too frequently one finds an attitude of unconcern bordering on contempt for the New Testament hermeneutical debates. It ought not to come as such a surprise when Schottroff applies to the prophets a principle so well known and widely accepted in New Testament as the criterion of dissimilarity.

c. *History or interpretation in Jeremiah?—An example*

We ask in conclusion what the effect would be on theological understanding of the Book Jeremiah if it were read out of the hermeneutical assumptions we have discussed, and take as a test case part of a book which deserves to be better known to English-speakers, Ulrich Mauser's *Gottesbild und Menschwerdung*.[43] Mauser takes up the question of biblical anthropomorphism, and his major thesis is that "the anthropomorphisms of the Old Testament are pointers to a God who is not alien to the human, but who by participating in human history takes on the human,"[44] the New

---

[41]Carl E. Braaten, *History and Hermeneutics, New Directions in Theology Today*, vol. II (Philadelphia, The Westminster Press, 1966), deals with both sets of problems in a single volume; but his division into chapters serves to show how distinct the discussions have been.

[42]Summarized by Braaten, ibid., 108–116.

[43]Ulrich Mauser, *Gottesbild und Menschwerdung, Beiträge zur historischen Theologie* 43 (Tübingen, J. C. B. Mohr, 1971). An English summary of Mauser's thesis, concentrating on the Hosea material, has appeared: "Image of God and Incarnation," *Int* 24 (1970) 336–356.

[44]Ibid., 17.

Testament showing the fulfillment of this in Christ. The final chapter deals with Paul and his view of incarnation, but the preceding two are on Hosea and Jeremiah as "parables" of God, partial incarnations of the divine humanity. The whole is an impressive essay in *biblical* theology, based on and contributing to a definite understanding of the relation between the Testaments.

Mauser's work on Jeremiah builds especially on that of A. Heschel.[45] Yahweh is not timeless, but has bound himself to human time. Yahweh is a god of pathos, not indifferent to Israel's situation. He longs and pleads for her repentance, but despairs of it. He punishes at the cost of inexpressible suffering to himself, because he has been left with no choice.[46] This is the god whose word the prophet delivers. But Jeremiah cannot be merely a mouthpiece; the pathos of his whole existence is the revelation and the incarnation of the divine suffering.[47] His anger is Yahweh's anger, and the scorn he suffers is scorn of Yahweh; the tension he experiences between himself and his task is the tension in Yahweh himself between what he feels for Israel and what he must do to her; the impossible waiting period which Jeremiah must face between his announcement of doom and its coming is Yahweh's own waiting for the vindication of his word.[48] Mauser rejects the view that Jeremiah, in being more than a mouthpiece, represents the end of prophecy in Israel—it is in being drawn into the divine history that Jeremiah truly *becomes* a prophet;[49] in him, prophecy takes on the priestly and the kingly aspects that properly belong to it.[50]

This brief summary does scant justice to the richness of Mauser's account of the Book of Jeremiah, and to the creative connecting of the Testaments under the category of "incarnation." But precisely at the point of method problems arise. Since Mauser's New Testament work is with Paul, who had either little knowledge of, or little interest in, the Jesus tradition, "incarnation" in the New Testament is studied at a distance from the Jesus tradition. Mauser starts from the proclamation *about* Jesus. But when he works with Jeremiah, he specifically confines himself to material "over the genuineness of (which) there is general agreement."[51] and in fact chooses Jeremiah for lengthy treatment because it contains "texts . . . which permit us an insight into the struggle in Jeremiah's soul."[52]

The difference in approach is startling—willingness to theologize about Jesus at a point quite remote from authentic historical tradition, but

---

[45]A. J. Heschel, *The Prophets* (New York and Evanston, Harper & Row, 1962), especially chapters 6, 12, and 15.

[46]Mauser, *Gottesbild,* 41–42.

[47]Ibid., 105.

[48]Ibid., 107–113.

[49]Ibid., 80–83.

[50]Ibid., 90–93.

[51]Ibid., 85.

[52]Ibid., 78.

unwillingness to theologize about Jeremiah at any point except the most authentic historical tradition available. To have begun from the herme-neutical presuppositions implied in the Jeremiah research we have outlined above, that is, to have assumed that the whole Book of Jeremiah comes from the hands of redactors serving a post-Jeremianic community, would, it seems, have enabled Mauser to avoid major problems. It would remove the inconsistency in his approach to Jesus and to Jeremiah. It would avoid making his conclusions dependent on the authenticity of this or that section, for, despite his claim that there is "general agreement" about the genuineness of the important passages with which he works, this agreement is rapidly breaking up.[53] But above all, it would relieve Jeremiah the individual of the weight of the concept of himself which his book contains: the new Moses, the one in whom Israel's sacred offices of prophet, priest and king are united,[54] the incarnation of the divine humanity. How far do we wish to go with the idea of Jeremiah's entertaining such self-understandings, at a time when *Jesus'* application to himself of any of the major christological titles of the Synoptics is being widely denied?[55] And can such concepts be worked out before the end is seen—*must* not the meaning of Jeremiah be formulated in retrospect?

The assumption and methods of modern historical Jesus research are not in every case applicable to Jeremiah or to other parts of the Old Testament; nor are they by any means to be taken over uncritically. The recent approaches to Jeremiah which we outlined in the first part of this article need to be tested on their merits, and compared with work being done elsewhere in the Old Testament. But, particularly in the light of our test case, we may conclude that such approaches hold promise of sounder exegesis and more firmly based theology of the Old Testament.

[53]For example, Mauser assumes (ibid., 98) the authenticity of 14:11 and 15:1–2. From Nicholson's point of view, *Preaching to the Exiles*, 87, 101–102, these passages are of deuteronomic origin. Many similar examples might be cited.

[54]Mauser, *Gottesbild*, 92.

[55]E.g. Hans Conzelmann, *Jesus*, trans. by J. R. Lord, edited with an introduction by John Reumann (Philadelphia, Fortress Press, 1973) 41–50; R. H. Fuller, *The Foundations of New Testament Christology* (New York, Scribner's, 1965) 108–131.

17

Overcoming the Israelite Crisis.
Remarks on the Interpretation of
the Book of Jeremiah*
Siegfried Herrmann

(Translated by Leo G. Perdue)

With this essay the future author of the *Biblischer Kommentar* Jeremiah commentary expresses his respect for the author of the Ezekiel commentary in the same series, Walther Zimmerli, whose comprehensive work has been in print now for quite some time.[1] This, of course, implies a proximity which continues to hold distinctive importance even to the present time. The look back at the completion of Zimmerli's significant work may be in some fashion also a glance towards the future, for we stand at the beginning of a similar endeavor, which must conquer, as it were, a rather large and extensive text. And yet one cannot escape the fact that the interpreter of the text, standing at the very beginning of his work, must achieve for himself some measure of clarity as regards both his principles of procedure and the nature of the critical questions to be addressed. Indeed these principles and questions will continue to accompany him in his work and should indicate even at a distance the primary goal toward which even the individual comments should ultimately point. This realization takes on added importance when one considers the fact that the volumes of the *Biblischer Kommentar* series appear in individual fascicles.

Preliminary considerations of this nature may not always be necessary in the same way for commentaries on other biblical books. However, when one casts a glance at the book of Jeremiah in its entirety, all the while not forgetting its proximity to Ezekiel, such reflections appear to be entirely in

---

*Originally appeared as "Die Bewältigung der Krise Israels. Bemerkungen zur Interpretation des Buches Jeremia," *Beiträge zur Alttestamentlichen Theologie* (FS Walther Zimmerli; ed. by H. Donner, R. Hanhart, and R. Smend. Göttingen: Vandenhoeck und Ruprecht, 1977), 164–178.

[1] W. Zimmerli, *Ezekiel* (BK XIII/1.2; Neukirchen, 1969). The treatment of the book of Jeremiah as Volume XII in this commentary series is planned by the author of the present essay.

order. For the book of Jeremiah in rather similar fashion to the book of Ezekiel offers to the observer the picture of an intended uniformity. This is true not only for the frequently detected overarching structure: Words of Disaster—Speeches concerning the Nations—and the Message of Salvation, but in a wider sense also for the nature of the process of collecting and editing the prophetic materials in general. The book is permeated with so-called "secondary" material. While the prophet himself was only indirectly involved in this material, it nonetheless served as his own supplements and interpretation. And in any case the admission of this material to the book itself resulted in its being placed under the prophet's authority.

The type of editing activity and the stratification of materials in Jeremiah both have unmistakable formal parallels with the book of Ezekiel, parallels which include features of content held in common. Thus, for instance, the materials taken up in Ezekiel 13–24 and 34–39 may in fact be considerably closer to the book of Jeremiah than has generally been assumed or even taken into account. The retrospective reflection in Jer 30–31 that pertains to Israel and Judah as two parts of a united country and to an eventual, reassuring future willed by Yahweh himself quite possibly for both parties demonstrates a conspicuously real and intentional correspondence with parts of the book of Ezekiel. For this reason the acceptance of common presuppositions for their conception is justified.[2] These presuppositions are most likely to be sought out at a time far beyond the catastrophe of 587/6 B.C. when efforts would be made to master Israel's fate. This would be the period when the prophetic word of both Jeremiah and Ezekiel began to be understood as the guarantee of the divine presence, a presence which one experienced afresh in crisis. However, in the sifting and fixing of traditional words and anecdotal reflections, there was no historical interest in the modern sense at work. These were not efforts that strove to achieve documentary and archival perfection. This is true even of those texts which some have attributed to Baruch and have characterized with the problematical designation "biography,"[3] texts which contain and narrate more than a little about the prophet and his fortunes. These texts

---

[2]Even the turn of expression so reminiscent of Ezekiel, "You shall know that my name is Yahweh," is found in the dispute over the problem of foreign gods in Jer 16:21. Character-istically, Zimmerli regards the passage as "no doubt post-deuteronomistic" ("Gottes Offen-barung," *ThB* 19 [1963] 73). The connecting of this expression of recognition with the "new heart" and the "covenant formula" in Jer 24:7 (similary 31:34) deserves no less attention. In regard to the differentiation of these and other expressions in Jeremiah, see Zimmerli, *ibid*, p. 73, note 48. Zimmerli stresses the closeness of Ezekiel to the book of Jeremiah in "Studien zur alttestamentlichen Theologie und Prophetie," *ThB* 51 (1974) 110f. Yet, he also has pointed to the very profound difference between the two personalities of Jeremiah and Ezekiel in BK XIII/1, 69*f.

[3]The expression "Biography of Baruch" is a familiar though recognizedly problematic one (cf. G. Wanke, *Untersuchungen zur sogenannten Baruchschrift* [BZAW 122, 1971]). In close proximity to the legend of the prophet, so judges K. Koch (*Was ist Formgeschichte?* [Neukirchen, 1974³] 245–50), is the biography of the prophet which Baruch may have initially composed. K. Baltzer (*Die Biographie der Propheten* [Neukirchen, 1975]) tends to use the

are more than the modern "in person" presentation of an "author" to his audience of interested readers. Rather it is in the fate of Jeremiah, a man who, though right, continued to be misunderstood even to the very end when he was led away to Egypt, that one experienced Yahweh anew and comprehended what Israel lost. Therefore it became necessary to continue to reflect on Jeremiah and to preserve his word as a deposit for future restoration.

It seems legitimate that the potential commentator, who is already to a certain extent conversant with the material and yet has in the main the rugged terrain still before him to search out, will want to detect the important purposes which gave this book its final shape. Of course, no one wishes to see in a prophetic book the chronologically exact, documentary precise, and untouched expression of prophetic speech in the nature, say, of a copied rough draft which from the beginning to the end reveals the prophet's own hand. That would certainly be a naive position to take. Nevertheless, the reader and the commentator continually feel the urge to hear the voice of the prophet himself and desire to detect the pulse beat of the prophetic experience. That such a temptation exists attests to the vivacity and originality of the tradition. However, this does not free the critical onlooker from the responsibility of questioning and then determining the task, intention, and objective of the tradents and the written tradition within the framework of the work of literature (i.e., the "prophetic book").

Already in the first chapter of Jeremiah, a text that describes the call of the prophet, one discovers superimposed and side by side blocks of tradition which neither could nor intend to originate from a single act of experience. Indeed the form and richness of expression preclude their being placed in the same time and place. Nonetheless, they stand together in the structure of the chapter and legitimate in different ways the speeches and words of the prophet which follow as his own. Here is played, as it were, an overture which may be heard under the key word "call" or "commission," but which in similar fashion to the opera overtures at least since the Age of Romanticism only suggests individual themes which either continue through the following work or resonate again more dramatically in a subsequent sequence.

Jeremiah 1:10 is the clearest instance to investigate, since it has for a long time been examined in considerable detail and valued for its proto-typical significance for both Jeremiah and his book.[4] However, is this verse

---

expression "biography" in referring to the large tradition complexes of the Old Testament in an unusually broad manner.

[4] I refer to R. Bach, *Bauen und Pflanzen, Studien zur Theologie der alttestamentlichen Überlieferungen* (Festschrift G. von Rad; Neukirchen, 1961) 7–32; W. Thiel, *Die deuteronomistische Redaktion von Jeremia 1–25* (WMANT 41, 1973) 69–71; cf. also S. Herrmann, *Die prophetischen Heilserwartungen im Alten Testament* (BWANT 85, 1965) 165–169. A comprehensive investigation of the series of expressions used in Jer 1:10 is offered by Helga Weippert, *Die Prosareden des Jeremiabuches* (BZAW 132, 1973) 191–202.

actually capable of sustaining itself against the warranted question as to when and where Jeremiah would have had occasion to attend to the message of "to tear down" and "to build and to plant." Not a single word of Jeremiah dealing with the future may without objection support such a suggested turn to a message of salvation.[5] Matters present themselves differently, however, if the expectations about the reconstruction of the land which are intimated in the book of Jeremiah are placed beside their similar sounding compositions pieced together in the book of Ezekiel, especially in chapters 34–37. One finds here an expansive, developed hope of reconstruction which clearly had been drawn up some time after 587/6. This, however, may be the same time in which the decisive redactions of the Jeremiah tradition occur.[6]

When one accepts a late date for the composition of Jer 1:10, the question that immediately comes to the fore is the date of the call report which begins in verse 4. One should see in this quite familiar schema,[7] not the record of prophetic experience,[8] but rather, on the basis of several

---

[5] It is typical that Bach, *op. cit.*, 32 as well as Weippert, *op cit.*, 196f. leave open the question of the dating of the verse and the series of expressions. Weippert is completely occupied with the extra-Jeremianic occurrences of the series of expressions employed. However, her investigation does not make use of evidence in the nature of datable strands of tradition, but rather is restricted primarily to the effort to exclude characteristic Deuteronomistic language (mainly against S. Herrmann, *op. cit.*). She does allow herself to use the expression, "the prophetic traditions" (*op. cit.*, 201f.), a surprisingly concrete classification!

[6] In his essay "Planungen für den Wiederaufbau nach der Katastrophe von 587" (1968, later in *ThB* 51 [1974] 165–191), W. Zimmerli chiefly takes up Ezek 40–48. However he lightly touches on Ezek 37:1–14 which he calls "unmistakably a viewpoint of Ezekiel" (p. 166) and argues against me and others, because "the weighty promise of the future in Ezek 37:1–14 may not be denied to the preaching of the prophet." I confess that I do not wish to deny this vision to the prophet for the very same reasons which Zimmerli names. However, I, as well as Zimmerli, must address the question about the earliest period that one may discover a concrete expectation of the restitution of Israel-Judah. In this regard Ezek 40–48 also offers difficulties which have hardly been overcome. It is exactly for this reason that the shaping and formation of the tradition in Ezek 34–37 and 40–48, two complexes which are strikingly different in regard to language and design, could not have occurred within a rather close time frame.

[7] The form of the call report has been investigated rather frequently in recent times. One may refer in brief to E. Kutsch, *ThLZ* 81 (1956) 75–84; N. Habel, *ZAW* 77 (1965) 297–323; W. Richter, *Traditionsgeschichtliche Untersuchungen zum Richterbuch* (BBB 18, 1966²) 152–55; *Die sogenannten vorprophetischen Berufungsberichte* (FRLANT 101, 1970); Marie-Louise Henry, *Prophet und Tradition* (BZAW 116, 1969) 11–41; and B. O. Long, "Prophetic Call Traditions and Reports of Visions," *ZAW* 84 (1972) 494–500.

[8] W. Rudolph deliberates over this in his *Jeremia* (HAT 1, 12; 1968³) 9f. Cf. further I. P. Seierstad's investigation that is oriented in the direction of a psychological analysis (*Die Offenbarungserlebnisse der Propheten Amos, Jesaja, und Jeremia* [Oslo, 1965²], especially pp. 66–70, 110–115). The two following studies in different ways attempt to deal with the call report of Jeremiah as the deposit of authentic prophetic experience: A. H. J. Gunneweg, "Ordinationsformular oder Berufungsbericht in Jeremia 1," *Glaube, Geist, Geschichte* (FS E. Benz; Leiden, 1967) 91–98; and J. M. Berridge, *Prophet, People, and the Word of Yahweh* (Zurich, 1970) 26–72. Gunneweg and Berridge have placed a critical distance between themselves and the work by H. Graf Reventlow (*Liturgie und prophetisches Ich bei Jeremia* [Gütersloh, 1963]).

characteristic topoi,[9] a text which seeks to place Jeremiah within the tradition of the great, true prophets. Nevertheless, one is still able to recognize in this report its unique elements that include the call from the mother's womb and the appointment to be a "prophet to the nations" (v. 5). The notion of the predestined election of the prophets, which was foreign to the classical period of the eighth century, took root during the course of the seventh century. This idea sprang forth during the time when, in reflecting on the prophetic experience itself, the person of the prophet as the mediator of the divine word received greater interest. Such considerations were prompted by Deut 18 with its conception that Yahweh now and then would raise up in Israel prophets like Moses himself (vv. 15–18). Thus there would come forth from the midst of Israel herself prophets in whose mouths Yahweh himself would place his divine word.[10] This idea presupposes that the appearance of prophets is to be understood as a planned action by God. It follows then that Yahweh on occasion would select some who even from their youth had already been created for their task. Jeremiah 1:5 goes a step farther and introduces at the same time the idea of Jeremiah as a prophet "to the nations." This means that the validity of the Jeremianic message should not be limited to Israel. This would be hard to conceive during the exilic period when significant parts of the people of God were dwelling outside the land and were in subjugation to foreign powers. The recording and collection of the prophet's message was thus designed equally so for the nations who should come to understand that he was right in predicting long beforehand that Judah would be destroyed. In this manner, the book of Jeremiah comes close to the horizons of Deutero-Isaiah whose Servant Songs in similar fashion contain the element of predestination.[11]

---

[9]In this regard, one would mainly have to take into account Jer 1:7b–9. Here the touching of the lips, an act of the physical approach of the otherwise only audibly perceived deity, is designed both to reduce the prophet's fear arising from the enormity of his task and to create in him the certainty that he is being confronted by Yahweh's word.

[10]The direct influences exerted by Deut 18 on the formation of Jer 1:7–9 (especially clear in the taking up of 18:18b in 7bβ and 9bβ) in connection with the entire shaping of 1:4–10 is treated by W. Thiel, *Die deuteronomistische Redaktion*, 66–72; cf. also the suggestion by W. L. Holladay, *VT* 25 (1975) 410.

[11]Isa 49:1,5. The Egyptian parallel to Jer 1:4,5 from the inscription of the Pi(anchi)-Stela (*Urk.* III, Breasted, *AR* IV §796ff.), frequently cited since the note by M. Gilula (*VT* 17 [1967] 114; cf. e.g. Rudolph, *op. cit.*, 5 and Berridge, *op. cit.*, 40), is of limited value for Jeremiah. This is due to the fact that the divine predetermination of the king belongs to the older segments of Egyptian royal ideology. Similar to Pianchi is the earlier statement by Amun to Thutmosis III (*Urk.* IV, 156f.) and the reference made by Sesostris I in regard to his creation by Re-Harachte in a well-known text from the Berlin leather manuscript. These and some other references, including the Pi(anchi) inscription (one now says simply Pi instead of Pianchi), are newly edited by H. Brunner (*Religionsgeschichtliches Textbuch zum Alten Testament* [ed. by W. Beyerlin; Göttingen, 1975] 53–56). Cf. also relevant texts in Elke Blumenthal, *Untersuchungen zum ägyptischen Königtum des Mittleren Reichs. I. Die Phraseologie* (AAL, Phil.-hist. Kl. Bd. 61/1, 1970) 35–37, 62–77. Significantly enough the formulation "to be chosen" or "to be called" from the womb has not entered into the Israelite-Jewish

Considerations and combinations of this type appear risky so long as one proceeds from the presupposition that he is obligated to mine the texts for their prophetic authenticity alone or to search out and find their earliest traditio-historical point of contact with the life of Jeremiah.[12] Certainly, such a procedure is not illegitimate. However, it all too easily tends to obstruct one's view when attempting to discover the continuing process of redaction of the prophetic words which had been deposited in the book. The additional elements of the first chapter of Jeremiah clearly point to a multiplicity of images which could hardly have originated either within the same circle of tradition or, for that matter, with the prophet himself. The two images of the "rod of almond" and the "boiling pot" (1:11–12, 13–14) are introduced by Yahweh's question directed to the prophet: "What do you see?" Afterwards, Yahweh himself explains the image which the prophet has identified. This technique of description is an old one. Its earliest prototype may be found in Amos,[13] while its most noteworthy development within the Old Testament occurs in the "Night Visions" of Zachariah.[14] While one cannot flatly deny that Jer 1:11–14 contains material from the prophet himself, neither can it be simply maintained. The "Enemy from the North" is mentioned here in prototypical fashion. However, while the employment of this prototype is unequivocally clear, its time of origin cannot be established with any certainty.[15]

---

royal ritual, in spite of the existence of dynastic linkages. Yahweh's election of a person to an office is certainly to be assessed as different from predestination before birth. This concept is not "implicit" for the Davidic dynasty (against O. Kaiser, *Der Königliche Knecht* [1959] 57). The kingship of Solomon according to 1 Kgs 3 rests, not on an "emphasized recourse to a physically conceived election" as in Egypt, but rather on the "authoritative-obligatory investiture with the office" (so in connection with the assessment of Egyptian material by M. Görg, *Gott-König-Reden in Israel und Ägypten* [BWANT 105, 1975] 76–81, especially 81). The prophet's being called from his mother's womb is not to be seen in the sense of a physical election, but rather in regard to the special task which Yahweh had handed over to him. The Egyptian parallel to which M. Gilula has pointed is comparable in wording, but is explained differently.

[12]In this regard I am referring to the seemingly endless efforts to determine the contents of the so-called *Urrolle*. However, the learned hypotheses have not been successful. In any case it does not reside within the purview of the text of Jer 36 to designate specific texts. Also hypothetical is C. Rietzschel's *Das Problem der Urrolle* (Gütersloh, 1966).

[13]Am 7:8, 8:2.

[14]In Zechariah it is generally the case that the prophet himself asks the interpreting angel the meaning of the things seen: Zech 1:9; 2:2,4; 4:4,11,12; 5:6,10; 6:4. The prophet is asked one time, however: "What do you see?" (5:2).

[15]The treatment of the "Enemy from the North" in the book of Jeremiah is to be kept separate from the "Land of the North" from where God will call home the scattered sons of his people. Destruction comes from the North (Jer 1:13,14; 4:6; 6:1,22; 10:21,22; 13:20). The call of Yahweh is made to the "tribes of the North" (Jer 25:9; 1:15 [is the word "kingdoms" redundantly placed beside "tribes"?]). The call to the North and the return from the North is mentioned in Jer 3:12,18. And in 16:15 and 23:8 one finds reference to the North and all the lands of the dispersion.

The subsequent picture of judgment should not be rashly joined to the visions, but rather is to be seen as something unique and apart. If the picture of the hostile nations appearing before the gates of Jerusalem is anchored in that strand of the Zion tradition which celebrates the breaking of the enemy forces at Zion and the triumph of Yahweh as world sovereign,[16] it is nevertheless presented in a significantly different manner. For here Jerusalem herself shall actually fall, and by this means Yahweh will have actualized his judgment against apostate Judah. This new development, which pieces together Deuteronomistic elements of language, accounts for the city's castastrophe exactly in the way that is typical for the exilic period. Yet it also allows this perspective chronologically as well as materially to appear in the field of vision at the very beginning of the book.[17]

The concluding section of the chapter, introduced by v. 17, speaks once again of the prophet's call and at all events intends to establish a connection with vv. 4–10 in a rather loose manner. Echoes and literary connections are clearly evident. In vv. 17f., after the summons to gird himself, vv. 7b–8 are almost entirely reproduced. A residue of these verses is found in v. 19b, thereby expanding the statement in v. 19a that pertains to the invincibility of the prophet. And 19a resonates rather well with the formerly independent, concrete images of v. 18 which, with its own distinctive diction, ruptures an original connection which existed between v. 17 and v. 19. Consequently, at the conclusion of the chapter the basic tenor of the material involving the call report in vv. 4–9 is substantially repeated: the prophet's hesitation to accept the divine commision. However, it is transformed into a variant that speaks of victory and triumph. Yahweh will stand by the prophet in his battle with his adversaries and will make him a fortified city, an iron pillar, and a bronze wall.[17a] The adversaries are enumerated. They turn out to be, not notorious, wicked wretches, but rather the kings of Judah, their officials and priests, and the people of the land.

The theme of the call comes to an end with v. 19. The divine word pertaining to the personal salvation of the prophet from possible situations of affliction brings the chapter to its conclusion. Even though this first chapter of Jeremiah does not present the record of a prophetic call, one still has at least in vv. 4–9 the reproduction of a well-known schema which is joined to verses (11–14) placed in the style of a prophetic vision report and promulgated with the summons and encouragement to gird on the

---

[16]E. Rohland, *Die Bedeutung der Erwählungstraditionen für die Eschatologie der alttestamentlichen Propheten* (Dissertation Heidelberg, 1956) 119–208, especially 190–193; G. von Rad, *Theologie des Alten Testaments* II (Munich, 1975⁶) 162–175.

[17]W. Thiel provides an informative table of comparison for Jer 1:16 (*Die deuteronomistische Redaktion*, 74–76).

[17a]As regards the pre-history of this picturesque image, see A. Alt, "Hic murus aheneus esto," *ZDMG* 85 (1932) 33–48; *PJB* 32 (1936) 10, note 3.

prophetic mantel. Chapter one provides a loose framework into which are placed certain demarcated units and thereby presents a program which anticipates and encompasses the activities of the man Jeremiah which are known to the redactors. But it also hastily sketches an entire perspective which the book of Jeremiah will present, a perspective which now and again will appear in a clearer fashion. The message which the reader anticipates is one of a predestined prophet who, in spite of his youth, has something extraordinary to say—the Word of the Lord which has been placed in his mouth. Destruction will unavoidably come to Judah and her inhabitants; the enemy has its origins in the North (v. 14). The kingdoms which Yahweh has called forth will rise up and not be deterred from reaching Jerusalem and helping to effectuate Yahweh's righteous work against the city and land (vv. 15–16). Further, what the prophet was commissioned to say has to do with the kings, officials, and priests of his land, and he will be victorious against them. Those who are to read and to hear afresh this word are in the first case those Jews who have experienced the catastrophe of their own nation. However, Jeremiah is now set forth as a prophet to the nations. And what he had already faithfully and openly executed forms as it were the necessary and boundless prototype, the example *par excellence* which is now intended for the nations. This should show them who Yahweh is, what he has done for Israel, and in addition what the nations have to expect from him. They are to come to understand this from the mouth of a predestined prophet of Yahweh.[18]

Seen in this larger perspective, the Book of Jeremiah is much more than the record of the man from Anathoth. It is in the utilization of numerous and varied materials the book that reckons with the past, presents a call to repentance, becomes a document of hope for Israel, and provides the future instruction of Yahweh for all nations. It is unmistakably the case that this is also the tenor of the over-arching shape of the composition of the book of Ezekiel.[19] It is also clear that the book stands in a thematic and intellectual proximity to Deutero-Isaiah. This understanding may emerge, however, only when the fixed gaze of the Jeremiah biographers with their search for the "authentic" is not allowed to pass the chapters in review. Rather it emerges only when one has in view that developing, intellectual process which is taking shape in the tradition, a process that

---

[18]Deutero-Isaiah illuminates also here the background, for it is finally the people who raise their hands in worship to the gods. However, these gods cannot reliably predict to them the future (cf. Isa 41: 21–29; 42:8,9; 43:9; 48:3–5, 6–8). Over against this, Jeremiah's authentic prophecy is evidenced by Yahweh's placing his word in the prophet's mouth. It has been fully validated.

[19]Strictly speaking this is so mainly for Ezek 1–39. This thought about the embracing of the nations does not present itself in 40–48. However, it is no less true for Jeremiah than it is for Ezekiel that the book stands "between the times" and has taken its stance at the threshold of a new beginning (W. Zimmerli, *Ezekiel. Gestalt und Botschaft* [BSt 62; Neukirchen, 1972] 153–155).

already in the first chapter is announced. As is the case with the book of Ezekiel and lastly with Deutero-Isaiah, one sees passing in succession how Israel understood and overcame its crisis, how she demonstrated full confidence in this last great prophet who remained in the land and survived the catastrophe, and how she brought together under his authority the tradition and thoughts which make up the book.

This manner of regarding the material enables the exegesis of the text not only to attain to new and appropriate insights, but also allows perhaps on a higher level a settling of the violent conflict that has continued to rage in the more recent Jeremiah criticism. This conflict exists between those groups which seek to attribute as much material as possible to Jeremiah himself and those who speak of a rather significant redactional casting of the word, whether it be named Deuteronomistic or something else. So long as only partial observations play a role, whether they are of a linguistic nature or limited to individual groups of tradition, one will from case to case most certainly discover ample material with which to establish one or another approach. But only too quickly one tends to regard such a partial view as one that is the correct one for the overall interpretation. Naturally, one can rather obstinately insist on delineating the text of an *Urrolle* or on defining the prose style in the book of Jeremiah as the literature emerging from the common language of the end of the seventh and the beginning of the sixth century.[20] However, as soon as the entire book with its observable slopes comes into view and the question concerning when the last hand was placed on the entire collection is asked, then points of view are yielded which, in comparison with other Old Testament traditions, compel one to treat the book of Jeremiah as a document in which Israel takes up the battle for her past as well as her future.[21] It is also of programmatic significance to consider the first independent saying in the book of Jeremiah (2:1–3). For these few verses address the entire fortune of the chosen nation in unusually succinct fashion. They outline its history, identify it as Yahweh's possession, and establish the consequences for all those who should attack or wound it. This small unit also points beyond itself and intends to prepare one for Jer 2:4ff.[22]

---

[20]In regard to the dispute over the idea of "artistic prose," see W. L. Holladay's discussion of the book by Helga Weippert (*VT* 25 [1975] 402–12).

[21]Peter K. D. Neumann's comprehensive Hamburg dissertation treats the linguistic and form critical details which link the book of Jeremiah with numerous other Old Testament writings (*Hört das Wort Jahwäs. Ein Beitrag zur Komposition alttestamentlicher Schriften* [Schriften der Stiftung Europa-Kolleg 30; Hamburg, 1975]).

[22]In connection with a detailed exegesis, W. Schottroff points out the significance of this piece as a preview to Jer 2:4–13 (indirectly also vv. 14–19) which goes back, not to a recension of the prophet, but rather in all probability to an exilic redaction. He combines in this article major reflections over the exegesis of the prophets with an analysis of the text and wishes to know, first of all, "the part that the redaction plays in a purported textual complex" before "questions are raised relative to the shaping of the individual traditions and their origin." Therefore, fundamental questions are asked which extend to the practical procedure to follow

Due to the limitations placed on the reflections which are set forth in this essay, we may point out the manner in which the details of the tradition are carried forth by resorting only to a single, specific example. The series of Jeremiah's opponents enumerated in 1:18b recurs in the same or similar way in the book and plays a rather pronounced role. Mentioned in v. 18 are "the kings of Judah, its princes, its priests, and the people of the land." This appears primarily to be a placing together of various groups which are listed only on the basis of a poetic literary style. Some degree of the dramatic, to be sure, is at work when the word "bones" is placed before each member of the series as occurs in 8:1. Here the prophet sees the day coming when the punishment of the worshippers of false gods will be consummated. Therefore, "the bones of the kings of Judah, the bones of its princes, the bones of the priests, the bones of the prophets, and the bones of the inhabitants of Jerusalem" are to be exhumed. The series in this context, in comparison to 1:18, is supplemented with the addition of the prophets, and one must ask whether it is only for stylistic reasons that this list of groups is repeated. More likely, however, is the impression that no one will be excluded from the coming judgment, not even the leading upper classes, the royal house included. Nevertheless, there are additional places which list these groups, though with noteworthy differences.

In Jer 36:11 Micaiah the son of Gemariah, the son of Shaphan, hears the words which Baruch reads at the gate of the upper forecourt in the temple precinct. Thereupon, he sets off to the royal palace and comes upon a meeting occurring in the highest official setting,[23] the "office chamber of the scribe" (*liškat hassōfēr*). Taking part in this meeting which was under the direction of the *sōfēr* Elishama are five specifically named officials "and all officials" (*wᵉkol-haśśārīm*). These men commission another official, Jehudi (who here is provided with a detailed family tree), to fetch Baruch in order that he may repeat to them the words previously read. This occurs, and those present "become afraid" (*pāḥᵃdū*). They prevail upon Baruch for additional details and then decide to make a report to the king. However, they recommend to Baruch and Jeremiah that they go into hiding.

Then follows the well-known scene in which Jehudi reads the scroll before King Jehoiakim and his close associates. Jehoiakim reacts by burning piece by piece the scroll upon the brazier. According to v. 24, neither the king nor "all his servants" (*wᵉkol-ᶜᵃbādāw*) become afraid, even though three of the officials present, namely Elnathan, Delaiah, and Gemariah, attempt to restrain the king from burning the scroll. This remark concerning these three officials is attached *post festum* in v. 25.

---

in the writing of commentaries on biblical books ("Jeremia 2, 1–3. Erwägungen zur Methode der Prophetenexegese," *ZThK* 67 (1970) 263–294, 293f).

[23] Cf. K. Galling, "Die Halle des Schreibers," *PJB* 27 (1931) 51–57, especially 55f.; differently W. Rudolph, *Jeremia* (1968³) 230.

From v. 26 on, the events run their course without any consideration of the preceeding verse (v. 25). Three other named officials, among them a son of the king, attempt to seize Baruch and Jeremiah on the basis of the royal order. However, Yahweh had hidden them.

There were, therefore, especially well-known officials who could "become afraid" at the reading of the prophetic word and even dare to restrain the king, though without result. These were the *śārīm* who certainly did not belong to the intimate circle of the *ᶜabādīm*. If one may be permitted to make a small observation, this explains at least the somewhat awkwardly inserted v. 25 which is placed here in order to name certain officials who undertook in the decisive hour to oppose the king. And by contrast one also finds mentioned by name those who carried out the radical mandates of the king.

Actually, this differentiated understanding of groups of officials may be placed on a broader foundation. After his temple sermon, the "priests and the prophets"[24] seize Jeremiah in order to put him to death (Jer 26:8). This process occasions the appearance of the "officials of Judah" (*śārē yᵉhūdā*) who come from the royal palace to the temple (v. 10). Then the priests and the prophets explain to them that Jeremiah should be sentenced to death. However, v. 16 indicates that the officials and all the people reprimand the priests and the prophets by saying that this man is not worthy of death, for he may have spoken in the name of Yahweh. Thereupon, men from the circle of the elders of the land stand forth and remind the entire assembly of people about the word of Micah of Moresheth which in like manner had as its contents the destruction of the temple. Nevertheless, King Hezekiah did not allow steps to be taken against this prophet (vv. 17–19). The following section (vv. 20–23) reports on the fate of Uriah the son of Shemaiah whose message of destruction admittedly cost him his life. Verse 22 names Elnathan the son of Achbor as the man who had the unhappy task of bringing Uriah back from Egypt where he had fled. This official may well have been the same man who belonged to the group of "fearful" officials in Jer 36:12. Only this time he was probably unable to disregard the royal command. In any event, v. 24 closes chapter 26 with the important note that Jeremiah stood under the protection of Ahikam the son of Shaphan who prevented the prophet from being killed.

Therefore, certain officials and portions of the population of Jerusalem were those who neither should nor ought to bear the large scale guilt for the downfall of the city and land. However, there were priests and prophets who were regularly exempted from such a lenient assessment.[25] One could

---

[24]The expression added here, "and all the people," does not harmonize with v. 11 where the priests and the prophets seek to justify their procedure before "the officials and all the people." Cf. especially also v. 16 where the officials and all the people stand over against the priests and the prophets.

[25]The prophets and priests are particularly singled out as guilty in Jer 5:30f., 6:13, 14:8, and 23:9–40. 5:12–13, the entire complex of Jer 27–29, and 37:19 are especially directed

naturally enough see in these remarks observations of a recorded nature and therefore conclude that they are based on historical facts. This would especially be the case, since the names of the officials are hardly mere inventions. In addition they are shoved to the fore as significant personalities in contrast to the undifferentiated reference to "the prophets and the priests." That this could have actually taken place is easily conceivable, since there well could have arisen factions and groups from the many different voices heard during the last turbulent years of Judah. However, it is hardly the case that the desire for recorded historical precision alone has preserved for us names and facts. The intention of the tradition may point in quite different directions. The guilt for the downfall of Judah and Jerusalem is borne mainly by the royal house, especially by Jehoiakim.[26] The conclusion of Jer 36 (vv. 29–31) leaves no doubt over this whatsoever. On the other hand, however, the tradition wishes to maintain that there were, in the midst of the people, upright individuals, personalities of high rank, who allowed themselves to be influenced by the prophetic word, who "became afraid," who protected Jeremiah, and who justified the authenticity of his prophetic speech on the basis of tradition by referring back to the century old message of the Judean prophet Micah. This is more than a recorded observation. It is a late justification, the expression of an inspired conviction that Judah was not indiscriminately destroyed and abandoned. These are the texts which, though they cannot at the present time be further elaborated, are found in exactly those contexts which summon people to repentance and to hear the Word of Yahweh, thereby setting forth the continuing validity of the prophetic word. They belong to the often treated prose sections of the book of Jeremiah which in a conscious taking up of older material wish to establish the appearance and word of Jeremiah as a valid, admonitory event which appears to offer possibilities of actualization far beyond its present occasion.

We return to our starting point. If the book of Jeremiah intended to determine and transmit not only the speeches of the prophet but also at the same time the far-reaching consequences of his appearance, then it became certainly necessary to enter into the conflict with the past even in regard to awkward details. Yet at the same time, this was to be done in a way so that the demonstration of guilt would not completely extinguish the hope in the

---

against the prophets. The prophets and priests play their roll besides kings and officials (in addition to the already cited passages, see Jer 1:18 [without the prophets]; 2:8; 4:9; 8:1; 13:13; 26:8, 11, 16; 32:32). In general 5:4–5 fits here also: the poor do not know the way of Yahweh; therefore the great bear an even heavier guilt, for they know it. In regard to the conduct of the prophets and priests in Jer 26, see the observations and conclusions offered by H. Graf Reventlow, "Gattung und Überlieferung in der 'Tempelrede Jeremias,' Jer 7 und 26," *ZAW* 81 (1969) 315–352, especially 344ff.

[26]The vacillating behavior of Zedekiah has found an appropriate place in the tradition. For that reason the judgment against him is not so completely negative as that against Jehoiakim.

coming restoration for those in the present. How could one explain otherwise the collection of such large literary corpora as those of Jeremiah and Ezekiel, if they should not in the final analysis serve to encourage future generations to continue to seek and to travel the way of the Lord. The differentiation of guilt, at which this small example of the assessment of the officials and their conduct could only hint, belongs, not last of all, to those convictions and insights which were discovered only when some distance was gained from the catastrophic event. Thus in this fact resides an indication that the book of Jeremiah was the product of several generations.

The different views of the Jeremiah tradition have increased in number during the last generations. Yet they have by no means led to uniform results, because it is so difficult to arrive at commonly accepted criteria of analysis.[27] This may also be partially due to the fact that scholars have very often limited themselves to the investigations of text complexes or tradition strata. All the more urgent then is the need for a comprehensive description that allows as many pertinent questions as possible to be asked in regard to the text and the interpretation of the whole book. This is possible only by a perspective that takes into view the entire tradition. A complete commentary, therefore, happily provides one with a welcome opportunity.

[27] It is certainly not easy to classify in suitable fashion even the monographs on Jeremiah which have appeared during the last twenty years. Still, there appears to be a prevailing tendency to see in the book of Jeremiah evidence of a long process which reached well into the period of the exile. In addition to the already cited works of Thiel and Wanke, one may name E. Janssen, *Juda in der Exilszeit* (FRLANT 69 [1956]); and E. W. Nicholson, *Preaching to the Exiles* (Oxford, 1970). See also the critical overview by R. E. Clements, *Prophecy and Tradition* (Oxford, 1975), especially 41–57.

18

The Background of
Jeremiah's Self-Understanding.
Moses, Samuel, and Psalm 22*
William L. Holladay

The call of the prophet Jeremiah in Jer 1, and his struggles against his call in his "confessions," offer us precious material by which we can enter into the prophet's own self-understanding. This material plainly shows us a very original prophet, and his very originality has tended to inhibit us from asking a prior question: Is it possible to discern any *background* to Jeremiah's self-understanding? Is it possible to discern some of the patterns of thinking upon which he drew in his view of himself?

Jer 15:1 might serve as a symbol of this inquiry. We read, "Then the Lord said to me, 'Though Moses and Samuel stood before me, yet my heart would not turn toward this people. Send them out of my sight, and let them go!'" Here, and only here, Jeremiah mentions earlier prophets by name. It can be shown, I believe, that it was in the light of the figure of Moses that Jeremiah lived out his own ministry, and that the figure of Samuel and the words of Psalm 22 also played a part in his self-understanding.

Let it be said immediately that it is not intended that this single verse be the basis for such a theory. The verse certainly offers its share of critical problems, though the mention of Moses and Samuel does seem to be authentic here to the prophet Jeremiah.[1] Rather, the verse serves to symbolize the heritage of which Jeremiah was conscious in the fulfillment of the demands of his own ministry.

---

*Originally published in the *Journal of Biblical Literature* 83 (1964) 153–164.
[1]J. P. Hyatt says of 15:1–4: "In its present form this passage is from the Deuteronomic editor, whose style and ideas pervade all the verses" (*Int. Bible*, 5, p. 936). Some of the material in these verses is certainly authentic, however. I have argued elsewhere the genuineness of the first three clauses of the poem in vs. 2 (*JBL*, 79 [1960], pp. 361 f.). While it is true that the phrase in vs. 1, "send them out of my sight," does sound suspiciously deuteronomic (cf. the similar phrase in I Kings 9:7, which is a deuteronomic passage), and while vs. 4 also betrays deuteronomic wording, the mention of the two prophets by name in vs. 1 is without parallel elsewhere in the deuteronomic material of Jeremiah, and I see no reason why their mention should be unoriginal to the prophet, even if the format of vs. 1 does betray deuteronomic editing.

There is firm evidence, I believe: parallels of word-association, phraseology, and idea-association in earlier biblical material likely to have been known to Jeremiah, so that we can penetrate the background of his self-understanding with some confidence; and I believe that the definition of this background will lead us to some surprising conclusions.

There are dangers, certainly, in "parallelomania."[2] Likeness of phrasing may not necessarily imply dependence of ideas. Some parallels may simply be common idioms otherwise unknown to us, or in some way commend themselves to two writers independently. At the same time, however, it seems clear that if a given phrase was already in use in specific earlier material which we suspect was known to Jeremiah, then his use of the phrase is likely to betray the bent of his thinking.

In section I we will assemble the parallels, postponing for the moment the task of demonstrating that Jeremiah must have had access to this other material. We will simply see where the parallels are, and then in section II we will deal with the critical problems of the dating and the accessibility of the material to Jeremiah. Finally, in section III we will try to summarize what the evidence can teach us about Jeremiah, and raise some further questions.

I

Let us begin with specific parallels between Jeremiah and Moses material, since it is Moses who seems to have loomed largest in the mind of Jeremiah.

Readers of the OT have long been conscious of the resemblance between the reactions of the two prophets to the call of God: both men wished to refuse the call (Jer 1:6; Exod 4). In the fourth century Ambrose of Milan wrote: "Moses and Jeremiah were called by the Lord to preach God's oracles to the people, as he enabled them by grace to do, but they pled timidity as an excuse."[3] Thus a reference to Moses is a commonplace of commentators in their treatment of Jer 1:6.[4]

---

[2] Samuel Sandmel, in *JBL*, 81 (1962), pp. 1–13.

[3] "Moyses et Hieremias, electi a Domino, ut oracula Dei praedicarent populo, quod poterant per gratiam, excusabant per verecundiam" (*de Off. Min.* 1, 66). We might note the possibility that the association of the two prophets may be even older, for the LXX rendering of Jer 1:6 hints at a recognition of it. The MT of Jer 1:6 begins with the interjection אהה, but the LXX translates here ὁ ὤν. This rendering immediately suggests the reading אהיה, the self-designation of God to Moses in Exod 3:14. Is the Alexandrian exegetical tradition associating Jeremiah's call here with the "I am" revelation to Moses? Note that the LXX rendering is consistent in Jer; ὁ ὤν also appears in 14:13 and 32:17=39:17. For this association of the LXX rendering with Exod 3:14, see P. A. Condamin, *Le Livre de Jérémie*, p. 3, and the literature cited there.

[4] So Wilhelm Rudolph (*HAT*); Artur Weiser (*ATD*).

But the parallelism goes well beyond the obvious similarity of reaction to God's call: there are specific verbal identities or resemblances in the two bodies of material.

First, there is the prophet's reaction to God's call. In Jer 1:6 Jeremiah says: אהה אדני יהוה הנה לא־ידעתי דבר כי־נער אנכי "Ah, Lord God! Behold, I do not know how to speak, for I am only a youth." In Exod 4:10 (JE) Moses says: בי אדני לא איש דברים אנכי "Oh, my Lord, I am not a man of words." Both responses begin with a precative interjection followed by אדני, both have a form of the root דבר preceded by לא, both end with אנכי. The response in Jeremiah nicely parallels that found in Exod 4:10, but employs the verb ידע, the verb which God has used to address him in the previous verse.

In Jer 1:7 we find two pairs of verbs, שלח and הלך ("send," "go") and צוה and דבר ("command," "speak"). The association of "send" and "go" is an obvious one, and is found not only in Exod 3:10–13 ("send" three times, "go" once) but also in the call of Isaiah (6:8, "Whom shall I send, and who will go for us?") and elsewhere.[5] But the pairing of "command" and "speak," at least in the pattern "all that I command you you shall speak," or the like, occurs, as far as I know, in only two other passages: Exod 7:2 (P) "You shall speak all that I command you," addressed to Moses, and Deut 18:18 "and he shall speak to them all that I command him."

This passage in Deut also shares a phraseological parallel with Jer 1:9; the Jer verse reads "Behold, I have put my words in your mouth," and the Deut verse reads "and I will put my words in his mouth." Though the phrase "put (God's) words in the mouth (of a prophet)" is rather common in the OT, the verb usually used is שום (ten times),[6] while the verb in Jer 1:9 is נתן, a verb occurring in this phrase only twice otherwise in the OT: Jer 5:14 (authentic to Jeremiah) and Deut 18:18.

Now Deut 18:18, containing parallels to both Jer 1:7 and 1:9 as it does, merits a closer examination. It forms part of a passage which is an oracle of God to Moses, and reads: "I will raise up for them a prophet like you from among their brethren; and I will put my words in his mouth, and he shall speak to them all that I command him." This verse has often been cited in association with the call of Jeremiah in a consideration of the relation between a prophet and the word of God,[7] but so far as I am aware, the verse has not been considered as a possible *source* for Jeremiah's own phrasing of his call, because of chronological difficulties.[8]

---

[5]E.g., Josh 1:16, where there are the following verbs: שלח, הלך, צוה, עשה.

[6]Exod 4:15, Num 22:38, 23:5 ('word' sg.), 23:12, 16, Deut 31:19, II Sam 14:3, 19, Isa 51:16, 59:21.

[7]E.g., Edmond Jacob, *Theology of the Old Testament*, p. 244; Weiser, *Das Buch des Propheten Jeremia*, p. 7, n. 1.

[8]See *infra* (n. 19 and the preceding paragraph of text).

Now let us turn in another direction. In Jer 1:5 there is the pairing of בטן ("belly"), a *hapax legomenon* in Jeremiah, and רחם ("womb"): "Before I formed you in the belly I knew you, and before you came forth from the womb I consecrated you." The parallelism of these two words, outside the present instance, occurs six times in the OT: four times in material later than Jeremiah,[9] and twice in the Psalms (22:11 and 58:4). Ps 58:4 speaks of the wicked as going astray from their birth and is thus not comparable here; but Ps 22:11 parallels Jeremiah's thought completely. Let us examine vss. 10–11:

> For thou art he who took me from the belly (מבטן),
>> He who made me secure upon the breasts of my mother (אמי).
> Upon thee was I cast (השלכתי) from the womb (מרחם),
>> From the belly (מבטן) of my mother (אמי) thou hast been my God.

Beyond Jeremiah's use of the parallelism of "belly" and "womb" in 1:5, he uses "womb" twice (20:17–18) in the midst of the "confession" in which he most keenly expresses a rejection of his call (vs. 18: "Why did I come forth from the womb to see toil and sorrow?"), an utterance which points directly back to 1:5.

The usage of "my mother," twice in the Psalm passage, is also reflected in Jeremiah. He uses the word three times: twice in the same "confession" (20:14, 17) and once in another "confession" with similar outlook (15:10): "Woe is me, my mother, that you bore me, a man of strife and contention to the whole land." These references to birth and mother are unparalleled in the extant pre-Jeremianic prophetic literature.

But if we consider the possibility that Jeremiah had understood Ps 22:10–11 in the light primarily of Moses, secondarily of Samuel also, then much becomes plain. In both the Moses and Samuel material, prominence is given to the prophet's mother. In both, mention is made of nursing the baby (ינק hiphil, four times in Exod 2:7, 9; once in I Sam 1:23) or of weaning it (גמל, four times in I Sam 1:22–24). The line in Ps 22:10, "He who made me secure upon the breasts of my mother," is peculiarly applicable to Moses, for in the Moses narrative God brought the baby back to its own mother's breast. And, most important, both narratives carry a strong sense of the undergirding protection of God as the child leaves his mother and prepares to serve God as a prophet.

Let us note three more possible parallelisms. The first may bind Moses and Samuel together with Jeremiah: both Moses and Samuel are spoken of as a נער: once in Exod 2:6, of the babe in the bulrushes ("Lo, the babe was crying"), and seven times in I Sam 1–3.[10] The use of this noun in these narratives in speaking of the childhood of the future prophets is a plausible

---

[9]Job 3:11; 10:18 f.; 31:15 (for a dating of Job subsequent to Jeremiah, see S. Terrien in *Int. Bible*, 3, p. 889); Isa 46:3.

[10]1:24; 2:11=18=3:1; 2:21, 26; 3:8.

source for Jeremiah's use of the term in 1:6–7, as if he were saying, "Oh Lord, not yet: I am not yet ready."

The second may bind together the Moses narrative and Ps 22: the verb שלך hophal appears in Ps 22:11, "upon thee *I was cast*," and in the hiphil in Exod 1:22, in which Pharaoh commands his people, "Every son that is born to the Hebrews *you shall cast* into the Nile." It is at least possible that such an association of phrase may have reinforced the association of Moses and Psalm 22 in the mind of Jeremiah.

The third seems to bind together the agony of Jeremiah with Ps 22: in Jer 20:7 we read כלה לעג לי ("everyone mocks me"), while in Ps 22:8 we read כל־ראי ילעגו לי ("all who see me mock at me").

In summary, there are some parallels which are unique, or nearly unique, to the cited material, and there are others which, though by no means unique, do seem to support the identification of this non-Jeremianic material with that of Jeremiah. The material is found on the one hand in the birth narrative of Moses (Exod 1–2, JE), in the birth narrative of Samuel (I Sam 1–3), in the call of Moses (Exod 3–4, JE; and 7, P) in a deuteronomic promise of God to Moses to raise up a prophet like himself (Deut 18:18), and in Psalm 22; and on the other hand in the call of Jeremiah (1:4–10) and in two "confessions" of Jeremiah which question the validity of his call (in 15 and 20).

II

The first critical problem before us is to inquire as to the authenticity of the call of Jeremiah. There are several possibilities: (1) The material in 1:4–10 might be Jeremiah's own verbalization of his call at the time of his response to God in his youth, as the passage itself seems to imply; (2) it might be authentic to Jeremiah but verbalized later in his ministry; (3) it might have been formulated by an editor like Baruch. It is also possible that the call is best explained as some combination of these: an early formulation by Jeremiah of his call, enlarged upon by him later; or a formulation by Jeremiah of his call, enlarged upon by an editor.

The critics in general assume the authenticity of the passage. The critic who is most zealous in cutting out so-called "unauthentic additions" is Giesebrecht, who has a theory of meter which is too strict for the type of material in this passage.[11] It is generally agreed that the two middle verbs of the sextet in vs. 10 are unoriginal[12] but that the passage otherwise stands.[13]

James Muilenburg suggests possibility (2): "The report of the call may well come from a later period in his life; like Isaiah's vision, it reflects, not

---

[11]*HKAT.*

[12]See Volz (*KAT*), Rudolph, Weiser, and my discussion of the problem in *JBL*, 79 (1960), p. 363 f.

[13]Volz omits מפניהם and נאם יהוה in vs. 8, but this would in no way threaten the conclusions reached in the present study.

only a profound awareness of the significance of his mission, but also a realization that he is called to prophesy to the nations."[14] One might add that the verbs "build and plant" in vs. 10 might also suggest a later "edition" of the call, when Jeremiah saw his task both before and after the fall of Jerusalem more clearly.

We can reject immediately possibility (3) above. The compactness, symmetry, and assonance of the poetry in vs. 5, the neat chiasmus and assonance of the original quartet of verbs in vs. 10, give all the marks of the master. There is likewise no good reason to suggest that any earlier form of the call, verbalized by the prophet, was supplemented by an editor to any crucial degree.

Possibility (2) is more plausible. It would not speak against the conclusion reached in this study except in the matter of Deut 18:18, for the other material which has been cited as parallel to Jeremiah's own words was presumably as available to him at the beginning as at a later moment of his ministry. But the matter of Deut 18:18 is crucial, and we must be prepared to understand the call as verbalized at a later point in Jeremiah's ministry in the light of the publishing of Deuteronomy. We will discuss this matter in a moment.

Now let us turn to the problem of the availability to Jeremiah of the parallel material. There is no reason for us to question the fact that the birth narratives of Moses and of Samuel were known to Jeremiah. Exod 1–2 is part of JE. Whether the material on the birth of Samuel in I Sam 1–3 (excepting the Song of Hannah, 2:1–10, which is not under discussion) is assigned to the so-called "late source,"[15] to "E,"[16] or simply to a "prophetic reworking of the history and its traditions" about Samuel,[17] it seems plain that the material concerning Samuel's birth was gathered prior to the historical work of the deuteronomists, and therefore well within the reach of the young Jeremiah.

Likewise the material concerning Moses' call: Exod 3–4 is JE, and if we deny the availability of Exod 7:2 (P) to Jeremiah, our conclusions will not be altered. The crucial questions then center around Ps 22 and Deut 18:18; were these known to Jeremiah, either at the beginning of his ministry or at a later moment of his life?

As to Ps 22, there would seem to be four possibilities: (1) that the psalm is quite unrelated to Jeremiah; (2) that he wrote Ps 22; (3) that the psalm is earlier than Jeremiah and influenced him; or (4) that the psalm is later than Jeremiah, the psalmist drawing on Jeremiah's experience in his phraseology.

---

[14]*Int. Dict. of the Bible*, 2, p. 825.

[15]So most commentators; cf. R. Pfeiffer, *Intro. to the O. T.*, p. 360.

[16]So O. Eissfeldt, *Einl. in das A. T.*[2], p. 328, by implication; and explicitly, S. Szikszai, in *Int. Dict. of the Bible*, 4, p. 206.

[17]Weiser, *The O. T.: Its Formation and Development*, p. 166.

Possibility (1) would seem to be ruled out completely; the resemblances are too close not only in situation but in wording and thought pattern (the polarity between mother and God). Possibility (2) is also out of the question. In the two bodies of material the "fathers" play a different rôle: in Ps 22:5–6 the fathers cried to Yahweh, while in Jeremiah's oracles (2:5; 14:20) the fathers have forgotten Yahweh. Furthermore, the psalm implies approval of temple worship; vs. 4 points in this direction, whether the difficult MT reading or the easier LXX reading is followed. Jeremiah's interests certainly lay in another direction than the cult. Possibility (4) is barely possible, though unlikely. That a psalmist would be sensitive enough to the agony which Jeremiah endured to reflect his words of desolation in a psalm while at the same time maintaining a conventional theology of history and a positive attitude toward the temple would seem unlikely.

There remains to us then alternative (3): that Jeremiah knew Ps 22 and used its phraseology as a clue to his own understanding of his situation. (This conclusion incidentally offers us a *terminus ad quem* for the psalm.)

Now what can be said in regard to Deut 18:18? Vss. 15–22 purport to be part of legislation by Moses for the institution of the prophet. As is well known, there is no parallel to this material in the other legal codes of the Pentateuch, and we may see it as a free composition in the light of the experience of Israel with the prophets. Though seeming to form part of Ur-Deuteronomium, it is quite conceivable that it forms an insertion into it.[18] Indeed we are faced with an array of possibilities identical to those we examined in regard to Ps 22: (1) that the Deuteronomy passage is unconnected in any way with Jeremiah; (2) that Jeremiah wrote the passage; (3) that Jeremiah was in some way influenced by the passage; or (4) that the passage is post-Jeremianic.

Again we must reject (1) and (2). The material is somehow related to the present form of the call of Jeremiah, but there is no indication that Jeremiah ever had anything to do with the compilation of Deuteronomy. As to possibility (4), it is of course possible that a prophetic passage, shaped by the influence of Jeremiah, was inserted into the deuteronomic material after the ministry of the prophet; but against this notion is the fact that the temple sermon would hardly have rendered Jeremiah a model to the deuteronomic school, and the fact that the passage is part of a section containing similar legislative material on the judges, kings, and priests (Deut 16:18 ff.), material which gives no indication of composition later than the remainder of Ur-Deuteronomium.

We are left, then, with the conclusion that Jeremiah knew Deut 18:18 and was influenced by it in the verbalization of his call. Since the traditional date for his call 626 (Jer 1:2), and since the publishing of Ur-Deuteronomium was five years later (II Kings 22:3), we are led to one of three conclusions: (1) that the date of Jeremiah's call in 1:2 is in error;

---

[18]So Eissfeldt, *op. cit.*, p. 269.

(2) that the date of the call is correct but the verbalization of the call was formulated later in the light of Deut 18:18; or (3) that the date in Jer 1:2 is the date of Jeremiah's *birth*, understood to be the date of the "true call."

Alternative (1) would seem to be only a last resort, although the suggestion has indeed been made.[19] But there is no other hint in our material either that an editor assigned an erroneous date to the call, or that our text needs emendation, and we should exhaust all other possibilities before we accept this alternative.

Now let us consider possibility (2), that the present form of Jeremiah's call represents his mature thinking at a later stage of his ministry, and let us see if we can work out a plausible hypothesis. Vss. 5–6, with the tight poem of the call of God, and Jeremiah's objection because of his youth, would seem inevitably a part of the original call. The disillusioned words of Jer 15 and 20 in the "confessions," which echo 1:5, make little sense unless they are a mocking reflection on the early promise of God. We might follow Giesebrecht and end the original form of vs. 7 with "I am only a youth"; it is conceivable, then, that the original form of God's reply to Jeremiah's demurrer, verbalized in his youth, contained the following portions of vss. 7–9: "Do not say, 'I am only a youth': be not afraid of them, for I am with you to deliver you, says the LORD. Then the Lord put forth his hand and touched my mouth." We could then theorize that the remaining material in vss. 7 and 9 was added later under the influence of Deut 18:18, and that vs. 10 represents a later word from God on the total task of the prophet, both to Israel and to the nations, both before the fall of Jerusalem and after it.

But alternative (3) has real plausibility, and it has the merit of saving the unity of 1:4–10. According to this alternative, Jeremiah would have been born in 626; and at a time in his youth (let us say at the time of the death of Josiah in 609, when Jeremiah would have been seventeen years old) would have become conscious of the call from God and responded to it. Jeremiah would then always have insisted that God had called him from his birth (626), but he would have verbalized his conscious awareness of God's call in words which were shaped in part by the prophet passage in Deuteronomy.

This revision of the chronology of Jeremiah has already been suggested by Hyatt[20] on other grounds: namely, that there are no oracles of Jeremiah which can be dated safely to the reign of Josiah. According to Hyatt, this dating banishes the Scythians forever as candidates for the identity of the "foe from the north," and these oracles can now be understood as applying to the Babylonians. If our alternative (3) is correct, then, we have uncovered new and independent evidence for this chronological revision of Hyatt's.

---

[19]T. C. Gordon and Hans Bardtke, cited by Hyatt in *Int. Bible*, 5, p. 797, propose that "thirteenth" in 1:2 is an error for "twenty-third"; on this hypothesis Jeremiah's call would, of course, fall in 616.

[20]*Int. Bible*, 5, p. 779.

And while a decision between alternatives (2) and (3) must fall short of certainty, (3) is here commended as offering a self-consistent and convincing reconstruction of Jeremiah's self-understanding.

III

Here, then, is such a reconstruction, a reasonable framework for the data we have isolated.

Jeremiah would have been born in 626 and have been five years old at the time of Josiah's reform. This reform reawakened the nation to the importance of Moses, to the covenant of Sinai, and to the response in Torah which God expected. The Passover was reinstituted after having been neglected for so long, and worship was reorganized and centralized in Jerusalem. In all this flurry of reform the figure of Moses loomed forth as the great mediator between God and Israel, and Moses would have been very much in the mind of the boy Jeremiah.

As interest in the reform died down, Jeremiah would have been keenly struck by the promise given to Moses that a new prophet, like Moses, would be called by God from among the Israelites (Deut 18:18), and the notion would have crossed his mind that the one whom God had intended might well be he. What would the fortune of this new prophet be, in such an age? Jeremiah would know the stories of Moses and Samuel, of their birth and childhood, and how God had shielded them from harm because of the great tasks to which he was calling them. But what would the fortune of this new prophet be? Some verses from Ps 22 would have stuck in his mind, verses which describe the way the future man of God is cast from his mother's arms into the care of God just as Moses and Samuel had been. But this psalm, most alarmingly, also describes the way enemies rise up to pursue and to persecute the man of God. Would this be the fortune of the prophet?

Then, when Jeremiah would have been seventeen years old, when Josiah was killed, hope for Israel's faithfulness to Yahweh diminished alarmingly. A deep void was left (not unlike the void left after the death of Uzziah which had stimulated Isaiah's experience of call). Jehoahaz was allowed to reign only a short time, and Jehoiakim, a protégé of Egypt, was certainly no devotee of Moses. Since the word of Moses in Deuteronomy was no longer a novelty to the nation, who could step forth as speaker of God's word to his people?

Jeremiah's mind would have crystallized in the conviction that the promised prophet was indeed he, frightened though he was both because of his youth and because of his uneasiness that enemies would pursue him. His very hesitation, however, would have reinforced in him the conviction that he was God's prophet, for had not Moses also begged off, feeling himself unsuitable for God's purposes?

But (as with Moses) God overruled Jeremiah, and specifically reassured him as to the protection he would have from his enemies. So Jeremiah said yes to God, overcome by the wonder of God's providence in having set him apart from his very birth, even as Moses and Samuel had been, and overcome also by uneasiness at the life that lay before him.

This, then, seems (to the present writer at least) to be the background of Jeremiah's self-understanding as he consciously responded to the call from God. And the doubt and bitterness which he felt in later years as enemies did rise up to pursue him were expressed in terms which recalled the words of the suffering psalmist, and the words of his own call.

If the conclusions reached here are sound, several other considerations come to mind regarding Jeremiah's message and ministry:

(1) The new chronology for Jeremiah's career should help clear the way to a solution of the vexed problem of his attitude toward the deuteronomic reform, and of the meaning and reliability of Jer 11:1–14. It is not intended that we should reach any definitive conclusions on these matters here, but the following observations seem plain: by the time Jeremiah was preaching, the external reforms were secure, while inner zeal for moral purity had lapsed; Jeremiah did not look upon the reform as a new thing, but as a re-establishment of the word of God to Moses; the phraseology of 11:1–14, though that of the prose editor, is not more so than that of the temple sermon, and the passage is therefore likely to preserve an accurate historical memory; and therefore the passage is likely to reflect Jeremiah's eagerness that the people continue to adhere to the terms of the Sinai covenant as understood in his age (and including the spirit of the reform of Josiah). Volz' conclusion, that Jeremiah asked for public rededication to "the covenant" (the only one there was, in his mind, at the beginning of the reign of Jehoiakim), may well be correct.[21]

(2) It is at least possible that Jeremiah's mention of the shrine at Shiloh (he is the only prophet to mention this shrine) in his temple sermon (7:12; 26:6) was in part stimulated by his interest in Samuel, who served God there. Jeremiah's reappropriation of the Samuel story would encourage his pondering the fate of the shrine where his predecessor had ministered.

(3) Jeremiah's "confessions" are unprecedented among the writings of the prophets. May we see Jeremiah's freedom in "talking back" to God as derivable in part from the freedom which the narrative portrays Moses as having had in speaking with God? Compare Exod 32:11 (JE): "But Moses entreated the Lord his God"; and Num 11:11 (JE): "Moses said to the Lord, 'Why hast thou dealt ill with thy servant? And why have I not found favor in thy sight, that thou dost lay the burden of this people upon me?'" This is precisely the same tone which Jeremiah manifests in his "confessions."

(4) This leads us to re-examine the intercessory rôle of Jeremiah. Moses and Samuel were great intercessors before God (Exod 32; Num 14:13–25; I Sam 7:5–11, 12:19), and this is of course why they are referred to by name in Jer 15:1. And although Amos also interceded for the nation

---

[21]Volz, p. 131.

(Amos 7:1–6), Jeremiah in particular seems to have felt moved to intercede more than once for the nation (8:23 by implication; 10:24 LXX;[22] 15:11;[23] 17:16; 18:20). The prose editor of Jeremiah insists that God specifically forbade Jeremiah to pray for the nation (7:16; 11:14), and this seems to be an authentic tradition (thus 15:1). It is unlikely that so much would have been made of Jeremiah's intercessions, and God's final refusal to hear them, if the figure of Moses had not reinforced this rôle in Jeremiah's mind.

(5) Finally we must consider the idea of the new covenant (31:31–34), an idea that is unprecedented, and authentic to Jeremiah, even though the passage in which it appears comes from the prose editor. Jeremiah taught that the old covenant which God had made at the time of the exodus from Egypt had been broken so completely by the people that God had no choice but to draw up a new covenant without the loopholes of the old. May it not be that it was Jeremiah's understanding of himself as the prophet like Moses which led him to the formulation of the new covenant idea? Moses had led the Israelites to God's first covenant, and thereby obedience to him and his gift to them of the land became correlates. But now in the eyes of Jeremiah the people had disobeyed, and the land was no longer theirs; and so, as the new Moses in the face of the new wilderness into which the people had been sent, Jeremiah dared to look forward to the time when God would draw up a new covenant, thereby to fulfill his ultimate purposes for his people. We may note here that Jer 31:2–6 is a genuine oracle of restoration from Jeremiah[24] and is a good poetic analogue to the new covenant passage. It is also saturated with imagery drawn from the exodus from Egypt. "Found favor in the wilderness" (vs. 2) reminds one of the intercession of Moses in Exod 33:12–17 (JE); the parallelism of "timbrels" and "dance" (vs. 4) reminds one of the introduction to the Song of Miriam in Exod 15:20.[25] The conclusion seems clear that Jeremiah dared to announce a new covenant for the people of God because of the work of Moses before him. The parallel is not perfect, of course, because Jeremiah did not see himself as the intermediary for the new covenant itself: that would be left for another to accomplish, when the punishment of God would be completed and the land could be repossessed again (Jer 31:27–30).

If our understanding of the evidence is sound, Jeremiah gives us an insight into the rôle Moses played in sensitive religious thinking of the late seventh century: uppermost in Jeremiah's mind was Moses' function as

---

[22]So Rudolph; Weiser, *Jer.*

[23]Cf. Hyatt, *Int. Bible, ad loc.*; Rudolph; Weiser, *Jer.*

[24]Note, for example, the coupling of the qal and niphal in vs. 4, a "signature" of Jeremiah's; cf. *JBL*, 81 (1962), p. 46.

[25]Besides these two passages, the words "timbrels" and "dance" are linked in four other passages in the OT: Judg 11:34 (Jephthah, the two words alone); I Sam 18:6 (David, in an extended phrase); and with other nouns in Pss 149:3 and 150:4.

prophet. (So it had been for Hosea before him; cf. Hos 12:14.) In Jeremiah's mind, the law of Moses was the vehicle for the intercourse between God and Israel, a vehicle which in Jeremiah's eyes had proved unavailing even in the flurry of reform under Josiah. In Jeremiah's eyes Moses was the prophet *par excellence*; and just as the deuteronomists would see Moses' rôle as one of bearing vicariously the sin of the people (Deut 1:37; 3:23–29, though the wording of these passages may not have been known to Jeremiah), so it was Jeremiah's fate to learn the lesson of innocent suffering (as Ps 22 set it forth for him) and to glimpse the renewal of the promised land only from afar, even as Moses himself was denied the chance to cross the Jordan.

19

A Prophet's Lament and
Its Answer: Jeremiah 15:10–21
John Bright

In an issue devoted to the psalms of lament it is appropriate that an article should be given to one of the so-called "confessions" of Jeremiah.* These little pieces have no parallel in any other prophetic book. In them the prophet speaks in his own name rather than God's and gives vent to his anguish, lamenting the abuse the prophetic office has brought him, bitterly cursing his enemies and crying out for his own vindication, and even accusing his God of having deceived him and failed him. Similarities between these complaints and the laments in the Psalter have been recognized for generations.[1] Both employ much of the same vocabulary and many of the same locutions; at times verbal parallels may be observed (cf., for example, Jer. 20:10 and Ps. 31:13). In an earlier day, when most of the psalms were assigned by critics to the post-exilic period, it was widely believed that Jeremiah's complaints had served as models for psalms of similar character.[2] But today, with the recognition that the psalm types had a long history behind them, and that many of the psalms are far older than Jeremiah's day, it has become the generally accepted opinion that Jeremiah composed in the form of the psalm of lament and that his "confessions" represent an adaptation by the prophet of that form.

This fact gives us a distinct advantage. In the laments of the Psalter the supplicant is, one might say, well-nigh faceless. Clearly he is in serious distress; but so lacking are these psalms for the most part in concrete details, and so filled with what appear to be stereotyped locutions, that it is seldom possible to say with assurance just who the supplicant is, or to determine the precise nature of the troubles that prompted his lament. All is different in the case of the "confessions" of Jeremiah. Here we know exactly who the complainant was.[3] We know—and sometimes by name—

---

*Originally published in *Interpretation* 28 (1974) 59–74.

[1]We cannot attempt to review the history of the discussion here. The basic treatment remains that of W. Baumgartner, *Die Klagegedichte des Jeremia* (BZAW 32, 1917).

[2]For a recent expression of a similar view, cf. P. E. Bonnard, *Le Psautier selon Jérémie* (Paris, Éditions du Cerf, 1960).

[3]It is assumed here, with the overwhelming majority of scholars, that the "confessions" are actual utterances of Jeremiah. Recently E. Gerstenberger, "Jeremiah's Complaints: Observa-

who his persecutors were, and we know why they persecuted him. And we know—thanks especially to the biographical portions of the book—some of the forms that that persecution took. True, we have no evidence for connecting any one of Jeremiah's laments with any one of the many occasions on which he was persecuted.[4] But the fact that we know both the identity of the sufferer and, at least in a general way, the cause and the nature of his sufferings lends to Jeremiah's laments a concreteness such as we seldom find in the laments of the Psalter.

Jeremiah in fact endured life-long persecution, and it fell upon him because of the word he was commissioned to proclaim. When he declared that God would destroy his temple (7:1–15; cf. chap. 26), he was set upon by a mob and narrowly escaped being put to death; when he announced the destruction of the city he was seized by a temple officer (and we know his name), beaten, and put in the stocks overnight (19:14–20:6). He dictated a scroll containing certain of his prophecies which his friend Baruch read publically in the temple; when it was brought to King Jehoiakim's attention, the king destroyed it and sought to have Jeremiah and Baruch arrested, undoubtedly with the intention of executing them (chap. 36). While Jerusalem was under attack by the Babylonians, Jeremiah was arrested on charges of treason (chaps. 37f.), hauled before a panel of nobles (whose names are given; 38:1), beaten, placed and left to die in a waterless cistern with deep mud at the bottom. And aside from such instances of physical abuse, there is abundant evidence that Jeremiah was widely hated, cursed, jeered at, ostracized, plotted against, and that his word was rejected and even flatly contradicted by prophets who opposed him.

Let it be repeated that none of Jeremiah's laments can be related to any one of the above incidents. But they may with confidence be regarded as expressing his reaction to persecution of this sort.[5] Though the fact that these pieces employ a conventional form, and conventional locutions, warns us against too hastily extracting psychological and biographical details from them, they present us with the picture of the prophet, abused

---

tions on Jer. 15:10–21," JBL, 82:393–408 (1963), has argued that this one "confession," at least, represents theological reflection on the part of exilic Deuteronomists. I do not find his arguments convincing.

[4] The laments in 11:18–12:6 are related to a plot on Jeremiah's life in which members of his own family were implicated. But we cannot say just when in the prophet's career this incident took place.

[5] The attempt of H. Graf Reventlow, *Liturgie und prophetisches Ich bei Jeremia* (Gütersloh, Gütersloher Verlagshaus Gerd Mohn, 1963), to interpret these laments corporately, and to see in them the prophet as he discharged an official function as cultic mediator for the people, cannot be regarded as successful. Cf. J. Bright, "Jeremiah's Complaints: Liturgy or Expressions of Personal Distress?" in J. I. Durham and J. R. Porter eds., *Proclamation and Presence; Old Testament Essays in Honour of Gwynne Henton Davies* (London, SCM Press; Richmond, John Knox Press, 1970), pp. 189–214; in greater detail, but reaching similar conclusions, J. M. Berridge, *Prophet, People, and the Word of Yahweh* (Zürich, EVZ-Verlag, 1970).

and in despair, as he laments his plight and lays his complaints before his God.

I

But let us turn to the passage that we have chosen, Jeremiah 15:10–21. The lament itself is found in verses 10–18. In common with perhaps the majority of commentators (and cf. NEB) we take verses 13f. to be an intrusion from another context. The verses are a damaged variant of 17:3f., where they seem to be in place, and they interrupt the "autobiographical" style of address of the lament (in verses 13f. Yahweh, not Jeremiah, is the speaker).[6] Verse 12 is likewise a problem. Most commentators confess to a certain unease (an unease which I certainly share) in trying to explain what it is supposed to mean in the context.[7] Whether or not the verse is to be regarded as a corruption of 17:1 is uncertain;[8] but it fits awkwardly where it is, seems textually corrupt, and is probably best taken as an intrusion like the two verses that follow it. In any event, it will be noted that verse 15 follows upon verse 11 splendidly.

We take it, then, that the lament consists of verses 10, 11, 15–18. It may be translated as follows:

10. Ah me, my mother, that you bore me
    [a]to accuse and indict the whole land![a]
    Neither lent I, nor loan received,
    [b]yet all of them curse me.[b]
11. [a]But I swear,[a] Yahweh, [b]for their good I have served you,[b]
    and with you [c]for the foe[c] interceded,
    in the time of his[d] trouble and woe.
    [e]Ah, but you know![e]
15. Remember me, Yahweh! Take note of me!
    [a]Avenge me[a] of those that harrass me!
    Do not through your patience[b] destroy me[b]!
    Consider! It's for your sake I suffer abuse.
16. [a]There were your words,[a] and I ate them;
    [b]and it was[b] my joy, my heart's delight,
    [c]that you claimed me as your own,[c]
    O Yahweh, God of Hosts.

[6] How these verses came to be intruded here is a question that is not without interest. But it is a question to which I can myself give no answer that I find satisfying; in view of the textual corruption in vs. 11–14 any answer must remain conjectural.

[7] Volz (KAT), pp. 171f. followed by Weiser (ATD), p. 136 reading $h^a r\bar{e}^c \bar{o}t\bar{\imath}$ for $h^a y\bar{a}r\bar{o}^{ca}$ and omitting "iron from the north," links the verse to the foregoing; he takes "I have broken iron and bronze" as Jeremiah's assertion that he has exerted every conceivable effort in behalf of the foe in his distress. But even if the emendation be accepted, the figure is somewhat forced, and, so far as I know, without parallel.

[8] So Rudolph (HAT), p. 90.

17. ^aNot for me to sit with the crowd,
    laughing and happy.^a
    ^bGripped by your hand^b I sat all alone,
    for with rage you did fill me.
18. O why is my pain without end,
    My wound ever worse, defying all cure?
    ^ayou are indeed^a a dry brook to me,
    whose waters have failed.

v. 10   a-a Lit., "a man of legal strife and (a man of) legal contention to the whole land."
      b-b Add *kî* (lost by haplography), redivide consonants and point *kull^ehem qil^elûnî*
      (cf. BHS).

v. 11   a-a Lit., "So be it (reading *'āmēn* with LXX), Yahweh, if I have not—" Jeremiah
      responds to curses with what amounts to an oath: let the curses take effect if he has not
      acted with integrity (which he swears that he has).
      b-b Pointing the verb as *šērattîkā* (cf. BHS). "For their good" is literally "for good,"
      which could have the force of "well" or "with good intent."
      c-c Transposing "the foe" from the end of the verse and reading before it *'el* or *l^e* (cf.
      LXX) in place of the sign of the accusative (cf. BHS).
      d Supply "his" following LXX.
      e-e The colon begins v. 15 in MT; LXX omits it.

v. 15   a-a More literally, "Avenge yourself for me—." But perhaps the verb *nqm* has rather
      the force of "get vindication," "obtain redress"; cf. G. E. Mendenhall, "The 'Vengeance'
      of Yahweh" (*The Tenth Generation* [Baltimore: The Johns Hopkins University Press,
      1973], pp. 69–104).
      b-b Lit., "take me away."

v. 16   a-a Lit., "Your words were found"; cf. the same verb in 2:34; 5:26.
      b-b Heb. "and your word (so Qre, MSS, Vrs; Ktib, "your words") was—." But perhaps
      it is better to omit "your word(s)" as a dittography from the preceding colon (Duhm,
      Giesebrecht).
      c-c Lit., "that your name was called over me."

v. 17   a-a Lit., "I did not sit in the company of merrymakers and (did not) rejoice."
      b-b Lit., "Because of your hand."

v. 18   a-a Taking *hāyô* as the infinitive absolute of the verb *hyh* (cf. LXX). The force of
      Jeremiah's accusation should not be weakened by emending the word to the inter-
      rogative particle (so RSV), or to *hôi* (So BHS).

    In spite of its textual difficulties the passage requires little explanation
in detail. Though it follows the form of a psalm of lament, it begins (v. 10a)
in a way no lament in the Psalter does, or could. These normally open with
an appeal to God for aid. Here the prophet apostrophizes his (presumably)
long-dead mother and cries, in effect, "O mother, why did you bring me
into the world?" Even allowing for the fact that in times of emotional stress
men will frequently exaggerate their feelings of frustration and despair, it is
clear that Jeremiah experienced moments when he found life more than he
could endure and wished that he had never been born (cf. 20:14–18). And
why was this so? No one who has read the accounts of the abuse that was
heaped upon him would have trouble divining the answer. He felt that he

had been condemned by his very birth to be like one who is perpetually at law with his people ("a man of legal strife and contention"), always accusing them, indicting them. He had felt himself predestined to the prophetic office even before he was born and, try as he did, he could not evade that office (1:4–10); and it was the faithful discharge of it that had earned him the enmity of all.

But Jeremiah protests his innocence (as the supplicant in the psalms of lament so often does): He has done nothing to deserve this (v. 10b). He has harmed nobody. He has been neither a foreclosing creditor nor a defaulting debtor (probably a proverbial saying, and certainly true to life, for few are more likely to earn the hatred of those with whom they have to deal than are these). Not only is he innocent of any wrong-doing; he vehemently declares (v. 11) that he has actively labored for the welfare of those who hate him, nay has interceded for them before God in their time of need. One is reminded of the words of Psalm 35:12–14. But the language here is no mere conventional formula, for we have ample evidence that Jeremiah did intercede for his people, and repeatedly (cf. 7:16; 11:14; 14:11–13; 18:20; 42:2–4). And what thanks did he get? Curses! But Jeremiah does not have to inform God of this, as though it were something he did not know; God is well aware that it is so ("Ah, but you know!" cf. Pss. 40:9; 69:19).

So Jeremiah must throw his case before the all-knowing God and appeal for redress (v. 15). It seems to him that God has forgotten him. "Remember me," he cries (cf. Pss. 74:2, 18, 22; 89:47, 50), "Take note of me!" The urgency of the appeal heightens. However much, and however earnestly, Jeremiah may have interceded for his persecutors, any thought of love toward the enemy vanishes. Let God take vengeance (or: get redress, vindication) for him—and for himself too ("avenge yourself for me"), for his own honor and justice are at stake, since it is his word that has been spurned. Let him destroy those who persecute his prophet, and let him do it quickly, for if God delays too long in punishing these villains, he, Jeremiah, is certain to lose his life ("Do not through your patience destroy me"). What is more, God owes him this. At his call (1:8, 17–19) had not God promised him that he would always be with him to come to his rescue? And has he not suffered all this abuse precisely in God's service ("for your sake") as he spoke the word that God had given him?

Jeremiah then goes on to protest that he has been completely faithful in the discharge of his calling (v. 16). God's words had come to him from the outside as something external to him, and he had taken them into himself; he "ate" them, as Ezekiel in some kind of visionary experience ate the scroll containing the words he was to proclaim (Ezek. 2:8–3:3). Moreover, it was to him a source of "joy," his "heart's delight," that God had "claimed" him as his own. The expression (lit. "your name was called over me") has a legal background, and means "to lay (legal) claim to something, to claim something or someone as one's property" (e.g., II Sam. 12:28; Isa. 4:1). In the Jeremiah book it is frequently applied to the temple to describe it as God's own special possession (7:10f., 14, 30; 32:34; 34:15).[9] Just as God claims ownership of the house where he dwells, and where men praise him, so, Jeremiah declares, God has claimed him as a special possession; and the knowledge that this was so brought him great happiness. This, incidentally, is the only place where Jeremiah allows us to see that he found any joy in his calling whatever. Yet he declares that it was so: he was happy to know that he was God's man.

But then (v. 17) the lament takes on a heightened intensity and vehemence. What has the prophetic office *not* cost him. It has brought him not only physical abuse, but bitter loneliness, indeed ostracism; he feels cut off from his fellowman. Jeremiah was in fact condemned from the outset to a life of loneliness. At God's command he had never married (16:1–4); and this had denied him the companionship and support of wife and family. And now the word he had been commmissioned to proclaim had made him so unpopular that men wished to have nothing to do with him; they shunned him, avoided him. But there was more to it than that. The word he must proclaim was such a terrible word that it robbed life of all joy; he simply could not take part in the normal, innocent pleasures that people enjoy—or in their occassions of sorrow either, for that matter (16:5–9). The "hand" of God (i.e., the compulsion of the divine power; Isa. 8:11; Ezek. 1:3; 3:14f., 22) was on him; he is filled with the divine wrath which he must pour out on his people (cf. 6:11). And it was this that made happiness, and a normal life, impossible for him. It was, in the final analysis, God who had put him in this predicament!

And he can no longer endure it (v. 18a)! He feels like a man in constant pain, suffering from an incurable wound (cf. 10:19; Pss. 38:5–8; 42:10). Is this to go on forever? Will it never end? He sees no hope; nothing helps. And (v. 18b) he finds no help in God! This is the climax. Here Jeremiah's complaint goes far beyond the bounds of a conventional lament and becomes a flat accusation directed at God. Jeremiah declares (and he does so with great emphasis; see textual notes) that God had been to him like a brook to which the thirsty traveler comes in search of life-giving water, only to find that it has run dry. This is all the more shocking when we recall that Jeremiah had once hailed his God as "the fountain of living water" (2:13) and had contrasted him with the false gods, who are like "cracked cisterns" that leak and allow the water to seep away. But now, in his despair, it seemed to him that his God was no better than they, for he too gives no help whatever when it is most needed. If Jeremiah had said in so many words, "God, you have failed me," he could have said no more. And on that note the lament ends.

---

[9]It is also used once of Jerusalem (25:29); and once (14:9), in a prayer, the people use it of themselves, claiming to be God's very own.

II

We have focused so far upon the lament in Jeremiah 15:10–18. But this lament should not be studied in isolation, for it is typical of various pieces of similar character which one finds in the Jeremiah book. Properly to appreciate Jeremiah's anguish and bitterness, his moments of despair, and the manner in which he felt free to address his God, the reader should examine them all. The most important are the following; we can do no more than summarize them here.

In 12:1–6 Jeremiah questions the justice of God.[10] Not only do wicked men prosper (as, of course, they should not), but it seems that God actually assists them in this. Outraged, Jeremiah calls on God to punish them, dragging them off "like sheep for the slaughter." He then receives an answering word from God telling him that he may expect worse injustice: members of his own family are plotting against his life. In 11:18–23 Jeremiah, having been appraised of a plot against him (presumably this very same one), cries out that he had been as unsuspecting as "an innocent lamb led to the slaughter" and once again demands vengeance. He receives a word from God telling him that the men of Anathoth will be destroyed without remnant. In 17:14–18 Jeremiah again cries out to God for aid. He has been mocked because his dire predictions had not come to pass. He protests that he had never wanted to make such predictions nor had he wished disaster to come—and God knows it very well. He then calls upon God to punish his tormentors, crying, "Smash them, then smash them again!" (literally, "With a double breaking break them"). Again, in 18:18–23 we learn that plots have been made against Jeremiah because of his preaching. Jeremiah indignantly calls on God to hear his case. He has been repaid evil for good, for, as God knows, he had frequently made intercession for the very men who would destroy him. He then calls down upon them a bloodcurdling curse concluding with words that sound like a parody of the words of our Lord spoken on the cross ("Father, forgive them—"): "Forgive not their crime, nor blot out their sin from your sight—Deal with them while you are angry." Then in 20:7–13 Jeremiah accuses God of having "seduced"[11] him in forcing him into the prophetic office. He has been the butt of jokes because of the word he has spoken, and plots have

---

[10]The first line of 12:1 should be read, "You are in the right (*ṣaddîq*), O Yahweh, whenever I lodge complaint (*rîb*) with you," or the like. In my Anchor Bible volume (New York, Doubleday, 1965, p. 83) I translated the final colon as, "Yet there are cases of which I would ask you." I am now inclined to believe that W. L. Holladay (JBL 81 [1962], pp. 49–51; *Interpretation* 17 [1963], pp. 280f.) is correct in reading, "Yet I would pass judgment on you." The locution employed has this force in each of its other occurrences (1:16; 4:12; 39:5; 52:9).

[11]Cf. v. 7. The word has this force in Exod. 22:16 (cf. Judg. 16:5) and probably does so here.

been made against his life. But when he resolved to speak in God's name no more, he found that he could not; the word was like a fire inside of him, and he could not hold it in, try as he might. This "confession," incidentally, unlike any of the others, ends on a note of confident trust, thanksgiving and praise, as the laments of the Psalter so frequently do. But it is followed in 20:14–18 by the most moving, and the most abject, of all. Here is nothing but the blackest despair, unrelieved by any ray of light. Cursing the day of his birth, and the miserable existence it had initiated for him, the prophet laments that he had ever been born.

The initial reaction of the sensitive reader to pieces of this kind might well be to regret that the prophet permitted himself to speak in this way, and to wonder why such words were preserved in his book. No other prophetic book contains anything comparable, as we have said. Others of the prophets to our knowledge suffered abuse and the rejection of their word, and we may take it that they were human beings with normal human sensitivities; but if any of them reacted with such outbursts of anger and despair no record of it has survived. Were they made of sterner stuff than he? Or did they in fact permit themselves similar outbursts, and did those who collected their sayings charitably suppress them? We do not know. We only know that laments and complaints of this sort are remembered only of Jeremiah. To be sure, one might agree that Jeremiah had ample reason to complain, perhaps more than any other one of the prophets. Only a saint or a man of steel could have endured what he was forced to endure with equanimity. Still, understandable though they may be under the circumstances, these expressions of anger and despair, and these accusations of God, can scarcely be said to reflect great credit on the prophet. Why were they preserved? Why were they included in his book? What function were they intended to serve?

These are interesting questions, and important ones. But we must begin—and end—by confessing that we cannot be sure of the answers. Too much is unknown. Not only do we not know the precise circumstances under which the "confessions" were first uttered; we cannot trace the process by which they were preserved and handed down, nor can we do more than guess the motives that caused Jeremiah's disciples to preserve them. Above all, we lack the omniscience to read the minds of those anonymous collectors who gathered them into the book and placed them where they are.

But one suspects that, in the final analysis, these pieces were included in the book because they were *there*, and were considered too precious to be left in the wastebasket, as it were. Future readers of the completed Jeremiah book would be forced to ponder the tragedy that befell the nation because of its rejection of the prophetic word; but they might also ponder the tragedy of the rejected prophet, whose word had now been shown to have been true.

But whatever considerations may have moved the collectors of the book to include these laments they certainly add to the book a dimension it otherwise would not have. Modern readers invariably find themselves fascinated by these pieces, and presumably it was no less the case with ancient readers as well. Thanks to the wealth of biographical and auto-biographical material which his book contains, Jeremiah would remain the best known of all the prophets even without these pieces. Not only would we know the details of the message he proclaimed; we would know of numerous occasions on which he was opposed and physically abused for proclaiming it. We would know that he could wheel in anger on those who would silence the word and pronounce God's judgment upon them (e.g., 20:3–6; 28:15f.; 29:31f.; 36:29–31). And we would even have intimations that he was capable of questioning God (32:16–17a, 24f.). But we would never have dreamed that he was so human. We would have thought that one who could preach such an obviously unpopular message, and do so unremittingly over a period of more than forty years in the face of persecution, must have been a man of iron courage and unshakeable faith. But we learn from his own words that he was not. Jeremiah was a weak mortal.

Now and then readers have been shocked to discover this, especially those who are accustomed to search their Bibles for edifying moral examples and who expect the heroes of the faith invariably to provide such examples. Such readers may be inclined to feel disappointed in Jeremiah and to find it a pity that so great a prophet should have exhibited such weakness. Now it certainly must be admitted that Jeremiah does not reveal himself to us in his "confessions" as an exemplary person. He neither loved his enemies nor forgave them, but rather called upon his God with vehemence to punish them, and to do so quickly. His faith was neither serene nor unshakeable; on the contrary, there were times when it crumbled beneath him and spilled him into the pit of despair. He addressed his God with utter honesty, yes; but it was an honesty that at times trod perilously close to blasphemy. No, Jeremiah does not reveal himself to the reader as an example to emulate but as a weak and angry mortal.

Yet the very presence of these laments in the book alongside Jeremiah's preached word and incidents from his life, reminds the reader—and reminds him forcibly—that this weak and angry mortal was nevertheless God's prophet. It was precisely this man who, for all his weakness and in his weakness, was God's chosen instrument to speak his word, his judging and saving word, to his people. Nor is this something that ought to surprise us, for it accords with the witness of the whole of Scripture. God does not make his call to his servants conditional upon their purging themselves of weakness and achieving a measure of perfection. He does not extend his call only to the brave, to the saintly, to those who are strangers to doubt and despair. Rather, it pleases him to entrust the treasure of his word to "earthen vessels." It is precisely *in* their weakness and frailty—even in their rebellion—that God calls his servants. So it was with Jeremiah; so it is through all the pages of Scripture; and so it is today.

But if we were to dismiss these complaints as no more than expressions of an all-too-human weakness on the prophet's part, we should do him less than justice. They were that, of course. But there is more. We must never allow ourselves to forget that the abuse that occasioned these laments fell on Jeremiah precisely because of his faithful discharge of the prophetic office. Jeremiah tells us that he had not wanted to be a prophet, and that when the call came to him he had tried to evade it, protesting that he was too young (1:5f.). But God overruled him. He was commanded to do exactly as he was told and to say exactly what he was told to say and he was promised that God would at all times be with him to come to his rescue (1:7f.). So Jeremiah became a prophet willy-nilly. And he had been absolutely obedient. Year after year he had faithfully proclaimed the word that was given him. When its fulfillment was delayed, his enemies mocked him; because it was an unwelcome word, they persecuted him. Persecution brought Jeremiah personal anguish; but God's word was also at stake.

In his anguish Jeremiah turned to his God in prayer. The "confessions" are the texts of such prayers, adaptations of a liturgical form. To whom else could he go but God? What he had endured had violated his understanding of God's justice and faithfulness to his word. After all, it was God whose call had gotten him all this misery; and it was God who had promised to come to his aid. Why does he not do so? Is it in accord with his justice that he should allow his prophet to suffer innocently at the hands of wicked men? Will he never vindicate his word? Could it be that he, Jeremiah, had been deluded and that the word he had spoken had *not* been given him by God? Unthinkable! But if it had been, then those enemies who abused him and tried to silence him were also enemies of God. Will God allow wicked men to spurn his word and abuse his prophet with impunity? Let him punish them and vindicate his prophet, and thus vindicate the word his prophet has spoken at his command! Let him take action! It was when it seemed to him that God would never take action that the prophet abandoned himself to despair—for he had no one to help him save God. The "confessions" do indeed show us a weak and angry mortal. But they also let us see a man utterly dependent upon God, utterly obedient to his calling and perplexed at its outcome, at the end of his resources, who with utter honesty lays himself bare before God, who alone can help—if help there is at all. And if at times his complaints heighten into angry accusations, it was always to God that he returned: He had nowhere else to go.

A further point: However much of anguish and despair the "confessions" may express, these were not the words of a quitter! Jeremiah's whole life seems to have been lived in tension with his calling. The only way in which he could have put an end to that tension would have been to quit the prophetic office—and that he never did. He expressed himself as wishing that he could (e.g., 9:2); indeed he hints (20:9) that there were times when he had taken all he could endure and had resolved to speak God's word no more. But the compulsion of the word was on him and he could not refrain from speaking it. So he went on till the end of his life faithfully proclaiming the word that was given him, and enduring abuse and suffering for doing so. Jeremiah may have spoken in weakness, but he acted in strength. His "confessions" show him at his lowest moments; but they must be read in the context of the whole book in which they are found, for here we learn of the message he proclaimed and continued to proclaim, of the suffering he endured and continued to endure, and of the steadfast loyalty to his calling which he exhibited to the very end. In that context the "confessions" remain the words of a weak mortal; but they may also be read as the words of a brave and devoted man.

III

The careful reader will have observed how often in the laments of the Psalter the tone suddenly shifts from one of abject distress, complaint and woeful pleading to one of confident assurance, thanksgiving, and praise.[12] A number of scholars have supposed that this is because in the course of the liturgy the supplicant has received a priestly oracle or a sign telling him that God has heard his prayer and will come to his aid.[13] The lament which we have been considering likewise has appended to it an answering oracle. But it can be called a *Heilsorakel* only with severe qualifications. Rather, it is a rebuke and a conditional promise. Because it adds to the passage a dimension that would otherwise not be found in Jeremiah's "confessions" it is important that we consider it. It reads as follows:

19. Therefore this is what Yahweh said:
    "ᵃIf you repent, I'll restore you,ᵃ
    ᵇbefore me you will stand.ᵇ
    ᶜIf you mix not the cheap and the precious,ᶜ
    as my mouth you will be.
    Let them turn back to you.
    Don't you turn back to them.
20. Then before this people I'll make you
    an impregnable wall of bronze.
    Attack you they will,
    overcome you they can't,

---

[12] As was noted above, this same feature may be observed in one of Jeremiah's laments (20:7–13).

[13] Whether or not the shift of mood can always be explained in this way is a question that cannot be debated here; cf. A. Weiser, *The Psalms* (Eng. tr., OTL, 1962), pp. 79–83. But it seems to be the case in certain Psalms; cf. Pss. 12:5; 60:6–8; 85:8.

for with you am I
to help you and save you—Yahweh's word.
21. From the grasp of the wicked I'll snatch you,
from the clutch of the ruthless release you."

v. 19   a-a Lit., "If you turn [from such talk as the foregoing] I'll return you [to the prophetic
office]." There is a play on the verb *šûb* which continues in the last two cola of the
verse.
b-b To "stand before" someone is to be in his personal service, to be in attendance
upon him; 1 Kings 1:2; 10:8; 12:8.
c-c Lit., "If you bring forth [i.e., separate] the precious from the worthless"; or, "If you
bring forth [i.e., utter] the precious, without the worthless."

The introductory formula ("Therefore—") is the one that normally
introduces a prophetic oracle of judgment. And what follows does indeed
pronounce judgment on the prophet, albeit at the same time it offers him a
way out. Jeremiah is summoned to repentance (v. 19). He who had all his
life called upon his people to repent must himself repent if he hopes to
continue in the prophetic office. As a prophet he was commissioned to
stand in God's service ("before me") and to act as his "mouth," that is, to
be his messenger to bring his "precious" word to the people. Instead of that
he has forgotten himself! His angry recriminations and accusations, far
from being recognized as legitimate, are bluntly branded as "cheap, worthless." Talking as he has (and we are intended to think of the lament
immediately preceding) he has descended to the level of the populace
generally, when he ought to have been proclaiming God's word to them
with the demand that they turn to it in obedience. And he has all but
forfeited the prophetic office! He will have to do a complete about-face,
purge himself of such talk and utter the word that is given him, and that
alone, or he cannot continue.

But the door is not closed. If he in fact repents, God will continue to
use him as his messenger. Moreover, God extends to him his promise (vs.
21f.). It is not a promise that harassment would end, or even that Jeremiah
would be given peace of mind in the midst of the struggle. Rather, he is
promised that he will be given the strength to endure whatever might be
laid upon him; God will make him like "an impregnable wall of bronze"
which no attack, however massive, can overwhelm. More than that, God
will be with him to rescue him out of the hands of those who persecute
him. Verbal similarities between verses 20f. and 1:8, 18f. (the account of
Jeremiah's call) are striking and have been noted by virtually every
commentator. We are undoubtedly intended to understand that at some
time in his life Jeremiah became aware that he had very nearly demitted the
prophetic office, but that he then underwent a second experience of call.

If we did not have verses 19–21 we should never have guessed that
Jeremiah regarded his angry outbursts and accusations of God as anything
but justifiable. But the presence of these verses is evidence that this was not
the case; Jeremiah knew, or came to know, that such talk was unworthy of
his calling and impermissible. Of course, we can say nothing further of the

experience that brought him to this realization. Jeremiah presents it as the reception of an objective word from God, something that came to him from outside; but factors in the prophet's own psyche must certainly have played a part. (It is possible that Jeremiah knew in his heart all along that he had no right to level accusations at God and that at some time of emotional stress the awareness exploded to the surface that God was rebuking him for doing so. But we cannot know.) Since the oracle in verses 19–21 is formally distinct from the lament that precedes it, we do not know whether Jeremiah underwent this experience immediately after he had accused God of having failed him or at some other time; the connection between the two parts of the passage could have been made secondarily. Nor do we know whether it was Jeremiah or another who gave the passage its present form, reduced it to writing and caused it to be preserved. If Jeremiah was responsible for this, as is by no means impossible, then we have before us a true *confessio*: The prophet lays bare before all who will read both his own weakness and the divine rebuke that it received.[14] But even if some anonymous collector brought the two parts of the passage together and gave it its place in the book, we are still intended to hear Jeremiah say, "In my weakness I spoke so; but I know that I sinned in doing so, for God rebuked me. And when he rebuked me, I repented, for, as you can see from my book, I continued in the prophetic office till the end."

But are we to assume that the experience reflected in this passage marked a turning point in Jeremiah's life in the sense that he was constrained by it to lay his complaints and recriminations aside once and for all? It is far from certain that it did. There is no evidence that Jeremiah ever underwent such a decisive "conversion experience," if we may put it so. Indeed, one may wonder if to the end of his life he ever escaped his inner struggle and found complete serenity in the discharge of his calling. Certainly the collectors of the book were not concerned to present matters in that light. Since we do not know when any of the "confessions" were uttered, 15:10–21 *could* have been the last chronologically; but if the collectors of the book had wished us to see it so, surely they would have placed it last (and perhaps commented upon it as well). We know that Jeremiah continued to meet persecution, and continued to see his word rejected, to the end of his life. It would be strange indeed if he had lamented no more. And, in fact, in the prose narrative passage in chapter 32—which is dated (v. 1) to the last year before the fall of Jerusalem, when Jeremiah was approaching old age—he is remembered as making complaint to God (vs. 16–17a, 24f.). The likelihood is that God's prophet remained a weak mortal and, like all weak mortals who are *simul iustus simul peccator*, experienced many occasions when he knew that repentance was needful. But the weak mortal also remained God's prophet, endowed by his God with the strength to carry on.

---

[14]Cf. Rudolph (HAT), p. 91.

20

The Confessions of Jeremiah
Gerhard von Rad

(Translated by Anne Winston and Gary Lance Johnson)

The confessions are the most singular feature in Jeremiah. Prophetic visions, oracles, and warnings against the misuse of the cultus can be found in other prophetic works, but Jeremiah's confessions, those most intimate, solitary discussions with God, have their equal in no other prophetic book. Let us turn now to the confessions and the particular theological problem they contain.[1] A complete examination of the restoration and interpretation of the text has not been attempted here.

Jeremiah 15:16–20
16. Thy words were found and I ate them, and thy words became to me a joy and the delight of my heart; for I am called by thy name, O Lord, God of hosts. 17. I did not sit in the company of merrymakers, nor did I rejoice; I sat alone, because thy hand was upon me, for thou hadst filled me with indignation. 18. Why is my pain unceasing, my wound incurable, refusing to be healed? Wilt thou be to me like a deceitful brook, like waters that fail? 19. Therefore thus says the Lord: "If you return, I will restore you, and you shall stand before me. If you utter what is precious, and not what is worthless, you shall be as my mouth. They shall turn to you, but you shall not turn to them. 20. And I will make you to this people a fortified wall of bronze; they will fight against you, for I am with you to save you and deliver you," says the Lord.

*Originally published as "Die Konfessionen Jeremias," *Evangelische Theologie* 3 (1936) 265–276.

[1]This short study utilizes the results of form criticism, Baumgartner's *Klagegedichte Jeremias* in particular, and intends to serve as an example of how a theological interpretation can and must connect with "the results of critical science." These confessions were considered inauthentic, because they appeared inconsistent with the image which one had of the prophet. Baumgartner has totally and convincingly rejected this proposition. New light has been shed on the picture of the prophet Jeremiah since this initially, purely literary-critical debate and a new situation now exists. Although the confessions strike us as an almost foreign element, nevertheless, they cannot be denied to him. In any respect, laments are distinct from prophetic speeches on behalf of God. Thus, much in the understanding of Old Testament scripture in recent times has shifted for us in various respects. Now, many things which appear unessential for the faith lie there available and ready for a new theological beginning.

This pericope falls into two formal divisions; an eloquent prayer of Jeremiah, and God's response. With verse 16, we are already in the middle of the confession. He "devoured" Yahweh's words when they came to him, and for him they were a "joy" and a "heart's-delight." From an Old Testament point of view, these statements are totally unusual. To Jeremiah, the revelation is an almost haunting force; he senses an innermost urgency for God that reaches down into the physical roots of his being. Without doubt, Jeremiah speaks at this point, not of the relationship of men to the revelation, but from his own experience as a prophet. Yes, there was for Jeremiah the possibility of a totally spontaneous ecstasy!

This alignment with God, however, has a negative side: he who is totally turned toward God is consequently turned away from men; it is just this inclination toward God that has isolated him from men. The simplicity of this truth is striking: those who are turned toward God are removed from human community; and this position has nothing to do with pride vis-a-vis other men. Jeremiah turns again to the notion of his loneliness; it has another basis: Yahweh has filled him with anger. Here, Jeremiah speaks of the meaning of his special prophetic calling. As a consequence of this, his relations with his fellowmen are disturbed. Like one who has been implanted with a foreign object, the prophet speaks of the anger, whose container and agent he now must be. He has relinquished the freedom of his natural emotions; now he must rebuke and threaten. "Joy" (שָׂשׂוֹן) toward God and "curses" (זַעַם) toward men is already a formula that summarizes the life of the prophet Jeremiah! The office which is given to him from God, however, causes him to suffer, a result which was not anticipated. Indeed, it is precisely this unexpected suffering which causes him to rebel; in this he sees a faithless god. The example of the deceitful winter stream is a dreadful reproach. Just as this kind of waterway attracts herds and tents, so has God attracted Jeremiah; for a while things went well, but then the deception became evident; a trust was broken.

In a concise and harsh manner, the divine answer dictates the conditions under which Jeremiah can return to his prophetic office. In content it is closely related to Jeremiah 1:18, and thus it becomes clear that Jeremiah must return to the place where God had started with him. It is significant that both a statement that Jeremiah has sinned with his words as well as a reproach of these words are missing; this is obvious in the very opening of the divine response. In taking the matter up again, the depth of his fall becomes apparent. He wanted to turn away from his prophetic office and become a common citizen among citizens. That would be wrong; Jeremiah should not make his fellowmen the standard. On the contrary, they should make him the standard to the degree that he utters what is "precious" and not what is "worthless." We should relate this last remarkable statement back to the entire previous complaint. What was "worthlessness" and "not precious" in the eyes of God was the fact that Jeremiah could take pleasure initially in his prophetic office, but was ready to cast it aside when it led him into complications and suffering.

In order to tie our problem together at this point, one simple observation is made: a God-speech, i.e., a prophetic proclamation in the strict sense of the word, is here only Yahweh's answer. It is clear that Jeremiah with the actual words of his confession has left his prophetic office. Without having examined the issues more closely, we still can say at this point that Jeremiah is speaking in no way as a prophet in the old sense of the word—in as much as one understands prophets to be men that have claimed a preaching commission directly from God. The direction of Jeremiah's words does not proceed from above to below, but from below to above, and what he bears witness to is primarily not a word of God, but his inner doubts, his suffering and his despair.

II

It is the same when we read Jeremiah 12:1–5. The torment of the grave question is noticeably revealed when Jeremiah, even before he states his case, gives away all the trumps in his hand.

> 1. Righteous art thou, O Lord, when I complain to thee; yet I would plead my case before thee.

He is not a partner of equal rank, but a sufferer still in the initial stages. Thus, Jeremiah writhes in a grinding conflict: on the one hand, there is the disturbingly unbroken chain of good fortune of the ungodly.

> 2. Thou plantest them, and they take root; they grow and bring forth fruit.

And, on the other hand, from this same God come suffering and sorrow. The ensuing answer of God once again breathes a critical harshness.

> 5. If you have raced with men on foot, and they have wearied you, how will you compete with horses? And if in a safe land you fall down, how will you do in the jungle of the Jordan?

This is no answer; it avoids going into the complicated question of the prophet; it is itself a question! The passage is magnificent and peculiarly secretive, almost a riddle of God, so that one suspects rather than grasps its extent and depth. O small, frail man, you are still a novice. Already you grow weary from walking, already you become afraid in a peaceful land. Jeremiah was almost overwhelmed by this question; now he must hear that he knows nothing at all of God, that he is still at the very beginning. In response to the human accusation about riddles in the divine world-order, God lifts the veil for a moment and opens a perspective on riddles and mysteries of an incomparably difficult nature, but without giving the slightest hint of an explanation. But just this last part is significant: it should not be a question of theoretical problems and their solution. With his question, God leads Jeremiah away from theory, away from brooding, to another question: that of the trial of life and suffering. For God, it is a question of standing firm, finally a question of obedience.

III

Jeremiah 8:18–23

18. My grief is beyond healing, my heart is sick within me. 19. Hark, the cry of the daughter of my people from the length and breadth of the land: "Is the Lord not in Zion? Is her King not in her?" "Why have they provoked me to anger with their graven images, and with their foreign idols?" 20. "The harvest is past, the summer is ended, and we are not saved." 21. For the wound of the daughter of my people is my heart wounded, I mourn, and dismay has taken hold on me. 22. Is there no balm in Gilead? Is there no physician there? Why then has the health of the daughter of my people not been restored? 23. O that my head were waters, and my eyes a fountain of tears, that I might weep day and night for the slain of the daughter of my people!

This section is full of disconcerting inner anxiety. Tormenting images thrust themselves before the soul of the prophet, but it is not a consistent picture. It is a collage, only pieces of pictures that position themselves in Jeremiah's sight: the cries for help of his people (19a), a possible divine answer (19b). Another thought strikes the prophet: is help to be found elsewhere, if healing is not to be found in Yahweh? But this thought is discarded as hopeless and the complaint fades away in unspeakable distress. But this is the significance: these restless, almost fragmenting elements of the picture are welded together into a seamless whole, framed and held together by great agony and the incredible ability to bear suffering. The poem begins with the expression of a very personal suffering and it closes with one, but inside this marked-off area, contained as if by the walls of his heart—incredible pictures are witnessed!

For the prophet, what crowds itself together in his vision, into a confined space, in disconnected images, is a tragedy that unfolds in many acts: distress leading to the questioning of God, the decision to obtain a divine judgement, and the God-speech announcing the rejection of the petition. After that, the situation disintegrates into hopelessness.

The summer is ended, the harvest is past . . .

The year is almost over and hope is gone. But still there is no surrender. His thoughts now run in another direction, and this time it is the prophet himself who seeks a way out (22). But this question also fades away, If until now the inner activity of the prophet in his questions was somewhat held back—during the search something strained in him—now, with the fading away of the last question, his distress is unleashed and he hopes only for the opportunity to pour out his sorrow.

It would seem that with this lamentation we are descending into a deeper, more basic level of Jeremiah's sufferings. This lamentation, above and beyond any other consideration, is an expression of compassion (a statement that makes us as theologians somewhat uneasy!). Here the God-speech is not the intellectual aim of the section; on the contrary, this confession serves alone and exclusively to describe a completely personal, emotional activity. It does not witness to God in the direct manner of previous prophetic announcements; on the contrary, it conveys a competely subjective expression of sorrow. Is Jeremiah still speaking here as a prophet? Before answering, we will let the poetry demonstrate the depth of his despair.

IV

Jeremiah 20:7–9

7 O Lord, thou hast deceived me, and I was deceived; thou art stronger than I, and thou has prevailed. I have become a laughingstock all the day; every one mocks me. 8. For whenever I speak, I cry out, I shout, "Violence and destruction." For the word of the Lord has become for me a reproach and derision all day long. 9. If I say, "I will not mention him, or speak any more in his name," there is in my heart as it were a burning fire shut up in my bones, and I am weary with holding it in, and I cannot.

The first verb in verse 7 strictly speaking means "entice" and is used in the sense of seducing a girl. The other verb suggests a wrestling match in which Jeremiah is inferior. How sweet you were to me and how strong.[2] This opening is frightening. The prophet complains to God of his frailty, certainly excusable; he could not have resisted. Thus, the accusation is immediately turned toward God, who has placed Jeremiah in a position of ridicule for all the world. Consequently, for Jeremiah it was a matter of the act of his appointment to prophetic office, not a question of right or wrong, and initially not a question of inner belief, but an elementary question of power. Thus, one can see the relationship between God and man as a frighteningly unequal power-relationship, and this arrangement probably is not yet at its most extreme form. The meaning of verse 8 is not certain; rather than meaning that outrages are happening to him, Jeremiah is probably summarizing his judicial indictment. Since he did not encounter serious opposition, but—what is naturally much worse—laughter and ridicule, Jeremiah confesses to us in magnificent candor those thoughts he has already had: God should seek another man; Jeremiah no longer wishes to concern himself with his prophetic office. This, however, does not remain just in his thoughts alone, but has been acted upon. The trial was

[2]Baumgartner, *loc. cit.*, p. 64.

unsuccessful; he would have been inwardly consumed if he had held back the burning words of God. The confession dies away; Jeremiah is exhausted to the point of death: "I am weary with holding it in, and I cannot." This belongs to the mightiest words that the Old Testament can express of the power that can come over a man from God. Once more we emphasize: here, the relationship of God to man is set within a deep level of human experience, where it is no longer a matter of free resolve ("choice"), or an intellectual agreement, or a conversion; here the question of the prophetic commission is perceived as one of human obedience and trial, simply a question of power.

V

Jeremiah 20:14–18

14. Cursed be the day on which I was born! The day when my mother bore me, let it not be blessed! 15. Cursed be the man who brought the news to my father, "A son is born to you," making him very glad. 16. Let the man be like the cities which the Lord overthrew without pity; let him hear a cry in the morning and an alarm at noon, because he did not kill me in the womb; so my mother would have been my grave, and her womb for ever great. 18. Why did I come forth from the womb to see toil and sorrow, and spend my days in shame?

Now the prophet is in total darkness. The pericope, also biographical, undoubtedly must have originated from one of the last phases of Jeremiah's sufferings. In terms of Old Testament and popular oriental religion, a curse like this functions as more than malicious, angry words. According to the ancients, there were demonic forces over which man had a certain control; he could call and enlist their aid because of their lustful willingness for destruction. Thus, the act of providence which determined the day of Jeremiah's birth to be an act of redemption should be cancelled and annulled. Jeremiah curses this day with all his strength and thereupon reaches back, so to speak, behind the empirical life and attacks the otherworldly act of providence. Certainly, the curse is so immense, so savage that it also strikes the unsuspecting man that had brought the news of the birth to Jeremiah's father; this fool who at the time only thought to announce good tidings. On that ill-fated day, Jeremiah could have died in his mother's womb. Was it true, did he afterall have to come forth from the womb of his mother? Then she would have remained pregnant with him forever; a grotesque thought! Nevertheless, we perceive precisely in this wish the sudden feeling of warmth for his mother: wishing still to be enclosed in her womb, even if she were to be his tomb in which he could rest! Jeremiah surveys his life as far as it lies before him: in hardship, sorrow and shame will it end.

One could describe this wish of Jeremiah as the lowest point of his sufferings. Now, all is devastated within him; he calls up the treasured images: mother, father, friend of the family, into the darkness of his despair.[3] It is useless to search for a lower depth of despair. Perhaps in the hour of his last martyrdom? One can say with caution, which here should be the first commandment of the interpreter, that physical death per se does not increase suffering, rather it provides a release.

*

Not only in the sense of an aesthetic judgement—that here only with difficulty may be repressed—let us first observe a few fundamental thoughts: the confessions of Jeremiah are unique in kind among prophetic literature, indeed, in the entire Old Testament. When we survey the contents of the prophetic books from Amos to Malachi, we find "proclamations" and indeed, usually in the direct prophetic sense of an urgent divine revelation (not just a witness of faith, as in the historical or poetic books). Jeremiah's confessions, however, are in no way prophetic proclamations; the direction of words does not proceed from above to below (nor is the prophet a bridge for God's word), but the words are directed from below to above. Jeremiah does not speak of God; on the contrary, he speaks of himself and the agitation in his soul. Now, perhaps one could be inclined to deal with the theological problem that unfolds itself before us by referring to some of the psalms,[4] in which, from time to time, the pious speak more of themselves and their circumstances than of God. In reality, why shouldn't Jeremiah speak to us once apart from his prophetic office—off the record, so to speak. Would we then have, consequently, a purely human piety that at one time pours itself out apart from the pressure of his prophetic calling, from beginning to end, so to speak, the *homo religiosus*? Those who know the direction of Jeremiah interpretations over the last fifty years, know with what preference and respect the interpreters followed this path. But it is the wrong direction. In his confessions, Jeremiah certainly does not speak off the record; on the contrary, he speaks out of the midst of his prophetic office. It is not true that we have, in reality, prophetic testimony and more general religious statements by Jeremiah side by side; rather the confessions come directly out of the center of his prophetic existence. Thus, we stand before the task: *to formulate anew the prophetic testimony of Jeremiah*.

A theological examination of these sections consequently, on the one hand, must begin with the assumption that they stem directly from the mouth of the prophet, and on the other hand, understand in the confessions that his soul, indeed his unique subjective life and experiences occupy the center. Thus, although 12:1–5 deals with a single problem, generally all of

[3]Volz, *Der Prophet Jeremia*, 1935, p. 211.
[4]Cf. G. Hölscher, *Die Propheten*, 1935, p. 399: "The presuppositions (of the confessions) are not different than those of most psalms of lamentation."

the emotional conflicts are evoked. Here we encounter the entire spectrum of human, emotional distress: fear of shame, fear of failure, loss of strength, doubting of faith, loneliness, pity, disappointment turning to hostility towards God. Very little is omitted here that can affect a human heart—and that "all" is suffering, disappointment, and despair of one's calling. Is it not possible then to understand Jeremiah as the conclusion of an historical line of prophetic figures? Isn't it true in these confessions that the prophetic office, in a very real sense, has come to an end? Although little is apparent of an outward prophetic tradition from Amos to Jeremiah, still much can be asserted: the mission and responsibility of Amos, Isaiah, Micah and Zephaniah are in Jeremiah, but also he bears their silent suffering and disappointments as an invisible, but real inheritance. However, Jeremiah is different from all his predecessors in that the prophetic office, which in the case of Amos was still intact, in Jeremiah breaks at a critical point and through this break darkness enters. And it is now clear: around this break in his prophetic office revolve all of his confessions.

The exegete is not called upon here to make value judgements; on the contrary, he must simply observe that the prophet Jeremiah, at the very least, is just as much occupied with that intrusion of dark desperation into his inner being as with his genuine prophetic mission of which we have said nothing here. Certainly, this despair visibly grows in his confessions and we see him occupied with it to the point of exhaustion. It is not enough to view this as simply a shattering of the prophetic office caused by subjective reflections or as a product of his individual spiritual inclination. Here there is more than subjective reflection and individual difference in temperament. Here is to be seen the ultimate hopelessness of the genuine prophetic mission. But it is not just seen, for the suffering has intruded itself into Jeremiah's life and now is part of his very existence. Isaiah and Micah were simply messengers of God's word. With Jeremiah a new element is announced in God's dealings through his prophets: Jeremiah serves God not only with the harsh proclamation of his mouth, but also with his person; his life becomes unexpectedly involved in the cause of God on earth. Thus, now—and in Jeremiah this is something new—the prophet not only becomes a witness of God through the strength of his charisma, but also in his humanity; but not as the one who triumphs over the sins of mankind, not as one overcoming, but as a messenger of God to mankind breaking under the strain. Hence, Jeremiah's life here becomes a forceful witness, his suffering soul and his life ebbing away in God's service become a testimony of God. The priestly office is introduced alongside the prophetic office. That is why Jeremiah is not only the end of a line, but also a beginning and with him an actual new chapter unfolds in the anticipation (*Weissagung*) of Jesus Christ.[5]

---

[5]The Baruch Narratives also belong here, which are not biography, but a history of suffering. What caused this man then to take pen in hand, if not the knowledge that Jeremiah

There is more! The prophets who preceded Jeremiah certainly can be correctly regarded theologically as intercessors. As an intercessor, Jeremiah not only confronts mankind in the manner of Hosea or Isaiah, but if we understand the confessions correctly—their expression of failure and rebellion—we arrive at a final observation: as intercessor, Jeremiah not only endures the suffering that men have caused him, but also he has taken upon himself all of their misery; they are present in his deepest struggles, and with these men for whom he suffers, Jeremiah must die in the sight of God, yes he dies many deaths with them until his own final, physical death. There is no "however" remaining, no consoling postscript, no final redeeming victory. Therefore, Jeremiah's confessions testify to the harshness of the divine wrath. These confessions know nothing whatever of an atoning, redeeming power; and this characteristic is not due to personal ignorance concerning the sense of his suffering.[6] Here we must be painfully honest with ourselves to guard against any over interpretation; his resistance, his rebellion and the awful curse at the end demonstrate clearly that he has reached the limit of his intercessory office. Furthermore, he is not "perfect" in the sense of the Letter of Hebrews, and therefore Jeremiah is only an indication of the One To Come who teaches us to perceive the intercessory role of Christ in its depth. What is depicted in the suffering which results from his intercessory office—being taken out of the joyful community of men, to the final journey into the night of "godforsakenness"—is a foreshadowing and an example of a future, perfect Intercessory Role.

---

not only became a witness through his words, but that his life's course which was slowly altered into suffering and despair also became a testimony in a new prophetic sense. To be sure, it lacks any martyr glorification, but also any notion of a sacrifice (*Imitatio*).

[6]H. Duhm, *Jeremia*, 1935, p. 168. "Jeremiah is the most subjective of all the prophets. He demonstrates this in the confessions. Also, he at no time betrays the faintest notion that his suffering could benefit the people. Actually, to others it is beneficial . . . "

21

The Fruit of the Tribulation
of the Prophet*
Walther Zimmerli

(Translated by Leo G. Perdue)

I

In a splendid mistranslation, Luther has rendered Isa. 28:19: "Tribulation teaches one to give attention to the word." This translation unmistakably issues forth from the reformer's own experience.[1] It expresses the valid recognition that tribulation, destructive when it is first experienced, has the capacity to produce rich fruit. Paul is aware of the dual nature of the tribulation of the messenger of God when, at the moment of his anxious awaiting of the arrival of Titus from Corinth, he characterizes his own situation in 2 Cor. 7:5, "being afflicted at every turn" (ἐν παντὶ θλιβόμενοι), with the twofold statment: "battles from without" (ἔξωθεν μάχαι), "fears within" (ἔσωθεν φόβοι).

The following study will not investigate in a general way the familiar, multifaceted nature of affliction common to human existence. Neither will it deal with the experience of Paul. Rather, this investigation will concern itself with the specific experiences of the Old Testament classical prophets. It is clear from many prophetic witnesses that prophecy (the communication of the word under the impress of the mysterious, direct seizure and call by Yahweh) especially has been a most trying charge. When a Paul, shortly after the passage cited above but in an altered context, says that divinely caused distress "produces repentance" (μετάνοιαν ἐργάζεται, 2 Cor. 7:10), then it may appear appropriate to ask in regard to the phenomenon of

---

*Walther Zimmerli, "Frucht der Anfechtung des Propheten," *Die Botschaft und die Boten* (FS Hans Walter Wolff; ed. J. Jeremias und L. Perlitt; Neukirchen-Vluyn: Neukirchener Verlag, 1981) 131–146.

[1]P. Th. Bühler, *Die Anfechtung bei Martin Luther*, Diss. Zürich 1942. Cf., e.g., p. 206, note 79: "Misery and persecution teach one the golden art" (*Weimar Aufgabe*. Tischreden 1, 1012). *Ibid.*, p. 222, note 94: "When one thinks that our Lord God has rejected a person, one should think that our Lord God has taken him into his arms and draws him to his heart" (*Weimar Ausgabe* 44, 111, 32–34).

prophetic affliction whether there is also something of the "tribulation which produces fruit" in the prophets. In this regard, Paul's statement in 2 Cor. 7:5 leads one not only to consider the external affliction of the prophets, but also their inner distress. Do the prophetic writings provide some insight in this regard?

II

The expression, "battles from without" (ἔξωθεν μάχαι), designates in an appropriate way the life of the Old Testament prophets from an early period. For example, one may point to the Elijah tradition as one in which this feature figures prominently. In regard to this, Steck's comprehensive monograph has demonstrated that a topos of the "violent destiny of the prophet" was shaped and as such was at work in the New Testament.[2]

In the same way, one recognizes in Amos, the earliest of the classical prophets, the opposition he faced during his preaching in the Northern Kingdom. The high priest, Amaziah of Bethel, not only denounced him but at the same time had him banished from the country.[3] This is a case of external affliction.

The Book of Amos initially provides us no answer to the question of the "fruits" of this tribulation. Nothing speaks against the assumption that Amos complied with the banishment and left Northern Israel. We do not know if he discontinued his prophetic activity and returned to his sheep herd from which Yahweh had taken him (7:15). The oracular material which derives from him does not suggest that he consequently undertook a prophetic office in Judah and there also may have announced an approaching destruction, as did Isaiah and Micah a short-time later.[4] The text of Amos remains disappointingly silent in regard to the type of complete, biographical information which interests modern inquiry.

Still one may ask with good reason whether this first emergence of the writing down of the prophetic word does not itself describe the tangible fruit of the external affliction of the prophet to which Amos 7:10-17 attests. Certainly, the matter at question is not present in the book as it presently exists. Hans Walter Wolff (to whom these expressions are fondly offered on his seventieth birthday as a sign of an old, long-standing

---

[2]O. H. Steck, *Israel und das gewaltsame Geschick der Propheten*, WMANT 23, 1967.

[3]The comparison of בְּרַח לְךָ (Am 7:12) with the identical expression in Num. 24:11 advises against seeing this only as a kind of benevolent advice which would allow Amos opportunity to flee away to safety before the intervention of the king. By contrast, such advice is found in Jer. 36:19.

[4]The strophe concerning Judah in 2:4f. could not issue forth from the prophet himself. In addition, the mentioning of "those who are at ease in Zion" (6:1) is subject to the suspicion that it is a later, Jewish adaptation; cf. in regard to this the detailed note in H. W. Wolff, *Amos*, BK XIV/2, 1969, note a). Against the authenticity of the oracle of salvation pertaining to the "booth of David that is fallen" in 9:11f. (W. Rudolph, *Amos*, KAT XIII, 2, 1971, 285f.), cf. the arguments by Wolff, *ibid*, 405f.

friendship) has impressively demonstrated that various, other hands during different periods have contributed to the compilation of materials in the present book.[5] However, that the first collector could have reached back to material recorded by Amos himself is compellingly suggested by the cycle of visions (7:1–8, 8:1–2 [9:1–4]) composed in the first person. This supposition is also suggested by the analogous cycle of oracles concerning the nations in Amos 1f. (although the first person form is avoided). And finally, there could reside a collection of the prophet's own speeches behind the materials in chapters 3–6.[6]

The suggestion that this first instance of the writing down of the prophetic word may have been the "fruits of the (outer) tribulation of the prophet" remains an assumption for the words of Amos. Yet it is defended by a consideration of the words of Isaiah which follow a short while later. At the same time, Isaiah also provides insight into the inner dynamic that results in the recording of the initially oral prophetic words.

Isaiah's proclamation is far more eventful and multi-layered than that of Amos. In periods of the apodictic announcement of judgment,[7] there follow situations where surprisingly he offers to the Davidic King Ahaz a "do not fear" and to Judah, evidently in later moments, a new cessation of Yahweh's judgment.[8] However, again and again Isaiah must come to experience the fact that Yahweh's outstretched hand is rejected, thereby once again demonstrating the stubbornness of the people. The call narrative already mentions that this stubbornness is a result of the prophet's preaching. Twice, however, the suggestion is found in the Book of Isaiah that the rejection of the message of God (this specific affliction of the messenger sent with the word) produces a new, in one case clearly, literary expression of the rejected message as the "fruit of (external) affliction."

In the gloomy concluding remark of the collection of words written down by the prophet's own hand from the period of the Syro-Ephraimitic war, one reads: "I intend to bind up the testimony, seal[9] the teaching among my disciples, and wait for the Lord, who is hiding his face from the house of Jacob, and I will hope in him" (8:16f.). This is clearly a speech pertaining to a message rejected by the people which is to be preserved for the distant future. How one understands the particulars of the preservation of this message is a controversial matter. Is there intended a writing down of the words which are entrusted to a circle of disciples, say in the manner

---

[5]Wolff, *ibid.*, 129–38.

[6]Wolff, *ibid.*, 130.

[7]The attempt by H. W. Hoffmann (*Die Intention der Verkündigung Jesajas*, BZAW 136 [1974]) to make Isaiah, up to the events of 701, into a preacher of conditional summons to repentance is not convincing. This understanding of an oracle being bound to a conditional situation (p. 80) does not do justice to Isa. 6:9–11.

[8]Cf., e.g., 14:32, 28:12. The mystery of the changing commission is reflected by the prophet in the parable of the farmer in 28:23–29.

[9]Here, in parallel to the analogue צוּר, the infinitive absolute, חָתוֹם, is to be read.

that Jeremiah (32:12, 16) transmits to his helper Baruch the sales contract for the farm in Anathoth by which he secures the farm for a future time? Or does the passage signify the oral transmission of the message and its preservation in the hearts of the "disciples?"[10] The text provides no unambiguous answer, not even when it adds that Isaiah and his children, who bear symbolic names for the prophet's proclamation, continue as "signs and portents in Israel (8:18)." Ought one to regard the education of the prophetic circle as the "fruit" of the opposition which the prophet publicly experienced ("the fruit of the [outer] tribulation of the prophet"), even though we find no similar class of prophetic circles expressly indicated by the remaining prophetic books?[11]

Isaiah 30:8 clearly speaks about the writing down of the prophetic message as a manifested result of the nation's unwillingnes to listen. In this context, Yahweh commissions the prophet: "And now, go, write it before them on a tablet, and inscribe[12] it in a book, that it may be for the time to come as a witness[13] forever, for they are a rebellious people, lying sons who will not hear the instruction of the Lord." As was the case in regard to the "instruction" (תּוֹרָה) in 8:16, this is a speech which the obstinate people are not prepared to accept. Since the prophet could not be certain that he would live long enough to witness Yahweh's effectuation of the announced judgment in the "latter days," his inscribed word would fulfill then the function of the prosecutor. That which is written down as the "testimony" of the present word is in this case the concrete "fruit" of the affliction of the prophet caused by a disobedient people. The woe oracle in 5:19 with its citation of the people's scornful provocation of God ("Let him make haste, let him speed his work that we may see it; let the purpose of the Holy One of Israel draw near and let it come that we know it") illustrates the prophet's trials as does the audible resistance in 30:10f.: "Prophesy not to us what is right . . . let us hear no more of the Holy One of Israel." Since the rejection of the prophetic word here is set forth as the entire reason for its recording, it may be that, in contrast to the recording of the enigmatic expression "the spoil speeds, the prey hastes" in 8:1f., it involves more than the simple writing down of the coded designation of Egypt as רהב המשבת[14] ("Rahab who sits still," RSV). Moreover, it turns out that in

---

[10]For this question, cf. H. Wildberger, *Jesaja*, *BK* X/1 (1972) on this section, where Duhm is incorrectly cited as a representative of the view that the words are written down.

[11]Baruch always appears as an individual alongside Jeremiah. The redactional analysis of the prophetic books, of course, leads very often to the assumption of circles of disciples functioning as tradents.

[12]חקק ("to cut into") must here in connection with סֵפֶר be understood in this more subdued way.

[13]Vocalizing the word as לְעֵד, over against the MT.

[14]The MT's רהב הם שבת may be read with an alternative division of words as רַהַב הַמָּשְׁבָּת. I desire to express in this setting a somewhat more definite judgment than I have made in my arguments concerning the theme "Vom Prophetenwort zum Prophetenbuch," *ThLZ* 104 (1979) 481–496 (484).

every mentioning of opposition against Isaiah's message from the Holy One of Israel,[15] the discussion is never one of an actual prohibition to speak or even of persecution by the priestly or governmental authorities, as was the case with Amos.

It would please us to know more of the destiny of the only truly northern prophet Hosea, who spoke in the final phase of the life of Northern Israel. Only in Hosea 9:7f. does one uncover the suggestion that he has experienced open persecution. After the antagonistic word of 9:7 ("The prophet is a fool, the man of the spirit is mad"), there follows in 9:8 the mentioning of the prophet's peril: "traps" and "snares" are set before him, "hatred in the house of his God." However, the precise nature of the external affliction of this prophet cannot be determined.

Even less is known about the external threat to Micah, from whom only a few authentic prophetic words have been preserved. According to 3:6f., he also engages in a lively exchange of words with opponents who want to silence him. However, the statement of the "elders of the land" in Jer. 26:17 appears nevertheless to demonstrate that even his uncompromising announcement of the destruction of the temple (Mic. 3:12) had endured in Judah, had been even to a certain extent obeyed, and had also received the attention of Hezekiah, king as well during the days of Isaiah. The assumption is that even Isaiah's relationship, not only with Ahaz (who as far as we know did not take steps against the prophet in spite of his sharp attacks against the king's political policies; Isa. 7:10f., especially v. 17), but also with Hezekiah, was characterized by friction, as was often the case, rather than serenity. From here on this assumption in my estimation appears to merit every consideration.[16]

III

The external threat to the life of the prophet is open to view in Jeremiah, during both the days of Jehoiakim and the final phase of the siege of Jerusalem. First of all, Jeremiah 36 may indicate that the writing down of Jeremiah's word is a "fruit" of the external tribulation of the prophet. True, the introduction of this chapter does not expressly say that Jeremiah may have recorded his words under the pressure of persecution. However, the fact that Baruch recites the written words in the temple instead of Jeremiah who was "hindered"[17] from doing so could well indi-

---

[15] Also the scene recognizable in Isa. 28:7ff. is to be mentioned in this connection.

[16] W. Zimmerli, "Jesaja und Hiskia," in *Wort und Geschichte*. Festschrift K. Elliger, AOAT 18 (1973) 199–208 (= TB 51, 88–103).

[17] The interpretation of עָצוּר in 36:5 is debated. Most probably it refers to a prohibition to enter the temple after the incident of 20:1–6 (so e.g. Volz, *Jeremia* KAT X [1922] 328; Rudolph, *Jeremia* HAT 12 (³1968) 233; and Bright, *Jeremiah*, AncB (1965) 179, who also mentions the other possibility: "perhaps it was simply that the authorities had him under observation and would stop him if he tried to speak there." Cf. also note 53).

cate an official debarring of the prophet. In connection with the report of
the tumult in the temple which had almost cost Jeremiah his life because
he had prophesied against the House of Yahweh, Jer. 26:20–23 contains a
brief section dealing with the fortune of Uriah, the prophet from Kiriath-
jearim. The execution of this prophet, after he had been successfully
extradited from Egypt where he had fled, illustrates along with other
reports in the Book of Jeremiah that during the final phase of the fall of
Jerusalem Jehoiakim's royal decision to silence prophetic criticism did not
shy away from taking the life of a prophet.

When we turn to Jeremiah, we are confronted with a novel, hitherto
unfamiliar feature in regard to the theme of the affliction of the prophet.
The "battles from without" (ἔξωθεν μάχαι) is a phrase no longer sufficient
to describe this prophet's tribulation. Much more now the phrase, "fears
within" (ἔσωθεν φόβοι), in association with external attack, carries its full
weight. Certainly, there is already some of this in Isaiah, when this prophet,
in what are probably his final, transmitted words in 22:4, says in reference
to Jerusalem's stubborn refusal to repent during the catastrophe of 701:
"Therefore I said: 'Look away from me, let me weep bitter tears; do not
labor to comfort me for the destruction of the daughter of my people.'"[18]

However, in Jeremiah the new development is complete: the outer and
inner distress of the prophet is prominently displayed in the collection of
words and narratives filled with both third person descriptions and first
person speeches, material which either originates with him or at least has
him as the subject.

Added to this is the recognition that the "fruit of tribulation" is not
simply an external process that leads to the development of the book from
the words of the prophet. This in turn leads in a hermeneutical direction
that goes beyond the posing of the question about external and internal
affliction to the underlying meaning of affliction which becomes a type of
meta-question.

It is significant that this novel question concerning the discovery of the
meaning of affliction in the Book of Jeremiah is clarified equally from two
different sides. On the one side, the shaping of the distinctive depiction of
the suffering, afflicted prophet in a way that is unparalleled by any other
prophetic book has been produced by a second hand. In dealing with this,
literary analyses by various individuals have resulted in different conclusions. Kremers[19] believed that the basic strand of Jer. 37–45, subsequently
embellished by various sorts of legendary material, must be understood as
the "passion narrative of Jeremiah" written by Baruch. Rietzschel[20] included

---

[18]There is no reason to deny 22:4 to Isaiah as does J. Vermeylen, *Du prophète Isaïe à
l'apocalyptique* I (1977) 337 ("v. 4 bears equally the mark of the Deuteronomic redactor").

[19]H. Kremers, "Leidensgemeinschaft mit Gott im Alten Testament. Eine Untersuchung
der 'biographischen' Berichte im Jeremiabuch," *EvTh* 13 (1953) 122–140.

[20]C. Rietzschel, *Das Problem der Urrolle. Ein Beitrag zur Redactionsgeschichte des
Jeremiabuches* (1966) 105–110.

in the "traditions-complex" Jer. 36, originally an independent piece, thus 36–44. Wanke,[21] on the other hand, brought together an only slightly abbreviated form of Jer. 36 with the basic strand of 27f. and regarded the entire section as the work of the same author. Wanke did the same thing in associating Jer. 45 with 51:59–64, though 37:1–43:7 was assessed to be a later narrative complex written by a person other than Baruch.[22]

On the other side, it has been recognized very early that the Psalm-like pieces, later coined the "Confessions" of Jeremiah, which are found sprinkled throughout 11:18–20:18, provide a type of material for assessing the prophet's character and that distinguishes him from older prophecy. It remains for the following section to determine the characteristic shape of these two groups of texts, to consider their redactional compilation, and in connection with that to ask to what extent one can, on the basis of these two kinds of texts, say something about the "fruit of tribulation" in Jeremiah.

IV

At first inspection, the text of Jer. 36–45 (to which one could also add 20:1–6; 26; 28; 29:24–32) has to do with the external affliction of the prophet: ἔξωθεν μάχαι ("battles from without"). What is told by a third person narrator about Amos in 7:10–17 and what appears to reside in the background of Hosea's oracle in 9:7f. accelerates in Jeremiah into a fully developed life threatening situation. The cause of this threat is the prophet's proclamation. The affliction grows out of his commission. What this tribulation entails for the prophet's inner turmoil and complaint against Yahweh is recognized with sufficient clarity from the confessions. The fact that the most despairing, confessional statements (20:7–18) have been directly connected to the narrative concerning the prophet's punishment resulting from a priestly directive (20:1–6) provides recognizable evidence of redactional shaping.

In regard to the question, "Why exactly does the book of Jeremiah contain this abundance of narratives about suffering?", the superficial statement that Jeremiah may well have historically experienced great suffering is not satisfactory. If this were so, would not the Uriah narrative have been told in a much harsher tone? Also unsatisfactory is the assertion that the increased interest in the individual during the twilight of the monarchy leads to a much more increased interest in biographical details. If this were the case, how could a biographically shaped interest so easily omit by

[21]G. Wanke, *Untersuchungen zur sogenannten Baruchschrift*, BZAW 122, 1971.

[22]K. F. Pohlmann, *Studien zum Jeremiabuch. Ein Beitrag zur Frage nach der Entstehung des Jeremiabuches*, FRLANT 118 (1978) 199. Pohlmann refuses in general to see as the main focus in Jer. 37–44 the question of "prophetic existence": "The central concern of the writer was to answer the question about the self-understanding of his fellow countrymen in Judah after 587/6."

chance the information about the end of the prophet's life?[23] It will lead to better results when one sees actively at work behind this shaping of the prophetic book the specific form of the prophetic preaching which, in Jeremiah, opens up new dimensions.

A look at the redactional structure of the complex of Jer. 37–44, which in its essence is to be regarded as the "passion narrative of the prophet," gives support to this assumption. In its present context, this passion narrative is framed by two pieces—Jer. 36 and 45. Whatever one may make of the literary origin of these two narrative frames, he should not overlook the fact that by means of the framework an intended hermeneutic for the narrative of the prophet's passion during the last phase of Jerusalem is in view.

The understanding of this is enhanced, if the two chapters are, to begin with, considered separately. As concerns Jer. 36, a more precise investigation yields the striking fact that this chapter in no way has as its subject the passion of Jeremiah. Rather the subject is the fate of the scroll on which were written the prophets's words of Yahweh. Even a cursory reading demonstrates that clearly. Throughout the thoroughly eventful narrative of Jer. 36 one knows, with the unraveling of each phase of the events, the exact location of the scroll. The same cannot be said of the prophet. Verses 1–4 describe the scroll of Baruch originating from the word of Yahweh. The second scene (vv. 5–10) tells how Baruch enters into the temple with the scroll, and then pinpoints in exact fashion the place where the scroll is recited. After Micaiah, the son of Gemariah, announced in the council what had happened (vv. 11–13), Baruch, who had previously read the scroll in the temple, is told: "Take in your hand the scroll that you read in the hearing of the people, and come."[24] So Baruch, the son of Neriah, took the scroll in his hand and came to them." After Baruch is politely invited to sit (the demonstration of respect is not primarily for him, but rather the scroll), he recites the words of the scroll. After the decision that the scroll must without question be read before the king, once again there is the meticulous inquiry about the history of the scroll's origin: "Tell us, how did you write all these words . . . ?"[25] And Baruch told them: "He dictated all these words to me while I wrote them with ink[26] on the scroll." Beyond that, however, after the instruction to Baruch and the absent Jeremiah to keep themselves concealed and after the ministers proceeded to go to the

---

[23]The late legend is more voluble here and speaks of a stoning of Jeremiah after he had returned to the land following the exile; cf. the [Christian edited] Paralipomena Jeremiae (P. Riessler, *Altjüdisches Schrifttum ausserhalb der Bibel*, 1928, 919).

[24]Instead of the MT וַלֵּךְ, perhaps one should read in 14a וַרֵד. Volz and Rudolph read וַיֵּלֶךְ and combine this with the narrated oracle which follows.

[25]מִפִּיו in the MT is intrusive, and should be omitted.

[26]This specific detail, absent in the LXX, is to be left in the text. It's inclusion demonstrates the extreme interest in the scroll.

king, it is carefully noted: "They placed, however, the scroll into the chamber of Elishama, the secretary, for safe-keeping." Again one knows even in this transition scene exactly where the scroll is, but not where Jeremiah and Baruch have hidden themselves. The scene before the king is then introduced by the statement that the scroll is brought to the king from the chamber of Elishama, the scribe (once more the location is expressly though superfluously mentioned, since this had just been stated). In a chilly scene, during which the king sits alone while his entire group of associates (probably including the reader of the scroll, Jehudi) stands before him, the sacrilege of the successive burning of the scroll containing the word of God by the king takes place. The prophet and Baruch remain in safety.[27] In the burning of the scroll, Yahweh himself experiences a fiery death, a means of death that was especially ignominious for Old Testament sensibilities.[28] The passion of God is not preceded by the passion of the prophet. A fifth scene, which reports a new preparation of a second scroll containing the written word of God, signifies to be sure that one cannot be rid of the word of Yahweh. It experiences its new, vital regeneration. The power of the king is incapable of negating Yahweh's living word.

What results from a careful examination of the emphases of Jer. 36 is confirmed in an equally surprising manner by a look at the concluding frame of the passion narrative of Jeremiah, chapter 45. Once again it is a matter of tribulation. But it is no longer the tribulation of the prophet, but rather that of his loyal companion Baruch. He had lamented (only here do we find a "Confession of Baruch") with the cry of woe: "Woe is me! for the Lord has added sorrow to my pain; I am weary with my groaning, and I find no rest." The actual statement of Yahweh himself is presented in Jeremiah's word of comfort which promises to Baruch during his lament that he would live through all persecution: "Behold, what I have built I am breaking down, and what I have planted I am plucking up. . . . And do you seek great things for yourself? Seek them not." Here is renewed the same expression heard earlier in Jer. 36, only now in a different context: the passion of God is not preceded by human passion. The suffering of the prophet and his companion is only to be understood as the pale reflection of the comprehensive suffering of Yahweh.

The deeper lying and more proper understanding of the suffering of the prophet is indicated by the framework of the narrative of Jeremiah 37–44 in which the prophet is the human figure whose suffering is reported. The biography of the prophet is not of interest in this passion narrative. The possibly undramatic end of Jeremiah in Egypt is not even mentioned.[29]

---

[27]In contrast to the MT וַיַּסְתִּרֵם יְהוָה, the LXX reads simply καὶ κατεκρύβησαν. Volz and Rudolph explain the MT reading as a scribal dittography resulting from וַיְהִי which follows in v. 27.

[28]Cf. Lev. 20:14, Amos 2:1.

[29]Cf. however the legendary tradition (n. 23).

What is intended in this narrative is the inner, human reflection of the much greater suffering of Yahweh himself. The history of divine suffering, expressed in Yahweh's dealings with his people and in the suffering of the prophet, becomes the hermeneutical key for understanding the tribulation of the prophet. This perception is the fruit, according to the narrator's report about this suffering, that issues forth from the tribulation of the prophet.

V

That this perception does not simply miss the mark in regard to the prophet's own words and intention is confirmed by the so-called confessions of Jeremiah. Since the fundamental, form-critical investigation by Baumgartner[30], the voices have fallen silent which said that the confessions were merely inserted, typical psalms that were later attributed to the prophet. In the same way, the opposite thesis, that Jeremiah may have been by means of his confessions the father of the poetry of the Psalms, has lost its supporters. G. von Rad[31] has attempted to demonstrate what Jeremiah himself came to hear in the trials of his office. More recent investigations have been obliged to reject this view as an inadmissible psychologizing of the prophet's suffering. Instead, they have maintained that the confessions, placed in the prophet's mouth, are not the immediate expressions of his own suffering, but rather exemplary expressions that are about prophetic suffering.[32] Such formulations may only be understood as a much later stage of reflection on this suffering.[33]

It is appropriate, first of all, to test the validity of these views before a judgment may be rendered about the significance of the confessions as the prophet's own statement.

In his interpretation of Jeremiah 11:18–12:6, 15:10–21, 17:(12) 14–18, 18:18–23, and 20:7–18 as secondarily shaped, "exemplary" expressions concerning the prophet's suffering, Gunneweg proceeds from the doubtlessly correct observation that the laments and thanksgivings of the Psalter as a rule may not simply be psychologically explained as the private expression of lament or thanksgiving issuing from an individual's own life experience. Rather, these psalms contain exemplary, deliberate, usually constant formulations. However, the further assumption is by no means established

---

[30]W. Baumgartner, *Die Klagegedichte des Jeremia*, BZAW 32, 1917.

[31]G. von Rad, "Die Konfessionen Jeremias, *Ev Th* 3 (1936) 265–276 (=TB 48, 1973, 224–235). (Translated and republished in this volume, Ed.).

[32]A. H. J. Gunneweg, "Konfession oder Interpretation im Jeremiabuch," *ZThK* 67 (1970) 395–416, in partial dependence on H. Graf Reventlow, *Liturgie und prophetisches Ich bei Jeremia* (1963), esp. 205–257. Against Reventlow: J. Bright, "Jeremiah's Complaints—Liturgy or Expressions of Personal Distress?" in: *Proclamation and Presence*. Festschrift G. H. Davies (1970) 189–214.

[33]P. Welten, "Leiden und Leidenserfahrung im Buch Jeremia," *ZThK* 74 (1977) 123–150.

with this observation, since, in a secondary usage of the exemplary fashioned materials of the Psalms, the individual experience of the one praying may well come to expression. The participation of his "psyche" by no means needs to be regarded as suspicious. Whoever models his prayer according to a prayer formula is not necessarily required to pray only in a formal manner.

Now, one recognizes in Jeremiah's speeches of judgment, speeches which are unquestionably the prophet's own, that a very deep-seated feeling may issue forth from his own personal experience. One should listen to the formulation of Jer. 4:19–21: "My anguish, my anguish! I writhe in pain! Oh, the walls of my heart! My heart is beating wildly; I cannot keep silent; for I hear the sound of the trumpet, the alarm of war. Disaster follows hard on disaster, the whole land is laid waste. Suddenly my tents are destroyed, my curtains in a moment. How long must I see the standard, and hear the sound of the trumpet?" The elemental auditory and visionary experience is here unmistakably reflected in the formulation of the prophet's words, even when one fails to hear in them the vocabulary of the exemplary language of the Psalms.[34]

If this is not a matter for debate in 4:19–21, then why should not very elemental, private experience be present in the confessions so that one finds conventional, borrowed psalmodic prayer modified here and there by unconventional expression?

In this context, one cannot engage in a complete literary, form-critical, and redactional analysis of all of the confessions of Jeremiah and take into consideration the valuable, preliminary work of Thiel[35] in a critical processing of the more specific analyses of Graf Reventlow,[36] Gunneweg,[37] Gerstenberger,[38] Hubmann,[39] Welten,[40] and others. It is sufficient for the present context to point to a couple of places in which, in my opinion, something that is unmistakably Jeremianic comes to expression, in which there is also to be recognized the stirring of the prophet's psyche. How could it be otherwise for living men? Thus, one may recognize in two answers of God that which is distinctively Jeremianic: in the first (12:5) the announcing to the weary prophet in a surprising "response" that he must carry an even heavier burden; and in the second (15:19[-21]) his being

---

[34]In regard to "cannot keep silent" (v. 19) cf., e.g., Ps. 32:3; cf. Ps. 39:3f. which has a different formulation. For עַד־מָתַי in v. 21, cf. Pss. 74:10, 80:5, *et passim*, as well as the repetition of עַד־אָנָא of Ps. 13:2f.

[35]W. Thiel, *Die deuteronomistische Redaktion von Jeremia 1–25*, WMANT 41, 1973.

[36]See above, note 32.

[37]See above, note 32.

[38]E. Gerstenberger, "Jeremiah's Complaint. Observations on Jer. 15:10–21," *JBL* 82 (1963) 393–408.

[39]F. D. Hubmann, *Untersuchungen zu den Konfessionen Jer 11, 18–12, 6 und Jer 15, 10–21*, 1978.

[40]See above, note 33.

called to return, a statement couched in the same words that Jeremiah himself had presented as a challenge to the people.[41]

This is also quite so in the ambivalent remark of Jer. 15:16f.[42] which combines the bliss of the experiencing of the word with the lament over the isolation caused by this same divine word. The first half of this lament has experienced a rather dire continuation in Ezek. 2:8–3:3,[43] and the second half has given occasion to the Deuteronomic speech in 16:1–9.[44] The same is true in regard to the harsh reproaches uttered against Yahweh in 15:18 and 20:7. In the first, Jeremiah accuses him of being a liar ("a deceitful brook"), while in the second the prophet openly calls God a seducer. Some will dare to exclude the cursing of the day of birth which has a "later history" in Job 3 where it is shaped and enlarged in a more powerful, literary fashion. In the same way they will dare to exclude the cry of woe directed toward the mother as one that is a later reflection of the prophetic experience. The fact that other pieces besides these, as e.g., the prayer for vengeance in 17:14–18 and 18:18–23, move along conventional paths does not invalidate the observations previously mentioned.

In regard to these, in my opinion, authentic "confessions" of the prophet which reach their final, harshest climax in the curse of 20:14–18, it is now to be determined how their redactional placement into their context gives them a definite meaning and thereby their deepest significance. It is remarkable at the same time how close this significance comes to the statement of God's word to Baruch in Jer. 45. However, is it erroneous to see in this a reflection of the perception which Jeremiah himself has grasped in his affliction from within (ἔσωθεν φόβοι) and without (ἔξωθεν μάχαι) and which only the written recording of these words of confession can truly make intelligible?

If the redactional connection of the last block of words of confession (20:7–18) to a report concerning persecution endured in the temple (20:1–6) is easily comprehensible, so the embedding of the first block (11:18–12:6) points to deep, enigmatic difficulties. First of all, redactionally speaking, it is conspicuous for this block, however this in itself may be literarily assessed, that the words of God are separated into two sections, the first preceded and the second followed by the key-word יְדִדוּת/יָדִיד ("beloved"), which for Jeremiah occurs only here. The preceding genuine word of Jeremiah (11:15f.)[45] is unfortunately difficult to understand in

---

[41] Jer. 3:12, 22; refusal of repentance 5:3.

[42] The treatment of this passage by Gerstenberger, op. cit., 401, is quite unsatisfactory.

[43] See BK XIII (²1979) 75–79.

[44] The analysis by Welten (note 33) yields the improbable result that the prose speech of 16:1–9 (131f.) is older (according to pp. 146f. exilic) than the poetic confession of 15:15f. which is attributed to post-exilic piety. This in spite of the fact v. 17 receives elaborate comment in 16:1–9; cf. Thiel, op. cit., 289.

[45] 11:1–17 describes according to Thiel, op. cit., p. 156, "a continuous section formulated by D, a section which has taken up and included a Jeremianic saying in the framing verses (14,17)." The relationship of the proverb of 11:15 to 12:7 is not noticed by Thiel.

detail. It is, however, in any case clear that Yahweh here announces a painful judgment over the "green olive tree, fair with goodly fruit.[46] Far more sharply focused is the continuation in 12:7ff. which expresses the personal suffering of Yahweh under the duress of having to hold judgment: "I have forsaken my house, I have abandoned my heritage; I have given the beloved of my soul into the hands of her enemies. My heritage has become to me like a lion in the forest, she has lifted up her voice against me, therefore I hate her. Is my heritage to make like a speckled bird of prey? Are the birds of prey against her round about? Go, assemble[47] all the wild beasts; bring[47] them to devour. Many shepherds have destroyed my vineyard, they have trampled down my portion, they have made my pleasant portion a desolate wilderness." The confession of the suffering of the prophet has been redacted in a corresponding way into the words about Yahweh's suffering in his judgment. Here we have the passion of God in exactly the same way as we have it in 45:4f. It envelops here the discussion about prophetic passion and intends thereby to become the interpreter of prophetic suffering. One will be justified in extending this hermeneutic also to the following confessions, since so many details still need further elucidation by means of text, literary, and redaction criticisms.

"The fruit of the tribulation of the prophet": in the redactional placement of the passion narrative of Jer. 37–44, narrated by one or more(?) third persons and in regard to the framework of 11:21–12:6, the impression is made that prophetic suffering provides a deep insight into the nature of Yahweh. In the background of the prophetic commission to proclaim judgment and its resultant suffering which may issue forth in a harsh attack against God, stands Yahweh's own suffering. Should this deep insight really only belong to a later redactor who then would also have had to have shaped Jer 45:4f.? Were this the case, this insight would have no basis in an authentic Jeremiah tradition, and thus would not be the prophet's own fruit which ripened in his suffering.[48]

VI

In regard to the question that has been posed and addressed thus far, the discussion must turn now to the anonymous prophet of the late post-exile who proclaimed a turning point in the history of salvation. Old

---

[46]The Zurich Bible: "a greening olive tree, wonderful to see."

[47]So MT. The Vulgate (LXX) appears to point, according to Rudolph, to an understanding of "gather yourself . . . come."

[48]One would expect in regard to so decisive a formulation by a later interpreter a direct address of God to Jeremiah, and hardly the roundabout way of the form of a unique word of God to Baruch through the mediation of Jeremiah. In the words of God to Ebed-Melech in 39:15–18, there exists in this regard a natural parallel for a word of Jeremia to one who helped him out of his circumstances. Cf. in addition J. Muilenburg, "Baruch the Scribe," in: Festschrift G. H. Davies (see above, note 32) 215–238, 235f. (Republished in this volume, Ed.).

Testament science is indebted to Duhm's commentary of 1892[49] for the recognition that four "Servant of Yahweh Songs" (42:1–4, 49:1–6, 50:4–9, 52:13–53:12) emerge from the text of Deutero-Isaiah as somewhat distinctive.[50] The first two are entirely given over to the thoughts of the universal extension of the message of salvation announced by the prophet. In the last two, however, this concern is conspicuously subdued. This allows instead to move toward the center something that the first two songs have scarcely anticipated: the aspect of the servant's suffering.[51] In the present context, our interest is directed to these final two songs and their theme—trial through suffering.

In the third song (50:4–9) it is difficult not to recognize that the servant (though this designation does not occur here) is understood as a prophetic figure. By tongue and ear, the specific organs of preparation and outfitting for prophetic office, the servant is made ready to be the proper disciple (לִמּוּד) so that he can rightly perform this task of "quickening"[52] the weary. Why he is spat upon, has his beard pulled, is struck, and is hurled into suffering during the performance of his task is not specified. Likewise, any concrete cause remains unstated in the fourth song which then speaks of the disfigurement of his appearance, humiliation, arrest,[53] judgment, abandonment in death, and ignominious burial. In the preceding, all the features of suffering are massed together in their enormity. Since several points of contact with Jeremiah are especially indicated in the servant songs, one can scarcely avoid the supposition that the suffering figure of the servant of God is not delineated without an awareness of the statements about Jeremiah's suffering. At the same time, however, one cannot fail to recognize, above all in the last song, that here everything has culminated in a most substantial, final figure of suffering. The speech of "exemplary suffering" is in place in Isaiah 53. The transcending of all "normal" experiences in the description of Isa. 53 is especially recognizable when the mouth of Yahweh speaks of a final exaltation and a renewed "seeing of light" by the servant who is given over to death (53:11f.).[54] The question, surrounded by riddles, concerning the interpretation of this servant in the framework of Deutero-Isaiah's own words needs not be further pursued

[49]B. Duhm, *Das Buch Jesaja*, HK III/1, 1892, [4]1922; with an accompanying word by W. Baumgartner [5]1967.

[50]The problem of the eventual relationship of 42:5–9 and 49:7, 8–13 to the Servant Songs does not need to be addressed here. Cf., e.g., J. Begrich, *Studien zu Deuterojesaja*, BWANT IV 25, 1938 (=TB 20, [2]1969).

[51]One could recognize at best remote traces in the statement of 42:4—"He will neither be extinguished nor broken (יָרוּץ)", and the despondent sigh of 49:4a.

[52]Read לַעֲנוֹת, instead of MT's לָעוּת.

[53]MT עֹצֶר (53:8) could remotely reflect the עָצוּר of Jer. 36:5, though of course a translation of "arrested" is forbidden by the context (see above, note 17).

[54]The addition of אוֹר after יִרְאֶה in 53:11, originally based on the LXX, has now been confirmed by QJes a and b.

here.[55] While one may be able to recognize in the first two songs something of the prophetic office of Deutero-Isaiah himself, still the statements about suffering and exaltation, especially in the last song, go far beyond what is biographically possible for Deutero-Isaiah.

In the present context, only the question concerning the "fruit of prophetic tribulation" is important. In regard to this formulation of the question, one will need to distinguish between the two final songs. In 50:4–9 the description of the mistreatment endured by the servant abruptly breaks off at v. 7 into a statement of trust. In imitation of the divine promise present in the call narrative of Ezek. 3:8f, the servant acknowledges that he has made his own face hard as flint[56] in order to continue with a triumphant defiance of the defendant, reminiscent of the style of other words in Deutero-Isaiah.[57] This defiance has found its echo in Rom. 8:33 One is tempted here, in regard to the question of the "fruit of prophetic tribulation," to point to the concatenation of Rom. 5:3f.: "Let us rejoice in our sufferings (θλίψεσιν), knowing that suffering produces (κατεργάζεται) endurance, and endurance produces character, and character produces hope, and hope does not disappoint us, because God's love has been poured into our hearts." Character, hope, and certainty of God's love are the fruit of affliction.

In Isa. 52:13–53:12, the servant himself does not speak. However, Yahweh, to be sure, in the framing sections (52:13–15 and 53:11aβ.b–12) confirms that he not only will bring his servant once again to a position of honor, but also that his hope will not be brought to shame.

On the other hand, an entirely different "perception" in regard to the suffering servant is expressed in the middle section (53:1–11aα) that is framed by the words of Yahweh. It is outwardly expressed by a human voice. A number of men (ought one to speak of a community of the servant's disciples?) confess that they themselves in an astonishing way have obtained a completely new understanding which is a different one to that found in Jeremiah. Here, there is nothing about a passion of God as the background for the passion of the prophet. The anguish of the figure of suffering who is "without form and beauty" (53:2) is hermeneutically construed and undertood in priestly categories. These help in this context to make transparent suffering in its divine sense. 53:10 speaks of this when it states that the servant has sacrificed his life as an אָשָׁם ("sin offering").[58] Already I Sam. 6:3f., 8 knows of this idea when it reports that the

---

[55]For the history of exegesis, see especially C. R. North, *The Suffering Servant in Deutero-Isaiah. An Historical and Critical Study*, [2]1956.

[56]Instead of the phrase כְשָׁמִיר חָזָק מִצֹּר ("like a diamond, harder than flint") found in Ezek. 3:9, Isa. 50:7 simply reads: כַּחַלָּמִישׁ ("like flint").

[57]Cf. the provocative, questioning מִי ("who") in 41:2, 4, 26; 43:9, 13, *et passim*, or the challenge to come forth in 41:1 and 45:21.

[58]This statement is clear, while the expression preceding 53:10 gives rise to questions.

Philistines, at the instruction of their priests and soothsayers, sent back "five golden tumors and five golden mice"[59] as an אָשָׁם ("sin offering, compensation, reparation")[60] with the ark to the Israelites. In general, אָשָׁם ("sin offering") has its place, though in a not entirely evident way, in the priestly system of sacrifice.[61] So, the suffering of the prophetic servant is "placed" (שִׂים) upon him as a sin-offering, reparation.

Corresponding to this are other categories of interpretation, including the linguistic, freely modified idiom נָשָׂא עָוֹן ("to bear guilt"). In the priestly source, this clearly defined, exactly employed formula describes in Lev. 16:22 the bearing away of the sin of Israel to the wilderness demon Azazel. The words of Ezekiel, which also have definite traces in the proclamation of Deutero-Isaiah,[62] prove that this conception had already become a familiar one to Ezekiel. So to some extent the powerful, later interpreted symbolic act in Ezek. 4:4–8 rests upon this conception as its proper category of interpretation.[63]

In terms of this interpretative category, the suffering of the servant of God has another side, though it points in a similar direction followed by the term אָשָׁם. The "reparation" accomplished by him in his suffering is described in this song as the act of guilt-bearing that produces righteousness for "the many" (53:11).

VII

The early Christian interpretation (with which H. W. Wolff in his Halle dissertation concerned himself in his exegesis of the text and its understanding in Judaism and beyond)[64] could no longer read pass the biblical discussion of the fruit of the tribulation of the servant of God as though the Christ event had not occurred. However, at the same time, the understanding of the passion of God obtained by Jeremiah and its conspicuous connection with the understanding obtained in Deutero-Isaiah lived on in the witness of the Christian community which recognized Jesus Christ in the suffering of the servant of God.

The observation is made in Heb. 1:1 that God has spoken previously to the fathers in many and various ways (πολυμερῶς καὶ πολυτρόπως) through the prophets, but now has spoken "in these last days" his complete word through his Son. This observation, which brings together the various

---

[59]So the MT. Probably one of these two elements is the result of secondary expansion.

[60]So D. Kellermann, ThWAT I, 465.

[61]For complete studies, see D. Kellermann, ibid., 413–472, "אָשָׁם"; and R. Knierim, THAT I 251–257, "אָשָׁם, Schuldverpflichtung."

[62]D. Baltzer, Ezekiel und Deuterojesaja. Berührungen in der Heilserwartung der beiden grossen Exilspropheten, BZAW 121, 1971.

[63]W. Zimmerli, "Zur Vorgeschichte von Jes 53," VTS 17 (1969) 236–244 (=TB 51, 1974, 213–221).

[64]H. W. Wolff, Jesaja 53 im Urchristentum. Die Geschichte der Prophetie 'Siehe, es siegt mein Knecht' bis zu Justin, 1942; ²1950; ³1953.

features previously discussed into a new unity, can appropriately receive under the inquiry concerning the "fruit of the tribulation of the prophet" its stirring confirmation.

22

"The Lord Has Created Something New": A Stylistic Study of Jer 31:15-22*

Bernhard W. Anderson

At the conclusion of a poem found in the "Little Book of Consolation" (Jeremiah 30–31) the announcement is made that Yahweh has created something new to signify the new age into which a sorrowing, despairing people is invited to enter. The received Hebrew text of Jer 31:22 reads:

kî bārāʾ YHWH ḥădāšâ bāʾāreṣ	For the Lord has created a new thing in the earth,
nĕqēbâ tĕsôbēb gāber	A woman shall compass a man.
	(KJV)

This announcement, introduced by the motive particle *kî* ("for"), is the climactic line of the poem. Here the poet speaks about God's innovation, something so marvellous that it should motivate a response to the gracious invitation. Unfortunately, however, the second colon, which specifies the "new thing" (*ḥădāšâ*) indicated in the first colon, is not clear. Weiser, though venturing a translation, observes that the final words constitute "ein ungelöstes Rätsel." Bright says that "the meaning is wholly obscure" and suggests that it would be wiser to leave the colon blank rather than try to translate it. Rudolph, among other scholars, maintains that the text in its present form makes no sense and should be emended.[1]

It may be that the Hebrew text has become corrupt in the course of transmission.[2] But before resorting to the desperate expedient of textual emendation, it may be worthwhile to take another look at the problem from the standpoint of a stylistic study of the text in its context.

---

*Originally published in the *Catholic Biblical Quarterly* 40 (1978) 463–78.

[1] A. Weiser, *Das Buch der Propheten Jeremia* (ATD 20/21; Göttingen: Vandenhoeck & Ruprecht, 1959) 290; J. Bright, *Jeremiah* (AB 21; Garden City, N.Y.: Doubleday) 282; W. Rudolph, *Jeremia* (HAT 12; Tübingen: Mohr, 1958) 290.

[2] The LXX at Jer 38:22 has a different reading: ἕως πότε ἀποστρέψεις θυγάτηρ ἠτιμωμένη; ὅτι ἔκτισεν κύριος σωτηρίαν εἰς καταφύτευσιν καινήν, ἐν σωτηρίᾳ. περιελεύσονται ἄνθρωποι. ("How long will you turn away, disgraced daughter? For the Lord has created salvation for a new planting; in salvation men will walk.")

The troublesome words occur in the immediate context of an appeal to Israel, addressed as "Virgin" or "Daughter," to return home (31:21–22). The summons to return involves a geographical movement: a movement away from captivity along the very route (marked with guideposts) of the journey into exile, and a movement toward her homeland, specifically "her cities" (v 21). There is also the suggestion that coming home involves a return to a faithful relationship to Yahweh, for the Virgin/Daughter is addressed: *habbat haššôbēbâ* ("O wandering daughter"). Thus she is asked, with double entendre, why she wanders to and fro (*ᶜadmātay tithammāqîn*),[3] both in the sense of getting lost on the homeward journey and in the sense of continuing in her faithless straying from the covenant relationship with Yahweh (v 22a). The appeal to "return," in the double sense of returning home to the land and of returning home to her covenant loyalty with Yahweh who gives his people a future, is followed by the inducement: "For Yahweh has created something new." Here the so-called "prophetic perfect" is used to announce the future that is already present, in the sense that it is anchored in the certainty of God's intention. Appropriately the creation verb *bārāʾ*, which is used only in connection with divine creativity (Gen 1:1; etc.), is employed here—as in Second Isaiah (Isa 48:6–7; cf. 65:17–18)—to announce the new creation, the new age that will be inaugurated "on the earth" or "in the land" (*bāʾāreṣ*).

The prophetic *novum* itself is described in three Hebrew words: 1. *nĕqēbâ*, a word that refers to a female, whether human or animal (Gen 1:27; 6:19); 2. a verb *tĕsôbēb* (polel of *sābab*, "to turn," "go around," "encircle"), which means to "encompass" in various senses, such as enemies surrounding a city (Ps 59:15 [ET 14]), a liturgical movement around the altar (Ps 26:6), or—in a theological sense—Yahweh's enfolding his people with protection (Deut 32:10) or with covenant faithfulness (Ps 32:7, 10); and finally, 3. an object *geber* which refers to a full-bodied male who is capable of military, sexual, and other responsibilities (Exod 12:37; Deut 22:5; Prov 30:19; etc.). It has long been recognized that the difficulty lies not in translating the three Hebrew words, but in understanding their meaning in the syntax of the sentence and, above all, their function in the given poetic context.

Special attention should be drawn to the translation of the Vulgate:

Usquequo deliciis dissolveris filia vaga?
quia creavit Dominus novum super terram:
femina circumdabit virum.

Jerome took the final words to be a mariological prophecy, referring to Mary's protective embrace of the Christ-child within her womb. He wrote:[4]

---

[3]The hithpael form is a *hapax legomenon* (cf. qal in Cant 5:6) and apparently means "to turn hither and thither," possibly to turn about in circles (like a lost person).

[4]Quoted in the annotation of *The New American Bible* (New York: Kenedy, 1970) 1136. See Jerome: *PL* 28, 255; 24, 880–81. My colleague, Karlfried Froehlich, has pointed out that

The Lord has created a new thing on earth without seed of man, without carnal union and conception, "a woman will encompass a man" within her womb—One who, though he will later appear to advance in wisdom and age through the stages of infancy and childhood, yet, while confined for the usual number of months in his mother's womb, will already be perfect man.

According to this interpretation, the words are not just eschatological but messianic in a specific Christian sense. In the history of interpretation this influential view has taken its place along with a variety of others.[5]

The difficulty of the text is evidenced by various modern English translations, each of which takes a hermeneutical stand. A few may be listed

Amer. Trans.	How long will you hesitate, O backturning daughter? For the Lord has created a new thing on the earth—The woman woos the man!
RSV	How long will you waver, O faithless daughter? For the Lord has created a new thing on the earth: a woman protects a man.
JB	How long will you hesitate, disloyal daughter? For Yahweh is creating something new on earth: the Woman sets out to find her Husband again.
NAB	How long will you continue to stray, rebellious daughter? The Lord has created a new thing upon the earth: the woman must encompass the man with devotion.
NEB	How long will you twist and turn, my wayward child? For the Lord has created a new thing in the earth: a woman turned into a man.
AB	How long dillydally, O turnabout daughter? For Yahweh has created a new thing on earth: [A female shall compass a man(?)]

The interpretations given in these translations may be divided into two general categories:

1. Some take *něqēbâ* and *geber* to refer generically to feminine and masculine human beings respectively. So according to one view (cf. *RSV*) there will be such peace and security in the new age that women will no longer need male protection but, on the contrary, will protect the men.

---

apparently the first patristic mariological interpretation of Jer 31:22 was given by Marcellus of Ancyra (d. ca. 374 A.D.); see *PG* 25, 250B (Ps. Athanasius). Following the translation of Aquila, not of LXX, he commented: "The Lord has created a new thing in the female [LXX: on the earth], that is, in Mary. For nothing new has been created in the female except that which was born from the Virgin Mary without intercourse, the body of the Lord."

[5]For a summary of the *Nachgeschichte* of this text to the mid-nineteenth century, see L. Reinke, *TQ* 33 (1851) 509–63, and *Beiträge zur Erklärung des Alten Testamentes* 3 (1855) 60–69, 318–406. Later brief updatings of the discussion are found in A. Condamin, *Le livre de Jérémie* (EBib; Paris: Lecoffre, 1920) 227–28, and C. Shedl, " 'Femina Circumdabit Virum,' oder 'Via Salutis'?" *ZKT* 83 (1961) 431–35.

Admittedly, the verb *tĕsôbēb* may connote protective encirclement, as in Deut 32:10, where it is said that Yahweh encircled his people and kept them as the apple of his eye; but this interpretation does not suit the context of the new age that is announced. A proper rejoinder is that if women need no protection in a time of peace and security, men should not need it either.[6] Others suggest that the new age will introduce a reversal of relationships, with the result that the woman will take the lead in "wooing" the man (cf. *Amer. Trans.*) or, by emending the verb, that the woman will "be turned into a man" (cf. *NEB*).[7] Even when these meanings are imputed to the verb, the sentence remains obscure. Are we to think that Israel, who had been acting like a timid woman, will act like a vigorous man? Or that there will be such a reversal of relationships that women will be the leaders? In none of these cases is the interpretation warranted by the context.

2. Other interpreters take the nouns *nĕqēbâ* and *geber* to refer to Israel and Yahweh respectively. In the new age there will be a great reversal: formerly, the Man (Yahweh) had encircled the Woman (Israel) with covenant fidelity, but the time will come when Israel will take the initiative to encompass Yahweh with devotion (cf. *NAB*).[8] Or the verb *tĕsôbēb* is construed as "to go looking for" (cf. JB) or is even emended to "return,"[9] with the resulting translation "the woman returns to the man," that is, "the faithless woman Israel finally does return to Yahweh, her man, even though this has never happened before."[10] These interpretations have the advantage of suiting the context. But it is doubtful that the verb, unless emended, can be so construed; and further, it is unusual for the word *geber* to be applied symbolically to Yahweh (cf. 3:20 [*rēa*ᶜ]; Hos. 2:2, 7 [*ʾîš*]).

In recent studies, William Holladay has offered a fresh interpretation.[11] He maintains that the verb *tĕsôbēb* is "plainly sexual" and that we should

---

[6]See J. Philip Hyatt, *IB* 5, 1034.

[7]Emending *tĕsôbēb* to *tissôb*, as proposed by Bernhard Duhm (*Das Buch Jeremia* [KHAT 11; Tübingen: Mohr, 1901] 251). Translating "the woman is turned into a man," he maintained that the sentence is a witty gloss, intended to remind the reader that Israel, who had been referred to shortly before as a man, is here regarded as a woman. Similarly J. Paterson (*Peake's Commentary on the Bible* [rev. ed.; New York: Nelson, 1962] 556) suggests that the sentence is "a grammatical gloss where the copyist is indicating that the masculine (son) has been changed to the feminine (daughter) in 20, 21, 22."

[8]In the annotation to the *NAB* translation it is pointed out that the words "with devotion" are not in the Hebrew text but "are added for the sense."

[9]The emendation of *tĕsôbēb geber* to *tāšûb lĕgeber* was proposed by A. Condamin, *Jérémie*, 228.

[10]N. C. Habel, *Jeremiah-Lamentations* (Concordia Commentary; St. Louis: Concordia, 1968) 241. This general view was advocated long ago by L. Reinke (*Beiträge*, 318–406) and has been freshly revived by E. Jacob ("Féminisme ou Messianisme? A propos de Jérémie 31, 32," *Beiträge zur alttestamentlichen Theologie, Walther Zimmerli Festschrift* [ed. H. Donner, R. Hanhart, and R. Smend; Göttingen: Vandenhoeck & Ruprecht, 1977] 179–84).

[11]W. L. Holladay, "Jer. xxxi Reconsidered: 'The Woman Encompasses the Man,'" *VT* 16 (1966) 236–39; "Jeremiah and Woman's Liberation,'" *Andover Newton Quarterly*, 12 (1972) 213–23; *Jeremiah: Spokesman Out of Time* (Philadelphia: Pilgrim Press, 1974) 116–21.

translate approximately: "the female embraces the he-man." The noun *geber*, he alleges, has the same meaning as in 30:5–7, which he interprets to mean that the soldiers of Judah are mocked for "acting like women" when God comes to wage battle against his people. In the passage at hand, Jeremiah is said to have used the motif of femininity in two ways: first, to portray Israel in the wilderness (exile) as innocent, vulnerable, and "giddy"; and second, to portray weakness under combat, like the "warriors-become-women" referred to in an earlier passage (30:5–7; cf. 50:37; Nah 3:13). "Israel is not only acting feminine in the wilderness but effeminate," and God intends to put a stop to such behavior. Therefore, in the new age God will reverse the masculine-feminine roles; he "will make the female rather than the male the initiator in sexual relations, so that the demoralized warriors-turned-to-women will no longer be under the curse. Next time the women will take the lead." Holladay, who is sensitive to changing human relations in our time, warns against hastily jumping to the conclusion that this text is "an early anticipation of the women's liberation." Rather, the prophet was using "the stock assumptions of his time" to portray hope for the people in their helplessness; for "God will make even the people's presumed effeminacy into strength."[12]

There are at least two problems with this novel interpretation. In the first place, the interpretation hinges on understanding 30:5–7 as the mockery or curse of warriors who had become, in the view of a male-oriented society, as weak as women.[13] The text at hand, however, does not lend itself easily to this understanding. Elsewhere, Jeremiah used the image of child-birth to portray the anguish of the times, for instance in 6:24 (cf. 4:31; 22:23) where the impending invasion of the foe from the north evokes the consternation of the people, portrayed as the daughter of Zion:

> We have heard the news of it,
>   our hands fall limp;
> anguish has seized us,
>   pain like a woman in labor [*yôlēdâ*].

Similarly in 30:5–6 we read that the pangs of "a woman in labor" (*yôlēdâ*) grip men—a metaphorical description of the general anguish and ashen fear in prospect of the Day of Yahweh, which will be unlike any other day. In the second place, while Holladay's interpretation is consonant with the movement of the poetry from despair to hope, from weakness to strength, it does not provide a persuasive identification of the enigmatic *něqēbâ* and *geber* mentioned in 31:22. The virile term *geber*, in view of its various usages in the Old Testament and in the prophecy of Jeremiah (see 30:6

---

[12]*Jeremiah*, 117, 120.

[13]Holladay alludes to D. Hillers, *Treaty-curses and the Old Testament Prophets* (BibOr 16; Rome: Pontifical Biblical Institute, 1964) where this theme is treated, and calls attention to Jer 50:37; 51:30; Nah 3:13, where this type of curse is reflected.

[parallel to *zākār*]; 22:30; 23:9 [parallel to *ʾîš*]), need not be restricted to "warrior."

A "pregnant" suggestion has been offered by Artur Weiser, who observes that two words in the line, *bārāʾ* ("create") and *nĕqēbâ* ("female"), are related to the creation account in Gen 1:27ff., a literary (or liturgical) tradition that reaches back into a time much earlier than the final formulation of the priestly work. He proposes that the final colon of 31:22 points to "the renewal of the creation-blessing of fertility (Gen 1:28; cf. Jer 31:27), from which the people will arise anew."[14] This potentially fruitful proposal, however, does not take sufficient account of the literary context of the poem in which the enigmatic words occur. Stylistic analysis of the poem, I submit, may illumine the exegetical problem and contribute to theological understanding.

Immediately the question arises: what is the literary unit with which we are dealing? Some literary critics maintain that the poetic unit is very brief: only two verses (vv 21–22). Weiser, for instance, remarks: "Previously it was Ephraim, the son, who was involved [31:18–20], but now it is the Virgin Israel; therefore v 21 begins a new utterance (*Spruch*) which, by virtue of its content, stands apart from the surrounding material as an independent unit."[15] On the other hand, other literary critics maintain that these two verses are the concluding strophe of a larger poem: 31:15–22.[16] Let us consider this important matter.

To begin with, it is noteworthy that 31:15–22 is surrounded on both sides by passages in which Yahweh speaks of his people in the third person plural, using the pronouns "they," "them," "their." On one side, this is true of the poem about homecoming in 31:7–9 (10–14) and, on the other side, of the oracle in 31:23–25—each of which is introduced by the formula, "thus says Yahweh." In the passage found between these units, however, Yahweh addresses his people as a Woman, using the second person singular *feminine*. There is no real exception to this prevailing mode of address in v 15 where weeping Rachel is referred to in the third person or in vv 18–19 where Ephraim, her son, speaks in the first person. To these matters we shall return presently. Notice, however, that the verbs and the pronouns at the end of the poem (vv 21–22a), as at the beginning (vv 16–17), all indicate feminine address.

The major reason for supposing that vv 21–22 represent an independent literary unit is that in v 22b Yahweh is referred to in the third person. Some

---

[14]Weiser, *Jeremia*, 290. He suggests that "die nicht wieder rekonstruirbare Uebersetzung" of LXX points in this direction.

[15]*Jeremia*, 289. This is also the view of Rudolph, *Jeremia*, 181, and of Holladay who maintains, in personal correspondence, that vv 21–22 are a separate poem that closes the whole cycle of chaps. 30–31 and do not belong closely with 31:15–20.

[16]So J. Muilenburg, "Jeremiah," *IDB* (1962) 834; also Bright (*AB*), Condamin (EBib), Duhm (*HKAT*), Habel (Concordia), Hyatt (*IB*).

go so far as to suggest that here the text should be emended to read "I will create" (*'ebrā'*);[17] but this is a purely conjectural way out of the difficulty. The reference to Yahweh in the third person stands securely in the text; and this has led scholars (e.g. Rudolph) to the conclusion that in these verses the prophet, not Yahweh, is the speaker, and therefore that this is a separate literary unit.

Admittedly, there is uncertainty about who the speaker is. However, we should guard against expecting strict distinctions in poetry, especially in a context where no sharp line can be drawn between the "words of Yahweh" and the prophetic bearer of those words (see 1:9). Sometimes the prophetic "I" fades imperceptibly into the Divine "I," as in 23:13–15, where "to me" (v 14b) seems to refer to Yahweh, not just to what the prophet "saw" (v 13). Moreover, it is not uncommon in prayerful address to Yahweh for the second person form to be used along with the third person (17:13), and the same flexibility is possible in God's address to his people. It is noteworthy that the poem in 31:7–9 (+ 10–14) displays an alternation of persons: Yahweh is spoken about (v 7) and is also the speaker (vv 8–9); and the prophet summons the nations to hear Yahweh's word (vv 10–12) but in the conclusion the divine "I" speaks (v 13). So the change of grammatical forms in 31:21–22, from second person feminine address to third person masculine (v 22b), is not conclusive proof that the prophet is the speaker here. In any case, a sudden change of speakers would not argue against the stylistic unity of the whole passage, 31:15–22, for this phenomenon is found elsewhere in Jeremiah's poetry (e.g. 5:1–14).[18] Even Rudolph, who maintains that the prophet is the speaker in vv 21–22, recognizes that "sachlich sind die Verse die Fortsetzung oder besser die Zusammenfassung alles Bisherigen."[19]

Under the assumption that the literary unit is 31:15–22, let us examine the structure of the passage in order to understand how the climactic strophe in vv 21–22 relates to the whole.

The poem falls into four strophes, each of which contributes to the dramatic movement toward the concluding exhortation to return home. The first strophe (v 15) is introduced by the formula, "thus says Yahweh." In this case, the formula serves to set off the passage from the preceding poem (31:7–9 [10–14]), for the strophe contains nothing to suggest that it is a word of Yahweh. Indeed, it is possible that this may have been an independent piece that was appropriated for an introduction to Jeremiah's poem. It speaks of the disconsolate weeping of Rachel, the ancestral

---

[17]See *BHK*. This textual change was advocated by F. Giesebrecht, *Das Buch Jeremia* 3/2 (Göttingen: Vandenhoeck & Ruprecht, 1907) 170. E. A. Leslie (*Jeremiah* [New York: Abingdon, 1954] 105) emends the text further and translates: "For I am about to create a new thing, in the land of [your] return."

[18]Jeremiah's fondness for changing speakers abruptly is discussed by W. L. Holladay, "The So-called 'Deuteronomic Gloss' in Jer. VIII 19b," *VT* 12 (1962) 494–98.

[19]*Jeremia*, 181.

mother of Joseph (Gen 30:24) and Benjamin (Gen 35:18), heard at her grave in Ramah with which Jeremiah, as a Benjaminite, was familiar.[20] The strophe is cast in a prevailing 3/2 *qînâ* (lamentation) meter:

> 1. Hark! In Ramah is heard lament,   31:15
>   bitter weeping;
>   Rachel is weeping for her sons,
>   refusing to be comforted for her sons,
>   for (*kî*) they are gone.

In rhythmic language the poet plays on the theme of Rachel's weeping (*běkî/měbakkâ*) and the loss of her sons (twice repeated: *bānêhā/bānêhā*). The motive (*kî*) for her disconsolate grief is stated in one emphatic Hebrew word: "they are not!" (*ʾênennû*). But unlike Matt 2:18, where Rachel's lament is remembered in a situation of abject motherly grief (Herod's slaying of the infants), here Rachel's refusal of consolation provides the occasion for Yahweh to speak, as indicated by the repetition of the formula, "thus says Yahweh," at the beginning of v 16.

The poem now shifts from the rhythm of lament to a prevailing 3/3 meter as Yahweh speaks comforting words to Mother Israel. Her sons are not gone forever, but they will come home. The opening imperative echoes sounds from the preceding lament (*miněʿî/mēʾănâ; qôlēk/qôl; mibbekî/běkî, měbakkâ*):

> 2. Restrain your voice from weeping,   31:16
>   your eyes from tears!
>   For (*kî*) there is reward for your labor:[21]
>   they will return from the enemy's land;
>
>   there is hope for your posterity:[21]   31:17
>   sons will return to their territory.

Here the key word—twice used—is *šûb*, "return." Clearly the poet refers to a concrete return—from the land (*ʾereṣ*) of the enemy to their own country (*gěbûl*), the land of Palestine. Thus there is hope for Rachel's future because she will have posterity (*ʾaḥărît*) and Israel will be rebuilt (cf. 31:4–5).

The third strophe is longer, for it contains a quotation within a quotation. At the beginning and end, Yahweh's words are cited (first person); but in between Yahweh quotes the confession of Rachel's son, Ephraim (first person), who penitently laments the folly of his youth:

---

[20] The tradition that Rachel's tomb was Ramah (I Sam 10:2) is at variance with the later tradition, based on the parenthetical scribal remark in Gen 35:19, which transferred it to the vicinity of Bethel (cf. Matt 2:18), where it is venerated today. Ephraim and Manasseh were Joseph's sons, though the former gained ascendancy.

[21] Omitting with the LXX the expression "oracle of Yahweh" (*něʾum YHWH*) at the end of the third and fifth cola.

3. I listened intently—   31:18
Ephraim was shaking with remorse:
"You disciplined me and I was corrected,
  like an untamed calf.
Restore me so that I may come back,
  for (*kî*) you are Yahweh, my God.

For after I turned away, I repented;   31:19
  after I came to my senses, I slapped my thigh.[22]
I blush with shame, feel humiliated,
  for (*kî*) I bear the disgrace of my youth."

Isn't Ephraim my precious son,   31:20
  a child in whom I delight,
For as often as I speak against him,[23]
  I am still very much concerned for him.
Therefore I yearn for him with my being,
  I am filled with compassion for him—the oracle of Yahweh.

Rhetorically, the last two lines display a wonderful balance and assonance, each being introduced by corresponding expressions ("as often as"/"therefore") and concluding with strengthened verbal forms (infinitive absolute + imperfect):

kî-middê dabbĕrî bô	*zāqōr ʾezkĕrennû ʿôd*
ʿal-kēn hāmû mēʿay lô	*raḥēm ʾăraḥămennû*

It is especially noteworthy, however, that the lament of Rachel's son adds another dimension to the verb *šûb* which occurs in various modulations (*hăšîbēnî*, "cause me to return," "restore me"; *ʾāšûbâ*, "I will return"; *šûbî*, "my turning away"). Like the NT parable of the prodigal son in the far country (Luke 15), the return in this case has a double dimension: it is a geographical return (from exile), and a return to a relationship that was spurned in the folly of youth.[24] Since Ephraim's confession is contained within Yahweh's speech, one may wonder whether repentance was the *condition* of Yahweh's restorative action. The passage itself, however, especially when understood in the larger context of Jeremiah's preaching, hardly warrants an affirmative answer to this question. Like Hosea (chap.

---

[22]This gesture of remorse is comparable to beating the breast or slapping the forehead.

[23]Bright (*Jeremiah*, 282) maintains that in v 20 *dabbĕrî bô* literally means "speak of him," not "speak against him" as usually translated, and he translates "as oft as I mention his name." Admittedly, the expression *dibbēr bô* may have either a friendly (cf. Num 12:8) or a hostile (cf. Num 12:1; 21:5, 7; Ps 78:19) meaning. In the context of Yahweh's discipline of his son, "against" is appropriate.

[24]Cf. W. L. Holladay (*The Root Šûbh in the Old Testament* [Leiden: Brill, 1958] 128–39, 152–53) who emphasizes the covenantal meaning of the verb ("repent"). He suggests (pp. 146–47) that the motif of return from exile in chaps. 30–31 is a later reinterpretation under the influence of Second Isaiah.

11), Jeremiah portrays Yahweh's tender affection for Rachel's son, Ephraim, who is also Yahweh's first-born (Jer 31:9c); and he says that even when Yahweh disciplines his son he nevertheless is concerned for him and eagerly waits for any sign of his return. Even in Ephraim's time of separation and alienation, he remained Yahweh's "son" and could confess, "You are Yahweh, my God."

Yahweh's moving soliloquy is not left hanging in the air. At its conclusion, the poem returns to the central theme of Yahweh's bringing Rachel's sons home. Once again in the fourth strophe the poet uses the language of address in the second person *feminine*, as in vv 16–17. Feminine language is dominant throughout the poem. Here, however, the poet shifts from the image of Mother Israel, to which the maternal ("womb") language in v 20c may correspond,[25] to the related prophetic imagery of Israel as the Virgin/Daughter (Amos 5:2; Isa 23:12; 37:22; Jer 14:17; 31:4; etc.). Portrayed as a Woman, Israel is summoned to return in the double meaning that has now become apparent in the poem: to return in a geographical sense from exile to the homeland along a well-marked highway, and to return in the deeper sense of coming home to the covenant relationship.

4. Establish for your path markers,   31:21
    set up for yourself guideposts [*tamrûrîm*]!
  Pay attention to the road,
    the path by which you went!
  Return, Virgin Israel,
    return to these cities of yours!

  How long will you go to and fro,   31:22
    O wandering daughter?
  For Yahweh has created something new,

  . . . .

For the time being we shall leave the final colon untranslated. Two matters, however, deserve special attention. First, the poet mixes the figural language of the sons of Israel returning home and of Israel, personified as a woman, coming back. This mixed figure, which may be disturbing to some readers, is present elsewhere in Jeremiah's poetry. An excellent example is found in Jer 3:12–13, 19–22a, poetry that is also addressed to the North (3:12a). The strophe begins in 3:12b with an address in the masculine singular, "Return faithless Israel!" (*šûbâ měšûbâ yiśrāʾēl*) and continues in v 13 with an address to Israel in the feminine singular, "Only, acknowledge your guilt . . ." (*ʾak děʿî ʿawōnēk*). In the ensuing strophe in 3:19–22a (taking the intervening verses to be a later supplement), Yahweh speaks of Israel as a daughter ("How I would set you [feminine singular] among my

---

[25]See P. Trible, "God, Nature of, in the OT," *IDBSup* 368–69, who discusses "womb imagery" (*reḥem* and related words) with special reference to Jer 31:20c.

sons . . . !" [v 19]) and at the same time as a faithless wife ("so you have been faithless [masculine plural] to me" [v 20]). Finally, in vv 21–22a it is the sons, whose weeping is heard on the bare heights (v 21a; compare Rachel's weeping), who receive the divine invitation: "Return, faithless sons!" (šûbû bānîm šôbābîm), whereupon they penitently confess their renewed faith in Yahweh (vv 22b–25).

Secondly, in the final strophe of the poem in 31:15–22 the poet plays on the motif of the road (mĕsillâ) or the path (derek), a motif also found in Isa 40:3. In the time of exile, this route led away from the promised land and away from the covenant relationship; in the time of restoration, on the other hand, the route will lead back to the land ("your cities") and to the relationship with Yahweh that is the basis of šālôm in the homeland. This observation adds force to the question in v 22a, addressed to Israel in feminine terms, as to why she turns this way and that (tithammāqîn), like one who is lost and goes in circles, both geographically and spiritually. Since Yahweh is gracious (cf. 3:12: kî ḥāsîd ʾănî), he summons his backturning (šôbēbâ) daughter to come back and to take part in the new age.

The invitation to return is motivated by the announcement that Yahweh will create (or, in the prophetic perfect, "has created") something new—the "new thing" (ḥădāšâ) of which the prophet of the exile also spoke (Isa 43:19; 42:9; 48:6–7). But what specifically is the future novum that is announced in Jer 31:22?

Let us approach this question by considering first of all the geographical locus of Yahweh's new act of creation: the innovation is to occur bāʾāreṣ, "in the earth" or "in the land." It is noteworthy that almost all modern translations render the Hebrew word as "on/in the earth," thereby implying the broad terrestial horizon of the creation story (Gen 1:1) or Jeremiah's vision of chaos (Jer 4:23–26). This consensus is surprising, for there is nothing to support it in the context of the Book of Consolation or in the poem itself. The theme of the collection as a whole is stated in the prefatory oracle (30:1–3):

> For lo! days are coming—the oracle of Yahweh—when I will restore the fortunes of Israel and Judah, says Yahweh; for I will bring them back to the land [hāʾāreṣ] which I gave to their ancestors and they will take possession of it.

It is generally recognized that this little book contains material that originally dealt with north Israel (Ephraim), the people who had gone into exile in 722 B.C. (e.g. the exquisite poem in 31:2–6). The preface indicates, however, that God's consolation is extended to Israel as a whole, north and south. The heart of the promise is the establishment of a new relationship, signified by the covenant formula, "You shall be my people and I will be your God" (30:22; 31:1; 31:33). But this promise is not purely spiritual; it involves return from exile and resettlement of the land of the ancestors

(31:5, 12), the blessing of fertility and increase for land and people (31:4–5, 12, 14), and a situation of security and peace (31:4, 13). Furthermore, the particular poem under consideration gives no hint of a wide meaning of ʾereṣ. On the contrary, the children of Rachel are summoned to come back from "the land of the enemy" (mēʾereṣ ʾôyēb) and are to return to their own territory (ligĕbûlām, v 16), to their own cities (v 21). Thus in the light of the total and immediate contexts there is every reason to suppose that the "new thing" pertains to life in the promised land (see also 3:14, "I will bring you to Zion," and 3:19, ". . . a pleasant land, a heritage most beauteous of all nations").[26] The poet announces that in the land Yahweh will create a "new thing" to signify the future that he opens up for his people, in reversal of their former condition.

The specific character of this reversal is clarified, in my judgment, when we consider the overall structure of the poem. A characteristic literary device of Israelite poets is to sound a motif at the end that was announced at the beginning, in the manner of *inclusio*. Recalling our previous summary, the design of the poem may be outlined as follows:

Mother Israel's grief (v 15)
Yahweh comforts Mother Israel (vv 16–17)
  The lost son, Ephraim, confesses (v 18–19)
  Yahweh's soliloquy of affection for the son (v 20)
Invitation to the Woman, Israel, to return (vv 21–22)

At the end, the poem returns to the theme struck at the beginning, but the correspondence is one of contrast. This is probably the reason for a striking play on words having the same sound but different meaning. At the beginning, Rachel's grief was characterized as *tamrûrîm* "bitter" (v 15a); but in the final strophe the poet uses *tamrûrîm* in a different and contrasting sense, namely, "road markers" that indicate the path of the homeward return (v 21a). Thus bitterness is converted into hope. Moreover, the poet juxtaposes and associates two images: Rachel who weeps disconsolately because her sons are no more, and Virgin/Daughter Israel who takes part in the homecoming and the rejoicing over family reunion. The promise to Rachel in her grief is quite specific: no longer will she be bereft of sons, for Ephraim is, in a special sense, God's beloved son and he will be restored to her at home. The motif of homecoming from exile is also found in 31:7–9, where Yahweh invites his returning people to sing aloud with joy.[27]

With weeping they will come,
  but with consolation I shall bring them.
I shall direct them to streams of water,

[26]Rudolph (*Jeremia*, 180) properly translates "im Lande."
[27]The following poem (31:10–14) may be a later expansion in the spirit of Second Isaiah. See, for instance, J. Muilenburg, "Jeremiah" (*IDB* 2, 830) and J. Bright, *Jeremiah*, 281.

in a smooth path where they will not stumble.
For ($k\hat{\imath}$) I am a father to Israel,
    and Ephraim is my first-born son. (31:9)

Viewed in this literary and theological context, the enigmatic concluding line about the *novum* begins to make sense. Weeping will be converted into rejoicing, for ($k\hat{\imath}$) Yahweh has created something new, as he did in the original creation when the blessing of fertility and posterity was conferred upon Man, consisting of "male and female" (*zākār ûnĕqēbâ*). Whereas Rachel, the Mother of Israel, was formerly deprived of her sons, she will have a posterity (*ʾaḥărît*), a future—as Yahweh explicitly promised in 31:17! It is probably true that the verb *tĕsôbēb* has a sexual—or, better, maternal—meaning: the Woman (Virgin Israel) will enfold a man (a son) as a sign of Yahweh's gracious gift of new life in the land. The use of *geber* (man) in a context of fertility also occurs, interestingly, in Job's lament that the Night had announced the conception of a "man-child" (Job 3:3). Furthermore, the enigmatic words in the final colon of v 22 may be analogous to the text of Gen 4:1 where Eve, after the birth of her firstborn, hailed the arrival of new life with the exclamation: "I have begotten [*qānîtî*] a man [*ʾîš*] with (the help of) Yahweh!" Like the English word "beget" in its original sense, the verb *qānâ* means both "to acquire, get" and "to bring into being," indicating that Eve, though a creature, engages in creative activity with divine assistance.[28] It is Yahweh who opens the womb and gives a future. So the Jeremianic text, when viewed in its poetic context, announces that the way into the future is opened by Yahweh who, in a miracle of creation, gives the people new life by restoring them to their land and giving them a posterity, a future (cf. " the seed of man . . . ," 31:27!). The old age, symbolized by Rachel weeping for her lost sons, will be superseded by a new age when Virgin Israel will be fruitful. The theme of Yahweh's "rebuilding" Virgin Israel is found also in the poem about "Grace in the Wilderness" (31:2–6), especially the central part where the language shifts from the masculine to the feminine and introduces a threefold emphatic "again" (*ʿôd*): *again* you shall be built up, *again* you shall take timbrels and go forth in the dance of the merrymakers,[29] *again* there will be fertile vineyards in the land (31:4–5).

---

[28]See I. M. Kikawada ("Two Notes on Eve," *JBL* 91 [1972] 35–37) who compares this passage to an Atra-ḫasis text where the goddess Mami creates life with the help of the god Enki. He argues that the preposition *ʾet* should be translated "together with," i.e. "with the help of."

[29]Possibly the motif of Virgin Israel taking timbrels and leading in "the dance of the merrymakers" (31:4) is a poetic allusion to the time of the Exodus when Miriam "took a timbrel in her hand, and all the women went out after her with timbrels and dancing" (Exod 15:20—as suggested by Holladay, *Jeremiah*, 114). The motif of the New Exodus and the New Entry into the land is prominent in the Book of Consolation, as it is also in the poems of Second Isaiah. See B. W. Anderson, "Exodus Typology in Second Isaiah," *Israel's Prophetic Heritage* (ed. by B. W. Anderson and W. Harrelson; New York: Harper, 1962) 177–95.

The contrast between the old and the new is suggested by a word-play in the final verse of the poem. On the one hand, the Woman is addressed as a "faithless one" (*haššôbēbâ*, v 22a); but, on the other, she will "encompass" or "enfold" (*tĕsôbēb*) a man. The latter verb seems to have been chosen because of its assonance with the adjective describing God's Daughter (*haššôbēbâ*/*tĕsôbēb*). The poetic juxtaposition of the two words draws a sharp contrast between Israel's faithlessness which led to divine judgment (exile from the land) and God's faithfulness to his people, despite their infidelity. In a miracle of divine grace, Rachel will receive her son back. The new life in the land, therefore, will be a gift of God, a new creation.

Attention was called earlier to Weiser's illuminating suggestion that the final line of this poem is reminiscent of the creation story, where God created (*bārā*ʾ) Man, consisting of "male [*zākār*] and female [*nĕqēbâ*]," in his image and endowed them with the power of procreation and dominion over "the earth" (Gen 1:27–28). If, however, the creation tradition is reflected here, the poet has reinterpreted it in a novel manner. For one thing, the word ʾ*ereṣ* no longer means "the earth" but "the land" of the promise. And further, here the emphasis is not on the equality of male and female in God's creation; rather, the poet boldly affirms that the Woman, in some sense, is the initiator. There is no basis for the notion, often expressed by commentators, that *nĕqēbâ* symbolizes weakness—"feminacy" in a pejorative sense. On the contrary, in the new age the Woman will be the agent of new life, new hope for a despairing, sorrowing people. But in the context of the poem, the Woman is Israel, typified by Rachel who wept for her lost sons and, through a juxtaposition of imagery, by the Virgin/ Daughter who is invited to return and, in the grace of God, to rebuild Israel. "The woman will enfold a man." Contextually this means that the bereaved Virgin Israel will have a son, a posterity, and therefore a future in the land promised to Israel's ancestors.[30]

---

[30]I am indebted to William Holladay for reading this essay with a critical eye. Subsequent to the completion of the study, I received Phyllis Trible's illuminating essay, "The Gift of a Poem: A Rhetorical Study of Jeremiah 31:15–22." *Andover Newton Quarterly* 17 (1977) 271– 80. Although her interpretive slant is different, she too agrees on the rhetorical unity of the poem.

23
Prophecy, Dissonance, and Jeremiah xxvi*
Robert P. Carroll

This paper is intended as an initial contribution to the study of the problems of consciousness and context in the prophetic tradition. The paucity of contextual information in the Old Testament makes the task of the historian extremely difficult in reconstructing the social ambience of the prophet in order to arrive at a fair understanding of his words. As Morton Smith has observed "form criticism has revealed an important gap between the documents in the Old Testament and the society from which they are supposed to derive."[1] If the reconstruction of the social context of the traditions is problematic then the contents of the prophetic books lack a necessary dimension for their interpretation. In this study I wish to limit myself to a consideration of the problem of unfulfilled prophecy in terms of a theoretical approach which I hope will illuminate some aspects of prophecy and, perhaps, provide some insights into the interaction between prophet and society.

The approach proposed is the application of dissonance theory to the prophetic books.[2] The theory of cognitive dissonance was propounded by Leon Festinger in 1957 and set out to describe social reactions to gaps between belief and behaviour or between expectations and reality.[3] Dissonance is said to exist where an attitude, e.g. smoking is bad for one's health, conflicts with the behavioural pattern, e.g. persistence in smoking. It characterises conflict in the relationship between cognitive elements where cognitive elements are defined as "the things a person knows about himself, about his behaviour, and about his surroundings."[4] Various attempts are made to resolve dissonance by ignoring it, or rethinking one's

---

*Originally published in the *Transactions of the Glasgow University Oriental Society* 25 (1976) 12–23.

[1] *Palestinian Parties and Politics that shaped the Old Testament* (London, 1971), p. 9.

[2] The notion of dissonance is usually associated with music, particularly in terms of harmony, e.g. concord, consonance: discord, dissonance. Apart from modern music it is perhaps best known in relation to Mozart's String Quartet in C, K. 465, nicknamed the "Dissonance Quartet."

[3] *A Theory of Cognitive Dissonance* (Evanston, 1957).

[4] *Ibid.*, p. 9.

attitudes or seeking out the companionship of like-minded people, or trying to convert critics to one's own point of view, or even giving up the attitude or the practice. Most of Festinger's work is concerned with structures of dissonance response whereby people come to terms with problems arising from post-decision making experiences.[5] Essential to the notion of dissonance theory is the view that man is not so much a rational creature as a rationalising creature.[6] In spite of ambiguities and the initial facileness of the theory it has been very influential in the field of social psychology and has given rise to a whole proliferation of studies and tests designed to support or modify its basic tenets.[7]

It is not possible in the limited space available to give a full analysis of how groups seek to construct cognitive consistency in response to the experience of dissonance but for my purposes an indication of the basic structures of response will be sufficient. The social group is of paramount importance as it provides social support for the individual and gives him a community of cognitive factors which protect him from dissonance producing opinions and situations.[8] Exclusivity of group loyalty with its concomitant control of exposure to dissonant factors helps to reduce or eliminate dissonance. The production of explanations or rationalisations which manipulate new evidence can reduce the problem. By gaining new converts to the movement or group new cognitive elements are introduced and these further modify dissonance. Thus dissonance is met by passive means through techniques of avoidance and active means through aggressive conversion programmes. As Festinger says elsewhere "if more and more people can be persuaded that the system of belief is correct, then clearly it must, after all, be correct."[9] To translate these response factors into terms suitable for application to the Bible may I suggest the traditional notions of hermeneutics, exclusivisation, and missionary activity.

In general terms the theory of cognitive dissonance may well have something to offer biblical studies but in particular terms it is Festinger's application of his theoretical approach to specific predictive expectations which has most to offer. In *When Prophecy Fails* he and his colleagues studied a group constructed around a belief that their part of the world was due for imminent destruction but the group would be saved by forces from outer space. When the expected disaster did not occur, the group did not

[5]See L. Festinger, *Conflict, Decision, and Dissonance* (London, 1964); J. W. Brehm and A. R. Cohen, *Explorations in Cognitive Dissonance* (London, 1962).

[6]So E. Aronson, "Dissonance Theory: Progress and Problems" in R. P. Abelson ed. *Theories of Cognitive Consistency: A Sourcebook* (Chicago, 1968), p. 6.

[7]See especially the volume edited by Abelson in note 6; for a bibliography of the first decade of dissonance theory studies see S. T. Margulis and E. Songer in *Psychological Reports* 24 (1969), pp. 923–35.

[8]Festinger, *Theory*, pp. 177–259.

[9]L. Festinger, H. W. Riecken, and S. Schachter, *When Prophecy Fails* (Minneapolis, 1956), p. 28.

break up but began to seek converts to their viewpoint. This reaction points to an important postulate of dissonance theory "when people are committed to a belief and a course of action, clear disconfirming evidence may simply result in deepened conviction and increased proselyting."[10] The first chapter of the book is a general consideration of unfulfilled prophecies and disappointed messiahs and so obviously comes within the range of biblical studies. However Festinger limits himself to discussing the second coming of Christ, the Sabbatai Zevi movement in the 17th century[11], and the Millerites in the 19th century so he has nothing to say directly about Old Testament prophecy.

To turn directly now to the Old Testament it should be said at the outset that the principle "disconfirming evidence results in increased preaching" might well constitute a paradigm for prophetic action. What evidence we have suggests that when prophetic groups experienced the dissonance caused by the failure of their expectations their reaction was to continue to proclaim their message but also to insist that failure was due to human activity rather than defects in the original message. A good example of this occurs in Is. 59 where the disciples of Second Isaiah account for the non-appearance of their master's triumphalist expectations by asserting the sinfulness of the community.[12] Continued or increased preaching backed up by explanations or rationalisations characterises the oracles of Third Isaiah. This explanatory approach belongs to the field of hermeneutics and constitutes one of the above suggested responses to dissonance. The notion of exclusivisation is more difficult to apply to the prophetic tradition but in terms of social support and retirement from public activity it is possible to see in Isaiah's withdrawal from active prophecy to seal his teaching among his disciples (Is. 8:16) an example of a prophet confounded by the lack of response to his proclamation. If this section of Isaiah is treated as a response to his failure to persuade Ahaz to follow his analysis of the Syro-Ephraimite situation (Is. 7:1–17) then we may regard Isaiah as having sought social support as a means of modifying the experience of dissonance.[13] The more general field of exclusivisation associated with Ezra and Nehemiah was structured by Torah and so does not come within the

[10] *Ibid.*, pp. 12, 28.

[11] *Ibid.*, pp. 8–23. There is a growing interest in the movement associated with Sabbatai Zevi and the notions of false messiah and salvation through sin; see esp. G. Scholem, "Shabbatai Zevi," *Encyclopedia Judaica* 14 (Jerusalem, 1971), cols. 1219–54; "Redemption Through Sin," *The Messianic Idea in Judaism* (London, 1971), pp. 78–141; *Sabbatai Sevi. The Mystical Messiah* (Princeton, 1973). For a fictional treatment of a situation similar to the one studied by Festinger see Alison Lurie's novel *Imaginary Friends* (London, 1967). For similar problems in clinical psychology see M. Rokeach, *The Three Christs of Ypsilanti* (London, 1964).

[12] On Is. 56–66 as reaction to the failure of Second Isaiah's hopes see P. D. Hanson, *The Dawn of Apocalyptic* (Philadelphia, 1975), pp. 32–208.

[13] Cf. H. W. Hoffmann, *Die Intention der Verkündigung Jesajas*, BZAW 136 (Berlin, 1974), pp. 77–80.

scope of this study. The role of missionary activity in the Old Testament is a controversial one and if it has any significance at all in the prophetic books, e.g. in Jonah and Second Isaiah, it can hardly be said to be the traditional one of gaining converts for a particular movement.[14] It is possible, however, that Second Isaiah's depiction of the activity of the servant (i.e. Israel?) is a resolution of dissonance caused by the initial rejection of the servant (cf. 49:1–7; 53:1–3, 11, 12).

The obvious difficulties in demonstrating the validity of viewing these aspects as reactions to dissonance suggest that the direction of investigation should be in the area of hermeneutics. When prophecy fails there must either be reinterpretation of the original prediction or a shifting of position must be undertaken. Either reaction will preserve the prophet's *amour-propre* and retain the loyalty of his followers. There is a good example of such a shift in position in the book of Jeremiah. An aspect of the conflict between Jeremiah and the other prophets concerned the future fate of Judah—for Jeremiah the future held invasion, destruction and exile but other prophets regarded the future as holding *šalom* or salvation (cf. Jer. 5:31; 6:9–15; 8:8–12). Yet when events appeared to vindicate Jeremiah's view, i.e. Nebuchadrezzar deported Jehoiachin, his companions and the sacred temple vessels, there is no evidence to suggest that the prophets radically altered their preaching. On the contrary, the prophetic oracles began to proclaim that the exile would be a very short one and that within two years king, exiles and vessels would all be restored to Jerusalem (Jer. 27–29). That shift in prophecy from non-destruction by the Babylonians to the brevity of the exile constitutes the principle of reinterpretation as reaction to dissonance.

It is the analysis of reactions to the predicament of unfulfilled predictions that is the core of the application of dissonance theory to biblical studies. However the lack of data in the Old Testament makes it difficult to work out the theory cogently. Not only is there the problem of little information about reception and reaction factors in prophecy and society there is also the problem of bias in reportage, e.g. the polemic between Jeremiah and the prophets is only presented from Jeremiah's point of view. Although there is the apparent absence in the Old Testament of a complete paradigm of prediction plus response to its failure it is the contention of this paper that certain texts are best explained as attempts at resolving dissonance, e.g. Is. 6:9–13; 8:16; Zec. 4:6–10; 6:10–14.

Apart from hermeneutics within the biblical text it is possible to posit response to dissonance in the hermeneutical systems used by translators of the Bible and also in commentaries on the biblical text. Communities that maintain the belief that prophecy is predictive and must always have

---

[14]On this controversial topic see H. M. Orlinsky, *Studies on the Second Part of the Book of Isaiah.* SVT 14 (Leiden, 1967), pp. 97–117.

specific fulfilment tend to be communities devoting a good deal of energy to apologetic stances. A substantial part of this activity is devoted to demonstrating how prophecy simply cannot fail and the construction of hermeneutical systems which appear to maintain such a proposition. Often these hermeneutical systems involve a cavalier treatment of the text in order to sustain dogmas of necessary fulfilment or biblical inspiration and tend to extend the warranty of prophecy by introducing typological, eschatological, messianic or christological principles. Thus the prophet is further divorced from the context of his time and his words cease to have any meaning other than as an apologetic for a theological system.

As an illustration of this point about the hermeneutics of translators and commentators we may consider a prophetic prediction that requires a specific fulfilment and would appear to have none. Taken from a set of five eschatological predictions in the book of Isaiah it is the statement in 19:24f.

> In that day Israel will be the third with Egypt and Assyria, a blessing in the midst of the earth, whom Yahweh of hosts has blessed, saying, "Blessed be my people Egypt, and the work of my hands Assyria, and my heritage Israel."

It seems to be a statement about the future role of Egypt, Assyria and Israel as the three powers sharing authority and blessing as the peoples of Yahweh. As the phrase "that day" indicates it is an "imminently certain" expectation.[15] Although the context of the oracles in 19:16–25 is usually regarded as non-Isaianic and post-exilic it may be possible to attribute verses 24, 25 to Isaiah.[16] There is little in the statement to preclude such an attribution and the reference to Assyria is more meaningful in a pre-exilic context (cf. Mic. 5:2–6). Also the note of implicit universalism in the idea of Egypt as the people of Yahweh and Assyria as the work of his hands is comparable to the notion expressed in Am. 9:7.[17] It might therefore be attributed to Isaiah and as such be part of his hopes for the future after the Assyrian crisis had passed. However estimating what Isaiah's opinion about the Assyrian issue was and how it might be related to the events of 701 B.C. and the legend of Sennacherib's destruction in 2 Kings 19 is a very

---

[15] So S. J. DeVries, *Yesterday, Today, and Tomorrow* (London, 1975), p. 331.

[16] It is taken as non-Isaianic by G. B. Gray, *Isaiah I–XXXIX*, ICC vol. 1 (London, 1912), p. 332; set between 3rd and early 2nd century B.C. by O. Kaiser, *Isaiah 13–39* (London, 1974), p. 105. Attributed to Isaiah by J. Mauchline, *Isaiah 1–39* (London, 1962), pp. 160–2; and described as "inimitably Isaianic" by Martin Buber, *The Prophetic Faith* (New York, 1960), p. 150.

[17] On universalism see J. Morgenstern, 'The Universalism of Amos,' *Essays presented to Leo Baeck* (London, 1954), pp. 106–26; also H. M. Orlinsky, "Nationalism—Universalism and Internationalism in Ancient Israel," *Translating and Understanding the Old Testament*, ed. H. T. Frank and W. L. Reed (Nashville, 1970), pp. 206–36. Orlinsky dates the Isaiah passage in the Seleucid-Ptolemaic period of Judean history, p. 223.

complicated and complex hermeneutical problem.[18] On the whole Is. 19:24f. appears to be a good example of a prediction that was never fulfilled and therefore constitutes a dissonance producing gap between expectation and reality.

When we turn to the translators a number of interesting points emerge. The LXX followed the Hebrew text closely for verse 24 but by modifying verse 25 transformed its meaning thus "Whom the Lord has blessed, saying, 'Blessed be my people *who are in* Egypt and *who are in* Assyria and my heritage Israel.' " This handling of the text avoids both the problem of dissonance and the issue of universalism.[19] The Targum simply translated verse 24 into Aramaic but completely changed verse 25 by an imaginative paraphrase "Whom the Lord of hosts has blessed, saying, 'Blessed be my people whom I have brought out of Egypt, because they sinned before me I carried them into exile to Assyria, but now that they have repented, they shall be called my people and my inheritance, even Israel.' "[20] This treatment of the words Egypt and Assyria as shorthand for the exodus and the deportation avoids or censors the notion of universalism implied by the Hebrew. It is extremely difficult to account for such textual changes especially as many exegetes do not attempt to explain them at all. Thus Qimhi in his commentary gives a very simple explanation of the Hebrew and then comments "Targum Jonathan refers it all to Israel."[21] The radical transformation of the text may have come about for ideological reasons, such as a retreat from the universalism hinted at by Amos and Isaiah or a generalisation of prediction to avoid the failure of the oracle after the collapse of Assyria. Thus the hermeneutics of the translators may avoid dissonance altogether by reinterpretation within their work.

The historical critical approach to the Bible accepts as normative the element of failure in the prophetic books but conventional or traditionalist approaches have to provide explanations which will maintain either the actuality or the necessity of fulfilment. Two examples of such hermeneutical principles may be cited as examples of dissonance avoidance by interpretation. In a book dealing with all the predictions in the Bible Barton Payne treats Is. 19:24f. as a typological prophecy and sees its fulfilment in "the equality of all nations in Jesus, Eph. 2:14, 19 (cf. Is. 44:5), but particularly the conversion of Egypt to become a leading Christian country, as it was

---

[18]See B. S. Childs, *Isaiah and the Assyrian Crisis*, SBT[2] 3 (London, 1967); cf. J. Bright, *A History of Israel* (London, 1960), pp. 282–7. Reaction to dissonance may have helped construct the tradition embodied in 2 Kings 19.

[19]R. R. Ottley, *The Book of Isaiah according to the Septuagint* vol. 2 (London, 1906) does not note the Greek addition to the Hebrew, unless he understood "who are in" to be the equivalent of the Hebrew, see p. 202 for the absence of comment.

[20]Cf. J. F. Stenning, *The Targum of Isaiah* (Oxford, 1949), pp. 62–5. He rightly notes that the Targum has "deliberately altered" the text, p. xvi.

[21]See L. Finkelstein, *The Commentary of David Kimhi on Isaiah* (New York, 1926), p. 116.

from the third to the seventh centuries."[22] After the lapse of a thousand years the prophet's words have a specific fulfilment for a few centuries and then presumably revert to the more general meaning of the Christianisation of the world. Another theologian of a similar school of futuristic interpretation of prophecy refers the prediction to an eschatological fulfilment "in the time of the Messiah, what in Isaiah's day were called Egypt and Assyria will serve the Lord."[23] In this case the time lapse is of the order of three thousand years and the prediction remains on the books as temporarily unfulfilled.

These approaches to the interpretation of prophecy protected all predictions from the problem of failure by asserting an eschatological verification principle which cannot be falsified.[24] As such the problem of dissonance is avoided by reinterpretation and the language of prophecy is emptied of meaning or manipulated to yield a predetermined meaning. In a sense such a technique of textual mishandling is not unlike a primitive version of the demythologisation approach to the biblical text—specific terms are drained of their cultural content and made to apply indiscriminately to vague existential realities. In addition to such hermeneutical avoidance of dissonance producing texts such groups also tend to be strongly exclusive in religious and social commitment and heavily committed to programmes of missionary activity. Such techniques are well designed to protect any group from the inroads dissonance may make on cognitive holdings.

For a more paradigmatic approach to the prophetic texts in terms of hermeneutical resolution of dissonance I have selected Jeremiah 26. The chapter is a prose account of his temple sermon, given in greater detail in 7:1–15, and the reaction to it of the authorities and the people.[25] Whether the prophet was charged with simply preaching against the city (v. 11) or preaching in the divine name (v. 16) and therefore of being in breach of the prophetic regulations laid down in Deut. 18:20 is not clear from the text.[26] But it is the defense offered by the elders of the land on Jeremiah's behalf against the death sentence that forms the kernel of this part of the paper.

---

[22] *Encyclopedia of Biblical Prophecy* (London, 1973), p. 304.

[23] E. J. Young, *The Book of Isaiah* vol. 2 (Grand Rapids, 1969), p. 43.

[24] For the notion of eschatological verification in the philosophy of religion see J. Hick, *Faith and Knowledge* (London, 1967[2]), pp. 169–99; for a brief criticism see A. Jeffner, *The Study of Religious Language* (London, 1972), p. 107. The biblicism of Payne and Young is not actually based on such philosophical notions but has its roots in an older dogmatic approach to biblical exegisis. For a very different view of the predictive element in prophecy see Buber, *op. cit.*, p. 178.

[25] For text and commentary see J. Bright, *Jeremiah*, Anchor Bible 21 (New York, 1965); W. Rudolph, *Jeremiah*, HAT 12 (Tübingen 1968[3]); A. Weiser, *Das Buch des Propheten Jeremia*, ATD 20, 21 (Göttingen, 1952, 1955).

[26] See the discussion in J. Skinner, *Prophecy and Religion* (Cambridge, 1922), pp. 171–4; cf. R. Davidson, "Orthodoxy and the Prophetic Word," *VT* 14 (1964), pp. 407–16.

They quoted the final lines of Micah's harangue against the religious and civil leaders of his day (Mic. 3:12) "Zion shall be ploughed as a field; Jerusalem shall become a heap of ruins, and the mountain of the house a wooded ruin" (v. 18). The quotation was used to show what the proper response to an oracle of judgment should be, namely repentance, Royal response led to the rescinding of the threat and the prediction remained unfulfilled. However nowhere in the prophecies of Micah is there any hint that repentance was a possibility. Thus the elders have provided an element lacking in Micah's prophecy and given it a conditionality not easily discerned in the text. There are two ways of accounting for this additional feature. Either the editors of Jeremiah understood all prophetic preaching to be essentially conditional, hence the call to repentance was implicit wherever it was not explicit. Or they are here attempting to deal with the problem of Micah's unfulfilled prediction; in other words, here is a good example of response to dissonance.

By all accounts Micah's vision of his day was faulty in that his trenchant criticism of the social evils of his time culminating in the destruction of Jerusalem (Mic. 1–3) was remembered at least a century later in the very city that should have been "a wooded height and a heap of ruins!" According to the rules of Deut. 18:21f. Micah was a prophet who had "spoken presumptuously" yet the quotation in Jer. 26:18 shows that he was revered as a prophet who spoke the divine word. This cluster of problems constitutes the heart of dissonance as applied to one aspect of prophecy. To rescue Micah from the charge of being a false prophet it is necessary to posit a public response to his preaching which obviated the prediction. Even Payne recognises the lack of conditionality and so concludes that the contrition of Hezekiah only postponed the devastation of Jerusalem rather than annulled it.[27]

The principle of response shaping the prophetic message is fairly well established for the Old Testament prophets. They were essentially moralists who preached "into the power of decision lying in the moment."[28] As such the response they sought could shape the message and transform it in positive or negative ways. The Immanuel prophecy in Is. 7 illustrates this principle of human response by showing how the king's refusal to trust the prophetic word transformed a sign of salvation into one of destruction (cf. vv. 13–17 with vv. 18–25).[29] The human response helped to structure the word and gave it its ultimate shape. In a similar way an oracle of judgment could be controlled by royal or popular repentance, e.g. Is. 1:16–19 and Jer. 26:18f. This notion of repentance or "turning" which is very important

---

[27] Op. cit., p. 427.

[28] Buber, op. cit., p. 103.

[29] An important principle for interpreting prophetic traditions is that of transformation, whether response transforming the word as in Is. 7 or the prophet transforming popular beliefs as in Am. 1, 2; 9:7; Is. 55:3. For a different view of the problematic Immanuel prophecy see W. McKane, "The Interpretation of Isaiah VII 14–25," VT 17 (1967), pp. 208–19.

in the prophetic tradition reaches a peak in Jeremiah and Ezekiel and is then taken up by the post-exilic priestly organisers of the community and used to help construct their expiatory regulations.[30]

There is an ambivalent element in the doctrine of repentance in the book of Jeremiah, as indeed there is in Is. 6:9–13, which reveals some of the tensions between prophet and society. Some of Jeremiah's fiercest attacks on the cult are modified by interpolation, e.g. the temple sermon as we now have it in 7:1–15 is made up of one strand which categorically rejects the evils of the day (vv. 8–15) and another strand which has a conditional element allowing for amendment of behaviour (vv. 3–7; cf. 26:4–5).[31] This conditional element is more in keeping with the deuteronomic view of history which permits repentance to save Hezekiah from destruction (2 Kings 19) and allows Josiah to die before judgment falls on Judah (2 Kings 22:18–20).[32] It is also similar to the Chronicler's view of history which even posits repentance of Manasseh (2 Chron. 33:10–20). The conditional element in Jeremiah may point towards a deuteronomic edition of the book which attempted to use Jeremiah as a demonstration of their theory of history as the outworking of prophecy.[33] Many of the later oracles of Jeremiah present a view of Judah as incapable of responding to the prophetic word. Thus the people do not know the *mišpaṭ* of Yahweh unlike the birds which know their seasons (8:7); no one speaks the truth, they refuse to know Yahweh (9:5f.); the people are so accustomed to doing evil that they can no more change their ways than an Ethiopian his skin or a leopard its spots (13:23). He may have started out as a preacher of response (cf. 4:1–4) but time and experience forced him to regard the people as incapable of such response. Perhaps the general failure of his peaching (cf. Jer. 25:1–7) could only be accounted for on the basis of an inability to repent in those he preached to and this explanation might well point towards his experience of dissonance.

Jer. 18:7–10 represents most clearly the general principle of repentance averting disaster and that "strange caricaturing of the prophet in the book

---

[30]See J. Milgrom, "The Priestly Doctrine of Repentance," *Revue Biblique* 82 (1975), pp. 186–205.

[31]For an analysis of the text see Bright, *op. cit.*, pp. 52–9; G. Fohrer, "Jeremias Tempelwort (Jeremia 7:1–15)," *Studien zur alttestamentliche Prophetie*, BZAW 99 (Berlin, 1967), pp. 190–203.

[32]The death of Josiah must have posed serious problems for the historians, see S. B. Frost, "The death of Josiah: a conspiracy of silence," *JBL* 87 (1968), pp. 369–82. If the main history had been completed before the death of Josiah then the absence of any reference to Jeremiah may be more easily understood. For the view that there were two editions, one pre-exilic and one exilic, of the history see F. M. Cross, *Canaanite Myth and Hebrew Epic* (Cambridge: Mass., 1973), pp. 285–9.

[33]On the problem of the prose sections in Jeremiah see E. W. Nicholson, *Preaching to the Exiles* (Oxford, 1970); H. Weippert, *Die Prosareden des Jeremiabuches*, BZAW 132 (Berlin, 1973).

of Jonah"[34] shows the prophet as essentially a preacher of repentance.[35] But by allowing the principle of repentance to stand as a means of exonerating a prophet from the charge of false prophecy (i.e. unfulfilled prediction) Deut. 18:20 has been effectively negated. At the same time a powerful resolution of dissonance has been provided for the unfulfilled predictions of salvation in most of the prophets. e.g. Am. 9:11–15; Hos. 2:14–23; Is. 9:2–7; 11:1–9; 35; Jer. 23:5, 6; 31:27–37; 33:12–26; Ez. 34:23–31; 37:15–28; Mic. 5:2–6; Hag. 2:21–23. For if man's response can transform the oracle of judgment and cause the deity to repent then the opposite may apply. Thus due to the lack of response the future has been cancelled! If we have proved too much here perhaps that is because at one level the idea of repentance was used to protect prophecy from failure and this usage should not be confused with the genuine prophetic call to repent. This symmetrical possibility may account for the absence of conditionality in the salvation oracles which posit a transcendental level of implementation beyond man's response. Yet it remains the case that without recourse to hermeneutics the non-fulfilment of oracles will posit a source of dissonance for the community. So at one level Jer. 26:18f. is a good example of how unfulfilled prophecy can be modified by a dissonance reducing hermeneutical principle.

When I first started research on Old Testament prophecy in the light of dissonance theory there was nothing in the field of biblical studies in the way of considerations of the subject or how it might be applied to traditional texts. I thought it should be able to yield useful insights into the biblical communities and even assist in the more specific areas of reaction to failed prophecies in both Old and New Testament. It seemed obvious that the theory might throw some light on such New Testament problems as the *Parousieverzögerung* "delay of the parousia" issue or what Kümmel calls "the most puzzling event of Jesus' life, his death on the cross."[36] Since this paper was read to the Society I have continued to work on the problems of relating a cross-disciplinary approach to the Bible and have put forward a number of theoretical considerations that would modify the use of dissonance theory in prophetic studies.[37] However I have found that the theory holds possibilities for treating various sets of texts, e.g. Is. 56–66; Zec. 1–8; and that, as one authority has it, "dissonance theory is helpful, not so much as an explanation of events, but rather as a way to

---

[34]R. E. Clements, *Prophecy and Tradition* (Oxford, 1975), p. 85.

[35]For the theme of Jonah as repentance see R. E. Clements, "The purpose of the Book of Jonah," *SVT* 28 (1975), pp. 16–28.

[36]*The Theology of the New Testament* (London, 1974), p. 116.

[37]See my "Ancient Israelite Prophecy and Dissonance Theory," *Numen* 24 (1977), 135–51. A brief paper entitled "Prophecy and Dissonance" was read to the Society for Old Testament Study at the Summer Meeting in Bangor in July 1974 but its contents were too generalized to make it worth publishing.

think about problems."[38] As a means of reflecting upon the problematics of prophecy in relation to society dissonance theory may well have something to say to biblical scholars. At the same time it is interesting to note that studies applying dissonance theory to the New Testament are beginning to appear. One such study has suggested that dissonance caused by the death of Jesus may be resolved by the christology of the gospels.[39] Another study sees the New Testament account of the resurrection as a possible response of people of strong faith to the problems caused by the crucifixion.[40] Ultimately dissonance theory is about reactions to information and the assimilation of new cognitive elements into already existing structures of knowledge. As such it should be helpful in working on the problematics of community and consciousness in the Bible.*

[38]K. E. Weick, "When Prophecy Pales: The Fate of Dissonance Theory," *Psychological Reports* 16 (1965), p. 1272.

[39]U. Wernik, "Frustrated beliefs and early Christianity," *Numen* 22 (1975), pp. 96–130.

[40]H. Jackson, "The Resurrection Belief of the Earliest Church: A Response to the Failure of Prophecy?," *Journal of Religion* 55 (1975), pp. 414–25.

*For further developments of this analysis see R. P. Carroll, *When Prophecy Failed* (London & New York 1979); "Prophecy and Dissonance," *ZAW* 92 (1980), 108–119; and the critical evaluation of Carroll's work in C. S. Rodd, "On Applying a Sociological Theory to Biblical Studies," *JSOT* 19 (1981), 95–106. On Jeremiah 26, see H. G. Reventlow, "Gattung und Überlieferung in der 'Tempelrede Jeremias.' Jer. 7 und 26," *ZAW* 81 (1969), 315–52; F. L. Hossfeld & I. Meyer, "Der Prophet vor dem Tribunal: Neuer Auslegungsversuch von Jer 26," ZAW 86 (1974), 30–50; and Carroll, *From Chaos to Covenant* (London & New York 1981), 91–95.

Index of Authors